CCNA
Cyber Ops
SECFND 210-250
Official Cert Guide

OMAR SANTOS, CISSP No. 463598
JOSEPH MUNIZ, CISSP No. 344594
STEFANO DE CRESCENZO CCIE No. 26025, CISSP 406579

Cisco Press

800 East 96th Street
Indianapolis, IN 46240

CCNA Cyber Ops SECFND 210-250 Official Cert Guide

Omar Santos
Joseph Muniz
Stefano De Crescenzo

Published by:
Cisco Press
800 East 96th Street
Indianapolis, IN 46240 USA

Printed in the United States of America

2   17

Library of Congress Control Number: 2017931952

ISBN-10: 1-58714-702-5

ISBN-13: 978-1-58714-702-9

Warning and Disclaimer

This book is designed to provide information about the CCNA Cyber Ops SECFND #210-250 exam. Every effort has been made to make this book as complete and accurate as possible, but no warranty or fitness is implied.

The information is provided on an "as is" basis. The authors, Cisco Press, and Cisco Systems, Inc., shall have neither liability nor responsibility to any person or entity with respect to any loss or damages arising from the information contained in this book or from the use of the discs or programs that may accompany it.

The opinions expressed in this book belong to the authors and are not necessarily those of Cisco Systems, Inc.

Trademark Acknowledgments

All terms mentioned in this book that are known to be trademarks or service marks have been appropriately capitalized. Cisco Press or Cisco Systems, Inc., cannot attest to the accuracy of this information. Use of a term in this book should not be regarded as affecting the validity of any trademark or service mark.

Special Sales

For information about buying this title in bulk quantities, or for special sales opportunities (which may include electronic versions; custom cover designs; and content particular to your business, training goals, marketing focus, or branding interests), please contact our corporate sales department at corpsales@pearsoned.com or (800) 382-3419.

For government sales inquiries, please contact governmentsales@pearsoned.com.

For questions about sales outside the United States, please contact intlcs@pearson.com.

Feedback Information

At Cisco Press, our goal is to create in-depth technical books of the highest quality and value. Each book is crafted with care and precision, undergoing rigorous development that involves the unique expertise of members from the professional technical community.

Readers' feedback is a natural continuation of this process. If you have any comments regarding how we could improve the quality of this book, or otherwise alter it to better suit your needs, you can contact us through email at feedback@ciscopress.com. Please make sure to include the book title and ISBN in your message.

We greatly appreciate your assistance.

Editor-in-Chief: Mark Taub

Product Line Manager: Brett Bartow

Managing Editor: Sandra Schroeder

Development Editor: Christopher Cleveland

Project Editor: Mandie Frank

Composition: Tricia Bronkella

Indexer: Ken Johnson

Alliances Manager, Cisco Press: Ron Fligge

Executive Editor: Mary Beth Ray

Technical Editors: Pavan Reddy, Ron Taylor

Copy Editor: Bart Reed

Designer: Chuti Prasertsith

Editorial Assistant: Vanessa Evans

Proofreader: The Wordsmithery LLC

Americas Headquarters
Cisco Systems, Inc.
San Jose, CA

Asia Pacific Headquarters
Cisco Systems (USA) Pte. Ltd.
Singapore

Europe Headquarters
Cisco Systems International BV
Amsterdam, The Netherlands

Cisco has more than 200 offices worldwide. Addresses, phone numbers, and fax numbers are listed on the Cisco Website at www.cisco.com/go/offices.

About the Authors

Omar Santos is an active member of the cyber security community, where he leads several industry-wide initiatives and standards bodies. His active role helps businesses, academic institutions, state and local law enforcement agencies, and other participants dedicated to increasing the security of their critical infrastructures.

Omar is the author of over a dozen books and video courses, as well as numerous white papers, articles, and security configuration guidelines and best practices. Omar is a principal engineer of the Cisco Product Security Incident Response Team (PSIRT), where he mentors and leads engineers and incident managers during the investigation and resolution of cyber security vulnerabilities. Additional information about Omar's current projects can be found at omarsantos.io, and you can follow Omar on Twitter @santosomar.

Joseph Muniz is an architect at Cisco Systems and security researcher. He has extensive experience in designing security solutions and architectures for the top Fortune 500 corporations and the U.S. government. Joseph's current role gives him visibility into the latest trends in cyber security, from both leading vendors and customers. Examples of Joseph's research include his RSA talk titled "Social Media Deception," which has been quoted by many sources (search for "Emily Williams Social Engineering"), as well as his articles in *PenTest Magazine* regarding various security topics.

Joseph runs The Security Blogger website, a popular resource for security, hacking, and product implementation. He is the author and contributor of several publications covering various penetration testing and security topics. You can follow Joseph at www.thesecurityblogger.com and @SecureBlogger.

Stefano De Crescenzo is a senior incident manager with the Cisco Product Security Incident Response Team (PSIRT), where he focuses on product vulnerability management and Cisco products forensics. He is the author of several blog posts and white papers about security best practices and forensics. He is an active member of the security community and has been a speaker at several security conferences.

Stefano specializes in malware detection and integrity assurance in critical infrastructure devices, and he is the author of integrity assurance guidelines for Cisco IOS, IOS-XE, and ASA.

Stefano holds a B.Sc. and M.Sc. in telecommunication engineering from Politecnico di Milano, Italy, and an M.Sc. in telecommunication from Danish Technical University, Denmark. He is currently pursuing an Executive MBA at Vlerick Business School in Belgium. He also holds a CCIE in Security #26025 and is CISSP and CISM certified.

About the Technical Reviewers

Pavan Reddy serves as a Security Principal in Cisco Security Services. Pavan has 20+ years of security and network consulting experience in Financial Services, Healthcare, Service Provider, and Retail arenas. Recent projects cover Technical Security Strategy and Architecture, Network Segmentation Strategy, Threat Intelligence Analytics, Distributed Denial-of-Service Mitigation Architectures, and DNS Architecture and Security. Pavan holds multiple CCIEs and BS in Computer Engineering.

Ron Taylor has been in the Information Security field for almost 20 years. Ten of those years were spent in consulting where he gained experience in many areas. In 2008, he joined the Cisco Global Certification Team as an SME in Information Assurance. In 2012, he moved into a position with the Security Research & Operations group (PSIRT), where his focus was mostly on penetration testing of Cisco products and services. He was also involved in developing and presenting security training to internal development and test teams globally. Additionally, he provided consulting support to many product teams as an SME on product security testing. In his current role, he is a Consulting Systems Engineer specializing in Cisco's security product line. Certifications include GPEN, GWEB, GCIA, GCIH, GWAPT, RHCE, CCSP, CCNA, CISSP, and MCSE. Ron is also a Cisco Security Blackbelt, SANS mentor, Cofounder and President of the Raleigh BSides Security Conference, and a member of the Packet Hacking Village team at Defcon.

Dedications

I would like to dedicate this book to my lovely wife, Jeannette, and my two beautiful children, Hannah and Derek, who have inspired and supported me throughout the development of this book.

I also dedicate this book to my father, Jose, and to the memory of my mother, Generosa. Without their knowledge, wisdom, and guidance, I would not have the goals that I strive to achieve today.

—Omar Santos

I would like to dedicate this book to the memory of my father, Raymond Muniz. He never saw me graduate from college or accomplish great things, such as writing this book. I would also like to apologize to him for dropping out of soccer in high school. I picked it back up later in life, and today play in at least two competitive matches a week. Your hard work paid off. Hopefully you somehow know that.

—Joseph Muniz

This book is dedicated to my wife, Nevena, and my beautiful daughters, Sara and Tea, who supported and inspired me during the development of this book. Specifically, Tea was born a few weeks before I started writing my first chapter, so she is especially connected with this book.

I would also like to mention my whole family: my mother, Mariagrazia, and my sister, Francesca, who supported my family and me while I was away writing. I also dedicate this book to the memory of my father, Cataldo.

—Stefano De Crescenzo

Acknowledgments

I would like to thank the technical editors, Pavan Reddy and Ron Taylor, for their time and technical expertise. They verified our work and contributed to the success of this book. I would also like to thank the Cisco Press team, especially Mary Beth Ray, Denise Lincoln, and Christopher Cleveland, for their patience, guidance, and consideration. Their efforts are greatly appreciated. Finally, I would like to acknowledge the Cisco Security Research and Operations teams, Cisco Advanced Threat Analytics, and Cisco Talos. Several leaders in the network security industry work there, supporting our Cisco customers, often under very stressful conditions, and working miracles daily. They are truly unsung heroes, and I am honored to have had the privilege of working side by side with them in the trenches while protecting customers and Cisco.

—Omar Santos

I would first like to thank Omar and Stefano for including me on this project. I really enjoyed working with these guys and hope we can do more in the future. I also would like to thank the Cisco Press team and technical editors, Pavan Reddy and Ron Taylor, for their fantastic support in making the writing process top quality and easy for everybody. Hey, Ron, you got this and the CTR comic. 2016 was great for you, Mr. Green.

I would also like to thank all the great people in my life who make me who I am.

Finally, a message for Raylin Muniz (age 7): Hopefully one day you can accomplish your dreams like I have with this book.

—Joseph Muniz

I would like to thank Omar and Joey for being fantastic mates in the development of this book. A special mention goes to my wife as well, for supporting me throughout this journey and for helping me by reviewing my work.

Additionally, this book wouldn't have been possible without the help of the Cisco Press team and in particular of Chris Cleveland. His guidance has been very precious. A big thanks goes to the technical reviewers, Pavan and Ron. Thanks for keeping me honest and to the point! A big thanks also to Eric Vyncke for his numerous suggestions.

—Stefano De Crescenzo

Contents at a Glance

Elements Available on the Book Website

Contents

Command Syntax Conventions

The conventions used to present command syntax in this book are the same conventions used in the IOS Command Reference. The Command Reference describes these conventions as follows:

- **Bold** indicates commands and keywords that are entered literally as shown. In actual configuration examples and output (not general command syntax), bold indicates commands that are manually input by the user (such as a **show** command).

- *Italic* indicates arguments for which you supply actual values.

- Vertical bars (|) separate alternative, mutually exclusive elements.

- Square brackets ([ ]) indicate an optional element.

- Braces ({ }) indicate a required choice.

- Braces within brackets ([{ }]) indicate a required choice within an optional element.

Introduction

Congratulations! If you are reading this, you have in your possession a powerful tool that can help you to:

- Improve your awareness and knowledge of cyber security fundamentals
- Increase your skill level related to the implementation of that security
- Prepare for the CCNA Cyber Ops SECFND certification exam

Whether you are preparing for the CCNA Cyber Ops certification or just changing careers to cyber security, this book will help you gain the knowledge you need to get started and prepared. When writing this book, we did so with you in mind, and together we will discover the critical ingredients that make up the recipe for a secure network and how to succeed in cyber security operations. By focusing on covering the objectives for the CCNA Cyber Ops SECFND exam and integrating that with real-world best practices and examples, we created this content with the intention of being your personal tour guides as we take you on a journey through the world of network security.

The CCNA Cyber Ops: Understanding Cisco Cybersecurity Fundamentals (SECFND) 210-250 exam is required for the CCNA Cyber Ops certification. This book covers all the topics listed in Cisco's exam blueprint, and each chapter includes key topics and preparation tasks to assist you in mastering this information. Reviewing tables and practicing test questions will help you practice your knowledge in all subject areas.

About the 210-250 CCNA Cyber Ops SECFND Exam

The CCNA Cyber Ops: Understanding Cisco Cybersecurity Fundamentals (SECFND) 210-250 exam is the first of the two required exams to achieve the CCNA Cyber Ops certification and is aligned with the job role of associate-level security operations center (SOC) security analyst. The SECFND exam tests candidates' understanding of cyber security's basic principles, foundational knowledge, and core skills needed to grasp the more advanced associate-level materials in the second required exam: Implementing Cisco Cybersecurity Operations (SECOPS).

The CCNA Cyber Ops: Understanding Cisco Cybersecurity Fundamentals (SECFND) 210-250 exam is a computer-based test that has 55 to 60 questions and a 90-minute time limit. Because all exam information is managed by Cisco Systems and is therefore subject to change, candidates should continually monitor the Cisco Systems site for exam updates at http://www.cisco.com/c/en/us/training-events/training-certifications/exams/current-list/secfnd.html.

You can take the exam at Pearson VUE testing centers. You can register with VUE at www.vue.com/cisco.

210-250 CCNA Cyber Ops SECFNC Exam Topics

Table I-1 lists the topics of the 210-250 SECFND exam and indicates the chapter in the book where they are covered.

Table I-1   *210-250 SECFND Exam Topics*

Exam Topic	Chapter
1.0 Network Concepts	
1.1 Describe the function of the network layers as specified by the OSI and the TCP/IP network models	Chapter 1
1.2 Describe the operation of the following:	
1.2.a IP	Chapter 1
1.2.b TCP	Chapter 1
1.2.c UDP	Chapter 1
1.2.d ICMP	Chapter 1
1.3 Describe the operation of these network services:	
1.3.a ARP	Chapter 1
1.3.b DNS	Chapter 1
1.3.c DHCP	Chapter 1
1.4 Describe the basic operation of these network device types:	
1.4.a Router	Chapter 1
1.4.b Switch	Chapter 1
1.4.c Hub	Chapter 1
1.4.d Bridge	Chapter 1
1.4.e Wireless access point (WAP)	Chapter 1
1.4.f Wireless LAN controller (WLC)	Chapter 1
1.5 Describe the functions of these network security systems as deployed on the host, network, or the cloud:	
1.5.a Firewall	Chapter 2
1.5.b Cisco Intrusion Prevention System (IPS)	Chapter 2
1.5.c Cisco Advanced Malware Protection (AMP)	Chapter 2
1.5.d Web Security Appliance (WSA) / Cisco Cloud Web Security (CWS)	Chapter 2
1.5.e Email Security Appliance (ESA) / Cisco Cloud Email Security (CES)	Chapter 2
1.6 Describe IP subnets and communication within an IP subnet and between IP subnets	Chapter 1
1.7 Describe the relationship between VLANs and data visibility	Chapter 1
1.8 Describe the operation of ACLs applied as packet filters on the interfaces of network devices	Chapter 2
1.9 Compare and contrast deep packet inspection with packet filtering and stateful firewall operation	Chapter 2

Exam Topic	Chapter
1.10 Compare and contrast inline traffic interrogation and taps or traffic mirroring	Chapter 2
1.11 Compare and contrast the characteristics of data obtained from taps or traffic mirroring and NetFlow in the analysis of network traffic	Chapter 2
1.12 Identify potential data loss from provided traffic profiles	Chapter 2
2.0 Security Concepts	
2.1 Describe the principles of the defense-in-depth strategy	Chapter 3
2.2 Compare and contrast these concepts:	
2.2.a Risk	Chapter 3
2.2.b Threat	Chapter 3
2.2.c Vulnerability	Chapter 3
2.2.d Exploit	Chapter 3
2.3 Describe these terms:	
2.3.a Threat actor	Chapter 3
2.3.b Runbook automation (RBA)	Chapter 3
2.3.c Chain of custody (evidentiary)	Chapter 3
2.3.d Reverse engineering	Chapter 3
2.3.e Sliding window anomaly detection	Chapter 3
2.3.f PII	Chapter 3
2.3.g PHI	Chapter 3
2.4 Describe these security terms:	
2.4.a Principle of least privilege	Chapter 3
2.4.b Risk scoring/risk weighting	Chapter 3
2.4.c Risk reduction	Chapter 3
2.4.d Risk assessment	Chapter 3
2.5 Compare and contrast these access control models:	
2.5.a Discretionary access control	Chapter 4
2.5.b Mandatory access control	Chapter 4
2.5.c Nondiscretionary access control	Chapter 4
2.6 Compare and contrast these terms:	
2.6.a Network and host antivirus	Chapter 4
2.6.b Agentless and agent-based protections	Chapter 4

Exam Topic	Chapter
3.9.b X.509 certificates	Chapter 6
3.9.c Key exchange	Chapter 6
3.9.d Protocol version	Chapter 6
3.9.e PKCS	Chapter 6
4.0 Host-based Analysis	
4.1 Define these terms as they pertain to Microsoft Windows:	
4.1.a Processes	Chapter 8
4.1.b Threads	Chapter 8
4.1.c Memory allocation	Chapter 8
4.1.d Windows Registry	Chapter 8
4.1.e WMI	Chapter 8
4.1.f Handles	Chapter 8
4.1.g Services	Chapter 8
4.2 Define these terms as they pertain to Linux:	
4.2.a Processes	Chapter 9
4.2.b Forks	Chapter 9
4.2.c Permissions	Chapter 9
4.2.d Symlinks	Chapter 9
4.2.e Daemon	Chapter 9
4.3 Describe the functionality of these endpoint technologies in regard to security monitoring:	
4.3.a Host-based intrusion detection	Chapter 10
4.3.b Antimalware and antivirus	Chapter 10
4.3.c Host-based firewall	Chapter 10
4.3.d Application-level whitelisting/blacklisting	Chapter 10
4.3.e Systems-based sandboxing (such as Chrome, Java, Adobe Reader)	Chapter 10
4.4 Interpret these operating system log data to identify an event:	
4.4.a Windows security event logs	Chapter 8
4.4.b Unix-based syslog	Chapter 9
4.4.c Apache access logs	Chapter 9
4.4.d IIS access logs	Chapter 8

Exam Topic	Chapter
5.0 Security Monitoring	
5.1 Identify the types of data provided by these technologies:	
5.1.a TCP Dump	Chapter 11
5.1.b NetFlow	Chapter 11
5.1.c Next-gen firewall	Chapter 11
5.1.d Traditional stateful firewall	Chapter 11
5.1.e Application visibility and control	Chapter 11
5.1.f Web content filtering	Chapter 11
5.1.g Email content filtering	Chapter 11
5.2 Describe these types of data used in security monitoring:	
5.2.a Full packet capture	Chapter 11
5.2.b Session data	Chapter 11
5.2.c Transaction data	Chapter 11
5.2.d Statistical data	Chapter 11
5.2.e Extracted content	Chapter 11
5.2.f Alert data	Chapter 11
5.3 Describe these concepts as they relate to security monitoring:	
5.3.a Access control list	Chapter 12
5.3.b NAT/PAT	Chapter 12
5.3.c Tunneling	Chapter 12
5.3.d TOR	Chapter 12
5.3.e Encryption	Chapter 12
5.3.f P2P	Chapter 12
5.3.g Encapsulation	Chapter 12
5.3.h Load balancing	Chapter 12
5.4 Describe these NextGen IPS event types:	
5.4.a Connection event	Chapter 11
5.4.b Intrusion event	Chapter 11
5.4.c Host or endpoint event	Chapter 11
5.4.d Network discovery event	Chapter 11
5.4.e NetFlow event	Chapter 11

Exam Topic	Chapter
5.5 *Describe the function of these protocols in the context of security monitoring:*	
5.5.a DNS	Chapter 12
5.5.b NTP	Chapter 12
5.5.c SMTP/POP/IMAP	Chapter 12
5.5.d HTTP/HTTPS	Chapter 12
6.0 Attack Methods	
6.1 *Compare and contrast an attack surface and vulnerability*	Chapter 13
6.2 *Describe these network attacks:*	
6.2.a Denial of service	Chapter 13
6.2.b Distributed denial of service	Chapter 13
6.2.c Man-in-the-middle	Chapter 13
6.3 *Describe these web application attacks:*	
6.3.a SQL injection	Chapter 13
6.3.b Command injections	Chapter 13
6.3.c Cross-site scripting	Chapter 13
6.4 *Describe these attacks:*	
6.4.a Social engineering	Chapter 13
6.4.b Phishing	Chapter 13
6.4.c Evasion methods	Chapter 13
6.5 *Describe these endpoint-based attacks:*	
6.5.a Buffer overflows	Chapter 13
6.5.b Command and control (C2)	Chapter 13
6.5.c Malware	Chapter 13
6.5.d Rootkit	Chapter 13
6.5.e Port scanning	Chapter 13
6.5.f Host profiling	Chapter 13
6.6 *Describe these evasion methods:*	
6.6.a Encryption and tunneling	Chapter 14
6.6.b Resource exhaustion	Chapter 14
6.6.c Traffic fragmentation	Chapter 14
6.6.d Protocol-level misinterpretation	Chapter 14

Exam Topic	Chapter
6.6.e Traffic substitution and insertion	Chapter 14
6.6.f Pivot	Chapter 14
6.7 Define privilege escalation	Chapter 13
6.8 Compare and contrast a remote exploit and a local exploit	Chapter 13

About the CCNA Cyber Ops SECFND 210-250 Official Cert Guide

This book maps to the topic areas of the 210-250 SECFND exam and uses a number of features to help you understand the topics and prepare for the exam.

Objectives and Methods

This book uses several key methodologies to help you discover the exam topics on which you need more review, to help you fully understand and remember those details, and to help you prove to yourself that you have retained your knowledge of those topics. So, this book does not try to help you pass the exams only by memorization, but by truly learning and understanding the topics. This book is designed to help you pass the SECFND exam by using the following methods:

- Helping you discover which exam topics you have not mastered

- Providing explanations and information to fill in your knowledge gaps

- Supplying exercises that enhance your ability to recall and deduce the answers to test questions

- Providing practice exercises on the topics and the testing process via test questions on the companion website

Book Features

To help you customize your study time using this book, the core chapters have several features that help you make the best use of your time:

- **"Do I Know This Already?" quiz**: Each chapter begins with a quiz that helps you determine how much time you need to spend studying that chapter.

- **Foundation Topics**: These are the core sections of each chapter. They explain the concepts for the topics in that chapter.

- **Exam Preparation Tasks**: After the "Foundation Topics" section of each chapter, the "Exam Preparation Tasks" section lists a series of study activities that you should do at the end of the chapter. Each chapter includes the activities that make the most sense for studying the topics in that chapter:

  - **Review All the Key Topics**: The Key Topic icon appears next to the most important items in the "Foundation Topics" section of the chapter. The "Review All the Key Topics" activity lists the key topics from the chapter, along with their page numbers.

Although the contents of the entire chapter could be on the exam, you should definitely know the information listed in each key topic, so you should review these.

■ **Complete the Tables and Lists from Memory:** To help you memorize some lists of facts, many of the more important lists and tables from the chapter are included in a document on the companion website. This document lists only partial information, allowing you to complete the table or list.

■ **Define Key Terms:** Although the exam is unlikely to ask you to define a term, the CCNA Cyber Ops exams do require that you learn and know a lot of networking terminology. This section lists the most important terms from the chapter, asking you to write a short definition and compare your answer to the glossary at the end of the book.

■ **Q&A:** Confirm that you understand the content you just covered.

■ **Web-based practice exam:** The companion website includes the Pearson Cert Practice Test engine, which allows you to take practice exam questions. Use it to prepare with a sample exam and to pinpoint topics where you need more study.

How This Book Is Organized

This book contains 14 core chapters—Chapters 1 through 14. Chapter 15 includes some preparation tips and suggestions for how to approach the exam. Each core chapter covers a subset of the topics on the CCNA Cyber Ops SECFND exam. The core chapters are organized into parts. They cover the following topics:

Part I: Network Concepts

■ **Chapter 1: Fundamentals of Networking Protocols and Networking Devices** covers the networking technology fundamentals such as the OSI model and different protocols, including IP, TCP, UDP, ICMP, DNS, DHCP, ARP, and others. It also covers the basic operations of network infrastructure devices such as routers, switches, hubs, wireless access points, and wireless LAN controllers.

■ **Chapter 2: Network Security Devices and Cloud Services** covers the fundamentals of firewalls, intrusion prevention systems (IPSs), Advance Malware Protection (AMP), and fundamentals of the Cisco Web Security Appliance (WSA), Cisco Cloud Web Security (CWS), Cisco Email Security Appliance (ESA), and the Cisco Cloud Email Security (CES) service. This chapter also describes the operation of access control lists applied as packet filters on the interfaces of network devices and compares and contrasts deep packet inspection with packet filtering and stateful firewall operations. It provides details about inline traffic interrogation and taps or traffic mirroring. This chapter compares and contrasts the characteristics of data obtained from taps or traffic mirroring and NetFlow in the analysis of network traffic.

Part II: Security Concepts

■ **Chapter 3: Security Principles** covers the principles of the defense-in-depth strategy and compares and contrasts the concepts of risks, threats, vulnerabilities, and exploits. This chapter also defines threat actor, runbook automation (RBA), chain of custody

(evidentiary), reverse engineering, sliding window anomaly detection, personally identifiable information (PII), protected health information (PHI), as well as the principle of
least privilege and how to perform separation of duties. It also covers the concepts of
risk scoring, risk weighting, risk reduction, and how to perform overall risk assessments.

- **Chapter 4: Introduction to Access Controls** covers the foundation of access control
  and management. It provides an overview of authentication, authorization, and accounting principles, and introduces some of the most used access control models, including
  discretionary access control (DAC), mandatory access control (MAC), role-based access
  control (RBAC), and attribute-based access control (ABAC). Also, this chapter covers
  the actual implementation of access control, such as AAA protocols, port security,
  802.1x, Cisco TrustSec, intrusion prevention and detection, and antimalware.

- **Chapter 5: Introduction to Security Operations Management** covers the foundation
  of security operations management. Specifically, it provides an overview of identity
  management, protocol and technologies, asset security management, change and configuration management, mobile device management, event and logging management,
  including Security Information and Event Management (SIEM) technologies, vulnerability management, and patch management.

Part III: Cryptography

- **Chapter 6: Fundamentals of Cryptography and Public Key Infrastructure (PKI)** covers the different hashing and encryption algorithms in the industry. It provides a comparison of symmetric and asymmetric encryption algorithms and an introduction of
  public key infrastructure (PKI), the operations of a PKI, and an overview of the IPsec,
  SSL, and TLS protocols.

- **Chapter 7: Introduction to Virtual Private Networks (VPNs)** provides an introduction
  to remote access and site-to-site VPNs, different deployment scenarios, and the VPN
  solutions provided by Cisco.

Part IV: Host-based Analysis

- **Chapter 8: Windows-Based Analysis** covers the basics of how a system running
  Windows handles applications. This includes details about how memory is used as well
  as how resources are processed by the operating system. These skills are essential for
  maximizing performance and securing a Windows system.

- **Chapter 9: Linux- and Mac OS X–Based Analysis** covers how things work inside a
  UNIX environment. This includes process execution and event logging. Learning how
  the environment functions will not only improve your technical skills but can also be
  used to build a strategy for securing these systems.

- **Chapter 10: Endpoint Security Technologies** covers the functionality of endpoint
  security technologies, including host-based intrusion detection, host-based firewalls,
  application-level whitelisting and blacklisting, as well as systems-based sandboxing.

Part V: Security Monitoring and Attack Methods

- **Chapter 11: Network and Host Telemetry** covers the different types of data provided
  by network and host-based telemetry technologies, including NetFlow, traditional and
  next-generation firewalls, packet captures, application visibility and control, and web

and email content filtering. It also provides an overview of how full packet captures, session data, transaction logs, and security alert data are used in security operations and security monitoring.

- **Chapter 12: Security Monitoring Operational Challenges** covers the different operational challenges, including Tor, access control lists, tunneling, peer-to-peer (P2P) communication, encapsulation, load balancing, and other technologies.

- **Chapter 13: Types of Attacks and Vulnerabilities** covers the different types of cyber security attacks and vulnerabilities and how they are carried out by threat actors nowadays.

- **Chapter 14: Security Evasion Techniques** covers how attackers obtain stealth as well as the tricks used to negatively impact detection and forensic technologies. Topics include encryption, exhausting resources, fragmenting traffic, manipulating protocols, and pivoting within a compromised environment.

Part VI: Final Preparation

- **Chapter 15: Final Preparation** identifies the tools for final exam preparation and helps you develop an effective study plan. It contains tips on how to best use the web-based material to study.

Part VII: Appendixes

- **Appendix A: Answers to the "Do I Know This Already?" Quizzes and Q&A Questions** includes the answers to all the questions from Chapters 1 through 14.

- **Appendix B: Memory Tables** (a website-only appendix) contains the key tables and lists from each chapter, with some of the contents removed. You can print this appendix and, as a memory exercise, complete the tables and lists. The goal is to help you memorize facts that can be useful on the exam. This appendix is available in PDF format at the book website; it is not in the printed book.

- **Appendix C: Memory Tables Answer Key** (a website-only appendix) contains the answer key for the memory tables in Appendix B. This appendix is available in PDF format at the book website; it is not in the printed book.

- **Appendix D: Study Planner** is a spreadsheet, available from the book website, with major study milestones, where you can track your progress throughout your study.

Companion Website

Register this book to get access to the Pearson Test Prep practice test software and other study materials, plus additional bonus content. Check this site regularly for new and updated postings written by the authors that provide further insight into the more troublesome topics on the exam. Be sure to check the box that you would like to hear from us to receive updates and exclusive discounts on future editions of this product or related products.

To access this companion website, follow these steps:

1. Go to www.pearsonITcertification.com/register and log in or create a new account.

2. Enter the ISBN 9781587147029.

3. Answer the challenge question as proof of purchase.

4. Click the "Access Bonus Content" link in the Registered Products section of your account page, to be taken to the page where your downloadable content is available.

Please note that many of our companion content files can be very large, especially image and video files.

If you are unable to locate the files for this title by following the steps, please visit www.pearsonITcertification.com/contact and select the "Site Problems/Comments" option. Our customer service representatives will assist you.

Pearson Test Prep Practice Test Software

As noted previously, this book comes complete with the Pearson Test Prep practice test software containing two full exams. These practice tests are available to you either online or as an offline Windows application. To access the practice exams that were developed with this book, please see the instructions in the card inserted in the sleeve in the back of the book. This card includes a unique access code that enables you to activate your exams in the Pearson Test Prep software.

Accessing the Pearson Test Prep Software Online

The online version of this software can be used on any device with a browser and connectivity to the Internet, including desktop machines, tablets, and smartphones. To start using your practice exams online, simply follow these steps:

1. Go to http://www.PearsonTestPrep.com.

2. Select **Pearson IT Certification** as your product group.

3. Enter your email/password for your account. If you don't have an account on PearsonITCertification.com or CiscoPress.com, you will need to establish one by going to PearsonITCertification.com/join.

4. In the My Products tab, click the **Activate New Product** button.

5. Enter the access code printed on the insert card in the back of your book to activate your product.

6. The product will now be listed in your My Products page. Click the **Exams** button to launch the exam settings screen and start your exam.

Accessing the Pearson Test Prep Software Offline

If you wish to study offline, you can download and install the Windows version of the Pearson Test Prep software. There is a download link for this software on the book's companion website, or you can just enter the following link in your browser:

http://www.pearsonitcertification.com/content/downloads/pcpt/engine.zip

To access the book's companion website and the software, simply follow these steps:

1. Register your book by going to PearsonITCertification.com/register and entering the ISBN 9781587147029.

2. Respond to the challenge questions.

3. Go to your account page and select the **Registered Products** tab.

4. Click the **Access Bonus Content** link under the product listing.

5. Click the **Install Pearson Test Prep Desktop Version** link under the Practice Exams section of the page to download the software.

6. Once the software finishes downloading, unzip all the files on your computer.

7. Double-click the application file to start the installation, and follow the onscreen instructions to complete the registration.

8. Once the installation is complete, launch the application and select **Activate Exam** button on the My Products tab.

9. Click the **Activate a Product button** in the Activate Product Wizard.

10. Enter the unique access code found on the card in the sleeve in the back of your book and click the **Activate** button.

11. Click **Next** and then the **Finish** button to download the exam data to your application.

12. You can now start using the practice exams by selecting the product and clicking the **Open Exam** button to open the exam settings screen.

Note that the offline and online versions will synch together, so saved exams and grade results recorded on one version will be available to you on the other as well.

Customizing Your Exams

Once you are in the exam settings screen, you can choose to take exams in one of three modes:

- Study mode
- Practice Exam mode
- Flash Card mode

Study mode allows you to fully customize your exams and review answers as you are taking the exam. This is typically the mode you would use first to assess your knowledge and identify information gaps. Practice Exam mode locks certain customization options, as it is presenting a realistic exam experience. Use this mode when you are preparing to test your exam readiness. Flash Card mode strips out the answers and presents you with only the question stem. This mode is great for late-stage preparation when you really want to challenge yourself to provide answers without the benefit of seeing multiple-choice options. This mode will not provide the detailed score reports that the other two modes will, so it should not be used if you are trying to identify knowledge gaps.

In addition to these three modes, you will be able to select the source of your questions. You can choose to take exams that cover all of the chapters or you can narrow your selection to just a single chapter or the chapters that make up a specific part in the book. All chapters are selected by default. If you want to narrow your focus to individual chapters, simply deselect all the chapters then select only those on which you wish to focus in the Objectives area.

You can also select the exam banks on which to focus. Each exam bank comes complete with a full exam of questions that cover topics in every chapter. The two exams printed in the book are available to you as well as two additional exams of unique questions. You can have the test engine serve up exams from all four banks or just from one individual bank by selecting the desired banks in the exam bank area.

There are several other customizations you can make to your exam from the exam settings screen, such as the time of the exam, the number of questions served up, whether to randomize questions and answers, whether to show the number of correct answers for multiple-answer questions, and whether to serve up only specific types of questions. You can also create custom test banks by selecting only questions that you have marked or questions on which you have added notes.

Updating Your Exams

If you are using the online version of the Pearson Test Prep software, you should always have access to the latest version of the software as well as the exam data. If you are using the Windows desktop version, every time you launch the software, it will check to see if there are any updates to your exam data and automatically download any changes that were made since the last time you used the software. This requires that you are connected to the Internet at the time you launch the software.

Sometimes, due to many factors, the exam data may not fully download when you activate your exam. If you find that figures or exhibits are missing, you may need to manually update your exam.

To update a particular exam you have already activated and downloaded, simply select the **Tools** tab and select the **Update Products** button. Again, this is only an issue with the desktop Windows application.

If you wish to check for updates to the Pearson Test Prep software, Windows desktop version, simply select the **Tools** tab and select the **Update Application** button. This will ensure you are running the latest version of the software engine.

This chapter covers the following topics:

- Introduction to TCP/IP and OSI models

- Wired LAN and Ethernet

- Frame switching

- Hub, switch, and router

- Wireless LAN and technologies

- Wireless LAN controller and access point

- IPv4 and IPv6 addressing

- IP routing

- ARP, DHCP, ICMP, and DNS

- Transport layer protocols

Fundamentals of Networking Protocols and Networking Devices

Welcome to the first chapter of the *CCNA Cyber Ops SECFND #210-250 Official Cert Guide*. In this chapter, we go through the fundamentals of networking protocols and explore how devices such as switches and routers work to allow two hosts to communicate with each other, even if they are separated by many miles.

If you are already familiar with these topics—for example, if you already have a CCNA Routing and Switching certification—this chapter will serve as a refresher on protocols and device operations. If, on the other hand, you are approaching these topics for the first time, you'll learn about the fundamental protocols and devices at the base of Internet communication and how they work.

This chapter begins with an introduction to the TCP/IP and OSI models and then explores link layer technologies and protocols—specifically the Ethernet and Wireless LAN technologies. We then discuss how the Internet Protocol (IP) works and how a router uses IP to move packets from one site to another. Finally, we look into the two most used transport layer protocols: Transmission Control Protocol (TCP) and User Datagram Protocol (UDP).

"Do I Know This Already?" Quiz

The "Do I Know This Already?" quiz helps you identify your strengths and deficiencies in this chapter's topics. The 13-question quiz, derived from the major sections in the "Foundation Topics" portion of the chapter, helps you determine how to spend your limited study time. You can find the answers in Appendix A Answers to the "Do I Know This Already?" Quizzes and Q&A Questions.

Table 1-1 outlines the major topics discussed in this chapter and the "Do I Know This Already?" quiz questions that correspond to those topics.

Table 1-1 "Do I Know This Already?" Section-to-Question Mapping

Foundation Topics Section	Questions
TCP/IP and OSI Model	1
Layer 2 Fundamentals and Technologies	2–5
Internet Protocol and Layer 3 Technologies	6, 7, 9
Domain Name System (DNS)	8
IPv6 Fundamentals	10–11
Transport Layer Technologies and Protocols	12–13

1. Which layer of the TCP/IP model is concerned with end-to-end communication and offers multiplexing service?

   a. Transport

   b. Internet

   c. Link layer

   d. Application

2. Which statement is true concerning a link working in Ethernet half-duplex mode?

   a. A collision cannot happen.

   b. When a collision happens, the two stations immediately retransmit.

   c. When a collision happens, the two stations wait for a random time before retransmitting.

   d. To avoid a collision, stations wait a random time before transmitting.

3. What is the main characteristic of a hub?

   a. It regenerates the signal and retransmits on all ports.

   b. It uses a MAC address table to switch frames.

   c. When a packet arrives, the hub looks up the routing table before forwarding the packet.

   d. It supports full-duplex mode of transmission.

4. Where is the information about ports and device Layer 2 addresses kept in a switch?

   a. MAC address table

   b. Routing table

   c. L2 address table

   d. Port table

5. Which of the following features are implemented by a wireless LAN controller? (Select all that apply.)

   a. Wireless station authentication

   b. Quality of Service

   c. Channel encryption

   d. Transmission and reception of frames

6. Which IP header field is used to recognize fragments from the same packet?

   a. Identification

   b. Fragment Offset

   c. Flags

   d. Destination Address

7. Which protocol is used to request a host MAC address given a known IP address?

   a. ARP

   b. DHCP

   c. ARPv6

   d. DNS

8. Which type of query is sent from a DNS resolver to a DNS server?

   a. Recursive

   b. Iterative

   c. Simple

   d. Type Q query

9. How many host IPv4 addresses are possible in a /25 network?

   a. 126

   b. 128

   c. 254

   d. 192

10. How many bits can be used for host IPv6 addresses assignment in the 2345::/64 network?

   a. 48

   b. 64

   c. 16

   d. 2^{64}

11. What is SLAAC used for?

   a. To provide an IPv6 address to a client

   b. To route IPv6 packets

   c. To assign a DNS server

   d. To provide a MAC address given an IP address

12. Which one of these protocols requires a connection to be established before transmitting data?

   a. TCP

   b. UDP

   c. IP

   d. OSPF

13. What is the TCP window field used for?

   a. Error detection

   b. Flow control

   c. Fragmentation

   d. Multiplexing

Foundation Topics

TCP/IP and OSI Model

Two main models are currently used to explain the operation of an IP-based network. These are the TCP/IP model and the Open System Interconnection (OSI) model. This section provides an overview of these two models.

TCP/IP Model

The TCP/IP model is the foundation for most of the modern communication networks. Every day, each of us uses some application based on the TCP/IP model to communicate. Think, for example, about a task we consider simple: browsing a web page. That simple action would not be possible without the TCP/IP model.

The TCP/IP model's name includes the two main protocols we will discuss in the course of this chapter: Transmission Control Protocol (TCP) and Internet Protocol (IP). However, the model goes beyond these two protocols and defines a layered approach that can map nearly any protocol used in today's communication.

In its original definition, the TCP/IP model included four layers, where each of the layers would provide transmission and other services for the level above it. These are the link layer, internet layer, transport layer, and application layer.

In its most modern definition, the link layer is split into two additional layers to clearly demark the physical and data link type of services and protocols included in this layer. Internet layer is also sometimes called the networking layer, which is based on another very known model, the OSI model, which is described in the next section. Figure 1-1 shows the TCP/IP stack model.

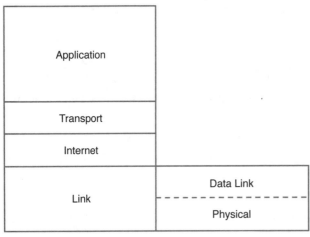

Figure 1-1 *TCP/IP Stack Model*

The TCP/IP model works on two main concepts that define how the layers interact:

■ On the same host, each layer works by providing services for the layer above it on the TCP/IP stack.

■ On different hosts, a same layer communication is established by using the same layer protocol.

For example, on your personal computer, the TCP/IP stack is implemented to allow networking communication. The link layer provides services for the IP layer (for example, encapsulation of an IP packet in an Ethernet frame). The IP layer provides services to the transport layer (for example, IP routing and IP addressing), and so on. These are all examples of services provided to the layer above it within the host.

Now imagine that your personal computer wants to connect to a web server (for example, to browse a web page). The web server will also implement the TCP/IP stack. In this case, the IP layer of your personal computer and the IP layer of the web server will use a common protocol, IP, for the communication. The same thing will happen with the transport protocol, where the two devices will use TCP, and so on. These are examples of the same layer protocol used on different hosts to communicate.

Later in this chapter, the "Networking Communication with the TCP/IP Model," section provides more detail about how the communication works between two hosts and how the TCP/IP stack is used on the same host.

The list that follows analyzes each layer in a bit more detail:

■ **Link layer:** The link layer provides physical transmission support and includes the protocols used to transmit information over a link between two devices. In simple terms, the link layer includes the hardware and protocol necessary to send information between two hosts that are connected by a physical link (for example, a cable) or over the air (for example, via radio waves). It also includes the notion of and mechanisms for information being replicated and retransmitted over several ports or links by dedicated devices such as switches and bridges.

Because different physical means are used to transmit information, there are several protocols that work at the link layer. One of the most popular is the Ethernet protocol. As mentioned earlier, nowadays the link layer is usually split further in the physical layer, which is concerned about physical bit transmission, and the data link layer, which provides encapsulation and addressing facilities as well as abstraction for the upper layers.

At link layer, the message unit is called a *frame*.

■ **Internet layer:** Of course, not all devices can be directly connected to each other, so there is a need to transmit the information across multiple devices. The Internet layer provides networking services and includes protocols that allow for the transmission of information through multiple hops. To do that, each host is identified by an Internet Protocol (IP) address, or a different address if another Internet Protocol type is used. Each hop device between two hosts, called *networking nodes*, knows how to reach the destination IP address and transmit the information to the next best node to reach the destination. The nodes are said to perform the *routing* of the information, and the way each node, also called *router*, determines the best next node to the destination is called the *routing protocol*.

At the Internet layer, the message unit is called a *packet*.

- **Transport layer:** When transmitting information, the sending host knows when the information is sent, but has no way to know whether it actually made it to the destination. The transport layer provides services to successfully transfer information between two end points. It abstracts the lower-level layer and is concerned about the end-to-end process. For example, it is used to detect whether any part of the information went missing. It also provides information about which type of information is being transmitted. For example, a host may want to request a web page and also start an FTP transaction. How do we distinguish between these two actions? The transport layer helps to separate the two requests by using the concept of a transport layer port. Each service is enabled on a different transport layer port—for example, port 80 for a web request or port 21 for an FTP transaction. So when the destination host receives a request on port 80, it knows that this needs to be passed to the application layer handling web requests. This type of service provided by the transport layer is called *multiplexing*.

  At this layer, the message unit is called a *segment*.

- **Application layer:** The application layer is the top layer and is the one most familiar to end users. For example, at the application layer, a user may use the email client to send an email message or use a web browser to browse a website. Both of these actions map to a specific application, which uses a protocol to fulfill the service.

  In this example, the Simple Message Transfer Protocol (SMTP) is used to handle the email transfer, whereas the Hypertext Transfer Protocol (HTTP) is used to request a web page within a browser. At this level, the protocols are not concerned with how the information will reach the destination, but only work on defining the content of the information being transmitted.

Table 1-2 shows examples of protocols working at each layer of the TCP/IP model.

Table 1-2   Protocols at Each Layer of the TCP/IP Model

TCP/IP Layer	Protocols
Link	Ethernet, Point-to-Point (PPP)
Internet	IP
Transport	TCP/UDP
Application	HTTP, SMTP, FTP

Table 1-3 summarizes what message units are referred to as at each layer.

Table 1-3   Message Unit Naming at Each Layer of the TCP/IP Model

TCP/IP Layer	Protocols
Link	Frame
Internet	Packet
Transport	Segment
Application	Application data

TCP/IP Model Encapsulation

In the TCP/IP model, each layer provides services for the level above it. Protocols at each layer include a protocol header and in some cases a trailer to the information provided by the upper layer. The protocol header includes enough information for the protocol to work toward the delivery of the information. This process is called *encapsulation*.

When the information arrives to the destination, the inverse process is used. Each layer reads the information present in the header of the protocol working at that specific layer, performs an action based on that information, and, if needed, passes the remaining information to the next layer in the stack. This process is called *decapsulation*.

Figure 1-2 shows an example of encapsulation.

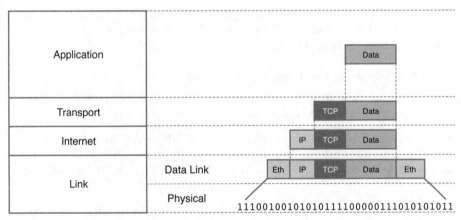

Figure 1-2   *Encapsulation*

Referring to Figure 1-2, let's assume that this represents the TCP/IP stack of a host, for example Host A, trying to request a web page using HTTP. Let's see how the encapsulation works, step by step:

Step 1.   In this example, the host has requested a web page using the HTTP application layer protocol. The HTTP application generates the information, represented as HTTP "data" in this example.

Step 2.   On the host, the TCP/IP implementation would detect that HTTP uses TCP at the transport layer and will send the HTTP data to the transport layer for further handling. The protocol at the transport layer, TCP, will create a TCP header, which includes information such as the service port (TCP port 80 for a web page request), and will send it to the next layer, the Internet layer, for further processing. The TCP header plus the payload forms a TCP segment.

Step 3.   The Internet layer receives the TCP information, attaches an IP header, and encapsulates it in an IP packet. The IP header will contain information to handle the packet at the Internet layer. This includes, for example, the IP addresses of the source and destination.

Step 4.   The IP packet is then passed to the link layer for further processing. The TCP/IP stack detects that it needs to use Ethernet to transmit the frame to the next device. It will add an Ethernet header and trailer and transmit the frame to the physical network interface card (NIC), which will take care of the physical transmission of the frame.

When the information arrives to the destination, the receiving host will start from the bottom of the TCP/IP stack by receiving an Ethernet frame. The link layer of the destination host will read and process the header and trailer, and then pass the IP packet to the Internet layer for further processing.

The same process happens at the Internet layer, and the TCP segment is passed to the transport layer, which will again process the TCP header information and pass the HTTP data for final processing to the HTTP application.

Networking Communication with the TCP/IP Model

Let's look back at the example of browsing a web page and see how the TCP/IP model is used to transmit and receive information through a networking connection path.

A *networking device* is a device that implements the TCP/IP model. The model may be fully implemented (for example, in the case of a user computer or a server) or partially implemented (for example, a router might implement the TCP/IP stack only up to the Internet layer).

Figure 1-3 shows the logical topology. It includes two hosts: Host A, which is requesting a web page, and Server B, which is the destination of the request. The network connectivity is provided by two routers: R1 and R2, which are connected via an optical link. The host and server are directly connected to R1 and R2, respectively, with a physical cable.

Host A   R1   R2   Server B

Figure 1-3   *Logical Topology Demonstrating Networking Communication with TCP/IP Model*

Figure 1-4 shows how each TCP/IP model layer interacts in this case.

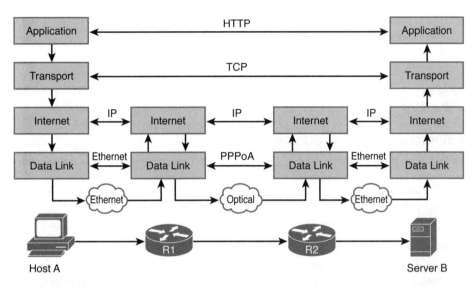

Figure 1-4 *Interaction of the TCP/IP Model Layers*

Referring to Figure 1-4, let's see how the steps are executed:

Step 1.   The HTTP application on Host A will create an HTTP Application message that includes an HTTP header and the contents of the request in the payload. This will be encapsulated up to the link layer, as described in Figure 1-2, and transmitted over the cable to R1.

Step 2.   The R1 link layer will receive the frame, extract the IP packet, and send it to the IP layer. Because the main function of the router is to forward the IP packet, it will not further decapsulate the packet. It will use the information in the IP header to forward the packet to the best next router, R2. To do that, it will encapsulate the IP packet in a new link layer frame—for example, Point-to-Point over ATM (PPPoA)—and send the frame on the physical link toward R2.

Step 3.   R2 will follow the same process that R1 followed in step 2 and will send the IP packet encapsulated in a new Ethernet frame to Host B.

Step 4.   Server B's link layer will decapsulate the frame and send it to the Internet layer.

Step 5.   The Internet layer detects that the packet is destined to Server B itself by looking into the IP header information (more specifically the value of the destination IP address). It strips the IP header and passes the TCP segment to the transport layer.

Step 6.   The transport layer uses the port information included in the TCP header to determine to which application to pass the data (in this case, the web service application).

Step 7. The application layer, the web service, finally receives the request and may decide to respond (for example, by providing the web page to Host A). The process will start again, with the web service creating some data and passing it to the HTTP application layer protocol for handling.

The example in Figure 1-4 is very simplistic. For example, TCP requires a connection to be established before transmitting data. However, it is important that the main idea behind the TCP/IP model is clear as a basis for understanding how the various protocols work.

Open System Interconnection Model

The Open System Interconnection (OSI) reference model is another model that uses abstraction layers to represent the operation of communication systems. The idea behind the design of the OSI model is to be comprehensive enough to take into account advancement in network communications and to be general enough to allow several existing models for communication systems to transition to the OSI model.

The OSI model presents several similarities with the TCP/IP model described in the previous section. One of the most important similarities is the use of abstraction layers. As with TCP/IP, each layer provides service for the layer above it within the same computing device, while it interacts at the same layer with other computing devices.

The OSI model includes seven abstract layers, each representing a different function and service within a communication network:

- **Physical layer—Layer 1 (L1):** Provides services for the transmission of bits over the data link.

- **Data link layer—Layer 2 (L2):** Includes protocols and functions to transmit information over a link between two connected devices. For example, it provides flow control and L1 error detection.

- **Network layer—Layer 3 (L3):** This layer includes the function necessary to transmit information across a network and provides abstraction on the underlying means of connection. It defines L3 addressing, routing, and packet forwarding.

- **Transport layer—Layer 4 (L4):** This layer includes services for end-to-end connection establishment and information delivery. For example, it includes error detection, retransmission capabilities, and multiplexing.

- **Session layer—Layer 5 (L5):** This layer provides services to the presentation layer to establish a session and exchange presentation layer data.

- **Presentation layer—Layer 6 (L6):** This layer provides services to the application layer to deal with specific syntax, which is how data is presented to the end user.

- **Application layer—Layer 7 (L7):** This is the last (or first) layer of the OSI model (depending on how you see it). It includes all the services of a user application, including the interaction with the end user.

The functionalities of the OSI layers can be mapped to similar functionalities provided by the TCP/IP model. It is sometimes common to use OSI layer terminology to indicate a protocol operating at a specific layer, even if the communication device implements the TCP/IP model instead of the OSI model.

Figure 1-5 shows how each layer of the OSI model maps to the corresponding TCP/IP layer.

OSI Model	TCP/IP
Application	Application
Presentation	
Session	
Transport	Transport
Network	Internet
Data Link	Link
Physical	

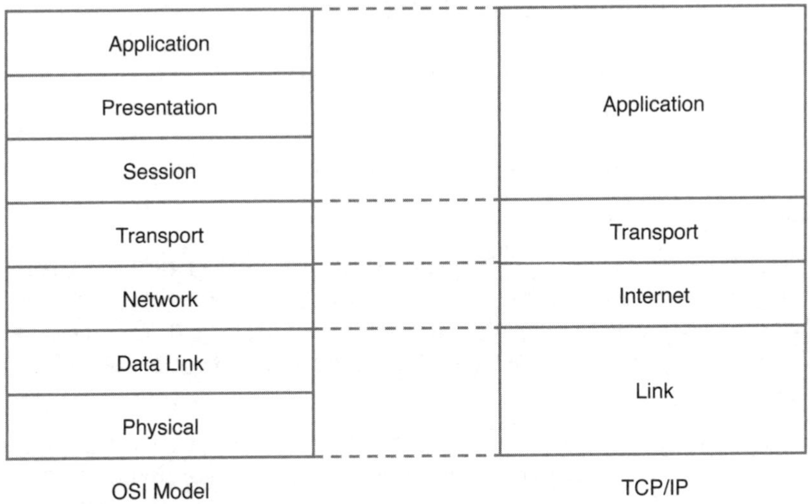

Figure 1-5   *Mapping the OSI Reference Model to the TCP/IP Model*

The physical and data link layers of the OSI model provide the same functions as the link layer in the TCP/IP model. The network layer can be mapped to the Internet layer, and the transport layer in OSI provides similar services as the transport layer in TCP/IP. The OSI session, presentation, and application layers map to the TCP/IP application layer.

Within the same host, each layer interacts with the adjacent layer in a way that is similar to the encapsulation performed in the TCP/IP model. The encapsulation is formalized in the OSI model as follows:

- Protocol control information (PCI) for a layer (N) is the information added by the protocol.
- A protocol data unit (PDU) for a layer (N) is composed by the data produced at that layer plus the PCI for that layer.
- A service data unit (SDU) for a layer (N) is the (N+1) layer PDU.

Figure 1-6 shows the relationship between PCI, PDU, and SDU.

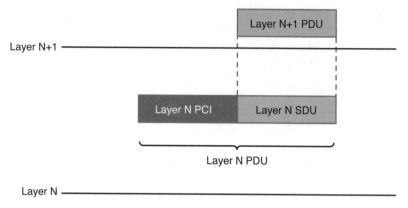

Figure 1-6 *Relationship Between PCI, PDU, and SDU*

For example, a TCP segment includes the TCP header, which maps to the L4PCI and a TCP payload, including the data to transmit. Together, they form a L4PDU. When the L4PDU is passed to the networking layer (for example, to be processed by IP), the L4PDU is the same as the L3SDU. IP will add an IP header, the L3PCI. The L3PCI plus the L3SDU will form the L3PDU, and so on.

The encapsulation process works in a similar way to the TCP/IP model. Each layer protocol adds its own protocol header and passes the information to the lower-layer protocol.

Figure 1-7 shows an example of encapsulation in the OSI model.

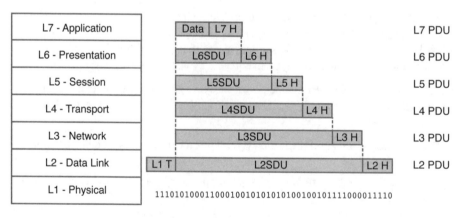

Figure 1-7 *Encapsulation in the OSI Model*

Table 1-4 shows examples of protocols and devices that work at a specific OSI layer. Note that each device is mapped to a level related to its main function capability. For example, a router's main function is forwarding packets based on L3 information, so it is usually referred to as an L3 device; however, it also needs to incorporate L2 and L1 functionalities. Furthermore, a router may implement the full OSI model (for example, because it implements some additional features such as firewalling or VPN). The same rationale could be applied to firewalls. They are usually classified as L4 devices; however, most of the time they are able to inspect traffic up to the application layer.

Table 1-4   Protocols and Devices Mapping to the OSI Layer Model and the TCP/IP Model

OSI Layer Model	TCP/IP Model	Protocols	Devices
Application	Application	FTP, HTTP, SMTP	Host, servers
Presentation			
Session			
Transport	Transport	TCP, UDP	Stateful firewalls
Network	IP	IP	Router
Data Link	Link	Ethernet, PPP, ATM	Switches
Physical		Ethernet (physical layer), cable, optical	Repeater

The flow of information through a network in the OSI model is similar to what's described in Figure 1-4 for the TCP/IP model. This is not by chance, because the OSI model has been designed to offer compatibility and enable the transition to the OSI model from multiple other communication models (for example, from TCP/IP).

Figure 1-8 shows a network implementing the OSI model.

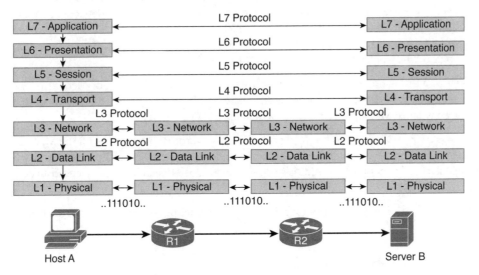

Figure 1-8   *Flow of Information Through a Network Implementing the OSI Model*

In the rest of this book, we will use the OSI model and TCP/IP model layer names interchangeably.

Layer 2 Fundamentals and Technologies

This section goes through the fundamentals of the link layer (or Layer 2). Although it is not required to know specific implementations and configurations, the CCNA Cyber Ops SECFND exam requires candidates to understand the various link layer technologies, such as hubs, bridges, and switches, and their behavior. Candidates also need to understand the protocols that enable the link layer communication. Readers interested in learning more about Layer 2 technologies and protocols can refer to CCNA Routing and Switching materials for more comprehensive information on the topic.

Two very well-known concepts used to describe communication networks at Layer 2 are local area network (LAN) and wide area network (WAN). As the names suggest, a LAN is a collection of devices, protocols, and technologies operating nearby each other, whereas a WAN typically deals with devices, protocols, and technologies used to transmit information over a long distance.

The next sections introduce two of the most used LAN types: wired LANs (specifically Ethernet-based LANs) and wireless LANs.

Ethernet LAN Fundamentals and Technologies

Ethernet is a protocol used to provide transmission and services for the physical and data link layers, and it is described in the IEEE 802.3 standards collection. Ethernet is part of the larger IEEE 802 standards for LAN communication. Another example of the IEEE 802 standards is 802.11, which covers wireless LAN.

The Ethernet collection includes standards specifying the functionality at the physical layer and data link layer. The Ethernet physical layer includes several standards, depending on the physical means used to transmit the information. The data link layer functionality is provided by the Ethernet Medium Access Control (MAC) described in IEEE 802.3, together with the Logical Link Control (LLC) described in IEEE 802.2.

Note that MAC is sometimes referred to as Media Access Control instead of Medium Access Control. Both ways are correct according to the IEEE 802. In the rest of this document we will use Medium Access Control or simply MAC.

LLC was initially used to allow several types of Layer 3 protocols to work with the MAC. However, in most networks in use today, there is only one type of Layer 3 protocol, which is the Internet Protocol (IP), so LLC is seldom used because IP can be directly encapsulated using MAC.

The following sections provide an overview of the Ethernet physical layer and MAC layer standards.

Ethernet Physical Layer

The physical layer includes several standards to account for the various physical means possibly encountered in a LAN deployment. For example, the transmission can happen over an optical fiber, copper, and so on.

1

Examples of Ethernet standards are 10BASE-T and 1000BASE-LX. Each Ethernet standard is characterized by the maximum transmission speed and maximum distance between two connected stations. Specifically, the transmission speed has seen (and is currently seeing) the biggest evolution.

Table 1-5 shows examples of popular Ethernet physical layer standards.

Table 1-5   Popular Ethernet Physical Layer Standards

Name	IEEE standard	Speed	Media	Maximum Distance
10BASE-T	802.3 (Ethernet)	10 Mbps	Twisted pair (copper)	100 m
100BASE-T	802.3u (FastEthernet)	100 Mbps	Twisted pair (copper)	100 m
1000BASE-T	802.3ab (GigaEthernet)	1000 Mbps	Twisted pair (copper)	100 m
1000BASE-LX	802.3z (GigaEthernet)	1000 Mbps	Long wavelength (single-mode fiber)	5 km
10GBASE-T	802.3an (10 Gigabit Ethernet)	10 GBps	Twisted pair (copper)	100 m

The Ethernet nomenclature is easy to understand. Each standard name follows this format:

   sTYPE-M

where:

- **s:** The speed (for example, 1000).
- **TYPE:** The modulation type (for example, baseband [BASE]).
- **M:** The information about the medium. Examples include T for twisted pair, F for fiber, L for long wavelength, and X for external sourced coding.

For example, with 1000BASE-T, the speed is 1000, the modulation is baseband, and the medium (T) is twisted-pair cable (copper).

An additional characteristic of a physical Ethernet standard is the type of cable and connector used to connect two stations. For example, 1000BASE-T would need a Category 6 (CAT 6) unshielded twisted-pair cable (UTP) and RJ-45 connectors.

Ethernet Medium Access Control

Ethernet MAC deals with the means used to transfer information between two Ethernet devices, also called stations, and it is independent from the physical means used for transmission.

The standard describes two modes of medium access:

- **Half duplex:** In half-duplex mode, two Ethernet devices share a common transmission medium. The access is controlled by implementing Carrier Sense Multiple Access with Collision Detection (CSMA/CD). In CSMA/CD, a device has the ability to detect whether there is a transmission occurring over the shared medium. When there is no transmission, a device can start sending. It can happen that two devices send nearly at the same time. In that case, there is a message collision. When a collision occurs, it is detected by CSMA/CD-enabled devices, which will then stop transmitting and will delay the transmission for a certain amount of time, called the *backoff time*. The jam signal is used by the station to signal that a collision occurred. All stations that can sense a collision are said to be in the same collision domain.

Half-duplex mode was used in early implementations of Ethernet; however, due to several limitations, including transmission performance, it is rarely seen nowadays. A network hub is an example of a device that can be used to share a common transmission medium across multiple Ethernet stations. You'll learn more about hubs later in this chapter in the "LAN Hubs and Bridges" section.

Figure 1-9 shows an example of CSMA/CD access.

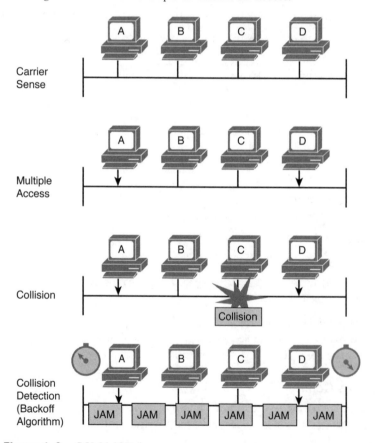

Figure 1-9   *CSMA/CD Access*

■ **Full duplex:** In full-duplex mode, two devices can transmit simultaneously because there is a dedicated channel allocated for the transmission. Because of that, there is no need to detect collisions or to wait before transmitting. Full duplex is called "collision free" because collisions cannot happen.

A switch is an example of a device that provides a collision-free domain and dedicated transmission channel. You'll learn more about switches later in this chapter in the "LAN Switches" section.

Ethernet Frame

Figure 1-10 shows an example of an Ethernet frame.

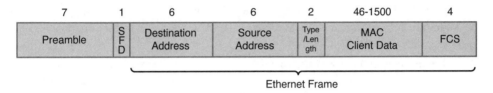

Figure 1-10 *Ethernet Frame*

The Ethernet frame includes the following fields:

- **Preamble:** Used for the two stations for synchronization purposes.
- **Start Frame Delimiter (SFD):** Indicates the start of the Ethernet frame. This is always set to 10101011.
- **Destination Address:** Contains the recipient address of the frame.
- **Source Address:** Contains the source of the frame.
- **Length/Type:** This field can contain either the length of the MAC Client Data (length interpretation) or the type code of the Layer 3 protocol transported in the frame payload (type interpretation). The latter is the most common. For example, code 0800 indicates IPv4, and code 08DD indicates IPv6.
- **MAC Client Data and Pad:** This field contains information being encapsulated at the Ethernet layer (for example, an LLC PDU or an IP packet). The minimum length is 46 bytes; the maximum length depends on the type of Ethernet frame:
    - 1500 bytes for basic frames. This is the most common Ethernet frame.
    - 1504 bytes for Q-tagged frames.
    - 1982 bytes for envelope frames.
- **Frame Check Sequence (FCS):** This field is used by the receiving device to detect errors in transmission. This is usually called the Ethernet trailer. Optionally, an additional extension may be present.

Ethernet Addresses

To transmit a frame, Ethernet uses source and destination addresses. The Ethernet addresses are called MAC addresses, or Extended Unique Identifier (EUI) in the new terminology, and they are either 48 bits (MAC-48 or EUI-48) or 64 bits (MAC-64 or EUI-64), if we consider all MAC addresses for the larger IEEE 802 standard.

The MAC address is usually expressed in hexadecimal. There are few ways it can be written for easier reading. The following two ways are the ones used the most:

- 01-23-45-67-89-ab (IEEE 802)
- 0123.4567.89ab (Cisco notation)

There are three types of MAC addresses:

- **Broadcast:** A broadcast MAC address is obtained by setting all 1s in the MAC address field. This results in an address like FFFF.FFFF.FFFF. A frame with a broadcast destination address is transmitted to all the devices within a LAN.
- **Multicast:** A frame with a multicast destination MAC address is transmitted to all frames belonging to the specific group.
- **Unicast:** A unicast address is associated with a particular device's NIC or port. It is composed of two sections. The first 24 bits contain the Organizational Unique Identifier (OUI) assigned to an organization. Although this is unique for an organization, the same organization can request several OUIs. For example, Cisco has multiple registered OUIs. The other portion of the MAC address (for example, the remaining 24 bits in the case of MAC-48) can be assigned by the vendor itself.

Figure 1-11 shows the two portions of a MAC address.

MAC-48 Address

24 Bits	24 Bits
OUI Assigned	Vendor Assigned

Figure 1-11 *MAC Address Portions*

Ethernet Devices and Frame-Forwarding Behavior

So far we have discussed the basic concepts of Ethernet, such as frame formats and addresses. It is now time to see how all this works in practice. We will start with the most basic case and progress toward a more complicated frame forwarding behavior and topology.

LAN Hubs and Bridges

As discussed previously, a collision domain is defined as two or more stations needing to share the same medium. This setup requires some algorithm to avoid two frames being sent at nearly the same time and thus colliding. When a collision occurs, the information is lost. CSMA/CD has been used to resolve the collision problem by allowing an Ethernet station to detect a collision and avoid retransmitting at the same time.

The simplest example of a collision domain is an Ethernet bus where all the stations are connected as shown in Figure 1-12.

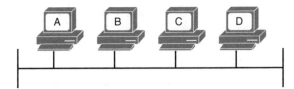

Figure 1-12 *Ethernet Bus*

Because the Ethernet signal will degrade across the distance between the stations, the same topology could be obtained by using a central LAN hub where all the stations connect. The role of the LAN hub or repeater was to regenerate the signal uniquely and transmit this signal to all its ports. This topology is typically half-duplex transmission mode and, as in the case of an Ethernet bus, defines a single collision domain.

Figure 1-13 shows how the information sent by Host A is repeated over all the hub's ports.

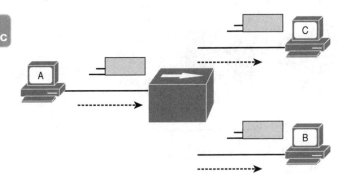

Figure 1-13 *A Network Hub Where the Electrical Signal of a Frame Is Regenerated and the Information Sent Out to All the Device Ports*

Before transmitting, a station senses the medium (also called *carrier*) to see if any frame is being transmitted. If the medium is empty, the station can start transmitting. If two stations start at nearly the same time, as is the case in this example, a collision occurs. All stations in the collision domain detect the collision and adopt a backoff algorithm to delay the transmission.

Figure 1-14 shows an example of a collision happening with a hub network. Note that B will also receive a copy of the frame sent from C, and C will receive a copy of the frame sent from B; although, this is not shown in the picture for simplicity.

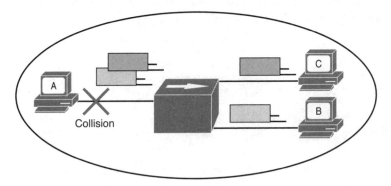

Figure 1-14 *Collision Domain with a Hub or Repeater*

Collision domains are highly inefficient because two stations cannot transmit at the same time. The performance becomes even more impacted as the number of stations connected to the same hubs increases. To partially overcome that situation, networking bridges are used. A *bridge* is a device that allows the separation of collision domain.

Unlike a LAN hub, which will just regenerate the signal, a LAN bridge typically implements some frame-forwarding decision based on whether or not a frame needs to reach a device on the other side of the bridge.

Figure 1-15 shows an example of a network with hubs and bridges. The bridges partition the network into two collision domains, thus allowing the size of the network to scale.

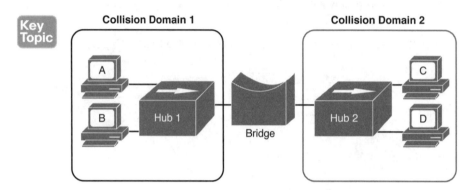

Figure 1-15   *A Bridge Creating Two Collision Domains*

LAN Switches

In modern networks, half-duplex mode has been replaced by full-duplex mode. Full-duplex mode allows two stations to transmit simultaneously because the transmission and receiver channels are separated. Because of that, in full duplex, CSMA/CD is not used because collisions cannot occur.

A LAN switch is a device that allows multiple stations to connect in full-duplex mode. This creates a separate collision domain for each of the ports, so collisions cannot happen. For example, Figure 1-16 shows four hosts connected to a switch. Each host has a separate channel to transmit and receive, so each port actually identifies a collision domain. Note that usually in this kind of scenario it does not make sense to refer to a port as collision domain, and it is usually more practical to assume that there is no collision domain—because no collision can occur.

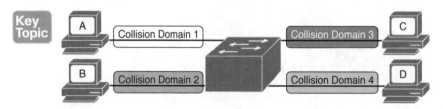

Figure 1-16   *A Switch Creating Several Collision Domains in Full-Duplex Mode*

How does a switch forward a frame? Whereas a hub would just replicate the same information on all the ports, a switch tries to do something a bit more intelligent and use the destination MAC address to forward the frame to the right station.

Figure 1-17 shows a simple example of frame forwarding.

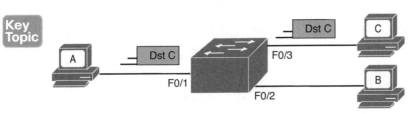

Figure 1-17 *Frame Forwarding with a Switch*

How does a switch know to which port to forward a frame? Before this forwarding mechanism can be explained, we need to discuss three concepts:

- **MAC address table:** This table holds the link between a MAC address and the physical port of the switch where frames for that MAC address should be forwarded.

  Figure 1-18 shows an example of a simplified MAC address table.

MAC Address	Port
0200.1111.1111	F0/1
0200.2222.2222	F0/2
0200.3333.3333	F0/3

Figure 1-18 *Simple MAC Address Table*

- **Dynamic MAC address learning:** It is possible to populate the MAC address table manually, but that is probably not the best use of anyone's time. Dynamic learning is a mechanism that helps with populating the MAC address table. When a switch receives an Ethernet frame on a port, it notes the source MAC address and inserts an entry in the MAC address table, marking that MAC address as reachable from that port.

- **Ethernet Broadcast domain:** A broadcast domain is formed by all devices connected to the same LAN switches. Broadcast domains are separated by network layer devices such as routers. An Ethernet broadcast domain is sometimes also called a *subnet*.

  Figure 1-19 shows an example of a network with two broadcast domains separated by a router.

Now that you have been introduced to the concepts of a MAC address table, dynamic MAC address learning, and broadcast domain, we can look at a few examples that explain how the forwarding is done.

The forwarding decision is uniquely done based on the destination MAC address. In this example, Host A with MAC address 0200.1111.1111, connected to switch port F0/1, is sending traffic (Ethernet frames) to Host C with MAC address 0200.3333.3333, connected to port F0/3.

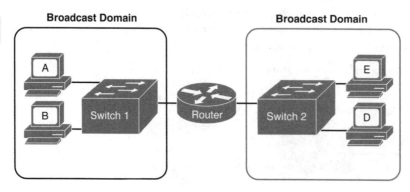

Figure 1-19 *A Router Dividing the Network into Two Broadcast Domains*

At the beginning, the MAC address table of the switch is empty. When the first frame is received on port F0/1, the switch does two things:

■ It looks up the MAC address table. Because the table is empty, it forwards the frame to all its ports except the one where the frame was received. This is usually called *flooding*.

■ It uses dynamic MAC address learning to update the MAC address table with the information that 0200.1111.1111 is reachable through port F0/1.

Figure 1-20 shows the frame flooding and the MAC address table updated with the information about Host A.

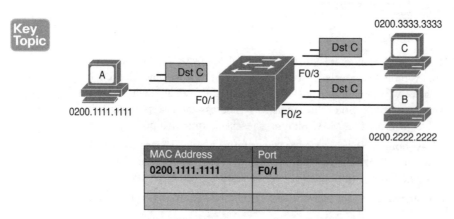

Figure 1-20 *Example of a MAC Address Table Being Updated as the Frame Is Received and Forwarded by the Switch*

Host B receives a copy of the frame; however, because the destination MAC address is not its own, it discards the frame. Host C receives the frame and may decide to respond. When Host C responds, the switch will look up the MAC address table. This time, it will find an entry for Host A and will just forward the frame on port F0/1 toward Host A. Like in the previous case, it will update the MAC address table to indicate that 0200.3333.3333 (Host C) is reachable through port F0/3, as shown in Figure 1-21.

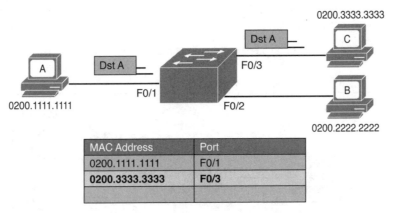

MAC Address	Port
0200.1111.1111	F0/1
0200.3333.3333	**F0/3**

Figure 1-21 *Dynamic Learning of the Host C MAC Address*

The flooding mechanism is also used when a frame has a broadcast destination MAC address. In that case, the frame will be forwarded to all ports in the Ethernet broadcast domain. In a more complex topology, switches may be connected to each other, sometimes with multiple ports to ensure redundancy; however, the basic forwarding principles do not change. All MAC addresses that are reachable via other switches will be marked in the MAC address table as reachable via the port where the switches are connected.

Figure 1-22 shows an example of Host A connected to port F0/1 of Switch 1 and sending traffic to Host E, connected to F0/1 of Switch 2. Switch 1 and Switch 2 are connected via port F0/10 on both sides.

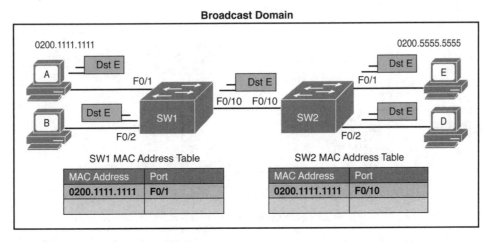

Figure 1-22 *Frame Forwarding and MAC Address Table Updates with Multiple Switches. Host A sends a frame for Host E.*

When Host A sends the first frame, Switch 1 will flood it on all ports, including on port F0/10 toward Switch 2. Switch 2 will also flood on all its ports because it does not know where Host E is located. Both Switch 1 and Switch 2 will use dynamic learning to update their own MAC address tables. Switch 1 will mark Host A as reachable via F0/1, while Switch 2 will mark Host A as reachable via F0/10.

If Host E responds to Host A, the same steps will be repeated, as shown in Figure 1-23.

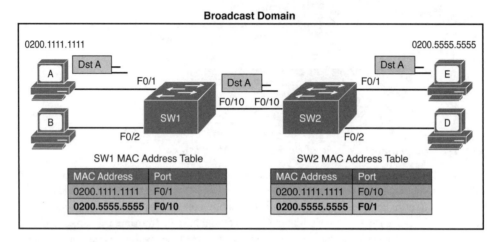

Figure 1-23 *Frame Forwarding and MAC Address Table Updates with Multiple Switches. Host E replies to a frame sent by Host A.*

Link Layer Loop and Spanning Tree Protocols

Let's now consider another example, shown in Figure 1-24, where three switches (SW1, SW2, and SW3) are interconnected.

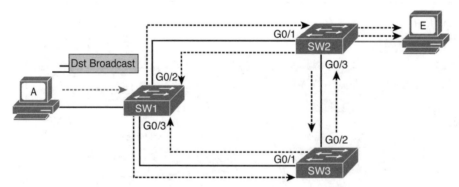

Figure 1-24 *Example of a Broadcast Storm Caused in a Network with Redundant Links*

Assume that Host A, connected to SW1, sends a broadcast frame. SW1 will forward the frame to SW2 and SW3 on ports G0/2 and G0/3. SW2 will receive the frame and forward it to SW3 and Host E. SW3 will do the same and forward the frame to SW2. SW3 will again receive the frame from SW2 and will forward it to SW1, and so on.

As you can see, the frame will loop indefinitely within the LAN, thus causing degradation of the network performance due to the useless forwarding of frames. This is called a *broadcast storm*. Other types of loops can happen—for example, if Host A would have sent a frame to a host that never replies (hence, no switches know where the host is). In general, link layer (or Layer 2) loops can happen every time there is a redundant link within the Layer 2 topology.

The second undesirable effect of Layer 2 loops is MAC table instability. SW1 in the preceding example will keep (incorrectly) updating the MAC address table, marking Host A on port G0/2 and G0/3 as it receives the looping frames with the source address of Host A on these two ports. So, whenever SW1 receives frames for Host A, it will incorrectly send them to the wrong port, making the problem worse.

The third effect of a Layer 2 loop is that a host (for example, Host E) will keep receiving a copy of the same frame that's circulating within the network. This can confuse the host and may result in higher-layer protocol failure.

Spanning Tree Protocols (STPs) are used to avoid Layer 2 loops. This section describes the fundamental concepts of STPs. Over the years, the concept has been enhanced to improve performance and to take into consideration the evolution of network complexity. In its basic function, the STP creates a logical Layer 2 topology that is loop free. This is done by allowing traffic on certain ports and blocking traffic on others. If the topology changes (for example, if a link fails), STP will recalculate the new logical topology (it is said to "reconverge") and unblock certain ports to adapt to the new topology.

Figure 1-25 shows STP applied to the previous example. Port G0/2 on SW3 is marked as blocked, and it will not forward traffic. This avoids frames looping. If the link between SW1 and SW3 goes down, STP will unblock the link between SW3 and SW2 to allow traffic to pass and provide redundancy.

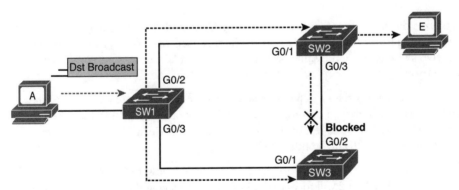

Figure 1-25 *Example of Layer 2 with STP Enabled*

STP uses a spanning tree algorithm (STA) to create a tree-like, loop-free logical topology. To understand how a basic STP works, we need to explore a few concepts:

- **Bridge ID (BID):** An 8-byte ID that is independently calculated on each switch. The first 2 bytes of the BID contain the priority, while the remaining 6 bytes includes the MAC address of the switch (of one of its ports).

- **Bridge PDU (BPDU):** Represents the STP protocol messages. The BPDU is sent to a multi-cast MAC address. The address may depend on the specific STP protocol in use.

- **Root switch:** Represents the root of the spanning tree. The spanning tree root is identified through a process called *root election*. The root switch BID is called the *root BID*.

- **Port cost:** A numerical value associated to each spanning tree port. Usually this value depends on the speed of the port. The higher the speed, the lower the cost. Table 1-6 reports the recommended values from IEEE (in IEEE 802.1Q-2014).

- **Root cost:** Represents the cost to reach the root switch. The root cost is given by summing all the costs of the ports on the shortest path to the root switch. The root cost value of the root switch is 0.

Table 1-6   Spanning Tree Port Costs

Port Speed	Recommended Cost
<=100 Kbps	200000000
1 Mbps	20000000
10 Mbps	2000000
100 Mbps	200000
1 Gbps	20000
10 Gbps	2000
100 Gbps	200
1 Tbps	20
10 Tbps	2

At initialization, an STP root switch needs to be identified. The root switch will be the switch with the lower BID. The BID priority field is used first to determine the lower BID; if two switches have the same priority, then the MAC address is used to determine the root.

The process to identify the switch with the lower BID is called *root election*. At the beginning, each switch tries to become the root and sends out a Hello BPDU to announce its presence in the network to the rest of the switches. The initial Hello BPDU includes its own switch BID as the root BID in the BPDU field.

When a switch receives a Hello BPDU with a better root BID (lower BID), it will stop sending its own Hello BPDU and will forward the Hello BPDU generated from the root switch. It will also update the root cost and add the cost of the port where the BPDU was received. The process continues until the root election is over and a root switch is identified. At this point, all switches on the network know which switch is the root and what the root cost is to that switch. Figure 1-26 shows an example of root election in our sample topology.

SW1 will send a BPDU to SW2 and SW3. When SW2 receives the BPDU from SW1, it will
see that the BID for SW1 is lower than its own BID, so it will update the Root BID entry to
include the BID of SW1. SW2 will then forward the BPDU to SW3 with a root cost of 4.

SW3 has also received the BPDU from SW1 and already updated the Root BID entry with
SW1's BID because it is lower than its own BID. It will then forward the BPDU to SW2 with
a root cost of 5. At the end, SW1 becomes the root within this topology.

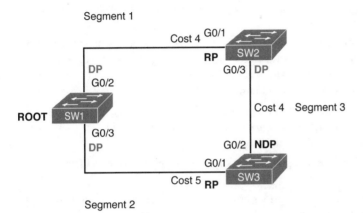

Figure 1-26 *STP Root Election*

As stated at the beginning of this section, the spanning tree is created by blocking a certain
port. Once the root switch is elected, the tree can start to be built. At this point, we need to
discuss the concepts of port role and port state:

- **Port role:** Depending on the STP-specific protocols, there are a few names and roles for
  ports; however, three main roles are important for understanding how STP works. Once
  that is clear, the nuances of the various STP protocols can be easily understood.

  - *Root port (RP)* is the port that offers the lowest path cost (root cost) to the root on
    non-root switches.

  - *Designated port (DP)* is the port that offers the lowest path to the root for a given
    LAN segment. For example, if a switch has a host attached to a port, that port be-
    comes a DP because it's the closest port to the root for that LAN segment. The switch
    is told to be the designated switch for that LAN segment. All ports on a root switch
    are DP.

  - *Non-designated ports* are all the other ports that are not either the RP or DP.
    Depending on the specific STP standards, they can assume various names, and the
    standard can define additional port categories.

Let's look again at our topology, but in a bit different way. Referring to Figure 1-26, we
can identify three segments. On the root switch, SW1, all ports are DPs because they
offer the shortest path to the root for Segments 1 and 2. What is the DP for Segment 3?
Port G0/3 on SW2 will become the DP because its cost to the root is 4, whereas Port
G0/2 on SW3 would have a cost of 5.

The RP identification is a bit easier. For each port on a non-root switch, we select the port with the lower path to the root. In this case, G0/1 on SW2 and G0/1 on SW3 become the RP. All remaining ports will be non-designated ports.

- **Port state:** The port state is related to the specific action a port can take while in that state. As in the port role definition, the name of the state depends on the STP protocol being used. Here are some common examples of port states:

  - **Blocking:** In this state, a port blocks all frames received except Layer 2 management frames (for example, BPDU).

  - **Listening:** A port transitions to this state from the blocking state when the STP determines that the port needs to participate in the forwarding. At this stage, however, the port is not fully functional. It can process BPDU and respond to Layer 2 management messages, but it does not accept frames.

  - **Learning:** The port transitions to learning after the listening phase. In this phase, the port still does not forward frames; however, it learns the MAC addresses via dynamic learning and fills in the MAC address table.

  - **Forwarding:** In this state, the port is fully operational and receives and forwards frames.

  - **Disabled:** A port in disable state does not forward and receive frames and does not participate in the STP process, so it does not process BPDU.

When the STP protocol has converged, which means the RPs and DPs are identified, each port transitions to a terminal state. Every RP and DP will be in the forwarding state, while all the other ports will be in the blocking state. Figure 1-27 shows the terminal state of the ports in our topology.

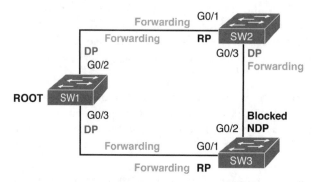

Figure 1-27   *STP Terminal State Applied to the Network Topology*

STP provides a critical function within communication networks, so a wrong design or implementation of the Spanning Tree Protocol (for example, an incorrect selection of the root switch) could lead to poor performance or even catastrophic failure in some cases.

Through the years, Spanning Tree Protocols have seen several updates and new standards have emerged. The most common versions of Spanning Tree Protocols in use today are Rapid STP, Per-VLAN STP+ (PVSTP+), and Multiple Spanning Tree (MST).

Virtual LAN (VLAN) and VLAN Trunking

So far, we have assumed that everything happens within a single LAN. In simple terms, a LAN can be identified as a part of the network within a single broadcast domain. LANs (and broadcast domains) are separated by Layer 3 devices such as routers.

As the network grows and becomes more complex, operating within a single broadcast domain degrades the network performance and adds complexity to management protocols, such as to the STP.

The concept of a virtual LAN (VLAN) has been introduced to overcome the issues created by a very large single LAN. A VLAN can exist within a switch, and each switch port can be assigned to a specific VLAN.

Figure 1-28 shows four hosts connected to the same switch. Host A and Host E are assigned to VLAN 101 whereas Host B and Host D are assigned to VLAN 102. The switch treats a host in one VLAN as being in a single broadcast domain. A packet from one VLAN cannot be forwarded to a different VLAN at Layer 2. As such, a VLAN provides Layer 2 network separation.

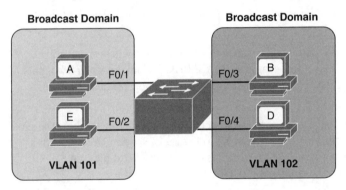

Figure 1-28 *Two Different VLANs Used to Separate Broadcast Domains within the Same Switch*

Here are some common benefits of using a VLAN:

- Reduces the number of devices receiving the broadcast frame and the related overhead
- Creates Layer 2 network separation
- Reduces management protocols' load and complexity
- Segments troubleshooting and failure areas, as failure in one VLAN will not be propagated to the rest of the network

How does frame forwarding work in VLANs? The same process we described for a single LAN applies for each VLAN. The switch knows which port is linked to which VLAN and will forward the frame accordingly. In the case of multiple switches, the VLAN concept can still work. Figure 1-29 shows the VLAN concept across two switches.

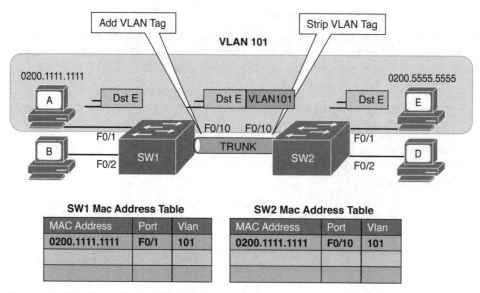

Figure 1-29 *Example of a VLAN and VLAN Trunk Used on a Topology with Multiple Switches*

In this case, Host A and Host E, although attached to two different switches, can still be configured within the same VLAN (for example, VLAN 101). The link between SW1 and SW2 is called a trunk, and it is a special link because it can transport frames belonging to several VLANs.

VLAN tagging is used to enable the forwarding between Host A and Host E within the same VLAN as well as across multiple switches. Referring to Figure 1-29, when Host A sends a frame to Host E, SW1 does not know where Host E is, so it will forward the frame to all ports in VLAN 101, including the trunk port to SW2.

As you can see, SW1 will not forward the frame to Host B because it is in a different VLAN. SW1, before sending the frame on the trunk link to SW2, will add a VLAN tag to the frame that carries the VLAN ID, VLAN 101. This tells SW2 that this frame should be forwarded to ports in VLAN 101 only.

SW2 receives the frame over the trunk link, strips the VLAN tagging, and forwards the frame to all its ports in VLAN 101 (in this case, only to F0/1). If Host E responds, the same process applies. SW2 will only send the packets over the trunk link (because SW2 now knows how to reach Host A) and will tag the packet with VLAN 101.

The VLAN information is added to the Ethernet frame. The way that it's done depends on the protocol used for trunking. The most known and used trunking protocol nowadays is defined in IEEE 802.1Q (dot1q). Another protocol is Inter-Switch Link (ISL), which is a Cisco proprietary protocol that was used in the past.

In IEEE 802.1Q, the VLAN tagging is obtained by adding an IEEE 802.1Q tag between the source MAC address and the Type field in the Ethernet frame.

Figure 1-30 shows an example of an IEEE 802.1Q tag. The tag includes the VLAN ID.

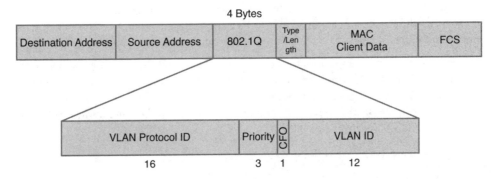

Figure 1-30 *IEEE 802.1Q Tag*

IEEE 802.1Q introduces the concept of a native VLAN. The difference between a native and non-native VLAN is that a native VLAN goes without tag over the trunk link. When the trunk is configured for IEEE 802.1Q, if a switch receives a frame without a tag over a trunk link, it will interpret it as belonging to the native VLAN and forward accordingly.

Cisco VLAN Trunking Protocol

Cisco VLAN Trunking Protocol (VTP) is a Cisco proprietary protocol used to manage VLAN distribution across switches. VTP should not be confused with protocols that actually handle the tagging of frames with VLAN information when being sent over a trunk link. VTP is used to distribute information about existing VLANs to all switches in a VTP domain so that VLANs do not have to be manually configured, thus reducing the burden of the administrator.

For example, when a new VLAN is created on one switch, the same VLAN may need to be created on all switches to enable VLAN trunking and consistent use of VLAN IDs. VTP facilitates the process by sending automatic advertisements about the state of VLAN databases across the VTP domain. Switches that receive advertisements will maintain the VLAN database, synchronized based on the information found in the VTP message.

VTP relies on protocols such as 802.1Q to transmit information. VTP defines three modes of operation:

- **Server mode:** In VTP server mode, the administrator can configure or remove a VLAN. VTP will take care of distributing the information to other switches in the VTP domain.

- **Client mode:** In VTP client mode, a switch receives updates about a VLAN and advertises the VLAN configured already; however, a VLAN cannot be added or removed.

- **Transparent mode:** In transparent mode, the switch does not participate in VTP, so it does not perform a VLAN database update and does not generate VTP advertisement; however, it forwards VTP advertisements from other switches.

Inter-VLAN Traffic and Multilayer Switches

As described in the previous section, VLANs provide a convenient way to separate broadcast domains. This means, however, that a Layer 3 device is needed to forward traffic between two VLANs even if they are on the same switch. We have defined switches as Layer 2 devices, so a switch by itself would not be able to forward traffic from one VLAN to the other, even if the source and destination host reside physically on the same switch.

Figure 1-31 shows an example of inter-VLAN traffic. Host A in VLAN 101 is sending traffic to Host B in VLAN 102. Both hosts are connected to SW1. Because SW1 is a switch operating at Layer 2, a Layer 3 device (for example, a router, R1) is needed to forward the traffic. In the figure, the router uses two different interfaces connected to the switch, where G0/1 is in VLAN 101 and G0/2 is in VLAN 102.

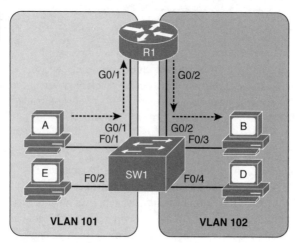

Figure 1-31 *Inter-VLAN Traffic*

Alternatively, R1 could have been configured with only one interface on the switch with trunking enabled. This alternative is sometimes defined as *router on a stick (ROAS)*, as illustrated in Figure 1-32.

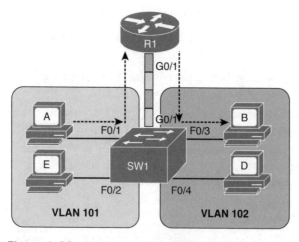

Figure 1-32 *Router on a Stick (ROAS)*

In both of the preceding examples, there is a waste of resources. For example, a packet needs to travel to the first router in the path, to then come back again to the same switch creating additional load on the links. Additionally, there is a loss in performance due to the encapsulation and upper-layer processing of the frame.

The solution is to integrate Layer 3 function within a classic Layer 2 switch. This type of switch is called a *Layer 3 switch* or sometimes a *multilayer switch*. Figure 1-33 shows an example of inter-VLAN flow with a multilayer switch.

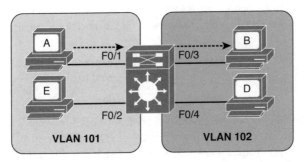

Figure 1-33 *Inter-VLAN Flow with a Multilayer Switch*

Wireless LAN Fundamentals and Technologies

Together with Ethernet, which is defined as wired access to a LAN, wireless LAN (WLAN) is one of the most used technologies for LAN access. This book covers the basics of WLAN fundamentals and technologies. Interested readers can refer to the *CCNA Wireless 200-355 Official Cert Guide* book for additional information.

Wireless LAN is defined within the IEEE 802.11 standards. While in some aspects WLANs resemble classic Ethernet technology, there are several significant differences.

The first and most notable difference is the medium. Here are several other characteristics that distinguish a wireless medium from a wire medium:

- There is no defined boundary.
- It is more prone to interference by other signals on the same medium.
- It is less reliable.
- The signal can propagate in asymmetric ways (for example, due to reflection).

The way stations access the medium is also different. In the previous section, you learned that Ethernet defines two operational modes: half duplex, where the stations can transmit one at time, and full-duplex, where stations can transmit simultaneously. In WLANs, network stations can only use half-duplex mode because they are not able to transmit and receive at the same time due to the limitation of the medium.

This means that two stations need to implement a way to detect if the medium (in this case, the radio frequency channel) is being used to avoid transmitting at the same time. This functionality is provided by a Carrier Sense Media Access with Collision Avoidance (CSMA/CA). Note that this is different from the CSMA/CD used in Ethernet. The main difference is in how a collision is handled. Wired devices can detect collisions over the medium, whereas wireless devices cannot.

Like we have seen for Ethernet, a wireless station senses the medium to determine whether is it possible to transmit. However, the way this is done is different for wired devices. In a wired technology, the device can sense an electrical signal on the wire and determine whether someone else is transmitting. This cannot happen in the case of wireless devices. There are mainly two methods for carrier sense:

■ **Physical carrier sense:** When the station is not transmitting, it can sense the channel for the presence of other frames. This is sometimes referred to as Clear Channel Assessment (CCA).

■ **Virtual carrier sense:** Stations when transmitting a frame include an estimated time for the transmission of the frame in the frame header. This value can be used to estimate how long the channel will be busy.

Collision detection is not possible for similar reasons. Wireless clients thus need to avoid collisions. To do that, they use a mechanism called Collision Avoidance. The mechanism works by using backoff timers. Each station waits a backoff period before transmitting. In addition to the backoff period, a station may need to wait for an additional time, called interframe space, which is used to reduce the likelihood of a collision and to allow an extra cushion of time between two frames.

802.11 defines several interframe space timers. The standard interframe timer is called Distributed Interframe Space (DIFS).

The basic process of transmitting frames includes three steps:

Step 1.   Sense the channel to see whether it is busy.

Step 2.   Select a delay based on the backoff timer. If, in the meantime, the channel gets busy, the backoff timer is stopped. When the channel is clear again, the backoff timer is restarted.

Step 3.   Wait for an additional DIFS time.

Figure 1-34 illustrates the process of transmitting frames in a WLAN. Client A is ready to transmit, it senses the medium, selects a backoff time, and then transmits. The duration of the frame is included in the frame header. Client B and Client C wait until the frame from Client A has been transmitted plus the DIFS, and then start the backoff timer. Client C's backoff timer expires before Client B's, so Client C transmits before Client B. Client B finds the channel busy, so it stops the backoff timer. Client B waits for the new transmission time, the DIFS period and the remaining backoff timer, and then it transmits.

One particularity of WLANs compared to wired networks is that a WLAN requires the other party to send an acknowledgement so that the sender knows the frame has been received.

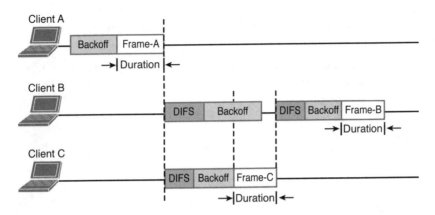

Figure 1-34 *Transmitting Frames in a WLAN*

802.11 Architecture and Basic Concepts

Unlike wired connections, where a station needs a physical connection to be able to transmit, the wireless medium is open, so any station can start transmitting. The IEEE 802.11 standards define the concept of Basic Service Set (BSS), which identifies a set of devices that share some common parameters and can communicate through a wireless connection. The most basic type of BSS is called Independent BSS (IBSS), and it is formed by two or more wireless stations communicating directly. IBSS is sometimes called *ad-hoc wireless network*.

Figure 1-35 shows an example of IBSS.

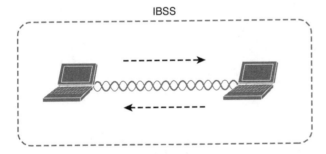

Figure 1-35 *Independent BSS*

Another type of BSS is called *infrastructure BSS*. The core of an infrastructure BSS is a wireless access point, or simply an access point (AP). Each station will associate to the AP, and each frame is sent to the AP, which will then forward it to the receiving station. The access point advertises a Service Set Identifier (SSID), which is used by each station to recognize a particular network.

To communicate with other stations that are not in the same BSS (for example, a server station in the organization's data center), access points can be connected in uplink with the rest of the organization's network (for example, with a wired connection). The uplink wired network is called a Distribution System (DS). The AP creates a boundary point between the BSS and the DS.

Figure 1-36 shows an example of infrastructure BSS with four wireless stations and an access point connected upstream with a DS.

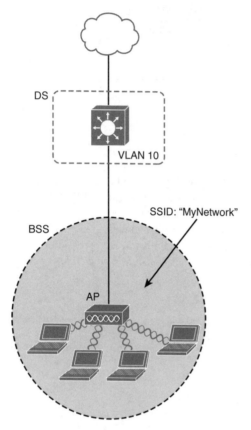

Figure 1-36   *Infrastructure BSS*

An access point has limited spatial coverage due to the wireless signal degradation. To extend the wireless coverage of a specific network (that is, a network identified by a single SSID), multiple BSSs can be linked together to form an Extended Service Set (ESS). A client can move from one AP to the other in a seamless way. The method to release a client from one AP and associate to the other AP is called *roaming*.

Figure 1-37 shows an example of an ESS with two APs connected to a DS and a user roaming between two BSSs.

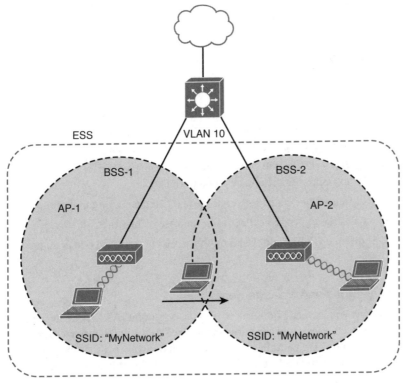

Figure 1-37 *Extended Service Set (ESS) Example*

802.11 Frame

An 802.11 frame is a bit different from the Ethernet frame, although there are some commonalities. Figure 1-38 shows an example of 802.11 frame.

Frame Control	Duration /ID	Address1	Address2	Address3	Sequence Control	Address4	Data	FCS
2 Bytes	2 Bytes	6 Bytes	6 Bytes	6 Bytes	2 Bytes	6 Bytes	0–2304 Bytes	4 Bytes

Protocol Version	Type	Subtype	To DS	From DS	More Frag	Retry	Pwr Mgmt	More Data	WEP	Order
Bits: 2	2	4	1	1	1	1	1	1	1	1

Figure 1-38 *802.11 Frame*

The 802.11 frame includes the following elements:

- **Frame control:** Includes some additional sub-elements, as indicated in Figure 1-37. It provides information on the frame type and whether this frame is directed toward the DS or is coming from the DS toward the wireless network.

- **Duration field:** Can have different meanings depending on the frame type. However, one common value is the expected time the frame will be traveling on the channel for the Virtual Carrier Sense functionality.

- **Address fields:** Contain addresses in 802 MAC format (for example, MAC-48). The following are the typical addresses included:

  - *Transmitter address (TA)* is the MAC address of the transmitter of the frame (for example, a wireless client).

  - *Receiver address (RA)* is the MAC address of the receiver of the frame (for example, the AP).

  - *Source address (SA)* is the MAC address of the source of the frame, if it is different from the TA. For example, if a frame is coming from the DS toward a wireless station, the SA would be the original Ethernet source address whereas the TA would be the AP.

  - *Destination address (DA)* is the MAC address of the final destination if different from the RA (for example, for a frame destined to the DS).

- **Sequence Control field:** This is used for sequence and fragmentation numbering.

- **Frame body:** Includes the upper-layer PDU, as in the case of Ethernet.

- **Frame Check Sequence (FCS) field:** Used by the receiving device to detect an error in transmission.

WLAN Access Point Types and Management

In the previous sections you learned about the wireless access point (AP). The main functionality of an AP is to bridge frames from the wireless interface to the wired interfaces so that a wireless station can communicate with the rest of the wired network. This means, for example, extracting the payload of an 802.11 frame and re-encapsulating it in an Ethernet frame.

The AP provides additional functionalities that are as important for the correct functionality of a wireless network. For example, an AP needs to manage the association or the roaming of wireless stations, implement authentication and security features, manage the radio frequency (RF), and so on.

The functionality provided by an access point can be classified in two categories:

- *Real-time functions* include all the functionality to actually transmit and receive frames, or to encrypt the information over the channel.

- *Management functions* include functions such as RF management, security management, QoS, and so on.

The access points also can be categorized based on the type of functionality provided:

- *Autonomous APs* are access points that implement both real-time and management functions. These are autonomous and thus work in a standalone mode. Each AP needs to be configured singularly.

- *Lightweight APs (LAPs)* only implement the real-time functions and work together with a management device called a *wireless LAN controller (WLC)*, which provides the management functions. The communication between LAPs and the WLC is done using the Control and Provision of Wireless Access Point (CAPWAP).

Figure 1-39 shows the difference between the two types of APs.

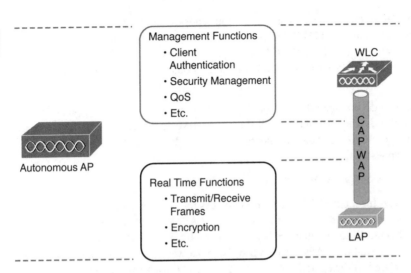

Figure 1-39 *Comparison Between an Autonomous Access Point and a Lightweight Access Point*

Depending on the type of AP, the network architecture and packet flow may change. In a network using autonomous AP, the packet flow is similar to a network with a switch, as seen in previous sections. Each wireless client will be associated to a VLAN, and the AP will be configured with a trunk on its DS interface. The AP can participate in STP and will behave much like a switch.

Autonomous APs can be managed singularly or through centralized management software. For example, Cisco Prime Infrastructure can be used to manage several autonomous access points. This type of architecture is called *autonomous architecture*.

Another option is to use autonomous access points that are managed from the cloud. This is called *cloud-based architecture*. An example of such a deployment is the Cisco Meraki cloud-based wireless network architecture.

A third option is to use LAPs and WLC. This type of deployment is called *split MAC* due to the splitting of functionalities between the LAPs and the WLC. The CAPWAP protocol is used for communication between the LAPs and the WLC. CAPWAP is a tunneling protocol described in RFC 5415. It is used to tunnel 802.11 frames from a LAP to the WLC for additional forwarding. The encapsulation is needed because the WLC can reside anywhere in the DS (for example, in a different VLAN than the LAP). CAPWAP encapsulates the 802.11 frame in an IP packet that can be used to reach the WLC regardless of its logical position. CAPWAP uses UDP to provide end-to-end connectivity between the LAP and WLC, and it uses DTLS to protect the tunnels.

CAPWAP consists of two logical tunnels:

■ *CAPWAP control messages*, which transport management frames

■ *CAPWAP data*, which transports the actual data to and from the LAP

When a LAP is added to the network, it establishes a tunnel to the WLC. After that, the WLC can push configuration and other management information.

In a split-MAC deployment, when a wireless station sends information, the AP will encapsulate the information using the CAPWAP specification and send it to the WLC. For example, in the case of a WLAN, it will use the CAPWAP protocol binding for 802.11 described in RFC 5416, which also specifies how the 802.11 frame should be encapsulated in a CAPWAP tunnel.

The WLC will then decapsulate the information and send it to the correct recipient. When the recipient responds, the information will flow in the reverse direction—first to the WLC and then through the CAPWAP data tunnel to the AP, which will finally forward the information to the wireless station.

There are two types of split-MAC architectures:

■ **Centralized architecture:** This architecture places the WLC in a central location (for example, closer to the core) so that the number of LAPs covered is maximized. One advantage of centralized architecture is that roaming between LAPs is simplified because one WLC controls all the LAPs a user is traversing. However, traffic between two wireless stations associated to the same LAP may need to travel through several links in order to reach the WLC and then back to the same LAP. This may reduce the efficiency of the network.

Figure 1-40 shows an example of a centralized WLC architecture and the frame path for a wireless-station-to-wireless-station transmission.

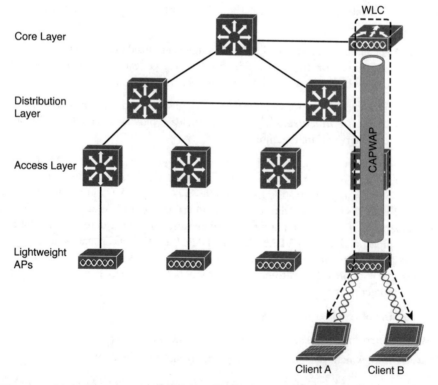

Figure 1-40   *Centralized WLC Architecture*

■ **Converged architecture:** With this architecture, the WLC is moved closer to the LAPs typically at the access layer. In this case, one WLC is covering fewer LAPs, so various WLCs need to work together in a distributed fashion. In a converged architecture, the WLC may be integrated into the access layer switch, which also provides WLC functionality. This type of architecture increases the performance of wireless-station-to-wireless-station communication, but makes roaming more complicated because the user must travel through several WLCs. Figure 1-41 shows an example of a converged architecture.

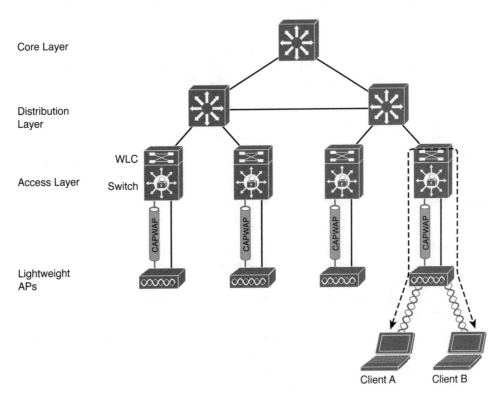

Figure 1-41   *Converged WLC Architecture*

Internet Protocol and Layer 3 Technologies

In previous sections, you learned how information is sent at the link layer, or Layer 2. In this section, we discuss how information is transmitted at Layer 3—that is, how a packet travels through a network, across several broadcast domains, to reach its destination.

Layer 3 protocols are used to enable communication without being concerned about the specific transportation medium or other Layer 2 properties (for example, whether the information needs to be transported on a wired network or using a wireless connection). The most-used Layer 3 protocol is the Internet Protocol (IP). As a security professional, it is fundamental that you master how IP works in communication networks.

IP comes in two different versions: IP version 4 (IPv4) and IP version 6 (IPv6). Although some of the concepts remain the same between the two versions, IPv6 could be seen as a completely different protocol rather than an update of IPv4. In this section, we mainly discuss IPv4. In the next section, we will discuss the fundamentals of IPv6 and highlight the differences between IPv4 and IPv6.

Before digging into more detail, let's look at the basic transmission of an IP packet, also referred to as *Layer 3 forwarding*. Figure 1-42 shows a simple topology where Host A is connected to a switch that provides LAN access to the host at Site A. Host B is also connected to an access switch at Site B. In the middle, two routers (R1 and R2) provide connectivity between the two sites.

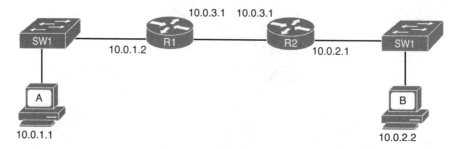

Figure 1-42 *Example of a Basic Network Topology*

Here are a few concepts you should be familiar with:

- An *IP address* is the means by which a device is identified by the IP protocol. An IP address can be assigned to a host or to a router interface.

  In the example in Figure 1-42, Host A is identified by IPv4 address 10.0.1.1, and Host B is identified by IPv4 address 10.0.2.2. IPv4 and IPv6 are different; we will look into the details of IPv4 and IPv6 addresses later in this section.

- The *routing table* or *routing database* is somewhat similar to the MAC address table discussed in the previous section. The routing table contains two main pieces of information: the destination IP or network and the next-hop IP address, which is the IP address of the next device where the IP packet should be sent.

- A *default route* is a special entry in the routing table that says to forward all packets, regardless of the destination to a specific next hop.

- *Packet routing* refers to the action performed by the Layer 3 device to transmit a packet. When a packet reaches one interface of the device, the device will look up the routing table to see where the packet should be sent. If the information is found, the packet is sent to the next-hop device.

- The *router* or *IP gateway* is a Layer 3 device that performs packet routing. It has two or more interfaces connected to a network segment—either a LAN segment or a WAN segment. Although a router is usually classified as Layer 3, most modern routers implement all layers of the TCP/IP model; however, their main function is to route packets at Layer 3. R1 and R2 in Figure 1-42 are examples of routers.

Referring to Figure 1-43, let's see how Host A can send information to Host B.

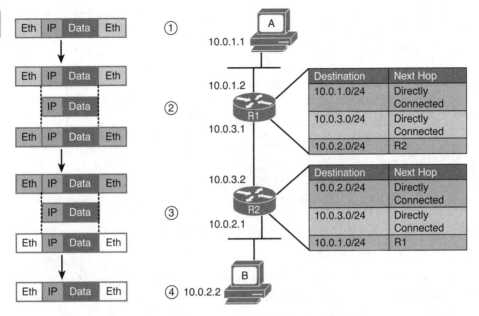

Figure 1-43 *Example of IP Packet Routing and a Routing Table*

Step 1.   Host A will encapsulate the data through the various TCP/IP layers up to the IP layer. The IP layer adds the IP header and sends it down to the link layer to encapsulate it in an Ethernet frame. After that, the frame is sent to R1.

Step 2.   R1 strips the Ethernet header and trailer and processes the IP packet header. It sees that this packet has Host B as its destination, so it looks to its routing table to find the next-hop device. In the routing table, Host B can be reached via R2, so R1 re-encapsulates the packet in a new link layer frame (for example, a new Ethernet frame) and sends it to R2.

Step 3.   R2 performs the same operation as R1. It strips the link layer information, processes the IP packet header, and looks to its routing table to find Host B. R2 sees that Host B is directly connected—that is, it is in the same broadcast domain as its F0/2 interface—so it encapsulates the packet in an Ethernet frame and sends it directly to Host B.

Step 4.   Host B receives the Ethernet frame, strips the information, and reads the IP packet header. Because Host B is the recipient of the packet, it will further process the IP packet to access the payload.

This process is somehow similar for IPv4 and IPv6. We will continue explaining the routing process using IPv4. IPv6 will be discussed a bit down the road.

IPv4 Header

An IP packet is formed by an IP header, which includes information on how to handle the packet from the IP protocol, and by the IP payload, which includes the Layer 4 PDU (for example, the TCP segment). The IP header is between 20 and 60 bytes long, depending on which IP header options are present.

Figure 1-44 shows an example of an IPv4 header.

4 Bits				
Version	Length	DS Field	Packet Length	
Identification			Flags	Fragment Offset
Time to Live		Protocol	Header Checksum	
Source IP Address				
Destination IP Address				

Figure 1-44 *IPv4 Header, Organized as 4 Bytes Wide, for a Total of 20 Bytes*

The IP header fields are as follows:

- **Version:** Indicates the IP protocol version (for example, IP version 4).

- **Internet Header Length:** It indicates the length of the header. A standard header, without options, is 20 bytes in length.

- **Notification (Differentiated Services Code Point [DSCP]) and Explicit Congestion (ECN):** Includes information about flow prioritization to implement Quality of Service and congestion control.

- **Total Length:** The length of the IP packet, which is the IP header plus the payload. The minimum length is 20 bytes, which is an IP packet that includes the basic IP header only.

- **Identification:** This field is mainly used when an IP packet needs to be fragmented due to constraint at the Layer 2 protocol. For example, Ethernet can transport, at a maximum, a 1500-byte IP packet.

- **Flags and Fragment Offset:** Fields to handle IP packet fragmentation.

- **Time to Live (TTL):** A field that's used to prevent IP packets from looping indefinitely. The TTL field is set when the IP packet is created, and each router on the path decrements it by one unit. If the TTL goes to zero, the router discards the packet and sends a message to the sender to tell it that the packet was dropped.

- **Protocol:** Indicates the type of protocol transported within the IP payload. For example, if TCP is transported, the value is 6; if UDP is transported, the value is 17.

Table 1-7 lists the common IP protocol codes. The protocol numbers are registered at IANA (http://www.iana.org/assignments/protocol-numbers/protocol-numbers.xhtml).

Table 1-7 Common IP Protocol Codes

Protocol Field Value	Protocol
1	ICMP
6	TCP
17	UDP

Protocol Field Value	Protocol
47	GRE
50	ESP
51	AH
88	EIGRP
89	OSPF

- **Header Checksum:** This is the checksum of the header. Every time a router modifies the header (for example, to reduce the TTL field), the header checksum needs to be recalculated.
- **Source Address:** This is the IP address of the sender of the IP packet.
- **Destination Address:** This is the IP address of the destination of the IP packet.

IPv4 Fragmentation

IP fragmentation is the process of splitting an IP packet into several fragments to allow the transmission by a Layer 2 protocol. In fact, the maximum length of a payload for a Layer 2 protocol depends on the physical medium used for transmission and on other factors. For example, Ethernet allows a maximum payload for the frame, also called the maximum transmission unit (MTU), of 1500 bytes in its basic frame, as you saw earlier. So what happens if a host sends an IP packet that is larger than that size? The packet needs to be fragmented.

Figure 1-45 shows an example of fragmentation. Host A sends an IP packet that is 2000 bytes, including 20 bytes of IP header. Before being transmitted via Ethernet, the packet needs to be split in two: one fragment will be 1500 bytes, and the other will be 520 bytes (500 bytes are due to the remaining payload, plus 20 bytes for the new IP header, which is added to the second fragment).

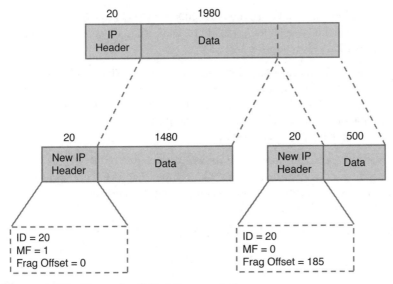

Figure 1-45 *Example of IPv4 Fragmentation*

The receiving host reassembles the original packet once all the fragments arrive. Two or more fragments of the same IP packet can be recognized because they will have the same value in the Identification field. The IP flags include a bit called More Fragments (MF), which indicates whether more fragments are expected. The last fragment will have this bit unset to indicate that no more fragments are expected. The Fragment Offset field is used to indicate at which point of the original unfragmented IP packet this fragment should start.

In the example in Figure 1-45, the first packet would have the following fields set:

- Identification = 20
- IP Flags MF = 1
- Fragment Offset = 0

The second fragment would have these fields set:

- Identification = 20 (which indicates that this is a fragment of the previous packet)
- IP Flags MF = 0 (which indicates that this is the last fragment)
- Fragment Offset = 1480 (to indicate that this fragment should start after 1480 bytes of the original packet)

NOTE   In reality, the fragment offset is expressed in multiples of 8. Therefore, the real value would be 185 (that is, 1480 / 8).

IPv4 Addresses and Addressing Architecture

An IPv4 address is a 32-bit-long number used to identify a device at Layer 3 (for example, a host or a router interface). In human-readable form, an IPv4 address is usually written in dotted decimal notation. The address is split in four parts of 8 bits each, and each part is represented in decimal form.

For example, an IPv4 address of 00000001000000010000000111111110 would be transformed into 00000001. 00000001. 00000001. 11111110, and each octet is transformed to decimal. Therefore, this address is written as 1.1.1.254.

You may be wondering how IP addresses are assigned? For example, who decided that 10.0.1.1 should be the IP address of Host A? Creating the IP address architecture is one of the most delicate tasks when designing an IP-based communication network. This section starts with a description of the basics of IP addressing and then delves into how the concept evolved and how it is commonly performed today.

One of the first architectures, called *classful addressing*, was based on IPv4 address classes, where the IPv4 address is logically divided into two components: a network part and a host part. The network prefix identifies the network (for example, an organization), while the host number identifies a host within that network.

The IPv4 address range was divided into five classes, as shown in Table 1-8.

Table 1-8   IPv4 Address Classes

Class Name	IP Address Range	Usage
Class A	1.0.0.0–127.255.255.255	Unicast
Class B	128.0.0.0–191.255.255.255	Unicast
Class C	192.0.0.0–223.255.255.255	Unicast
Class D	224.0.0.0–239.255.255.255	Multicast
Class E	240.0.0.0–255.255.255.255	Reserved

Class A, B, and C IP addresses can be assigned to hosts or interfaces for normal IP unicast usage; Class D IP addresses can be used as multicast addresses; Class E is reserved and cannot be used for IP routing. The network prefix length and host numbering length vary depending on the class.

Class A allots the first 8 bits for the network prefix and the remaining 24 bits for host addresses. This means Class A includes 256 (2^8) distinct networks, each capable of providing an address to 16,777,216 (2^{24}) hosts. For example, address 1.1.1.1 and address 2.2.2.2 would be in two different networks, whereas address 1.1.1.1 and address 1.4.1.1 would be in the same 1.x.x.x Class A network.

Class B allots the first 16 bits for the network prefix and the remaining 16 for host addresses. Class B includes 65,536 (2^{16}) distinct networks and 65,536 (2^{16}) host addresses within a single network.

Class C allots the first 24 bits for the network prefix and the remaining 8 for host addresses. Class C includes 16,777,216 (2^8) distinct networks and 256 (2^8) host addresses within one network.

Figure 1-46 summarizes the network and host portions for each class.

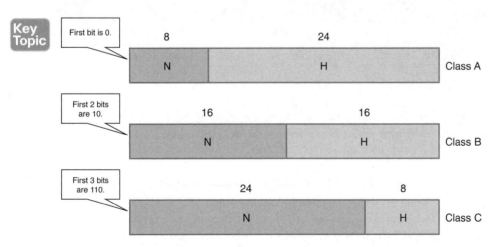

Figure 1-46   *Network and Host Portion for IPv4 Address Classes*

For each network, there are two special addresses that are usually not assigned to a single host:

- **Network address:** An address where the host portion is set to all 0s. This address is used to identify the whole network.

- **Broadcast network address:** An address where the host portion is set to all 1s in binary notation, which correspond to 255 in decimal notation.

For example, in the network 1.x.x.x, the network address would be 1.0.0.0 and the broadcast address would be 1.255.255.255. To indicate the bits used for the network portion and the bits used for the host portion, each IP address is followed by a network mask.

A network mask is a binary number that has the same length as an IP address: 32 bits. In a network mask, the network portion is indicated with all 1s and the host portion with all 0s. The network mask can also be read in dotted decimal format like an IP address. For example, the network mask for a Class A network would be 11111111000000000000000000000000, or 255.0.0.0.

The network mask sometimes is abbreviated as a backslash character (/) followed by the number of bits of the network portion of the IP address. For example, the same Class A network mask can be written as /8. This is sometime called Classless Interdomain Routing (CIDR) notation. Although it may seem that a network mask is unnecessary because the IP address range already provides the same info (for example, 3.3.3.3 would fall under the Class A addresses range, which would imply a network prefix of 8 bits), network masks are important to the concept of subnets, which we discuss in the next section.

Table 1-9 shows the default network mask for Classes A, B, and C. Classes D and E do not have any predefined mask because they are not used for unicast traffic.

Table 1-9   Default Network Masks for IPv4 Classes A, B, and C

Class	Number of Networks	Number of Hosts per Network	Network Mask
Class A	256	16,777,216 – 2	255.0.0.0 or /8
Class B	65,536	65,536 – 2	255.255.0.0 or /16
Class C	16,777,216	256 – 2	255.255.255.0 or /24

Keep in mind that two hosts are subtracted from the totals in this table because we need to remove the host address reserved for the network address as well as the address reserved for the broadcast network address.

IP Network Subnetting and Classless Interdomain Routing (CIDR)

In the classful addressing model, an organization would need to send a request to an Internet registry authority for a network within one of the classes, depending on the number of hosts needed. However, this method is highly inefficient because organizations receive more addresses than they actually need due to the structure of the classes. For example, an organization that only needs to assign an address to 20 hosts would get a Class C network, thus wasting 234 addresses (that is, 256 – 20 – 2). A more intelligent approach is introduced with Classless Interdomain Routing (CIDR).

CIDR moves away from the concept of class and introduces the concept of a network mask or prefix, as mentioned in the previous section. By using CIDR, the IANA or any local registry can assign to an organization a smaller number of IP addresses instead of having to assign a full class range. With this method, IP addresses can be saved because an organization can request an IP address range that actually fits its requirements, which means other addresses can be allocated to a different organization.

In the previous example, the organization would receive a /27 network mask instead of a full Class C network (/24). In the following pages, we explore how an organization can further partition the received address space to adapt to organizational needs using the concept of subnets.

You were already introduced to the term *subnet* or *network segment* when we discussed Layer 2 technologies. A subnet can be identified with a broadcast domain. In Figure 1-47, we can identify three subnets, each representing a separate broadcast domain. Each subnet includes a number of IP addresses that are assigned to the hosts and interfaces within that subnet. In this example, Subnet 1 would need a minimum of three IP addresses (Host A, Host B, and the R1 interface), and Subnet 2 at least two IP addresses (one for each router interface). Subnet 3 also would need at least two IP addresses (one for Host C and one for the R2 interface). Remember than on each subnet, we also need to reserve one address for the network ID and one for the broadcast network address.

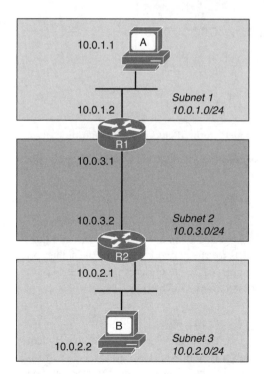

Figure 1-47 *Example of Addressing in a Topology with Three Subnets*

When subnets are used, an IP address is logically split into three parts: the network prefix, the subnet ID, and the host portion, as shown in Figure 1-48. The network prefix is assigned by the IANA (or by any other assignment authority) and cannot be changed. Network administrators, however, can use the subnet prefix to split the address space into various smaller groups.

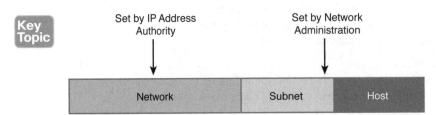

Figure 1-48   *IP Address Format with Subnet*

For example, an organization receiving a Class B range of IP addresses, 172.1.0.0/16, could use Subnets to further split the address range. Using 8 bits for the subnet ID, for example, they could create 255 subnets, 172.1.1.0/24, 172.1.2.0/24, 172.1.3.0/24 etc., as shown in Figure 1-49 each with 253 (255 − 2) IP addresses that could be assigned to hosts within the subnet.

Network	Subnet	Host
10101100. 00000001	00000001.	00000000
172 1	1	0

Figure 1-49   *Example of IP Address and Subnet*

There are two fundamental rules when using subnets in the IP address architecture:

- Hosts within the same subnet should be assigned only IP addresses provided by the host portion of that subnet.

- Traffic between subnets needs a router or a Layer 3 device to flow. This is because each subnet represents a broadcast domain.

So how do you know how a network has been subnetted? You use network masks. In the case of subnets, the network mask would set all 1s for the network part plus the subnet prefix, while the host part would be all 0s. For example, each subnet derived from the Class B network in Figure 1-49 would get a network mask of 255.255.255.0, or /24.

Variable-Length Subnet Mask (VLSM)

Classic subnetting splits a network into equal parts. This might not be completely efficient because, for example, one subnet may require fewer IP addresses than others. Let's suppose we have three subnets: SubA, SubB, and SubC. Each subnet has a different number of devices that require an IP address, as shown in Figure 1-50.

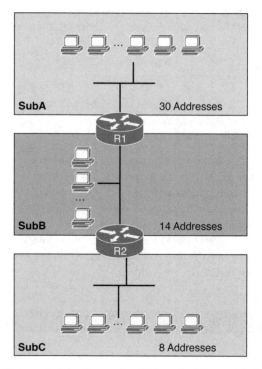

Figure 1-50   *Example of Three Subnets with Different Requirements for IP Addresses*

Let's assume that the subnets have the following requirements in terms of IP addresses:

■ SubA requires 30 IP addresses.

■ SubB requires 14 IP addresses.

■ SubC requires eight IP addresses.

Because of the requirement of SubA, in classic subnetting, we would use a subnet mask of /27 so that 30 hosts can be assigned an IP address. However, all the other subnets will also receive a /27 address because of the fixed way a subnet is split. For example, we would create and assign the addresses and subnets as detailed in Table 1-10.

Table 1-10   Classic Subnetting

Subnet	Network	Number of IP addresses
SubA	172.16.1.0/27	30
SubB	172.16.1.32/27	30
SubC	172.16.1.64/27	30
SubD	172.16.1.96/27	30
SubE	172.16.1.128/27	30
SubE	172.16.1.160/27	30

Subnet	Network	Number of IP addresses
SubF	172.16.1.192/27	30
SubG	172.16.1.224/27	30

The first subnet, SubA, will consume all the IP addresses; however, SubB will only use 14 out of the 30 provided, SubC will only use eight out of 30, and SubD through SubG will be unused, thus wasting 30 IP addresses each.

The variable-length subnet mask (VLSM) method allows you to subnet a network with subnets of different sizes. The size will be calculated based on the actual need for IP addresses in each subnet. Table 1-11 shows how the VLSM approach can be used in our example. SubA will still need 30 hosts, so it will keep the former subnet mask. SubB only needs 14 IP addresses, so it can use a /28 subnet mask, which allows for up to 14 IP addresses. SubC needs eight IP addresses, so it will also use a /28 subnet mask, because a /29 subnet mask would allow only six IP addresses—that is, 8 − 2 (for the network and broadcast addresses). There is no need to create other subnets, which further saves IP addresses.

Table 1-11   Subnetting with VLSM

Subnet	Network	Number of IP addresses
SubA	172.16.1.0/27	30
SubB	172.16.1.32/28	14
SubC	172.16.1.48/28	14

Public and Private IP Addresses

Based on the discussion so far, it is probably clear that IP addresses are scarce resources and that reducing the number of unused IP addresses is a priority due to the exponential growth of the use of TCP/IP and the Internet. CIDR, subnets, and VLSM have greatly helped with optimizing the IP addressing architecture, but by themselves have not been enough to handle the amount of requests for IP addresses.

In most organizations, probably not all the devices need to be reachable from the Internet. Some or even most of them just need to be reached within the organization. For example, an internal database might need to be reached by applications within the organization boundaries, but there is no need to make it accessible for everyone on the Internet.

A *private IP addresses range* is a range that can be used by any organization without requiring a specific assignment from an IP address assignment authority. The rule is, however, that these ranges can be used only within the organization and should never be used to send traffic over the Internet.

Figure 1-51 shows two organizations using IP address ranges. RFC 1918 defines three IP address ranges for private use:

- 10.0.0.0/8 network
- 172.16.0.0/12 network
- 192.168.0.0/16 network

Be careful not to confuse these address ranges with Class A, B, or C because the network masks are different.

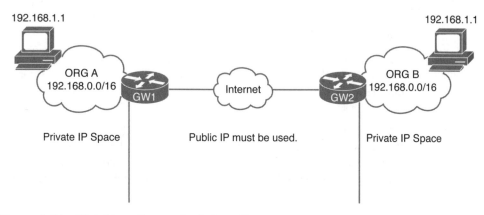

Figure 1-51 *IP Address Ranges for Private Use*

Organizations can pick one of these ranges and assign IP addresses internally (for example, using classic subnetting or VLSM). You may have noticed that when you connect to your home router (for example, over Wi-Fi), you may get an IP address that looks like 192.168.x.x. This is because your home router is using the 192.168.0.0/16 network to provide addresses for the local LAN.

Because two organizations can use the same network range, there could be two devices with the same IP address within these two organizations. What if these two devices want to send and receive traffic to and from each other? Recall that we said that private IP addresses should never be used on the Internet. So how can a host with a private IP address browse a web server on the Internet?

The method that is used to solve this problem is *network address translation (NAT)*. NAT uses the concept of a local IP address and a global (or public) IP address. The local IP address is the IP address assigned to a host within the organization, and it is usually a private address. Other devices within the organization will use this address to communicate with that device. The global IP address is the IP address used outside the organization, and it is a public IP address.

NOTE Two hosts are not permitted to have the same IP address within a subnet. If, within an organization, two hosts have the same IP address, then NAT needs to be performed within the organization to allow traffic.

The following example shows how NAT is used to allow communication between two hosts with the same IP address belonging to two different organizations (see Figure 1-52):

Step 1.   Host A initiates the traffic with the source IP address 192.168.1.1, which is the local IP address, and the destination 2.2.2.2, which is the global IP address of Host B.

Step 2.   When the packet reaches the Internet gateway of Organization A, the router notices that Host A needs to reach a device on the Internet. Therefore, it will perform an address translation and change the source IP address of the packet with the global IP address of Host A (for example, to 1.1.1.1). This is needed because the 192.168.1.1 address is only locally significant and cannot be routed over the Internet.

Step 3.   The Internet gateway of Organization B receives a packet for Host B. It notices that this is the global IP address of Host B, so it will perform an address translation and change the destination IP address to 192.168.1.1 which is the local IP address for Host B.

Step 4.   If Host B replies, it will send a packet with the source IP address of its local IP address, 192.168.1.1, and a destination of the global IP address of Host A (1.1.1.1). The Internet gateway at Organization B would follow a similar process and translate the source IP address of the packet to match the global IP address of Host B.

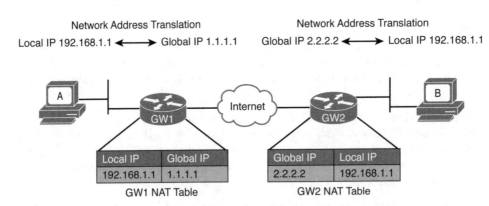

Figure 1-52 *Using NAT to Allow Communication Between Two Hosts with the Same IP Addresses Belonging to Two Different Organizations*

How do Internet gateways know about the link between global and local IP addresses? The information is included in a table, which is called the NAT table. This is a simple example of how NAT works. NAT is described in more detail in Chapter 2, "Network Security Devices and Cloud Services."

Special and Reserved IPv4 Addresses

Besides the private addresses, additional IPv4 addresses have been reserved and cannot be used to route traffic over the Internet. Table 1-12 provides a summary of IPv4 unicast special addresses based on RFC 6890. For example, 169.254.0.0/16 is used as the link local address and can be used to communicate only within a subnet (that is, it cannot be routed).

Table 1-12 IPv4 Unicast Special Addresses

Address Range	Use
0.0.0.0/8	This host on this network
10.0.0.0/8	Private use
100.64.0.0/10	Shared address space
127.0.0.0/8	Loopback
169.254.0.0/16	Link local
172.16.0.0/12	Private use
192.0.0.0/24	IETF protocol assignments
192.0.0.0/29	DS-Lite
192.0.2.0/24	Documentation (TEST-NET-1)
192.88.99.0/24	6to4 Relay Anycast
192.168.0.0/16	Private use
198.18.0.0/15	Benchmarking
198.51.100.0/24	Documentation (TEST-NET-2)
203.0.113.0/24	Documentation (TEST-NET-3)
240.0.0.0/4	Reserved
255.255.255.255/32	Limited broadcast

IP Addresses Assignment and DHCP

So far you have learned that each device in a subnet must receive an IP address so it can send and receive IP packets. How do we assign an IP address to a device or interface?

Two methods are available for assigning IP addresses:

- **Static address assignment:** With this method, someone needs to log in to the device and statically assign an IP address and network mask. The advantage of this method is that the IP address will not change because it is statically configured on the device. The disadvantage is that this is a manual configuration. This is typically used on networking devices or on a server where it is important that the IP address is always the same. For example, the following commands can be used to assign an IP address to the F0/0 interface of a Cisco IOS router:

  ```
  Interface FastEthernet 0/0
  ip address 10.0.0.2 255.255.255.0
  ```

- **Dynamic address assignment:** If there are hundreds or thousands of devices, configuring each of them manually is probably not the best use of anyone's time. Additionally, if for some reason the network administrator changes something in the network mask, network topology, and so on, all devices might need to be reconfigured. Dynamic address assignment allows automatic IP address assignment for networking devices. The Dynamic Host Configuration Protocol (DHCP) is used to provide dynamic address assignment and to provision additional configuration to networking devices. An older protocol not in use anymore and that provided similar services was the BOOTP protocol.

Let's explore how DHCP works.

DHCP, which is described in RFC 2131, is a client-server protocol that allows for the automatic provisioning of network configurations to a client device. The DHCP server is configured with a pool of IP addresses that can be assigned to devices. The IP address is not statically assigned to a client, but the DHCP server "leases" the address for a certain amount of time. When the duration of the leasing period is close to expiring, the client can request to renew the leasing. Together with the IP addresses, the DHCP server can provide other configurations.

Here are some examples of network configurations that can be provisioned via DHCP:

- IP address
- Network mask
- Default gateway address
- DNS server address
- Domain name

DHCP uses UDP as the transport protocol on port 67 for the server and port 68 for the client. DHCP defines several types of messages:

- **DHCPDISCOVERY**: Used by a client to discover DHCP servers within a LAN. It can include some preferences for addresses or lease period. It is sent to the network broadcast address or to the broadcast address 255.255.255.255 and usually carries as a source IP of 0.0.0.0.

- **DHCPOFFER**: Sent by a DHCP server to a client. It includes a proposed IP address, called YIADDR, and a network mask. It must also include the server ID, which is the IP address of the server. This is also called SIADDR. There could be multiple DHCP servers within a LAN, so multiple DHCPOFFER messages can be sent in response to a DHCPDISCOVERY.

- **DHCPREQUEST**: Sent from the client to the broadcast network. This message is used to confirm the offer from a particular server. It includes the SIADDR of the DHCP server that has been selected. This is broadcast and not unicast because it provides information to the DHCP servers that have not been chosen about the choice of the client.

- **DHCP ACKNOWLEDGEMENT (DHCPACK)**: Sent from the server to the client to confirm the proposed IP address and other information.

- **DHCP Not ACKNOWLEDGED (DHCPNACK)**: Sent from the server to the client in case some issues with the IP address assignment are raised after the DHCPOFFER.

- **DHCPDECLINE**: Sent from the client to the server to highlight that the IP address assigned is in use.

- **DHCPRELEASE:** Sent from the client to the server to release the allocation of an IP address and to end the lease.
- **DHCPINFORM:** Sent from the client to the server. It is used to request additional network configuration; however, the client already has an IP address assigned.

The following steps provide an example of a basic DHCP IP address request (see Figure 1-53):

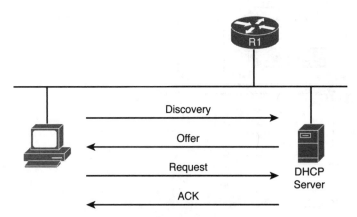

Figure 1-53   *Basic DHCP IP Address Assignment Process*

Step 1.   When a host first connects to a LAN, it does not have an IP address. It will send a DHCPDISCOVERY packet to discover the DHCP servers within a LAN. In one LAN there could be more than one DHCP server.

Step 2.   Each DHCP server responds with DHCPOFFER message.

Step 3.   The client receives several offers, picks one of them, and responds with a DHCPREQUEST.

Step 4.   The DHCP server that has been selected responds to the client with a DHCPACK to confirm the leasing of the IP address.

What happens if there is no DHCP server within a subnet? To make it work, the Layer 3 device needs to be configured as DHCP relay or DHCP helper. In that case, the router will take the broadcast requests (for example, DHCPDISCOVERY and DHCPREQUEST) and unicast them to the DHCP server configured in the relay, as shown in Figure 1-54. When the DHCP server replies, the router will forward it to the client.

Figure 1-54 shows an example of DHCP relay. The host sends a DHCP DISCOVERY broadcast in the network segment where it is directly connected, 10.0.1.0/24. The router R1 is configured with a helper address, 10.0.1.1, within that subnet. Because of that, R1 picks up the DHCP REQUEST and forwards it to the DHCP server configured. The server will answer the DHCP DISCOVERY with a DHCP OFFER, which is sent directly to the IP helper address of R1. When R1 receives the answer from the DHCP server, it will forward the answer to the host.

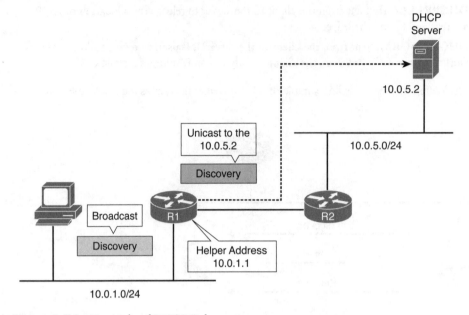

Figure 1-54 *Example of DHCP Relay*

IP Communication Within a Subnet and Address Resolution Protocol (ARP)

In the previous section, you learned how each device in a subnet gets its own IP address. So let's see how devices communicate in a subnet first, and then in the next section we will discuss how devices communicate across multiple subnets. Let's imagine Host A with IP address 10.0.0.1 wants to communicate with Host B in the same subnet with IP address 10.0.0.3. At this point, Host A knows the IP address of Host B; however, Layer 2 still requires the MAC destination address for Host B. How can Host A get this information? Host A will use the Address Resolution Protocol (ARP) to get the MAC address of Host B.

ARP includes two messages:

- **ARP request:** This is used to request the MAC address given an IP address. It includes the IP address and MAC address of the device sending the request and only the IP address of the destination.

- **ARP reply:** This is used to provide information about a MAC address. It includes the IP address and MAC address of the device responding to the ARP request and the IP address and MAC address of the device that sent the ARP request.

When Host A needs to send a message to Host B for the first time, it will send an ARP request message using the Layer 2 broadcast address so that all devices within the broadcast domain receive the request. Host B will see the request and recognize that the request is looking for its IP address. It will respond with an ARP reply indicating its own MAC address. Host A stores this information in an ARP table, so the next time it does not have to go through the ARP exchanges.

Figure 1-55 shows an example of an ARP message exchange.

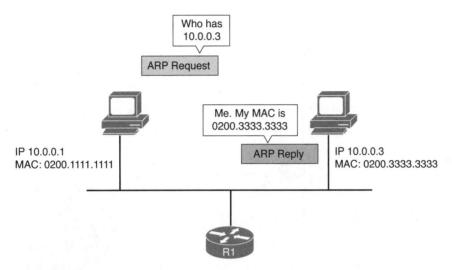

Figure 1-55 *ARP Message Exchange*

Once the MAC address of the destination is known, Host A can send packets directly to Host B by encapsulating the IP packet within an Ethernet frame, as discussed in the previous sections.

Intersubnet IP Packet Routing

In the previous sections, you learned how IP communication works within a subnet. In this section, we analyze how packets move across subnets. As stated in the previous sections, each subnet is divided by a Layer 3 device (for example, a router). Figure 1-56 shows two hosts, Host A and Host B, which belong to different subnets, and Host C, which is in the same subnet as Host A. The two routers, R1 and R2, provide Layer 3 connectivity, and R3 is the gateway to the rest of the network. The table shown in this figure includes the IP addresses for the relevant interfaces and hosts.

When Host A needs to send a packet, it must make a decision on where to send the packet. The logic implemented by the host is simple:

■ If the destination IP address is in the same subnet as the interface IP address, the packet is sent directly to the device.

■ If the destination IP address is in a different subnet, it is sent to the default gateway.

The default gateway for a host is the router that allows the packet to exit the host subnet (in this example, R1). The logic is implemented in Host A's routing table. Host A will see network 10.0.1.1/24 as directly connected and will have an entry saying that packets for any other IP addresses go to the default gateway.

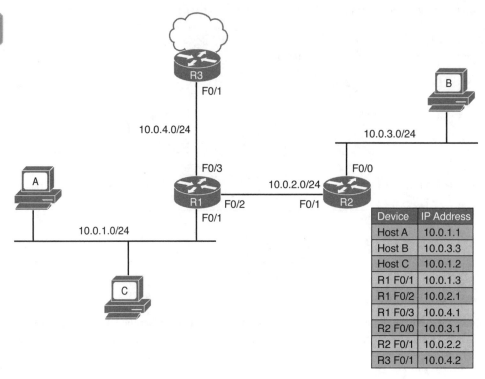

Figure 1-56 *Example of a Network Topology with Three Routers*

Figure 1-57 shows the routing table for Host A.

```
❌ ⚫ ⚪  cisco@HostA:~

cisco@HostA:~$ route -n
Kernel IP routing table
Destination    Gateway      Genmask          Flags Metric Ref    Use Iface
0.0.0.0        10.0.1.3     0.0.0.0          UG    0      0        0 eht0
10.0.1.0       0.0.0.0      255.255.255.0    U     0      0        0 eth0
cisco@HostA:~$ ▮
```

Figure 1-57 *Host A's Routing Table*

Let's assume Host A needs to send a packet to Host B; it will check its routing table and decide that the packet's next hop (which means the next Layer 3 device to handle this packet) is R1 F0/1, with an IP address of 10.0.1.3/24. If Host A does not know the Layer 2 address of R1, it will send an ARP request, as discussed in the previous section.

R1 receives the packets from Host A on the F0/1 interface. At this point, R1 will do a routing table lookup to check where packets with the destination 10.0.3.3 should be sent. Table 1-13 shows what the R1 routing table might look like.

Table 1-13   Example of the R1 Routing Table

Network	Next-Hop	Interface
10.0.1.0/24	Directly connected	F0/1
10.0.2.0/24	Directly connected	F0/2
10.0.4.0/24	Directly connected	F0/3
10.0.3.0/24	10.0.2.2	F0/2
0.0.0.0/0	10.0.4.2	F0/3

Networks 10.0.1.0/24, 10.0.2.0/24, and 10.0.4.0/24 are directly connected to the router. Network 10.0.3.0/24, which is the network of the destination IP address, has a next hop of R2. The last network, 0.0.0.0/0, is called the default network. This means that, if there is no better match, R1 will send the packet to 10.0.4.2, which is the F0/1 interface of R3. R1 is said to have a default route via R3.

When looking up the routing table, the router will use the interface with the best matching network, which is the network with the longest prefix match. For example, imagine that the router includes the two entries in its routing table outlined in Table 1-14.

Table 1-14   Example of the Longest Prefix Match to Decide the Next Hop

Network	Next Hop	Interface
10.0.3.0/24	10.0.2.2	F0/2
10.0.0.0/16	10.0.4.2	F0/3

Where would a packet with a destination of IP 10.0.3.3 be sent? In this case, 10.0.3.0/24 is a closer match than 10.0.0.0/16 (longest prefix match), so the router will select 10.0.2.2 via the F0/2 interface.

Let's go back to our example. R1 identified R2 as the next hop for this packet. R1 will update the IP header information (for example, it will reduce the TTL field by one and recalculate the checksum). After that, it will encapsulate the packet in an Ethernet frame and send it to R2. Remember that R1 does not modify the IP addresses of the packet. When R2 receives the IP packet on F0/1, it will again perform a routing table lookup to understand what to do with the packet. The R2 routing table might look something like Table 1-15.

Table 1-15   Example of the R2 Routing Table

Network	Next Hop	Interface
10.0.3.0/24	Directly connected	F0/0
10.0.2.0/24	Directly connected	F0/1
0.0.0.0/0	10.0.2.1	F0/1

Because the destination IP address matches a directly connected network, R2 can send the packet directly to Host B via the F0/0 interface. If Host B replies to Host A, it will send an IP packet with a destination of IP 10.0.1.1 to R2, which is the default gateway for Host B.

R2 does not have a match for the 10.0.1.1 address; however, it is configured to send anything for which it does not have a match to 10.0.2.1 (R1) via the F0/1 interface. R2 has a default route via R1. R2 will send the packet to R1, which will then deliver to Host A.

Routing Tables and IP Routing Protocols

The routing table is a key component of the forwarding decision. How is this table populated? The connected network will be automatically added when the interface is configured. In fact, the device can determine the connected network from the interface IP address and network mask. The host default gateway can also be configured statically or, as you saw in the "IP Addresses Assignment and DHCP" section, dynamically assigned via DHCP.

For the other entries, there are two options:

- **Static routes:** Routes that have been manually added by the device administrator. Static routes are used when the organization does not use an IP routing protocol or when the device cannot participate in an IP routing protocol.

- **Dynamic routes:** Routes that are dynamically learned using an IP routing protocol exchange.

An *IP routing protocol* is a protocol that allows the exchange of information among Layer 3 devices (for example, among routers) in order to build up the routing table and thus allow the routing of IP packets across the network. A *routed protocol* is the protocol that actually transports the information and allows for packet forwarding. For example, IPv4 and IPv6 are routed protocols.

Each routing protocol has two major characteristics that need to be defined by the protocol itself:

- How and which type of information is exchanged, and when it should be exchanged
- What algorithm is used by each device to calculate the best path to destination

This book does not go into the details of all the routing protocols available; however, it is important that you are familiar at least with the basic functioning of how an IP routing protocol works.

The first classification of a routing protocol is based on where it operates in a network:

- Interior gateway protocols (IGPs) operate within the organization boundaries. Here are some examples of IGPs:
  - Open Shortest Path First (OSPF)
  - Intermediate System to Intermediate System (IS-IS)

- Enhanced Interior Gateway Routing Protocol (EIGRP)

- Routing Information Protocol Version 2 (RIPv2)

- Exterior gateway protocols (EGPs) operate between service providers or very large organizations. An example of an EGP is the Border Gateway Protocol (BGP).

An autonomous system (AS) is a collection of routing information under the administration of a single organization entity. Usually the concept coincides with a single organization. Each AS is identified by an AS number (ASN). IGPs run within an autonomous system, whereas EGPs run across autonomous systems.

Figure 1-58 shows an example of autonomous systems interconnected with EGPs and running IGPs inside.

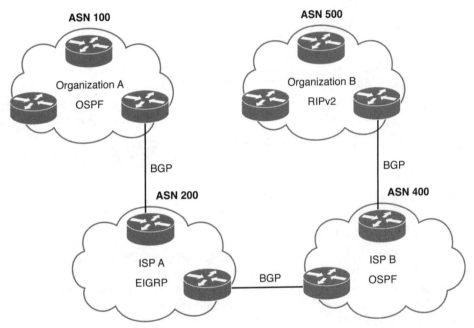

Figure 1-58 *Autonomous Systems Interconnected with EGPs and IGPs Running Inside*

The other common way of classifying IP routing protocols is based on the algorithm used to learn routes from other devices and choose the best path to a destination. The most common algorithms for IGP protocols are distance vector (used in RIPv2), link-state (used in OSPF or IS-IS), and advanced distance vector (also called hybrid, used in EIGRP).

Distance Vector

Distance vector (DV) is one of the first algorithms used for exchanging routing information, and it is usually based on the Bellman-Ford algorithm. The most well-known IP routing protocol using DV is RIPv2. To better understand how DV works, let's introduce two concepts:

- *Neighbors* are two routers or Layer 3 devices that are directly connected.

- *Hop count* is a number that represents the distance (that is, the number of routers on the path) between a router and a specific network.

A device running a DV protocol will send a "vector of distances," which is a routing protocol message to the neighbors, that contains the information about all the networks the device can reach and the cost.

In Figure 1-59, R2 will send a message to R1 saying that it can reach NetB 10.0.3.0/24 with a cost of 0, because it is directly connected, while it can reach NetC 10.0.5.0/24 with a cost of 1. R3 also sends a message to R1 saying that it can reach NetC 10.0.5.0/24 with a cost of 2 and NetB 10.0.3.0/24 with a cost of 1. R1 receives the information and updates its routing table. It will add both NetB and NetC as reachable via R2 because it has the lowest hop count to the destinations.

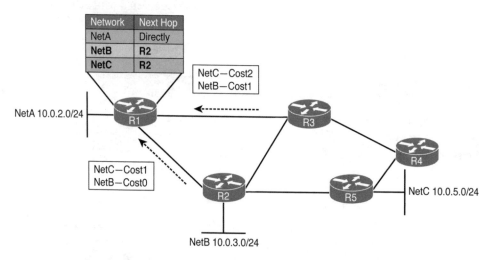

Figure 1-59   *Example of a Distance Vector Exchange*

The exchange continues until all routers have a stable routing table. At this point, the routing protocol has converged. Neighbor routers also exchange periodic messages. If the link to a neighbor goes down, both router will detect the situation and inform the other neighbors about the situation. Each neighbor will inform its own neighbors, and the routing tables will be updated accordingly until the protocol converges again.

There are several issues with DV protocols:

■ Using hop count as the cost to determine the best path to a destination is not the best method. For example, you may have three routers operating with a bandwidth of 1 Gbps and two routers operating with a bandwidth of 1 Mbps. It is probably better for the packet to travel through one more router but with a better bandwidth.

■ Routers do not have full visibility into the network topology (they know only what the neighbor routers tell them), so calculating the best path might not be optimal.

■ Each update includes an exchange of the full list of networks and costs, which can consume bandwidth.

■ It is not loop free. Because of how the algorithm works, in some scenarios packets might start looping in the network. This problem is known as *count to infinity*. To solve this issue, routing protocols based on DV implement split-horizon and reverse-poison techniques. These techniques, however, increase the time the routing protocol takes to converge to a stable situation.

Advanced Distance Vector or Hybrid

To overcome most of the downside of legacy DV protocols such as RIPv2, there is a class of protocols that are based on DV but that implement several structural modifications to the protocol behavior. These are sometimes called advanced distance vector or hybrid protocols, and one of the most known is Cisco EIGRP.

Figure 1-60 shows an example of an EIGRP message exchange between two neighbors. At the beginning, the two routers discover each other with Neighbor Discovery hello packets. Once neighborship is established, the two routers exchange the full routing information, in a similar way as in DV. When an update is due (for example, because of a topology change), only specific information is sent rather than the full update.

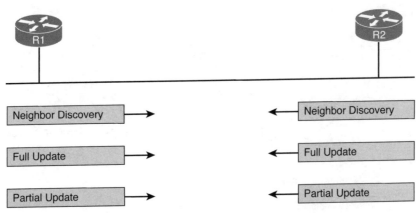

Figure 1-60 *Example of EIGRP Message Exchange*

Here are the main enhancements of these types of protocols:

- They do not use hop count as a metric to determine the best path to a network. Bandwidth and delay are typically used to determine the best path; however, other metrics can be used in combination, such as load on the link and the reliability of the link.

- The full database update is only sent at initialization, and partial updates are sent in the event of topology changes. This reduces the bandwidth consumed by the protocol.

- They include a more robust method to avoid loops and reduce the convergence time. For example, EIGRP routers maintain a partial topology table and include an algorithm called Diffused Update Algorithm (DUAL), which is used to calculate the best path to a destination and provides a mechanism to avoid loops.

Link-State

Link-state algorithms operate in a totally different way than DV, and the fundamental difference is that devices that participate in an IP routing protocol based on a link-state algorithm will have a full view of the network topology; therefore, they can use an algorithm such as Dijkstra or Shortest Path First (SPF) to calculate the best path to each network. The most well-known IP routing protocols using link-state are OSPF and IS-IS.

This section describes the basic functioning of link-state by using OSPF as the basis for the examples. In link-state routing protocols, the concept of router neighbors is maintained while the cost to reach a specific network is based on several parameters. For example, in OSPF, the higher the bandwidth, the lower the cost.

During the initiation phase, each router will send a link-state advertisement (LSA) to the neighbors, which will then forward it to all other neighbors. In Figure 1-61, R2 will send an LSA containing information about its directly connected network and the cost to R1, R3, and R5. Both R3 and R5 will forward this information to their neighbor routers (in this case, R1 and R4). This process is called *LSA flooding*.

Each router will collect all the LSAs and store them in a database called a link-state database (LSDB).

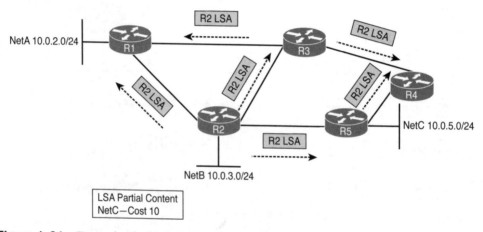

Figure 1-61   *Example of a Link-State Advertisement Exchange*

In this example, R1 receives the same LSA from both R2 and R3. Because there is already one LSA present in the R1 LSDB from R2, the one received from R3 is discarded. At the end of the flooding process, each router should have an identical view of the network topology.

A router can now use an SPF algorithm to calculate the best way to reach each of the networks. Once that is done, the information is added to the router's routing table. When a link goes down, the neighbor routers that detect it will again flood an LSA with the updated information. Each router will receive the LSA, update the LSDB with that information, recalculate the best path, and update the routing table accordingly.

Advantages of a link-state algorithm include the following:

- A better way to calculate the cost to a destination
- Less protocol overhead compared to DV because updates do not require sending the full topology

- Better best-path calculation because each router has a view of the full topology
- Loop-free

Using Multiple Routing Protocols

An organization can run more than one routing protocol within a network; for example, they can use a combination of static routes and dynamic routes learned via a routing protocol. What happens if the same destination is provided by two routing protocols with a different next hop?

Routers may assign a value, called an *administrative distance* in Cisco routers, that is used to determine the precedence based on the way the router has learned about a specific network. For example, we may want the router to use the route information provided by OSPF instead of the one provided by RIPv2.

Table 1-16 summarizes the default administrative distance of a Cisco IOS router. These values can be modified to tweak the route selection if needed.

Table 1-16   Cisco IOS Router Default Administrative Distances

Route Source	Default Distance Values
Connected interface	0
Static route	1
Enhanced Interior Gateway Routing Protocol (EIGRP) summary route	5
External Border Gateway Protocol (BGP)	20
Internal EIGRP	90
IGRP	100
OSPF	110
Intermediate System-to-Intermediate System (IS-IS)	115
Routing Information Protocol (RIP)	120
Exterior Gateway Protocol (EGP)	140
On Demand Routing (ODR)	160
External EIGRP	170
Internal BGP	200
Unknown	255

Internet Control Message Protocol (ICMP)

The Internet Control Message Protocol (ICMP) is part of the Internet Protocol suite, and its main purpose is to provide a way to communicate that an error occurred during the routing of IP packets.

ICMP packets are encapsulated directly within the IP payload. An IP packet transporting an ICMP message in its payload sets the Protocol field in the header to 1. The ICMP packet starts with an ICMP header that always includes the Type and Code fields of the ICMP message, which define what that message is used for. ICMP also defines several Message types. Each Message type can include a code.

Table 1-17 provides a summary of the most used values for ICMP Type and Code fields. A full list can be found at http://www.iana.org/assignments/icmp-parameters/icmp-parameters. xhtml.

Table 1-17 Most Used ICMP Types and Codes

Type	Code	Description
0 – Echo Reply	0	
3 – Destination Unreachable	0	Network unreachable
	1	Host unreachable
	2	Protocol unreachable
	3	Port unreachable
	4	Fragmentation required, and DF flag set
8 – Echo Request	0	
11 – Time Exceeded	0	TTL Exceed in transit
	1	Fragment reassembly time exceeded

Probably the most known use of an ICMP message is Ping, which is a utility implemented in operating systems using TCP/IP and used to confirm the reachability of a remote host at Layer 3. Ping uses ICMP to perform the task. When you ping a remote destination, an ICMP Echo Request (type 8 code 0) is sent to the destination. If the packet arrives at the destination, the destination sends an ICMP Echo Reply (type 0 code 0) back to the host. This confirms connectivity at Layer 3.

Figure 1-62 shows an example of an ICMP Echo Request and Echo Reply exchange.

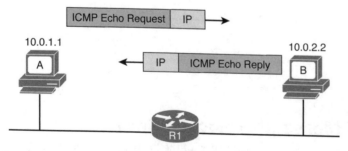

Figure 1-62 *ICMP Echo Request and Echo Reply Exchange*

Another very popular ICMP message is Destination Unreachable. This is used for a number of cases, as you can see by the large number of codes for this type. For example, if Host A pings a remote host, but your default gateway does not have information on how to route the packet to that destination, it will send back an ICMP Destination Unreachable – Network Unreachable message (type 3 code 0) back to Host A to communicate that the packet was dropped and could not be delivered.

An ICMP Time Exceeded message is instead generated when a router receives an IP packet with an expired TTL value. The router will drop the packet and send back to the IP packet source an ICMP Time Exceeded – TTL Exceed in Transit message (type 11 code 0).

Domain Name System (DNS)

In all the examples so far, we always had Host A sending a packet to Host B using its IP address. However, having to remember IP addresses is not very convenient. Imagine if you had to remember 72.163.4.161 instead of www.cisco.com when you wanted to browse resources on the Cisco web server.

The solution is called the Domain Name System (DNS). DNS is a hierarchical and distributed database that is used to provide a mapping between an IP address and the name of the device where that IP is assigned.

This section introduces DNS and describes its basic functionalities. DNS works at TCP/IP application layer; however, it is included in this section to complete the overview of how two hosts communicate.

DNS is based on a hierarchical architecture called domain namespace. The hierarchy is organized in a tree structure, where each leaf represents a specific resource and is uniquely identified by its fully qualified domain name (FQDN). The FQDN is formed by linking together the names in the hierarchy, starting from the leaf name up to the root of the tree.

Figure 1-63 shows an example of a DNS domain namespace. The FQDN of the host www. cisco.com is composed, starting from the root, by its top-level domain (TLD), which is *com*, then the second level domain, *cisco*, and finally by the resource name or host name, *www*, which is the name for a server used to provide world-wide web services. Another resource within the same second-level domain could be, for example, a server called *tools*, in which case the FQDN would be tools.cisco.com.

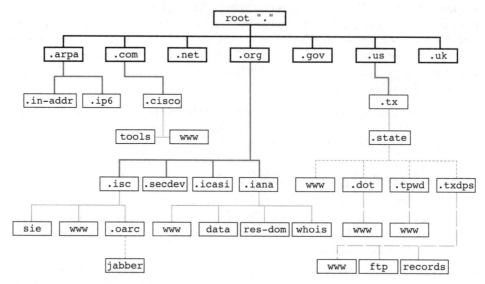

Figure 1-63 *DNS Domain Namespace*

Table 1-18 summarizes the types of domain names.

Table 1-18   Domain Names

Type	Use
Root	The root domain is usually indicated by a dot (.), and it indicates the top of DNS hierarchy.
Top-level domains	This type of domain is maintained by IANA. Several types of TLDs exist. For example, the TLD could be *.com*, which usually refers to commercial organizations, or, for example, .it, which is a country code for Italy.
Second-level domains	The second-level domains (for example, *cisco*).
Subdomains	Any subdomains within the same second-level domain.
Resource name	The hostname of the resource (for example, w*ww*).

Each entry in the DNS database is called a *resource record* (RR) and includes several fields. Figure 1-64 shows an example of a resource record structure.

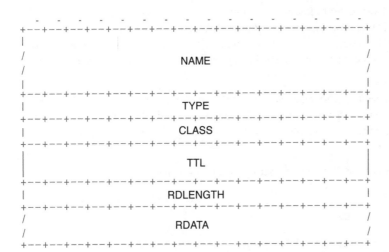

Figure 1-64 *RR Structure*

The Type field of the RR indicates which type of resources are included in the RDATA field. For example, the RR type "A" refers to the address record and includes the hostname and the associated IP address. This RR is used for the main functionality of DNS, which is to provide an IP address based on an FQDN.

Table 1-19 summarizes other common RRs.

Table 1-19 Common RRs

Type	Description	Use
A	Address record IPv4	Mapping between IPv4 and FQDN
AAAA	Address record IPv6	Mapping between IPv6 and FQDN
MX	Mail Exchange record	Includes information about mail exchange servers in a domain
NS	Name Server record	Indicates the authoritative servers for a DNS zone
SOA	Start of Authority record	Includes information about the zone, such as the authoritative name server for that zone

The DNS database is divided into DNS zones. A *zone* is a portion of the DNS database that is managed by an entity. Each zone must have an SOA RR that includes information about the management of the zone and the primary authoritative name server. Each DNS zone must have an authoritative name server. This server is the one that has the information about the resources present in the DNS zone and can respond to queries concerning those resources.

So how then does Host A get to know the IP address of the www.cisco.com server? The process is very simple. Host A will ask its configured DNS server about the IP address of www.cisco.com. If its DNS knows the answer, it will reply. Otherwise, it will reach the authoritative DNS server for www.cisco.com to get the answer. Let's see the process in a bit more detail.

Host A needs to query the DNS database to find the answer. In the context of DNS, Host A, or in general any entity that requests a DNS service, is called a DNS *resolver*. The DNS resolver sends queries to its own DNS server that is configured (for example, via DHCP), as in the previous section.

There are two types of DNS queries, sometimes called lookups:

■ Recursive queries
■ Iterative queries

Recursive queries are sent from the DNS resolver to its own DNS server. Iterative queries are sent from the DNS server to other DNS servers in case the initial DNS server does not have the answer to the recursive query.

Figure 1-65 shows an example of the DNS resolution process, as detailed in the following steps:

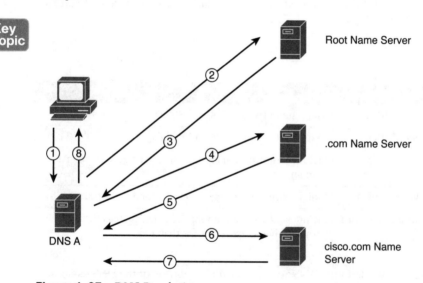

Figure 1-65   *DNS Resolution*

Step 1.   Host A sends a recursive DNS query for a type A record (remember, a type A RR is used to map IPv4 IP addresses to FQDN) to resolve www.cisco.com to its own DNS server, DNS A.

Step 2.   DNS A checks its DNS cache but does not find the information, so it sends an iterative DNS query to the root DNS server, which is authoritative for all of the Internet.

Step 3.   The root DNS server is not authoritative for that host, so it sends back a referral to the .com DNS server, which is the authoritative server for the .com domain.

Steps 4 and 5.   The .com DNS server performs a similar process and sends a referral to the cisco.com DNS server.

Steps 6 and 7.   The cisco.com DNS server is the DNS authoritative server for www.cisco.com, so it can reply to DNS A with the information.

Step 8.   DNS A receives the information and stores it in its DNS cache for future use. The information is stored in the cache for a finite time, which is indicated by the Time To Live (TTL) value in the response from the cisco.com DNS server. DNS A can now reply to the recursive DNS query from Host A.

Host A receives the information from DNS A and can start sending packets to www.cisco.com using the correct IP address. Additionally, it will store the information in its own DNS cache for a time indicated in the TTL field.

The DNS protocol, described in RFC 1035, uses one message format for both queries and replies. A DNS message includes five sections: Header, Question, Answer, Authority, and Additional.

The DNS protocol can use UDP or TCP as the transport protocol, and the DNS server is typically listening on port 53 for both UDP and TCP. According to RFC 1035, UDP port 53 is recommended for standard queries, whereas TCP is used for DNS zone transfer.

IPv6 Fundamentals

So far we have analyzed how two or more hosts can communicate using a routed protocol (for example, IP), mainly using IPv4. In this section, we cover the newer version of the IP protocol: IPv6.

With the growth of the Internet and communication networks based on TCP/IP, the number of IPv4 addresses quickly became a scarce resource. Using private addressing with NAT or CIDR has been fundamental to limiting the impact of the issue; however, a long-term solution was needed. IPv6 has been designed with that in mind, and its main purpose is to provide a larger IP address space to support the growth of the number of devices needing to communicate using the TCP/IP model.

Most of the concepts we have discussed in the sections on the Internet Protocol and Layer 3 technologies, such as the routing of a packet and routing protocols, work in a similar way with IPv6. Of course, some modifications need to be taken into account due to structural differences with IPv4 (for example, the IP address length).

This book will not go into detail on the IPv6 protocol; however, it is important that security professionals and candidates for the CCNA Cyber Ops SECFND certification have a basic understanding of IPv6 address, how IPv6 works, and its differences and commonalities with IPv4.

Table 1-20 summarizes the main differences and commonalities between IPv6 and IPv4.

Table 1-20   Comparing IPv6 and IPv4

	IPv6	IPv4
Address	Uses a 128-bit address.	Uses a 32-bit address.
Address type	Uses unicast, anycast, and multicast address types. Broadcast communication happens via a special multicast address.	Uses unicast, multicast, and broadcast address types.
Subnetting and prefix	Subnets can be used, and the network prefix is indicated as /nnn after the IP address.	Subnets can be used, and the network prefix is indicated as /nn after the IP address.
Address assignment	Supports several IP address assignment methods: ■ Static ■ Static prefix with EUI-64 and other methods ■ Stateless address auto-configuration (SLAAC) ■ Stateful DHCPv6	Supports static and dynamic address assignment via DHCP.
Private IP addresses	Supports the concept of private addresses in a similar way as IPv4. These types of addresses are called *unique-local addresses* and are described in RFC 4193. These address have similar properties as the IPv4 private IP addresses, cannot be routed over the Internet, and do not require Internet registries to assign them. Due to a different design and addressing concept in IPv6, private addresses are not used as they are for IPv4.	Supports private IP address as described in RFC 1918. Private IP addresses cannot be routed over the Internet.
Link-local address	Uses the FE80::/10 network.	Uses the 169.254.0.0/16 network.
Interface IP address	Can have multiple IPv6 addresses.	Can only have one address.
DNS	Uses AAAA type resource record.	Uses A type resource record.
IP header	Fixed length of 40 bytes. It does not support IP options but uses extension headers to carry information for Layer 3 protocols.	Varies between 20 and 60 bytes, depending on the IP options.
Reserved IP addresses	Described in RFC 6890.	Described in RFC 6890.
Routing protocols	Supports distance vector, link-state, and hybrid. It requires a new version of protocols specific for IPv6, such as RIPng, OSPFv3, EIGRP for IPv6. BGP-4 needs a multiprotocol extension (MP-BGP).	Supports distance vector, link-state, and hybrid. Commonly used protocols are RIPv2, OSPFv2, EIGRP, IS-IS for IGP, and BGP-4 for EGP.

	IPv6	IPv4
Management protocol	Uses ICMPv6.	Uses ICMP.
Address resolution	Uses Neighbor Discovery Protocol in a combination with ICMPv6. NDP security can be improved using SeND.	Uses the ARP protocol.
NAT	The IPv6 address architecture increases the address space, and each host is capable of receiving an Internet routable address, so NAT is not needed.	Uses NAT in conjunction with private addresses as a way to alleviate the issue with the scarce number of public IP addresses.

Figure 1-66 shows an example of communications between Host A and Host B using IPv6. Similar to the example we saw in the IPv4 section, Host A and Host B would have an IP address that can identify the device at Layer 3. Each router interface would also have an IPv6 address.

Host A will send the IPv6 packet encapsulated in an Ethernet frame to its default gateway, R1 (step 1).

R1 decapsulates the IPv6 packet, looks up the routing table, and finds that the next hop is R2. It encapsulates the packet in a new Layer 2 frame and sends it to R2 (step 2). R2 will follow a similar process and finally deliver the packet to Host B.

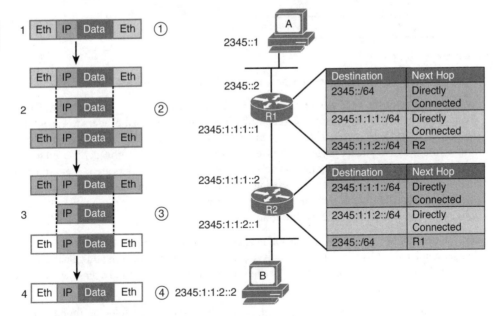

Figure 1-66 *Communication Between Hosts Using IPv6*

In the example in Figure 1-66, probably the most notable difference is the format of the IPv6 address. However, there are additional differences that are not visible. For example, how does an IPv6 host know about the default gateway? Is ARP needed to find out the MAC address given an IP address for intra-subnet traffic?

As discussed at the beginning of this section, several protocols that work for IPv4 could work with IPv6 with just a few modifications. Some others are not necessary with IPv6, and some new protocols had to be created. For example, ICMP and DHCP could not be used "as is," so new versions have been created: ICMPv6 and DHCPv6. The functionality of ARP has been replaced with a new protocol called IPv6 Neighbor Discovery. OSPF, EIGRP, and other routing protocols have been modified to work with IPv6, and new versions have been proposed, such as OSPFv3, EIGRPv6, and RIPng.

IPv6 Header

IPv6 has been designed to provide similar functionality to IPv4; however, it is actually a separate and new protocol rather than an improvement to IPv4. As such, RFC 2460 defines a new header for IPv6 packets.

Figure 1-67 shows an IPv6 header.

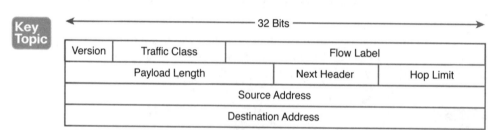

Figure 1-67 *IPv6 Header*

Most of the fields serve the same purpose as their counterparts in IPv4.

With IPv6, one of the core differences with IPv4 is the introduction of extension headers. Besides the fixed header, shown in Figure 1-67, IPv6 allows additional headers to carry information for Layer 3 protocols. The extension header is positioned just after the fixed header and before the IPv6 packet payload. The Next Header field in the IPv6 header is used to determine what the next header in the packet is. If no extension headers are present, the field will point to the Layer 4 header that is being transported (for example, the TCP header). This is similar to the IP protocol field in IPv4. If an extension header is present, it will indicate which type of extension header will follow.

IPv6 allows the use of multiple extension headers in a chained fashion. Each extension header contains a Next Header field that is used to determine whether an additional extension header follows. The last extension header in the chain indicates the Layer 4 header type being transported (for example, TCP).

Figure 1-68 shows examples of chained extension headers. The first shows an IPv6 header without any extension headers. This is indicated by the Next Header field set to TCP. In the third example of Figure 1-68, instead, the IPv6 header is followed by two extension headers: the Routing extension header and the Fragmentation extension header. The Fragmentation header's Next Header field is indicating that a TCP header will follow.

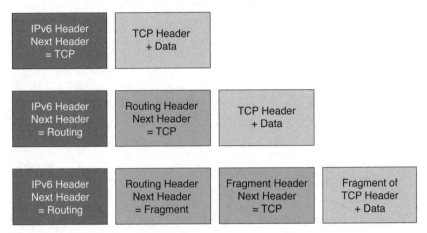

Figure 1-68 *Chained Extension Header*

IPv6 Addressing and Subnets

The most notable difference between IPv4 and IPv6 is the IP address and specifically the IP address length. The IPv6 address is 128 bits long, whereas the IPv4 address is only 32 bits. This is because IPv6 is aimed at increasing the IP address space to resolve the IPv4 address exhaustion issue and cope with the growth in demand of IP addresses. Similar to IPv4, writing an IPv6 address in binary is not convenient. IPv6 uses a different convention than IPv4 when it comes to writing down the IP address.

IPv6 addresses are represented by using four hexadecimal digits, which represent 16 bits, followed by a colon (:) An example of an IPv6 address is as follows:

2340:1111:AAAA:0001:1234:5678:9ABC:1234

Some additional simplification can be done to reduce the complexity of writing down an IPv6 address:

■ For each block of four digits, the leading zeros can be omitted.

■ If two or more consecutive blocks of four digits are 0000, they can be substituted with two colons (::). This, however, can only happen one time within an IPv6 address.

Let's use FE00:0000:0000:0001:0000:0000:0000:0056 as an example. The first rule will transform it as follows:

FE00:0:0:1:0:0:0:56

The second rule can be applied either to the second and third blocks or to the fifth, sixth, and seventh blocks, but not to both. The shortest form would be to apply it to the fifth, sixth, and seventh blocks, which results in the following:

FE00:0:0:1::56

Like IPv4, IPv6 supports prefix length notation to identify subnets. For example, an address could be written as 2222:1111:0:1:A:B:C:D/64, where the /64 indicates the prefix length. To find the network ID, you can use the same process we used for IPv4; that is, you can take the first *n* bits (in this case, 64) from the IPv6 address and set the remaining bits to zeros. Figure 1-69 illustrates the process.

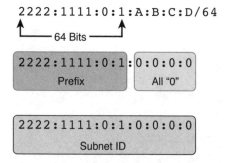

Figure 1-69   *Finding the Network ID of an IPv6 Address*

The resulting IPv6 address indicates the prefix or network for that IPv6 address. In our example, this would be 2222:1111:0:1:0:0:0:0 or 2222:1111:0:1::.

IPv6 also defines three types of addresses:

- **Unicast:** Used to identify one specific interface.

- **Anycast:** Used to identify a set of interfaces (for example, on multiple nodes). When this address is used, packets are usually delivered to the nearest interface with that address.

- **Multicast:** Used to identify a set of interfaces. When this address is used, packets are usually delivered to all interfaces identified by that identifier.

In IPv6, there is no concept of broadcast address as we have seen for IPv4. To send packets in broadcast, IPv6 uses a multicast address. Several types of addresses are defined within these three main classes. In this book, we will not analyze all types of addresses and instead will focus on two particular types defined within the Unicast class: global unicast and link-local unicast addresses (LLA).

In very simple terms, the difference between global unicast and link-local unicast is that the former can be routed over the Internet whereas the latter is only locally significant within the local link, and it is used for specific operations such as for the Neighbor Discovery Protocol process.

One concept that is unique for IPv6 is that one interface can have multiple IPv6 addresses. For example, the same interface can have a link-local and a global unicast address. Actually, this is one of the most common cases. In fact, IPv6 mandates that all interfaces have at least one link-local address.

The global unicast address is very similar to a public IPv4 address. A global unicast IPv6 address can be split in three parts (or prefixes), as shown in Figure 1-70.

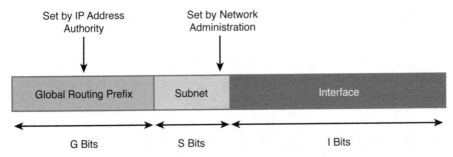

Figure 1-70 *Global Unicast IPv6 Address*

The first one is called the global routing prefix and identifies the address block, as assigned to an organization, the subnet ID, used to identify a subnet within that block space, and the interface ID, which identifies an interface within that subnet.

The assignment of the global routing prefix is provided by IANA or by any of its delegation, such as a regional Internet registry organization. The subnet part is decided within the organization and is based on the IP address schema adopted.

The link-local address (LLA) is a special class of unicast address that is only locally significant within a link or subnet. In IPv6, at least one LLA needs to be configured per interface. The LLA is used for a number of functions, such as by the Neighbor Discovery Protocol or as the next-hop address instead of the global unicast address. Any IPv6 packet that includes an LLA should not be forwarded by a router outside of the subnet.

An LLA address should always start with the first 10 bits set to 1111111010 (FF80::/10), followed by 54 bits set to all 0s. This means that an LLA address always starts with FE80:0000:0000:0000 for the first 64 bits, and the interface ID is determined by the EUI-64 method, which we discuss in the next section.

Figure 1-71 shows an example of an IPv6 LLA.

Figure 1-71 *IPv6 LLA*

IPv6 multicast addresses are also very important for the correct functioning of IPv6 (for example, because they replace the network broadcast address and are used in a number of protocols to reach other devices). An IPv6 multicast address always starts with the first 8 bits set to 1s, which is equivalent to FF00::/8.

Figure 1-72 shows the format of an IPv6 multicast address.

Figure 1-72 *IPv6 Multicast Address Format*

The FLGS and SCOP fields are used to communicate whether the address is permanently assigned (and thus well known) or not, and for which scope the address can be used (for example, only for local-link).

Table 1-21 summarizes some of most common IPv6 multicast addresses. A list of reserved IPv6 multicast addresses can be found at http://www.iana.org/assignments/ipv6-multicast-addresses/ipv6-multicast-addresses.xhtml.

Table 1-21   Common IPv6 Multicast Addresses

Short Name	Address
All-Nodes	FF02:0:0:0:0:0:0:1
All-Routers	FF02:0:0:0:0:0:0:2
All-OSPF-Routers	FF02:0:0:0:0:0:0:5
All-OSPF-Designated-Routers	FF02:0:0:0:0:0:0:6
All-EIGRPv6-Routers	FF02:0:0:0:0:0:0:A
All-RIPng-Routers	FF02:0:0:0:0:0:0:9
All-DHCP-Relay-Agent-and-Server	FF02:0:0:0:0:0:1:2
Solicited-Node Address	FF02::1:FF00:0000/104

Special and Reserved IPv6 Addresses

Like IPv4, IPv6 includes some reserved addresses that should not be used for interface assignment. Table 1-22 provides a summary of the special and reserved unicast addresses and prefixes for IPv6 based on RFC 6890.

Table 1-22   Special and Reserved Unicast Addresses and Prefixes for IPv6

Address	Use
::1/128	loopback address
::/128	unspecified address
64:ff9b::/96	IPv4–IPv6 translation
::ffff:0:0/96	IPv4-mapped address
100::/64	Discard-only address block
2001::/23	IETF protocol assignments
2001::/32	TEREDO
2001:2::/48	Benchmarking
2001:db8::/32	Documentation
2001:10::/28	ORCHID[1]

Address	Use
2002::/16	6to4
fc00::/7	Unique-local
fe80::/10	Linked-scoped unicast

[1]This address was reserved until March 2014.

IPv6 Addresses Assignment, Neighbor Discovery Protocol, and DHCPv6

IPv6 supports several methods for assigning an IP address to an interface:

- Static

- Static prefix with EUI-64 method

- Stateless address auto-configuration (SLAAC)

- Stateful DHCPv6

With static assignment, the IP address and prefix are configured by the device administrator. In some devices, such as Cisco IOS routers, it is possible just to configure the IPv6 prefix, the first 64 bits, and let the router automatically calculate the interface ID portion of the address, the last 64 bits. The method to calculate the interface ID is called the *EUI-64 method*.

The EUI-64 method, described in RFC 4291, uses the following rules to build the interface ID:

1. Split the interface MAC address in two.

2. Add FFFE in between. This makes the address 64-bits long.

3. Invert the 7th bit (for example, if the bit is 1, write 0, and vice versa).

Figure 1-73 shows an example of the EUI-64 method to calculate the interface ID portion of an IPv6 address. In this example, the MAC address of the interface is 0200.1111.1111. We first split the MAC address and add FFFE in the middle. We then flip the 7th bit from 1 to 0. This results in an interface ID of 0000.11FF.FE11.1111.

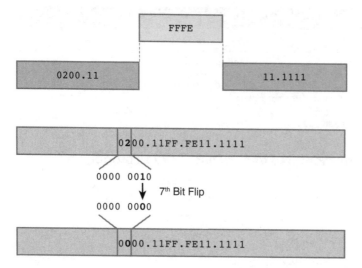

Figure 1-73 *Calculating the Interface ID Portion of an IPv6 Address with EUI-64*

The EUI-64 method is also used to calculate the interface ID for an LLA address, as explained in the previous section.

The third method, SLAAC, allows for automatic address assignment when the IPv6 network prefix and prefix length are not known (for example, if they are not manually configured). To understand how SLAAC works, we need to look at a new protocol that is specific for IPv6: the Neighbor Discovery Protocol (NDP).

NDP is used for several functionalities:

- **Router discovery:** Used to discover routers within a subnet.

- **Prefix discovery:** Used to find out the IPv6 network prefix in a given link.

- **Address auto-configuration:** Supports SLAAC to provide automatic address configuration.

- **Address resolution:** Similar to ARP for IPv4, address resolution is used to determine the link layer address, given an IPv6 address.

- **Next-hop determination:** Used to determine the next hop for a specific destination.

- **Neighbor unreachability detection (NUD):** Used to determine whether a neighbor is reachable. It is useful, for example, to determine whether the next-hop router is still available or an alternative router should be used.

- **Duplicate address detection (DAD):** Used to determine whether the address a node decided to use is already in use by some other node.

- **Redirect:** Used to inform nodes about a better first-hop node for a destination.

NDP uses ICMP version 6 (ICMPv6) to provide these functionalities. As part of the NDP specification, five new ICMPv6 messages are defined:

- **Router Solicitation (RS):** This message is sent from hosts to routers and is used to request a Router Advertisement message. The source IP address of this message is either the host-assigned IP address or the unspecified address ::/128 if an IP address is not assigned yet. The destination IP address is the all-routers multicast address FF01::2/128.

- **Router Advertisement (RA):** This message is sent from routers to all hosts, and it is used to communicate information such as the IP address of the router and information about network prefix and prefix length, or the allowed MTU. This can be sent at regular intervals or to respond to an RS message.

  The source IP of this message is the link-local IPv6 address of the router interface, and the destination is either all-nodes multicast address FF01::1 or the address of the host that sent the RS message.

- **Neighbor Solicitation (NS):** This message is used to request the link-layer address from a neighbor node. It is also used for NUD and DUD functionality. The source IP address would be the IPv6 address of the interface, if already assigned, or the unspecified address ::/128.

- **Neighbor Advertisement (NA):** This message is sent in response to an NS or can be sent unsolicited to flag a change in the link-layer address. The source IP address is the interface IP, while the destination is either the IP address of the node that sent the NS or the all-nodes address FF01::1.

- **Redirect:** This message is used to inform the hosts about a better first hop. The source IP address is the link-local IP of the router, and the destination IP address is the IP address of the packet that triggered the redirect.

Figure 1-74 shows an example of an RS/RA exchange to get information about the router. In this example, Host A sends a Router Solicitation to all routers in the subnet to get the network prefix and prefix length.

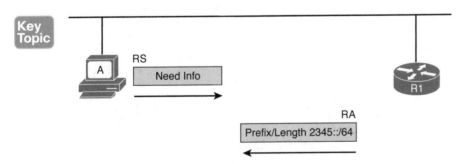

Figure 1-74 *RS/RA Exchange*

Figure 1-75 shows an example of an NS/NA exchange to get information about the link-layer address. This process replaces the ARP process in IPv4. Host A needs to have the MAC address of Host B so it can send frames. It sends an NS asking who has 2345::2, and Host B responds with an NA, indicating its MAC address.

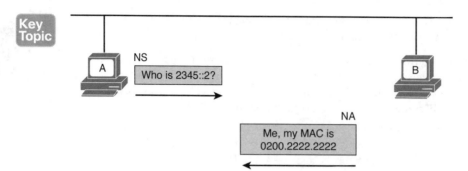

Figure 1-75 *NS/NA Exchange to Get Link-Layer Address Information*

Due to the criticality of the NDP operation, RFC 3971 describes the Secure Neighbor Discovery (SeND) protocol to improve the security of NDP. SeND defines two ND messages—Certification Path Solicitation (CPS) and Certification Path Answer (CPA)—an additional ND option, and an additional auto-configuration mechanism.

Now that you know how NDP works, you can better understand the SLAAC process. In the following example, we assume the host uses the EUI-64 method to generate an LLA. At the start, the host generates an LLA address. This provides link-local connectivity to neighbors.

At this point, the host can receive RAs from the neighbor's routers, or, optionally, it can solicit an RA by sending an RS message. The RA message contains the network prefix and prefix length information that can be used by the host to create a global unicast IP address.

The prefix part of the address is provided by the information included in the RA. The interface ID, instead, is provided by using EUI-64 or other methods (for example, randomly). This depends on how the host has implemented SLAAC. For example, a host may implement a privacy extension (described in RFC 4941) or a cryptographically generated address (CGA) when SeND is used. Before the address can be finally assigned to the interface, the host can use the DAD functionality of NDP to find out whether any other host is using the same IP.

The following steps detail address assignment via SLAAC. In Figure 1-76, Host A has a MAC address of 0200.2211.1111.

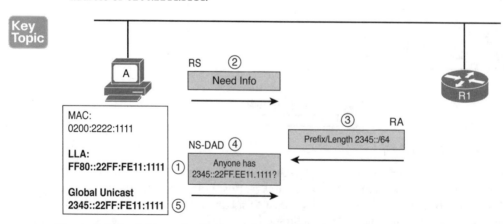

Figure 1-76 *Address Assignment via SLAAC*

Step 1.   The SLAAC process starts by calculating the LLA. This is done by using the EUI-64 method. This will result in an LLA address of FF80::22FF:FE11:1111.

Step 2.   At this point, Host A has link-local connectivity and can send an RS message to get information from the local routers.

Step 3.   R1 responds with information about the prefix and prefix length, 2345::/64.

Step 4.   Host A uses this information to calculate its global unicast address 2345::22FF:FE11:1111. Before using this address, Host A uses DAD to check whether any other device is using the same address. It sends an NS message asking whether anyone is using this address.

Step 5.   Since no one responded to the NS message, Host A assumes it is the only one with that address. This terminates the SLAAC configuration.

The fourth method we look at in this section is stateful DHCPv6. As with many other protocols, a new version of DHCP has been defined to make it work with IPv6. DHCP version 6 uses UDP as the transport protocol with port 546 for clients and 547 for servers or relays.

Two modes of operation have been defined:

- **Stateful DHCPv6:** Works pretty much like DHCPv4, where a server assigns IP addresses to clients and can provide additional network configuration. The server keeps track of which IP addresses have been leased and to which clients. The difference is that stateful DHCPv6 does not provide information about the default route; that functionality is provided by NDP.

- **Stateless DHCPv6:** Used to provide network configuration only. It is not used to provide IP address assignment. The term *stateless* comes from the fact that the DHCPv6 server does not need to keep the state of the leasing of an IPv6 address. Stateless DHCPv6 can be used in combination with static or SLAAC IPv6 assignments to provide additional network configuration such as for a DNS server or NTP server.

DHCPv6 defines several new messages as well, and some of the messages present in DHCPv4 have been renamed.

The following steps show a basic stateful DHCPv6 exchange for IPv6 address assignment (see Figure 1-77):

Step 1.   The client sends a DHCPv6 Solicit message to the IPv6 multicast address All_ DHCP_Relay_Agents_and_Servers FF02::1:2 and uses its link-local address as the source.

Step 2.   The DHCPv6 servers reply with a DHCPv6 Advertise message back to the client.

Step 3.   The client picks a DHCPv6 server and sends a DHCPv6 Request message to request the IP address and additional configuration.

Step 4.   The DHCPv6 server sends a DHCPv6 Reply message with the information.

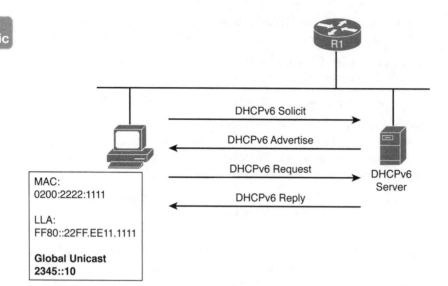

Figure 1-77 *Stateful DHCPv6 Exchange for IPv6 Address Assignment*

If an IP address has been assigned using a different method, a host can use stateless DHCPv6 to receive additional configuration information. This involves only two messages instead of four, as shown here (see Figure 1-78):

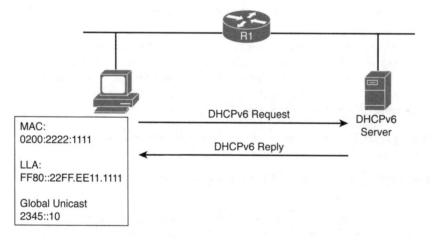

Figure 1-78 *Stateless DHCPv6*

Step 1.   The client sends a DHCPv6 Information Request message to the IPv6 multicast address All_DHCP_Relay_Agents_and_Servers FF02::1:2.

Step 2.   The server sends a DHCPv6 Reply with the information.

Just like DHCPv4, DHCPv6 includes the relay functionality to allow clients to access DHCPv6 servers outside of a subnet.

Transport Layer Technologies and Protocols

The last concept to discuss in this chapter is how two hosts (Host A and Host B) can establish end-to-end communication. The end-to-end communication service is provided by the transport layer or Layer 4 protocols. These protocols are the focus of this section.

Several protocols work at the transport layer and offer different functionalities. In this section, we focus on two of the most used protocols: User Datagram Protocol (UDP) and Transmission Control Protocol (TCP).

Before we get into the protocol details, we need to discuss the concept of multiplexing, which is at the base of the functionality of UDP and TCP. On a single host, there may be multiple applications that want to use the transport layer protocols (that is, TCP and UDP) to communicate with remote hosts. In Figure 1-79, for example, Host B supports a web server and an FTP server. Let's imagine that Host A would like to browse and use the FTP services from Host B. It will send two TCP requests to Host B. The question is, how does Host B differentiate between the two requests and forward the packets to the correct application?

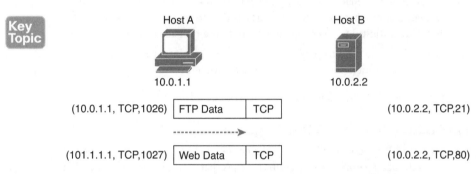

Figure 1-79   *Example of TCP Multiplexing*

The solution to this problem is provided by multiplexing, which relies on the concept of a socket. A socket is a combination of three pieces of information:

- The host IP address
- A port number
- The transport layer protocol

The first two items are sometimes grouped together under the notion of a socket address. A socket (in the case of this example, a TCP socket) is formed by the IP address of the host and a port number, which is used by the host to identify the connection. The pair of sockets on the two hosts, Host A and Host B, uniquely identify a transport layer connection.

For example, the Host A socket for the FTP connection would be (10.0.1.1, 1026), where 10.0.1.1 is the IP address of Host A and 1026 is the TCP port used for the communication. The Host B socket for the same connection would be (10.0.2.2, 21), where 21 is the standard port assigned to FTP services.

Similarly, the Host A socket for the HTTP connection (web service) would be (10.0.1.1, 1027), whereas the Host B socket would be (10.0.2.2, 80), where 80 is the standard port assigned to HTTP services.

The preceding example illustrates the concepts of multiplexing and sockets as applied to a TCP connection, but the same holds for UDP. For example, when a DNS query is made to a DNS server, as detailed earlier in the section "Domain Name System (DNS)" of this chapter, a UDP socket is used on the DNS resolver and on the DNS server.

An additional concept that's generally used to describe protocols at the transport layer is whether a formal connection needs to be established before a device can send data. Therefore, the protocols can be classified as follows:

- **Connection oriented:** In this case, the protocol requires that a formal connection be established before data can be sent. TCP is a connection-oriented protocol and provides connection establishment by using three packets prior to sending data. Generally, connection-oriented protocols have a mechanism to terminate a connection. Connection-oriented protocols are more reliable because the connection establishment allows the exchange of settings and ensures the receiving party is able to receive packets. The drawback is that it adds additional overhead and delay to the transmission of information.

- **Connectionless:** In this case, the protocol allows packets to be sent without any need for a connection. UDP is an example of a connectionless protocol.

We will now examine how TCP and UDP work in a bit more detail.

Transmission Control Protocol (TCP)

The Transmission Control Protocol (TCP) is a reliable, connection-oriented protocol for communicating over the Internet. *Connection oriented* means that TCP requires a connection between two hosts to be established through a specific packet exchange before any data packets can be sent. This is the opposite of connectionless protocols (such as UDP), which don't require any exchange prior to data transmission.

As mentioned in RFC 793, which specifies the TCP protocol, TCP assumes it can obtain simple and potentially unreliable datagrams (IP packets) from lower-level protocols. TCP provides most of the services expected by a transport layer protocol. This section explains the following services and features provided by TCP:

- Multiplexing
- Connection establishment and termination
- Reliability (error detection and recovery)
- Flow control

You may wonder why we don't use TCP for all applications due to these important features. The reason is that the reliability offered by TCP is done at the cost of lower speed and the need for increased bandwidth, in order to manage this process. For this reason, some applications that require fast speed but don't necessarily need to have all the data packets received to provide the requested level of quality (such as voice/video over IP) rely on UDP instead of TCP.

Table 1-23 summarizes the services provided by TCP.

Table 1-23   TCP Services

Service	Description
Multiplexing	Allows multiple transport layer connections between the same hosts. Sockets are used to distinguish to which application a connection belongs.
Connection establishment and termination	A connection is established before data is sent. This ensures that the other host is ready to receive data. The connection is also terminated through a formal data exchange.
Reliability	Data lost due to error or from the underlying datagram can be recovered by asking the remote device to send the information again.
Flow control	TCP uses a windowing system to adjust the speed of transmission.

TCP Header

Application data is encapsulated in TCP segments by adding a TCP header to the application data. These segments are then passed to IP for further encapsulation, thus ensuring that the packets can be routed on the network, as shown on Figure 1-80.

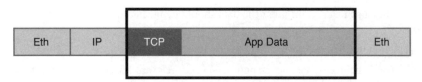

Figure 1-80   *Application Data Encapsulated in TCP Segments*

The TCP header is more extensive compared to the UDP header; this is because it needs additional fields to provide additional services and features. Figure 1-81 shows the TCP header structure.

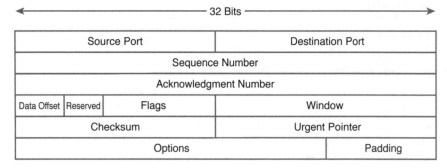

Figure 1-81   *TCP Header Structure*

The main TCP header fields are as follows:

- **Source and Destination Port:** These are used to include the source and destination port for a given TCP packet. They are probably the most important fields within the TCP header and are used to correctly identify a TCP connection and TCP socket.

- **Sequence Number (32 bits):** When the SYN flag bit is set to 1, this is the initial sequence number (ISN) and the first data byte is ISN+1. When the SYN flag bit is set to 0, this is the sequence number of the first data byte in this segment.

- **Acknowledgment Number (32 bits):** Once the connection is established, the ACK flag bit is set to 1, and the acknowledgment number provides the sequence number of the next data payload the sender of the packet is expecting to receive.

- **Control Flags (9 bits, 1 bit per flag):** This field is used for congestion notification and to carry TCP flags.

  - **ECN (Explicit Congestion Notification) Flags (3 bits):** The first three flags (NS, CWR, ECE) are related to the congestion notification feature that has been recently defined in RFC 3168 and RFC 3540 (following RFC 793 about the TCP protocol in general). This feature supports end-to-end network congestion notification, in order to avoid dropping packets as a sign of network congestion.

  - TCP flags include the following:

    - **URG:** The Urgent flag signifies that Urgent Pointer data should be reviewed.

    - **ACK:** The Acknowledgment bit flag should be set to 1 after the connection has been established.

    - **PSH:** The Push flag signifies that the data should be pushed directly to an application.

    - **RST:** The Reset flag resets the connection.

    - **SYN:** The Synchronize (sequence numbers) flag is relevant for connection establishment, and should only be set within the first packets from both of the hosts.

    - **FIN:** This flag signifies that there is no more data from sender.

- **Window (16 bits):** This field indicates the number of data bytes the sender of the segment is able to receive. This field enables flow control.

- **Urgent pointer (16 bits):** When the URG flag is set to 1, this field indicates the sequence number of the data payload following the urgent data segment. The TCP protocol doesn't define what the user will do with the urgent data; it only provides notification on urgent data pending processing.

TCP Connection Establishment and Termination

As mentioned at the beginning of this section, the fact that the TCP protocol is connection oriented means that before any data is exchanged, the two hosts need to go through a process of establishing a connection. This process is often referred to as "three-way-handshake" because it involves three packets and the main goal is to synchronize the sequence numbers so that the hosts can exchange data, as illustrated in Figure 1-82.

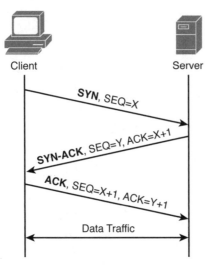

Figure 1-82   *TCP Three-way Handshake*

Let's examine the packet exchange in more detail:

- **First packet (SYN):** The client starts the process of establishing a connection with a server by sending a TCP segment that has the SYN bit set to 1, in order to signal to the peer that it wants to synchronize the sequence numbers and establish the connection. The client also sends its initial sequence number (here X), which is a random number chosen by a client.

- **Second packet (SYN-ACK):** The server responds with a SYN-ACK packet where it sends its own request for synchronization and its initial sequence number (another random number; here Y). Within the same packet, the server also sends the acknowledgment number X+1, acknowledging the receipt of a packet with the sequence number X and requesting the next packet with the sequence number X+1.

- **Third packet (ACK):** The client responds with a final acknowledgment, requesting the next packet with the sequence number Y+1.

In order to terminate a connection, peers go through a similar packet exchange, as shown in Figure 1-83.

The process starts with the client's application notifying the TCP layer on the client side that it wants to terminate the connection. The client sends a packet with the FIN bit set, to which the server responds with an acknowledgment, acknowledging the receipt of the packet. At that point, the server notifies the application on its side that the other peer wishes to terminate the connection. During this time, the client will still be able to receive traffic from the server, but will not be sending any traffic to the server. Once the application on the server side is ready to close down the connection, it signals to the TCP layer that the connection is ready to be closed, and the server sends a FIN packet as well, to which the client responds with an acknowledgment. At that point, the connection is terminated.

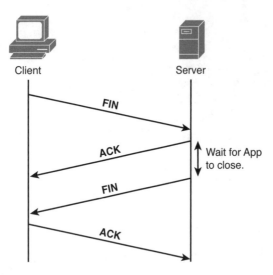

Figure 1-83   *TCP Connection Termination*

TCP Socket

The concept of multiplexing has already been introduced as a way to enable multiple applications to run on the same host and sockets by uniquely identifying a connection with an IP address, transport protocol, and port number.

There are some "well-known" applications that use designated port numbers (for example, WWW uses TCP port 80). This means that the web server will keep its socket for TCP port 80 open, listening to requests from various hosts. When a host tries to open a connection to a web server, it will use TCP port 80 as a destination port, and it will choose a random port number (greater than 1024) as a source port. Random port numbers need to be greater than 1024 because the ones up to 1024 are reserved for well-known applications.

Table 1-24 shows a list of some of the most used applications and their port numbers. A full list of ports used by known services can be found at http://www.iana.org/assignments/service-names-port-numbers/service-names-port-numbers.xhtml.

Table 1-24   Commonly Used TCP Applications and Associated Port Numbers

Application Name	Port Number
FTP Data	20
FTP Control	21
SSH	22
Telnet	23
SMTP	25
DNS Zone Transfer	53
HTTP	80

Application Name	Port Number
IMAP	143
BGP	179
HTTPS	443

FTP (File Transfer Protocol) usesTCP port 20 for transferring the data and a separate connection on port 21 for exchanging control information (for example, FTP commands). Depending on whether the FTP server is in active or passive mode, different port numbers can be involved.

SSH (Secure Shell) is a protocol used for remote device management by allowing a secure (encrypted) connection over an unsecure medium. Telnet can also be used for device management; however, this is not recommended because FTP is not secure—data is sent in plaintext.

SMTP (Simple Mail Transfer Protocol) is used for email exchange. Typically, the client would use this protocol for sending emails, but would use POP3 or IMAP to retrieve emails from the mail server.

DNS (Domain Name System) uses UDP port 53 for domain name queries from hosts that allow other hosts to find out about the IP address for a specific domain name, but it uses TCP port 53 for communication between DNS servers for completing DNS zone transfers.

HTTP (Hypertext Transfer Protocol) is an application-based protocol that is used for accessing content on the Web. HTTPS (HTTP over Secure Socket Layer) is basically HTTP that uses TLS (Transport Layer Security) and SSL (Secure Sockets Layer) for encryption. HTTP is widely used on the Internet for secure communication because it allows encryption and server authentication.

BGP (Border Gateway Protocol) is an exterior gateway protocol used for exchanging routing information between different autonomous systems. It's the routing protocol of the Internet.

TCP Error Detection and Recovery

TCP provides reliable delivery because the protocol is able to detect errors in transmission (for example, lost, damaged, or duplicated segments) and recover from such errors. This is done through the use of sequence numbers, acknowledgments, and checksum fields in the TCP header.

Each segment transmitted is marked with a sequence number, allowing the receiver of the segments to order them and provide acknowledgment on which segments have been received. If the sender doesn't get acknowledgment, it will send the data again.

Figure 1-84 shows an example of sequence numbers and acknowledgments in a typical scenario.

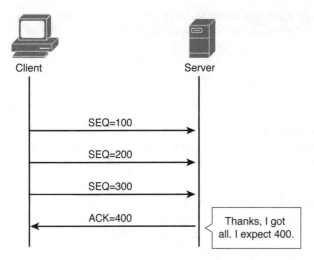

Figure 1-84 *Example of TCP Acknowledgement and Sequence Numbers*

In this example, the client is sending three segments, each with 100 bytes of data. If the server has received all three segments in order, it would send a packet with the acknowledgment set to 400, which literally means "I've received all the segments with sequence numbers up to 399, and I am now expecting a segment with the sequence number 400."

The fact that the segments have sequence numbers will allow the server to properly align the data upon receipt—for example, if for any reason it receives the segments in a different order or if it receives any duplicates.

Figure 1-85 shows how TCP detects and recovers from an error.

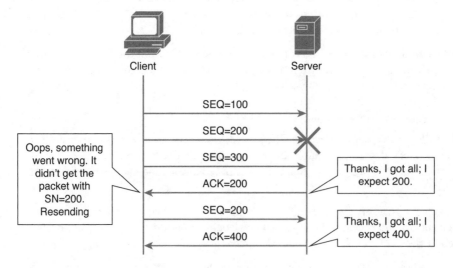

Figure 1-85 *TCP Error Detection and Recovery*

Imagine now that the client sends three packets with sequence numbers 100, 200, and 300. Due to some error in the transmission, the packet with the sequence number 200 gets lost or damaged. If the segment gets damaged during transmission, the TCP protocol would be able to detect this through the checksum number available within the TCP header. Because the packet with the sequence number 200 has not been received properly, the server will only send acknowledgement up to 200. This indicates to the client that it needs to resend that packet. When the server receives the missing packet, it will resume the normal acknowledge to 400, because it already received the packet with sequence numbers 300 and 400. This indicates to the client that it can send packets with sequence 500 and so on. It is worth mentioning that if the receiver doesn't receive the packet with the sequence number 200, it will continue to send packets with acknowledgment number 200, asking for the missing packet.

TCP Flow Control

The TCP protocol ensures flow control through the use of "sliding windows," by which a receiving host "tells" the sender how many bytes of data it can handle at a given time before waiting for an acknowledgment—this is called the window size. This mechanism works for both the client and server. For example, the client can ask the server to slow down, and the server can use this mechanism to ask the client to slow down or even to increase the speed. This allows the TCP peers to increase or reduce the speed of transmission depending on the conditions on the network and processing capability, and to avoid the situation of having a receiving host overwhelmed with data. The size of the receiving window is communicated through the "Window" field within the TCP header. Figure 1-86 shows how the window size gets adjusted based on the capability of the receiving host.

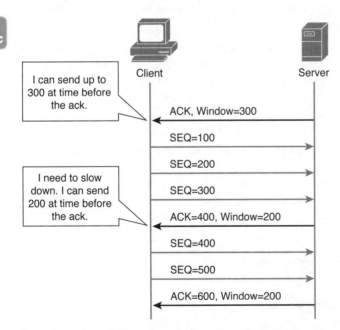

Figure 1-86   *Example of TCP Flow Control*

Initially, the server notifies the client that it can handle a window size of 300 bytes, so the client is able to send three segments of 100 bytes each, before getting the acknowledgment. However, if for some reason the server becomes overwhelmed with data that needs to be processed, it will notify the client that it can now handle a smaller window size.

The receiving host (for example, the server) has a certain buffer that it fills in with data received during a TCP connection, which could determine the size of this window. In ideal conditions, the receiving host may be able to process all the received data instantaneously, and free up the buffer again, leaving the window at the same size. However, if for some reason it is not able to process the data at that speed, it will reduce the window, which will notify the client of the problem. In Figure 1-86, the receiving party (the server) notifies the client that it needs to use a smaller window size of 200 bytes instead of the initial 300-byte window. The client adjusts its data stream accordingly. This process is dynamic, meaning that the server could also increase the window size.

The Window field in TCP header is 16 bits long, which means that the maximum window size is 65,535 bytes. In order to use higher window sizes, a scaling factor within the TCP Options field can be used. This TCP option will get negotiated within the initial three-way handshake.

User Datagram Protocol (UDP)

Like TCP, the User Datagram Protocol (UDP) is one of the most used transport layer protocols. Unlike TCP, however, UDP is designed to reduce the number of protocol iterations and complexity. It in fact does not establish any connection channel and in essence just wraps higher-layer information in a UDP segment and passes it to IP for transmission. UDP is usually referred as a "connectionless" protocol.

Due to its simplicity, UDP does not implement any mechanism for error control and retransmission; it leaves that task to the higher-layer protocols if required. Generally, UDP is used in applications where the low latency and low jitter are more important than reliability. A well-known use case for UDP is Voice over IP. UDP is described in RFC 768.

UDP Header

The UDP header structure is shorter and less complex than TCP's. Figure 1-87 shows an example of a UDP header.

← 32 Bits →	
Source Port	Destination Port
Length	Checksum

Figure 1-87 *UDP Header*

The UDP header includes the following fields:

■ **Source and Destination Port:** Similar to the TCP header, these fields are used to determine the socket address and to correctly send the information to the higher-level application.

- **Length:** Includes the length of the UDP segment.
- **Checksum:** It is built based on a pseudo header which includes information from the IP header (source and destination addresses) and information from the UDP header. Refer to the RFC for more information on how the checksum is calculated.

UDP Socket and Known UDP Application

As described earlier, UDP uses the same principle of multiplexing and sockets that's used by TCP. The protocol information on the socket determines whether it is a TCP or UDP type of socket. As with TCP, UDP has well-known applications that use standard port numbers while listening for arriving packets. Table 1-25 provides an overview of known applications and their standard ports.

Table 1-25 Commonly Used UDP Applications and Associated Port Numbers

Application Name	Port
DNS	53
DHCP	67/68
Network Time Protocol (NTP)	123
SNMP	161/162
IKEv1/IKEv2	500
IKEv1/IKEv2 (NAT)	4500
Syslog	514
DHCPv6	546/547
RADIUS	1812/1813

This concludes the overview of networking fundamentals. The next chapter introduces the concepts of network security devices and cloud services.

Exam Preparation Tasks

Review All Key Topics

Review the most important topics in the chapter, noted with the Key Topic icon in the outer margin of the page. Table 1-26 lists these key topics and the page numbers on which each is found.

Table 1-26   Key Topics

Key Topic Element	Description	Page
Figure 1-1	TCP/IP stack model	6
Summary	Description of how the TCP/IP model works	7
List	TCP/IP model layers	7
Table 1-2	Protocols at each layer of the TCP/IP model	8
Table 1-3	Message unit naming at each layer of the TCP/IP model	9
Figure 1-2	Encapsulation in the TCP/IP model	9
Figure 1-4	Interaction between layers of the TCP/IP model	11
List	Description of the OSI reference model layers	12
Figure 1-5	Mapping of the OSI model to the TCP/IP model	13
Figure 1-7	Encapsulation in the OSI model	14
Table 1-4	Protocols and devices at each layer of the OSI and TCP/IP models	15
List	Description of the two modes of medium access	17
List	Types of MAC addresses	20
Figure 1-11	Portions of a MAC address	20
Section	Description of LAN hubs and bridges	20
Figure 1-13	How information is repeated over hub ports	21
Figure 1-15	Collision domains in a hub/bridge network	22
Summary	Description of LAN switches	22
Figure 1-16	"Collision domains" in a switch	22
Figure 1-17	Frame forwarding in a switch	23
List	Switch forwarding concepts	23
Figure 1-19	Network broadcast domains	24
Figure 1-20	MAC address table population during forwarding	24
Figure 1-21	Dynamic learning of host MAC addresses	25

Key Topic Element	Description	Page
Figure 1-31	Inter-VLAN traffic	34
Summary	Multilayer switches	35
List	Characteristics of wireless media	35
Summary	Infrastructure Basic Service Set	37
Figure 1-36	Infrastructure Basic Service Set topology	38
List	Access point functionality	40
List	Access point categories	40
Figure 1-39	Differences in APs	41
Summary	Autonomous AP management options	41
Summary	Description of CAPWAP	42
List	Description of basic network concepts	44
Figure 1-43	IP packet routing and routing table	45
Figure 1-44	IPv4 header	46
Figure 1-45	Packet fragmentation	47
Summary	IPv4 addresses and addressing structure	48
Figure 1-46	IPv4 network and host portions for Class A, B, and C addresses	49
List	Description of network and broadcast network addresses	50
Summary	Description of network masks	50
Table 1-9	Default networks masks for Class A, B, and C networks	50
Summary	Description of CIDR	51
Summary	Description of subnets	51
Figure 1-48	IP address format with a subnet	52
Figure 1-49	Example of an IP address with a subnet	52
Summary	VLSM	54
List	IP address ranges	55
Summary	NAT	55
List	IP addressing methods	57
Summary	Description of DHCP	58
Summary	Description of ARP	60
Figure 1-56	Inter-subnet IP packet routing	62
List	Static routes versus dynamic routes	64

Key Topic Element	Description	Page
Summary	Routing protocols versus routed protocols	64
List	Routing protocol classifications	64
Section	Distance vector algorithm	65
List	Advantages of link-state routing protocols	68
Summary	ICMP packet flow	70
Summary	DNS hierarchy	71
Figure 1-65 and List	DNS resolution process	74
Table 1-20	Comparison of IPv6 and IPv4	76
Figure 1-66	Communication between hosts using IPv6	77
Figure 1-67	IPv6 header	78
Summary and Figure 1-68	IPv6 extension header	78
List	IPv6 address types	80
Summary	Description of global unicast and link-local unicast addresses	80
Figure 1-70	Global unicast IPv6 address format	81
Summary	Description of link-local addresses (LLA)	81
Section	IPv6 methods to assign an IP address to an interface	83
List	NDP functions	84
Figure 1-74	RS/RA exchange	85
Figure 1-75	NS/NA exchange	86
Figure 1-76	Address assignment via SLAAC	86
Figure 1-77	Stateful DHCPv6 exchange to IPv6 address assignment	88
Summary	Description of multiplexing	89
Figure 1-79	Example of TCP multiplexing	89
Summary	Description of sockets	89
List	Routing protocol classification by connection type	90
List	TCP services and features	90
Table 1-23	TCP services	91
Summary	TCP header	91
Figure 1-82 and List	TCP three-way handshake	93
Section	TCP error detection and recovery	95
Figure 1-86	TCP flow control	97
Figure 1-87	UDP header	97

Complete Tables and Lists from Memory

Print a copy of Appendix B, "Memory Tables," (found on the book website), or at least the section for this chapter, and complete the tables and lists from memory. Appendix C, "Memory Tables Answer Key," also on the website, includes completed tables and lists to check your work.

Define Key Terms

Define the following key terms from this chapter, and check your answers in the glossary:

TCP/IP model, OSI model, local area network, Ethernet, collision domain, half duplex, full duplex, MAC address, LAN hub, LAN bridge, LAN switch, MAC address table, dynamic MAC address learning, Ethernet broadcast domain, VLAN, trunk, multilayer switch, wireless LAN, access point, lightweight access point, autonomous access point, Internet Protocol, IP address, private IP addresses, routing table, router, Classless Interdomain Routing (CIDR), variable-length subnet Mask (VLSM), routing protocol, Dynamic Host Configuration Protocol (DHCP), address resolution, Domain Name System, stateless address auto-configuration (SLAAC), transport protocol socket, connectionless communication, connection-oriented communication

Q&A

The answers to these questions appear in Appendix A, "Answers to the 'Do I Know This Already?' Quizzes and Q&A Questions." For more practice with exam format questions, use the exam engine on the website.

1. At which OSI layer does a router typically operate?

   a. Transport

   b. Network

   c. Data link

   d. Application

2. What are the advantages of a full-duplex transmission mode compared to half-duplex mode? (Select all that apply.)

   a. Each station can transmit and receive at the same time.

   b. It avoids collisions.

   c. It makes use of backoff time.

   d. It uses a collision avoidance algorithm to transmit.

3. How many broadcast domains are created if three hosts are connected to a Layer 2 switch in full-duplex mode?

   a. 4

   b. 3

   c. None

   d. 1

4. What is a trunk link used for?

   a. To pass multiple virtual LANs

   b. To connect more than two switches

   c. To enable Spanning Tree Protocol

   d. To encapsulate Layer 2 frames

5. What is the main difference between a Layer 2 switch and a multilayer switch?

   a. A multilayer switch includes Layer 3 functionality.

   b. A multilayer switch can be deployed on multiple racks.

   c. A Layer 2 switch is faster.

   d. A Layer 2 switch uses a MAC table whereas a multilayer switch uses an ARP table.

6. What is CAPWAP used for?

   a. To enable wireless client mobility through different access points

   b. For communication between a client wireless station and an access point

   c. For communication between a lightweight access point and a wireless LAN controller

   d. For communication between an access point and the distribution service

7. Which of the following services are provided by a lightweight access point? (Select all that apply.)

   a. Channel encryption

   b. Transmission and reception of frames

   c. Client authentication

   d. Quality of Service

8. Which of the following classful networks would allow at least 256 usable IPv4 addresses? (Select all that apply).

   a. Class A

   b. Class B

   c. Class C

   d. All of the above

9. What would be the maximum length of the network mask for a network that has four hosts?

   a. /27

   b. /30

   c. /24

   d. /29

10. Which routing protocol exchanges link state information?

    a. RIPv2

    b. RIP

    c. OSPF

    d. BGP

11. What is an advantage of using OSPF instead of RIPv2?

    a. It does not have the problem of count to infinity.

    b. OSPF has a higher hop-count value.

    c. OSPF includes bandwidth information in the distance vector.

    d. OSPF uses DUAL for optimal shortest path calculation.

12. What are two ways the IPv6 address 2345:0000:0000:0000:0000:0000:0100:1111 can be written?

    a. 2345:0:0:0:0:0:0100:1111

    b. 2345::1::1

    c. 2345::0100:1111

    d. 2345::1:1111

13. In IPv6, what is used to replace ARP?

    a. ARPv6

    b. DHCPv6

    c. NDP

    d. Route Advertisement Protocol

14. What would be the IPv6 address of a host using SLAAC with 2345::/64 as a network prefix and MAC address of 0300.1111.2222?

    a. 2345::100:11FF:FE11:2222

    b. 2345:0:0:0:0300:11FF:FE11:2222

    c. 2345:0:0:0:FFFE:0300:1111:2222

    d. 2345::0300:11FF:FE11:2222

15. What is a DNS iterative query used for?

    a. It is sent from a DNS server to other servers to resolve a domain.

    b. It is sent from a DNS resolver to the backup DNS server.

    c. It is sent from a DNS server to the DNS client.

    d. It is sent from a client machine to a DNS resolver.

16. Which TCP header flag is used by TCP to establish a connection?

    a. URG

    b. SYN

    c. PSH

    d. RST

17. What information is included in a network socket? (Select all that apply.)

    a. Protocol

    b. IP address

    c. Port

    d. MAC address

References and Further Reading

"Requirements for Internet Hosts – Communication Layers," https://tools.ietf.org/html/rfc1122

ISO/IEC 7498-1 – Information technology – Open System Interconnection – Basic Reference Model: The Basic Model

David Hucaby, *CCNA Wireless 200-355 Official Cert Guide*, Cisco Press (2015)

DNS Best Practices, Network Protections, and Attack Identification

http://www.cisco.com/c/en/us/about/security-center/dns-best-practices.html

Wendell Odom, *CCENT/CCNA ICND1 100-105 Official Cert Guide*, Cisco Press (2016)

Wendell Odom, *CCNA Routing and Switching ICND2 200-105 Official Cert Guide*, Cisco Press (2016)

Cisco ICND1 Foundation Learning Guide: LANs and Ethernet

http://www.ciscopress.com/articles/article.asp?p=2092245&seqNum=2

IEEE Std 802.1D – IEEE Standard for Local and Metropolitan Area Networks – Media Access Control (MAC) Bridges

IEEE Std 802.1Q – IEEE Standard for Local and Metropolitan Area Networks – Bridges and Bridged Networks

IEEE Std 802 – IEEE Standard for Local and Metropolitan Area Networks: Overview and Architecture

"Address Allocation for Private Internets," https://tools.ietf.org/html/rfc1918

"Special-Purpose IP Address Registries," https://tools.ietf.org/html/rfc6890

"Dynamic Host Configuration Protocol," https://www.ietf.org/rfc/rfc2131.txt

"An Ethernet Address Resolution Protocol," https://tools.ietf.org/html/rfc826

"INTERNET CONTROL MESSAGE PROTOCOL," https://tools.ietf.org/html/rfc792

"Domain Names - Implementation and Specification," https://www.ietf.org/rfc/rfc1035.txt

"Internet Protocol, Version 6 (IPv6)," Specification https://tools.ietf.org/html/rfc2460

"Unique Local IPv6 Unicast Addresses," https://tools.ietf.org/html/rfc4193

"IP Version 6 Addressing Architecture," https://tools.ietf.org/html/rfc4291

"IPv6 Secure Neighbor Discovery," http://www.cisco.com/en/US/docs/ios-xml/ios/sec_data_acl/configuration/15-2mt/ip6-send.html

"Privacy Extensions for Stateless Address Autoconfiguration in IPv6," https://tools.ietf.org/html/rfc4941

"SEcure Neighbor Discovery (SEND)," https://tools.ietf.org/html/rfc3971

"Cryptographically Generated Addresses (CGA)," https://tools.ietf.org/html/rfc3972

"IPv6 Stateless Address Autoconfiguration," https://tools.ietf.org/search/rfc4862

"Transmission Control Protocol," https://tools.ietf.org/html/rfc793

"User Datagram Protocol," https://tools.ietf.org/html/rfc768

1

This chapter covers the following topics:

- The different network security systems used in today's environments

- What the benefits of security cloud-based solutions are and how they work

- Details about Cisco NetFlow and how it plays a great role in cyber security

- Data loss prevention systems and solutions

Network Security Devices and Cloud Services

Welcome to the second chapter! In this chapter, you will learn the different types of network security devices and cloud services in the industry. This chapter compares traditional and Next-Generation Firewalls, as well as traditional and Next-Generation Intrusion Prevention Systems (IPS). You will learn details about the Cisco Web Security and Cisco Email Security solutions, as well as what is Advanced Malware Protection (AMP), what are identity management systems, Cisco NetFlow, and details about data loss prevention (DLP).

"Do I Know This Already?" Quiz

The "Do I Know This Already?" quiz helps you identify your strengths and deficiencies in this chapter's topics. The ten-question quiz, derived from the major sections in the "Foundation Topics" portion of the chapter, helps you determine how to spend your limited study time. You can find the answers in Appendix A Answers to the "Do I Know This Already?" Quizzes and Q&A Questions.

Table 2-1 outlines the major topics discussed in this chapter and the "Do I Know This Already?" quiz questions that correspond to those topics.

Table 2-1 "Do I Know This Already?" Foundation Topics Section-to-Question Mapping

Foundation Topics Section	Questions Covered in This Section
Network Security Systems	1–5
Security Cloud-based Solutions	6–7
Cisco NetFlow	8–9
Data Loss Prevention	10

1. Which of the following are examples of network security devices that have been invented throughout the years to enforce policy and maintain network visibility?

   a. Routers

   b. Firewalls

   c. Traditional and next-generation intrusion prevention systems (IPSs)

   d. Anomaly detection systems

   e. Cisco Prime Infrastructure

2. Access control entries (ACE), which are part of an access control list (ACL), can classify packets by inspecting Layer 2 through Layer 4 headers for a number of parameters, including which of the following items?

   a. Layer 2 protocol information such as EtherTypes

   b. The number of bytes within a packet payload

   c. Layer 3 protocol information such as ICMP, TCP, or UDP

   d. The size of a packet traversing the network infrastructure device

   e. Layer 3 header information such as source and destination IP addresses

   f. Layer 4 header information such as source and destination TCP or UDP ports

3. Which of the following statements are true about application proxies?

   a. Application proxies, or proxy servers, are devices that operate as intermediary agents on behalf of clients that are on a private or protected network.

   b. Clients on the protected network send connection requests to the application proxy to transfer data to the unprotected network or the Internet.

   c. Application proxies can be classified as next-generation firewalls.

   d. Application proxies always perform network address translation (NAT).

4. Which of the following statements are true when referring to network address translation (NAT)?

   a. NAT can only be used in firewalls.

   b. Static NAT does not allow connections to be initiated bidirectionally.

   c. Static NAT allows connections to be initiated bidirectionally.

   d. NAT is often used by firewalls; however, other devices such as routers and wireless access points provide support for NAT.

5. Which of the following are examples of next-generation firewalls?

   a. Cisco WSA

   b. Cisco ASA 5500-X

   c. Cisco ESA

   d. Cisco Firepower 4100 Series

6. Which of the following are examples of cloud-based security solutions?

   a. Cisco Cloud Threat Security (CTS)

   b. Cisco Cloud Email Security (CES)

   c. Cisco AMP Threat Grid

   d. Cisco Threat Awareness Service (CTAS)

   e. OpenDNS

   f. CloudLock

7. The Cisco CWS service uses web proxies in the Cisco cloud environment that scan traffic for malware and policy enforcement. Cisco customers can connect to the Cisco CWS service directly by using a proxy auto-configuration (PAC) file in the user endpoint or through connectors integrated into which of the following Cisco products?

   a. Cisco ISR G2 routers

   b. Cisco Prime LMS

   c. Cisco ASA

   d. Cisco WSA

   e. Cisco AnyConnect Secure Mobility Client

8. Depending on the version of NetFlow, a network infrastructure device can gather different types of information, including which of the following?

   a. Common vulnerability enumerators (CVEs)

   b. Differentiated services code point (DSCP)

   c. The device's input interface

   d. TCP flags

   e. Type of service (ToS) byte

9. There are several differences between NetFlow and full-packet capture. Which of the following statements are true?

   a. Full-packet capture provides the same information as NetFlow.

   b. Full-packet capture is faster.

   c. One of the major differences and disadvantages of full-packet capture is cost and the amount of data to be analyzed.

   d. In many scenarios, full-packet captures are easier to collect and require pretty much the same analysis ecosystem as NetFlow.

10. Which of the following is an example of a data loss prevention solution?

   a. Cisco Advanced DLP

   b. Cisco CloudLock

   c. Cisco Advanced Malware Protection (AMP)

   d. Cisco Firepower 4100 appliances

Foundation Topics

Network Security Systems

Many network security devices have been invented throughout the years to enforce policy and maintain visibility of everything that is happening in the network. These network security devices include the following:

- Traditional and next-generation firewalls
- Personal firewalls
- Intrusion detection systems (IDSs)
- Traditional and next-generation intrusion prevention systems (IPSs)
- Anomaly detection systems
- Advanced malware protection (AMP)
- Web security appliances
- Email security appliances
- Identity management systems

In the following sections, you will learn details about each of the aforementioned network security systems.

Traditional Firewalls

Typically, firewalls are devices that are placed between a trusted and an untrusted network, as illustrated in Figure 2-1.

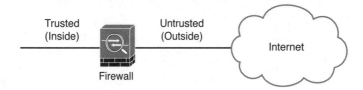

Figure 2-1 *Traditional Firewall Deployment*

In Figure 2-1, a firewall is deployed between two networks: a trusted network and an untrusted network. The trusted network is labeled as the "inside" network, and the untrusted network is labeled as the "outside" network. The untrusted network in this case is connected to the Internet. This is the typical nomenclature you'll often see in Cisco and non-Cisco documentation. When firewalls are connected to the Internet, they are often referred to as *Internet edge firewalls*. A detailed understanding of how firewalls and their related technologies work is extremely important for all network security professionals. This knowledge not only helps you to configure and manage the security of your networks accurately and effectively, but also allows you to gain an understanding of how to enforce policies and achieve network segmentation suitable for your environment.

Several firewall solutions offer user and application policy enforcement in order to supply protection for different types of security threats. These solutions often provide logging capabilities that enable the security administrators to identify, investigate, validate, and mitigate such threats.

Additionally, several software applications can run on a system to protect only that host. These types of applications are known as *personal firewalls*. This section includes an overview of network firewalls and their related technologies. Later in this chapter, you will learn the details about personal firewalls.

Network-based firewalls provide key features that are used for perimeter security, such as network address translation (NAT), access control lists (ACLs), and application inspection. The primary task of a network firewall is to deny or permit traffic that attempts to enter or leave the network based on explicit preconfigured policies and rules. Firewalls are often deployed in several other parts of the network to provide network segmentation within the corporate infrastructure and also in data centers. The processes used to allow or block traffic may include the following:

- Simple packet-filtering techniques
- Application proxies
- Network address translation
- Stateful inspection firewalls
- Next-generation context-aware firewalls

Packet-Filtering Techniques

The purpose of packet filters is simply to control access to specific network segments by defining which traffic can pass through them. They usually inspect incoming traffic at the transport layer of the Open System Interconnection (OSI) model. For example, packet filters can analyze Transmission Control Protocol (TCP) or User Datagram Protocol (UDP) packets and compare them against a set of predetermined rules called access control lists (ACLs). They inspect the following elements within a packet:

- Source address
- Destination address
- Source port
- Destination port
- Protocol

ACLs are typically configured in firewalls, but they also can be configured in network infrastructure devices such as routers, switches, wireless access controllers (WLCs), and others.

Each entry of an ACL is referred to as an access control entry (ACE). These ACEs can classify packets by inspecting Layer 2 through Layer 4 headers for a number of parameters, including the following:

- Layer 2 protocol information such as EtherTypes
- Layer 3 protocol information such as ICMP, TCP, or UDP

- Layer 3 header information such as source and destination IP addresses
- Layer 4 header information such as source and destination TCP or UDP ports

After an ACL has been properly configured, you can apply it to an interface to filter traffic. The firewall or networking device can filter packets in both the inbound and outbound direction on an interface. When an inbound ACL is applied to an interface, the security appliance analyzes packets against the ACEs after receiving them. If a packet is permitted by the ACL, the firewall continues to process the packet and eventually passes the packet out the egress interface.

The big difference between a router ACL and a Cisco ASA (a stateful firewall) ACL is that only the first packet of a flow is subjected by an ACL in the security appliance. After that, the connection is built, and subsequent packets matching that connection are not checked by the ACL. If a packet is denied by the ACL, the security appliance discards the packet and generates a syslog message indicating that such an event has occurred.

If an outbound ACL is applied on an interface, the firewall processes the packets by sending them through the different processes (NAT, QoS, and VPN) and then applies the configured ACEs before transmitting the packets out on the wire. The firewall transmits the packets only if they are allowed to go out by the outbound ACL on that interface. If the packets are denied by any one of the ACEs, the security appliance discards the packets and generates a syslog message indicating that such an event has occurred.

Following are some of the important characteristics of an ACL configured on a Cisco ASA or on a Cisco IOS zone-based firewall:

- When a new ACE is added to an existing ACL, it is appended to the end of the ACL.
- When a packet enters the firewall, the ACEs are evaluated in sequential order. Hence, the order of an ACE is critical. For example, if you have an ACE that allows all IP traffic to pass through, and then you create another ACE to block all IP traffic, the packets will never be evaluated against the second ACE because all packets will match the first ACE entry.
- There is an implicit deny at the end of all ACLs. If a packet is not matched against a configured ACE, it is dropped and a syslog is generated.
- Each interface is assigned a security level. The higher the security level, the more secure. In traditional Cisco ASA firewalls, the security levels go from 0 (less secure) to 100 (more secure). By default, the outside interface is assigned a security level of 0 and the inside interface is assigned a security level of 100. In the Cisco ASA, by default, you do not need to define an ACE to permit traffic from a high-security-level interface to a low-security-level interface. However, if you want to restrict traffic flows from a high-security-level interface to a low-security-level interface, you can define an ACL. If you configure an ACL to a high-security-level interface to a low-security-level interface, it disables the implicit permit from that interface. All traffic is now subject to the entries defined in that ACL.
- Also in the Cisco ASA, an ACL must explicitly permit traffic traversing the security appliance from a lower- to a higher-security-level interface of the firewall. The ACL must be applied to the lower-security-level interface.

- The ACLs (Extended or IPv6) must be applied to an interface to filter traffic that is passing through the security appliance.

- You can bind one extended and one EtherType ACL in each direction of an interface at the same time.

- You can apply the same ACL to multiple interfaces. However, this is not considered to be a good security practice because overlapping and redundant security policies can be applied.

- You can use ACLs to control traffic through the security appliance, as well as to control traffic to the security appliance. The ACLs controlling traffic to the appliance are applied differently than ACLs filtering traffic through the firewall. The ACLs are applied using access groups. The ACL controlling traffic to the security appliance are called *controlled plane ACLs*.

- When TCP or UDP traffic flows through the security appliance, the return traffic is automatically allowed to pass through because the connections are considered established and bidirectional.

- Other protocols such as ICMP are considered unidirectional connections and therefore you need to allow ACL entries in both directions. There is an exception for the ICMP traffic when you enable the ICMP inspection engine.

The Cisco ASA supports five different types of ACLs to provide a flexible and scalable solution to filter unauthorized packets into the network:

- Standard ACLs
- Extended ACLs
- IPv6 ACLs
- EtherType ACLs
- Webtype ACLs

Standard ACLs

Standard ACLs are used to identify packets based on their destination IP addresses. These ACLs can be used in scenarios such as split tunneling for the remote-access VPN tunnels and route redistribution within route maps for dynamic routing deployments (OSPF, BGP, and so on). These ACLs, however, cannot be applied to an interface for filtering traffic. A standard ACL can be used only if the security appliance is running in routed mode. In routed mode, the Cisco ASA routes packets from one subnet to another subnet by acting as an extra Layer 3 hop in the network.

Extended ACLs

Extended ACLs, the most commonly deployed ACLs, can classify packets based on the following attributes:

- Source and destination IP addresses
- Layer 3 protocols

- Source and/or destination TCP and UDP ports
- Destination ICMP type for ICMP packets

An extended ACL can be used for interface packet filtering, QoS packet classification, packet identification for NAT and VPN encryption, and a number of other features. These ACLs can be set up on the Cisco ASA in the routed and the transparent mode.

EtherType ACLs

EtherType ACLs can be used to filter IP and non-IP-based traffic by checking the Ethernet type code field in the Layer 2 header. IP-based traffic uses an Ethernet type code value of 0x800, whereas Novell IPX uses 0x8137 or 0x8138, depending on the Netware version.

An EtherType ACL can be configured only if the security appliance is running in transparent mode. Just like any other ACL, the EtherType ACL has an implicit deny at the end of it. However, this implicit deny does not affect the IP traffic passing through the security appliance. As a result, you can apply both EtherType and extended ACLs to each direction of an interface. If you configure an explicit deny at the end of an EtherType ACL, it blocks IP traffic even if an extended ACL is defined to pass those packets.

Webtype ACLs

A Webtype ACL allows security appliance administrators to restrict traffic coming through the SSL VPN tunnels. In cases where a Webtype ACL is defined but there is no match for a packet, the default behavior is to drop the packet because of the implicit deny. On the other hand, if no ACL is defined, the security appliance allows traffic to pass through it.

An ACL Example

Example 2-1 shows the command-line interface (CLI) configuration of an extended ACL. The ACL is called **outside_acl_in**, and it is composed of four ACEs. The first two ACEs allow HTTP traffic destined for 10.10.20.111 from the two client machines, whereas the last two ACEs allow SMTP access to 10.10.20.112 from both machines. Adding remarks to an ACL is recommended because it helps others to recognize its function. In Example 2-1 the system administrator has added the ACL remark: "*ACL to block inbound traffic except HTTP and SMTP.*"

Example 2-1 *Configuration Example of an Extended ACL*

```
ASA# configure terminal
ASA(config)# access-list outside_access_in remark ACL to block inbound traffic except
HTTP and SMTP
ASA(config)# access-list outside_access_in extended permit tcp host 10.10.10.1 host
10.10.202.131 eq http
ASA(config)# access-list outside_access_in extended permit tcp host 10.10.10.2 host
209.165.202.131 eq http
ASA(config)# access-list outside_access_in extended permit tcp host 10.10.10.1 host
10.10.20.112 eq smtp
ASA(config)# access-list outside_access_in extended permit tcp host 10.10.10.2 host
10.10.20.112 eq smtp
```

Always remember that there is an implicit deny at the end of any ACL.

Packet filters do not commonly inspect additional Layer 3 and Layer 4 fields such as sequence numbers, TCP control flags, and TCP acknowledgment (ACK) fields. The firewalls that inspect such fields and flags are referred to as *stateful firewalls*. You will learn how stateful firewalls operate later in this chapter in the "Stateful Inspection Firewalls" section.

Various packet-filtering firewalls can also inspect packet header information to find out whether the packet is from a new or an existing connection. Simple packet-filtering firewalls have several limitations and weaknesses:

- Their ACLs or rules can be relatively large and difficult to manage.
- They can be deceived into permitting unauthorized access of spoofed packets. Attackers can orchestrate a packet with an IP address that is authorized by the ACL.
- Numerous applications can build multiple connections on arbitrarily negotiated ports. This makes it difficult to determine which ports are selected and used until after the connection is completed. Examples of this type of application are multimedia applications such as streaming audio and video applications. Packet filters do not understand the underlying upper-layer protocols used by this type of application, and providing support for this type of application is difficult because the ACLs need to be manually configured in packet-filtering firewalls.

Application Proxies

Application proxies, or proxy servers, are devices that operate as intermediary agents on behalf of clients that are on a private or protected network. Clients on the protected network send connection requests to the application proxy to transfer data to the unprotected network or the Internet. Consequently, the application proxy (sometimes referred to as a *web proxy*) sends the request on behalf of the internal client. The majority of proxy firewalls work at the application layer of the OSI model. Most proxy firewalls can cache information to accelerate their transactions. This is a great tool for networks that have numerous servers that experience high usage. Additionally, proxy firewalls can protect against some web-server-specific attacks; however, in most cases, they do not provide any protection against the web application itself.

Network Address Translation

Several Layer 3 devices can supply network address translation (NAT) services. The Layer 3 device translates the internal host's private (or real) IP addresses to a publicly routable (or mapped) address.

Cisco uses the terminology of "real" and "mapped" IP addresses when describing NAT. The real IP address is the address that is configured on the host, before it is translated. The mapped IP address is the address to which the real address is translated.

TIP Static NAT allows connections to be initiated bidirectionally, meaning both to the host and from the host.

Figure 2-2 demonstrates how a host on the inside of a firewall with the private address of 10.10.10.123 is translated to the public address 209.165.200.227.

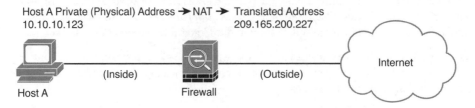

Figure 2-2 *NAT Example*

NAT is often used by firewalls; however, other devices such as routers and wireless access points provide support for NAT. By using NAT, the firewall hides the internal private addresses from the unprotected network and exposes only its own address or public range. This enables a network professional to use any IP address space as the internal network. A best practice is to use the address spaces that are reserved for private use (see RFC 1918, "Address Allocation for Private Internets"). Table 1-1 lists the private address ranges specified in RFC 1918.

Table 2-1   RFC 1918 Private Address Ranges

Class	IP Address Range	Networks	Number of Hosts
Class A	10.0.0.0 to 10.255.255.255	1	16,777,214
Class B	172.16.0.0 to 172.31.255.255	16	65,534
Class C	192.168.0.0 to 192.168.255.255	256	254

It is important to think about the different private address spaces when you plan your network (for example, the number of hosts and subnets that can be configured). Careful planning and preparation lead to substantial time savings if changes are encountered down the road.

> **TIP**   The whitepaper titled "A Security-Oriented Approach to IP Addressing" provides numerous tips on planning and preparing your network IP address scheme. You can find this whitepaper here: http://www.cisco.com/web/about/security/intelligence/security-for-ip-addr.html.

Port Address Translation

Typically, firewalls perform a technique called port address translation (PAT). This feature, which is a subset of the NAT feature, allows many devices on the internal protected network to share one IP address by inspecting the Layer 4 information on the packet. This shared address is usually the firewall's public address; however, it can be configured to any other available public IP address. Figure 2-3 shows how PAT works.

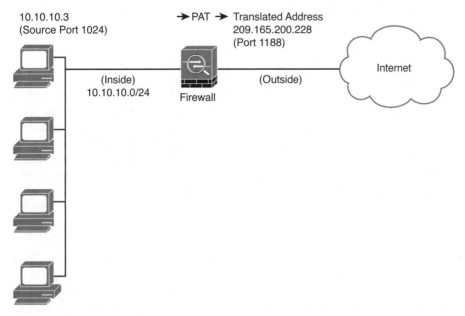

Figure 2-3 *PAT Example*

As illustrated in Figure 2-3, several hosts on a trusted network labeled "inside" are configured with an address from the network 10.10.10.0 with a 24-bit subnet mask. The ASA is
performing PAT for the internal hosts and translating the 10.10.10.x addresses into its own
address (209.165.200.228). In this example, Host A sends a TCP port 80 packet to the web
server located in the "outside" unprotected network. The ASA translates the request from the
original 10.10.10.8 IP address of Host A to its own address. It does this by randomly selecting a different Layer 4 source port when forwarding the request to the web server. The TCP
source port is modified from 1024 to 1188 in this example.

Static Translation

A different methodology is used when hosts in the unprotected network need to initiate
a new connection to specific hosts behind the NAT device. You configure the firewall to
allow such connections by creating a static one-to-one mapping of the public (mapped) IP
address to the address of the internal (real) protected device. For example, static NAT can be
configured when a web server resides on the internal network and has a private IP address
but needs to be contacted by hosts located in the unprotected network or the Internet.
Figure 2-2 demonstrated how static translation works. The host address (10.10.10.123) is
statically translated to an address in the outside network (209.165.200.227, in this case). This
allows the outside host to initiate a connection to the web server by directing the traffic to
209.165.200.227. The device performing NAT then translates and sends the request to the
web server on the inside network.

Firewalls like the Cisco ASA, Firepower Threat Defense (FTD), Cisco IOS zone-based firewalls and others can perform all these NAT operations. On the other hand, address translation is not limited to firewalls. Nowadays, all sorts of lower-end network devices such as

simple small office, home office (SOHO) and wireless routers can perform different NAT techniques.

Stateful Inspection Firewalls

Stateful inspection firewalls provide enhanced benefits when compared to simple packet-filtering firewalls. They track every packet passing through their interfaces by ensuring that they are valid, established connections. They examine not only the packet header contents but also the application layer information within the payload. Subsequently, different rules can be created on the firewall to permit or deny traffic based on specific payload patterns. A stateful firewall monitors the state of the connection and maintains a database with this information, usually called the state table. The state of the connection details whether such a connection has been established, closed, reset, or is being negotiated. These mechanisms offer protection for different types of network attacks.

Demilitarized Zones

Firewalls can be configured to separate multiple network segments (or zones), usually called *demilitarized zones (DMZs)*. These zones provide security to the systems that reside within them with different security levels and policies between them. DMZs can have several purposes; for example, they can serve as segments on which a web server farm resides or as extranet connections to a business partner. Figure 2-4 shows a Cisco ASA with a DMZ.

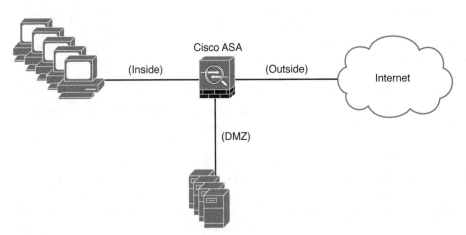

Figure 2-4   *DMZ example*

DMZs minimize the exposure of devices and clients on your internal network by allowing only recognized and managed services on those hosts to be accessible from the Internet. In Figure 2-4, the DMZ hosts web servers that are accessible by internal and Internet hosts. In large organizations, you can find multiple firewalls in different segments and DMZs.

Firewalls Provide Network Segmentation

Firewalls can provide network segmentation while enforcing policies between those segments. In Figure 2-5, a firewall is segmenting and enforcing policies between three networks in the overall corporate network. The first network is the finance department, the second is the engineering department, and the third is the sales department.

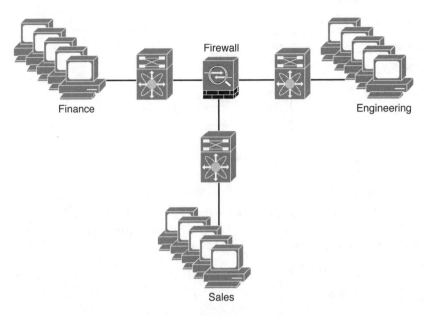

Figure 2-5 *Firewall Providing Network Segmentation*

High Availability

Firewalls such as the Cisco ASA provide high availability features such as the following:

- Active-standby failover
- Active-active failover
- Clustering

Active-Standby Failover

In an active-standby failover configuration, the primary firewall is always active and the secondary is in standby mode. When the primary firewall fails, the secondary firewall takes over. Figure 2-6 shows a pair of Cisco ASA firewalls in an active-standby failover configuration.

The configuration and stateful network information is synchronized from the primary firewall to the secondary.

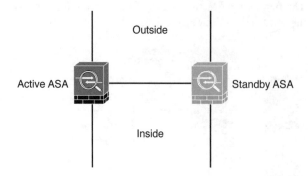

Figure 2-6   *Firewalls in Active-Standby Failover Mode*

Active-Active Failover

In an active-active failover configuration, both of the firewalls are active. If one fails, the other will continue to pass traffic in the network. Figure 2-7 shows a pair of Cisco ASA firewalls in an active-active failover configuration.

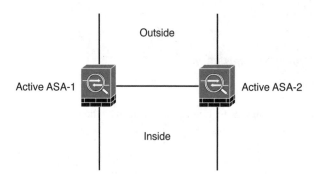

Figure 2-7   *Firewalls in Active-Active Failover Mode*

Clustering Firewalls

Firewalls such as the Cisco ASA can also be clustered to provide next-generation firewall protection in large and highly scalable environments. For example, the Cisco ASA firewalls can be part of a cluster of up to 16 firewalls. Figure 2-8 shows a cluster of three Cisco ASAs. One of the main reasons to cluster firewalls is to increase packet throughput and to scale in a more efficient way.

In Figure 2-8, the Cisco ASAs have 10 Gigabit Ethernet interfaces in an Etherchannel configuration to switches in both inside and outside networks. An Etherchannel involves bundling together two or more interfaces in order to scale and achieve bigger bandwidth.

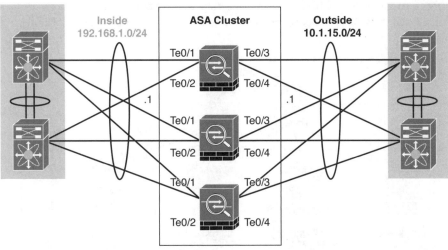

Figure 2-8   *Cisco ASAs in a Cluster*

Firewalls in the Data Center

Firewalls can also be deployed in the data center. The placement of firewalls in the data center will depend on many factors, such as how much latency the firewalls will introduce, what type of traffic you want to block and allow, and in what direction the traffic will flow (either north to south or east to west).

In the data center, traffic going from one network segment or application of the data center to another network segment or application within the data center is often referred to as east-to-west (or west-to-east) traffic. This is also known as *lateral traffic*. Figure 2-9 demonstrates east-west traffic.

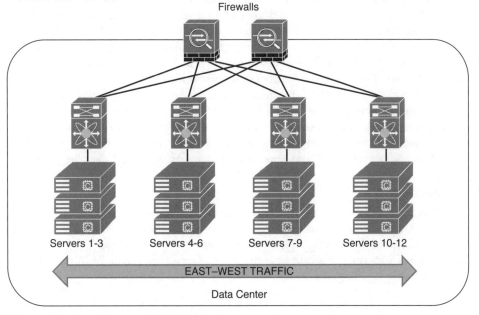

Figure 2-9   *Data Center East-West Traffic*

Similarly, traffic going to and from the data center and the rest of the corporate network is often referred to as north-to-south (or south-to-north) traffic. Figure 2-10 demonstrates north-south traffic.

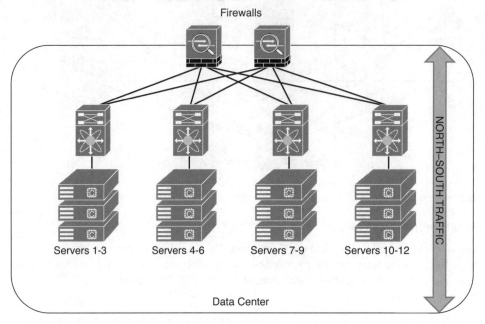

Figure 2-10 *Data Center North-South Traffic*

Another example of advanced segmentation and micro-segmentation in the data center is the security capabilities of the Cisco Application Centric Infrastructure (ACI). Cisco ACI is a software-defined networking (SDN) solution that has a very robust policy model across data center networks, servers, storage, security, and services. This policy-based automation helps network administrators to achieve micro-segmentation through the integration of physical and virtual environments under one policy model for networks, servers, storage, services, and security. Even if servers and applications are "network adjacent" (that is, on the same network segment), they will not communicate with each other until a policy is configured and provisioned. This is why Cisco ACI is very attractive to many security-minded network administrators. Another major benefit of Cisco ACI is automation. With such automation, you can reduce application deployment times from weeks to minutes. Cisco ACI policies are enforced and deployed by the Cisco Application Policy Infrastructure Controller (APIC).

Virtual Firewalls

Firewalls can also be deployed as virtual machines (VMs). An example of a virtual firewall is the Cisco ASAv. These virtual firewalls are often deployed in the data center to provide segmentation and network protection to virtual environments. They are typically used because traffic between VMs often does not leave the physical server and cannot be inspected or enforced with physical firewalls.

> **TIP**   The Cisco ASA also has a featured called *virtual contexts*. This is not the same as the virtual firewalls described previously. In the Cisco ASA security context feature, one physical appliance can be "virtualized" into separate contexts (or virtual firewalls). Virtual firewalls such as the Cisco ASAv run on top of VMware or KVM on a physical server such as the Cisco UCS.

Figure 2-11 shows two virtual firewalls providing network segmentation between several VMs deployed in a physical server.

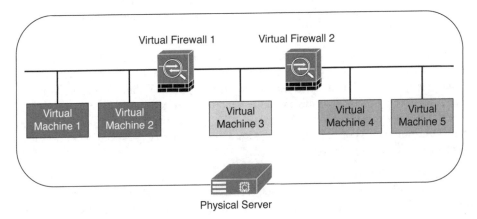

Figure 2-11   *Virtual Firewalls Example*

Deep Packet Inspection

Several applications require special handling of data packets when they pass through firewalls. These include applications and protocols that embed IP addressing information in the data payload of the packet or open secondary channels on dynamically assigned ports. Sophisticated firewalls and security appliances such as the Cisco ASA and Cisco IOS Firewall offer application inspection mechanisms to handle the embedded addressing information to allow the previously mentioned applications and protocols to work. Using application inspection, these security appliances can identify the dynamic port assignments and allow data exchange on these ports during a specific connection.

With deep packet inspection, firewalls can look at specific Layer 7 payloads to protect against security threats. For example, you can configure a Cisco ASA running version 7.0 or later to not allow peer-to-peer (P2P) applications to be transferred over the HTTP protocol. You can also configure these devices to deny specific FTP commands, HTTP content types, and other application protocols.

> **TIP**   The Cisco ASA provides a Modular Policy Framework (MPF) that offers a consistent and flexible way to configure application inspection and other features to specific traffic flows in a manner similar to the Cisco IOS Software modular quality-of-service (QoS) command-line interface (CLI).

Next-Generation Firewalls

The proliferation of mobile devices and the need to connect from any place are radically changing the enterprise security landscape. Social networking sites such as Facebook and Twitter long ago moved beyond mere novelty sites for teens and geeks and have become vital channels for communicating with groups and promoting brands.

Security concerns and fear of data loss are leading reasons why some businesses don't embrace social media, but many others are adopting social media as a vital resource within the organization. Some of the risks associated with social media can be mitigated through the application of technology and user controls. However, there's no doubt that criminals have used social media networks to lure victims into downloading malware and handing over login passwords.

Before today's firewalls grant network access, they need to be aware of not only the applications and users accessing the infrastructure but also the device in use, the location of the user, and the time of day. Such context-aware security requires a rethinking of the firewall architecture. Context-aware firewalls extend beyond the next-generation firewalls on the market today. They provide granular control of applications, comprehensive user identification, and location-based control. The Cisco ASA 5500-X Series next-generation firewalls are examples of context-based firewall solutions.

The Cisco ASA family provides a very comprehensive set of features and next-generation security capabilities. For example, it provides capabilities such as simple packet filtering (normally configured with access control lists, or ACLs) and stateful inspection. The Cisco ASA also provides support for application inspection/awareness. It can listen in on conversations between devices on one side and devices on the other side of the firewall. The benefit of listening in is so that the firewall can pay attention to application layer information.

The Cisco ASA also supports network address translation (NAT), the capability to act as a Dynamic Host Configuration Protocol (DHCP) server or client, or both. The Cisco ASA supports most of the interior gateway routing protocols, including Routing Information Protocol (RIP), Enhanced Interior Gateway Routing Protocol (EIGRP), and Open Shortest Path First (OSPF). It also supports static routing. The Cisco ASA also can be implemented as a traditional Layer 3 firewall, which has IP addresses assigned to each of its routable interfaces. The other option is to implement a firewall as a transparent (Layer 2) firewall, in which the actual physical interfaces receive individual IP addresses, but a pair of interfaces operate like a bridge. Traffic that is going across this two-port bridge is still subject to the rules and inspection that can be implemented by the ASA. Additionally, the Cisco ASA is often used as a head-end or remote-end device for VPN tunnels for both remote-access VPN users and site-to-site VPN tunnels. It supports IPsec and SSL-based remote access VPNs. The SSL VPN capabilities include support for clientless SSL VPN and the full AnyConnect SSL VPN tunnels.

Cisco Firepower Threat Defense

The Cisco Firepower Threat Defense (FTD) is unified software that includes Cisco ASA features, legacy FirePOWER Services, and new features. FTD can be deployed on Cisco Firepower 4100 and 9300 appliances to provide next-generation firewall (NGFW) services.

In addition to being able to run on the Cisco Firepower 4100 Series and the Firepower 9300 appliances, FTD can also run natively on the ASA 5506-X, ASA 5506H-X, ASA 5506W-X, ASA 5508-X, ASA 5512-X, ASA 5515-X, ASA 5516-X, ASA 5525-X, ASA 5545-X, and ASA 5555-X. It is not supported in the ASA 5505 or the 5585-X. FTD can also run as a virtual machine (Cisco Firepower Threat Defense Virtual, or FTDv).

NOTE   Cisco spells the word FirePOWER (uppercase "POWER") when referring to the Cisco ASA FirePOWER Services module. The word Firepower (lowercase "power") is used when referring to all other software, such as FTD, Firepower Management Center (FMC), and Firepower appliances.

Cisco Firepower 4100 Series

The Cisco Firepower 4100 Series appliances are next-generation firewalls that run the Cisco FTD software and features. There are four models:

- Cisco Firepower 4110, which supports up to 20 Gbps of firewall throughput
- Cisco Firepower 4120, which supports up to 40 Gbps of firewall throughput
- Cisco Firepower 4140, which supports up to 60 Gbps of firewall throughput
- Cisco Firepower 4150, which supports over 60 Gbps of firewall throughput

All of the Cisco Firepower 4100 Series models are one rack-unit (1 RU) appliances and are managed by the Cisco Firepower Management Center.

Cisco Firepower 9300 Series

The Cisco Firepower 9300 appliances are designed for very large enterprises or service providers. They can scale beyond 1 Tbps and are designed in a modular way, supporting Cisco ASA software, Cisco FTD software, and Radware DefensePro DDoS mitigation software. Radware DefensePro DDoS mitigation software is provided by Radware, a Cisco partner.

NOTE   The Radware DefensePro DDoS mitigation software is available and supported directly from Cisco on Cisco Firepower 4150 and Cisco Firepower 9300 appliances.

Radware's DefensePro DDoS mitigation software provides real-time analysis to protect the enterprise or service provider infrastructure against network and application downtime due to distributed denial of service (DDoS) attacks.

Cisco FTD for Cisco Integrated Services Routers (ISRs)

The Cisco FTD can run on Cisco Unified Computing System (UCS) E-Series blades installed on Cisco ISR routers. Both the FMC and FTD are deployed as virtual machines. There are two internal interfaces that connect a router to a UCS E-Series blade. On ISR G2, Slot0 is a Peripheral Component Interconnect Express (PCIe) internal interface, and UCS E-Series Slot1 is a switched interface connected to the backplane Multi Gigabit Fabric (MGF). In Cisco ISR 4000 Series routers, both internal interfaces are connected to the MGF.

A hypervisor is installed on the UCS E-Series blade, and the Cisco FTD software runs as a virtual machine on it. FTD for ISRs is supported on the following platforms:

- Cisco ISR G2 Series: 2911, 2921, 2951, 3925, 3945, 3925E, and 3945E
- Cisco ISR 4000 Series: 4331, 4351, 4451, 4321, and 4431

Personal Firewalls

Personal firewalls are popular software applications that you can install on end-user machines or servers to protect them from external security threats and intrusions. The term *personal firewall* typically applies to basic software that controls Layer 3 and Layer 4 access to client machines. Today, sophisticated software is available that not only supplies basic personal firewall features but also protects the system based on the behavior of the applications installed on such systems.

Intrusion Detection Systems and Intrusion Prevention Systems

Intrusion detection systems (IDSs) are devices that detect (in promiscuous mode) attempts from an attacker to gain unauthorized access to a network or a host, to create performance degradation, or to steal information. They also detect distributed denial-of-service (DDoS) attacks, worms, and virus outbreaks. Figure 2-12 shows how an IDS device is configured to promiscuously detect security threats.

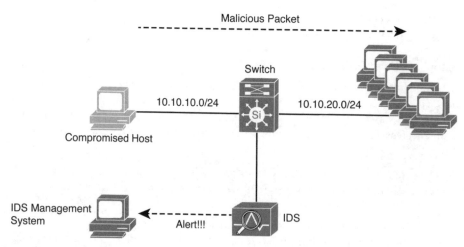

Figure 2-12   *IDS Example*

In Figure 2-12, a compromised host sends a malicious packet to a series of hosts in the 10.10.20.0/24 network. The IDS device analyzes the packet and sends an alert to a monitoring system. The malicious packet still successfully arrives at the 10.10.20.0/24 network.

Intrusion prevention system (IPS) devices, on the other hand, are capable of not only detecting all these security threats, but also dropping malicious packets inline. IPS devices may be initially configured in promiscuous mode (monitoring mode) when you are first deploying them in the network. This is done to analyze the impact to the network infrastructure. Then they are deployed in inline mode to be able to block any malicious traffic in your network.

Figure 2-13 shows how an IPS device is placed inline and drops the noncompliant packet while sending an alert to the monitoring system.

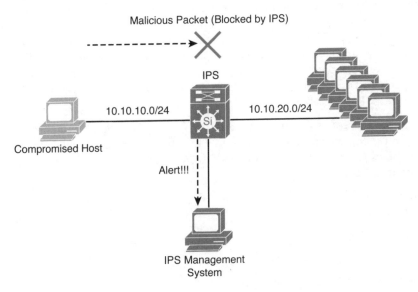

Figure 2-13 *IPS Example*

A few different types of IPSs exist:

■ Traditional network-based IPSs (NIPSs)

■ Next-generation IPS systems (NGIPSs)

■ Host-based IPSs (HIPSs)

Examples of traditional NIPSs are the Cisco IPS 4200 sensors and the Catalyst 6500 IPS module. These devices have been in the end-of-life (EoL) stage for quite some time. Examples of NGIPSs are the Cisco Firepower IPS systems.

The Cisco ASA 5500 Series FirePOWER Services provide intrusion prevention, firewall, and VPN services in a single, easy-to-deploy platform. Intrusion prevention services enhance firewall protection by looking deeper into the flows to provide protection against threats and vulnerabilities. The Cisco Firepower Threat Defense (FTD) provides these capabilities in a combined software package.

Network-based IDSs and IPSs use several detection methodologies, such as the following:

■ Pattern matching and stateful pattern-matching recognition

■ Protocol analysis

■ Heuristic-based analysis

■ Anomaly-based analysis

■ Global threat correlation capabilities

Pattern Matching and Stateful Pattern-Matching Recognition

Pattern matching is a methodology in which the intrusion detection device searches for a fixed sequence of bytes within the packets traversing the network. Generally, the pattern is aligned with a packet that is related to a specific service or, in particular, associated with a source and destination port. This approach reduces the amount of inspection made on every packet. However, it is limited to services and protocols that are associated with well-defined ports. Protocols that do not use any Layer 4 port information are not categorized. Examples of these protocols are Encapsulated Security Payload (ESP), Authentication Header (AH), and Generic Routing Encapsulation (GRE).

This tactic uses the concept of signatures. A *signature* is a set of conditions that point out some type of intrusion occurrence. For example, if a specific TCP packet has a destination port of 1234 and its payload contains the string ff11ff22, a signature can be configured to detect that string and generate an alert.

Alternatively, the signature could include an explicit starting point and endpoint for inspection within the specific packet.

Here are some of the benefits of the plain pattern-matching technique:

- Direct correlation of an exploit
- Trigger alerts on the pattern specified
- Can be applied across different services and protocols

One of the main disadvantages is that pattern matching can lead to a considerably high rate of *false positives*, which are alerts that do not represent a genuine malicious activity. In contrast, any alterations to the attack can lead to overlooked events of real attacks, which are normally referred as *false negatives*.

To address some of these limitations, a more refined method was created. This methodology is called *stateful pattern-matching recognition*. This process dictates that systems performing this type of signature analysis must consider the chronological order of packets in a TCP stream. In particular, they should judge and maintain a stateful inspection of such packets and flows.

Here are some of the advantages of stateful pattern-matching recognition:

- The capability to directly correlate a specific exploit within a given pattern
- Supports all non-encrypted IP protocols

Systems that perform stateful pattern matching keep track of the arrival order of non-encrypted packets and handle matching patterns across packet boundaries.

However, stateful pattern-matching recognition shares some of the same restrictions as the simple pattern-matching methodology, which was discussed previously, including an uncertain rate of false positives and the possibility of some false negatives. Additionally, stateful pattern matching consumes more resources in the IPS device because it requires more memory and CPU processing.

Protocol Analysis

Protocol analysis (or protocol decode-base signatures) is often referred to as an extension to stateful pattern recognition. A network-based intrusion detection system (NIDS) accomplishes protocol analysis by decoding all protocol or client-server conversations. The NIDS identifies the elements of the protocol and analyzes them while looking for an infringement. Some intrusion detection systems look at explicit protocol fields within the inspected packets. Others require more sophisticated techniques, such as examination of the length of a field within the protocol or the number of arguments. For example, in SMTP, the device may examine specific commands and fields such as HELO, MAIL, RCPT, DATA, RSET, NOOP, and QUIT. This technique diminishes the possibility of encountering false positives if the protocol being analyzed is properly defined and enforced. On the other hand, the system can generate numerous false positives if the protocol definition is ambiguous or tolerates flexibility in its implementation.

Heuristic-Based Analysis

A different approach to network intrusion detection is to perform heuristic-based analysis. Heuristic scanning uses algorithmic logic from statistical analysis of the traffic passing through the network. Its tasks are CPU and resource intensive, so it is an important consideration while planning your deployment. Heuristic-based algorithms may require fine tuning to adapt to network traffic and minimize the possibility of false positives. For example, a system signature can generate an alarm if a range of ports is scanned on a particular host or network. The signature can also be orchestrated to restrict itself from specific types of packets (for example, TCP SYN packets). Heuristic-based signatures call for more tuning and modification to better respond to their distinctive network environment.

Anomaly-Based Analysis

A different practice keeps track of network traffic that diverges from "normal" behavioral patterns. This practice is called *anomaly-based analysis*. The limitation is that what is considered to be normal must be defined. Systems and applications whose behavior can be easily considered as normal could be classified as heuristic-based systems.

However, sometimes it is challenging to classify a specific behavior as normal or abnormal based on different factors, which include the following:

■ Negotiated protocols and ports

■ Specific application changes

■ Changes in the architecture of the network

A variation of this type of analysis is profile-based detection. This allows systems to orchestrate their alarms on alterations in the way that other systems or end users interrelate on the network.

Another kind of anomaly-based detection is protocol-based detection. This scheme is related to, but not to be confused with, the protocol-decode method. The protocol-based detection technique depends on well-defined protocols, as opposed to the protocol-decode method, which classifies as an anomaly any unpredicted value or configuration within a field in the respective protocol. For example, a buffer overflow can be detected when specific strings are identified within the payload of the inspected IP packets.

> **TIP**   A buffer overflow occurs when a program attempts to stock more data in a temporary storage area within memory (buffer) than it was designed to hold. This might cause the data to incorrectly overflow into an adjacent area of memory. An attacker could thus craft specific data inserted into the adjacent buffer. Subsequently, when the corrupted data is read, the target computer executes new instructions and malicious commands.

Traditional IDS and IPS provide excellent application layer attack-detection capabilities. However, they do have a weakness. For example, they cannot detect DDoS attacks where the attacker uses valid packets. IDS and IPS devices are optimized for signature-based application layer attack detection. Another weakness is that these systems utilize specific signatures to identify malicious patterns. Yet, if a new threat appears on the network before a signature is created to identify the traffic, it could lead to false negatives. An attack for which there is no signature is called a *zero-day attack*.

Although some IPS devices do offer anomaly-based capabilities, which are required to detect such attacks, they need extensive manual tuning and have a major risk of generating false positives.

You can use more elaborate anomaly-based detection systems to mitigate DDoS attacks and zero-day outbreaks. Typically, an anomaly detection system monitors network traffic and alerts or reacts to any sudden increase in traffic and any other anomalies. Cisco delivers a complete DDoS-protection solution based on the principles of detection, diversion, verification, and forwarding to help ensure total protection. Examples of sophisticated anomaly detection systems are the Cisco CRS Carrier-Grade Services Engine Module DDoS mitigation solution and the Cisco Firepower 9300 appliances with Radware's software.

You can also use NetFlow as an anomaly detection tool. NetFlow is a Cisco proprietary protocol that provides detailed reporting and monitoring of IP traffic flows through a network device, such as a router, switch, or the Cisco ASA.

Global Threat Correlation Capabilities

Cisco NGIPS devices include global correlation capabilities that utilize real-world data from Cisco Talos. Cisco Talos is a team of security researchers who leverage big-data analytics for cyber security and provide threat intelligence for many Cisco security products and services. Global correlation allows an IPS sensor to filter network traffic using the "reputation" of a packet's source IP address. The reputation of an IP address is computed by Cisco threat intelligence using the past actions of that IP address. IP reputation has been an effective means of predicting the trustworthiness of current and future behaviors from an IP address.

> **NOTE**   You can obtain more information about Cisco Talos at https://talosintel.com.

Next-Generation Intrusion Prevention Systems

As a result of the Sourcefire acquisition, Cisco expanded its NGIPS portfolio with the following products:

- **Cisco Firepower 8000 Series appliances:** These high-performance appliances running Cisco FirePOWER Next-Generation IPS Services support throughput speeds from 2 Gbps up to 60 Gbps.

- **Cisco Firepower 7000 Series appliances:** These appliances comprise the base platform for the Cisco FirePOWER NGIPS software. The base platform supports throughput speeds from 50 Mbps up to 1.25 Gbps.

- **Virtual next-generation IPS (NGIPSv) appliances for VMware:** These appliances can be deployed in virtualized environments. By deploying these virtual appliances, security administrators can maintain network visibility that is often lost in virtual environments.

Firepower Management Center

Cisco Firepower Management Center (FMC) provides a centralized management and analysis platform for the Cisco NGIPS appliances, the Cisco ASA with FirePOWER Services, and Cisco FTD. It provides support for role-based policy management and includes a fully customizable dashboard with advanced reports and analytics. The following are the models of the Cisco FMC appliances:

- **FS750:** Supports a maximum of ten managed devices (NGIPS or Cisco ASA appliances) and a total of 20 million IPS events.

- **FS2000:** Supports a maximum of 70 managed devices and up to 60 million IPS events.

- **FS4000:** Supports a maximum of 300 managed devices and a total of 300 million IPS events.

- **FMC virtual appliance:** Allows you to conveniently provision on your existing virtual infrastructure. It supports a maximum of 25 managed devices and up to 10 million IPS events.

Advance Malware Protection

Cisco provides advanced malware protection (AMP) capabilities for endpoint and network security devices. In the following sections, you will learn the details about AMP for Endpoints and the integration of AMP in several Cisco security products.

AMP for Endpoints

Numerous antivirus and antimalware solutions on the market are designed to detect, analyze, and protect against both known and emerging endpoint threats. Before diving into these technologies, you should understand viruses and malicious software (malware). The following are the most common types of malicious software:

- **Computer virus:** Malicious software that infects a host file or system area to produce an undesirable outcome such as erasing data, stealing information, or corrupting the integrity of the system. In numerous cases, these viruses multiply again to form new generations of themselves.

- **Worm:** A virus that replicates itself over the network, infecting numerous vulnerable systems. In most cases, a worm executes malicious instructions on a remote system without user interaction.

- **Mailer or mass-mailer worm:** A type of worm that sends itself in an email message. Examples of mass-mailer worms are Loveletter.A@mm and W32/SKA.A@m (a.k.a. the Happy99 worm), which sends a copy of itself every time the user sends a new message.

- **Logic bomb:** A type of malicious code that is injected into a legitimate application. An attacker can program a logic bomb to delete itself from the disk after it performs the malicious tasks on the system. Examples of these malicious tasks include deleting or corrupting files or databases and executing a specific instruction after certain system conditions are met.

- **Trojan horse:** A type of malware that executes instructions to delete files, steal data, or otherwise compromise the integrity of the underlying operating system. Trojan horses typically use a form of social engineering to fool victims into installing such software on their computers or mobile devices. Trojans can also act as back doors.

- **Back door:** A piece of malware or a configuration change that allows an attacker to control the victim's system remotely. For example, a back door can open a network port on the affected system so that the attacker can connect to and control the system.

- **Exploit:** A malicious program designed to exploit, or take advantage of, a single vulnerability or set of vulnerabilities.

- **Downloader:** A piece of malware that downloads and installs other malicious content from the Internet to perform additional exploitation on an affected system.

- **Spammer:** Malware that sends spam, or unsolicited messages sent via email, instant messaging, newsgroups, or any other kind of computer or mobile device communications. Spammers send these unsolicited messages with the primary goal of fooling users into clicking malicious links, replying to emails or other messages with sensitive information, or performing different types of scams. The attacker's main objective is to make money.

- **Key logger:** A piece of malware that captures the user's keystrokes on a compromised computer or mobile device. A key logger collects sensitive information such as passwords, personal ID numbers (PINs), personally identifiable information (PII), credit card numbers, and more.

- **Rootkit:** A set of tools used by an attacker to elevate his or her privilege to obtain root-level access in order to completely take control of the affected system.

- **Ransomware:** A type of malware that compromises a system and then demands that the victim pay a ransom to the attacker in order for the malicious activity to cease or for the malware to be removed from the affected system. Two examples of ransomware are Crypto Locker and CryptoWall; they both encrypt the victim's data and demand that the user pay a ransom in order for the data to be decrypted and accessible again.

The following are just a few examples of the commercial and free antivirus software options available today:

- Avast
- AVG Internet Security Bitdefender Antivirus Free

- ZoneAlarm PRO Antivirus+, ZoneAlarm PRO Firewall, and ZoneAlarm Extreme Security
- F-Secure Anti-Virus
- Kaspersky Anti-Virus
- McAfee AntiVirus
- Panda Antivirus
- Sophos Antivirus
- Norton AntiVirus
- ClamAV
- Immunet AntiVirus

There are numerous other antivirus software companies and products.

NOTE   ClamAV is an open source antivirus engine sponsored and maintained by Cisco and non-Cisco engineers. You can download ClamAV from www.clamav.net. Immunet is a free community-based antivirus software maintained by Cisco Sourcefire. You can download Immunet from www.immunet.com.

Personal firewalls and host intrusion prevention systems (HIPSs) are software applications that you can install on end-user machines or servers to protect them from external security threats and intrusions. The term *personal firewall* typically applies to basic software that can control Layer 3 and Layer 4 access to client machines. HIPS provides several features that offer more robust security than a traditional personal firewall, such as host intrusion prevention and protection against spyware, viruses, worms, Trojans, and other types of malware.

Today, more sophisticated software makes basic personal firewalls and HIPS obsolete. For example, Cisco Advanced Malware Protection (AMP) for Endpoints provides granular visibility and control to stop advanced threats missed by other security layers. Cisco AMP for Endpoints takes advantage of telemetry from big data, continuous analysis, and advanced analytics provided by Cisco threat intelligence to be able to detect, analyze, and stop advanced malware across endpoints.

Cisco AMP for Endpoints provides advanced malware protection for many operating systems, including Windows, Mac OS X, Android, and Linux.

Attacks are getting very sophisticated and can evade detection of traditional systems and endpoint protection. Today, attackers have the resources, knowledge, and persistence to beat point-in-time detection. Cisco AMP for Endpoints provides mitigation capabilities that go beyond point-in-time detection. It uses threat intelligence from Cisco to perform retrospective analysis and protection. Cisco AMP for Endpoints also provides device and file trajectory capabilities to allow a security administrator to analyze the full spectrum of an attack. Device trajectory and file trajectory support the following file types in the Windows and Mac OS X operating systems:

- MSEXE
- PDF

- MSCAB

- MSOLE2

- ZIP

- ELF

- MACHO

- MACHO_UNIBIN

- SWF

- JAVA

AMP for Networks

Cisco AMP for Networks provides next-generation security services that go beyond point-in-time detection. It provides continuous analysis and tracking of files and also retrospective security alerts so that a security administrator can take action during and after an attack. The file trajectory feature of Cisco AMP for Networks tracks file transmissions across the network, and the file capture feature enables a security administrator to store and retrieve files for further analysis.

The network provides unprecedented visibility into activity at a macro-analytical level. However, to remediate malware, in most cases you need to be on the host. This is why AMP has the following connectors: AMP for Networks, AMP for Endpoints, and AMP for Content Security Appliances.

You can install AMP for Networks on any Cisco Firepower security appliance right along-side the firewall and IPS; however, there are dedicated AMP appliances as well. When it comes down to it, though, AMP appliances and Firepower appliances are actually the same. They can all run all the same services. Are you thoroughly confused? Stated a different way, Cisco AMP for Networks is the AMP service that runs on the appliance examining traf-fic flowing through a network. It can be installed in a standalone form or as a service on a Firepower IPS or even a Cisco ASA with FirePOWER Services.

AMP for Networks and all the AMP connectors are designed to find malicious files, provide retrospective analysis, illustrate trajectory, and point out how far malicious files may have spread.

The AMP for Networks connector examines, records, tracks, and sends files to the cloud. It creates an SHA-256 hash of the file and compares it to the local file cache. If the hash is not in the local cache, it queries the Firepower Management Center (FMC). The FMC has its own cache of all the hashes it has seen before, and if it hasn't previously seen this hash, the FMC queries the cloud. Unlike with AMP for Endpoints, when a file is new, it can be analyzed locally and doesn't have to be sent to the cloud for all analysis. Also, the file is examined and stopped in flight, as it is traversing the appliance.

Figure 2-14 illustrates the many AMP for Networks connectors sending the file hash to the FMC, which in turn sends it to the cloud if the hash is new. The connectors could be run-ning on dedicated AMP appliances, as a service on a Cisco next-generation IPS (NGIPS), on an ASA with FirePOWER Services, or on the next-generation firewall (NGFW) known as Firepower Threat Defense (FTD).

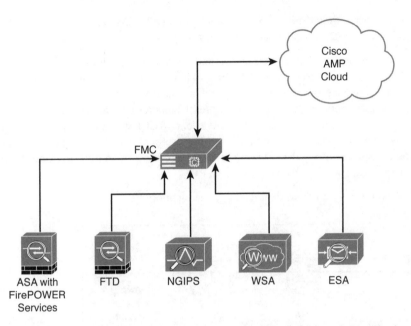

Figure 2-14 *AMP Connectors Communicating to the FMC and the Cloud*

It's very important to note that only the SHA-256 hash is sent unless you configure the policy to send files for further analysis in Threat Grid.

AMP can also provide retrospective analysis. The AMP for Networks appliance keeps data from what occurred in the past. When a file's disposition is changed, AMP provides an historical analysis of what happened, tracing the incident/infection. With the help of AMP for Endpoints, retrospection can reach out to that host and remediate the bad file, even though that file was permitted in the past.

Web Security Appliance

For an organization to be able to protect its environment against web-based security threats, security administrators need to deploy tools and mitigation technologies that go far beyond traditional blocking of known bad websites. Today, you can download malware through compromised legitimate websites, including social media sites, advertisements in news and corporate sites, and gaming sites. Cisco has developed several tools and mechanisms to help customers combat these threats, including and Cisco Web Security Appliance (WSA), Cisco Security Management Appliance (SMA), and Cisco Cloud Web Security (CWS). These solutions enable malware detection and blocking, continuous monitoring, and retrospective alerting.

A Cisco WSA uses cloud-based intelligence from Cisco to help protect an organization before, during, and after an attack. This "lifecycle" is referred to as the *attack continuum*. The cloud-based intelligence includes web (URL) reputation and zero-day threat intelligence from the Talos Cisco security intelligence and research group. This threat intelligence helps security professionals stop threats before they enter the corporate network and also enables file reputation and file sandboxing to identify threats during an attack. Retrospective attack analysis allows security administrators to investigate and provide protection after an attack, when advanced malware might have evaded other layers of defense.

A Cisco WSA can be deployed in explicit proxy mode or as a transparent proxy, using the Web Cache Communication Protocol (WCCP). In explicit proxies, clients are aware of the requests that go through a proxy. On the other hand, in transparent proxies, clients are not aware of a proxy in the network; the source IP address in a request is that of the client. In transparent proxies, configuration is needed on the client. WCCP was originally developed by Cisco, but several other vendors have integrated this protocol into their products to allow clustering and transparent proxy deployments on networks using Cisco infrastructure devices (routers, switches, firewalls, and so on).

Figure 2-15 illustrates a Cisco WSA deployed as an explicit proxy.

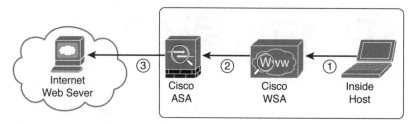

Figure 2-15 *WSA Explicit Proxy Configuration*

The following are the steps illustrated in Figure 2-15:

1. An internal user makes an HTTP request to an external website. The client browser is configured to send the request to the Cisco WSA.

2. The Cisco WSA connects to the website on behalf of the internal user.

3. The firewall (Cisco ASA) is configured to only allow outbound web traffic from the Cisco WSA, and it forwards the traffic to the web server.

Figure 2-16 shows a Cisco WSA deployed as a transparent proxy.

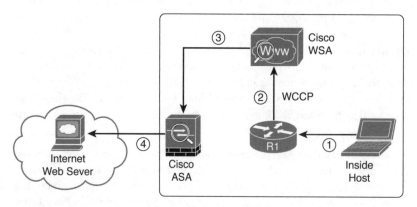

Figure 2-16 *WSA Transparent Proxy Configuration*

The following are the steps illustrated in Figure 2-16:

1. An internal user makes an HTTP request to an external website.

2. The internal router (R1) redirects the web request to the Cisco WSA, using WCCP.

3. The Cisco WSA connects to the website on behalf of the internal user.

4. The firewall (Cisco ASA) is configured to only allow outbound web traffic from the WSA. The web traffic is sent to the Internet web server.

Figure 2-17 demonstrates how the WCCP registration works. The Cisco WSA is the WCCP client, and the Cisco router is the WCCP server.

Figure 2-17 *WCCP Registration*

During the WCCP registration process, the WCCP client sends a registration announcement ("Here I am") every 10 seconds. The WCCP server (the Cisco router, in this example) accepts the registration request and acknowledges it with an "I see you" WCCP message. The WCCP server waits 30 seconds before it declares the client as "inactive" (engine failed). WCCP can be used in large-scale environments. Figure 2-18 shows a cluster of Cisco WSAs, where internal Layer 3 switches redirect web traffic to the cluster.

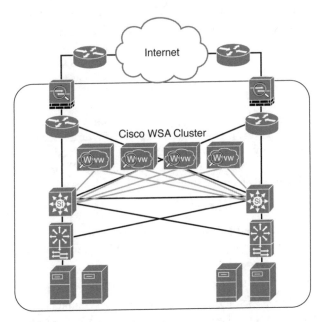

Figure 2-18 *Cisco WSA Cluster*

The Cisco WSA runs the Cisco AsyncOS operating system. Cisco AsyncOS supports numerous features, including the following, that help mitigate web-based threats:

■ **Real-time antimalware adaptive scanning:** The Cisco WSA can be configured to dynamically select an antimalware scanning engine based on URL reputation, content type, and scanner effectiveness. Adaptive scanning is a feature designed to increase the "catch rate" of malware embedded in images, JavaScript, text, and Adobe Flash files. Adaptive scanning is an additional layer of security on top of Cisco WSA web reputation filters that include support for Sophos, Webroot, and McAfee.

■ **Layer 4 traffic monitor:** The Cisco WSA is used to detect and block spyware. It dynamically adds IP addresses of known malware domains to databases of sites to block.

■ **Third-party DLP integration:** The Cisco WSA redirects all outbound traffic to a third-party DLP appliance, allowing deep content inspection for regulatory compliance and data exfiltration protection. It enables an administrator to inspect web content by title, metadata, and size, and to even prevent users from storing files to cloud services such as Dropbox and Google Drive.

■ **File reputation:** Using threat information from Cisco Talos, this file reputation threat intelligence is updated every 3 to 5 minutes.

■ **File sandboxing:** If malware is detected, the Cisco AMP capabilities can put files in a sandbox to inspect the malware's behavior and combine the inspection with machine-learning analysis to determine the threat level. Cisco Cognitive Threat Analytics (CTA) uses machine-learning algorithms to adapt over time.

■ **File retrospection:** After a malicious attempt or malware is detected, the Cisco WSA continues to cross-examine files over an extended period of time.

■ **Application visibility and control:** The Cisco ASA can inspect and even block applications that are not allowed by the corporate security polity. For example, an administrator can allow users to use social media sites such as Facebook but block micro-applications such as Facebook games.

Email Security Appliance

Users are no longer accessing email only from the corporate network or from a single device. Cisco provides cloud-based, hybrid, and on-premises solutions based on the Email Security Appliance (ESA) that can help protect any dynamic environment. This section introduces these solutions and technologies and explains how users can use threat intelligence to detect, analyze, and protect against both known and emerging threats.

The following are the most common email-based threats:

■ **Spam:** Unsolicited email messages that advertise a service, a scam (typically), or a message with malicious intent. Email spam continues to be a major threat because it can be used to spread malware.

■ **Malware attachments:** Email messages containing malicious software (malware).

■ **Phishing:** An attacker's attempt to fool a user into thinking that the email communication comes from a legitimate entity or site, such as a bank, social media website, online payment processor, or even the corporate IT department. The goal of a phishing email is to steal a user's sensitive information, such as user credentials, bank account information, and so on.

- **Spear phishing:** This involves phishing attempts that are more targeted. Spear-phishing emails are directed to specific individuals or organizations. For instance, an attacker might perform a passive reconnaissance on an individual or organization by gathering information from social media sites (for example, Twitter, LinkedIn, and Facebook) and other online resources. Then the attacker might tailor a more directed and relevant message to the victim to increase the probability that the user will be fooled into following a malicious link, clicking an attachment containing malware, or simply replying to the email and providing sensitive information. Another phishing-based attack, called *whaling*, specifically targets executives and high-profile users.

The Cisco ESA runs the Cisco AsyncOS operating system. Cisco AsyncOS supports numerous features that help mitigate email-based threats. The following are examples of the features supported by the Cisco ESA:

- **Access control:** Controlling access for inbound senders, according to a sender's IP address, IP address range, or domain name.

- **Anti-spam:** Multilayer filters based on Cisco SenderBase reputation and Cisco antispam integration. The antispam reputation and zero-day threat intelligence are fueled by the Cisco security intelligence and research group named Talos.

- **Network antivirus:** Network antivirus capabilities at the gateway. Cisco partnered with Sophos and McAfee, supporting their antivirus scanning engines.

- **Advanced Malware Protection (AMP):** Allows security administrators to detect and block malware and perform continuous analysis and retrospective alerting.

- **Data loss prevention (DLP):** The ability to detect any sensitive emails and documents leaving the corporation. The Cisco ESA integrates RSA email DLP for outbound traffic.

- **Email encryption:** The ability to encrypt outgoing mail to address regulatory requirements. The administrator can configure an encryption policy on the Cisco ESA and use a local key server or hosted key service to encrypt the message.

- **Email authentication:** A few email authentication mechanisms include Sender Policy Framework (SPF), Sender ID Framework (SIDF), and DomainKeys Identified Mail (DKIM) verification of incoming mail, as well as DomainKeys and DKIM signing of outgoing mail.

- **Outbreak filters:** Preventive protection against new security outbreaks and email-based scams using Cisco's Security Intelligence Operations (SIO) threat intelligence information.

NOTE Cisco SenderBase (see www.senderbase.org) is the world's largest email and web traffic monitoring network. It provides real-time threat intelligence powered by Cisco SIO.

The Cisco ESA acts as the email gateway for an organization, handling all email connections, accepting messages, and relaying messages to the appropriate systems. The Cisco ESA can service email connections from the Internet to users inside a network and from systems inside the network to the Internet. Email connections use Simple Mail Transfer Protocol (SMTP). The ESA services all SMTP connections, by default acting as the SMTP gateway.

> **TIP**   Mail gateways are also known as *mail exchangers* (MX).

The Cisco ESA uses listeners to handle incoming SMTP connection requests. A listener defines an email processing service that is configured on an interface in the Cisco ESA. Listeners apply to email entering the appliance from either the Internet or internal systems.

The following listeners can be configured:

- Public listeners for email coming in from the Internet.
- Private listeners for email coming from hosts in the corporate (inside) network. (These emails are typically from internal groupware, Exchange, POP, or IMAP email servers.)

Cisco ESA listeners are often referred to as SMTP daemons, and they run on specific Cisco ESA interfaces. When a listener is configured, the following information must be provided:

- Listener properties such as a specific interface in the Cisco ESA and the TCP port that will be used. The listener properties must also indicate whether the listener is public or private.
- The hosts that are allowed to connect to the listener, using a combination of access control rules. An administrator can specify which remote hosts can connect to the listener.
- The local domains for which public listeners accept messages.

Cisco Security Management Appliance

Cisco Security Management Appliance (SMA) is a Cisco product that centralizes the management and reporting for one or more Cisco ESAs and Cisco WSAs. Cisco SMA enables you to consistently enforce policy and enhance threat protection. Figure 2-19 shows a Cisco SMA that is controlling Cisco ESAs and Cisco WSAs in different geographic locations (New York, Raleigh, Paris, and London).

The Cisco SMA can be deployed with physical appliances or as virtual appliances.

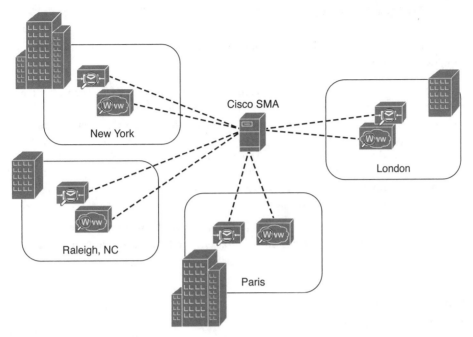

Figure 2-19   *Cisco SMA*

Cisco Identity Services Engine

The Cisco Identity Services Engine (ISE) is a comprehensive security identity management solution designed to function as a policy decision point for network access. It allows security administrators to collect real-time contextual information from a network, its users, and devices. Cisco ISE is the central policy management platform in the Cisco TrustSec solution. It supports a comprehensive set of AAA (authentication, authorization, and accounting), posture, and network profiler features in a single device. Cisco ISE provides the AAA functionality of legacy Cisco products such as the Cisco Access Control Server (ACS).

Cisco ISE allows security administrators to provide network guest access management and wide-ranging client provisioning policies, including 802.1X environments. The support of TrustSec features such as security group tags (SGTs) and security group access control lists (SGACLs) make the Cisco ISE a complete identity services solution. Cisco ISE supports policy sets, which let a security administrator group sets of authentication and authorization policies.

Cisco ISE provides Network Admission Control (NAC) features, including posture policies, to enforce configuration of end-user devices with the most up-to-date security settings or applications before they enter the network. The Cisco ISE supports the following agent types for posture assessment and compliance:

- **Cisco NAC Web Agent:** A temporary agent that is installed in end-user machines at the time of login. The Cisco NAC Web Agent is not visible on the end-user machine after the user terminates the session.

- **Cisco NAC Agent:** An agent that is installed permanently on a Windows or Mac OS X client system.

- **Cisco AnyConnect Secure Mobility Client :** An agent that is installed permanently on a Windows or Mac OS X client system.

Cisco ISE provides a comprehensive set of features to allow corporate users to connect their personal devices—such as mobile phones, tablets, laptops, and other network devices—to the network. Such a bring-your-own-device (BYOD) system introduces many challenges in terms of protecting network services and enterprise data. Cisco ISE provides support for multiple mobile device management (MDM) solutions to enforce policy on endpoints. ISE can be configured to redirect users to MDM onboarding portals and prompt them to update their devices before they can access the network. Cisco ISE can also be configured to provide Internet-only access to users who are not compliant with MDM policies.

Cisco ISE supports the Cisco Platform Exchange Grid (pxGrid), a multivendor, cross-platform network system that combines different parts of an IT infrastructure, such as the following:

- Security monitoring
- Detection systems
- Network policy platforms
- Asset and configuration management
- Identity and access management platforms

Cisco pxGrid has a unified framework with an open application programming interface (API) designed in a hub-and-spoke architecture. pxGrid is used to enable the sharing of contextual-based information from a Cisco ISE session directory to other policy network systems, such as Cisco IOS devices and the Cisco ASA.

The Cisco ISE can be configured as a certificate authority (CA) to generate and manage digital certificates for endpoints. Cisco ISE CA supports standalone and subordinate deployments.

Cisco ISE software can be installed on a range of physical appliances or on a VMware server (Cisco ISE VM). The Cisco ISE software image does not support the installation of any other packages or applications on this dedicated platform.

Security Cloud-based Solutions

Several cloud-based security solutions are also available in the market. For example, Cisco provides the following cloud-based security services:

- Cisco Cloud Web Security (CWS)
- Cisco Cloud Email Security (CES)
- Cisco AMP Threat Grid
- Cisco Threat Awareness Service

- OpenDNS

- CloudLock

The following sections describe these cloud-based security services.

Cisco Cloud Web Security

Cisco Cloud Web Security (CWS) is a cloud-based security service that provides worldwide threat intelligence, advanced threat defense capabilities, and roaming user protection. The Cisco CWS service uses web proxies in the Cisco cloud environment that scan traffic for malware and policy enforcement. Cisco customers can connect to the Cisco CWS service directly by using a proxy auto-configuration (PAC) file in the user endpoint or through connectors integrated into the following Cisco products:

- Cisco ISR G2 routers

- Cisco ASA

- Cisco WSA

- Cisco AnyConnect Secure Mobility Client

NOTE   Cisco is always adding more functionality to their products. The number of connectors may increase throughout time. Those in the preceding list are the ones available at the time of writing.

Organizations using the transparent proxy functionality through a connector can get the most out of their existing infrastructure. In addition, the scanning is offloaded from the hardware appliances to the cloud, thus reducing the impact to hardware utilization and reducing network latency. Figure 2-20 illustrates how the transparent proxy functionality through a connector works.

In Figure 2-20, the Cisco ASA is enabled with the Cisco CWS connector at a branch office, and it protects the corporate users at the branch office with these steps:

1. An internal user makes an HTTP request to an external website (example.org).
2. The Cisco ASA forwards the request to the Cisco CWS global cloud infrastructure.
3. Cisco CWS notices that example.org has some web content (ads) that is redirecting the user to a known malicious site.
4. Cisco CWS blocks the request to the malicious site.

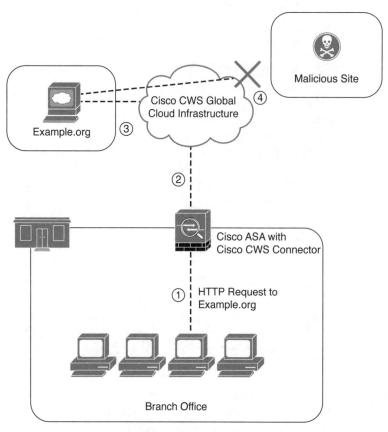

Figure 2-20 *Cisco CWS Example*

Cisco Cloud Email Security

Cisco Cloud Email Security (CES) provides a cloud-based solution that allows companies to outsource the management of their email security. The service provides email security instances in multiple Cisco data centers to enable high availability.

The Cisco Hybrid Email Security solution combines both cloud-based and on-premises ESAs. This hybrid solution helps Cisco customers reduce their onsite email security footprint and outsource a portion of their email security to Cisco, while still allowing them to maintain control of confidential information within their physical boundaries. Many organizations must comply with regulations that require them to keep sensitive data physically on their premises. The Cisco Hybrid Email Security solution allows network security administrators to remain compliant and to maintain advanced control with encryption, DLP, and onsite identity-based integration.

Cisco AMP Threat Grid

Cisco acquired a security company called Threat Grid that provides cloud-based and on-premises malware analysis solutions. Cisco integrated Cisco AMP and Threat Grid to provide a solution for advanced malware analysis with deep threat analytics. The Cisco AMP Threat Grid integrated solution analyzes millions of files and correlates them with hundreds of millions of malware samples. This provides a look into attack campaigns and how malware is distributed. This solution provides a security administrator with detailed reports of indicators of compromise and threat scores that help prioritize mitigations and recover from attacks. Cisco AMP Threat Grid crowdsources malware from a closed community and analyzes all samples using highly secure proprietary techniques that include static and dynamic analysis. These are different from traditional sandboxing technologies. The Cisco AMP Threat Grid analysis exists outside the virtual environment, identifying malicious code designed to evade analysis. There is a feature in Cisco AMP Threat Grid called *Glovebox* that helps you interact with the malware in real time, recording all activity for future play-back and reporting. Advanced malware uses numerous evasion techniques to determine whether it is being analyzed in a sandbox. Some of these samples require user interaction. Glovebox dissects these samples without infecting your network while the samples are being analyzed. Glovebox is a powerful tool against advanced malware that allows analysts to open applications and replicate a workflow process, see how the malware behaves, and even reboot the virtual machine.

NOTE The Mac OS X connector does not support SWF files. The Windows connector does not scan ELF, JAVA, MACHO, and MACHO_UNIBIN files at the time of this writing. The Android AMP connector scans APK files.

Cisco Threat Awareness Service

The Cisco Threat Awareness Service (CTAS) is a threat intelligence service that provides Cisco customers with network visibility by making security information available 24 hours a day, 7 days a week. CTAS is a cloud-based service that is accessed via a web browser. It allows Cisco customers to maintain visibility into inbound and outbound network activity from the outside and displays potential threats requiring additional attention by the network security staff. CTAS requires no configuration changes, network infrastructure, or new software, as it tracks the domain names and IP addresses of Cisco customer premises to alert on suspicious activity or requests. CTAS also provides remediation recommendations through its web portal.

Cisco provides a base offer of the CTAS service with Cisco Smart Net Total Care Service at no additional cost. A premium offer is available as a yearly subscription for customers looking to track an unlimited number of domain names and IP addresses.

NOTE You can obtain more information about CTAS at http://www.cisco.com/c/en/us/products/security/sas-threat-management.html.

OpenDNS

Cisco acquired a company called OpenDNS that provides DNS services, threat intelligence, and threat enforcement at the DNS layer. OpenDNS has a global network that delivers advanced security solutions (as a cloud-based service) regardless of where Cisco customer offices or employees are located. This service is extremely easy to deploy and easy to manage. Cisco has also incorporated the innovative advancements to threat research and threat-centric security that OpenDNS has developed to block advanced cyber security threats with other security and networking products. Millions of people use OpenDNS, including thousands of companies, from Fortune 500 enterprises to small businesses.

OpenDNS provides a free DNS service for individuals, students, and small businesses. You can just simply configure your endpoint (laptop, desktop, mobile device, server, or your DHCP server) to point to OpenDNS servers: 208.67.222.222 and/or 208.67.220.220.

It also provides the following premium services:

- **OpenDNS Umbrella:** An enterprise advanced network security service to protect any device, anywhere. This service blocks known malicious sites from being "resolved" in DNS. It provides an up-to-the-minute view and analysis of at least 2% of the world's Internet activity to stay ahead of attacks. This service provides threat intelligence by seeing where attacks are being staged on the Internet.

- **OpenDNS Investigate:** This is a premium service that provides you information on where attacks are forming, allowing you to investigate incidents faster and prioritize them better. With the Investigate service, you can see up-to-the-minute threat data and historical context about all domains on the Internet and respond quickly to critical incidents. It provides a dynamic search engine and a RESTful API that you can use to automatically bring critical data into the security management and threat intelligence systems deployed in your organization. It also provides predictive threat intelligence using statistical models for real-time and historical data to predict domains that are likely malicious and could be part of future attacks.

CloudLock

Cisco acquired a company called CloudLock that creates solutions to protect their customers against data breaches in any cloud environment and application (app) through a highly configurable cloud-based data loss prevention (DLP) architecture. CloudLock has numerous out-of-the-box policies and a wide range of automated, policy-driven response actions, including the following:

- File-level encryption
- Quarantine
- End-user notifications

These policies are designed to provide common data protection and help with compliance. CloudLock also can monitor data at rest within platforms via an API and provide visibility of user activity through retroactive monitoring capabilities. This solution helps organizations defend against account compromises with cross-platform User and Entity Behavior Analytics (UEBA) for Software as a Service (SaaS), Infrastructure as a Service (IaaS), Platform as a Service (PaaS), and Identity as a Service (IDaaS) environments. CloudLock uses advanced machine learning to be able to detect anomalies and to identify activities in different countries that can be whitelisted or blacklisted in the platform. CloudLock Apps Firewall is a feature that discovers and controls malicious cloud apps that may be interacting with the corporate network.

Cisco NetFlow

NetFlow is a Cisco technology that provides comprehensive visibility into all network traffic that traverses a Cisco-supported device. Cisco invented NetFlow and is the leader in IP traffic flow technology. NetFlow was initially created for billing and accounting of network traffic and to measure other IP traffic characteristics such as bandwidth utilization and application performance. NetFlow has also been used as a network capacity planning tool and to monitor network availability. Nowadays, NetFlow is used as a network security tool because its reporting capabilities provide nonrepudiation, anomaly detection, and investigative capabilities. As network traffic traverses a NetFlow-enabled device, the device collects traffic flow data and provides a network administrator or security professional with detailed information about such flows.

NetFlow provides detailed network telemetry that can be used to see what is actually happening across the entire network. You can use NetFlow to identify DoS attacks, quickly identify compromised endpoints and network infrastructure devices, and monitor network usage of employees, contractors, or partners. NetFlow is also often used to obtain network telemetry during security incident response and forensics. You can also take advantage of NetFlow to detect firewall misconfigurations and inappropriate access to corporate resources.

NetFlow supports both IP Version 4 (IPv4) and IP Version 6 (IPv6).

There's also the Internet Protocol Flow Information Export (IPFIX), which is a network flow standard led by the Internet Engineering Task Force (IETF). IPFIX was designed to create a common, universal standard of export for flow information from routers, switches, firewalls, and other infrastructure devices. IPFIX defines how flow information should be formatted and transferred from an exporter to a collector. IPFIX is documented in RFC 7011 through RFC 7015 and RFC 5103. Cisco NetFlow Version 9 is the basis and main point of reference for IPFIX. IPFIX changes some of the terminologies of NetFlow, but in essence they are the same principles of NetFlow Version 9.

Traditional Cisco NetFlow records are usually exported via UDP messages. The IP address of the NetFlow collector and the destination UDP port must be configured on the sending device. The NetFlow standard (RFC 3954) does not specify a specific NetFlow listening port. The standard or most common UDP port used by NetFlow is UDP port 2055, but other ports, such as 9555, 9995, 9025, and 9026, can also be used. UDP port 4739 is the default port used by IPFIX.

What Is the Flow in NetFlow?

A *flow* is a unidirectional series of packets between a given source and destination. Figure 2-21 shows an example of a flow between a client and a server.

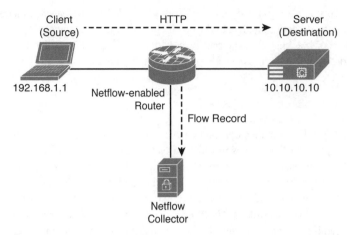

Figure 2-21   *Flow Example*

In a flow, the same source and destination IP addresses, source and destination ports, and IP protocol are shared. This is often referred to as the *five-tuple*.

In Figure 2-21, the client (source) establishes a connection to the server (destination). When the traffic traverses the router (configured for NetFlow), it generates a flow record. At the very minimum, the five-tuple is used to identify the flow in the NetFlow database of flows kept on the device. This database is often called the NetFlow cache. Here is the five-tuple for the basic flow represented in Figure 2-21:

- **Source address:** 192.168.1.1
- **Destination IP address:** 10.10.10.10
- **Source port:** 15728
- **Destination port:** 80
- **Protocol:** TCP (since HTTP is carried over TCP)

Many people often confuse a flow with a session. All traffic in a flow is going in the same direction; however, when the client establishes the HTTP connection (session) to the server and accesses a web page, it represents two separate flows. The first flow is the traffic from the client to the server, and the other flow is from the server to the client.

There are different versions of NetFlow. Depending on the version of NetFlow, the router can also gather additional information, such as type of service (ToS) byte, differentiated services code point (DSCP), the device's input interface, TCP flags, byte counters, and start and end times.

Flexible NetFlow, Cisco's next-generation NetFlow, can track a wide range of Layer 2, IPv4, and IPv6 flow information, such as the following:

- Source and destination MAC addresses
- Source and destination IPv4 or IPv6 addresses
- Source and destination ports

- ToS
- DSCP
- Packet and byte counts
- Flow timestamps
- Input and output interface numbers
- TCP flags and encapsulated protocol (TCP/UDP) and individual TCP flags
- Sections of a packet for deep packet inspection
- All fields in an IPv4 header, including IP-ID and TTL
- All fields in an IPv6 header, including Flow Label and Option Header
- Routing information, such as next-hop address, source autonomous system number (ASN), destination ASN, source prefix mask, destination prefix mask, Border Gateway Protocol (BGP) next hop, and BGP policy accounting traffic index

NetFlow vs. Full Packet Capture

A substantial difference exists between a full packet capture and the information collected in NetFlow. Think about NetFlow as being a technology to collect metadata on all transactions/ flows traversing the network.

Collecting packet captures in your network involves "tapping" or capturing a mirror image of network packets as they move through the network. Cisco switches allow for the setup of mirror ports that do not impact network performance. Typically, a deep packet inspection (DPI) application is connected to a mirror port, and certain information is extracted from the packets so that you can find out what is happening on your network. DPI solutions range from open source packet capture software such as Wireshark to commercial applications that can provide more detailed analysis.

You may be asking, "How does NetFlow compare to traditional packet capture technologies that leverage SPAN ports or Ethernet taps?" The cost and the amount of data that needs to be analyzed is much higher with packet captures. In a lot of scenarios and in most cases, you don't need heavyweight packet capture technology everywhere throughout your network if you have an appropriate NetFlow collection and analysis ecosystem. In fact, you probably couldn't afford it even if you did need it. For instance, the storage and compute power needed to analyze full packet captures can lead to much higher costs. However, there is definitely also a good benefit to collecting full packet capture data.

If you really must have latency and packet capture capabilities, Cisco through its Lancope acquisition offers a device called a FlowSensor that plugs into a SPAN, tap, or mirror port to generate NetFlow suitable for consumption by any NetFlow v9–capable collector.

The NetFlow Cache

The three types of NetFlow cache are as follows:

- Normal cache
- Immediate cache
- Permanent cache

The "normal cache" is the default cache type in many infrastructure devices enabled with NetFlow and Flexible NetFlow. The entries in the flow cache are removed (aged out) based on the configured timeout active seconds and timeout inactive seconds settings.

In the immediate cache, the flows account for a single packet. This type of NetFlow cache is desirable for real-time traffic monitoring and distributed DoS (DDoS) detection. The immediate NetFlow cache is used when only very small flows are expected (for example, sampling).

> **TIP**   You have to keep in mind that the immediate cache may result in a large amount of export data.

The permanent cache is used to track a set of flows without expiring the flows from the cache. The entire cache is periodically exported (update timer). Another thing to highlight is that the cache is a configurable value. After the cache is full, new flows will not be monitored. The permanent cache uses update counters rather than delta counters.

Data Loss Prevention

Data loss prevention (DLP) is the ability to detect any sensitive emails, documents, or information leaving your organization. Several products in the industry inspect for traffic to prevent data loss in an organization. Several Cisco security products integrate with third-party products to provide this type of solution. For example, the Cisco ESA integrates RSA email DLP for outbound email traffic. Also, the Cisco Cloud Email Service and the Cisco Hybrid Email Security solution allow network security administrators to remain compliant and to maintain advanced control with encryption, DLP, and onsite identity-based integration. Another product family that integrates with other DLP solutions is the Cisco WSA, which redirects all outbound traffic to a third-party DLP appliance, allowing deep content inspection for regulatory compliance and data exfiltration protection. It enables an administrator to inspect web content by title, metadata, and size and even to prevent users from storing files to cloud services such as Dropbox and Google Drive.

Cisco CloudLock is also another DLP solution. CloudLock is designed to protect organizations of any type against data breaches in any type of cloud environment or application (app) through a highly configurable cloud-based DLP architecture.

CloudLock is an API-driven solution that provides a deep level of integration with monitored SaaS, IaaS, PaaS, and IDaaS solutions. It provides advanced cloud DLP functionality that includes out-of-the-box policies designed to help administrators maintain compliance. Additionally, CloudLock can monitor data at rest within platforms via APIs and provide a comprehensive picture of user activity through retroactive monitoring capabilities. Security administrators can mitigate risk efficiently using CloudLock's configurable, automated response actions, including encryption, quarantine, and end-user notification.

Data loss doesn't always take place because of a complex attack carried out by an external attacker; many data loss incidents have been carried out by internal (insider) attacks. Data loss can also happen because of human negligence or ignorance—for example, an internal employee sending sensitive corporate email to their personal email account, or uploading sensitive information to an unapproved cloud provider. This is why maintaining visibility into what's coming as well as leaving the organization is so important.

Exam Preparation Tasks

Review All Key Topics

Review the most important topics in the chapter, noted with the Key Topic icon in the outer margin of the page. Table 2-2 lists a reference of these key topics and the page numbers on which each is found.

Table 2-2 Key Topics

Key Topic Element	Description	Page
Summary	Network firewalls	113
Summary	Access control lists (ACLs)	113
Summary	Extended ACLs	115
Summary	Application proxies	117
Summary	Network address translation	117
Summary	Port address translation	118
Summary	Static translation	119
Summary	Demilitarized zones	120
Summary	Next-generation firewalls	126
Summary	Cisco Firepower Threat Defense	126
Summary	Next-generation IPS	133
Summary	Advanced malware protection (AMP)	133
Summary	Cisco WSA	137
Summary	Cisco ESA	141
Summary	Cisco ISE	143
Summary	Security cloud-based solutions	144
Summary	Cisco CES	146
Summary	Cisco AMP Threat Grid	147
Summary	OpenDNS	148
Summary	Cisco NetFlow	149
Summary	What is a flow?	149
Summary	NetFlow vs. full packet capture	151
Summary	Data loss prevention	152

Complete Tables and Lists from Memory

Print a copy of Appendix B, "Memory Tables," (found on the book website), or at least the section for this chapter, and complete the tables and lists from memory. Appendix C, "Memory Tables Answer Key," also on the website, includes completed tables and lists to check your work.

Define Key Terms

Define the following key terms from this chapter, and check your answers in the glossary:

network firewalls, ACLs, network address translation, DLP, AMP, IPS, NetFlow

Q&A

The answers to these questions appear in Appendix A, "Answers to the 'Do I Know This Already?' Quizzes and Q&A Questions." For more practice with exam format questions, use the exam engine on the website.

1. Which of the following explains features of a traditional stateful firewall?

    a. Access control is done by application awareness and visibility.

    b. Access control is done by the five-tuple (source and destination IP addresses, source and destination ports, and protocol).

    c. Application inspection is not supported.

    d. Traditional stateful firewalls support advanced malware protection.

2. Which of the following describes a traditional IPS?

    a. A network security appliance or software technology that resides in stateful firewalls

    b. A network security appliance or software technology that supports advanced malware protection

    c. A network security appliance or software technology that inspects network traffic to detect and prevent security threats and exploits

    d. A virtual appliance that can be deployed with the Cisco Adaptive Security Manager (ASM)

3. Which of the following is true about NetFlow?

    a. NetFlow can be deployed to replace IPS devices.

    b. NetFlow provides information about network session data.

    c. NetFlow provides user authentication information.

    d. NetFlow provides application information.

4. What is DLP?

   a. An email inspection technology used to prevent phishing attacks

   b. A software or solution for making sure that corporate users do not send sensitive or critical information outside the corporate network

   c. A web inspection technology used to prevent phishing attacks

   d. A cloud solution used to provide dynamic layer protection

5. Stateful and traditional firewalls can analyze packets and judge them against a set of predetermined rules called access control lists (ACLs). They inspect which of the following elements within a packet?

   a. Session headers

   b. NetFlow flow information

   c. Source and destination ports and source and destination IP addresses

   d. Protocol information

6. Which of the following are Cisco cloud security solutions?

   a. CloudDLP

   b. OpenDNS

   c. CloudLock

   d. CloudSLS

7. Cisco pxGrid has a unified framework with an open API designed in a hub-and-spoke architecture. pxGrid is used to enable the sharing of contextual-based information from which devices?

   a. From a Cisco ASA to the Cisco OpenDNS service

   b. From a Cisco ASA to the Cisco WSA

   c. From a Cisco ASA to the Cisco FMC

   d. From a Cisco ISE session directory to other policy network systems, such as Cisco IOS devices and the Cisco ASA

8. Which of the following is true about heuristic-based algorithms?

   a. Heuristic-based algorithms may require fine tuning to adapt to network traffic and minimize the possibility of false positives.

   b. Heuristic-based algorithms do not require fine tuning.

   c. Heuristic-based algorithms support advanced malware protection.

   d. Heuristic-based algorithms provide capabilities for the automation of IPS signature creation and tuning.

9. Which of the following describes the use of DMZs?

   a. DMZs can be configured in Cisco IPS devices to provide additional inspection capabilities.

   b. DMZs can automatically segment the network traffic.

   c. DMZs can serve as segments on which a web server farm resides or as extranet connections to business partners.

   d. DMZs are only supported in next-generation firewalls.

10. Which of the following has the most storage requirements?

   a. NetFlow

   b. Syslog

   c. Full packet captures

   d. IPS signatures

This chapter covers the following topics:

- Describe the principles of the defense-in-depth strategy.

- What are threats, vulnerabilities, and exploits?

- Describe Confidentiality, Integrity, and Availability.

- Describe risk and risk analysis.

- Define what personally identifiable information (PII) and protected health information (PHI) are.

- What are the principles of least privilege and separation of duties?

- What are security operation centers (SOCs)?

- Describe cyber forensics.

CHAPTER 3

Security Principles

This chapter covers the principles of the defense-in-depth strategy and compares and contrasts the concepts of risk, threats, vulnerabilities, and exploits. This chapter also defines what are threat actors, run book automation (RBA), chain of custody (evidentiary), reverse engineering, sliding window anomaly detection, Personally Identifiable Information (PII), Protected Health Information (PHI), as well as what is the principle of least privilege, and how to perform separation of duties. It also covers concepts of risk scoring, risk weighting, risk reduction, and how to perform overall risk assessments.

"Do I Know This Already?" Quiz

The "Do I Know This Already?" quiz helps you identify your strengths and deficiencies in this chapter's topics. The 11-question quiz, derived from the major sections in the "Foundation Topics" portion of the chapter, helps you determine how to spend your limited study time. You can find the answers in Appendix A Answers to the "Do I Know This Already?" Quizzes and Q&A Questions.

Table 3-1 outlines the major topics discussed in this chapter and the "Do I Know This Already?" quiz questions that correspond to those topics.

Table 3-1 "Do I Know This Already?" Foundation Topics Section-to-Question Mapping

Foundation Topics Section	Questions Covered in This Section
The Principles of the Defense-in-Depth Strategy	1–2
What Are Threats, Vulnerabilities, and Exploits?	3–6
Risk and Risk Analysis	7
Personally Identifiable Information and Protected Health Information	8
Principle of Least Privilege and Separation of Duties	9
Security Operation Centers	10
Forensics	11

1. What is one of the primary benefits of a defense-in-depth strategy?

   a. You can deploy advanced malware protection to detect and block advanced persistent threats.

   b. You can configure firewall failover in a scalable way.

   c. Even if a single control (such as a firewall or IPS) fails, other controls can still protect your environment and assets.

   d. You can configure intrusion prevention systems (IPSs) with custom signatures and auto-tuning to be more effective in the network.

2. Which of the following planes is important to understand for defense in depth?

    a. Management plane

    b. Failover plane

    c. Control plane

    d. Clustering

    e. User/data plane

    f. Services plane

3. Which of the following are examples of vulnerabilities?

    a. Advanced threats

    b. CVSS

    c. SQL injection

    d. Command injection

    e. Cross-site scripting (XSS)

    f. Cross-site request forgery (CSRF)

4. What is the Common Vulnerabilities and Exposures (CVE)?

    a. An identifier of threats

    b. A standard to score vulnerabilities

    c. A standard maintained by OASIS

    d. A standard for identifying vulnerabilities to make it easier to share data across tools, vulnerability repositories, and security services

5. Which of the following is true when describing threat intelligence?

    a. Threat intelligence's primary purpose is to make money by exploiting threats.

    b. Threat intelligence's primary purpose is to inform business decisions regarding the risks and implications associated with threats.

    c. With threat intelligence, threat actors can become more efficient to carry out attacks.

    d. Threat intelligence is too difficult to obtain.

6. Which of the following is an open source feed for threat data?

    a. Cyber Squad ThreatConnect

    b. BAE Detica CyberReveal

    c. MITRE CRITs

    d. Cisco AMP Threat Grid

7. What is the Common Vulnerability Scoring System (CVSS)?

   a. A scoring system for exploits.

   b. A tool to automatically mitigate vulnerabilities.

   c. A scoring method that conveys vulnerability severity and helps determine the urgency and priority of response.

   d. A vulnerability-mitigation risk analysis tool.

8. Which of the following are examples of personally identifiable information (PII)?

   a. Social security number

   b. Biological or personal characteristics, such as an image of distinguishing features, fingerprints, x-rays, voice signature, retina scan, and geometry of the face

   c. CVE

   d. Date of birth

9. Which of the following statements are true about the principle of least privilege?

   a. Principle of least privilege and separation of duties can be considered to be the same thing.

   b. The principle of least privilege states that all users—whether they are individual contributors, managers, directors, or executives—should be granted only the level of privilege they need to do their job, and no more.

   c. Programs or processes running on a system should have the capabilities they need to "get their job done," but no root access to the system.

   d. The principle of least privilege only applies to people.

10. What is a runbook?

   a. A runbook is a collection of processes running on a system.

   b. A runbook is a configuration guide for network security devices.

   c. A runbook is a collection of best practices for configuring access control lists on a firewall and other network infrastructure devices.

   d. A runbook is a collection of procedures and operations performed by system administrators, security professionals, or network operators.

11. Chain of custody is the way you document and preserve evidence from the time you started the cyber forensics investigation to the time the evidence is presented at court. Which of the following is important when handling evidence?

   a. Documentation about how and when the evidence was collected

   b. Documentation about how evidence was transported

   c. Documentation about who had access to the evidence and how it was accessed

   d. Documentation about the CVSS score of a given CVE

Foundation Topics

In this chapter, you will learn the different cyber security principles, including what threats, vulnerabilities, and exploits are. You will also learn details about what defense in depth is and how to perform risk analysis. This chapter also provides an overview of what runbooks are and how to perform runbook automation (RBA).

When you are performing incident response and forensics tasks, you always have to be aware of how to collect evidence and what the appropriate evidentiary chain of custody is. This chapter provides an overview of chain of custody when it pertains to cyber security investigations. You will learn the details about reverse engineering, forensics, and sliding window anomaly detection. You will also learn what personally identifiable information (PII) and protected health information (PHI) are, especially pertaining to different regulatory standards such as the Payment Card Industry Data Security Standard (PCI DSS) and the Health Insurance Portability and Accountability Act (HIPAA).

In this chapter, you will also learn the concepts of principle of least privilege. It is important to know how to perform risk scoring and risk weighting in the realm of risk assessment and risk reduction. This chapter provides an overview of these risk assessment and risk reduction methodologies.

The Principles of the Defense-in-Depth Strategy

If you are a cyber security expert, or even an amateur, you probably already know that when you deploy a firewall or an intrusion prevention system (IPS) or install antivirus or advanced malware protection on your machine, you cannot assume you are now safe and secure. A layered and cross-boundary "defense-in-depth" strategy is what is needed to protect your network and corporate assets. One of the primary benefits of a defense-in-depth strategy is that even if a single control (such as a firewall or IPS) fails, other controls can still protect your environment and assets. Figure 3-1 illustrates this concept.

The following are the layers illustrated in Figure 3-1 (starting from the top):

- Nontechnical activities such as appropriate security policies and procedures, and end-user and staff training.

- Physical security, including cameras, physical access control (such as badge readers, retina scanners, and fingerprint scanners), and locks.

- Network security best practices, such as routing protocol authentication, control plane policing (CoPP), network device hardening, and so on.

- Host security solutions such as advanced malware protection (AMP) for endpoints, antiviruses, and so on.

- Application security best practices such as application robustness testing, fuzzing, defenses against cross-site scripting (XSS), cross-site request forgery (CSRF) attacks, SQL injection attacks, and so on.

- The actual data traversing the network. You can employ encryption at rest and in transit to protect data.

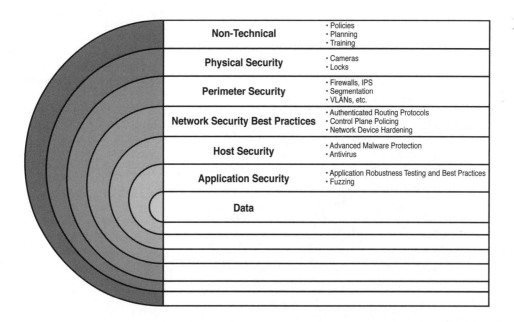

Non-Technical	• Policies • Planning • Training
Physical Security	• Cameras • Locks
Perimeter Security	• Firewalls, IPS • Segmentation • VLANs, etc.
Network Security Best Practices	• Authenticated Routing Protocols • Control Plane Policing • Network Device Hardening
Host Security	• Advanced Malware Protection • Antivirus
Application Security	• Application Robustness Testing and Best Practices • Fuzzing
Data	

Figure 3-1 *Defense in Depth*

TIP   Each layer of security introduces complexity and latency, while requiring that someone manage it. The more people are involved, even in administration, the more attack vectors you create, and the more you distract your people from possibly more important tasks. Employ multiple layers, but avoid duplication—and use common sense.

The first step in the process of preparing your network and staff to successfully identify security threats is achieving complete network visibility. You cannot protect against or mitigate what you cannot view/detect. You can achieve this level of network visibility through existing features on network devices you already have and on devices whose potential you do not even realize. In addition, you should create strategic network diagrams to clearly illustrate your packet flows and where, within the network, you could enable security mechanisms to identify, classify, and mitigate the threats. Remember that network security is a constant war. When defending against the enemy, you must know your own territory and implement defense mechanisms.

In some cases, onion-like diagrams are used to help illustrate and analyze what "defense-in-depth" protections and enforcements should be deployed in a network. Figure 3-2 shows an example of one of these onion diagrams, where network resources are protected through several layers of security.

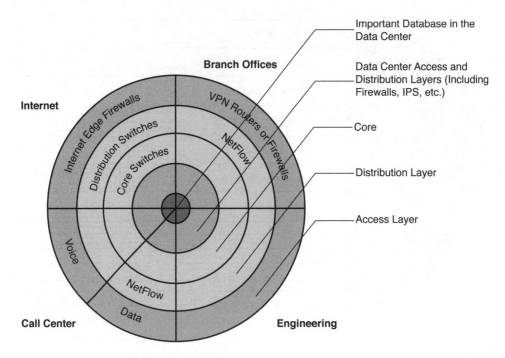

Figure 3-2   *Layered Onion Diagram Example*

You can create this type of diagram, not only to understand the architecture of your organization, but also to strategically identify places within the infrastructure where you can implement telemetry mechanisms such as NetFlow and identify choke points where you can mitigate an incident. Notice that the access, distribution, and core layers/boundaries are clearly defined.

These types of diagrams also help you visualize operational risks within your organization. The diagrams can be based on device roles and can be developed for critical systems you want to protect. For example, identify a critical system within your organization and create a layered diagram similar to the one in Figure 3-2. In this example, an "important database in the data center" is the most critical application/data source for this company. The diagram includes the database in the center.

You can also use this type of diagram to audit device roles and the types of services they should be running. For example, you can decide in what devices you can run services such as Cisco NetFlow or where to enforce security policies. In addition, you can see the life of a packet within your infrastructure, depending on the source and destination. An example is illustrated in Figure 3-3.

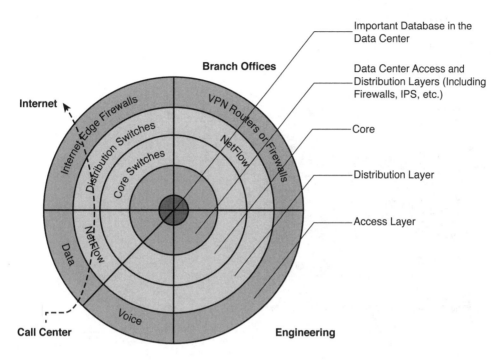

Figure 3-3 *Layered Onion Diagram Example*

In Figure 3-3, you can see a packet flow that occurs when a user from the call center accesses an Internet site. You know exactly where the packet is going based on your architecture as well as your security and routing policies. This is a simple example; however, you can use this concept to visualize risks and to prepare your isolation policies.

When applying defense-in-depth strategies, you can also look at a roles-based network security approach for security assessment in a simple manner. Each device on the network serves a purpose and has a role; subsequently, you should configure each device accordingly. You can think about the different planes as follows:

■ **Management plane:** This is the distributed and modular network management environment.

■ **Control plane:** This plane includes routing control. It is often a target because the control plane depends on direct CPU cycles.

■ **User/data plane:** This plane receives, processes, and transmits network data among all network elements.

■ **Services plane:** This is the Layer 7 application flow built on the foundation of the other layers.

■ **Policies:** The plane includes the business requirements. Cisco calls policies the "business glue" for the network. Policies and procedures are part of this section, and they apply to all the planes in this list.

You should also view security in two different perspectives, as illustrated in Figure 3-4:

- Operational (reactive) security
- Proactive security

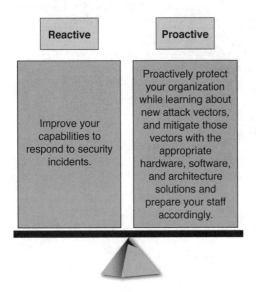

Figure 3-4   *Reactive vs. Proactive Security*

You should have a balance between proactive and reactive security approaches. Prepare your network, staff, and organization as a whole to better identify, classify, trace back, and react to security incidents. In addition, proactively protect your organization while learning about new attack vectors, and mitigate those vectors with the appropriate hardware, software, and architecture solutions.

What Are Threats, Vulnerabilities, and Exploits?

In this section, you will learn the difference between vulnerabilities, threats, and exploits.

Vulnerabilities

A *vulnerability* is an exploitable weakness in a system or its design. Vulnerabilities can be found in protocols, operating systems, applications, hardware, and system designs. Vulnerabilities abound, with more discovered every day. You will learn many examples of vulnerability classifications in Chapter 13, "Types of Attacks and Vulnerabilities." However, the following are a few examples:

- SQL injection vulnerabilities
- Command injections
- Cross-site scripting (XSS)
- Cross-site request forgery (CSRF)
- API abuse vulnerabilities

- Authentication vulnerabilities
- Privilege escalation vulnerabilities
- Cryptographic vulnerabilities
- Error-handling vulnerabilities
- Input validation vulnerabilities
- Path traversal vulnerabilities
- Buffer overflows
- Deserialization of untrusted data
- Directory restriction error
- Double free
- Password management: hardcoded password
- Password plaintext storage

Vendors, security researchers, and vulnerability coordination centers typically assign vulnerabilities an identifier that's disclosed to the public. This identifier is known as the *Common Vulnerabilities and Exposures (CVE)*. CVE is an industry-wide standard. CVE is sponsored by US-CERT, the office of Cybersecurity and Communications at the U.S. Department of Homeland Security. Operating as DHS's Federally Funded Research and Development Center (FFRDC), MITRE has copyrighted the CVE List for the benefit of the community in order to ensure it remains a free and open standard, as well as to legally protect the ongoing use of it and any resulting content by government, vendors, and/or users. MITRE maintains the CVE list and its public website, manages the CVE Compatibility Program, oversees the CVE Naming Authorities (CNAs), and provides impartial technical guidance to the CVE Editorial Board throughout the process to ensure CVE serves the public interest.

The goal of CVE is to make it easier to share data across tools, vulnerability repositories, and security services.

More information about CVE is available at http://cve.mitre.org.

Threats

A *threat* is any potential danger to an asset. If a vulnerability exists but has not yet been exploited—or, more importantly, it is not yet publicly known—the threat is latent and not yet realized. If someone is actively launching an attack against your system and successfully accesses something or compromises your security against an asset, the threat is realized. The entity that takes advantage of the vulnerability is known as the *malicious actor*, and the path used by this actor to perform the attack is known as the *threat agent* or *threat vector*.

A *countermeasure* is a safeguard that somehow mitigates a potential risk. It does so by either reducing or eliminating the vulnerability, or it at least reduces the likelihood of the threat agent to actually exploit the risk. For example, you might have an unpatched machine on your network, making it highly vulnerable. If that machine is unplugged from the network and ceases to have any interaction through exchanging data with any other device, you have successfully mitigated all those vulnerabilities. You have likely rendered that machine no longer an asset, though—but it is safer.

Threat Actors

Threat actors are the individuals (or group of individuals) who perform an attack or are responsible for a security incident that impacts or has the potential of impacting an organization or individual. There are several types of threat actors:

- **Script kiddies:** People who uses existing "scripts" or tools to hack into computers and networks. They lack the expertise to write their own scripts.

- **Organized crime groups:** Their main purpose is to steal information, scam people, and make money.

- **State sponsors and governments:** These agents are interested in stealing data, including intellectual property and research-and-development data from major manufacturers, government agencies, and defense contractors.

- **Hacktivists:** People who carry out cyber security attacks aimed at promoting a social or political cause.

- **Terrorist groups:** These groups are motivated by political or religious beliefs.

Threat Intelligence

Threat intelligence is referred to as the knowledge about an existing or emerging threat to assets, including networks and systems. Threat intelligence includes context, mechanisms, indicators of compromise (IoCs), implications, and actionable advice. Threat intelligence is referred to as the information about the observables, indicators of compromise (IoCs) intent, and capabilities of internal and external threat actors and their attacks. Threat intelligence includes specifics on the tactics, techniques, and procedures of these adversaries. Threat intelligence's primary purpose is to inform business decisions regarding the risks and implications associated with threats.

Converting these definitions into common language could translate to threat intelligence being evidence-based knowledge of the capabilities of internal and external threat actors. This type of data can be beneficial for the security operations center (SOC) of any organization. Threat intelligence extends cyber security awareness beyond the internal network by consuming intelligence from other sources Internet-wide related to possible threats to you or your organization. For instance, you can learn about threats that have impacted different external organizations. Subsequently, you can proactively prepare rather than react once the threat is seen against your network. Providing an enrichment data feed is one service that threat intelligence platforms would typically provide.

Forrester defines a five-step threat intelligence process (see Figure 3-5) for evaluating threat intelligence sources:

Step 1.   Planning and direction

Step 2.   Collection

Step 3.   Processing

Step 4.   Analysis and production

Step 5.   Dissemination

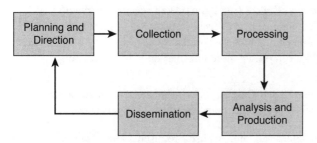

Figure 3-5   *Threat Intelligence*

Many different threat intelligence platforms and services are available in the market nowadays. Cyber threat intelligence focuses on providing actionable information on adversaries, including indicators of compromise (IoCs). Threat intelligence feeds help you prioritize signals from internal systems against unknown threats. Cyber threat intelligence allows you to bring more focus to cyber security investigation because instead of blindly looking for "new" and "abnormal" events, you can search for specific IoCs, IP addresses, URLs, or exploit patterns. The following are a few examples:

- **Cyber Squad ThreatConnect:** An on-premises, private, or public cloud solution offering threat data collection, analysis, collaboration, and expertise in a single platform. You can obtain more details at http://www.threatconnect.com.

- **BAE Detica CyberReveal:** A multithreat monitoring, analytics, investigation, and response product. CyberReveal brings together BAE Systems Detica's heritage in network intelligence, big-data analytics, and cyber threat research. CyberReveal consists of three core components: platform, analytics, and investigator. Learn more at http://www.baesystems.com.

- **Lockheed Martin Palisade:** Supports comprehensive threat collection, analysis, collaboration, and expertise in a single platform. Learn more at http://www.lockheedmartin.com.

- **MITRE CRITs:** Collaborative Research Into Threats (CRITs) is an open source feed for threat data. Learn more at https://crits.github.io.

- **Cisco AMP Threat Grid:** Combines static and dynamic malware analysis with threat intelligence into one unified solution.

A number of standards are being developed for disseminating threat intelligence information. The following are a few examples:

- **Structured Threat Information eXpression (STIX):** An express language designed for sharing of cyber attack information. STIX details can contain data such as the IP address of command-and-control servers (CnC), malware hashes, and so on. STIX was originally developed by MITRE and is now maintained by OASIS. You can obtain more information at http://stixproject.github.io.

- **Trusted Automated eXchange of Indicator Information (TAXII):** An open transport mechanism that standardizes the automated exchange of cyber threat information. TAXII was originally developed by MITRE and is now maintained by OASIS. You can obtain more information at http://taxiiproject.github.io.

- **Cyber Observable eXpression (CybOX):** A free standardized schema for specification, capture, characterization, and communication of events of stateful properties that are observable in the operational domain. CybOX was originally developed by MITRE and is now maintained by OASIS. You can obtain more information at https://cyboxproject.github.io.

- **Open Indicators of Compromise (OpenIOC):** An open framework for sharing threat intelligence in a machine-digestible format. Learn more at http://www.openioc.org.

It should be noted that many open source and non-security-focused sources can be leveraged for threat intelligence as well. Some examples of these sources are social media, forums, blogs, and vendor websites.

Exploits

An *exploit* is software or a sequence of commands that takes advantage of a vulnerability in order to cause harm to a system or network. There are several methods of classifying exploits; however, the most common two categories are remote and local exploits. A *remote exploit* can be launched over a network and carries out the attack without any prior access to the vulnerable device or software. A *local exploit* requires the attacker or threat actor to have prior access to the vulnerable system.

> **NOTE** Exploits are commonly categorized and named by the type of vulnerability they exploit.

There is also the concept of exploit kits. An *exploit kit* is a compilation of exploits that are often designed to be served from web servers. Their main purpose is identifying software vulnerabilities in client machines and then exploiting such vulnerabilities to upload and execute malicious code on the client. The following are a few examples of known exploit kits:

- Angler
- MPack
- Fiesta
- Phoenix
- Blackhole
- Crimepack
- RIG

> **NOTE** Cisco Talos has covered and explained numerous exploit kits in detail, including Angler. You can obtain more information about these type of threats at Talos's blog, http://blog.talosintel.com, and specifically for Angler at http://blog.talosintel.com/search/label/angler.

Confidentiality, Integrity, and Availability: The CIA Triad

Confidentiality, integrity and availability, is often referred to as the CIA triad. This is a model that was created to define security policies. In some cases, you may also see this model referred to as the AIC triad (availability, integrity and confidentiality) to avoid confusion with the United States Central Intelligence Agency.

The idea is that confidentiality, integrity and availability should be guaranteed in any system that is considered secured.

Confidentiality

The ISO 27000 standard has a very good definition: "confidentiality is the property, that information is not made available or disclosed to unauthorized individuals, entities, or processes." One of the most common ways to protect the confidentiality of a system or its data is to use encryption. The Common Vulnerability Scoring System (CVSS) uses the CIA triad principles within the metrics used to calculate the CVSS base score.

> **NOTE**   You will learn more about CVSS throughout the following chapters, and you can obtain more information about CVSS at: https://www.first.org/cvss/specification-document

Integrity

Integrity is the ability to make sure that a system and its data has not been altered or compromised. It ensures that the data is an accurate and unchanged representation of the original secure data. Integrity applies not only to data, but also to systems. For instance, if a threat actor changes the configuration of a server, firewall, router, switch or any other infrastructure device, it is considered that he or she impacted the integrity of the system.

Availability

Availability refers that a system or application must be "available" to authorized users at all times. According to the CVSS version 3 specification, the availability metric "measures the impact to the availability of the impacted component resulting from a successfully exploited vulnerability. While the Confidentiality and Integrity impact metrics apply to the loss of confidentiality or integrity of data (e.g., information, files) used by the impacted component, this metric refers to the loss of availability of the impacted component itself, such as a networked service (e.g., web, database, email). Since availability refers to the accessibility of information resources, attacks that consume network bandwidth, processor cycles, or disk space all impact the availability of an impacted component."

A common example of an attack that impacts availability is a denial of service (DoS) attack.

Risk and Risk Analysis

According to the Merriam-Webster dictionary, risk is "the possibility that something bad or unpleasant will happen." In the world of cyber security, risk can be defined as the possibility of a security incident (something bad) happening. There are many standards and methodologies for classifying and analyzing cyber security risks. The Federal Financial Institutions Examination Council (FFIEC) developed the Cybersecurity Assessment Tool (Assessment)

to help financial institutions identify their risks and determine their cyber security preparedness. This guidance/tool can be useful for any organization. The FFIEC tool provides a repeatable and measurable process for organizations to measure their cyber security readiness.

According to the FFIEC, the assessment consists of two parts:

- **Inherent Risk Profile and Cybersecurity Maturity**: The Inherent Risk Profile identifies the institution's inherent risk before implementing controls. The Cybersecurity Maturity includes domains, assessment factors, components, and individual declarative statements across five maturity levels to identify specific controls and practices that are in place. Although management can determine the institution's maturity level in each domain, the Assessment is not designed to identify an overall cyber security maturity level.

- **The International Organization for Standardization (ISO) 27001**: This is the international standard for implementing an information security management system (ISMS). ISO 27001 is heavily focused on risk-based planning to ensure that the identified information risks (including cyber risks) are appropriately managed according to the threats and the nature of those threats. ISO 31000 is the general risk management standard that includes principles and guidelines for managing risk. It can be used by any organization, regardless of its size, activity, or sector. Using ISO 31000 can help organizations increase the likelihood of achieving objectives, improve the identification of opportunities and threats, and effectively allocate and use resources for risk treatment.

The ISO/IEC 27005 standard is more focused on cyber security risk assessment. It is titled "Information technology—Security techniques—Information security risk management."

The following is according to ISO's website:

"The standard doesn't specify, recommend or even name any specific risk management method. It does however imply a continual process consisting of a structured sequence of activities, some of which are iterative:

- Establish the risk management context (e.g. the scope, compliance obligations, approaches/methods to be used and relevant policies and criteria such as the organization's risk tolerance or appetite);

- Quantitatively or qualitatively assess (i.e. identify, analyze and evaluate) relevant information risks, taking into account the information assets, threats, existing controls and vulnerabilities to determine the likelihood of incidents or incident scenarios, and the predicted business consequences if they were to occur, to determine a 'level of risk;'

- Treat (i.e. modify [use information security controls], retain [accept], avoid and/or share [with third parties]) the risks appropriately, using those 'levels of risk' to prioritize them;

- Keep stakeholders informed throughout the process; and

- Monitor and review risks, risk treatments, obligations and criteria on an ongoing basis, identifying and responding appropriately to significant changes."

There are also standards to score the overall "risk" of a vulnerability. The most commonly used is the Common Vulnerability Scoring System (CVSS) developed by the Forum of Incident Response and Security Teams (FIRST). CVSS is a standards-based scoring method that conveys vulnerability severity and helps determine the urgency and priority of response. CVSS is used by many Product Security Incident Response Teams (PSIRTs), vulnerability coordination centers, security researchers, and consumers of security vulnerability information.

> **NOTE**   You will learn about CVSS in more detail in Chapter 5, "Introduction to Security Operations Management," and can obtain more information at FIRST's website, https://www.first.org/cvss.

There are also several additional scoring systems:

- **Common Weakness Scoring System (CWSS):** A methodology for scoring software weaknesses. CWSS is part of the Common Weakness Enumerator (CWE) standard. More information about CWSS is available at http://cwe.mitre.org/cwss.

- **Common Misuse Scoring System (CMSS):** A standardized way to measure software feature misuse vulnerabilities. More information about CMSS is available at http://scap.nist.gov/emerging-specs/listing.html#cmss.

- **Common Configuration Scoring System (CCSS):** More information about CCSS can be found at http://csrc.nist.gov/publications/nistir/ir7502/nistir-7502_CCSS.pdf.

Personally Identifiable Information and Protected Health Information

Many regulations as well as the United States government require organizations to identify personally identifiable information (PII) and protected health information (PHI) and handle them in a secure manner. Unauthorized release or loss of such data could result in severe fines and penalties for the organization. Given the importance of PII and PHI, regulators and the government want to oversee the usage more efficiently. This section explains what PII and PHI are.

PII

According to the Executive Office of the President, Office of Management and Budget (OMB) and the U.S. Department of Commerce, Office of the Chief Information Officer, PII refers to "information which can be used to distinguish or trace an individual's identity." The following are a few examples:

- The individual's name
- Social security number
- Biological or personal characteristics, such as an image of distinguishing features, fingerprints, x-rays, voice signature, retina scan, and the geometry of the face
- Date and place of birth
- Mother's maiden name
- Credit card numbers
- Bank account numbers

- Driver license number
- Address information, such as email addresses or street addresses, and telephone numbers for businesses or personal use

PHI

The Health Insurance Portability and Accountability Act (HIPAA) requires health care organizations and providers to adopt certain security regulations for protecting health information. The Privacy Rule calls this information "protected health information," or PHI. This information includes, but is not limited to, the following:

- Individual's name (that is, patient's name)
- All dates directly linked to an individual, including date of birth, death, discharge, and administration
- Telephone and fax numbers
- Email addresses and geographic subdivisions such as street addresses, ZIP Codes, and county.
- Medical record numbers and health plan beneficiary numbers
- Certificate numbers or account numbers
- Social security number
- Driver license number
- Biometric identifiers, including voice or fingerprints
- Photos of the full face or recognizable features
- Any unique number-based code or characteristic
- The individual's past, present, and future physical or mental health or condition
- The provision of health care to the individual, or the past, present, or future payment for the provision of health care to the individual

Principle of Least Privilege and Separation of Duties

Two additional key concepts in information security are the principle of least privilege and separation of duties. This section defines these two key concepts.

Principle of Least Privilege

The principle of least privilege states that all users—whether they are individual contributors, managers, directors, or executives—should be granted only the level of privilege they need to do their jobs, and no more. For example, a sales account manager really has no business having administrator privileges over the network, or a call center staff member over critical corporate financial data.

The same concept of principle of least privilege can be applied to software. For example, programs or processes running on a system should have the capabilities they need to "get their job done," but no root access to the system. If a vulnerability is exploited on a system that runs "everything as root," the damage could extend to a complete compromise of the system. This is why you should always limit users, applications, and processes to access and run as the least privilege they need.

> **TIP**   Somewhat related to the principle of least privilege is the concept of "need to know," which means that users should get access only to data and systems that they need to do their job, and no other.

Separation of Duties

Separation of duties is an administrative control that dictates that a single individual should not perform all critical- or privileged-level duties. Additionally, important duties must be separated or divided among several individuals within the organization. The goal is to safeguard against a single individual performing sufficiently critical or privileged actions that could seriously damage a system or the organization as a whole. For instance, security auditors responsible for reviewing security logs should not necessarily have administrative rights over the systems. Another example is that a network administrator should not have the ability to alter logs on the system. This is to prevent such individuals from carrying out unauthorized actions and then deleting evidence of such action from the logs (in other words, covering their tracks).

Think about two users having two separate keys in order to open a safety deposit box. Separation of duties is similar to that concept, where the safety deposit box cannot be opened by a user without the other key.

Security Operation Centers

Security operation centers (SOCs) are facilities where an organization's assets, including applications, databases, servers, networks, desktops, and other endpoints, are monitored, assessed, and protected. Establishing SOC capabilities requires careful planning. The planning phase helps you decide on and formalize yourself with the objectives that justify having an SOC, and to develop a roadmap you can use to track your progress against those predefined objectives. The success of any security program (including the SOC) depends on proper planning. There are always challenges that are specific to an organization, and these challenges are introduced because of issues related to governance, collaboration, lack of tools, lack of automation, lack of threat intelligence, skill sets, and so on. Such challenges must be identified and treated, or at least acknowledged, at an early stage of an SOC establishment program. SOCs are created to be able to address the following challenges:

- How can you detect a compromise in a timely manner?
- How do you triage a compromise to determine the severity and the scope?
- What is the impact of the compromise to your business?
- Who is responsible for detecting and mitigating a compromise?
- Who should be informed or involved, and when do you deal with the compromise once detected?
- How and when should you communicate a compromise internally or externally, and is that needed in the first place?

To build and operate an effective SOC, you must have the following:

■ Executive sponsorship.

■ SOC operating as a program. Organizations should operate the SOC as a program rather than a single project. Doing so depends on the criticality and the amount of resources required to design, build, and operate the various services offered by the SOC. Having a clear SOC service strategy with clear goals and priorities will shape the size of the SOC program, timeline, and the amount of resources required to deliver the program objectives.

■ A governance structure. Metrics must be established to measure the effectiveness of the SOC capabilities. These metrics should provide sufficient and relevant visibility to the organization's management team on the performance of the SOC and should identify areas where improvements and investments are needed.

■ Effective team collaboration.

■ Access to data and systems.

■ Applicable processes and procedures.

■ Team skill sets and experience.

■ Budget (for example, will it be handled in-house or outsourced?).

Runbook Automation

Organizations need to have capabilities to define, build, orchestrate, manage, and monitor the different operational processes and workflows. This is achieved by implementing runbooks and runbook automation (RBA). A *runbook* is a collection of procedures and operations performed by system administrators, security professionals, or network operators. According to Gartner, "the growth of RBA has coincided with the need for IT operations executives to enhance IT operations efficiency measures." Gartner, Inc. is an American research and advisory firm providing information technology related insight for IT and other business leaders.

Here are some of the metrics to measure effectiveness:

■ Mean time to repair (MTTR)

■ Mean time between failures (MTBF)

■ Mean time to discover a security incident

■ Mean time to contain or mitigate a security incident

■ Automating the provisioning of IT resources

Many different commercial and open source RBA solutions are available in the industry. An example of a popular open source RBA solution is Rundeck (http://rundeck.org/). Rundeck can be integrated with configuration management platforms such as Chef, Puppet, and Ansible. A commercial RBA example is the Cisco Workload Automation (CWA), which can manage different business processes across a comprehensive set of applications and systems. You can obtain more information about Cisco CWA at http://www.cisco.com/c/en/us/products/analytics-automation-software/tidal-enterprise-scheduler/index.html.

Forensics

The United States Computer Emergency Response Team (CERT) defines cyber forensics as follows:

> "If you manage or administer information systems and networks, you should understand cyber forensics. Forensics is the process of using scientific knowledge for collecting, analyzing, and presenting evidence to the courts. (The word forensics means 'to bring to the court.') Forensics deals primarily with the recovery and analysis of latent evidence. Latent evidence can take many forms, from fingerprints left on a window to DNA evidence recovered from blood stains to the files on a hard drive."

Cyber forensics is often referred to as "computer forensics." However, "cyber forensics" is a more appropriate term than "computer forensics."

The two primary objectives in cyber forensics are to find out what happened and to collect data in a manner that is acceptable to the court. Any device that can store data is potentially the object of cyber forensics, including, but not limited to, the following:

- Computers (servers, desktop machines, and so on)
- Smartphones
- Tablets
- Network infrastructure devices (routers, switches, firewalls, intrusion prevention systems)
- Network management systems
- Printers
- Even vehicle GPSs

Chain of custody is critical to forensics investigations. The following section describes chain of custody in detail.

Evidentiary Chain of Custody

Chain of custody is the way you document and preserve evidence from the time that you started the cyber forensics investigation to the time the evidence is presented at court. It is extremely important to be able to show clear documentation of the following:

- How the evidence was collected
- When it was collected
- How it was transported
- How is was tracked
- How it was stored
- Who had access to the evidence and how it was accessed

TIP   If you fail to maintain proper chain of custody, it is likely you cannot use that evidence in court. It is also important to know how to dispose of evidence after an investigation.

When you collect evidence, you must protect its integrity. This involves making sure that nothing is added to the evidence and that nothing is deleted or destroyed (this is known as *evidence preservation*).

> **TIP**   A method often used for evidence preservation is to only work with a copy of the evidence—in other words, not directly working with the evidence itself. This involves creating an image of any hard drive or any storage device.

Several forensics tools are available on the market. The following are two of the most popular:

- Guidance Software's EnCase (https://www.guidancesoftware.com/)
- AccessData's Forensic Toolkit (http://accessdata.com/)

Another methodology used in evidence preservation is to use write-protected storage devices. In other words, the storage device you are investigating should immediately be write-protected before it is imaged and should be labeled to include the following:

- Investigator's name
- The date when the image was created
- Case name and number (if applicable)

Additionally, you must prevent electronic static or other discharge from damaging or erasing evidentiary data. Special evidence bags that are antistatic should be used to store digital devices. It is very important that you prevent electrostatic discharge (ESD) and other electrical discharges from damaging your evidence. Some organizations even have cyber forensic labs that control access to only authorized users and investigators. One method often used involves constructing what is called a "Faraday cage." This "cage" is often built out of a mesh of conducting material that prevents electromagnetic energy from entering into or escaping from the cage. Also, this prevents devices from communicating via Wi-Fi or cellular signals.

What's more, transporting the evidence to the forensics lab or any other place, including the courthouse, has to be done very carefully. It is critical that the chain of custody be maintained during this transport. When you transport the evidence, you should strive to secure it in a lockable container. It is also recommended that the responsible person stay with the evidence at all times during transportation.

Reverse Engineering

Reverse engineering is the methodology for acquiring architectural information about anything originally created by someone else. Reverse engineering has been around since long before computers or modern technology. Nowadays, reverse engineering is not only used to steal or counterfeit technology and to "reverse" cryptographic algorithms, but also to perform malware analysis and cyber security forensics. Reverse engineering can even be useful to software developers to discover how to interoperate with undocumented or partially documented software, or even to develop competing software (which in some cases may be illegal).

Reverse engineering can be used for exploit development to locate vulnerabilities in a system and compromise the system, but it also can be used on malware. Security researchers and forensics experts can trace every step the malware takes and assess the damage it could cause, the expected rate of infection, how it could be removed from infected systems, and how to potentially proactively defend against such a threat. Malware analysis extends to identifying whether malware is present on a given system and studying the malware to understand how it functions. Doing this can reveal the purpose of the malware, and even its author.

Two additional uses of reverse engineering are to "reverse" cryptographic algorithms to decrypt data as well as Digital Rights Management (DRM) solutions. Threat actors use DRM reverse-engineering techniques to steal music, movies, books, and any other content protected by DRM solutions.

Many tools are available for performing reverse engineering. The following are a few examples:

- **System-monitoring tools:** Tools that sniff, monitor, explore, and otherwise expose the program being reversed.

- **Disassemblers:** Tools that take a program's executable binary as input and generate textual files that contain the assembly language code for the entire program or parts of it.

- **Debuggers:** These tools allow reverse engineers to observe the program while it is running and to set breakpoints; they also provide the ability to trace through code. Reverse engineers can use debuggers to step through the disassembled code and watch the system as it runs the program, one instruction at a time.

- **Decompilers:** Programs that take an executable binary file and attempt to produce readable high-level language code from it.

Exam Preparation Tasks

Review All Key Topics

Review the most important topics in the chapter, noted with the Key Topic icon in the outer margin of the page. Table 3-2 lists a reference of these key topics and the page numbers on which each is found.

Table 3-2   Key Topics

Key Topic Element	Description	Page
Summary	Describe what are vulnerabilities	166
Summary	Define what are threats	167
Summary	Define threat actors	168
Summary	Describe what is threat intelligence and why is it useful	168
Summary	Define what are exploits	170
Summary	Describe confidentiality, integrity, and availability	171
Summary	Describe risk and risk analysis	171
Summary	Define and provides examples of PII	173
Summary	Define and provides examples of PHI	174
Summary	Decribe the principle of least privilege	174
Summary	Define what is a security operations center	175
Summary	Describe runbook automation	176
Summary	Define and describe chain of custody	177
Summary	Describe what is reverse engineering	178

Define Key Terms

Define the following key terms from this chapter, and check your answers in the glossary:

Vulnerabilities, threats, threat actors, exploits

Q&A

The answers to these questions appear in Appendix A, "Answers to the 'Do I Know This Already?' Quizzes and Q&A Questions." For more practice with exam format questions, use the exam engine on the website.

1. Which of the following statements are true about vulnerabilities?

   a. A vulnerability is a threat on a system.

   b. A vulnerability is an exploitable weakness in a system or its design.

   c. Vulnerabilities can be found in protocols, operating systems, applications, hardware, and system designs.

   d. Vulnerabilities are exploits that are discovered every day in software and hardware products.

2. On which of the following can exploit kits be run from?

   a. Web servers

   b. Email servers

   c. NTP servers

   d. Firewalls

3. Which of the following are examples of exploit kits?

   a. Angler

   b. Mangler

   c. Blackhole

   d. Black ICE

4. Which of the following describe what a threat is?

   a. Threats and vulnerabilities are the same.

   b. A threat is an exploit against a patched vulnerability.

   c. A threat is any potential danger to an asset.

   d. A threat is a piece of software aimed at exploiting a vulnerability.

5. What is an IoC?

   a. An indicator of compromise

   b. An indicator of containment

   c. An intrusion operating control

   d. An intrusion of compromise

6. Which of the following are provided by threat intelligence feeds?

   a. Indicators of compromise

   b. IP addresses of attacking systems

   c. The overall risk score of all vulnerabilities in the corporate network

   d. The overall risk score of threats in the corporate network

7. The way you document and preserve evidence from the time you start the cyber forensics investigation to the time the evidence is presented in court is referred to as which of the following?

   a. Chain of compromise

   b. Custody of compromise

   c. Chain of forensics

   d. Chain of custody

8. What are decompilers?

   a. Programs that take an executable binary file and attempt to produce readable high-level language code from it

   b. Programs that take a non-executable binary file and attempt to produce compiled code from it

   c. Programs that take a non-executable binary file and attempt to produce encrypted code from it

   d. Programs that execute a binary file and attempt to crack the encryption of it

9. Which of the following are metrics that can measure the effectiveness of a runbook?

   a. Mean time to repair (MTTR)

   b. Mean time between failures (MTBF)

   c. Mean time to discover a security incident

   d. All of the above

10. What is PHI?

   a. Protected HIPAA information

   b. Protected health information

   c. Personal health information

   d. Personal human information

The following are the learning objectives for this chapter:

- Understand the concepts of subject, object, and access controls

- Define identification, authentication, authorization, and accounting

- Understand the access control process and asset protection

- Explain the difference among the access control types

- Compare and contrast discretionary access controls, mandatory access controls, and nondiscretionary access controls

- Describe RADIUS, TACACS+, and Diameter

- Describe the implementation of port access control technologies, network access list, and Cisco TrustSec

- Understand network and host-based intrusion prevention and protection

- Understand network and host-based antivirus protection

CHAPTER 4

Introduction to Access Controls

One of the foundational topics of information security is access controls. *Access controls* is a broad term used to define the administrative, physical, and technical controls that regulate the interaction between a subject and an object. More simply, access controls help with defining and enforcing policy for who is authorized to access what and in which way.

"Do I Know This Already?" Quiz

The "Do I Know This Already?" quiz helps you determine your level of knowledge on this chapter's topics before you begin. Table 4-1 details the major topics discussed in this chapter and their corresponding quiz sections. You can find the answers in Appendix A Answers to the "Do I Know This Already?" Quizzes and Q&A Questions.

Table 4-1 "Do I Know This Already?" Section-to-Question Mapping

Foundation Topics Section	Questions
Subject and Object Definition	1
Access Control Fundamentals	2–4
Access Control Process	5–6
Information Security Roles and Responsibilities	7
Access Control Types	8
Access Control Models	9–12
Identity and Access Control Implementation	13–17

1. What entity requests access to a resource?
   a. Object
   b. Subject
   c. File
   d. Database

2. In which phase of the access control does a user need to prove his or her identity?
   a. Identification
   b. Authentication
   c. Authorization
   d. Accounting

3. Which of the following authentication methods can be considered examples of authentication by knowledge? (Select all that apply.)

   a. Password

   b. Token

   c. PIN

   d. Fingerprint

4. When a biometric authentication system rejects a valid user, which type of error is generated?

   a. True positive

   b. False positive

   c. False rejection

   d. Crossover error

5. In military and governmental organizations, what is the classification for an asset that, if compromised, would cause severe damage to the organization?

   a. Top Secret

   b. Secret

   c. Confidential

   d. Unclassified

6. What is a common way to protect "data at rest"?

   a. Encryption

   b. Transport Layer Security

   c. Fingerprint

   d. IPSec

7. Who is ultimately responsible for security control of an asset?

   a. Senior management

   b. Data custodian

   c. User

   d. System administrator

8. Which type of access controls are used to protect an asset before a breach occurs? (Select all that apply.)

   a. Preventive

   b. Deterrent

   c. Corrective

   d. Recovery

9. Which access control model uses environmental information to make an access decision?

   a. Discretionary access control

   b. Attribute-based access control

   c. Role-based access control

   d. Mandatory access control

10. What is the main advantage of using a mandatory access control (MAC) model instead of a discretionary access control (DAC) model?

   a. MAC is more secure because the operating system ensures security policy compliance.

   b. MAC is more secure because the data owner can decide which user can get access, thus providing more granular access.

   c. MAC is more secure because permissions are assigned based on roles.

   d. MAC is better because it is easier to implement.

11. Which of the following are part of a security label used in the mandatory access control model? (Select all that apply.)

   a. Classification

   b. Category

   c. Role

   d. Location

12. Which access control model uses the function of a subject in an organization?

   a. Discretionary access control

   b. Attribute-based access control

   c. Role-based access control

   d. Mandatory access control

13. Which IDS system can detect attacks using encryption?

   a. Network IDS deployed in inline mode

   b. Network IDS deployed in promiscuous mode

   c. Host-based IDS

   d. Network IPS deployed in inline mode

14. Which of the following is not a disadvantage of host-based antimalware?

   a. It requires updating multiple endpoints.

   b. It does not have visibility into encrypted traffic.

   c. It does not have visibility of all events happening in the network.

   d. It may require working with different operating systems.

15. Which type of access list works better when implementing RBAC?

   a. Layer 2 access list

   b. MAC access list

   c. VLAN map

   d. Security group access list

16. Which of the following is not a true statement about TACACS+?

   a. It offers command-level authorization.

   b. It is proprietary to Cisco.

   c. It encrypts the TACACS+ header.

   d. It works over TCP.

17. What is used in the Cisco TrustSec architecture to provide link-level encryption?

   a. MACSec

   b. IPSec

   c. TLS

   d. EAP

Foundation Topics

Information Security Principles

Before we delve into access control fundamentals, processes, and mechanisms, it is important to revisit the concepts of confidentiality, integrity, and availability, which were explored in Chapter 3, "Security Principles," and understand their relationship with access controls:

- **Confidentiality:** Access controls are used to ensure that only authorized users can access resources. An example of such control would be a process that ensures that only authorized people in an engineering department are able to read the source code of a product under development. Attacks to access controls that protect the confidentiality of a resource would typically aim to steal sensitive or confidential information.

- **Integrity:** Access controls are used to ensure that only authorized users can modify the state of a resource. An example of this control would be a process that would allow only authorized people in an engineering department to be able to change the source code of a product under development. Attacks to access controls that protect the integrity of a resource would typically aim at changing information. In some cases, when the changes are disruptive, the same attack would also have an impact on the availability of the resource. For example, an attack that causes the delete of a user from a database would have an impact on the integrity but also a secondary impact on the availability, as that user would not be able to access the system.

- **Availability:** Access controls would typically ensure that the resource is available to users that are authorized to access it, in a reasonable amount of time. Attacks that would affect the availability would typically aim at disabling access to a resource. Denial of Service (DoS) attacks are simple examples of attacks to the availability of a resource.

Subject and Object Definition

As stated earlier, *access controls* is a broad term used to define the administrative, physical, and technical controls that regulate the interaction between a subject and an object. A *subject* is defined as any active entity that requests access to a resource (also called an object). An *object* is defined as the passive entity that is, or contains, the information needed by the subject.

The role of the subject or object is purely determined on the entity that requests the access. The same entity could be considered a subject or an object, depending on the situation. For example, a web application could be considered an object when a user runs the browser program (the subject requesting information). The web application, however, would need to query an internal database before being able to provide the requested information. In this latter case, the web application would be the subject and the database would be considered the object in the transaction.

Access controls are any type of controls that regulate and make authorization decisions based on the access rights assigned to a subject for a specific object. The goal of an access control is to grant, prevent, or revoke access to a given object.

The list that follows highlights the key concepts about subject and object definition:

- A *subject* is the active entity that requests access to a resource.

- An *object* is the passive entity that is (or contains) the information needed by the subject and for which access is requested.

- *Access controls* are used in the process of granting, preventing, or revoking access to an object.

Figure 4-1 shows how the subject, object, and access control interact.

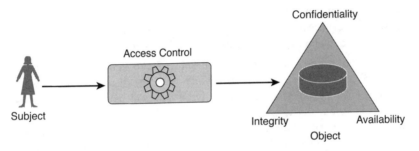

Figure 4-1 *Interaction Between a Subject, Object, and Access Control*

Access Control Fundamentals

As described earlier, access controls help in defining and enforcing policies that regulate who can access a resource and what can be done with that resource once accessed. Four building blocks or processes characterize access controls: *identification, authentication, authorization,* and *accounting.* Although these have similar definitions and applicability, each uniquely defines a specific requirement of an access control system.

Identification

Identification is the process of providing the identity of a subject or user. This is the first step in the authentication, authorization, and accounting process. Providing a username, a passport, an IP address, or even pronouncing your name is a form of identification. A secure identity should be *unique* in the sense that two users should be able to identify themselves unequivocally. This is particularly important in the context of account monitoring. Duplication of identity is possible if the authentication systems are not connected. For example, a user can use the same user ID for his corporate account and for his personal email account. A secure identity should also be *nondescriptive,* so that information about the user's identity cannot be inferred. For example, using "Administrator" as the user ID is generally not recommended. An identity should also be issued in a secure way. This includes all processes and steps in requesting and approving an identity request. This property is usually referred to as *secure issuance.*

TIP   Identity should not be considered secret.

The list that follows highlights the key concepts of identification.

- Secure identities should be **unique**. Two users with the same identity should not be allowed.

- Secure identities should be **nondescriptive**. It should not be possible to infer the role or function of the user. For example, a user called Admin represents a descriptive identity, while a user called c122eert represents a nondescriptive identity.

- Secure identities should be **securely issued**. A secure process for issuing an identity to a user needs to be established.

Authentication

Authentication is the process of proving the identity of a subject or user. Once a subject has identified itself in the identification step, the enforcer has to validate the identity—that is, be sure that the subject (or user) is the one it is claiming to be. This is done by requesting that the subject (or user) provide something that is unique to the requestor. This could be something known only by the user, usually referred to as *authentication by knowledge*, or owned only by the user, usually referred to as *authentication by ownership*, or it could be something specific to the user, usually referred to as *authentication by characteristic*.

Authentication by Knowledge

Authentication by knowledge is where the user provides a secret that is only known by him. An example of authentication by knowledge would be a user providing a password, a personal identification number (PIN) code, or answering security questions.

The disadvantage of using this method is that once the information is lost or stolen (for example, if a user's password is stolen), an attacker would be able to successfully authenticate.

Authentication by Ownership

With this type of authentication, the user is asked to provide proof that he owns something specific—for example, a system might require an employee to use a badge to access a facility. Another example of authentication by ownership is the use of a token or smart card.

Similar to the previous method, if an attacker is able to steal the object used for authentication, he would be able to successfully access the system.

Authentication by Characteristic

A system that uses authentication by characteristic authenticates the user based on some physical or behavioral characteristic, sometimes referred to as a *biometric attribute*. Here are the most used physical or physiological characteristics:

- Fingerprints
- Face
- Retina and iris

- Palm and hand geometry
- Blood and vascular information
- Voice

Here are examples of behavioral characteristics:

- Signature dynamic
- Keystroke dynamic/pattern

The drawback of a system based on this type of authentication is that it's prone to accuracy errors. For example, a signature-dynamic-based system would authenticate a user by requesting that the user write his signature and then comparing the signature pattern to a record in the system. Given that the way a person signs his name differs slightly every time, the system should be designed so that the user can still authenticate even if the signature and pattern is not exactly the one in the system. However, it should also not be too loose and thus authenticate an unauthorized user attempting to mimic the pattern.

Two types of errors are associated with the accuracy of a biometric system:

- A **Type I error**, also called *false rejection*, happens when the system rejects a valid user who should have been authenticated.
- A **Type II error**, also called *false acceptance*, happens when the system accepts a user who should have been rejected (for example, an attacker trying to impersonate a valid user).

The crossover error rate (CER), also called the equal error rate (EER), is the point where the rate of false rejection errors (FRR) and the rate of false acceptance error (FAR) are equal. This is generally accepted as an indicator of the accuracy (and hence the quality) of a biometric system.

Table 4-2 lists the three authentication methods described in this section and provides a short description and examples of each.

Table 4-2   Authentication Methods

Authentication Method	Description	Examples
Authentication by knowledge	Something the user knows	Password, PIN
Authentication by ownership	Something the user owns	Smart card, badge, token
Authentication by characteristic	Something the user is or does	Fingerprint, hand geometry, keystroke dynamic

Multifactor Authentication

An authentication system may use more than one of the methods outlined in Table 4-2 (for example, a password and a badge). The system is said to use one-, two-, or three-factor authentication depending on how many authentication methods are requested. The higher the number of factors, the stronger the authentication system is. An authentication system is considered strong if it uses at least two different authentication methods.

TIP Identification and authentication are often performed together; however, it is important to understand that they are two different operations. Identification is about establishing who you are, whereas authentication is about proving you are the entity you claim to be.

Authorization

Authorization is the process of granting a subject access to an object or resource. This typically happens after the subject has completed the authentication process. A policy or rule needs to be established to describe in which cases a subject should be able to access the resource.

Additionally, when granting access, the authorization process would check the permissions associated with the subject/object pair so that the correct access right is provided. The object owner and management usually decide (or give input on) the permission and authorization policy that governs the authorization process.

The authorization policy and rule should take various attributes into consideration, such as the identity of the subject, the location from where the subject is requesting access, the subject's role within the organization, and so on. Access control models, which are described in more detail later in this chapter, provide the framework for the authorization policy implementation.

An authorization policy should implement two concepts:

- **Implicit deny:** If no rule is specified for the transaction of the subject/object, the authorization policy should deny the transaction.
- **Need to know:** A subject should be granted access to an object only if the access is needed to carry out the job of the subject.

The permission could be abstract, such as "open the door," or more formal, such as read, write, or execute a specific resource.

Accounting

Accounting is the process of auditing and monitoring what a user does once a specific resource is accessed. This process is sometimes overlooked; however, as a security professional, it is important to be aware of accounting and to advocate that it be implemented due to the great help it provides during detection and investigation of cyber security breaches.

When accounting is implemented, an audit trail log is created and stored that details when the user has accessed the resource, what the user did with that resource, and when the user stopped using the resource. Given the potential sensitive information included in the auditing logs, special care should be taken in protecting them from unauthorized access.

Access Control Fundamentals: Summary

The following example summarizes the four-step process described in this section. In this example, the user wants to withdraw some money from an Automated Teller Machine (ATM).

Step 1.   When the user approaches the machine and inserts his bank card, he is identifying himself to the system.

Step 2.   Once the user is identified, the system will ask him to confirm his identity, usually requesting a PIN code. This is the authentication step, and it's performed by using authentication by knowledge (PIN code) and by ownership (the user owns the bank card).

Step 3.   Once the user is authenticated, he is allowed to withdraw money from his account. He does not have the right, however, to withdraw more than $500. This is controlled by the authorization process, which will not authorize transactions larger than $500.

Step 4.   After the user has withdrawn the money, the ATM system will log the information about the transaction, which includes information about the user, the location of the ATM and identification number, the user's account number, the amount withdrawn, the date and time, and so on.

Table 4-3 summarizes the four phases of access control and includes examples of each phase.

Table 4-3   Access Control Process Phases

Phase	Questions It Answers	Examples
Identification	Who are you?	User ID, IP address.
Authentication	Can you prove you are who you claim to be?	Password, badge, fingerprint.
Authorization	Can you access a resource? What can you do with that resource?	User A can access Resource B in read and write mode.
Accounting	What have you done with that resource?	User A has modified Resource B on August 31, 2016.

The list that follows highlights the key concepts of identification, authentication, authorization, and accounting:

- *Identification* is the process of providing identity.

- *Authentication* is the process of proving the identity.

- *Authorization* is the process of providing access to a resource with specific access rights.

- *Accounting* is the process of auditing and monitoring user operations on a resource.

Access Control Process

As described in the previous sections, the access control process governs the granting, preventing, or revoking of access to a resource. The core of an access control process is the establishment of an access control policy or rule that determines which type of access to assign and when.

To determine an access control policy, the policy owner needs an evaluation of the asset or data—that is, he needs to understand the importance of an organization's asset so that adequate controls can be established. Then, the asset should be properly marked so that its classification is clear to everyone, and a disposal policy needs to be established for when the access is not needed anymore.

The list that follows highlights the key terminology related to the access control process:

- *Asset* or *data classification* is the process of classifying data based on the risk for the organization related to a breach on the confidentiality, integrity, and availability of the data.

- *Asset marking* is the process of marking or labeling assets or data so that its classification is clear to the user.

- *Access policy definition* is the process of defining policies and rules to govern access to an asset.

- *Data disposal* is the process of disposing or eliminating an asset or data.

Asset Classification

To protect an asset, an organization first needs to understand how important that asset is. For example, the unauthorized disclosure of the source code of a product might be more impactful on an organization than the disclosure of a public configuration guide. The first step in implementing an access control process is to classify assets or data based on the potential damage a breach to the confidentiality, integrity, or availability of that asset or data could cause.

This process is called asset or data classification, and there are several ways to classify assets. For example, military and governmental organizations commonly use the following classification definitions:

- **Top Secret:** Unauthorized access to top-secret information would cause grave damage to national security.

- **Secret:** Unauthorized access to secret information would cause severe damage to national security.

- **Confidential:** Unauthorized access to confidential information would cause damage to national security.

- **Unclassified:** Unauthorized access to unclassified information would cause no damage to national security.

The commercial sector has more variety in the way data classification is done—more specifically, to the label used in the classification. Here are some commonly used classification labels in the commercial sector:

- **Confidential or Proprietary:** Unauthorized access to confidential or proprietary information could cause grave damage to the organization. Examples of information or assets that could receive this type of classification include source code and trade secrets.

- **Private:** Unauthorized access to private information could cause severe damage to the organization. Examples of information or assets that could receive this type of classification are human resource information (for example, employee salaries), medical records, and so on.

- **Sensitive:** Unauthorized access to sensitive information could cause some damage to the organization. Examples of information or assets that could receive this type of classification are internal team email, financial information, and so on.

- **Public:** Unauthorized access to public information does not cause any significant damage.

Although the classification schema will differ from one company to another, it is important that all departments within a company use the schema consistently. For each label there should be a clear definition of when that label should be applied and what damage would be caused by unauthorized access. Because the classification of data may also be related to specific times or other contextual factors, the asset-classification process should include information on how to change data classification.

Table 4-4 summarizes the typical classification schemas for the two types of organizations discussed in this section.

Table 4-4   Classification Schema

Military/Government Classification	Commercial Classification	Damage Degree
Top Secret	Confidential	Grave damage
Secret	Private	Severe damage
Confidential	Sensitive	Damage
Unclassified	Public	Not significant damage

Asset Marking

Once an asset has been classified with a specific category, a mark or label needs to be applied to the asset itself so that the classification level is clear to the user accessing the asset. Putting a stamp on a document with the label "Top Secret" and watermarking a digital document with the label "Confidential" are examples of the marking process.

Access Control Policy

The next step of an access control process is to establish the access control policy for each asset or data. This will be based on the label the asset received in the classification and marking steps described in the preceding sections. The access control policy should include information on who can access the asset or data, when, and in which mode. The access control policy will also describe how the access should be protected, depending on its state, which could be any of the following:

■ *Data at rest* refers to data that resides in a storage device such as a hard drive, CD or DVD, or magnetic drive. Data is in this state most of its lifetime. Data at rest is usually protected by using strong access controls and encryption.

■ *Data in motion* refers to data moving between two parties, meaning it is in transit. When in this state, the data is subject to higher risk because it goes outside of the security perimeter where the data owner might not have control. End-to-end encryption and VPN technologies are usually used to protect data in motion.

■ *Data in use* refers to data being processed by applications or programs and stored in a temporary or volatile memory such as random access memory (RAM), a CPU register, and so on.

Data Disposal

An access control process should include information on how to dispose of an asset or data once it is not needed anymore, as defined by the organization's data retention policy.

Data disposal may take several steps and use different technology. In fact, having a strong process for disposing data is equally important as setting up a process to protect the data when still in use. For example, one type of technique malicious actors use is called dumpster diving. In simple terms, dumpster divers try to find useful information for an attack by looking in the trash, hoping to find useful documents, network diagrams, and even passwords to access systems.

Depending on the classification level, data may be subject to sanitization before it can be disposed. Sanitization methods include the following:

■ **Clearing:** This technique should ensure protection against simple and noninvasive data-recovery techniques.

■ **Purging:** This technique should ensure protection against recovery attempts using state-of-the-art laboratory techniques.

■ **Destroying:** This technique should ensure protection against recovery attempts using state-of-the-art laboratory techniques and should also make the storage media unusable.

Information Security Roles and Responsibilities

The previous section described the pillars of an access control process and emphasized the importance of correctly classifying data and assets. Who decides whether a set of data should be considered confidential? Who is ultimately responsible in the case of unauthorized disclosure of such data?

Because data is handled by several people at different stages, it is important that an organization build a clear role and responsibility plan. By doing so, accountability and responsibility is maintained within the organization, reducing confusion and ensuring that security requirements are balanced with the achievement of business objectives.

Regardless of the user's role, one of the fundamental principles in security is that maintaining the safekeeping of information is the responsibility of everyone.

Key Topic

The list that follows highlights the key concepts related to security roles and responsibilities:

■ The definition of roles is needed to maintain clear responsibility and accountability.

■ Protecting the security of information and assets is everyone's responsibility.

The following roles are commonly used within an organization, although they might be called something different, depending on the organization. Additionally, depending on the size of the organization, an individual might be assigned more than one role.

■ **Executives and senior management:** They have the ultimate responsibility over the security of data and assets. They should be involved in and approve access control policies.

■ **Data owner:** The data owner, also called the information owner, is usually part of the management team and maintains ownership of and responsibility over a specific piece or subset of data. Part of the responsibility of this role is to determine the appropriate classification of the information, ensure that the information is protected with controls, to periodically review classification and access rights, and to understand the risk associated with the information.

■ **Data custodian:** The data custodian is the individual who performs day-to-day tasks on behalf of the data owner. Their main responsibility is to ensure that the information is available to the end user and that security policies, standards, and guidelines are followed.

■ **System owner:** The system owner is responsible for the security of the systems that handle and process information owned by different data owners. Their responsibility is to ensure that the data is secure while it is being processed by the system they own. The system owner works closely with the data owner to determine the appropriate controls to apply to data.

■ **Security administrator:** The security administrator manages the process for granting access rights to information. This includes assigning privileges, granting access, and monitoring and maintaining records of access.

■ **End user:** The role is for the final users of the information. They contribute to the security of the information by adhering to the organization's security policy.

Besides these roles, several others could be seen in larger organizations, including the following:

■ **Security officer:** In charge of the design, implementation, management, and review of security policies and organizing and coordinating information security activities

■ **Information system security professional:** Responsible for drafting policies, creating standards and guidelines related to information security, and providing guidance on new and existing threats

■ **Auditor:** Responsible for determining whether owners, custodians, and systems are compliant with the organization's security policies and providing independent assurance to senior management

Access Control Types

There are several types of access controls. For example, a policy that provides information on who is authorized to access a resource and an access list implemented on a firewall to limit access to a resource are two types of access controls. In this case, the policy would be an administrative access control, whereas the access list would be a technical or logical access control.

Controls can be classified into three main categories:

■ **Administrative controls:** Sometime called *management controls*, these include the policies, procedures around the definition of access controls, definitions of information classifications, roles and responsibilities, and in general anything that is needed to manage access control from the administrative point of view. Administrative controls are usually directly overseen by senior management. Administrative controls include the following subcategories:

   ■ **Operational and security policies and procedures:** These could include policies about change control, vulnerability management, information classification, product lifecycle management, and so on.

   ■ **Policies around personnel or employee security:** These could include the level of clearance needed to access specific information, background checks on new hires, and so on. Generally, this category includes policies on all the controls that need to be in place before access is granted to a resource.

   ■ **Security education and training:** This subcategory includes all the policies and efforts needed to implement end-user training and education.

   ■ **Auditing and monitoring policies:** These might include policies on how to perform employee monitoring, system and compliance auditing, and so on.

■ **Physical controls:** This type of control is aimed at protecting the physical boundaries and ensuring employee safety. These types of controls are usually deployed in various layers in accordance to the concept of defense in depth described in Chapter 3. Examples of these controls are the fence at the entrance of the building, fire alarms, surveillance systems, and security guards. Physical access controls are usually designed by defining security zones (for example, Data Center) and implementing physical controls, depending on the classification of the assets. For example, entering the data center area may require additional privileges versus entering the building facilities.

■ **Technical controls:** These controls, also called *logical controls*, are all the logical and technological systems in place to implement and enforce the controls included in the security policy and, in general, dictated by the administrative controls. A firewall, an intrusion detection system, a remote access server, an identity management system, and encryption are all examples of technical controls.

Besides the administrative, physical, and technical classifications, access controls can also be classified based on their purpose. Access controls can be categorized as having preventive, detective, corrective, deterrent, recovery, and compensating capacities, as detailed in the following list. Both classification approaches can work at the same time. For example, encrypting data when it is at rest is a technical control aimed at preventing unauthorized access to the data itself.

- *Preventive controls* enforce security policy and should prevent incidents from happening. The only way to bypass a preventive control is to find a flaw in its implementation or logic. These controls are usually not optional. Examples of preventive controls are access lists, passwords, and fences.

- *Deterrent controls* are similar to preventive controls in the sense that the primary objective is to prevent an incident from occurring. Unlike preventive controls, however, the rationale behind deterrent controls is to discourage an attacker from proceeding just because a control is in place. For example, a system banner warning that any unauthorized attempt to log in will be monitored and punished is a type of deterrent control. In fact, it would probably discourage a casual user from attempting to access the system; however, it might not block a determined attacker from trying to log in to the system.

- *Detective controls* aim at monitoring and detecting any unauthorized behavior or hazard. These types of controls are generally used to alert a failure in other types of controls such as preventive, deterrent, and compensating controls. Detective controls are very powerful while an attack is taking place, and they are useful in the post-mortem analysis to understand what has happened. Audit logs, intrusion detection systems, motion detection, and Security Information and Event Management are examples of detective controls.

- *Corrective controls* include all the controls used during an incident to correct the problem. Quarantining an infected computer, sending a guard to block an intruder, and terminating an employee for not having followed the security policy are all examples of corrective controls.

- *Recovery controls* are used after the environment or system has been modified because of an unauthorized access or due to other reasons; they're aimed at restoring the initial behavior. Performing a backup, implementing a redundant system, and creating a disaster recovery plan are all examples of recovery controls.

- *Compensating controls* complement or offer an alternative to the primary control. These types of controls are generally used as temporary measures until the primary control is implemented, or to increase the efficacy of the primary control. Overall, the goal of compensating controls is to reduce the risk to an acceptable level. For example, a security guard checking your badge because the badge reader is temporarily out of order would be an example of a compensating control.

It is sometimes hard to properly classify a control. For example, an access list could be classified as preventive; however, it might also be a deterrent, because if you know that your access is blocked, you would probably not attempt to access a resource. An access list could also be used as a detective control if it is implemented in a way that permits traffic and logs when someone has actually accessed a resource.

Generally, it is important to get information about the context in which the control is used, but you should also think of the main purpose of the control itself. For example, an access list should probably be classified as preventive rather than as a deterrent. Table 4-5 provides examples of various access controls and how they map to each access control type.

Table 4-5   Mapping Access Controls to Access Control Types

	Administrative	Physical	Technical
Preventive			Firewall
Deterrent		Fence	
Detective			Intrusion detection system
Corrective	Employee termination policy		
Recovery			Data backup
Compensating		Manual user screening	

Figure 4-2 shows how each type of control maps to the Cisco Attack Continuum. Preventive and deterrent controls can be used before an attack occurs to harden and avoid an attack. Detective and corrective controls are used during an attack to detect the attack and mitigate its impact. Recovery controls are used after the attack to return to a normal situation. Compensating controls span the attack continuum and can be used before, during, and after an attack.

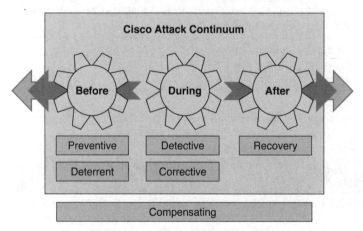

Figure 4-2   *Mapping Access Controls to the Cisco Attack Continuum*

Access Control Models

An access control model is a conceptual framework that describes how the access control should be designed (that is, how a subject interacts with an object). There are several access control models; for example, access controls that authorize access to resources based on the identity of the subject are called identity-based access controls (IBACs).

However, any access controls can usually be categorized as discretionary access controls and nondiscretionary access controls. The key differentiator between the two is based on the entity that decides how to enforce a policy. With discretionary access controls, the object owner has the right to decide who can access an object. Nondiscretionary access control is a broad category that includes all types of access control models where the authorization is decided by a central administrator instead of by the object owner.

In this section, we discuss in detail the following access control models:

- Discretionary access control (DAC)
- Mandatory access control (MAC)
- Role-based access control (RBAC)
- Attribute-based access control (ABAC)

Table 4-6 provides an overview of the access control models described in this section.

Table 4-6 Overview of Access Control Models

Access Control Model	Access Decision	Reference
DAC	Access decisions and permissions are decided by the object owner.	DoD – Trusted Computer System Evaluation Criteria
MAC	Access decision is enforced by the access policy enforcer (for example, the operating system). It uses security labels.	DoD – Trusted Computer System Evaluation Criteria
RBAC	Access decisions are based on the role or function of the subject.	ANSI INCITS 359-2004
ABAC	Access decisions are based on the attributes or characteristics of the subject, object, and environment.	NIST SP 800-162

Table 4-7 summarizes the pros and cons of each access control model.

Table 4-7 Pros and Cons of Access Control Models

Access Control Model	Pros	Cons
DAC	Simpler than the other models	Security policy can be bypassed. No centralized control.
MAC	Strict control over information flow	Complex administration.
RBAC	Scalable and easy to manage	Increase in role definition.
ABAC	Flexible	More complex compared to DAC or RBAC.

Discretionary Access Control

In a DAC model, each resource has a clearly identified owner. For example, a user creating a file becomes the owner of that file. The owner of a resource can decide at his discretion to allow other users or subjects access to that resource. The owner discretion is the main characteristic of DAC. In fact, when assigning permission, the owner should comply with the organization's security policy; however, security policy compliance is not enforced by the operating system. When the owner allows access to a different user, he would also set access permission (for example, read, write, or execute) for the resource specific to the user.

In a DAC model, users can also be organized in groups. The owner can grant access to a resource to the entire group instead of the individual user. Also, permission attributes are assigned to a resource for the specific group. A simple way to implement the DAC model is to use an access control list that is associated with each object. Most of the commercial operating systems in use today implement a form of the DAC model.

One of the drawbacks of using a DAC model is that the security policy is left to the discretion of the data owner, and the security administrator has limited control over it. Additionally, with the number of subjects (users, processes, programs, and so on) accessing a large number of objects, maintaining permissions by respecting the need-to-know and least-privileges concepts becomes a complex administrative task. *Authorization creep* or *privilege creep* describes an issue that's common in a large organization of privileges being assigned to a user and never being revoked when the user does not need them anymore, which goes against the need-to-know and least-privileges principles.

TIP Privilege creep, which happens more often in organizations using discretionary access controls, is not specific to this control model and may very well happen in organizations using nondiscretionary access controls. The best way to avoid privilege creep is to adopt strong account lifecycle and management practices. These are explored more in depth in Chapter 5, "Introduction to Security Operations Management."

The list that follows highlights the key concepts related to the DAC model:

- With discretionary access controls, authorization is decided by the owner of the object.
- In a DAC system, access permissions are associated with the object.
- Access control is usually enforced with access control lists.

Figure 4-3 shows an example of DAC implemented via an access control list associated with a resource. In this example, User A tries both read and write operations over the resource File A. The access control list associated with the resource (File A) provides the access control function and determines which user can access the resource and with which access rights.

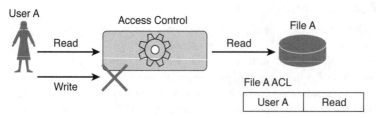

Figure 4-3 *DAC Implementation*

Mandatory Access Control

In a MAC model, the access authorization is provided by the operating system itself, and the owner has no control over who can access the resource. Each resource receives a sensitivity or security label that is determined during the classification steps outlined in the previous sections and includes two components: the security classification of the object, and the compartment or category to which the object belongs. For example, a file can be given the security classification "Top Secret" and be associated with the categories Engineering, ProjectA, and TopicB.

A label is also attached to each subject and indicates the clearance level of that subject.

Examples of security classifications are Top Secret, Secret, Confidential, and Unclassified for military and governmental environments; and Confidential, Private, Sensitive, and Public for the commercial sector. Categories, on the other hand, can be anything that is meaningful for the organization. These can be workgroup, projects, business units, and so on.

The system using a MAC model would authorize access to an object only if a subject has a label that is equal to or, for hierarchical systems, superior to the label attached to the object. In a hierarchical system, a label is superior if it has the same or higher classification and includes all categories included in the object's security label.

Systems based on a MAC model are considered more secure than systems based on a DAC model because the policy is enforced at the operating system, thus reducing the risk of mishandled permissions. The drawback of a MAC-based system, however, is that it does not offer the same degree of flexibility offered by a DAC-based system.

Due to the issues of less flexibility and more complicated administration, MAC systems have historically been used in environments where high security is needed, such as in a military environment. Regardless, MAC-based systems are being used increasingly in the commercial sector. SELinux is an example of an operating system that implements the MAC model.

The list that follows highlights the key concepts related to the mandatory access control model:

■ With mandatory access controls, the operating system or policy enforcer decides on whether to grant access.

■ The data owner does not have control and cannot decide to grant access to a resource.

■ The security policy is enforced by using security labels.

Figure 4-4 shows an example of a MAC-based system. Security labels are associated with User A and User B and with File A, which is the resource the users are attempting to access. In the example, User A has the clearance level and category matching the classification and category of File A, so access is granted. User B does not have the clearance necessary to access File A, so access is denied.

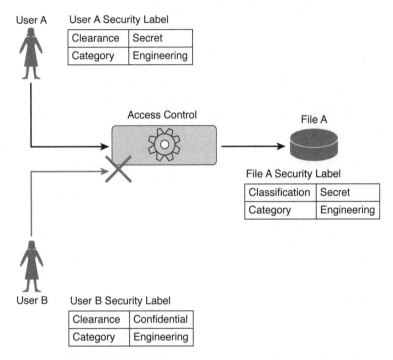

Figure 4-4   *MAC Implementation*

Role-Based Access Control

The RBAC model uses a subject role to make authorization decisions. Each subject needs to be assigned to a role; however, the assignment is done by the system administrator. This is called *user assignment* (UA). Each role is then assigned permission over an object. This is called *permission assignment* (PA).

The RBAC model greatly improves scalability and simplifies administration because a subject can just be assigned to a role without the permission over an object needing to be changed. For example, when a user changes jobs or roles, he is simply removed from that role, instead of having permissions removed for all the objects that user was interacting with before the change.

A subject can be assigned to several roles, and a role can include multiple subjects. In the same way, a role can have multiple permissions, and the same permissions can be assigned to multiple roles. This creates a many-to-many relationship. The RBAC model supports the principles of least privileges, separation of duties, and data abstraction.

The least-privileges principle is provided by configuring the RBAC system to assign only the privileges that are needed to execute a specific task to a role. Separation of duties is obtained by configuring the system so that two roles that are mutually exclusive are needed to finish a task. Data abstraction is achieved by using abstract permissions (for example, open and close if the object is a lock instead of the typical read, write, and execute).

According to the RBAC standard proposed by NIST, there are three components of the RBAC model:

- **Core RBAC**: This is the fundamental component of the RBAC model, and it implements the basic authorization based on the user roles. A session in the context of RBAC is the way a subject or user activates a subset of roles. For example, if a user is assigned to two roles (guest and administrator), then using a session as guest will activate only the permission given to the guest role. Using a session as administrator will give the user permission based on the administrator role.

- **Hierarchical RBAC**: This component introduces hierarchy within the RBAC model and is added on top of the core RBAC. This component facilitates the mapping to an organization, which is usually structured in a hierarchical way. In simple terms, hierarchical RBAC allows permission inheritance from one role to the other. For example, the head of multiple business units may inherit all the permissions assigned to each business unit, plus have the permission assigned to the "head of business units" role itself. Within hierarchical RBAC, two models are defined: *general role hierarchy*, which allows for multiple role inheritance, and *limited role hierarchy*, when the model includes restriction on the type of inheritance.

- **Constraint RBAC**: This component introduces the concept of separation of duties. The main goal of this component is to avoid collusion and fraud by making sure that more than one role is needed to complete a specific task. It comes in two subcomponents:

  - **Static Separation of Duty (SSoD)**: This subcomponent puts constraints on the assignment of a user to a role. For example, the same user whose role is to implement the code of a product should not also be part of the auditor or assurance role. If this component is built on top of a hierarchical RBAC, it will take permission inheritance in consideration when the constraint is formulated.

  - **Dynamic Separation of Duty (DSoD)**: This subcomponent also limits the subject or user access to certain permissions; however, it does so in a dynamic way during a user session rather than forbidding a user/role relationship. That is, it uses a session to regulate which permissions are available to a user. For example, a user could be in the role of code implementer and the role of code auditor, but will not be able to get permission as code auditor for code that he implemented himself.

Although the RBAC model offers higher scalability than a DAC-based system, in complex organizations the RBAC model would lead to a great expansion of roles, which would increase the administration and management burden. This is one of the drawbacks of this model.

The list that follows highlights the key concepts related to the role-based access control model:

- With role-based access controls, the access decision is based on the role or function of the subject.
- The role assignment is not discretionary, so users get assigned to a role based on the organization's policies.
- Permissions are connected to the roles, not directly to the users.

Figure 4-5 shows an example of an RBAC system. Users can map to multiple roles, and vice versa. Each role has permissions assigned, which are sets of operations that can be executed on resources (objects).

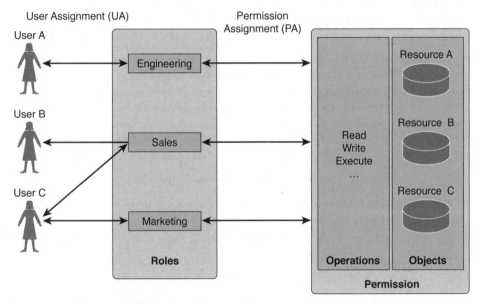

Figure 4-5 *RBAC Implementation*

Attribute-Based Access Control

Attribute-based access control (ABAC) is a further evolution in access control models that takes into consideration factors besides identity or role. These factors could include the location of access, time or temporal constraints, the level of risk or threat, and so on.

With the ABAC model, the authorization decision is based on attributes assigned to subjects and objects, environmental conditions, and a set of policies linked to these attributes and conditions. Attributes are defined as characteristics that belong to a subject (user), object (resource), or environment. For example, a subject attribute could be name, nationality, organization, role, ID, security clearance, and so on. Examples of object attributes are name, owner, data creation, and so on.

Environment conditions are contextual information associated with the access request. Location of the access, time of the access, and the threat level are all examples of environmental attributes. Every object should also be associated with at least one policy that regulates which operations a subject with certain attributes, given some environmental constraints, can perform on the object. For example, a policy could be formulated as "all *Engineers* who work in the *Security Business Unit* and are assigned to the *Next-Gen Firewall Project* are allowed to *Read* and *Write* all the *Design Documents* in the *Next-Gen Firewall Project* folder when connecting from *Building A*."

In this example, being an engineer, belonging to the security business unit, and being assigned to the next-gen firewall project are all attributes that could be assigned to a subject. Being a design document within the next-gen firewall project folder are attributes that could be assigned to the object (the document). Read and write are the operations allowed by the subject over the object. Building A is an environmental condition.

Because roles and identities could be considered attributes, RBAC and IBAC systems could be considered instances of an ABAC system. One of the best known standards that implements the ABAC model is the eXtensible Access Control Markup Language (XACML).

Another model that can be considered a special case of ABAC is called *rule-based access control*. In reality, this is not a well-defined model and includes any access control model that implements some sort of rule that governs the access to a resource. Usually rule-based access controls are used in the context of access list implementation to access network resources, for example, where the rule is to provide access only to certain IP addresses or only at certain hours of the day. In this case, the IP addresses are attributes of the subject and object, and the time of day is part of the environment attribute evaluation.

The list that follows highlights the key concepts related to the ABAC model:

- With attribute-based access controls, the access decision is based on the attributes associated with subjects, objects, or the environment.
- Attributes are characteristics that belong to a subject (user), object (resource), or environment.
- User role, identity, and security classification can be considered attributes.

Figure 4-6 shows an example of ABAC. User A has several attributes, including a role, a business unit, and assigned projects. File A also has several attributes, including the file category and the project folder. An environmental attribute (the user location) is also considered in this scenario.

The access control rule is defined as follows:

"All *Engineers* who work in the *Security Business Unit* and are assigned to the *Next-Gen Firewall Project* are allowed to *Read* and *Write* all the *Design Documents* in the *Next-Gen Firewall Project* folder when connecting from *Building A*."

All *Engineers* that work in the *Security Business Unit* and are assigned to *Next-Gen Firewall Projects* are allowed to *Read* and *Write* all the *Design Documents* in the *Next-Gen Firewall Project* folder when connecting from *Building A*.

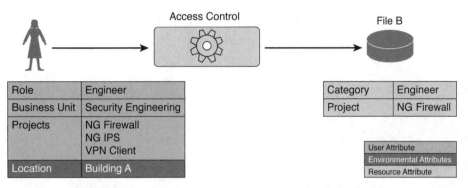

Role	Engineer
Business Unit	Security Engineering
Projects	NG Firewall NG IPS VPN Client
Location	Building A

Category	Engineer
Project	NG Firewall

User Attribute
Environmental Attributes
Resource Attribute

Figure 4-6 *ABAC Implementation*

In this example, the conditions are satisfied and access is granted. In Figures 4-7 and 4-8, however, access is denied because User B's attributes and the environmental condition, respectively, do not satisfy the access rule.

All *Engineers* that work in the *Security Business Unit* and are assigned to *Next-Gen Firewall Projects* are allowed to *Read* and *Write* all the *Design Documents* in the *Next-Gen Firewall Project* folder when connecting from *Building A*.

User B   Access Control   File A

Role	Sales
Business Unit	**Security Sales**
Projects	NG Firewall Sales
Location	Building A

Category	Engineer
Project	NG Firewall

User Attribute
Environmental Attributes
Resource Attribute

Figure 4-7 *ABAC Implementation: Access Denied Due to User Attributes*

All *Engineers* that work in the *Security Business Unit* and are assigned to *Next-Gen Firewall Projects* are allowed to *Read* and *Write* all the *Design Documents* in the *Next-Gen Firewall Project* folder when connecting from *Building A*.

User D   Access Control   File A

Role	Engineering
Business Unit	Security Engineering
Projects	NG Firewall NG IPS VPN Client
Location	**Connecting from Home**

Category	Engineer
Project	NG Firewall

User Attribute
Environmental Attributes
Resource Attribute

Figure 4-8   *ABAC Implementation: Access Denied Due to User Environmental Condition*

Access Control Mechanisms

An access control mechanism is, in simple terms, a method for implementing various access control models. A system may implement multiple access control mechanisms. In some modern systems, this notion of access control mechanism may be considered obsolete because the complexity of the system calls for more advanced mechanisms. Nevertheless, here are some of the most known methods:

■ **Access control list:** This is the simplest way to implement a DAC-based system. The key characteristic of an access control list is that it is assigned to the object that it is protecting. An access control list, when applied to an object, will include all the subjects that can access the object and their specific permissions. Figure 4-9 shows an example of an ACL applied to a file.

File A

File A ACL

User A	Read
User B	Read, Execute
User C	Read, Write

Figure 4-9   *ACL Applied to a File*

■ **Capability table:** This is a collection of objects that a subject can access, together with the granted permissions. The key characteristic of a capability table is that it's subject centric instead of being object centric, like in the case of an access control list. Figure 4-10 shows a user capability table.

User A

User A Capability Table

File A	Read
File B	Read, Execute
File C	Read, Write

Figure 4-10 *User Capability Table*

- **Access control matrix (ACM):** This is an access control mechanism that is usually associated with a DAC-based system. An ACM includes three elements: the subject, the object, and the set of permissions. Each row of an ACM is assigned to a subject, while each column represents an object. The cell that identifies a subject/object pair includes the permission that subject has on the object. An ACM could be seen as a collection of access control lists or a collection of capabilities table, depending on how you want to read it. Figure 4-11 shows an example of access controls using an ACM.

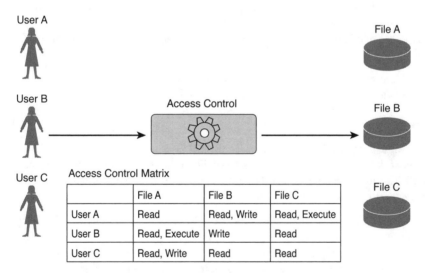

User A

User B   Access Control   File B

User C   Access Control Matrix   File C

	File A	File B	File C
User A	Read	Read, Write	Read, Execute
User B	Read, Execute	Write	Read
User C	Read, Write	Read	Read

Figure 4-11 *Access Controls Using an ACM*

- **Restricted interface:** This type of control limits the operations a subject can perform on an object by not providing that option on the interface that the subject uses to access the object. Typical examples of this type of control are menus, shells, physical constraint interfaces, and so on. For example, a menu could offer more options if a user is a system administrator, and fewer options if the user is a guest.

- **Content-dependent access control:** This type of control uses the information (content) within a resource to make an authorization decision. This type of control is generally used in database access controls. A typical example is a database view.

> **TIP** A database view could also be considered a type of restricted interface because the available information is restricted depending on the identity of the user.

- **Context-dependent access control:** This type of control uses contextual information to make an access decision, together with other information such as the identity of the subject. For example, a system implementing a context-dependent control may look at events preceding an access request to make an authorization decision. A typical system that uses this type of control is a stateful firewall, such as Cisco ASA or Cisco IOS configured with the Zone-Based Firewall feature, where a packet is allowed or denied based on the information related to the session the packet belongs to.

Identity and Access Control Implementation

Several methods, technologies, and protocols can be used to implement identity and access technical controls. This section explores some of the most common ones that are relevant to the CCNA CyberOps Security Fundamentals Exam.

Authentication, Authorization, and Accounting Protocols

Several protocols are used to grant access to networks or systems, provide information about access rights, and provide capabilities used to monitor, audit, and account for user actions once authenticated and authorized. These protocols are called authentication, authorization, and accounting (AAA) protocols.

The most well-known AAA protocols are RADIUS, TACACS+, and Diameter. The sections that follow provide some background information about each.

RADIUS

The Remote Authentication Dial-In User Service (RADIUS) is an AAA protocol mainly used to provide network access services. Due to its flexibility, it has been adopted in other scenarios as well. The authentication and authorization parts are specified in RFC 2865, while the accounting part is specified in RFC 2866.

RADIUS is a client-server protocol. In the context of RADIUS, the client is the access server, which is the entity to which a user sends the access request. The server is usually a machine running RADIUS services and that provides authentication and authorization responses containing all the information used by the access server to provide service to the user.

The RADIUS server can act as proxy for other RADIUS servers or other authentication systems. Also, RADIUS can support several types of authentication mechanisms, such as PPP PAP, CHAP, and EAP. It also allows protocol extension via the attribute field. For example, vendors can use the attribute "vendor-specific" (type 26) to pass vendor-specific information.

Figure 4-12 shows a typical deployment of a RADIUS server.

Figure 4-12 *RADIUS Server Implementation*

RADIUS operates in most cases over UDP protocol port 1812 for authentication and authorization, and port 1813 for accounting, which are the officially assigned ports for this service. In earlier implementations, RADIUS operated over UDP port 1645 for authentication and authorization, and port 1646 for accounting. The authentication and authorization phase consists of two messages:

1. The access server sends an ACCESS-REQUEST to the RADIUS server that includes the user identity, the password, and other information about the requestor of the access (for example, the IP address).

2. The RADIUS server may reply with three different messages:

    a. ACCESS-ACCEPT if the user is authenticated. This message will also include in the Attribute field authorization information and specific vendor information used by the access server to provide services.

    b. ACCESS-REJECT if access for the user is rejected.

    c. ACCESS-CHALLENGE if additional information is needed, RADIUS server needs to send an additional challenge to the access server before authenticating the user. The ACCESS-CHALLENGE will be followed by a new ACCESS-REQUEST message.

Figure 4-13 shows an example of a RADIUS exchange for authentication and authorization.

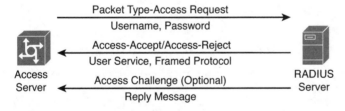

Figure 4-13 *RADIUS Exchange for Authentication/Authorization*

The accounting exchange consists of two messages: ACCOUNTING-REQUEST and ACCOUNTING-RESPONSE. Accounting can be used, for example, to specify how long a user has been connected to the network (the start and stop of a session).

The RADIUS exchange is authenticated by using a shared secret key between the access server and the RADIUS server. Only the user password information in the ACCESS-REQUEST is encrypted; the rest of the packets are sent in plaintext.

TACACS+

Terminal Access Controller Access Control System Plus (TACACS+) is a proprietary protocol developed by Cisco. It also uses a client-server model, where the TACACS+ client is the access server and the TACACS+ server is the machine providing TACACS+ services (that is, authentication, authorization, and accounting).

Similar to RADIUS, TACACS+ also supports protocol extension by allowing vendor-specific attributes and several types of authentication protocols. TACACS+ uses TCP as the transport protocol, and the TACACS+ server listens on port 49. Using TCP ensures a more reliable connection and fault tolerance.

TACACS+ has the authentication, authorization, and accounting processes as three separate steps. This allows the use of different protocols (for example, RADIUS) for authentication or accounting. Additionally, the authorization and accounting capabilities are more granular than in RADIUS (for example, allowing specific authorization of commands). This makes TACACS+ the preferred protocol for authorization services for remote device administration.

The TACACS+ exchange requires several packets;

- START, REPLY and CONTINUE packets are used during the authentication process.
- REQUEST and RESPONSE packets are used during the authorization and accounting process.

The following is an example of an authentication exchange:

1. The access server sends a START authentication request.
2. The TACACS+ server sends a REPLY to acknowledge the message and ask the access server to provide a username.
3. The access server sends a CONTINUE with the username.
4. The TACACS+ server sends a REPLY to acknowledge the message and ask for the password.
5. The access server sends a CONTINUE with the password.
6. The TACACS+ server sends a REPLY with authentication response (pass or fail).

Figure 4-14 shows an example of a TACACS+ authentication, authorization, and accounting exchange.

TACACS+ offers better security protection compared to RADIUS. For example, the full body of the packet may be encrypted.

Table 4-8 summarizes the main differences between RADIUS and TACACS+.

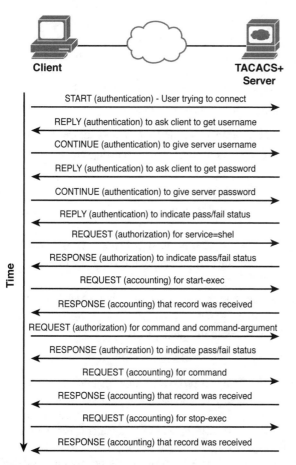

Figure 4-14 *TACACS+ Message Exchange for Authentication, Authorization, and Accounting*

Table 4-8 RADIUS vs. TACACS+ Comparison

	RADIUS	TACACS+
Transport protocol	UDP.	TCP.
Security	Encrypts user password in ACCESS-REQUEST packets.	Can optionally encrypt the full payload.
AAA phases	Authentication and authorization are performed with the same exchange. Accounting is done with a separate exchange.	Authentication, authorization, and accounting are performed with separate exchanges.
Command authorization	There is no support for granular command authorization.	Allows command authorization.
Accounting	Implements strong accounting capabilities.	Provides basic accounting capabilities.
Standard	RFC 2865 (authentication and authorization) and RFC 2866 (accounting)	Cisco proprietary.

Diameter

RADIUS and TACACS+ were created with the aim of providing AAA services to network access via dial-up protocols or terminal access. Due to their success and flexibility, they have been used in several other scopes. To respond to newer access requirements and protocols, the IETF has proposed a new protocol called Diameter, which is described in RFC 6733.

Diameter has been built with the following functionality in mind:

- **Failover:** Diameter implements application-level acknowledgement and failover algorithms.
- **Transmission-level security:** Diameter protects the exchange of messages by using TLS or DTLS.
- **Reliable transport:** Diameter uses TCP or STCP as the transport protocol.
- **Agent support:** Diameter specifies the roles of different agents such as proxy, relay, redirect, and translation agents.
- **Server initiated messages:** Diameter makes mandatory the implementation of server-initiated messages. This enables capabilities such as on-demand re-authentication and re-authorization.
- **Transition support:** Diameter allows compatibility with systems using RADIUS.
- **Capability negotiation:** Diameter includes capability negotiations such as error handling as well as mandatory and nonmandatory attribute/value pairs (AVP).
- **Peer discovery:** Diameter enables dynamic peer discovery via DNS.

The main reason for the introduction of the Diameter protocol is the capability to work with applications that enable protocol extension. The main Diameter application is called *Diameter base* and it implements the core of the Diameter protocol. Other applications are Mobile IPv4 Application, Network Access Server Application, Diameter Credit-Control Application, and so on. Each application specifies the content of the information exchange in Diameter packets. For example, to use Diameter as AAA protocol for network access, the Diameter peers will use the Diameter Base Application and the Diameter Network Access Server Application.

The Diameter header field *Application ID* indicates the ID of the application. Each application, including the Diameter Base application, uses command code to identify specific application actions. Diameter is a peer-to-peer protocol, and entities in a Diameter context are called Diameter nodes. A Diameter node is defined as a host that implements the Diameter protocol.

The protocol is based on two main messages: a REQUEST, which is identified by setting the R bit in the header, and an ANSWER, which is identified by unsetting the R bit. Each message will include a series of attribute/value pairs (AVPs) that include application-specific information.

In its basic protocol flow, after the transport layer connection is created, the Diameter initiator peer sends a Capability-Exchange-Request (CER) to the other peer that will respond with a Capability-Exchange-Answer (CEA). The CER can include several AVPs, depending on the application that is requesting a connection. Once the capabilities are exchanged, the Diameter applications can start sending information.

Diameter also implements a keep-alive mechanism by using a Device-Watchdog-Request (DWR), which needs to be acknowledged with a Device-Watchdog-Answer (DWA). The communication is terminated by using a Disconnect-Peer-Request (DPR) and Disconnect-Peer-Answer (DPA). Both the Device-Watchdog and Disconnect-Peer can be initiated by both parties.

Figure 4-15 shows an example of a Diameter capability exchange and communication termination.

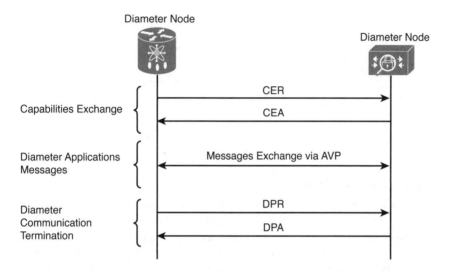

Figure 4-15 *Diameter Capability Exchange/Communication Termination*

The following is an example of protocol flows where Diameter is used to provide user authentication service for network access (as defined in the Network Access Server Application RFC 7155):

1. The initiator peer, the access server, sends a CER message with the Auth-Application-Id AVP set to 1, meaning that it supports authentication capabilities.

2. The Diameter server sends a CEA back to the access server with the Auth-Application-Id AVP set to 1.

3. The access server sends an AA-Request (AAR) to the Diameter server that includes information about the user authentication, such as username and password.

4. The access server will reply with an AA-Answer (AAA) message including the authentication results.

Figure 4-16 shows an example of a Diameter exchange for network access services.

Diameter is a much more complex protocol and is used mainly in a mobile service provider environment.

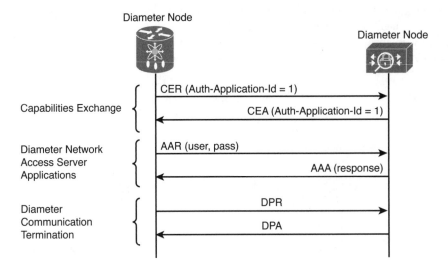

Figure 4-16 *Diameter Exchange for Network Access Services*

Port-Based Access Control

Port-based access controls are associated with a specific access port, such as an access layer switch port, for example. The idea behind this type of control is to allow or deny a device that is physically connected to a network port with access to a specific resource. In this section, we discuss two types of port-based access controls implemented in Cisco devices: port security and 802.1x. Both types of access controls are based on the ABAC model (sometimes also described as identity-based or rule-based access control).

Port Security

Port security is a security feature present in most Cisco routers and switches, and it is used to provide access control by restricting the medium access control (MAC) addresses that can be connected to a given port. This differs from a MAC access list because it works only on the source MAC address without matching the MAC destination.

> **TIP** The medium access control (MAC) address should not be confused with the mandatory access control (MAC) model. The former is the address of the Ethernet card and has been discussed in the "Ethernet Addresses" section of Chapter 1, "Fundamentals of Networking Protocols and Networking Devices." The latter is a type of access control model and has been discussed in the "Mandatory Access Control" section of this chapter.

Port security works by defining a pool of MAC addresses that are allowed to transmit on a device port. The pool can be statically defined or dynamically learned. Compared to a MAC access list, which would need to be implemented on each port and have static entries, the dynamically learned method reduces the administrative overhead related to the port access control implementation.

When a frame is received on the port, the port security feature checks the source MAC address of the frame. If it matches an allowed MAC address, the frame will be forwarded; otherwise, the frame will be dropped.

In addition to drop frames coming from an unauthorized MAC address, port security will raise a security violation. A security violation is raised under the following circumstances:

- If a MAC address that is configured or dynamically learned on one port is seen on a different port in the same VLAN. This is referred to as a *MAC move*.

- If the maximum number of MAC addresses allowed for a port is reached and the incoming MAC is different from the one already learned.

802.1x

802.1x is an IEEE standard that is used to implement port-based access control. In simple terms, an 802.1x access device will allow traffic on the port only after the device has been authenticated and authorized.

Figure 4-17 shows an example of traffic allowed before and after an 802.1x authentication and authorization.

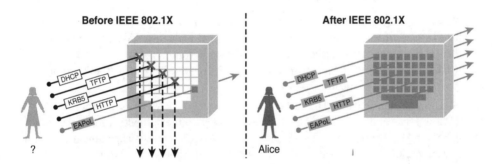

Figure 14-17 *Traffic Allowed Before/After 802.1x Authentication and Authorization*

In an 802.1x-enabled network, three main roles are defined:

- **Authentication server:** An entity that provides an authentication service to an authenticator. The authentication server determines whether the supplicant is authorized to access the service. This is sometimes referred to as the Policy Decision Point (PdP). Cisco ACS and Cisco ISE are examples of an authentication server.

- **Supplicant:** An entity that seeks to be authenticated by an authenticator. For example, this could be a client laptop connected to a switch port.

- **Authenticator:** An entity that facilitates authentication of other entities attached to the same LAN. This is sometimes referred to as the Policy Enforcement Point (PeP). Cisco switches and access points are examples of authenticators.

Other components, such as an identity database or a PKI infrastructure, may be required for a correct deployment.

Figure 4-18 shows an example of an authentication server, supplicant, and authenticator. The supplicant is connected to the switch port via a wired connection.

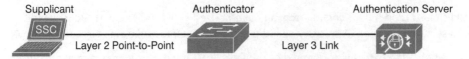

Figure 4-18 *Authentication Server, Supplicant, and Authenticator Topology*

802.1x uses the following protocols:

- **EAP over LAN (EAPoL):** An encapsulation defined in 802.1x that's used to encapsulate EAP packets to be transmitted from the supplicant to the authentication server.

- **Extensible Authentication Protocol (EAP):** An authentication protocol used between the supplicant and the authentication server to transmit authentication information.

- **RADIUS or Diameter:** The AAA protocol used for communication between the authenticator and authentication server.

The 802.1x port-based access control includes four phases (in this example, RADIUS is used as the protocol and a Cisco switch as the authenticator):

1. **Session initiation:** The session can be initiated either by the authenticator with an EAP-Request-Identity message or by the supplicant with an EAPoL-Start message. Before the supplicant is authenticated and the session authorized, only EAPoL, Cisco Discovery Protocol (CDP), and Spanning Tree Protocol (STP) traffic is allowed on the port from the authenticator.

2. **Session authentication:** The authenticator extracts the EAP message from the EAPoL frame and sends a RADIUS Access-Request to the authentication server, adding the EAP information in the AV pair of the RADIUS request. The authenticator and the supplicant will use EAP to agree on the authentication method (for example, EAP-TLS).

   Depending on the authentication method negotiated, the supplicant may provide a password, a certificate, a token, and so on.

3. **Session authorization:** If the authentication server can authenticate the supplicant, it will send a RADIUS Access-Accept to the authenticator that includes additional authorization information such as VLAN, downloadable access control list (dACL), and so on.

   The authenticator will send an EAP Success to the supplicant, and the supplicant can start sending traffic.

4. **Session accounting:** This represents the exchange of accounting RADIUS packets between the authenticator and the authentication server.

Figure 4-19 shows an example of 802.1x port access control exchange.

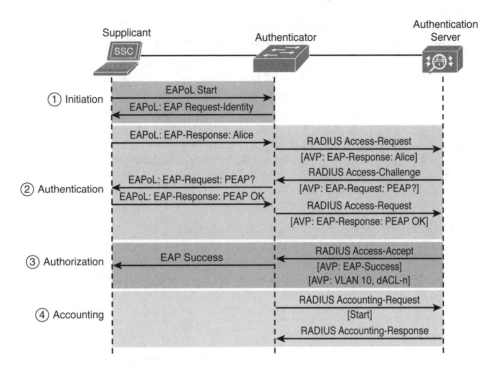

Figure 4-19 *802.1x Port Access Control Exchange*

In addition to these four phases, it is also very important that the session is correctly terminated. In the standard scenario, where the supplicant terminates the connection, it will send an EAPoL-Logoff message.

Network Access Control List and Firewalling

The most basic implementation of an access control is an access control list (ACL). When an ACL is applied to network traffic, it is called a *network ACL*. Cisco networking devices such as routers, switches, and firewalls include network ACL capabilities to control access to network resources. As for port-based access controls, network ACLs and firewalling are usually seen as special cases of the ABAC model and also sometimes classified as identify-based or rule-based access control because they base the control decision on attributes such as IP or MAC addresses or Layer 4 information. Security group ACLs, on the other hand, are access lists based on the role of the subject trying to access a resource, and they implement role-based access control.

Network ACLs can be implemented at various levels of the OSI model:

■ A Layer 2 ACL operates at the data link layer and implements filters based on Layer 2 information. An example of this type of access list is a MAC access list, which uses information about the MAC address to create the filter.

■ A Layer 3 ACL operates at the networking layer. Cisco devices usually allow Layer 3 ACLs for different Layer 3 protocols, including the most used ones nowadays—IPv4 and

IPv6. In addition to selecting the Layer 3 protocol, a Layer 3 ACL allows the configuration of filtering for a protocol using raw IP, such as OSPF or ESP.

■ A Layer 4 ACL operates at the transport layer. An example of a Layer 4 ACL is a TCP- or UDP-based ACL. Typically, a Layer 4 ACL includes the source and destination. This allows filtering of specific upper-layer packets.

VLAN Map

VLAN ACLs, also called VLAN maps, are not specifically Layer 2 ACLs; however, they are used to limit the traffic within a specific VLAN. A VLAN map can apply a MAC access list, a Layer 3 ACL, and a Layer 4 ACL to the inbound direction of a VLAN to provide access control.

Security Group–Based ACL

A security group–based ACL (SGACL) is an ACL that implements access control based on the security group assigned to a user (for example, based on his role within the organization) and the destination resources. SGACLs are implemented as part of Cisco TrustSec policy enforcement. Cisco TrustSec is described in a bit more detail in the sections that follow. The enforced ACL may include both Layer 3 and Layer 4 access control entries (ACEs).

Figure 4-20 shows an example of SGACL.

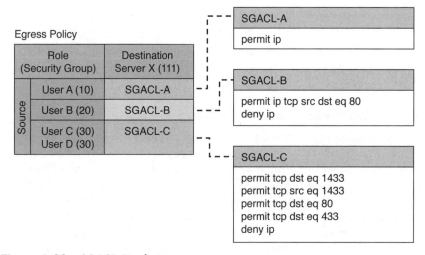

Figure 4-20 *SGACL Deployment*

Downloadable ACL

A downloadable ACL (dACL), also called a *per-user ACL*, is an ACL that can be applied dynamically to a port. The term *downloadable* stems from the fact that these ACLs are pushed from the authenticator server (for example, from a Cisco ISE) during the authorization phase.

When a client authenticates to the port (for example, by using 802.1x), the authentication server can send a dACL that will be applied to the port and that will limit the resources the client can access over the network.

Firewalling

ACLs are stateless access controls because they do not maintain the state of a session or a connection. A more advanced implementation of access control is provided by stateful firewalls, which are able to implement access control based on the state of a connection. Cisco offers several firewalling solutions, which have been discussed in Chapter 2, "Network Security Devices and Cloud Services."

Firewalls often implement inspection capabilities that enforce application layer protocol conformance and dynamic access control based on the state of the upper-layer protocol.

Next-generation firewalls go one step further and implement context-aware controls, where not only the IP address or specific application information are taken into account, but other contextual information, such as the location, the type of device requesting access, and the sequence of events, are taken into consideration when allowing or denying a packet.

Identity Management and Profiling

Cisco offers a number of management products that help the security administrator to implement identity management and access control enforcement:

- **Cisco Secure Access Control Server:** Cisco Secure Access Control Server (ACS) is AAA and policy enforcement software running on Cisco Secure Network Server or as a virtual appliance. It offers RADIUS and TACACS+ services and can be integrated with other backend identity databases such as Microsoft Active Directory and RSA SecureID. It supports the most used authentication protocols, both for wired and wireless access, and includes the ability to pass authorization policies such as downloadable ACLs or VLAN assignment to the enforcer device (for example, a Cisco switch).

- **Cisco Identity Service Engine:** Cisco Identity Service Engine (ISE) is a comprehensive secure identity management solution designed to function as a policy decision point for network access. It allows security administrators to collect real-time contextual information from a network, its users, and devices. Cisco ISE is the central policy management platform in the Cisco TrustSec solution. It supports a comprehensive set of authentication, authorization, and accounting (AAA); posture; and network profiler features in a single device. Cisco ISE is described in more detail in Chapter 2.

- **Cisco Prime Access Registrar:** Cisco Prime Access Registrar is software that provides RADIUS- and Diameter-based AAA services for a wide range of network access implementation, including Wi-Fi (SP Wi-Fi), Vo-Wi-Fi, femtocell, Connected Grid, LTE, DSL, Code Division Multiple Access (CDMA), General Packet Radio Service (GPRS), Universal Mobile Telecommunications Service (UMTS), WLAN, and WiMAX.

Network Segmentation

Network segmentation is a technique that is used in access controls design to separate resources either physically or logically. Logical network segmentation can be implemented in several ways. For example, a careful choice of IP addressing schema is one way to implement network segmentation. Network segmentation by itself will not provide access control functionality, but facilitate the enforcement of access control policy at the ingress/egress points.

Network Segmentation Through VLAN

As described in Chapter 1, a VLAN is a Layer 2 broadcast domain. A careful plan of how ports or users are assigned to a specific VLAN can allow network segmentation and facilitate the implementation of access policy (for example, via network ACLs for traffic that needs to be routed across VLAN segments).

VLAN ACLs, also called VLAN maps, are not specifically Layer 2 ACLs; however, they work to limit traffic within a specific VLAN. VLAN maps can apply MAC access lists or Layer 3 and Layer 4 access lists to the inbound direction of a VLAN to provide access control.

Private VLANs can also be used to implement VLAN partitioning and control the communication among ports belonging to the same VLAN. A private VLAN includes three types of ports:

- **Promiscuous:** Devices attached to a promiscuous port can communicate with all ports within the switch, including isolated and community ports.
- **Isolated:** Devices attached to an Isolated port can only communicate with the promiscuous port.
- **Community:** Devices attached to a community port can communicate with the promiscuous port and with other devices in the same community.

Figure 4-21 shows how the communication happens between various types of ports.

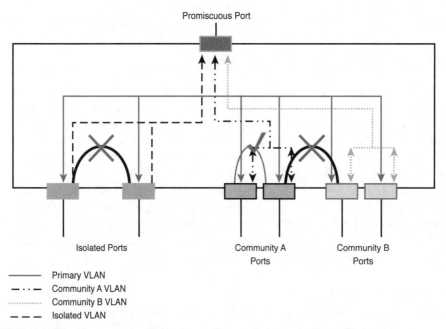

Figure 4-21 *Communication Between Ports in a Private VLAN Environment*

Firewall DMZ

Firewalls can be configured to separate multiple network segments (or zones), usually called demilitarized zones (DMZs). These zones provide security to the systems that reside within them with different security levels and policies between them. DMZs can have several purposes; for example, they can serve as segments on which a web server farm resides or as extranet connections to a business partner. DMZs and firewalls are described in more detail in Chapter 2.

Cisco TrustSec

Cisco TrustSec is a security architecture that allows network segmentation and enables access controls primarily based on a role or attribute of the user requesting access to the network. The Cisco TrustSec architecture includes three key concepts:

- **Authenticated networking infrastructure:** Each networking device in a TrustSec environment is authenticated by its peers. This creates a trusted domain.

- **Security group-based access control:** The access control does not happen, as with a normal ACL, based on the IP addresses of the source and destination, but based on the role of the source and destination. This is done by assigning a security group tag (SGT) to sources and destinations.

- **Encrypted communication:** Communication on each link is encrypted by using 802.1AE Media Access Control Security (MACSec).

Similar to 802.1x, Cisco TrustSec defines the roles of supplicant, authentication server, and authenticator. Before a supplicant can send packets to the network, it needs to join the TrustSec domain. This involves the following steps:

1. The supplicant authenticates by using 802.1x with the authentication server. In the authentication phase, the authentication server authenticates both the supplicant and authenticator. Both the supplicant device and user may need to be authenticated.

2. The authentication server sends authorization information to the authenticator and supplicant. The information includes the SGT to be assigned to the supplicant traffic.

3. The security association is negotiated and link encryption is established between the supplicant and the authenticator (the rest of the domain already has link encryption set up as part of the network device enrollment).

Figure 4-22 shows how an SGT is embedded within a Layer 2 frame.

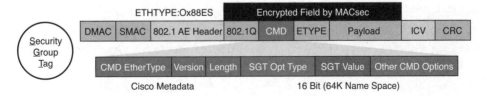

Figure 4-22 *Embedding and SGT Within a Layer 2 Frame*

The access control is provided by ingress tagging and egress enforcement. This means that a packet is tagged based on its source once it enters the Cisco TrustSec domain and the access control happens at the egress point based on the destination. The access decision is based on SGACL implemented at the egress point.

The following example, shown in Figure 4-23, explains the ingress tagging and egress enforcement:

1. A host sends packets to a destination (the web server).

2. The TrustSec authenticator (the ingress switch to the TrustSec domain) modifies the packet and adds a source SGT—for example, Engineering, which corresponds to ID 3.

3. The packet travels through the TrustSec domain and reaches the egress point. The egress point will check the SGACL to see whether Engineering group (3) is authorized to access the web server, which also receives an destination SGT (DGT) with ID 4.

4. If the packet is allowed to pass, the egress point will remove the SGT and transmit to the destination.

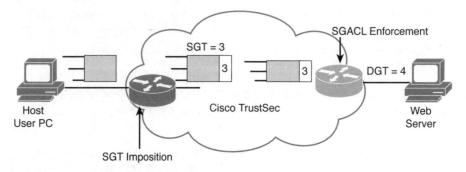

Figure 4-23 *Ingress Tagging and Egress Enforcement*

Adding the SGT requires the ingress point to have hardware enabled for TrustSec. Although most of the latest Cisco devices are enabled for TrustSec, in legacy environments there may be some issues with adopting TrustSec.

The SGT Exchange Protocol (SXP) allows software-enabled devices to still participate in the TrustSec architecture and expand the applicability of Cisco TrustSec. It uses an IP-address-to-SGT method to forward information about the SGT to the first Cisco TrustSec-enabled hardware on the path to the destination. Once the packet reaches that point, the device will tag in the packet, which will then continue its trip to the destination.

Figure 4-24 shows how SXP can be used to exchange SGT between an access device with only Cisco TrustSec capability in software and a device with Cisco TrustSec hardware support.

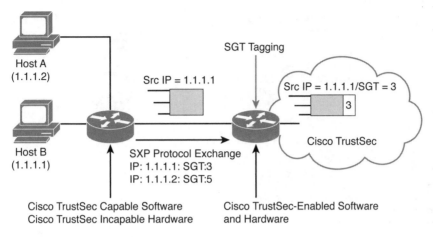

Figure 4-24 *Use of SXP*

Intrusion Detection and Prevention

Intrusion detection and intrusion prevention controls can be administrative, physical, or technical. This section discusses the technical type of controls.

Intrusion detection systems (IDSs) and intrusion prevention systems (IPSs) implement detection and prevention capabilities for unauthorized access to the network or to an information system. IDSs focus more on detection whereas IPSs focus on threat or unauthorized access prevention. The main difference between an IDS and IPS is the deployment mode. IDS usually works on a copy of the packet and is mainly used to detect an issue or anomaly and alert the security analyst. This is called promiscuous mode. IDS may also include capabilities to enforce corrective action through other devices (for example, a firewall or a router that works as an enforcement point).

For example, an IDS can communicate with a firewall device and ask the firewall to reset a connection. Because the IDS does not intercept the real packet, the response time to block a threat is lower than in an IPS system; thus, some malicious packets may enter the network.

An IPS, on the other hand, is deployed inline, which means it has visibility of the packets or threats as they flow through the device. Because of that, it is able to block a threat as soon as it is detected—for example, by dropping a malicious packet. The drawback of having an IPS inline is that it adds additional latency due to the packet processing, and it may drop legitimate traffic in the case of a false positive.

Figure 4-25 and Figure 4-26 show examples of IDS and IPS deployment.

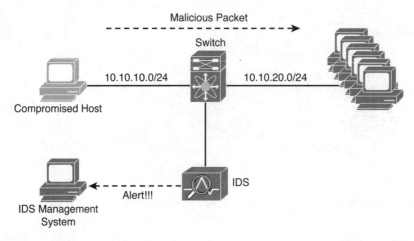

Figure 4-25 *IDS Deployment*

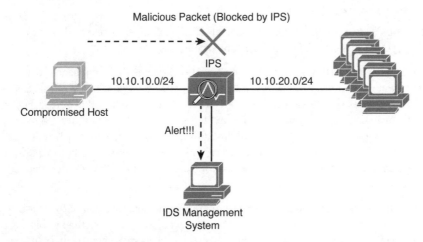

Figure 4-26 *IPS Deployment*

The lists that follow summarize the key topics regarding intrusion detection and prevention systems:

IDS:

■ Works on a copy of the packet (promiscuous mode).

■ Does not introduce delay due to packet inspection.

■ Cannot stop a packet directly but can work with other devices, such as firewalls, to drop malicious packets.

■ Some malicious packets may pass through even if they are flagged as malicious.

IPS:

- Intercepts and processes real traffic (inline mode).
- Introduces delay due to packet processing and inspection.
- Can stop packet as they come through.
- Packets that are recognized to be malicious can be dropped right away.

Table 4-9 summarizes the differences between an IPS and IDS.

Table 4-9 IDS vs. IPS Comparison

IDS	IPS
Works on a copy of the packet (promiscuous mode).	Intercepts and processes real traffic (inline mode).
No latency added.	Adds latency due to packet processing.
Cannot stop malicious packets directly. Can work together with other devices.	Can stop malicious packets.
Some malicious packets may pass through (for example, the first packet).	Malicious packets always can be dropped.

The basic purpose of any intrusion detection or prevention system is to produce an event based on something that is observed. When an event is triggered, the system is configured to produce an action (for example, create an alert or drop a packet).

Different types of events can be generated by an IPS or IDS:

- **False positive:** Happens when the system raises an event against legitimate traffic that is not malicious. The IPS or IDS administrator's goal is to minimize false positive events because these types of the events can cause unneeded investigation.
- **False negative:** Happens when the system fails to recognize a malicious event. This is usually very dangerous because it would allow malicious events to reach the target unnoticed.
- **True positive:** Refers to the correct behavior of the system when an actual threat has been detected.
- **True negative:** Refers to the correct behavior of the system when no event is triggered for legitimate traffic.

Another relevant distinction is done based on where an IDS or IPS is deployed. They can be installed on the network or on a host system.

Network-Based Intrusion Detection and Protection System

Network IDSs and IPSs (NIDSs and NIPSs) are specialized networking devices deployed at important network segments and have visibility on all traffic entering or exiting a segment. Network-based IDS and IPS use several detection methodologies, such as the following:

- Pattern matching and stateful pattern-matching recognition
- Protocol analysis

- Heuristic-based analysis
- Anomaly-based analysis
- Global threat correlation capabilities

NIDS and NIPS capabilities and detection methodologies are discussed in detail in Chapter 2.

Host-Based Intrusion Detection and Prevention

A host-based IDS (HIDS) or IPS (HIPS) is specialized software that interacts with the host operating system to provide access control and threat protection. In most cases, it also includes network detection and protection capabilities on the host network interface cards. Additionally, HIDS and HIPS are used for end-host security policy enforcement and for compliance and audit control.

In its basic capabilities, an HIDS or HIPS usually inserts itself between the application and the operating system kernel functionality and monitors the application calls to the kernel. It adopts most of the detection techniques mentioned for an NIDS/NIPS, such as anomaly based, heuristic based, and so on.

HIDS and HIPS are able to check for file integrity, registry monitoring, log analysis, and malware detection. The main advantages of HIDS compared to NIDS are that it will have visibility on all traffic on a specific host and can determine and alert on whether an attack was successful. It also works on attacks that employ encryption or fragmentation to evade network-based detection.

A disadvantage of a host-based system is that it has visibility only on traffic or attacks hitting the host and ignores anything else that happens in the network. Many commercial products, however, offer management control facilities and integration to network-based intrusion systems to overcome this limitation. Additionally, a host-based system adds latency on the CPU and packet processing on the host where it is installed. Most security architecture will adopt both network-based and host-based solutions.

Table 4-10 summarizes the differences between a network-based solution and a host-based solution. Later in Chapter 10, "Endpoints Security Technologies," we will provide additional details about the technologies to implement HIDS and HIPS.

Table 4-10 Network-Based Vs. Host-Based Detection/Prevention Systems

NIDS/NIPS	HIDS/HIPS
Software is deployed on a dedicated machine.	Software is installed on top of the host (end user) operating system (OS). It may require support for several OSs.
Easy to maintain and update.	May require an update of several endpoints.
Have visibility on all network traffic; therefore, can offer better event correlation.	Have visibility only on traffic hitting the host.
Can introduce delay due to packet processing.	Can slow down the operating system of the host.

NIDS/NIPS	HIDS/HIPS
Do not have visibility into whether an attack was successful.	Can verify whether an attack has been successful on a host.
Do not have visibility into encrypted packets.	Have visibility after encryption and can block an attack delivered via encrypted packets.
Can block an attack at the entry point.	The attacker is able to reach the target before being blocked.

Antivirus and Antimalware

The terms *antivirus* and *antimalware* are generally used interchangeably to indicate software that can be used to detect and prevent the installation of computer malware and in some cases quarantine affected computers or eradicate the malware and restore the operation of the system.

In its initial concept, antivirus was signature-based software that scanned a system or a downloaded file looking for a match on the signature database. The signature usually resided on the host itself, and the user was required to download new signatures to keep up the protection. most modern antimalware integrates the initial functionality of antivirus and expands it to cope with most modern attack techniques and malware.

The signature-based functionality has been kept and expanded with cloud-based monitoring, where the antimalware checks with a cloud-based system on the security reputation of a given file. Most antimalware also includes heuristic-based and anomaly-based detection, which are similar to the intrusion detection and prevention systems discussed in the previous section.

Similar to IDS and IPS, antimalware technologies can be implemented in two modes: host based and network based. Host-based and network-based antimalware share most of the same benefits and limitations of HIDS and NIDS. For example, network-based antimalware might not be able to determine whether malware actually reached an endpoint, whereas host-based antimalware might be able to block the malware only on the system where it is installed. In a well-planned security design, the two technologies are deployed together to maximize protection and apply the concept of layered security.

Network-based antimalware can be integrated with other functional devices such as email gateways, web proxies, or intrusion prevention systems. For example, Cisco ESA, Cisco WSA, and Cisco FirePower Next-Gen IPS all include antimalware features.

Cisco Anti-Malware Protection (AMP) comes as host-based antimalware, known as AMP for Endpoints, and network-based antimalware, known as AMP for Networks. Both use cloud-based signature detection, heuristic-based detection, and machine learning methodologies to protect the host.

An example of a network-based antivirus and antimalware solution that is integrated into other devices is the antivirus scanning offered on the Cisco Email Security Appliance (ESA), which integrates the antivirus engines from known antivirus vendors such as McAfee and Sophos. In the context of an email gateway, the antivirus engine is used to scan the content of email to prevent the delivery of a virus sent via email. Without this solution, the user would have to rely on the host-based antivirus solution. Refer to Chapter 2 for additional information about Cisco AMP and Cisco ESA. In Chapter 10, we will dig a bit more into antimalware technologies for endpoints.

Table 4-11 summarizes the differences between a network-based antimalware solution and a host-based one.

Table 4-11   Network-Based Vs. Host-Based Antivirus/Antimalware Systems

Network-based Antivirus/Antimalware	Host-based Antivirus/Antimalware
Software is deployed on a dedicated machine.	Software is installed on top of the host (end user) operating system (OS). It may require support for several OSs.
Easier to maintain and update.	May require updating of several endpoints.
Have visibility into all network traffic; therefore, can offer better event correlation.	Have visibility only into traffic hitting the host.
Can introduce delay due to packet processing.	Can slow down the operating system of the host.
Do not have visibility into whether an attack was successful.	Can verify whether an attack has been successful on a host.
Do not have visibility into encrypted packets.	Have visibility after encryption and can block an attack delivered via encrypted packets.
Can block an attack at the entry point.	The attacker is able to reach the target before being blocked.

Exam Preparation Tasks

Review All Key Topics

Review the most important topics in the chapter, noted with the Key Topic icon in the outer margin of the page. Table 4-12 lists these key topics and the page numbers on which each is found.

Table 4-12   Key Topics

Key Topic Element	Description	Page
List	Differences and definitions of subject, object, and access controls	190
List	Secure Identity attributes	191
Table 4-2	Authentication methods	192
Summary	Multifactor authentication	192
Table 4-3	Access control process phases (identification, authentication, authorization, and accounting)	194
List	Access Control Process key terminology	195
List	Security roles and responsibilities	198
List	Describe access control types based on purpose	199
List	Describe access control types based on preventive, detective, corrective, deterrent, recovery, and compensating capacities	200
Table 4-6	Discuss the different types of access control models	202
Table 4-7	Understand the advantages and disadvantages of access control models	202
List	Describe the main characteristics of DAC	203
List	Describe the main characteristics of MAC	204
List	Describe the main characteristics of RBAC	207
List	Describe the main characteristics of ABAC	208
Table 4-8	Discuss the differences between TACACS+ and RADIUS	215
List	Discuss the main characteristics of IPS/IDS	228
Table 4-9	Discuss the advantages and disadvantages between IPS and IDS	229
List	Properly categorize IPS/IDS events	229
List	Describe the main characteristics of network IDS/IPS	229
Summary	Describe the main characteristics of host-based IDS/IPS	230
Table 4-10	Discuss the differences between network- and host-based intrusion prevention systems	230
Table 4-11	Discuss the differences between network- and host-based antivirus	232

Complete Tables and Lists from Memory

Print a copy of Appendix B, "Memory Tables," (found on the book website), or at least the section for this chapter, and complete the tables and lists from memory. Appendix C, "Memory Tables Answer Key," also on the website, includes completed tables and lists to check your work.

Define Key Terms

Define the following key terms from this chapter, and check your answers in the glossary:

subject and object, access controls, identification, authentication, authorization, accounting, asset classification, information or data owner, discretionary access control, mandatory access control, role-based access control, attribute-based access control, network-based intrusion prevention, host-based intrusion prevention, antivirus, antimalware

Q&A

The answers to these questions appear in Appendix A, "Answers to the 'Do I Know This Already?' Quizzes and Q&A Questions." For more practice with exam format questions, use the exam engine on the website.

1. In which phase of access control is access granted to a resource with specific privileges?

   a. Identification

   b. Authentication

   c. Authorization

   d. Accounting

2. Which of the following are characteristics of a secure identity? (Select all that apply.)

   a. Uniqueness

   b. Nondescriptiveness

   c. Secured issuance

   d. Length

3. Which of the following authentication methods is considered strong?

   a. Authentication by knowledge

   b. Authentication by characteristic

   c. Authentication by ownership

   d. Any combination of these methods

4. Who assigns a security classification to an asset?

   a. Asset owner

   b. Senior management

   c. Asset custodian

   d. Security administrator

5. Which technique ensures protection against simple and noninvasive data-recovery techniques?

   a. Clearing

   b. Purging

   c. Destroying

   d. Erasing

6. Which type of control includes security training?

   a. Administrative

   b. Physical

   c. Logical

   d. None of the above

7. Which type of control best describes an IPS dropping a malicious packet?

   a. Preventive

   b. Corrective

   c. Compensating

   d. Recovery

8. Which type of controls best describe a fence?

   a. Administrative, preventive

   b. Administrative, logical

   c. Physical, deterrent

   d. Logical, compensating

9. What is included in a capability table?

   a. Several objects with user access rights

   b. Several subjects with user access rights

   c. Objects and subjects with their access rights

   d. Access rights

10. Where does the RADIUS exchange happen?

    a. Between the user and the network access server

    b. Between the network access server and the authentication server

    c. Between the user and the authentication server

    d. None of the above

11. Which AAA protocol allows for capabilities exchange?

    a. RADIUS

    b. TACACS+

    c. Diameter

    d. Kerberos

12. Which port access control technology allows dynamic authorization policy to be downloaded from the authentication server?

   a.   VLAN map

   b.   Port security

   c.   802.1x

   d.   MAC access list

13. Where is EAPoL traffic seen?

   a.   Between the supplicant and the authentication server

   b.   Between the supplicant and the authenticator

   c.   Between the authenticator and the authentication server

   d.   None of the above

14. What is the Security Group Tag Exchange (SXP) protocol used for?

   a.   To transmit SGT to the egress point for enforcement

   b.   To send SGT information to a hardware-capable Cisco TrustSec device for tagging

   c.   To send SGT information from the authentication server to the authenticator

   d.   To send SGT information to the supplicant

15. A host on an isolated port can communicate with which of the following?

   a.   A host on another isolated port

   b.   A host on a community port

   c.   A server on a community port

   d.   With the promiscuous port only

16. What is a disadvantage of using an IPS compared to an IDS?

   a.   It may add latency due to packet processing.

   b.   It is not able to drop a packet.

   c.   To stop an attack, it relies on external devices such as a firewall.

   d.   It is more difficult to maintain.

17. What is an advantage of network-based antimalware compared to a host-based solution?

   a.   It can block malware at the entry point.

   b.   It can check the integrity of a file on the host.

   c.   It can receive a signature and reputation from the cloud.

   d.   It can use a heuristic engine for malware detection.

18. According to the attribute-based access control (ABAC) model, what is the subject location considered?

   a.   Part of the environmental attributes

   b.   Part of the object attributes

   c.   Part of the access control attributes

   d.   None of the above

19. Which of the following access control models use security labels to make access decisions?

   a. Discretionary access control (DAC)

   b. Mandatory access control (MAC)

   c. Role-based access control (RBAC)

   d. Identity-based access control (IBAC)

20. What is one of the advantages of the mandatory access control (MAC) model?

   a. Complex to administer.

   b. Stricter control over the information access.

   c. Easy and scalable.

   d. The owner can decide whom to grant access to.

21. In a discretionary access control (DAC) model, who can authorize access to an object?

   a. The object owner

   b. The subject

   c. The system

   d. None of the above

References and Additional Reading

Harris and Maymi, *CISSP All-in-One Exam Guide, Seventh Edition*, McGraw-Hill Education (2016)

Darril Gibson, Mike Chapple, James M. Stewart, *CISSP (ISC)2 Certified Information Systems Security Professional Official Study Guide, Seventh* Edition, Sybex (2015)

Adam Gordon, *Official (ISC)2 Guide to the CISSP CBK*, Fourth Edition, Auerbach Publications (2015)

NIST SP 1800-3b -ATTRIBUTE BASED ACCESS CONTROL https://nccoe.nist.gov/sites/default/files/library/sp1800/abac-nist-sp1800-3b-draft.pdf

ANSI INCITS 359-2004 available at: http://profsandhu.com/journals/tissec/ANSI+INCITS+359-2004.pdf

NIST SP 800-18 Revision 1 - Guide for Developing Security Plans for Federal Information Systems - http://nvlpubs.nist.gov/nistpubs/Legacy/SP/nistspecialpublication800-18r1.pdf

DoD 5200.28-STD - DEPARTMENT OF DEFENSE TRUSTED COMPUTER SYSTEM EVALUATION CRITERIA - http://csrc.nist.gov/publications/history/dod85.pdf

Introduction to Computer Security Access Control and Authorization - http://www.ra.cs.uni-tuebingen.de/lehre/ss11/introsec/06-access.pdf

UNIX/Linux : Access control lists (ACLs) basics - http://thegeekdiary.com/unix-linux-access-control-lists-acls-basics/

NIST Role Based Access Control - Frequently Asked Questions - http://csrc.nist.gov/groups/SNS/rbac/faq.html

OASIS - eXtensible Access Control Markup Language (XACML) Version 3.0 - http://docs.oasis-open.org/xacml/3.0/xacml-3.0-core-spec-os-en.html

NIST Special Publication 800-162 - Guide to Attribute Based Access Control (ABAC) Definition and Considerations - http://nvlpubs.nist.gov/nistpubs/specialpublications/NIST.sp.800-162.pdf

Diameter Base Protocol - https://tools.ietf.org/html/rfc6733

Diameter Network Access Server Application - https://tools.ietf.org/html/rfc7155

Diameter Protocol Explained - http://diameter-protocol.blogspot.in/2012/10/diameter-network-access-server_8.html

Remote Authentication Dial In User Service (RADIUS) - https://tools.ietf.org/html/rfc2865

RADIUS Accounting - https://tools.ietf.org/html/rfc2866

The TACACS+ Protocol Version 1.78 - https://tools.ietf.org/html/draft-grant-tacacs-02

TACACS+ and RADIUS Comparison - http://www.cisco.com/c/en/us/support/docs/security-vpn/remote-authentication-dial-user-service-radius/13838-10.html#comp_udp_tcp

How Does RADIUS Work? - http://www.cisco.com/c/en/us/support/docs/security-vpn/remote-authentication-dial-user-service-radius/12433-32.html

Diameter Mobile IPv4 Application - https://tools.ietf.org/html/rfc4004

http://www.cisco.com/c/en/us/td/docs/switches/lan/catalyst6500/ios/12-2SX/configuration/guide/book/port_sec.html

Cisco TrustSec Switch Configuration Guide - http://www.cisco.com/c/en/us/td/docs/switches/lan/trustsec/configuration/guide/trustsec/arch_over.html

Andrew Hay, Daniel Cid, and Rory Bray, *OSSEC Host-Based Intrusion Detection Guide 1st edition*, Syngress (2008)

Wired 802.1X Deployment Guide - http://www.cisco.com/c/en/us/td/docs/solutions/Enterprise/Security/TrustSec_1-99/Dot1X_Deployment/Dot1x_Dep_Guide.html

Extensible Authentication Protocol (EAP) - https://tools.ietf.org/html/rfc3748

Configuring Private VLAN - Cisco Nexus 5000 Series NX-OS Software Configuration Guide - http://www.cisco.com/c/en/us/td/docs/switches/datacenter/nexus5000/sw/configuration/guide/cli/CLIConfigurationGuide/PrivateVLANs.html

This chapter covers the following topics:

- Introduction to identity and access management

- Enterprise Mobility management

- Events and Logs management

- Asset management

- Configuration and change management

- Vulnerability management

- Patch management

CHAPTER 5

Introduction to Security Operations Management

Security operations management is a key task within information security. Security professionals need to understand the foundation of the various management activities performed to enable effective security controls.

"Do I Know This Already?" Quiz

The "Do I Know This Already?" quiz helps you determine your level of knowledge on this chapter's topics before you begin. Table 5-1 details the major topics discussed in this chapter and their corresponding quiz sections. You can find the answers in Appendix A Answers to the "Do I Know This Already?" Quizzes and Q&A Questions.

Table 5-1 "Do I Know This Already?" Section-to-Question Mapping

Foundation Topics Section	Questions
Introduction to Identity and Access Management	1–5
Security Events and Log Management	6
Asset Management	7
Introduction to Enterprise Mobility Management	8–9
Configuration and Change Management	10–11
Vulnerability Management	12–13
Patch Management	14

1. In which phase of the identity and account lifecycle are the access rights assigned?

   a. Registration

   b. Access review

   c. Privileges provisioning

   d. Identity validation

2. What is an advantage of a system-generated password?

   a. It is easy to remember.

   b. It complies with the organization's password policy.

   c. It is very long.

   d. It includes numbers and letters.

3. Which of the following is a password system that's based on tokens and uses a challenge-response mechanism?

   a. Synchronous token system

   b. Asynchronous token system

   c. One-time token system

   d. Time-base token system

4. In the context of the X.500 standard, how is an entity uniquely identified within a directory information tree?

   a. By its distinguish name (DN)

   b. By its relative distinguish name (RDN)

   c. By its FQDN

   d. By its DNS name

5. What is the main advantage of single sign-on?

   a. The user authenticates with SSO and is authorized to access resources on multiple systems.

   b. The SSO server will automatically update the password on all systems.

   c. The SSO server is a single point of failure.

   d. SSO is an open source protocol.

6. What is the main advantage of an SIEM compared to a normal log collector?

   a. It provides log storage.

   b. It provides log correlation.

   c. It provides a GUI.

   d. It provides a log search functionality.

7. In asset management, what is used to create a list of assets owned by the organization?

   a. Asset inventory

   b. Asset acceptable use

   c. Asset disposal

   d. Asset category

8. Which of the following are advantages of a cloud-based mobile device manager compared to an on-premises model? (Select all that apply.)

   a. Higher control

   b. Flexibility

   c. Scalability

   d. Easier maintenance

9. Which of the following is a typical feature of a Mobile Device Management solution?

    a. Device jailbreak

    b. PIN lock enforcement

    c. Call forwarding

    d. Speed dial

10. In the context of configuration management, which of the following best defines a security baseline configuration?

    a. A configuration that has been formally reviewed and approved

    b. The default configuration from the device vendor

    c. A configuration that can be changed without a formal approval

    d. The initial server configuration

11. A change that is low risk and might not need to follow the full change management process is classified as which of the following?

    a. Standard

    b. Emergency

    c. Normal

    d. Controlled

12. In which type of penetration assessment is all information about the systems and network known?

    a. White box approach

    b. Black box approach

    c. Gray box approach

    d. Silver box approach

13. In which type of vulnerability disclosure approach is the vulnerability exploit not disclosed?

    a. Partial disclosure

    b. Full disclosure

    c. Responsible disclosure

    d. Initial disclosure

14. Which of the following are required before a patch can be applied? (Select all that apply.)

    a. Formally start a request for change.

    b. Perform a security assessment.

    c. Verify that the patch works correctly.

    d. Test the patch in the lab.

Foundation Topics

Introduction to Identity and Access Management

Identity and access management (IAM) has a very broad definition and in general includes all policies, processes, and technologies used to manage the identity, authentication, and authorization of an organization's resources. Several disciplines and technologies are usually covered under the umbrella of IAM: access controls (which were described in detail in Chapter 4, "Introduction to Access Controls"), password management, the IAM lifecycle, directory management, and single sign-on (SSO), among others. This section provides an introduction to the main topics of IAM. Although IAM is not currently part of the SECFND blueprint, understanding the main topics of IAM is important for any security professional.

Phases of the Identity and Access Lifecycle

As discussed in Chapter 4, one of the properties of a secure identity is the secure issuance of that identity. Additionally, access privileges should be associated with an identity, and the identity's validity and permissions should be constantly reviewed. At times, an identity and permissions should be revoked, and a process should be established to do this in a secure way. These processes are called identity proof and registration, account provisioning, access review, and access revocation. All of this goes under the umbrella of identity and account lifecycle management.

Figure 5-1 shows the four phases of the identity and access lifecycle, which are described in the list that follows:

- **Registration and identity validation:** A user provides information and registers for a digital identity. The issuer will verify the information and securely issue a unique and nondescriptive identity.

- **Privileges provisioning:** The resource owner authorizes the access rights to a specific account, and privileges are associated with it.

- **Access review:** Access rights are constantly reviewed to avoid privilege creep.

- **Access revocation:** Access to a given resource may be revoked due, for example, to account termination.

Let's review each of these phases in a bit more detail.

Figure 5-1 *Identity and Access Lifecycle*

Registration and Identity Validation

The first step in a secure identity lifecycle is the user registration. During this phase, the user registers his data to request an identity. The second step of this process would be to verify the identity. This can be done in several ways, depending on the privileges associated with that identity. For example, starting the identity validation for a system administrator may require additional steps compared to a normal user. During this phase, a user could be asked to provide a copy of his identity card, HR could perform a background check, proof of a specific clearance level could be requested, and so on. Finally, the identity assigned will be unique and nondescriptive.

Privileges Provisioning

Once an identity has been assigned, privileges or access rights should be provisioned to that account. The privileges should be assigned by using the main security principles discussed in previous chapters of this book—that is, least privileges, separation of duty, and need to know. In general, privileges will be assigned in accordance with the organization's security policy.

Depending on the access control model applied, the process might need to ensure that an authorization request is sent to the resource owner and that privileges are not assigned until the access has been approved. A temporal limit should also be applied to the privileges assigned.

For highly sensitive privileges, a more formal process might need to be established. For example, users may be asked to sign a specific nondisclosure agreement. Provisioning could also apply to existing accounts requesting access to additional resources, for example, due to a job change within the organization.

> **NOTE** The registration, identity validation, and privileges provisioning phases are grouped together under the account provisioning step.

Access Review

Access rights and privileges associated with an account should be constantly reviewed to ensure that there is no violation to the organization's security policy. The process should ensure a regular review of privileges as well as an event-driven review, such as when a user changes roles.

One of the issues in large organizations is the unneeded assignment of privileges, which brings up the *privileges creep* issue discussed in Chapter 4.

Access Revocation

When an employee changes jobs or leaves the organization, there may be a need to partially or completely revoke his associated access rights. A formal process should be established to make sure this is done properly. In some cases, privileges may need to be revoked before the actual event (for example, an involuntarily job termination) to ensure the employee does not cause damage to the organization before officially leaving.

Password Management

A password is a combination of characters and numbers that should be kept secret, and it is the most common implementation of the authentication-by-knowledge concept described in Chapter 4. Password authentication is usually considered one of the weakest authentication methods, yet it's one of the most used due to its implementation simplicity.

The weakness of password authentication is mainly due to the human factor rather than technological issues. Here's a list of some typical issues that lead to increased risk when using passwords as the sole authentication method:

- Users tend to use the same password across all systems and accounts.
- Users tend to write down passwords (for example, on a sticky note).
- Users tend to use simple passwords (for example, their child's name or 12345).
- Users tend to use the default system password given at system installation.

Password management includes all processes, policies, and technologies that help an organization and its users to improve the security of their password-authentication systems. Password management includes policies and technologies around password creation, password storage, and password reset, as described in the sections that follow.

Password Creation

One of the most important steps in password management is creating a standard to define secure password requirements. This needs to be applied across the organization and for all systems. An organization should take into consideration the following requirements when building policies, processes, and standards around password creation:

- **Strength:** Establishing a policy about the password strength is very important to reduce the risk of users setting up weak passwords, which are easier to compromise via brute-force attacks, for example. Complexity and length requirements contribute to increasing the strength of a password. Complexity is usually enforced by asking the user to use a combination of characters, numbers, and symbols. Password length increases the difficulty of cracking a password. The shorter the password, the higher the risk. The strength and entropy of a password are the main factors used to measure the quality of a password. NIST SP 800-63 provides more information about password entropy and how passwords can be used in electronic authentication systems.

- **Age:** The age of a password (or better, the maximum age of a password) is an important attribute. Changing a password frequently is considered a best practice. The longer a password is used, the higher the risk of password compromise. The password requirement policy should dictate the maximum age of a password. Changing passwords frequently is better for security; however, it creates additional administrative overhead for users and systems.

- **Reusability:** Reusing the same password or part of it also increases the risk of password compromise. It is common practice to change just the last digit of a password or to use only two passwords repeatedly and just swap them when the time comes. Policy around reusability should ensure that passwords are not reused within a given amount of time.

The policies around the creation of a password should also specify whether the password is created by the user or is automatically generated by the system. A hybrid approach would use both methods by combining a user-chosen password with a system-generated one. Table 5-2 summarizes the pros and cons of each of these methods.

Table 5-2 Summary of Password-Generation Methods

Method	Description	Pros	Cons
User-generated password	The user generates the password himself.	Simple to remember.	Usually leads to an easily guessable password. Users may reuse the same password on multiple systems.
System-generated password	The password is generated by the system.	Strong password. Compliant with security policy.	Difficult to remember. Users tend to write down the password, thus defeating the purpose.
OTP and token	The password is generated by an external entity (such as hardware or software) that is synchronized with internal resources. The device is usually protected by a user-generated password.	Users do not need to remember a difficult password.	More complicated infrastructure. It makes use of hardware or software to generate the token, which increases maintenance and deployment costs.

User-Generated Password

Using passwords created by the users is the easiest method but is the riskiest from a security point of view. Users tend to use easy passwords, reuse the same passwords, and, in some cases, disclose password to others. Enforcing password requirements helps reduce the risk.

System-Generated Password

Using system-generated passwords is a stronger method than using user-created passwords because the password requirements are directly enforced. In most cases, the system can create the passwords by using a random password generator, which ensures higher entropy and is usually more difficult to compromise. The drawback of this method is that these types of passwords are more difficult to remember. Users, therefore, tend to write them down, which defeats the purpose of having a secure password.

One-Time Password and Token

A one-time password is a randomly generated password that can be used only once. One of the most used methods for implementing one-time password authentication is through a token device. The token device can be either a hardware device or implemented in software (soft-token), and it is basically a one-time password generator. For example, most of the authentication systems for online banking use token technologies.

A token device can work in two ways: synchronously and asynchronously. In most cases, the token generator is protected through a password or PIN. In synchronous token authentication, the token generator is synchronized with the authenticator server (for example, via time synchronization). When a user needs to authenticate, she will use the token to generate a one-time password that's be used to authenticate to the system. In an asynchronous token system, the authenticator will produce a challenge. The user inputs the challenge in the token generator, which will use that information to generate the one-time password.

Password Storage and Transmission

Password management should ensure that policies and controls are in place to securely store passwords and that passwords are securely transmitted when used. Encrypting files that include passwords, storing hashes of the passwords instead of the passwords themselves, and implementing tight access controls on systems storing passwords are all methods that contribute to the secure storage of passwords. In addition, all external means of accessing passwords, such as a removable hard drive used to store passwords and even any documents that include passwords, should be appropriately secured.

Because passwords are used in the authentication process, they need to be transmitted over the network (for example, over the Internet). Policies should be in place to ensure passwords are protected while in transit. Network segmentation and encryption usually help with increasing the secure transmission of passwords. For example, HTTP can be used for normal website browsing, but HTTPS or an equivalent secure protocol should be required when performing authentication.

Password Reset

Password management should include policies and technologies to allow the resetting of passwords in a secure way. If an attacker is able to reset a password, all the rest of the things discussed so far are meaningless. Password reset is usually a task assigned to help desk personnel. In a large organization, with many users, accounts, and systems, the administration around resetting passwords can become cumbersome. Many organizations nowadays offer their employees and affiliates automatic ways to reset their passwords. This is usually done by requiring the user to provide an additional form of authentication (for example, by answering a security questionnaire) or token. Alternatively, a reset link can be sent to the user's personal email address.

Password Synchronization

In large organizations, having to create an account on each system and for each user can be complicated both for the system administrator and the final user. For example, users might need to remember several passwords, depending on the systems they access, which in turn may foster the bad habit of writing down passwords on sticky notes. This can also cause increased calls to the help desk due to forgotten passwords. Additionally, when passwords need to be changed, due to a maximum-age password policy, for example, the user would need to change his password for each system.

Password synchronization technologies allow the user to set his password once, and then the management system will automatically push the password to all systems that are part of the synchronization process. This largely reduces the administration overhead around password management. The drawback of this method, however, is that once the password is compromised, the attacker is able to access all the systems. The organization should evaluate this risk as part of its security risk management.

Figure 5-2 shows an example of a password synchronization system. The user can change his password on the password synchronization manager, and the password will be updated on all the systems that are part of the synchronization domain.

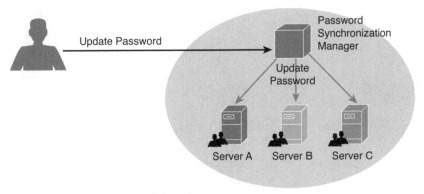

Figure 5-2 *Password Synchronization System*

Directory Management

Directories are repositories used by an organization to store information about users, systems, networks, and so on. Information stored in directories can be used for the purposes of identifying and authenticating users, as well applying security policies and authorization.

Using directory services for IAM offers a centralized place where all applications and processes can connect to get information about the organization's resources. This reduces the overhead of having to replicate information across all systems. The disadvantage is that not all the systems are able to interface with directory services, and the directory server becomes a single point of failure for the IAM system. Replicated and distributed directory services may help overcoming these disadvantages.

One of the most known implementations of directory services is the ITU-T X.500 series, which is a collection of standards that includes information on directory organization and the protocols to access the information within directories. In this implementation, the directory is organized in a hierarchical way. The data is represented in a directory information tree (DIT), and the information is stored in a directory information base (DIB).

Each entity is uniquely identified by its distinguish name (DN), which is obtained by attaching to the relative distinguish name (RDN) of the specific object the DN of the parent entity. Each entity contains several attributes. Here are some examples of attributes described in the X.500 schema:

- Country (C)
- Organization (O)
- Organization unit (OU)
- Common name (CN)
- Location (L)

Figure 5-3 shows an example of a hypothetical DIT.

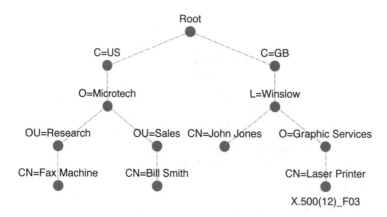

Figure 5-3 *Directory Information Tree (DIT) Example*

Figure 5-4 shows the difference between an RDN and a DN. For example, at the OU level, the RDN is OU=Security, whereas the DN includes all of the RDN up to the ROOT, so it is C=US, O=Cisco, OU=Security.

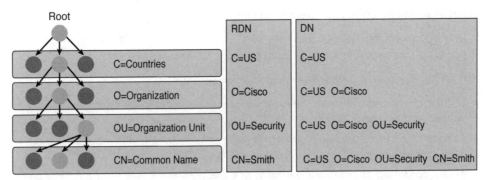

Figure 5-4 *Comparing Distinguish Name (DN) and Relative Distinguish Name (RDN)*

In the X.500 standards, the directory service agent (DSA) is the process that provides access to the information in the DIB and is where the directory user agent (DUA) component connects to request services. In a distributed directory environment, multiple DSAs exist that can interact with each other to provide services to the DUA.

The Directory Access Protocol (DAP) is used between a DUA and DSA to interrogate and modify the contents of the directories. Other protocols are part of the standard, such as the Directory System Protocol (DSP), which is used between two DSAs, the Directory Information Shadowing Protocol (DISP), and the Directory Operational Binding Management Protocol (DOP).

Figure 5-5 shows an example of interaction between a DUA and a DSA. The DUA uses DAP to query the directory. DISP is used between two DSAs.

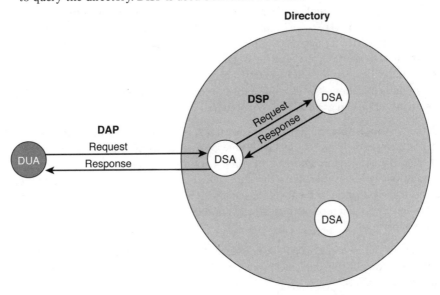

Figure 5-5 *Directory User Agent (DUA) and Directory Service Agent (DSA) Interaction*

If you think that this is too complex, you are not the only one. Due to the complexity of the X.500 directory, a lightweight version called the Lightweight Directory Access Protocol (LDAP) was created. As with X.500, in an LDAP system, directories and systems are organized hierarchically and use the same naming convention (that is, the distinguished name of an object is used to identify an object within the information tree).

In an LDAP system, the DUA is called the LDAP client, while the DSA is called the LDAP server. LDAP can coexist with and be used to query X.500-based systems.

Here are the key concepts related to directory management:

- *Directories* are repositories of information about an organization's resources, including people, hardware, and software.

- *Directory services* uses directories to provide an organization with a way to manage identity, authentication, and authorization services.

- *ITU-T X.500* is a collection of standards that specify how to implement directory services.

- *LDAP* is based on X.500 and maintains the same directory structure and definition. It simplifies the directory queries and has been designed to work with the TCP/IP stack.

Single Sign-On

The idea behind single sign-on (SSO) is that a user needs to authenticate with only one system and only once to get access to the organization's resources. This concept is different from using the same password on all systems, like in the password synchronization systems described in the Password Management section of this chapter. In that case, the user needs to authenticate against each of the systems but provides the same password. In an SSO system, typically the authentication is done by providing proof that the user has been authenticated. This avoids the need to input the credentials multiple times.

Figure 5-6 shows a simple example of SSO. A user is accessing resources on Server A; for example, the user sends an HTTP GET request for a web page (step 1). SSO is used to provide authentication service for Server A. When Server A receives the request for a web page, it redirects the user to the SSO server of the organization for authentication (steps 2 and 3). The user will authenticate to the SSO server, which will redirect the user back to Server A with proof of authentication—for example a token (steps 4 and 5). Server A will validate the proof of authentication and grant access to resources.

Although the concept is very simple, its implementation is very difficult due to the high diversity of systems usually present in a large enterprise. Effectively, organizations implementing SSO are usually implementing it only in part of the network on a subset of their systems. Additionally, SSO suffers from the same limitations as other centralized authentication systems: namely, that the authentication server can become a single point of failure and that once an account is compromised, an attacker is able to access all the systems for which that user has access rights.

Directory systems (for example, LDAP-based systems) are usually considered a type of SSO implementation. Other known implementations of SSO are Kerberos, SESAME, OpenID, and OAuth, to name a few.

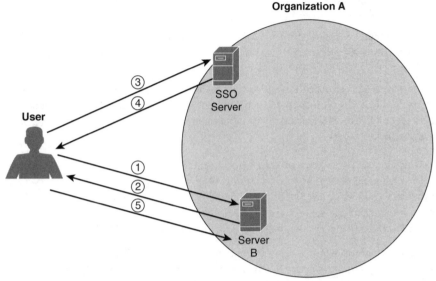

Figure 5-6 *Single Sign-On (SSO) System*

Here are the key concepts related to SSO, all of which are described in more detail in the sections that follow. Again, these topics are not part of the blueprint; however, having a basic understanding of them would be beneficial in your work as a security professional.

- *Single sign-on* is an authentication method in which a user authenticates to an authentication server, also called an SSO server. The SSO server provides proof of authentication, which can be used to access other systems within the organization without the need to authenticate again.
- *Kerberos* is a protocol used to implement SSO. It uses the notion of ticket to contain the proof of authentication.
- *Federated SSO* extends the concept of SSO to multiple organizations. A user can authenticate with an SSO server within one organization, and the proof of authentication will be valid to authenticate on a system within a different organization.
- *SAML, OAuth,* and *OpenID Connect* are known frameworks used to implement federated SSO.

Kerberos

Kerberos is one well-known authentication protocol that provides single sign-on capabilities. It was proposed by MIT and in its last version (v5) is described in RFC 4120. Here are the main entities or objects involved in the Kerberos protocol:

- **Key Distribution Server (KDC):** The main component of a Kerberos system. It includes three components, the *authentication server (AS)*, which provides the initial authentication ticket; the *ticket-granting service (TGS)*, which provides ticket-granting ticket (TGT), also called the service ticket; and the *Kerberos database*, which includes all the information about users, hosts, servers (principals), and so on.
- **Principal:** A client or server entity that participates in the Kerberos realm.

- **Ticket:** A record that proves the identity of the client when authenticating to a server. This needs to be used together with an authenticator.

- **Authenticator:** Further proof of identity that is used to reduce the likelihood of a replay-based attack. The authenticator message includes information about the principal and a session key.

- **Realm:** Identifies an authentication and authorization domain where the authentication service has authority to provide its service. Authentication of a principal can also happen outside a realm, if there is a trusted relation between realms. This is called *cross-realm authentication*.

In its basic implementation, when a principal (for example, a user) requests access to another principal (for example, a server), it sends a request (AS_REQ) to the authentication server (AS) that includes its identity and the principal identifier of the server it wants to access. The AS checks that the client and server exist in the Kerberos database, generates a session key, and creates a response (AS_RES) that includes a ticket-granting ticket (TGT).

At this point, the client principal is ready to send a request (TGS_REQ) to the TGS to obtain a session ticket. This request includes the TGT and the authenticator. The TGS verifies that the principal server exists in the Kerberos database and then issues a service ticket that is then sent with its reply (TGS_REP) to the client principal that also includes a session key. The client principal can now request access to the server principal (AP_REQ), which includes the service ticket and the new authenticator built based on the new session key. The server may reply with an AP_REP that has information proving the server's identity, if mutual authentication is required.

Figure 5-7 shows an example of authentication and authorization using Kerberos.

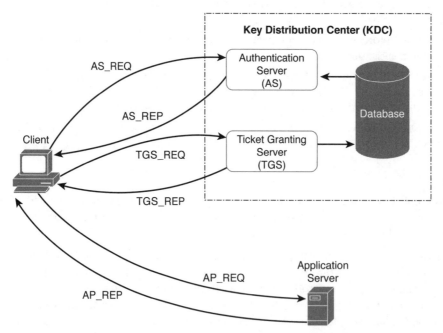

Figure 5-7 *Authentication and Authorization Using Kerberos*

Federated SSO

A further evolution of the SSO model within a single organization is a model where a user can authenticate once and then have access to resources across multiple organizations not managed under the same IAM system. A *federation* is a collection of distinct organizations that agree to allow users to use one set of credential for authentication and authorization purposes. The identity used by the users across organizations is called a *federated identity*.

At the base of the federation is the concept of *trust* between the organization entities. In fact, each organization should trust that the authentication and authorization process is carried out in a secure way by the party providing that service.

The concept of federation has been further formalized by introducing the following concepts:

- **Principal:** The end user who requests service from a service provider and whose identity can be authenticated.

- **Service provider (SP):** In some cases also called the *relying party (RP)*. Defined as the system entity that provides service to the principal or other entities in the federation.

- **Identity provider (IdP):** The service provider that also manages the authentication and authorization process on behalf of the other systems in the federation.

- **Assertion:** The information produced by the authentication authority (for example, the IdP). It is usually provided to the SP to allow the user to access its resource. The assertion proves that the user has been authenticated and includes additional user attributes and authorization directives.

In a federation context, an SP can rely on multiple IdPs, and one IdP can serve multiple SPs. When a user wants to access resources with one SP, the SP determines which IdP to use to authenticate the user. The choice happens based on the user identifier or preference (for example, the user may indicate a specific IdP), or the choice happens based on the domain name associated with the user email address. This process is called *discover of identity*.

The SP will then redirect the user to the IdP for the authentication process. Once the user is authenticated, the IdP will generate an assertion that proves the identity and includes additional info about the user and authorization information.

Figure 5-8 shows a similar example as Figure 5-6; however, in this case, the user will authenticate with an SSO server that is in a different organization than the one in Server B, which will provide service to the user it belongs to. In this case, the SSO server acts as the IdP, and Server B is the SP.

As in Figure 5-6, the user sends a request to Server B (step 1), which redirects the user to the SSO server for authentication (steps 2 and 3). The user then authenticates with the SSO server and receives proof of authentication, the assertion, which is provided to Server B (steps 4 and 5). Server B, after verifying the information in the assertion, grants access to resources.

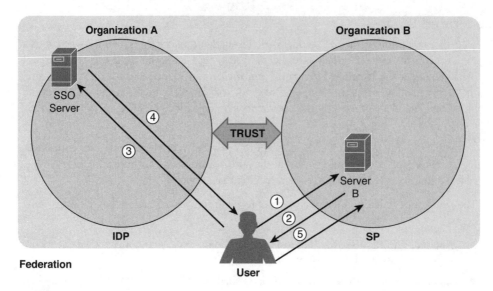

Figure 5-8 *Federated SSO*

Several protocols and frameworks are currently used to implement SSO and identity federation: SAML, OAuth2, and OpenID Connect are popular examples.

Security Assertion Markup Language

The OASIS Security Assertion Markup Language (SAML) standard is currently the most used standard for implementing federated identity processes. SAML is an XML-based framework that describes the use and exchange of SAML assertions in a secure way between business entities. The standard describes the syntax and rules to request, create, use, and exchange these assertions.

The SAML process involves a minimum two entities, the *SAML assertion party* (or *SAML authority*), which is the entity that produces the assertion, and the *SAML relying party*, which is the entity that uses the assertion to make access decisions.

An assertion is the communication of security information about a subject (also called a principal) in the form of a statement. The basic building blocks of SAML are the SAML assertion, SAML protocol, SAML binding, and SAML profile. SAML assertions can contain the following information:

- **Authentication statement:** Includes the result of the authentication and additional info such as the authentication method, timestamps, and so on
- **Attribute statement:** Includes attributes about the principal
- **Authorization statement:** Includes information on what the principal is allowed to do

An example of an assertion would be User A, who has the email address usera@domain.com authenticated via username and password, is a platinum member and is authorized for a 10% discount.

SAML protocols define the protocols used to transfer assertion messages. SAML bindings include information on how lower-level protocols (such as HTTP or SOAP) transport SAML protocol messages. SAML profiles are specific combinations of assertions, protocols, and bindings for specific use cases. Examples of profiles include Web Browser Single Sign-On, Identity Provider Discovery, and Enhanced Client and Proxy (ECP).

Figure 5-9 shows the SAML building blocks.

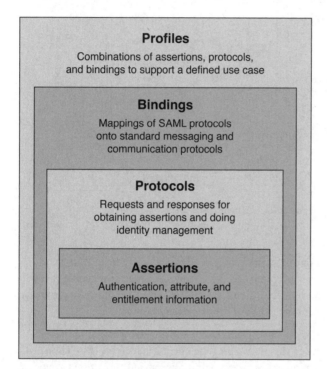

Figure 5-9   *SAML Building Blocks*

SAML also defines the concepts of identity provider and service provider.

SAML can work in two different ways:

- In IdP initiated mode, a user is already authenticated on the IdP and requests a service from the SP (for example, by clicking a link on the IdP website). The IdP will build an assertion that is sent to the SP within the user request to the SP itself.

  For example, a user who is authenticated on an airline website decides to book a rental car by clicking a link on the airline website. The airline IAM system, which assumes the role of an IdP, will send assertion information about the user to the rental car IAM, which in turn will authenticate the user and provide access rights based on the information in the assertion.

- In SP initiated mode, a user initiates an access request to some resource on the SP. Because the federated identity is managed by a different IdP, the SP redirects the user to log in at the IdP. After the login, the IdP will send a SAML assertion back to the SP.

Figure 5-10 shows an example of IdP initiated mode (on the right) and SP initiated mode (on the left).

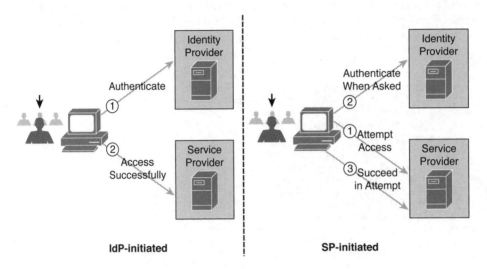

Figure 5-10 *SAML IdP Initiated Mode and SP Initiated Mode*

OAuth

OAuth is a framework that provides authorization to a third-party entity (for example, a smartphone application) to access resources hosted on a resource server. In a classic client-server authorization framework, the third-party entity would receive the credentials from the resource owner (user) and then access the resource on the resource server.

The main issue OAuth resolves is providing the third-party entity authorization to access restricted resources without passing to this third party the client credentials. Instead of getting the user credentials, the entity requesting access will receive an authorization token that includes authorization information, such as scope, duration, and so on, and that will be used to request access to a resource hosted by the resource server. The OAuth schema is usually called *delegation of access*.

OAuth2, defined in RFC 6749, includes four main roles:

- **Resource owner:** The party that owns the resource (for example, a user) and that will grant authorization to access some of its resources
- **Client:** The party that requires access to a specific resource
- **Resource server:** The party that hosts or stores the resource
- **Authorization server:** The party that provides an authorization token

In the basic scenario, the authorization is done with six messages:

1. The client sends an authorization request to the resource owner or indirectly to the authorization server.

2. The resource owner (or the authorization server on behalf of the resource owner) sends an authorization grant to the client.

3. The client sends the authorization grant to the authorization server as proof that authorization was granted.

4. The authorization server authenticates the client and sends an access token.

5. The client sends the access token to the resource server as proof of authentication and authorization to access the resources.

6. The resource server validates the access token and grants access.

For example, a user (the resource owner) may grant access to her personal photos hosted at some online storage provider (the resource server) to an application on her mobile phone (the client) without directly providing her credentials to the application but instead by directly authenticating with the authorization server (in this case, also the online storage provider) and authorizing the access.

Figure 5-11 shows an example of an OAuth exchange.

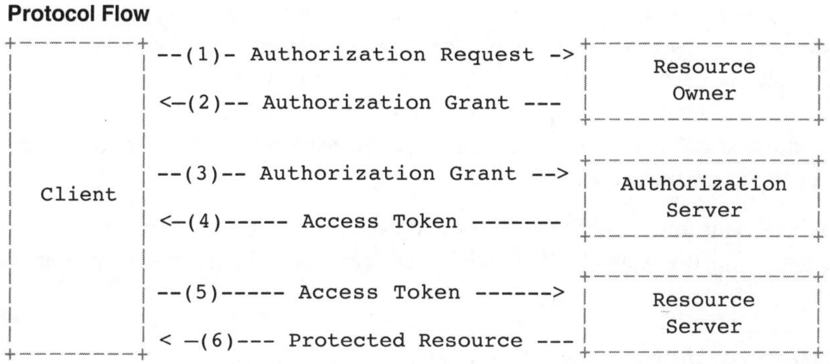

Protocol Flow

```
+---------+                               +----------------------+
|         |  --(1)- Authorization Request ->|                      |
|         |                               |     Resource         |
|         |  <-(2)-- Authorization Grant ---|     Owner            |
|         |                               +----------------------+
|         |
|         |                               +----------------------+
|         |  --(3)-- Authorization Grant -->|                     |
| Client  |                               |   Authorization      |
|         |  <-(4)----- Access Token -------|     Server           |
|         |                               +----------------------+
|         |
|         |                               +----------------------+
|         |  --(5)----- Access Token ------>|                     |
|         |                               |     Resource         |
|         |  < -(6)--- Protected Resource ---|    Server           |
+---------+                               +----------------------+
```

Figure 5-11 *OAuth Exchange*

OpenID Connect

OpenID has been a very popular SSO protocol for federated systems for quite some time. In the 2.0 version, the authentication and authorization process is similar to the one in SAML. OpenID also defines an IdP, called the OpenID provider (OP), and a relying party (RP), which is the entity that holds the resource the user wants to access. In OpenID, a user is free to select an OP of her choice, and the initial identity is provided in a form of a URL.

Version 2.0 has been superseded by OpenID Connect. This version drops the authorization functionality present in version 2.0 and is designed to work with OAuth 2.0 for deployments. In practice, OpenID Connect operates as an authentication profile for OAuth. In OpenID Connect, when a user tries to access resources on an RP, the RP will send an authentication request to the OP for that user. In practice, this is an OAuth 2.0 authorization request to access the user's identity at the OP. The authentication request can be of three types:

■ Authorization code flow (the most commonly used)

■ Implicit flow

■ Hybrid flow

In an authorization code flow scenario, once the user authenticates with the OP, the OP will ask the user for consent and issue an authorization code that the user will then send to the RP. The RP will use this code to request an ID token and access token from the OP, which is the way the OP provides assertion to the RP.

Security Events and Logs Management

Systems within an IT infrastructure are often configured to generate and send information every time a specific event happens. An event, as described in NIST SP 800-61r2, is any observable occurrence in a system or network, whereas a security incident is an event that violates the security policy of an organization. One important task of a security operation center analyst is to determine when an event constitutes a security incident. An event log (or simply a log) is a formal record of an event and includes information about the event itself. For example, a log may contain a timestamp, an IP address, an error code, and so on.

Event management includes administrative, physical, and technical controls that allow for the proper collection, storage, and analysis of events. Event management plays a key role in information security because it allows for the detection and investigation of a real-time attack, enables incident response, and allows for statistical and trending reporting. If an organization lacks information about past events and logs, this may reduce its ability to investigate incidents and perform a root-cause analysis.

An additional important function of monitoring and event management is compliance. Many compliance frameworks (for example, ISO and PCI DSS) mandate log management controls and practices.

Logs Collection, Analysis, and Disposal

One of the most basic tasks of event management is log collection. Many systems in the IT infrastructure are in fact capable of generating logs and sending them to a remote system that will store them. Log storage is a critical task for maintaining log confidentiality and integrity. Confidentiality is needed because the logs may contain sensitive information. In some scenarios, logs may need to be used as evidence in court or as part of an incident response. The integrity of the logs is fundamental for them to be used as evidence and for attribution.

The facilities used to store logs need to be protected against unauthorized access, and the logs' integrity should be maintained. Enough storage should be allocated so that the logs are not missed due to lack of storage.

The information collected via logs usually includes, but is not limited to, the following:

- User ID
- System activities
- Timestamps
- Successful or unsuccessful access attempts
- Configuration changes
- Network addresses and protocols
- File access activities

Different systems may send their log messages in various formats, depending on their implementation. According to NIST SP 800-92, three categories of logs are of interest for security professionals:

- **Logs generated by security software:** This includes logs and alerts generated by the following software and devices:
  - Antivirus/antimalware
  - IPS and IDS
  - Web proxies
  - Remote access software
  - Vulnerability management software
  - Authentication servers
  - Infrastructure devices (including firewalls, routers, switches, and wireless access points)
- **Logs generated by the operating system:** This includes the following:
  - System events
  - Audit records
- **Logs generated by applications:** This includes the following:
  - Connection and session information
  - Usage information
  - Significant operational action

Once collected, the logs need to be analyzed and reviewed to detect security incidents and to make sure security controls are working properly. This is not a trivial task because the analyst may need to analyze an enormous amount of data. It is important for the security professional to understand which logs are relevant and should be collected for the purpose of security administration, event, and incident management.

Systems that are used to collect and store the logs usually offer a management interface through which the security analyst is able to view the logs in an organized way, filter out unnecessary entries, and produce historical reporting. At some point, logs may not be needed anymore. The determination of how long a log needs to be kept is included in the log retention policy. Logs can be deleted from the system or archived in separate systems.

Syslog

One of the most used protocols for event notification is syslog, which is defined in RFC 5424. The syslog protocol specifies three main entities:

- **Originator:** The entity that generates a syslog message (for example, a router)
- **Collector:** The entity that receives information about an event in syslog format (for example, a syslog server)
- **Relay:** An entity that can receive messages from originators and forward them to other relays or collectors

The syslog protocol is designed not to provide acknowledgement and can use both UDP on port 514 and TCP on port 514 as transport methods. Security at the transport layer can be added by using DTLS or TLS. Two additional concepts that are not part of the RFC but are commonly used are the facility code and the severity code. The facility code indicates the system, process, or application that generated the syslog. The syslog facilities are detailed in Table 5-3.

Table 5-3   Syslog Facilities

Numerical Code	Facility
0	Kernel messages
1	User-level messages
2	Mail system
3	System daemons
4	Security/authorization messages
5	Messages generated internally by Syslogd
6	Line printer subsystem
7	Network news subsystem
8	UUCP subsystem
9	Clock daemon
10	Security/authorization messages
11	FTP daemon
12	NTP subsystem
13	Log audit
14	Log alert
15	Clock daemon
16	Local use 0 (local0)
17	Local use 1 (local1)
18	Local use 2 (local2)

Numerical Code	Facility
19	Local use 3 (local3)
20	Local use 4 (local4)
21	Local use 5 (local5)
22	Local use 6 (local6)
23	Local use 7 (local7)

The syslog server can use the facility number to classify the syslog message. Usually applications that do not map to a predefined facility can use any of the local use facilities (local0 through local7). For example, Cisco ASA allows the user to set the facility number, meaning the user can specify which local facility to use. The default facility used by Cisco ASA is 20 (local4).

The severity code represents the severity of the message. Table 5-4 shows the severity code associated to each severity level.

Table 5-4   Severity Codes

Integer	Severity
0	Emergency: System is unusable.
1	Alert: Action must be taken immediately.
2	Critical: Critical conditions.
3	Error: Error conditions.
4	Warning: Warning conditions.
5	Notice: Normal but significant condition.
6	Informational: Informational messages.
7	Debug: Debug-level messages.

The header of a syslog message contains, among other things, the following important information:

- **Priority (PRI):** The priority is obtained by combining the numerical code of the facility and the severity. The formula to obtain the PRI is as follows:

  Facility × 8 + Severity

  For example, a message with a facility code of security/authorization messages (code 4) and a severity code of critical (code 2) will receive a PRI of 34.

- **Timestamp**
- **Hostname**
- **Application name**
- **Process ID**

The message carried within the syslog can be any text message. The following shows an example of a syslog message generated from a Cisco ASA following the detection of a malicious pattern in an SMTP message:

```
Aug 19 2016 18:13:29 ASACCNA : %ASA-2-108003: Terminating ESMTP/SMTP connection;
malicious pattern detected in the mail address from
source_interface:source_address/source_port to
dest_interface:dest_address/dset_port. Data: string
```

The message starts with the timestamp "Aug 19 2016 18:13:29" and the hostname. Both are not sent by default but can be configured. Also, "%ASA-2-108003" specifies the syslog severity (2) and a specific message identifier (108003). The last part includes the text message with the information about the event.

Security Information and Event Manager

The Security Information and Event Manager (SIEM) is a specialized device or software for security event management. It typically allows for the following functions:

- **Log collection:** This includes receiving information from devices with multiple protocols and formats, storing the logs, and providing historical reporting and log filtering.

- **Log normalization:** This function extracts relevant attributes from logs received in different formats and stores them in a common data model or template. This allows for faster event classification and operations. Non-normalized logs are usually kept for archive, historical, and forensic purposes.

- **Log aggregation:** This function aggregates information based on common information and reduces duplicates.

- **Log correlation:** This is probably one of most important functions of an SIEM. It refers to the ability of the system to associate events gathered by various systems, in different formats and at different times, and create a single actionable event for the security analyst or investigator. Often the quality of an SIEM is related to the quality of its correlation engine.

- **Reporting:** Event visibility is also a key functionality of an SIEM. Reporting capabilities usually include real-time monitoring and historical base reports.

Most modern SIEMs also integrate with other information systems to gather additional contextual information to feed the correlation engine. For example, they can integrate with an identity management system to get contextual information about users or with NetFlow collectors to get additional flow-based information. Respectively, Cisco ISE and Cisco Stealthwatch are examples of an identity management system and flow collector that are able to integrate with most of the SIEM systems.

Several commercial SIEM systems are available. Cisco partners with several vendors that offer seamless integration with Cisco products. Here's a list of some SIEM solutions from Cisco partners:

- HP ArcSight
- BlackStratus

- EiQ Networks
- Hawk Network Defense
- Log Rhythm
- NetIQ
- IBM QRadar
- RSA
- Splunk
- Symantec
- TrustWave

Figure 5-12 shows a typical deployment of an SIEM and summarizes the SIEM key capabilities.

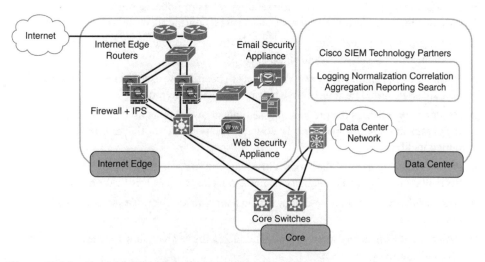

Figure 5-12   *Typical SIEM Deployment/Key Capabilities*

The following summarizes the key concepts of log collection and SIEM:

- *Logs collection* is the process of collecting and organizing logs for analysis. A log collector is software that is able to receive logs from multiple sources and in some cases offers storage capabilities and log analysis functionality.
- *SIEM* is a specialized device or software for security event management. It increases the normal log collector functionality by providing log collection, normalization, aggregation, correlation, and reporting capabilities.

Assets Management

Assets are key components of an organization and, as such, should be protected. An asset can be defined as anything that has value for the organization. In simple terms, an asset can be any organization resource, including personnel, hardware, software, building, and data.

Assets should be protected appropriately against unauthorized access and from any threat that could compromise the confidentiality, integrity, and availability. *Asset management* is a broad term that defines procedures and policies to manage an organization's assets throughout their lifecycle. In information security, asset management refers to administrative, physical, and technical control to protect assets within an organization.

ISO 27001 mandates several controls that are applicable to asset management. In the context of information security, asset management usually includes policies and processes around assets inventory, ownership of the assets, acceptable use and return policies, assets classification, asset labeling, asset and information handling, and media management.

A high-level view of asset management in the context of access controls that was provided in Chapter 4.

The following list summarizes the key concepts and phases of secure assets management:

- *Assets management* in information security refers to policies, processes, and technologies to manage and protect an organization's assets during their lifecycle.

- *Assets inventory* deals with collecting and storing information about assets, such as location, security classification, and owner.

- *Assets acceptable use and return policies* specify how users can use an asset and how an asset should be returned when it is not needed anymore.

- *Assets ownership* is the process of assigning an owner to an asset. Each asset within the organization needs an owner. The owner is responsible for the security of the asset during its lifecycle.

- *Assets classification* is the process of evaluating the risk of an asset in terms of confidentiality, integrity, and availability and assigning a security classification to an asset.

- *Assets labeling* is the process of assigning a label to an asset that includes its security classification.

- *Assets handling* refers to procedures and technologies that allow for the secure storage, use, and transfer of an asset.

- *Media management* deals with the secure management of the media lifecycle, which includes media access, media marking, media storage, media use, media transport, media downgrading, and media sanitization and disposal.

Let's review each of these items in more detail.

Assets Inventory

Organizations need to have a clear understanding of which assets are part of the organization and what they are used for. According to ISO 27005, assets can be classified as primary and supporting assets. Primary assets include the following:

- Business processes and activities (for example, processes or activities that enable the organization or business to deal with secret and proprietary information)

- Information (for example, personal or strategic information)

Supporting assets include the following:

- Hardware (for example, laptops)
- Software (for example, operating systems and licenses)
- Network (for example, infrastructure devices such as routers and switches)
- Personnel (for example, users)
- Sites (for example, locations)
- Organizational structure (for example, external organizations)

Not all assets need to be part of an inventory of security assets, and the security profession-al would need to provide feedback on what should and should not be part of the inventory. Asset inventory should be as accurate as possible and may need regular review to reflect the current state. It should include information about the location of the asset, the asset descrip-tion, the asset owner, the asset classification, and the asset configuration. An asset inventory should include both physical and virtual assets and on-premises and cloud-based assets. An asset inventory is also a component of other management processes, such as configuration management, which is described later in this chapter.

Assets Ownership

Each asset should have an owner. The owner can be an individual or an entity within the organization. The owner is assigned at asset creation, asset acquisition, or when the asset is transferred. The asset owner is responsible for the following tasks:

- Ensuring proper inventory of the assets she owns
- Asset classification
- Ensuring that the assets are protected appropriately
- Periodically reviewing the asset classification and access control policies, including privi-leges on the assets
- Ensuring proper disposal of the assets

The asset owner, together with senior management, is responsible for the asset through its entire lifecycle. The owner can delegate day-to-day operations to a custodian. Roles and duties within information security were discussed in more detail in Chapter 4.

Assets Acceptable Use and Return Policies

Users of an asset should receive information about rules for accessing and using a specific asset. The rules should describe user responsibility and expected behavior. An organization may ask users to sign an acknowledgment that they have read and understood the acceptable use rules before being granted access to the asset. The user may be held responsible for any misuse of the assets or use against the security organization policy.

A return policy and process should be established for the time when the asset is not needed anymore by the user. For example, this may be due to employee termination or transfer to another organization, ending of a contract agreement, and so on. The Return policy should consider physical assets and assets in electronic form. If a user uses personal devices for business, the policy should include information on how to properly transfer the information contained on these devices.

Assets Classification

Assets should be classified based on the risk to the organization that an unauthorized access can cause to the confidentiality, integrity and availability. The asset classification is assigned by the asset owner, and it influences the level of protection the asset receives.

The classification policies and processes should include information on the classification schema (for example, the name of the labels) and about the process for changing the classification when the value and risk associated with an asset changes. The classification schema should include labels that are associated with the related risk for the organization. For example, the label "Top Secret" is associated with "grave damage to the organization."

Table 5-5 outlines a sample classification schema that's generally used in military and governmental organizations. Assets classification was discussed in more detail in Chapter 4.

Table 5-5   Classification Schema

Classification Label	Organization Risk
Top Secret	Grave damage
Secret	Severe damage
Confidential	Damage
Unclassified	No significant damage

Assets Labeling

Assets labeling includes processes for marking an asset with information about its security classification. The label should be visible so that users are aware of a specific classification and can handle the asset accordingly. The process can also include exceptions (for example, in which occasion a label can be omitted).

Assets and Information Handling

The asset owner should identify procedures and processes for securely handling assets. The cases of an asset at rest, an asset in use, and an asset being transferred (in motion) need to be taken into consideration. The handling processes usually include the following:

- Access controls and restrictions to match the security classification
- Maintenance of access records and auditing
- Protection of any temporary copies of the assets
- Storage of the assets that conforms with vendor guidelines

Access controls were discussed in Chapter 4.

Media Management

Media is a category of asset used to store information. If the information stored is sensitive, the media needs to be handled with special care. Media management deals with policies and procedures for protecting and securely handling media. It includes information on media access, media marking, media storage, media use, media transport, media downgrading, and media sanitization and disposal.

Removable media refers to media that can be used and removed while the system is still in use. Examples of removable media are USB, DVD, and external HD. These constitutes a higher risk for the organization because they are easily portable, so there is a higher chance of media theft or loss. The media management should include procedures for handling removable media, including processes for securely erasing the information stored, mitigating the risk of media degradation, cryptographic technology for information storage, and registration of removable media.

Media sanitization and disposal are also important parts of media management. At the end of the media lifecycle, the media should be sanitized and disposed of securely to avoid theft of any information that might still be present on the media. Depending on the classification of the information stored on the media, different methods of sanitization and disposal might be required.

Additional information about media and asset disposal is provided in Chapter 4.

Introduction to Enterprise Mobility Management

Mobile assets are a special class of assets that allow mobility and seamless connectivity to an organization's infrastructure. Mobile assets or devices usually include laptops, tablets, smartphones, and mobile phones. In the last few years, the security of mobile assets has become a hot topic due to the increased use of mobile devices to perform business tasks. In addition, organizations are more and more adopting the bring-your-own-device (BYOD) philosophy that allows employees to use their own personal device to access and consume an organization's assets.

There are several reasons for the spread of the BYOD philosophy across organizations; however, the primary reason is that BYOD increases employee and organizational productivity because employees are empowered to work from wherever and at whatever time they want. The spread of the use of mobile devices and specifically personally owned devices, however, has created several security gaps and new threats to the organization.

NIST SP 800-124 identifies several threats to the organization due to the use of mobile devices:

- **Lack of physical security controls:** Mobile devices can be used anywhere outside of the organization, including in coffee shops, at home, in a hotel, and on a train. The risk of a device being stolen or lost is much higher compared to assets that cannot be used outside the organization's perimeter.

- **Use of untrusted devices:** Mobile devices, especially those that are personally owned, may not be fully trusted. For example, a personal mobile device could be rooted or jailbroken, thus increasing the risk for device compromise.

- **Use of untrusted networks:** Mobile devices can connect from everywhere, including untrusted networks, for Internet access. For example, an employee might attempt to connect to a public Wi-Fi hotspot from a coffee shop that could be compromised.

- **Use of untrusted applications:** Mobile devices and especially smartphones enable users to install third-party applications that in some cases interact with corporate information stored on the device itself, or with organization resources over the network. These applications are untrusted and potentially dangerous.

- **Interaction with other systems:** Mobile devices often interact with other systems for data exchange. For example, a smartphone can connect to a laptop for backup or even perform a data backup via the network with various cloud backup systems. These systems are often not under the control of the organization and are potentially untrusted. The risk of data loss for an organization is, therefore, increased.

- **Use of untrusted content:** Mobile devices can access content in various ways that are not available for other types of devices. For example, a website URL can be specified in the form of a Quick Response (QR) code. This increases the risk because the user, who might understand the risk of clicking an untrusted URL link, might not understand the risk of scanning an untrusted QR code.

- **Use of location services:** Location services used by mobile devices allow tracking of information and user location. This could help an attacker locate a specific asset or person and use the information to build up an attack.

In response to organizations implementing BYOD and the corresponding need to manage the new threats inherited by this choice, several new technologies have emerged. Enterprise Mobility Management (EMM) includes policies, processes, and technologies that allow for the secure management of mobile devices. Technologies that enable BYOD, Mobile Device Management (MDM), and Mobile Applications Management (MAM) are examples of areas covered by an organization's EMM.

NIST SP 800-124 proposes a five-phase lifecycle model for an enterprise mobile device solution:

1. **Initiation:** Includes the activities an organization needs to perform before designing a mobile device solution. This includes selecting the strategy for implementation, determining how the strategy matches the organization's mission, developing a mobile device security policy, and so on.

2. **Development:** In this phase, the technical characteristics and deployment plan of the mobile solution are specified. It includes which authentication or encryption strategy will be used, the type of mobile brands that will be allowed, and so on.

3. **Implementation:** In this phase, mobile devices are being provisioned to meet the security policy requirements. This phase includes the testing and the production deployment of the solution.

4. **Operation and maintenance:** This includes ongoing security tasks that need to be performed during the mobile device's lifecycle. Examples are reviewing access controls, managing patches, threat detection and protection, and so on.

5. **Disposal:** This includes all the activities around media disposal, such as media sanitization and destruction. Asset disposal was discussed in the Asset Management section of this chapter.

Figure 5-13 shows the five phases of an EMM solution lifecycle.

Figure 5-13 *EMM Solution Lifecycle Based on NIST SP 800-124*

Mobile Device Management

Mobile device management (MDM) controls the deployment, operations, and monitoring of mobile devices used to access organization resources. It is used to enforce an organization's security policy on mobile devices. It includes all or part of the following capabilities:

- Restrict user or application access to mobile device hardware, such as digital cameras, network interfaces, GPS, and services or native applications such as the built-in web browser or email client.

- Limit or prevent access to organization resources based on the device profile and security posture (for example, a device that is rooted should not be able to access certain resources).

- Monitor, alert, and report on policy violation (for example, if a user is trying to root the mobile device).

- Encrypt data communication between the device and the organization as well as data stored on the device or in removable storage.

- Provide the ability to remotely wipe the device in case the device is lost or stolen, and in case of device reuse.

- Enforce strong password or PIN code authentication for accessing the device and/or organization resources. This includes password strength policies, clipping level, and so on.

- Remotely lock the device and remotely reset the password.

- Enable the enforcement of data loss prevention (DLP) on mobile devices.

- Restrict the type of applications that can be installed (for example, via whitelisting or blacklisting) and which resources the applications can use. Due to the large threat untrusted applications may pose to the organization, application management is usually handled within a mobile application management (MAM) framework.

Mobile device management capabilities could be offered by the mobile vendor or provided by a third-party management tool that offers multivendor support. The second option is currently the most used due to the increased adoption of BYOD and heterogeneous types of devices used within an organization.

One of the characteristics of an MDM solution is the use of over-the-air (OTA) device management. OTA historically refers to the deployment and configuration performed via a messaging service, such as Short Message Service (SMS), Multimedia Messaging Service (MMS), or Wireless Application Protocol (WAP). Nowadays it's used to indicate remote configuration and deployment of mobile devices.

The Cisco Unified Access validated design recommends two different deployment models for an MDM solution. In the *on-premises model*, the MDM server and application reside inside the organization perimeter, usually in a DMZ close to the Internet edge or in the organization's data center. The organization's IT department is responsible for operating the MDM solution. This model suits most organizations with experienced IT units. In the *cloud-based model*, the MDM solution is deployed as a service and operated by a third party from the cloud. The advantages of a cloud-based model are as follows:

- The cost of the solution and deployment
- The flexibility
- Speed of deployment
- Scalability
- Easy to use and maintain

And here are the advantages of the on-premises model:

- Higher level of control
- Intellectual property retention
- Regulatory compliance (for example, if it is not possible to store data on the cloud)

In terms of security, both solutions have pros and cons, as outlined in Table 5-6; however, the security depends largely on the security maturity level of the IT workforce for the on-premises model or the security maturity level of the third party that operates the cloud-based MDM.

Table 5-6   Comparing Cloud-Based MDM and On-Premises MDM

Cloud-Based MDM Characteristics	On-Premises MDM Characteristics
Deployed as a service and operated by a third party from the cloud	Deployed and managed within the organization
Lower cost of the solution and deployment	Higher level of control
Flexibility	Intellectual property retention
Fast deployment	Regulatory compliance
Scalability	
Easier to maintain	

Cisco BYOD Architecture

The Cisco Unified Access validated design offers an end-to-end architecture for implementing BYOD within an organization. Here are the main components of the BYOD architecture:

- **Mobile devices:** These can be any corporate-owned or personally-owned mobile devices that require access to corporate resources. Examples are laptops, smartphones, and tablets.

- **Wireless access points (APs):** Cisco wireless APs provide wireless connectivity to the corporate network.

- **Wireless LAN (WLAN) controllers:** Cisco WLAN controllers (WLCs) serve as a centralized point for the configuration, management, and monitoring of the Cisco WLAN solution. These are also used to enforced authorization policies to the endpoints that require access.

- **Identity Services Engine (ISE):** The Cisco ISE is the critical component of a BYOD solution and provides identity management and profiling services, including authentication, authorization, accounting, and access controls.

- **Cisco AnyConnect Secure Mobility Client:** The software installed on the mobile device that provides client-side authentication and authorization services by using 802.1x when on the premises and enabling VPN access when used outside the premises.

- **Integrated Services Routers (ISRs):** Cisco ISRs provide Internet access for home offices and branch locations.

- **Image Aggregation Services Routers (ASRs):** Cisco ASRs provide aggregation and Internet gateway functionality for campus networks and function as aggregators for home offices and branches that connect back to the corporate campus.

- **Cloud Web Security (CWS):** CWS provides worldwide threat intelligence, advanced threat defense capabilities, and roaming user protection. The Cisco CWS service uses web proxies in the Cisco cloud environment that scan traffic for malware and policy enforcement.

- **Adaptive Security Appliance (ASA):** The Cisco ASA provides all the standard security functions for the BYOD solution at the Internet edge, including VPN servers, next-gen firewall services, and next-gen IPS services.

Here are some additional elements typically found in BYOD deployments:

- Cisco Converged Access Switches
- Cisco Mobility Service Engine
- Cisco switches (Catalyst and Nexus series family)
- Cisco Prime Infrastructure
- Corporate Directory Service (for example, AD or LDAP server)
- Certificate authority and PKI services

Figure 5-14 provides an example of a BYOD infrastructure with an on-premises MDM solution.

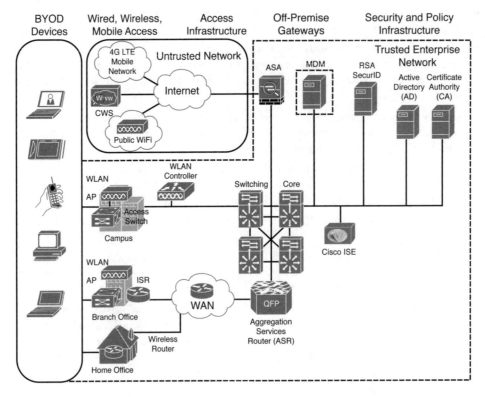

Figure 5-14   *BYOD Infrastructure with an On-Premises MDM Solution*

Cisco ISE and MDM Integration

At press time, Cisco ISE does not include MDM functionality; however, it allows seamless integration with third-party MDM services and commercial tools both for on-premises and cloud-based deployments. Cisco ISE allows MDM integration via the Cisco MDM API and can be used to enforce mobile device policy and compliance.

By using the Cisco MDM API, the Cisco ISE is capable of pulling information from the MDM server (for example, for additional data points regarding an endpoint) or pushing administrative actions to the endpoint via the MDM service capabilities.

Here are some examples of supported capabilities:

- PIN lock check
- Jailbreak check
- Data encryption check
- Device augmentation information check
- Registration status check
- Compliance status check
- Periodic compliance status check

- MDM reachability check
- (Full/Partial) remote wipe
- Remote PIN lock

Cisco ISE supports a variety of third-party MDM vendors as well as Cisco Meraki device management. Figure 5-15 provides an example of Cisco ISE integration with cloud-based MDM solutions.

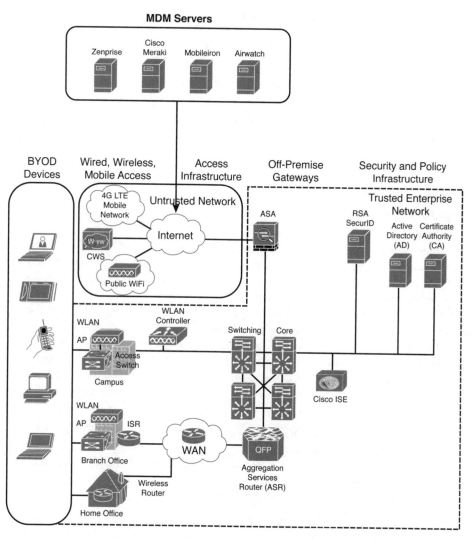

Figure 5-15 *Cisco ISE Integration with Cloud-Based MDM Solutions*

Cisco Meraki Enterprise Mobility Management

Cisco Meraki Enterprise Mobility Management (EMM) it is a cloud-based EMM solution that offers unified management, diagnostics, and monitoring of multiple types of mobile devices, including smartphones and laptops. It allows security policy enforcement, scalable configuration deployment, device classification and inventory, and device geolocation. It also allows for several types of secure device enrollment, such as fully automated, partially automated, and manual, and granular MDM access rights configuration.

Configuration and Change Management

Configuration and change management is a broad term that can have different meanings depending on the context in which it is used. In this book, we will define them as follows:

- Configuration management is concerned with all policies, processes, and technologies used to maintain the integrity of the configuration of a given asset.

- Change management is concerned with all policies, processes, and technologies that handle a change to an asset's lifecycle.

In some cases, configuration and change management are described as part of asset management.

Configuration Management

NIST SP 800-128 defines configuration management as a set of activities used to maintain organizational resource integrity through the control of processes for initializing, changing, and monitoring the resource configuration. A *configuration item (CI)* is defined as an identifiable part of the system that is the target of the configuration control process. A CI can be an information system component such as a router, application, server, or a group of components (for example, a group of routers sharing the same operating system and configuration), or it can be a noncomponent such as documentation or firmware. Each CI includes a set of attributes; for example, the attributes for a CI describing a server could be the firmware version and applications installed. If these attributes are configured as individual CIs, then two CIs are said to be "in relation." For example, a Cisco router could be considered a CI, and the router operating system, IOS-XE 16.1.1, could be considered a separate CI. These two CIs are said to be "in relation."

The set of attributes and relationships for a CI create a configuration record. The configuration record is stored in the configuration management database (CMDB). The main goal of configuration management is to manage the lifecycle of the CIs. An important step is the inventory of CIs. The inventory process is about identifying all the CIs and capturing the configuration records in the configuration management database.

Another important concept in configuration management is the baseline configuration. A *baseline configuration* is a set of attributes and CIs related to a system, which has been formally reviewed and approved. It can only be changed with a formal change process.

While configuration management goes beyond information security, it is an important part of the management of secure configurations, as well as to enable security and facilitate the assessment of the risk for an organization. Security-focused configuration management

(SecCM), as described in NIST SP 800-128, should be built on top of normal configuration management and includes four main activities:

- Identification and recording of configurations that impact the security posture of a resource
- Consideration of the security risk when approving the initial configuration
- Analysis of the security risk involved in a configuration change
- Documentation and approval of changes

The process described in SecCM includes four main phases:

- **Planning:** Includes the definition of SecCM policies and procedures and the integration of these procedures within the IT and information security policy of an organization.
- **Identifying and implementing the configuration:** Includes the development and establishment of security baseline configuration and the implementation of the baseline on CIs.
- **Controlling the configuration changes:** Includes the management of changes to keep the baseline configuration secure. Change management is further detailed in the next section.
- **Monitoring:** Used to validate and ensure that the CIs are compliant with the organization's security policy and to maintain a secure baseline configuration.

Planning

The main items of the planning phase include the following:

- Establish an organization-wide SecCM program.
- Develop an organizational SecCM policy.
- Develop organizational SecCM procedures.
- Develop the SecCM monitoring strategy.
- Define the types of changes that do not require configuration change control.
- Develop SecCM training.
- Identify approved IT products.
- Identify tools.
- Establish a configuration test environment and program.
- Develop a SecCM plan for the information system.
- Create or update the information system component inventory.
- Determine the configuration items.
- Establish the relationship between an information system and its configuration items and information system components.
- Establish a configuration control board (CCB) for the information system.

Identifying and Implementing the Configuration

Identifying and implementing the configuration requires, for example, setting secure baseline values (such as the use of secure protocols, OS and application features, and methods for remote access), applying vendor patches, using approved signed software, implementing end-user protection, implementing network protections, and maintaining documentation. Implementation includes prioritizing and testing configurations, approving and recording the baseline, and deploying the baseline. The main items of this phase are as follows:

- Establishing a secure configuration
- Implementing a secure configuration

Controlling the Configuration Changes

This phase includes the management of changes to maintain a secure baseline configuration. Change management is further detailed in the next section. The main items of this phase are as follows:

- Implementing access restrictions for changes
- Implementing a configuration change control process
- Conducting a security impact analysis
- Recording and archiving

Monitoring

Monitoring is used to validate and ensure that the CIs are in compliance with the organization's security policy and to maintain a secure baseline configuration. This may include scanning to find components that are not present in the inventory, identifying the difference between the actual configuration and the configuration baseline, implementing change-monitoring tools, running integrity checks, and so on. The main items of this phase are as follows:

- Assessing and reporting
- Implementing and managing the tool for monitoring

Change Management

A *change* is defined as any modification, addition, or removal of an organizational resource (for example, of a configuration item). Change management includes all policies, processes, and technologies for handling a change's lifecycle.

In ITIL Service Transition, changes are categorized as follows:

- **Standard change:** A common change that has already been authorized and is low risk. This type of change might not need to follow a formal change management process.
- **Emergency change:** A change that needs to be implemented on an urgent basis. This type of change usually has a separate procedure.

- **Normal change:** A change that is not a standard change or an emergency change. This is the type of change that will go through the full change management procedure.

A *request for change (RFC)* is a formal request that usually includes a high-level description of the change, the reason for the change, and other information. Change management should also account for emergency and nonscheduled changes. A process should be created for situations when the normal change management process cannot be implemented.

According to ITIL Service Transition, a change control process includes the following steps:

Step 1. **Create an RFC.** In this step, an RFC is created with a high-level plan for the change and its motivation.

Step 2. **Record the RFC.** In this step, the RFC is formally recorded in the change management system.

Step 3. **Review the RFC.** In this step, the RFC is reviewed to see whether the change makes sense and whether it is necessary to proceed further in the process.

Step 4. **Assess and evaluate the change.** In this step, the change review board will determine whether the change requires change control (for example, if it was already preapproved). In this step, the security impact of the change is also determined.

Step 5. **Authorize the change's build and test.** The change authority is appointed and the change test plan is formally authorized. The test may be built before the actual authorization and authorization decision is taken based on the outcome of the test. The test should confirm the security impact anticipated in step 4 or highlight additional impacts.

Step 6. **Coordinate the change's build and test.** The authorized change is passed to the technical group for the change's build and testing.

Step 7. **Authorize deployment.** If the change's build and testing phase goes fine, the change is authorized for deployment. The change authority may request additional tests and send the change back to previous steps.

Step 8. **Implement the change.** The change is implemented.

Step 9. **Review and close the change record.** After the change is deployed, the system is tested to make sure the change was deployed correctly. If all goes well, the change record is updated in the change management system and the request is closed.

Figure 5-16 summarizes the ITIL change management process.

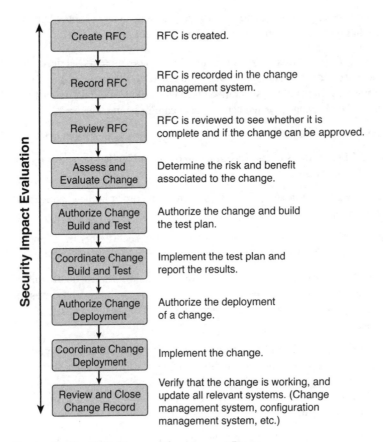

Create RFC	RFC is created.
Record RFC	RFC is recorded in the change management system.
Review RFC	RFC is reviewed to see whether it is complete and if the change can be approved.
Assess and Evaluate Change	Determine the risk and benefit associated to the change.
Authorize Change Build and Test	Authorize the change and build the test plan.
Coordinate Change Build and Test	Implement the test plan and report the results.
Authorize Change Deployment	Authorize the deployment of a change.
Coordinate Change Deployment	Implement the change.
Review and Close Change Record	Verify that the change is working, and update all relevant systems. (Change management system, configuration management system, etc.)

Figure 5-16 *ITIL Change Management Process*

As a security professional, an important step to perform is the security impact analysis of the change. According to NIST SP 800-128, the change security impact analysis includes the following steps:

Step 1.   **Understand the change.** Develop a high-level view of what the change will look like.

Step 2.   **Identify vulnerabilities.** This step includes looking for information on vulnerabilities from the vendor or other vulnerability information providers. This step might also include performing a security analysis of the code.

Step 3.   **Assess risks.** This step includes identifying possible threats and calculating the impact and likelihood of the threats exploiting the system vulnerabilities identified in the previous step. The risk can be accepted, mitigated with the use of additional countermeasures, or avoided, in which case the change request is rejected.

Step 4.   **Assess the impact on existing security controls.** This includes the evaluation of how the change would impact other security controls. For example, a deployment of new application on a server might require a change to a firewall rule.

Step 5. **Plan safeguards and countermeasures.** This step deals with any safeguards and countermeasures that need to be put in place to mitigate any risk determined by the change request.

Vulnerability Management

A *vulnerability*, as defined in Chapter 3, "Security Principles," is an exploitable weakness in a system or its design. *Vulnerability management* is the process of identifying, analyzing, prioritizing, and remediating vulnerabilities in software and hardware.

As for the other security operations management process discussed in this chapter, vulnerability management intersects with asset management, risk management, configuration and change management, and patch management. For example, to remediate a vulnerability, a patch should be installed on the system, which requires using the patch management process.

There are several frameworks used to describe the vulnerability management processes. For example, in the white paper, "Vulnerability Management: Tools, Challenges and Best Practices" published by the SANS Institute, a six-steps process is proposed that includes asset inventory, information management, risk assessment, vulnerability assessment, report and remediate, and respond. At its core, vulnerability management includes three main phases, as illustrated in Figure 5-17 and described in detail in the sections that follow.

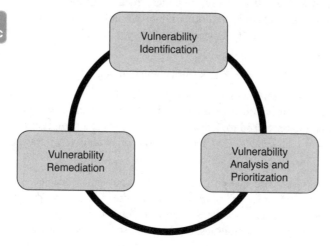

Figure 5-17 *Vulnerability Management Phases*

Vulnerability Identification

One important process that is part of vulnerability management is the identification of a vulnerability. There are several ways to identify vulnerabilities in systems. Security professionals need to be aware of these methods and understand the underlying concepts.

Each vendor may identify vulnerabilities based on its own tracking systems and identifiers. This creates several issues in the vulnerability management process. For example, the same vulnerability might be tracked by several identifiers depending on the specific vendor. This, in turn, increases the chance for security gaps.

Common Vulnerabilities and Exposures (CVE) from MITRE is a dictionary of vulnerabilities and exposures in products and systems. It is an industry-standard method for identifying vulnerabilities. Each vulnerability is identified by a CVE identifier (CVE-ID).

Anyone, including researchers, incident response teams, and vendors can request a CVE identifier upon the discovery and disclosure of a vulnerability. The CVE can be requested from one of several CVE numbering authorities (CNAs), which are the only entities authorized to assign a CVE. Cisco is a CNA and can assign a CVE ID directly upon finding any vulnerability in Cisco products. More information about CVE can be found at https://cve.mitre.org.

Finding Information about a Vulnerability

Several sources provide information about vulnerabilities in software and hardware.

Vendor's Vulnerability Announcements

Most vendors have a vulnerability disclosure policy that is used to provide information about vulnerabilities found in their products. The announcement, usually called a security advisory, includes information such as the vulnerability identifier (both vendor and CVE-ID), the affected products list, a security impact evaluation, and remediation steps. For example, Cisco publishes information about security vulnerabilities on a publicly accessible website. The vendor security vulnerabilities policy will also describe under which condition the vendor will release information, any specific schedule, and other important information about vulnerabilities announcements. The Cisco Security Vulnerability Policy is available via the following URL:

http://www.cisco.com/c/en/us/about/security-center/security-vulnerability-policy.html

Besides providing information on a website, vendors may also provide information via other means (for example, an API) to enable automatic consumption of vulnerability information. Currently, two formats are most commonly used for automatic vulnerability consumption: Open Vulnerability and Assessment Language (OVAL) and Common Vulnerability Reporting Framework (CVRF).

OVAL is an international community standard that promotes open and publicly available security content and standardizes the transfer of this information in security tools and services. It uses a language, the OVAL language, to standardize information such as system configuration, system states (for example, vulnerabilities, patches, and so on), and reporting. It includes three schemas:

- **OVAL systems characteristic:** Used for representing system information
- **OVAL definition:** Used to represent the state of a system
- **OVAL result:** Used to represent reporting on the assessment

OVAL definitions are XML files that contain information about how to check a system for the presence of vulnerabilities, configuration issues, patches, installed applications, or other characteristics. For vulnerability checks, definitions are written to check for a vulnerability identified by a specific CVE identifier.

There are four main use cases, also called "classes," of OVAL definitions:

- **Vulnerability:** This class determines the presence of a vulnerability on the system being tested
- **Compliance:** This class validates a device configuration against a known or approved valid configuration
- **Inventory:** This class checks for specific software installed on the system
- **Patches:** This class finds a specific patch on the system

Cisco provides an OVAL definition to enable vulnerability information consumption for certain products. More information about OVAL can be found at https://oval.mitre.org/. The following white paper provides an overview on how to use OVAL for security vulnerability automation:

http://www.cisco.com/c/en/us/about/security-center/oval-security-automation.html

Common Vulnerability Reporting Framework (CVRF) from ICASI is an XML-based standard that enables security professionals and organizations to share security vulnerability information in a single format, speeding up information exchange and digestion. Cisco has been a major contributor to this standard. CVRF is a common and consistent framework for exchanging not just vulnerability information, but any security-related documentation. The CVRF section of the XML schema is built following a mind map approach with sections that are set as mandatory and optional. More information about CVRF are available at https://cvrf.github.io/. Cisco publishes security advisories in CVRF format as well. They are available here:

https://tools.cisco.com/security/center/cvrfListing.x

Besides providing information in common standard format, some vendors may provide APIs for direct consumption of vulnerability information. Cisco provides an API for vulnerability through the Cisco PSIRT openVuln program. The Cisco PSIRT openVuln API is a RESTful API that allows customers to obtain Cisco security vulnerability information in different machine-consumable formats. It supports industry-wide security standards such as CVRF and OVAL. This API allows technical staff and programmers to build tools that help them do their jobs more effectively. In this case, it enables them to easily keep up with security vulnerability information specific to their networks.

Vulnerabilities Information Repositories and Aggregators

Following up on vulnerability disclosures and security advisories on vendor websites or via APIs is not a trivial task, especially in a highly heterogeneous and multivendor environment. Security professionals can opt to use vulnerability aggregator services and public vulnerability repositories to find information about vulnerabilities in products.

Here are some public vulnerability information repositories:

- **cve.mitre.org:** Includes a repository of CVE IDs and the descriptions associated with them.
- **nvd.nist.gov:** The U.S. national vulnerability database is maintained by the NIST. It provides a search engine for CVE and detailed vulnerability information, including vulnerability assessments via Common Vulnerability Scoring System (CVSS; more on CVSS later in this section) and an external reference to the vendor announcement.

- **us-cert.gov:** Maintained by the U.S. Computer Emergency Readiness Team (CERT). Provides a weekly summary in the form of a bulletin for all vulnerabilities disclosed during the period covered.

- **cert.europa.eu:** Maintained by the European CERT (CERT-EU). Provides security advisories to various European institutions and aggregates vulnerability information per vendor base.

- **jpcert.or.jp:** Maintained by the Japan Computer Emergency Response Team. Provides alerts and bulletins about vulnerabilities from several vendors.

- **auscert.org.au:** The Australian Cyber Emergency Response Team provides security bulletins organized by operating system/environment.

This list is not exhaustive. In most cases, national CERTs also provide relevant vulnerabilities information organized per vendor. Many consultant firms also offer vulnerability aggregator and advisory services that can be customized to provide information only on devices and systems present in the customer environment. Information about vulnerabilities can also be found on security-focused mailing lists. Full Disclosure and Bugtraq are two examples of this type of mailing list.

Vulnerability Scan

Another popular method for identifying vulnerabilities in systems and devices is through a vulnerability scan. A vulnerability scanner is software that can be used to identify vulnerabilities on a system. The scan can be done in two ways:

- **Active scanner:** Sends probes to the system and evaluates a vulnerability based on the system response. An active scanner can be used together with some type of system credentials or without them.

- **Passive scanner:** Deployed on the network, a passive scanner observes network traffic generated by a system and determines whether or not the system may be affected by a specific vulnerability.

Generally speaking, a vulnerability scanner will not try to exploit a vulnerability but rather base its response on information gathered from the system. For example, a scanner may conclude that a system is affected by a vulnerability because the system banner shows an operating system version that is reported vulnerable by the vendor. However, vulnerability scanners might usually not be able to specify whether that vulnerability can be actually exploited. This, however, largely depends on the scanner capabilities.

Vulnerability scanners usually report on known vulnerabilities with already assigned CVE IDs and are not used to find unknown vulnerabilities in the system. Most modern scanning tools, however, integrate part of the functionality.

Scanners can also be classified as *network vulnerability scanners* and *web vulnerability scanners*. Network vulnerability scanners focus on network infrastructure devices and probe the network stack of the target system. Web vulnerability scanners, on the other hand, work at the application level and probe the web services of a target system.

The workflow followed by most security practitioners using vulnerability scanners is as follows:

Step 1.   Identify the set of systems that are the targets of the vulnerability scan. The systems are identified either by their IP address or DNS name.

Step 2.   Alert the system owners, users, and any other stakeholders of the system. Although vulnerability scanners usually do not cause downtime, it is good practice to run scanners during a maintenance window.

Step 3.   Run the scanner.

Step 4.   Perform the report analysis.

Vulnerability scanners have become very popular both as part of vulnerability management and as tools for compliance and assurance fulfillment. For example, PCI DSS requires you to perform regular internal and external vulnerability scans. There are several commercial vulnerability scanner tools. Popular commercial vulnerability scanners include the following:

- Nessus from Tenable
- Retina from Beyond Trust
- Nexpose from Rapid7
- AppScan from IBM
- AVDS from Beyond Security

Penetration Assessment

A penetration assessment or pen test goes one step further and is used to test an exploit of a vulnerability. Besides trying to exploit known vulnerabilities, penetration tests also can find unknown vulnerabilities in a system. Penetration assessment may also make use of vulnerability scanners to get a list of vulnerabilities that can be used to exploit the system.

A pen test requires advanced skills to be performed properly, and it requires a mixture of automatic and manual tools, especially to find unknown security gaps. Sometimes pen testing is referred to as *ethical hacking*, and the people performing a pen test are called white hats.

Pen testers try to exploit a single vulnerability or get full control of the system by chaining multiple vulnerabilities, security gaps, and misconfigurations. *Vulnerability chaining* is the process of exploiting vulnerabilities in sequence so that the exploit of the first vulnerability enables the possible exploitation of a second vulnerability. There are several types of penetration assessments. A popular classification is based on the amount of information received by the pen tester prior to the test:

- **White box:** With this approach, the pen tester has access to inside information and has the possibility to receive documentation about systems, system versions and patch levels, and so on. In some cases, they may also get information on the source code of applications or credentials to access some systems. This approach is generally used to simulate an insider threat.

- **Black box:** This approach is the opposite of white box, and the pen tester does not have any information about the system they are trying to breach. This is more accurate in simulating an external attack. This type of test, however, is less complete than a white box approach because the pen tester needs to find by himself all the information needed in order to prepare the attack. Because these activities are performed during a limited amount of time, not all the security gaps are usually found.

- **Gray box:** This is halfway between a white box and a black box approach. In this approach, the pen tester has some information available, but not all.

Because penetration assessment can be a very intrusive operation and may cause system outages, or make it completely unavailable, special care should be taken by management and the risk assessment board to make sure the pen test is not disruptive for the business. Usually a compromise needs to be found between performing a realistic test and the risk of affecting normal business operations.

Table 5-7 summarizes the main characteristics of a vulnerability scan and penetration assessment.

Table 5-7   Comparing Vulnerability Scan and Penetration Assessment

Vulnerability Scan	Penetration Assessment
Works by assessing known vulnerabilities.	Can find unknown vulnerabilities.
Can be fully automated.	Mixture of automated and manual process.
Minimal impact on the system.	May completely disable the system.
Main goal is to report any hits on known vulnerabilities.	Main goal is to compromise the system.

Product Vulnerability Management

The vulnerability management process is followed by an organization's security department and incident response team (IRT) to manage vulnerabilities in products present in the organization's infrastructure. Product vendors also need a process so that vulnerabilities in products they produce are correctly handled and that information about these vulnerabilities is communicated to affected customers.

The product vulnerability management process is usually handled by the organization Product Security Incident Response Team (PSIRT). This can be a different team than the company's Computer Security Incident Response Team (CSIRT) or can be integrated with it.

For example, Cisco has PSIRT and CSIRT teams that work on two different aspects of vulnerability management. PSIRT handles the vulnerability management process for vulnerabilities on all Cisco products, whereas CSIRT handles the vulnerability management related to the Cisco IT infrastructure.

The main responsibilities of the PSIRT team are as follows:

- Provide a point of contact for vulnerability communication found in Cisco products.
- Provide evaluation, prioritization, and risk information about vulnerabilities.

- Help internal stakeholders (for example, product business units) with technical information about vulnerabilities and exploits.

- Handle external communication of vulnerability information.

According to the Cisco Security Vulnerability Policy, the Cisco PSIRT process includes seven phases:

1. **Awareness:** PSIRT receives notification of a security incident.

2. **Active management:** PSIRT prioritizes and identifies resources.

3. **Fix determined:** PSIRT coordinates a fix and impact assessment.

4. **Communication plan:** PSIRT sets the timeframe and notification format.

5. **Integration and mitigation:** PSIRT engages experts and executives.

6. **Notification:** PSIRT notifies all customers simultaneously.

7. **Feedback:** PSIRT incorporates feedback from customers and Cisco internal input.

Figure 5-18 shows the Cisco PSIRT process.

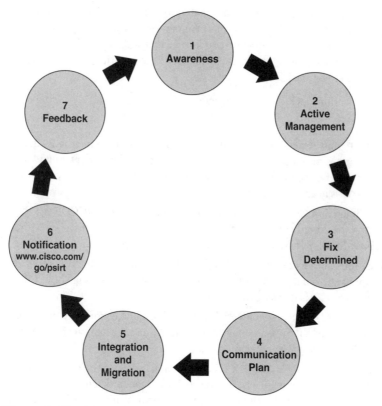

Figure 5-18   *Cisco PSIRT Process*

Responsible Disclosure versus Full Disclosure

The disclosure of vulnerability information is one of the most critical tasks of a PSIRT. There are two approaches to vulnerability disclosure. In a *full disclosure approach*, all the details about a vulnerability are disclosed. While that could help the incident response team to evaluate the vulnerability better and may provide more information for temporary remediation (for example, via network-based mitigation), it usually includes enough details for anyone with the right skill to build exploits. This increases the risk and urgency to implement patches.

In a *responsible disclosure approach*, relevant information about the vulnerability is disclosed; however, information that could help an attacker to build an exploit is omitted. This provides a good compromise between giving out too much information and allowing a correct analysis from incident response teams and security departments within an organization. Most of the vendors, including Cisco, and national CERTs use a responsible disclosure approach.

Security Content Automation Protocol

Security Content Automation Protocol (SCAP) was created to provide a standardized solution for security automation. The SCAP mission is to maintain system security by ensuring security configuration best practices are implemented in the enterprise network, verifying the presence of patches, and maintaining complete visibility of the security posture of systems and the organization at all times.

The current SCAP specifications include the following:

- **Languages:**
    - **Open Vulnerability and Assessment Language (OVAL):** OVAL is an international community standard to promote open and publicly available security content and to standardize the transfer of this information in security tools and services. More information about OVAL is available at http://oval.mitre.org.
    - **Extensible Configuration Checklist Description Format (XCCDF):** XCCDF is a specification for a structured collection of security checklists and benchmarks. More information about XCCDF is available at http://scap.nist.gov/specifications/xccdf.
    - **Open Checklist Interactive Language (OCIL):** OCIL is a framework for collecting and interpreting responses from questions offered to users. More information about OCIL is available at http://scap.nist.gov/specifications/ocil.
    - **Asset Identification (AI):** AI is a specification designed to quickly correlate different sets of information about enterprise computing assets. More information about AI is available at http://scap.nist.gov/specifications/ai.
    - **Asset Reporting Format (ARF):** ARF is a specification that defines the transport format of information about enterprise assets and provides a standardized data model to streamline the reporting of such information. More information about ARF is available at http://scap.nist.gov/specifications/arf.

> **NOTE** Two emerging languages are **Asset Summary Reporting** (ASR) and the **Open Checklist Reporting Language** (OCRL). More information about ASR is available at http://scap.nist.gov/specifications/asr/, and more information about OCRL is available at http://ocrl.mitre.org/.

- Enumerations:
  - **Common Vulnerabilities and Exposures (CVE):** CVE assigns identifiers to publicly known system vulnerabilities. Cisco assigns CVE identifiers to security vulnerabilities according to the Cisco public vulnerability policy at http://www.cisco.com/web/about/security/psirt/security_vulnerability_policy.html.
    More information about CVE is available at http://cve.mitre.org.
  - **Common Platform Enumeration (CPE):** CPE is a standardized method of naming and identifying classes of applications, operating systems, and hardware devices. More information about CPE is available at http://nvd.nist.gov/cpe.cfm.
  - **Common Configuration Enumeration (CCE):** CCE provides unique identifiers for configuration guidance documents and best practices. The main goal of CCE is to enable organizations to perform fast and accurate correlation of configuration issues in enterprise systems. More information about CCE is available at http://nvd.nist.gov/cce/index.cfm.

> **NOTE** Other community-developed enumerators, such as the Common Weakness Enumeration (CWE), are currently being expanded and further developed. CWE is a dictionary of common software architecture, design, code, or implementation weaknesses that could lead to security vulnerabilities. More information about CWE is available from http://cwe.mitre.org. Another emerging enumerator is the Common Remediation Enumeration (CRE). More information about CRE is available at http://scap.nist.gov/specifications/cre.

- Metrics:
  - **Common Vulnerability Scoring System (CVSS):** CVSS is a standards-based scoring method that conveys vulnerability severity and helps determine the urgency and priority of response.
  - **Common Configuration Scoring System (CCSS):** More information about CCSS is available in the following PDF document: http://csrc.nist.gov/publications/nistir/ir7502/nistir-7502_CCSS.pdf.

> **NOTE** Two emerging metrics specifications are the *Common Weakness Scoring System* (CWSS) and the *Common Misuse Scoring System* (CMSS). CWSS is a methodology for scoring software weaknesses. CWSS is part of CWE. More information about CWSS is available at http://cwe.mitre.org/cwss. CMSS is a standardized way to measure software feature misuse vulnerabilities. More information about CMSS is available at http://scap.nist.gov/emerging-specs/listing.html#cmss.

■ **Integrity:** Provided by the *Trust Model for Security Automation Data* (TMSAD), which is a trust model for maintaining integrity, authentication, and traceability of security automation data. More information about TMSAD is available in the following PDF document: http://csrc.nist.gov/publications/nistir/ir7802/NISTIR-7802.pdf.

Figure 5-19 summarizes the SCAP components.

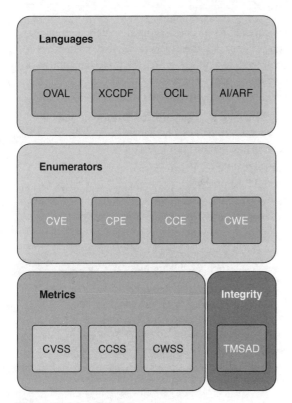

Figure 5-19   *SCAP Components*

Vulnerability Analysis and Prioritization

Once vulnerabilities are identified on a system, the organization needs to perform an analysis and assign a priority based on the impact on the business. The analysis of a reported vulnerability is aimed at confirming that the system is vulnerable and trying to better understand the characteristics of the vulnerability (for example, the technical details around the trigger and the impact).

Vulnerability analysis typically includes the following tasks:

■ Determining whether the vulnerability applies to the system based on the actual configuration

■ Removing any false positives

- Contacting the product vendor for additional information
- Reproducing the vulnerability in-house

If the vulnerability is confirmed, a vulnerability risk assessment should be done so that remediation actions can be properly prioritized. The risk assessment is done based on the severity of the vulnerability and the criticality of the vulnerable system. For example, a medium severity vulnerability on a mission-critical server may receive the same prioritization as a severe vulnerability on a non-mission-critical system.

How organizations determine the severity of a vulnerability and criticality of a system depends on the organization security policy and asset classification. For example, a typical classification for vulnerability severity is *Critical, High, Medium, Low*, and it is based on the impact the exploitation of the vulnerability can cause on the confidentiality, integrity, and availability of the system.

Common Vulnerability Scoring System (CVSS) is an industry standard used to convey information about the severity of vulnerabilities. In CVSS, a vulnerability is evaluated under three aspects, and a score is assigned to each of them.

- The *base* group represents the intrinsic characteristics of a vulnerability that are constant over time and do not depend on a user-specific environment. This is the most important information and the only mandatory information to obtain for a vulnerability score.
- The *temporal* group assesses the vulnerability as it changes over time.
- The *environmental* group represents the characteristic of a vulnerability taking into account the organization's environment.

The CVSS score is obtained by taking into account the base, temporal, and environmental group information.

The score for the base group is between 0 and 10, where 0 is the least severe and 10 is assigned to highly critical vulnerabilities (for example, for vulnerabilities that could allow an attacker to remotely compromise a system and get full control). Additionally, the score comes in the form of a vector string that identifies each of the components used to make up the score. The formula used to obtain the score takes into account various characteristics of the vulnerability and how the attacker is able to leverage these characteristics. At press time, the latest version of the CVSS framework is version 3 (CVSSv3). CVSSv3 defines several characteristics for the base, temporal, and environmental groups.

The base group defines exploitability metrics that measure how the vulnerability can be exploited, and impact metrics that measure the impact on confidentiality, integrity, and availability. In addition to these two, a metric called *scope change* (S) is used to convey the impact on systems that are affected by the vulnerability but do not contain vulnerable code.

Exploitability metrics include the following:

- **Attack Vector (AV):** Represents the level of access an attacker needs to have to exploit a vulnerability. It can assume four values:
  - Network (N)
  - Adjacent (A)

- Local (L)
- Physical (P)

- **Attack Complexity (AC):** Represents the conditions beyond the attacker's control that must exist in order to exploit the vulnerability. The values can be one of the following:
  - Low (L)
  - High (H)

- **Privileges Required (PR):** Represents the level of privileges an attacker must have to exploit the vulnerability. The values are as follows:
  - None (N)
  - Low (L)
  - High (H)

- **User Interaction (UI):** Captures whether user interaction is needed to perform an attack. The values are as follows:
  - None (N)
  - Required (R)

- **Scope (S):** Captures the impact on other systems other than the system being scored. The values are as follows:
  - Unchanged (U)
  - Changed (C)

The Impact metrics include the following:

- **Confidentiality Impact (C):** Measures the degree of impact to the confidentiality of the system. It can assume the following values:
  - Low (L)
  - Medium (M)
  - High (H)

- **Integrity Impact (I):** Measures the degree of impact to the integrity of the system. It can assume the following values:
  - Low (L)
  - Medium (M)
  - High (H)

- **Availability Impact (A):** Measures the degree of impact to the availability of the system. It can assume the following values:
  - Low (L)
  - Medium (M)
  - High (H)

The temporal group includes three metrics:

- **Exploit code maturity (E):** Measures whether or not public exploits are available.
- **Remediation Level (RL):** Indicates whether a fix or workaround is available.
- **Report Confidence (RC):** Indicates the degree of confidence in the existence of the vulnerability.

The environmental group includes two main metrics:

- **Security Requirements (CR, IR, AR):** Indicate the importance of confidentiality, integrity, and availability requirements for the system.
- **Modified Base Metrics (MAV, MAC, MAPR, MUI, MS, MC, MI, MA):** Allow the organization to tweak the base metrics based on specific characteristics of the environment.

For example, a vulnerability that could allow a remote attacker to crash the system by sending crafted IP packets would have the following values for the base metrics:

- Access Vector (AV) would be Network because the attacker can be anywhere and can send packets remotely.
- Attack Complexity (AC) would be Low because it is trivial to generate malformed IP packets (for example, via the Scapy tool).
- Privilege Required (PR) would be None because no privileges are required by the attacker on the target system.
- User Interaction (UI) would also be None because the attacker does not need to interact with any user of the system in order to carry out the attack.
- Scope (S) would be Unchanged if the attack does not cause other systems to fail.
- Confidentiality Impact (C) would be None because the primary impact is on the availability of the system.
- Integrity Impact (I) would be None because the primary impact is on the availability of the system.
- Availability Impact (A) would be High because the device becomes completely unavailable while crashing and reloading.

The base score vector for this vulnerability is AV:N/AC:L/PR:N/UI:N/S:U/C:N/I:N/A:H, which results in a quantitative score of 7.5. Additional examples of CVSSv3 scoring are available at the FIRST website https://www.first.org/cvss.

Figure 5-20 summarizes the CVSS base, temporal, and environmental metrics.

5

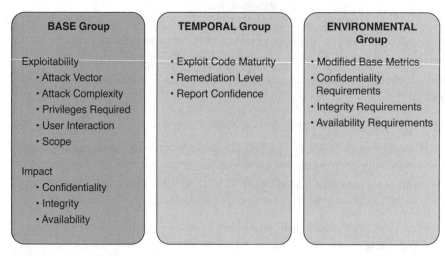

Figure 5-20 *CVSS Base, Temporal, and Environmental Metrics*

CVSSv3 also defines a mapping between a CVSSv3 Base Score quantitative value and a qualitative score. Table 5-8 provides the qualitative-to-quantitative score mapping.

Table 5-8 Qualitative-to-Quantitative Score Mapping

Rating	CVSS Score
None	0.0
Low	0.1–3.9
Medium	4.0–6.9
High	7.0–8.9
Critical	9.0–10.0

Organizations can use the CVSS score as input to their own risk management processes in order to evaluate the risk related to a vulnerability and then prioritize the vulnerability remediation. Risk management and risk evaluation methods are discussed in Chapter 3.

Vulnerability Remediation

The third phase of vulnerability management is to remediate a vulnerability. The most common way to remediate a vulnerability is by applying a patch or system update that includes the fix for the flaw that caused the vulnerability. Applying a patch or a system update may require extensive testing, organizing the maintenance window, and getting approval for deployment. The process that governs patch and system update deployment is defined within "Patch Management" later in this chapter.

Patching a system may take some time (for example, due to the extensive testing the patch needs to undertake in order to be qualified for production deployment). The risk management board needs to find a compromise between leaving the system unprotected and performing a complete test of the patch. Workarounds and vulnerability mitigations might be used, when available, to temporarily reduce the likelihood or the impact of a vulnerability while the patch goes through the formal patch management process.

A *vulnerability workaround* is a technical solution that can avoid an exploit of a vulnerability without affecting the service or feature that is affected by the vulnerability itself. For example, creating an access list on a device and dropping a specific malicious packet that triggers the vulnerability is considered a workaround.

Mitigations are technical solutions that limit the exposure or the impact of a vulnerability. Limiting the number of hosts that can send the affected packet via an access control list is an example of a mitigation. It does not eliminate the risk of exploiting a vulnerability, but constrains the attacker's implementation of the exploit. In this example, the attacker would need to be able to spoof one of the allowed hosts' IP addresses.

Both workaround and mitigation can be applied on the vulnerable device itself and/or on other systems (for example, on the network infrastructure that provides connectivity to the affected device).

Examples of workarounds and network-based mitigations include the following:

- Infrastructure access control lists (iACLs)
- Transit access control lists (tACLs)
- Unicast Reverse Path Forwarding (uRPF)
- Layer 2 security (IP Source Guard, Port Security)
- NetFlow
- Firewalls (for example, Cisco ASA and Cisco IOS Zone-Based Firewall)
- Intrusion prevention systems (for example, FirePower)

This list is not exhaustive, and the mitigation largely depends on the vulnerability analysis performed in the previous phase.

Patch Management

Patch management is defined in NIST SP 800-40r3 as the process of identifying, acquiring, installing, and verifying patches for products and systems. In the context security operations management, patch management typically comes as a result of the vulnerabilities remediation phase. As such, patch management sometimes is described as part of vulnerability management. However, the need to install a patch or a system update may span beyond vulnerability remediation (for example, the patch may need to be applied to resolve an operational bug in the software).

Regardless of the reason why a patch needs to be installed, patch management takes care of establishing a process around it. The operational part of the patch process can be considered a case of change management—that is, a request for change (RFC) is raised to request for a system to be patched.

A *patch* usually fixes a specific software bug or vulnerability, and it is usually applied on top of a software release. A *system update* refers to a full software package that is installed instead of the existing software release. A system update includes all the patches that have been issued before the update package is created. In some cases, is not possible to provide a point patch; rather, the code needs to be rebuilt with the fix for a specific issue. In that case, the patch will be released with a system upgrade.

Several compliance frameworks require patch management (for example, PCI DSS sets requirements not only about the patch itself but also about the timeframe for installing the patch for vulnerability mitigation).

The patching process includes several steps:

Step 1. **Identify the systems.** This is where the patch should be installed. A patch may need to be installed, for example, because of a vendor announcement of a new vulnerability, as a result of a vulnerability assessment. Asset inventory and configuration record databases are important to correctly identifying systems that run a version of software that needs to be patched. Other methods for identifying systems are discussed later in this section.

Step 2. **Prioritize the systems that need to be patched.** Installing a patch or a system update is not a trivial task and requires several resources within the organization. When a new patch is released, it may apply to several systems; however, not all systems may need to be patched immediately. For example, some systems need to be patched immediately because they are mission critical or because they are highly exposed to the vulnerability covered by that patch. Other systems might need to be patched, but there is no immediate danger.

Step 3. **Evaluate countermeasures.** In some cases, additional compensative controls can be deployed while the patch request goes through the change management process (for example, while the patch is being qualified in the test environment). At the discretion of the system owner and risk profile, a workaround could be deployed instead of a patch, when available.

Step 4. **Start the change process.** Filing a request for change formally starts the change process to request the installation of a patch. After this point, the process will follow the steps described in the change management process, which includes the following:

■ Review the RFC.

■ Assess whether the patch deployment needs to follow the formal process.

■ Test the patch.

■ Perform security impact analysis.

■ Authorize and deploy the patch.

■ Verify that the system works correctly.

Testing the patch prior to deployment is one of the most sensitive tasks in the patch management process. Installing a patch could potentially disrupt normal business operation (for example, because of new bugs introduced by the patch).

It is very important that the patch is tested in an environment that represents a real business environment. A rollback strategy should also be implemented in case the patch deployment is not done successfully.

Step 5.   **Update configuration records.** Once the patch has been deployed and successfully verified, the configuration record database needs to be updated with the information about the new patch installed and related documentation (such as the time and date for completion, Service Level Agreement [SLA] milestones, issues found during the deployment, and so on).

> **NOTE**   In most of cases, steps 1, 2, and 3 may have already been performed during the vulnerability management process.

Identifying the systems that need to be patched is a complex task; however, it can be greatly simplified by maintaining accurate information in the configuration record database and asset inventory. Enterprise patch management can also help with this task. According to NIST SP 800-40r3, there are three typical deployment models that an enterprise patch management can use:

- **Agent based:** This model uses an agent, which is software installed on the system that communicates with a patch management server. The agent constantly communicates with the server to check whether a new patch is available, and it would retrieve the patch and install it in automatic fashion. The server acts as the patch repository and process orchestrator.

  This solution offers better protection compared to the other methods; however, because it requires installation of specific software, it might not be suitable for some deployment or appliances.

- **Agentless:** This model includes one device that constantly scans the infrastructure and determines which host to patch. It usually requires administrative access to the target host to be able to perform the scanning. This is a lighter approach compared to the agent-based model; however, it might not work in situations where the host is not always present in the network (for example, mobile devices and laptops).

- **Passive network monitoring:** This model uses network traffic monitoring to determine which version of operating system a host is running. This is the least intrusive method but it's the least reliable as well. Because it does not require any privileges on the system, it is generally used to check systems that are not under control of the organization (for example, visitor systems).

Prioritization is also a critical step due to the finite resource an organization can assign to the patch management process. The prioritization task is strictly bound to the security risk assessment that needs to be done every time a new vulnerability is announced.

The Cisco Risk Vulnerability Response Model provides a step-by-step approach on how to prioritize the patch and system update deployment whenever information about new vulnerabilities are released by Cisco.

Figure 5-21 illustrates the Cisco recommended approach to patch deployment prioritization.

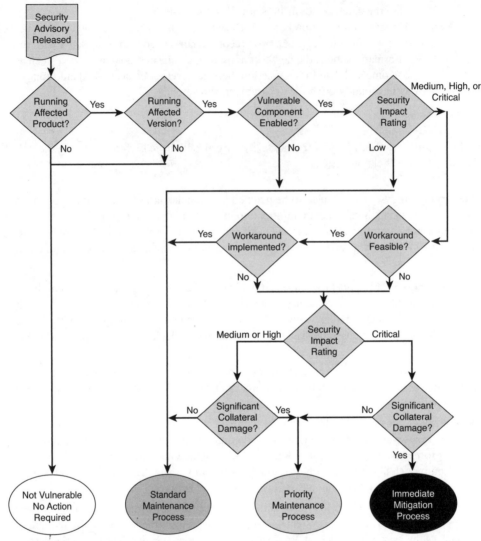

Figure 5-21 *Patch Deployment Prioritization*

A patch deployment can be done with various approaches:

■ **Update all or phased deployment:** The patch can be deployed at once to all systems that require it, or a phased approach can be used based on prioritization and risk assessment.

■ **Pull or push deployment:** The patch can be pushed to the system (for example, in enterprise patch management using an agent-based method), or the user can be asked to install a patch.

■ **Manual or automatic deployment:** The patch can be pushed and installed automatically, or the user may be asked to choose to install the patch manually or semi-manually (for example, by requesting the user click an Install button).

References and Additional Readings

ITU-T X.500: Information Technology – Open Systems Interconnection – The Directory: Overview of concepts, models and services

ITU-T X.519: Information Technology – Open Systems Interconnection – The Directory: Protocol specifications

NIST Special Publication 800-128: Guide for Security-Focused Configuration Management of Information Systems, http://nvlpubs.nist.gov/nistpubs/Legacy/SP/nistspecialpublication800-128.pdf

NIST Special Publication 800-53 Revision 4: Security and Privacy Controls for Federal Information Systems and Organizations, http://nvlpubs.nist.gov/nistpubs/SpecialPublications/NIST.SP.800-53r4.pdf

NIST Framework for Improving Critical Infrastructure Cybersecurity, http://www.nist.gov/cyberframework/upload/cybersecurity-framework-021214.pdf

Kerberos Protocol Tutorial, http://www.kerberos.org/software/tutorial.html

The Kerberos Network Authentication Service (V5), https://tools.ietf.org/html/rfc4120

OASIS – Assertions and Protocols for the OASIS Security Assertion Markup Language (SAML) V2.0, http://docs.oasis-open.org/security/saml/v2.0/saml-core-2.0-os.pdf

OASIS – Glossary for the OASIS Security Assertion Markup Language (SAML) V2.0, http://docs.oasis-open.org/security/saml/v2.0/saml-glossary-2.0-os.pdf

OASIS – Security Assertion Markup Language (SAML) V2.0 Technical Overview, http://docs.oasis-open.org/security/saml/Post2.0/sstc-saml-tech-overview-2.0.html

An Introduction to OAuth 2, https://www.digitalocean.com/community/tutorials/an-introduction-to-oauth-2

OpenID Connect Explained, http://connect2id.com/learn/openid-connect

The OAuth 2.0 Authorization Framework, https://tools.ietf.org/html/rfc6749

OpenID Connect Core 1.0 incorporating errata set 1, http://openid.net/specs/openid-connect-core-1_0.html

OpenID Connect, http://openid.net/connect/

OpenID Authentication 2.0 – Final, https://openid.net/specs/openid-authentication-2_0.html

Federated Identities: OpenID vs SAML vs OAuth, https://softwaresecured.com/federated-identities-openid-vs-saml-vs-oauth/

INTERNATIONAL STANDARD ISO/IEC 27001 – Information technology – Security techniques – Information security management systems – Requirements

Gupta, Das Smith, and Sharman, *Digital Identity and Access Management*, IGI Global (2011)

Cisco Security Information Event Management Deployment Guide, http://www.cisco.com/c/dam/en/us/solutions/collateral/enterprise/design-zone-security-technology-partners/bn_cisco_siem.pdf

5

NIST SPECIAL PUBLICATION 1800-5b – IT ASSET MANAGEMENT – Approach, Architecture, and Security Characteristics, https://nccoe.nist.gov/sites/default/files/library/sp1800/fs-itam-nist-sp1800-5b-draft.pdf

INTERNATIONAL STANDARD ISO/IEC 27002 – Information technology – Security techniques – Code of practice for information security controls

INTERNATIONAL STANDARD ISO/IEC 27005 Information technology – Security techniques – Information security risk management

Rance, *Key Element Guide ITIL Service Transition*, Stationery Office (2012)

Risk Triage for Security Vulnerability Announcements, http://www.cisco.com/c/en/us/about/security-center/vulnerability-risk-triage.html

NIST Special Publication 800-40 Revision 3 – Guide to Enterprise Patch Management Technologies, http://nvlpubs.nist.gov/nistpubs/SpecialPublications/NIST.SP.800-40r3.pdf

SANS Institute, "Three Different Shades of Ethical Hacking: Black, White and Gray," https://www.sans.org/reading-room/whitepapers/hackers/shades-ethical-hacking-black-white-gray-1390

Gatford, Gold, and Manzuik, *Network Security Assessment: From Vulnerability to Patch*, Singress (2006)

What is the Open Vulnerability and Assessment Language (OVAL)?, https://communities.cisco.com/docs/DOC-63158

I Can't Keep Up with All These Cisco Security Advisories: Do I Have to Upgrade?, http://blogs.cisco.com/security/i-cant-keep-up-with-all-these-cisco-security-advisories-do-i-have-to-upgrade

Common Vulnerability Scoring System v3.0: User Guide, https://www.first.org/cvss/cvss-v30-user_guide_v1.1.pdf

Cisco Security Vulnerability Policy, http://www.cisco.com/c/en/us/about/security-center/security-vulnerability-policy.html

Introducing the Cisco PSIRT openVuln API, http://blogs.cisco.com/security/psirt-open-vuln-api

Help! I Need to Respond to All These Cisco IOS Software Vulnerabilities and I Cannot Scale!!!, http://blogs.cisco.com/security/help-i-need-to-respond-to-all-these-cisco-ios-software-vulnerabilities-and-i-cannot-scale

Cisco Unified Access (UA) and Bring Your Own Device (BYOD) CVD, http://www.cisco.com/c/en/us/td/docs/solutions/Enterprise/Borderless_Networks/Unified_Access/BYOD_Design_Guide/BYOD_MDMs.html

Stuppi and Santos, *CCNA Security 210-260 Official Cert Guide*, Cisco Press (2015)

NIST Special Publication 800-124 Revision 1, http://nvlpubs.nist.gov/nistpubs/SpecialPublications/NIST.SP.800-124r1.pdf

Enterprise Deployment Guide and Best Practices, https://documentation.meraki.com/SM/Deployment_Guides/Enterprise_Deployment_Guide_and_Best_Practices

Solutions: Mobile device management, https://meraki.cisco.com/solutions/mobile-device-management

Cisco Identity Services Engine Administrator Guide, Release 2.0, http://www.cisco.
com/c/en/us/td/docs/security/ise/2-0/admin_guide/b_ise_admin_guide_20/b_ise_admin_
guide_20_chapter_01000.html#ID397

NIST Special Publication 800-92 – Guide to Computer Security Log Management, http://
csrc.nist.gov/publications/nistpubs/800-92/SP800-92.pdf

The Syslog Protocol, https://tools.ietf.org/html/rfc5424

NIST Special Publication 800-61 Revision 2, http://nvlpubs.nist.gov/nistpubs/
SpecialPublications/NIST.SP.800-61r2.pdf

Vulnerability Management: Tools, Challenges and Best Practices - SANS Institute Infosec
Reading Room - https://www.sans.org/reading-room/whitepapers/threats/vulnerability-
management-tools-challenges-practices-1267

5

Exam Preparation Tasks

Review All Key Topics

Review the most important topics in the chapter, noted with the Key Topic icon in the outer margin of the page. Table 5-9 lists these key topics and the page numbers on which each is found.

Table 5-9   Key Topics

Key Topic Element	Description	Page
List	Identity and account lifecycle management phases	244
Summary	Password management	246
Figure 5-6	Single sign-on system	253
Summary	Security Events and Logs Management	260
Summary	Logs Collection, Analysis, and Disposal	260
List	SIEM capabilities	264
List	Difference between log collection and SIEM	265
List	Summary of assets management phases	266
List	Threats to organization using BYOD	269
List	Enterprise mobile management phases	270
List	Capabilities of an MDM system	271
Table 5-6	Comparison of on-premises and cloud-based MDM	272
Summary	Configuration management and terminology	276
List	Secure configuration management phases	276
Summary	Change definition and changes classification	277
List	Configuration and Change Management definitions	278
List	Request for Change process	279
List	Change security impact analysis	280
Figure 5-17	Vulnerability management phases	281
Summary	Vulnerability identification and CVE ID	282
Summary	Vulnerability scan	284
Summary	Penetration assessment	285
List	Types of pen tests	285
Table 5-7	Comparison of vulnerability scanner and penetration assessment	286
Summary	Responsible versus full disclosure	288
Summary	CVSS system	291

Key Topic Element	Description	Page
List	Vulnerabilities workarounds and mitigations	295
List	Patch management steps	296
List	Patch deployment methods	297
Figure 5-21	Patch prioritization using Cisco Vulnerability Risk Management framework	298
List	Patches deployment approaches	298

Complete Tables and Lists from Memory

Print a copy of Appendix B, "Memory Tables," (found on the book website), or at least the section for this chapter, and complete the tables and lists from memory. Appendix C, "Memory Tables Answer Key," also on the website, includes completed tables and lists to check your work.

Define Key Terms

Define the following key terms from this chapter, and check your answers in the glossary:

identity and access management (IAM), password management, one-time password, directory, directory service, ITU-T X.500, LDAP, single sign-on (SSO), federated SSO, log collection, Security Information and Event Manager (SIEM), asset, asset management, asset inventory, asset ownership, asset classification, asset handling, enterprise mobile management, mobile device management (MDM), configuration management, configuration item (CI), configuration record, configuration management database, security baseline configuration, change management, change, request for change (RFC), vulnerability management, Common Vulnerabilities and Exposures (CVE), vulnerability scanner, penetration assessment, Common Vulnerability Scoring System (CVSS), patch management

Q&A

The answers to these questions appear in Appendix A, "Answers to the 'Do I Know This Already?' Quizzes and Q&A Questions." For more practice with exam format questions, use the exam engine on the website.

1. Which of the following are properties of a secure digital identity? (Select all that apply.)

   a. Unique

   b. Nondescriptive

   c. Encrypted

   d. Nominative

2. Why is a periodic access rights and privileges review important?

   a. To avoid privilege creep

   b. To verify a user's security clearance

   c. To ensure credentials are encrypted

   d. To assign a security label

3. In which cases can access be revoked? (Select all that apply.)

   a. After job termination

   b. When a user moves to another job

   c. When creating an administrative user

   d. Due to a security violation

4. Which of the following are responsibilities of an asset owner? (Mark all that apply)

   a. Implementation of security controls

   b. Asset security classification

   c. Asset disposal

   d. Analysis of the access logs

5. What is the relative distinguished name at the organizational unit level of the following entity? C=US, O=Cisco, OU=CCNA Learning, CN=Jones?

   a. OU=CCNA Learning

   b. C=US, O=Cisco, OU=CCNA Learning

   c. CN=Jones

   d. OU=CCNA Learning, CN=Jones

6. In which case should an employee return his laptop to the organization?

   a. When moving to a different role

   b. Upon termination of the employment

   c. As described in the asset return policy

   d. When the laptop is end of lease

7. Where are configuration records stored?

   a. In a CMDB

   b. In a MySQL DB

   c. In a XLS file

   d. There is no need to store them

8. Which type of vulnerability scanner probes the target system to get information?

   a. Intrusive

   b. Direct

   c. Passive

   d. Active

9. In which enterprise patch management model can the system can install a patch automatically?

    a. Agentless

    b. Passive

    c. Agent based

    d. Install based

10. What is the syslog priority (PRI) of a message from facility 20 with a severity of 4?

    a. 164

    b. 160

    c. 24

    d. 52

11. What is the log normalization functionality used for?

    a. It provides a way to archive logs.

    b. It aggregates information based on common information and reduces duplicates.

    c. It provides reporting capabilities.

    d. It extracts relevant attributes from logs received in different formats and stores them in a common data model or template.

12. Which of the following functions are typically provided by an SIEM? (Select all that apply.)

    a. Log correlation

    b. Log archiving

    c. Log normalization

    d. Log correction

13. Which elements are found in a typical Cisco BYOD architecture? (Select all that apply.)

    a. Mobile device management (MDM) server

    b. Cisco ISE

    c. Cisco MARS

    d. Cisco ASR5000

14. At which step of the change process is the configuration database updated?

    a. In the review and close change record

    b. When the request for change is created

    c. During the change implementation

    d. During the request for change review

5

15. Which of the following are true statements regarding vulnerability scanners and penetration assessments? (Select all that apply.)

    a. Vulnerability scanners can crash a device; penetration assessments do not.

    b. Vulnerability scanners usually work with known vulnerabilities.

    c. Penetration assessment is typically fully automated.

    d. Vulnerability scanners can work in active mode and passive mode.

16. What is an OVAL definition?

    a. An XML file that contains information about how to check a system for the presence of vulnerabilities.

    b. It is synonymous with the OVAL language.

    c. An XML file used to represent reporting on the vulnerability assessment.

    d. A database schema.

The learning objectives of this chapter are as follows:

- Describe the uses of a hash algorithm
- Explore the uses of encryption algorithms
- Compare and contrast symmetric and asymmetric encryption algorithms
- Describe the processes of digital signature creation and verification
- Describe the operation of a PKI
- Describe the security impact of the commonly used hash algorithms (SHA and MD5)

CHAPTER 6

Fundamentals of Cryptography and Public Key Infrastructure (PKI)

This chapter discusses the fundamental components of cryptography, including algorithms for hashing, encryption, and key management, which may be used by virtual private networks, secure web connections, and many other applications.

"Do I Know This Already?" Quiz

The "Do I Know This Already?" quiz helps you identify your strengths and deficiencies in this chapter's topics. The eight-question quiz, derived from the major sections in the "Foundation Topics" portion of the chapter, helps you determine how to spend your limited study time. You can find the answers in Appendix A Answers to the "Do I Know This Already?" Quizzes and Q&A Questions.

Table 6-1 outlines the major topics discussed in this chapter and the "Do I Know This Already?" quiz questions that correspond to those topics.

Table 6-1   "Do I Know This Already?" Foundation Topics Section-to-Question Mapping

Foundation Topics Section	Questions Covered in This Section
Cryptography	1–4
Fundamentals of PKI	5–8

1. Which of the following are examples of common methods used by ciphers?

   a. Transposition

   b. Substitution

   c. Polyalphabetic

   d. Polynomial

2. Which of the following are examples of symmetric block cipher algorithms?

   a. Advanced Encryption Standard (AES)

   b. Triple Digital Encryption Standard (3DES)

   c. DSA

   d. Blowfish

   e. ElGamal

3. Which of the following are examples of hashes?

   a. ASH-160

   b. SHA-1

   c. SHA-2

   d. MD5

4. Which of the following are benefits of digital signatures?

   a. Authentication

   b. Nonrepudiation

   c. Encryption

   d. Hashing

5. Which of the following statements are true about public and private key pairs?

   a. A key pair is a set of two keys that work in combination with each other as a team.

   b. A key pair is a set of two keys that work in isolation.

   c. If you use the public key to encrypt data using an asymmetric encryption algorithm, the corresponding private key is used to decrypt the data.

   d. If you use the public key to encrypt data using an asymmetric encryption algorithm, the peer decrypts the data with that public key.

6. Which of the following entities can be found inside of a digital certificate?

   a. FQDN

   b. DNS server IP address

   c. Default gateway

   d. Public key

7. Which of the following is true about root certificates?

   a. A root certificate contains information about the user.

   b. A root certificate contains information about the network security device.

   c. A root certificate contains the public key of the CA.

   d. Root certificates never expire.

8. Which of the following are public key standards?

   a. IPsec

   b. PKCS #10

   c. PKCS #12

   d. ISO33012

   e. AES

Foundation Topics

Cryptography

The word *cryptography* or *cryptology* comes from the Greek word *kryptós*, which means a secret. It is the study of the techniques used for encryption and secure communications. Cryptographers are the people who study and analyze cryptography. Cryptographers are always constructing and analyzing protocols for preventing unauthorized users from reading private messages as well as the following areas of information security:

- Data confidentiality
- Data integrity
- Authentication
- Nonrepudiation

Cryptography is a combination of disciplines, including mathematics and computer science. Examples of the use of cryptography include virtual private networks (VPNs), ecommerce, secure email transfer, and credit card chips. You may also often hear the term *cryptanalysis*, which is the study of how to crack encryption algorithms or their implementations.

Ciphers and Keys

Understanding the terminology is a large part of understanding any technology, so let's begin with some fundamentals.

Ciphers

A *cipher* is a set of rules, which can also be called an *algorithm*, about how to perform encryption or decryption. Literally hundreds of encryption algorithms are available, and there are likely many more that are proprietary and used for special purposes, such as for governmental use and national security.

Common methods that ciphers use include the following:

- **Substitution:** This type of cipher substitutes one character for another.
- **Polyalphabetic:** This is similar to substitution, but instead of using a single alphabet, it can use multiple alphabets and switch between them by some trigger character in the encoded message.
- **Transposition:** This method uses many different options, including the rearrangement of letters. For example, if we have the message "This is secret," we could write it out (top to bottom, left to right) as shown in Example 6-1.

Example 6-1 *Transposition Example*

```
T S S R
H I E E
I S C T
```

We then encrypt it as RETCSIHTSSEI, which involves starting at the top right and going around like a clock, spiraling inward. In order for someone to know how to encrypt/decrypt this correctly, the correct key is needed.

Keys

The key in Example 6-1 refers to the instructions for how to reassemble the characters. In this case, it begins at the top-right corner and moves clockwise and spirals inward.

A one-time pad (OTP) is a good example of a key that is only used once. Using this method, if we want to encrypt a 32-bit message, we use a 32-bit key, also called the *pad*, which is used one time only. Each bit from the pad is mathematically computed with a corresponding bit from our message, and the results are our cipher text, or encrypted content. The key in this case is the one-time use pad. The pad must also be known by the receiver if he or she wants to decrypt the message. (Another use of the acronym OTP is for a user's *one-time password*, which is a different topic altogether.)

Block and Stream Ciphers

Encryption algorithms can operate on blocks of data at a time, or bits and bytes of data, based on the type of cipher. Let's compare the two methods.

Block Ciphers

A block cipher is a symmetric key cipher (meaning the same key is used to encrypt and decrypt) that operates on a group of bits called a *block*. A block cipher encryption algorithm may take a 64-bit block of plaintext and generate a 64-bit block of ciphertext. With this type of encryption, the key to encrypt is also used to decrypt. Examples of symmetric block cipher algorithms include the following:

- Advanced Encryption Standard (AES)
- Triple Digital Encryption Standard (3DES)
- Blowfish
- Digital Encryption Standard (DES)
- International Data Encryption Algorithm (IDEA)

Block ciphers may add padding in cases where there is not enough data to encrypt to make a full block size. This might result is a very small amount of wasted overhead, because the small padding would be processed by the cipher along with the real data.

Stream Ciphers

A stream cipher is a symmetric key cipher (meaning the same key is used to encrypt and decrypt), where the plaintext data to be encrypted is done a bit at a time against the bits of the key stream, also called a *cipher digit stream*. The resulting output is a ciphertext stream. Because a cipher stream does not have to fit in a given block size, there may be slightly less overhead than with a block cipher that requires padding to complete a block size.

Symmetric and Asymmetric Algorithms

As you build your vocabulary, the words *symmetric* and *asymmetric* are important ones to differentiate. Let's look at the options of each and identify which of these requires the most CPU overhead and which one is used for bulk data encryption.

Symmetric Algorithms

As mentioned previously, a symmetric encryption algorithm, also known as a symmetric cipher, uses the same key to encrypt the data and decrypt the data. Two devices connected via a VPN both need the key (or keys) to successfully encrypt and decrypt the data protected using a symmetric encryption algorithm. Common examples of symmetric encryption algorithms include the following:

- DES
- 3DES
- AES
- IDEA
- RC2, RC4, RC5, RC6
- Blowfish

Symmetric encryption algorithms are used for most of the data we protect in VPNs today because they are much faster to use and take less CPU than asymmetric algorithms. As with all encryption, the more difficult the key, the more difficult it is for someone who does not have the key to intercept and understand the data. We usually refer to keys with VPNs by their length. A longer key means better security. A typical key length is 112 bits to 256 bits. The minimum key length should be at least 128 bits for symmetric encryption algorithms to be considered fairly safe. Again, bigger is better.

Asymmetric Algorithms

An example of an asymmetric algorithm is a public key algorithm. There is something magical about asymmetric algorithms because instead of using the same key for encrypting and decrypting, they use two different keys that mathematically work together as a pair. Let's call these keys the *public key* and the *private key*. Together they make a key pair. Let's put these keys to use with an analogy.

Imagine a huge shipping container that has a special lock with two keyholes (one large keyhole and one smaller keyhole). With this magical shipping container, if we use the small keyhole with its respective key to lock the container, the only way to unlock it is to use the big keyhole with its larger key. Another option is to initially lock the container using the big key in the big keyhole, and then the only way to unlock it is to use the small key in the small keyhole. (I told you it was magic.) This analogy explains the interrelationship between the public key and its corresponding private key. (I'll let you decide which one you want to call the big key and which one you want to call the little key.) There is a very high CPU cost when using key pairs to lock and unlock data. For that reason, we use asymmetric algorithms sparingly. Instead of using them to encrypt our bulk data, we use asymmetric algorithms for things such as authenticating a VPN peer or generating keying material that we can use for our symmetric algorithms. Both of these tasks are infrequent compared to encrypting all the user packets (which happens consistently).

With public key cryptography, one of the keys in the key pair is published and available to anyone who wants to use it (the public key). The other key in the key pair is the private key, which is known only to the device that owns the public-private key pair. An example of when a public-private key pair is used is visiting a secure website. In the background, the public-private key pair of the server is being used for the security of the session. Your PC has access to the public key, and the server is the only one that knows its private key.

Here are some examples of asymmetric algorithms:

- **RSA:** Named after Rivest, Shamir, and Adleman, who created the algorithm. The primary use of this asymmetric algorithm today is for authentication. It is also known as public key cryptography standard (PKCS) #1. The key length may be from 512 to 2048, and a minimum size for good security is at least 1024. Regarding security, bigger is better.

- **DH:** The Diffie-Hellman key exchange protocol is an asymmetric algorithm that allows two devices to negotiate and establish shared secret keying material (keys) over an untrusted network. The interesting thing about DH is that although the algorithm itself is asymmetric, the keys generated by the exchange are symmetric keys that can then be used with symmetric algorithms such as Triple Digital Encryption Standard (3DES) and Advanced Encryption Standard (AES).

- **ElGamal:** This asymmetric encryption system is based on the DH exchange.

- **DSA:** The Digital Signature Algorithm was developed by the U.S. National Security Agency.

- **ECC:** Elliptic Curve Cryptography is a public-key cryptography based on the algebraic structure of elliptic curves over finite fields.

Asymmetric algorithms require more CPU processing power than symmetric algorithms. Asymmetric algorithms, however, are more secure. A typical key length used in asymmetric algorithms can be anywhere between 2048 and 4096. A key length that is shorter than 2048 is considered unreliable or not as secure as a longer key.

A commonly asymmetric algorithm used for authentication is RSA (as in RSA digital signatures).

Hashes

Hashing is a method used to verify data integrity. For example, you can verify the integrity of a downloaded software image file from Cisco, and then verify its integrity using a tool such as the **verify md5** command in a Cisco IOS device or a checksum verification in an operating system such as Microsoft Windows, Linux, or Mac OS X.

SHA512 checksum (512 bits) output is represented by 128 characters in hex format, whereas MD5 produces a 128-bit (16-byte) hash value, typically expressed in text format as a 32-digit hexadecimal number. Example 6-2 provides a comparison of the output of an SHA512 checksum with an MD5 checksum for a Cisco ASA software image (asa941-smp-k8.bin).

Example 6-2   *Hash Verification of a Cisco ASA Software Image*

```
SHA512 checksum
1b6d41e893868aab9e06e78a9902b925227c82d8e31978ff2c412c18ac99f49f7035471544
1385e0b96e4bd3e861d18fb30433d52e12b15b501fa790f36d0ea0
MD5 checksum
6ddc5129d43a22490a3c42d93f058ffe
```

> **NOTE**   You can find a blog post explaining hash verification of Cisco software at http://
> blogs.cisco.com/security/sha512-checksums-for-all-cisco-software.

A cryptographic hash function is a process that takes a block of data and creates a small fixed-sized hash value. It is a one-way function, meaning that if two different computers take the same data and run the same hash function, they should get the same fixed-sized hash value (for example, a 12-bit long hash). Message Digest 5 (MD5) algorithm is an example of a cryptographic hash function. It is not possible (at least not realistically) to generate the same hash from a different block of data. This is referred to as *collision resistance*. The result of the hash is a fixed-length small string of data, and is sometimes referred to as the digest, message digest, or simply the hash.

An example of using a hash to verify integrity is the sender running a hash algorithm on a packet and attaching that hash to it. The receiver runs the same hash against the packet and compares his results against the results the sender had (which are attached to the packet as well). If the hash generated matches the hash that was sent, they know that the entire packet is intact. If a single bit of the hashed portion of the packet is modified, the hash calculated by the receiver will not match, and the receiver will know that the packet had a problem—specifically with the integrity of the packet.

Example 6-3 is another example that verifies the integrity of three files, as well as compares the contents of each one. In Example 6-3, three files are shown (file_1.txt, file_2.txt, and file_3.txt). The **shasum** Linux command is used to display the hashes of all three files. Files file_1.txt and file_3.txt have exactly the same contents; that's why you see the same SHA-512 hash.

Example 6-3   *File Hash Verification*

```
bash-3.2$ ls -l
-rw-r--r--  1 omar   staff    32 Dec  7 12:30 file_1.txt
-rw-r--r--  1 omar   staff   288 Dec  7 12:31 file_2.txt
-rw-r--r--  1 omar   staff    32 Dec  7 12:30 file_3.txt

bash-3.2$ shasum -a 512 *
815e1cbe6556ba31d448c3e30df3f1942d2f05a85ce2dd9512604bfbc9336fcb8ad0ea688597003b1806
cf98ce7699bd58c48576ccd1010451154afa37814114  file_1.txt
72ff6c32b9d2b0ff288382f8f07a8556fa16ccb3ef4672c612a1ec4a9a397b195b4ac993dca710d-
bebbd72b7f72da3364da444d7d64580f035db405109b6f6e1  file_2.txt
815e1cbe6556ba31d448c3e30df3f1942d2f05a85ce2dd9512604bfbc9336fcb8ad0ea688597003b1806
cf98ce7699bd58c48576ccd1010451154afa37814114  file_3.txt
```

Hashes are also used when security experts are analyzing, searching, and comparing malware. A hash of the piece of malware is typically exchanged instead of the actual file, in order to avoid infection and collateral damage. For example, Cisco Advanced Malware Protection (AMP) uses malware hashes in many of its different functions and capabilities.

The three most popular types of hashes are as follows:

- **Message Digest 5 (MD5):** This hash creates a 128-bit digest.
- **Secure Hash Algorithm 1 (SHA-1):** This hash creates a 160-bit digest.
- **Secure Hash Algorithm 2 (SHA-2):** Options include a digest between 224 bits and 512 bits.

With encryption and cryptography, and now hashing, bigger is better, and more bits equals better security. There are several vulnerabilities in the MD5 hashing protocol, including collision and pre-image vulnerabilities. Attackers use collision attacks in order to find two input strings of a hash function that produce the same hash result. This is because hash functions have infinite input length and a predefined output length. Subsequently, there is the possibility of two different inputs producing the same output hash.

There are also several vulnerabilities and attacks against SHA-1. Subsequently, it is recommended that SHA-2 with 512 bits be used when possible.

> **TIP** During the last few years there has been a lot of discussion on quantum computers and their potential impact on current cryptography standards. This is an area of active research and growing interest. The industry is trying to label what are the post-quantum ready and next-generation cryptographic algorithms. AES-256, SHA-384, and SHA-512 are believed to have post-quantum security. Other public key algorithms are believed to also be resistant to post-quantum security attacks; however, not many standards support them.
>
> Cisco provides a great resource that explains the next-generation encryption protocols and hashing protocols at http://www.cisco.com/c/en/us/about/security-center/next-generation-cryptography.html.

Hashed Message Authentication Code

Hashed Message Authentication Code (HMAC) uses the mechanism of hashing, but it kicks it up a notch. Instead of using a hash that anyone can calculate, it includes in its calculation a secret key of some type. Thus, only the other party who also knows the secret key and can calculate the resulting hash can correctly verify the hash. When this mechanism is used, an attacker who is eavesdropping and intercepting packets cannot inject or remove data from those packets without being noticed because he cannot recalculate the correct hash for the modified packet because he does not have the key or keys used for the calculation.

Once again, MD5 is a hash function that is insecure and should be avoided. SHA-1 is a legacy algorithm and therefore is adequately secure. SHA-256 provides adequate protection for sensitive information. On the other hand, SHA-384 is required to protect classified information of higher importance.

Digital Signatures

When you sign something, this often represents a commitment to follow through, or at least proves that you are who you say you are. In the world of cryptography, a digital signature provides three core benefits:

- Authentication
- Data integrity
- Nonrepudiation

Digital Signatures in Action

One of the best ways to understand how a digital signature operates is to remember what you learned in the previous sections about public and private key pairs, hashing, and encryption. Digital signatures involve each of these elements.

In most security books, three fictional characters are used to explain encryption and PKI: Bob, Alice, and Eve. Bob and Alice typically are the two entities that exchange a secured message over a public or untrusted network, and Eve is the person who tries to "eavesdrop" and steal the information being exchanged. In this book, let's make it more entertaining and use Batman, Robin, and the Joker. In Figure 6-1, all three entities are illustrated. Batman wants to send an encrypted message to Robin without the Joker being able to read it.

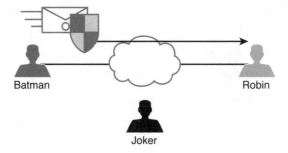

Figure 6-1 *Fundamentals of Encrypted Communications*

Batman and Robin are two people who want to establish a VPN connection to each other, and to do so they want to use digital signatures to verify each other to make sure they are talking to the right entity. This concept is illustrated in Figure 6-2.

Both Batman and Robin want to verify each other, but for simplicity let's focus on one entity: Batman wanting to prove its identity to the other device, Robin. (This could also be phrased as Robin asking Batman to prove Batman's identity.)

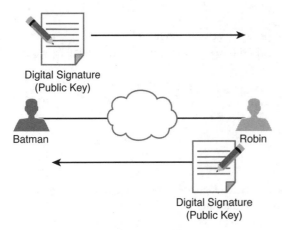

Figure 6-2 *Digital Signature Verification*

As a little setup beforehand, you should know that both Batman and Robin have generated public-private key pairs, and they both have been given digital certificates from a common certificate authority (CA). A CA is a trusted entity that hands out digital certificates. This concept is illustrated in Figure 6-3.

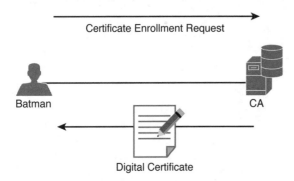

Figure 6-3 *Digital Certificate Enrollment with a CA*

In Figure 6-3, Batman requests a digital certification from (enrolls with) a CA, and the CA assigns one to Batman. If you and I were to open the digital certificate, we would find the name of the entity (in this case, Batman). We would also find Batman's public key (which Batman gave to the CA when applying for the digital certificate). Figure 6-4 shows an example of a digital certificate. In this case, Cisco's website (cisco.com) digital certificate is shown. Also, the digital signature of the CA is shown.

> **NOTE**   You will learn more about CAs and the certificate enrollment process later in the "Certificate Authorities" section.

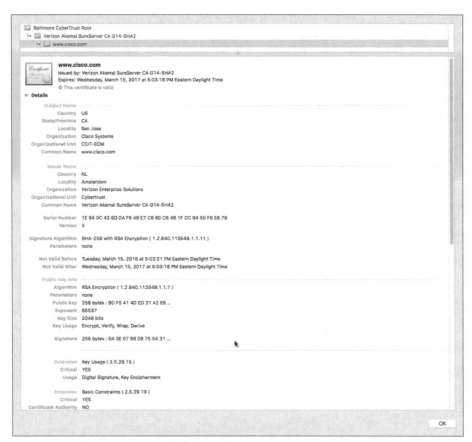

Baltimore CyberTrust Root
　　Verizon Akamai SureServer CA G14-SHA2
　　　　www.cisco.com

www.cisco.com
Issued by: Verizon Akamai SureServer CA G14-SHA2
Expires: Wednesday, March 15, 2017 at 5:03:18 PM Eastern Daylight Time
ⓧ This certificate is valid

▼ **Details**

Subject Name
　Country   US
　State/Province   CA
　Locality   San Jose
　Organization   Cisco Systems
　Organizational Unit   CCIT-ECM
　Common Name   www.cisco.com

Issuer Name
　Country   NL
　Locality   Amsterdam
　Organization   Verizon Enterprise Solutions
　Organizational Unit   Cybertrust
　Common Name   Verizon Akamai SureServer CA G14-SHA2

　Serial Number   1E 94 0C 43 8D 0A F6 49 E7 C6 60 C6 4B 1F CC 94 50 F6 E6 79
　Version   3

　Signature Algorithm   SHA-256 with RSA Encryption (1.2.840.113549.1.1.11)
　Parameters   none

　Not Valid Before   Tuesday, March 15, 2016 at 5:03:21 PM Eastern Daylight Time
　Not Valid After   Wednesday, March 15, 2017 at 5:03:18 PM Eastern Daylight Time

Public Key Info
　Algorithm   RSA Encryption (1.2.840.113549.1.1.1)
　Parameters   none
　Public Key   256 bytes : BD F5 41 4D ED 21 A2 E8 ...
　Exponent   65537
　Key Size   2048 bits
　Key Usage   Encrypt, Verify, Wrap, Derive

　Signature   256 bytes : 64 3E 07 88 09 75 54 31 ...

　Extension   Key Usage (2.5.29.15)
　Critical   YES
　Usage   Digital Signature, Key Encipherment

　Extension   Basic Constraints (2.5.29.19)
　Critical   YES
Certificate Authority   NO

OK

Figure 6-4   *Digital Certificate Enrollment with a CA*

Both Batman and Robin trust the CA and have received their certificates.

Batman takes a packet and generates a hash. Batman then takes this small hash and encrypts it using Batman's private key. (Think of this as a shipping container, and Batman is using the small key in the small keyhole to lock the data.) Batman attaches this encrypted hash to the packet and sends it to Robin. The fancy name for this encrypted hash is *digital signature*.

When Robin receives this packet, it looks at the encrypted hash that was sent and decrypts it using Batman's public key. (Think of this as a big keyhole and the big key being used to unlock the data.) Robin then sets the decrypted hash off to the side for one moment and runs the same hash algorithm on the packet it just received. If the hash Robin just calculated matches the hash just received (after Robin decrypted it using the sender's public key), then Robin knows two things: that the only person who could have encrypted it was Batman with Batman's private key, and that the data integrity on the packet is solid, because if one bit had been changed, the hashes would not have matched. This process is called authentication, using digital signatures, and it normally happens in both directions with an IPsec VPN tunnel if the peers are using digital signatures for authentication (referred to as *rsa-signatures* in the configuration).

At this point you might be wondering how Robin got Batman's key (Batman's public key) to begin with. The answer is that Batman and Robin also exchanged digital certificates that contained each other's public keys. Batman and Robin do not trust just any certificates, but they do trust certificates that are digitally signed by a CA they trust. This also implies that to verify digital signatures from the CA, both Batman and Robin also need the CA's public key. Most browsers and operating systems today have the built-in certificates and public keys for the mainstream CAs on the Internet. Figure 6-5 shows the "System Roots" keychain on Mac OS X.

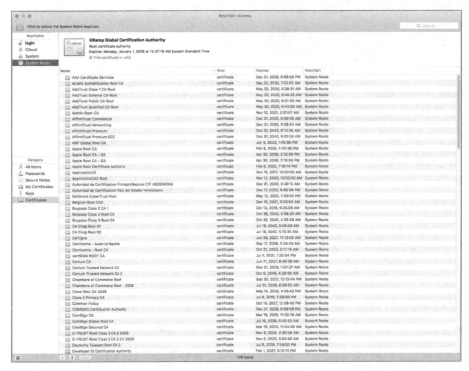

Figure 6-5 *Mac OS X System Roots*

Key Management

Key management is huge in the world of cryptography. We have symmetric keys that can be used with symmetric algorithms for hashing and encryption. We have asymmetric keys such as public-private key pairs that can be used with asymmetric algorithms such as digital signatures, among other things. You could say that the key to security with all these algorithms we have taken a look at is the keys themselves.

Key management deals with generating keys, verifying keys, exchanging keys, storing keys, and at the end of their lifetime, destroying keys. An example of why this is critical is when two devices that want to establish a VPN session send their encryption keys over at the beginning of their session in plaintext. If that happens, an eavesdropper who sees the keys could use them to change ciphertext into understandable data, which would result in a lack of confidentiality within the VPN.

Keyspace refers to all the possible values for a key. The bigger the key, the more secure the algorithm will be. The only negative of having an extremely long key is that the longer the key, the more the CPU is used for the decryption and encryption of data.

Next-Generation Encryption Protocols

The industry is always looking for new algorithms for encryption, authentication, digital signatures, and key exchange to meet escalating security and performance requirements. The U.S. government selected and recommended a set of cryptographic standards called Suite B because it provides a complete suite of algorithms designed to meet future security needs. Suite B has been approved for protecting classified information at both the secret and top-secret levels. Cisco participated in the development of some of these standards. The Suite B next-generation encryption (NGE) includes algorithms for authenticated encryption, digital signatures, key establishment, and cryptographic hashing, as listed here:

- Elliptic Curve Cryptography (ECC) replaces RSA signatures with the ECDSA algorithm, and replaces the DH key exchange with ECDH. ECDSA is an elliptic curve variant of the DSA algorithm, which has been a standard since 1994. The new key exchange uses DH with P-256 and P-384 curves.
- AES in the GaRobin/Counter Mode (GCM) of operation.
- ECC digital signature algorithm.
- SHA-256, SHA-384, and SHA-512.

IPsec and SSL

IPsec is a suite of protocols used to protect IP packets and has been around for decades. It is in use today for both remote-access VPNs and site-to-site VPNs. SSL is the new kid on the block in its application with remote-access VPNs. Let's take a closer look at both these options.

IPsec

IPsec is a collection of protocols and algorithms used to protect IP packets at Layer 3—hence the name IP Security (IPsec). IPsec provides the core benefits of confidentiality through encryption, data integrity through hashing and HMAC, and authentication using digital signatures or using a pre-shared key (PSK) that is just for the authentication, similar to a password. IPsec also provides anti-replay support. The following is a high-level explanation of IPsec components (protocols, algorithms, and so on):

- **ESP and AH:** These are the two primary methods for implementing IPsec. ESP stands for Encapsulating Security Payload, which can perform all the features of IPsec. AH stands for Authentication Header, which can do many parts of the IPsec objectives, except for the important one (the encryption of the data). For that reason, we do not frequently see AH being used.
- **Encryption algorithms for confidentiality:** DES, 3DES, and AES.
- **Hashing algorithms for integrity:** MD5 and SHA.
- **Authentication algorithms:** Pre-shared keys (PSKs) and RSA digital signatures.

6

■ **Key management:** Examples of key management include Diffie-Hellman (DH), which can be used to dynamically generate symmetric keys to be used by symmetric algorithms; PKI, which supports the function of digital certificates issued by trusted CAs; and Internet Key Exchange (IKE), which does a lot of the negotiating and management needed for IPsec to operate.

SSL

Information transmitted over a public network needs to be secured through encryption to prevent unauthorized access to that data. An example is online banking. Not only do you want to avoid an attacker seeing your username, password, and codes, you also do not want an attacker to be able to modify the packets in transit during a transaction with the bank. This would seem to be a perfect opportunity for IPsec to be used to encrypt the data and perform integrity checking and authentication of the server you are connected to. Although it is true that IPsec can do all this, not everyone has an IPsec client or software running on their computer. What's more, not everyone has a digital certificate or a PSK they could successfully use for authentication.

You can still benefit from the concepts of encryption and authentication by using a different type of technology called Secure Sockets Layer (SSL). The convenient thing about SSL is that almost every web browser on every computer supports it, so almost anyone who has a computer can use it.

To use SSL, the user connects to an SSL server (that is, a web server that supports SSL) by using HTTPS rather than HTTP (the *S* in HTTPS stands for Secure). Depending on whom you talk to, SSL may also be called Transport Layer Security, or TLS. To the end user, it represents a secure connection to the server, and to the correct server.

Even if the user does not type in HTTPS, the website can redirect him or her behind the scenes to the correct URL. Once there, the browser requests that the web server identify itself. (Be aware that everything that is about to happen is occurring in the background and does not require user intervention.) The server sends the browser a copy of its digital certificate, which may also be called an SSL certificate. When the browser receives the certificate, it checks whether it trusts the certificate. Using the method for verifying a digital signature discussed earlier, the browser determines whether the certificate is valid based on the signature of the CA. Assuming the certificate is trusted, the browser now has access to the server's public key contained in the certificate.

> **NOTE** If the signature is not valid, or at least if the browser does not think the certificate is valid, a pop-up is usually presented to the user asking whether he or she wants to proceed. This is where user training is important. Users should be trained never to accept a certificate that the browser does not trust.

Most of the time, the server does not require the browser to prove who it is. Instead, the web server uses some type of user authentication, such as a username and password, as required, to verify who the user is.

After the authentication has been done, several additional exchanges occur between the browser and the server as they establish the encryption algorithm they will use as well as the keys they will use to encrypt and decrypt the data. You learn more about that exact process in the next section, "Fundamentals of PKI."

As mentioned previously, understanding the terminology is important for you in mastering encryption and VPN technologies. Figure 6-6 explains the key components and their functions as well as provides examples of their implementation.

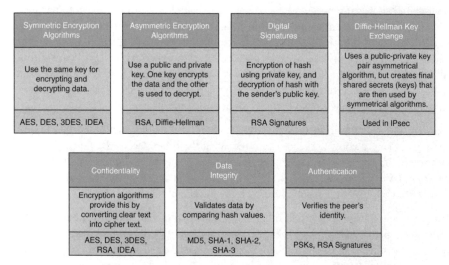

Figure 6-6 *Fundamental Encryption Components*

Fundamentals of PKI

Public key infrastructure (PKI) is a set of identities, roles, policies, and actions for the creation, use, management, distribution, and revocation of digital certificates. The reason that PKI exists is to enable the secure electronic transfer of information for many different purposes. You probably know that using simple passwords is an inadequate authentication method. PKI provides a more rigorous method to confirm the identity of the parties involved in the communication and to validate the information being transferred.

PKI binds public keys with the identities of people, applications, and organizations. This "binding" is maintained by the issuance and management of digital certificates by a certificate authority (CA).

Public and Private Key Pairs

A key pair is a set of two keys that work in combination with each other as a team. In a typical key pair, you have one public key and one private key. The public key may be shared with everyone, and the private key is not shared with anyone. For example, the private key for a web server is known only to that specific web server. If you use the public key to encrypt data using an asymmetric encryption algorithm, the corresponding private key is used to decrypt the data. The inverse is also true. If you encrypt with the private key, you then decrypt with the corresponding public key. Another name for this asymmetric encryption is *public key cryptography* or *asymmetric key cryptography*. The uses for asymmetric algorithms are not just limited to authentication, as in the case of digital signatures discussed in the previous sections, but that is one example of an asymmetric algorithm.

RSA Algorithm, the Keys, and Digital Certificates

Keys are the secrets that allow cryptography to provide confidentiality. Let's take a closer look at the keys involved with RSA and how they are used.

With RSA digital signatures, each party has a public-private key pair because both parties intend on authenticating the other side. Going back to the analogy in the previous sections, let's use two users named Batman and Robin. As you saw in Figures 6-2 and 6-3, they both generated their own public-private key pair, and they both enrolled with a certificate authority (CA). That CA took each of their public keys as well as their names and IP addresses and created individual digital certificates, and the CA issued these certificates back to Batman and Robin, respectively. The CA also digitally signed each certificate.

When Batman and Robin want to authenticate each other, they send each other their digital certificates (or at least a copy of them). Upon receiving the other party's digital certificate, they both verify the authenticity of the certificate by checking the signature of a CA they currently trust. (When you *trust* a certificate authority, it means that you know who the CA is and can verify that CA's digital signature by knowing the public key of that CA.)

Now that Batman and Robin have each other's public keys, they can authenticate each other. This normally happens inside of a VPN tunnel in both directions (when RSA signatures are used for authentication). For the purpose of clarity, we focus on just one of these parties (for example, the computer Batman) and proving its identity to the other computer (in this case, Robin).

Batman takes some data, generates a hash, and then encrypts the hash with Batman's private key. (Note that the private key is not shared with anyone else—not even Batman's closest friends have it.) This encrypted hash is inserted into the packet and sent to Robin. This encrypted hash is Batman's digital signature.

Robin, having received the packet with the digital signature attached, first decodes or decrypts the encrypted hash using Batman's public key. It then sets the decrypted hash to the side for a moment and runs a hash against the same data that Batman did previously. If the hash that Robin generates matches the decrypted hash, which was sent as a digital signature from Batman, then Robin has just authenticated Batman—because only Batman has the private key used for the creation of Batman's digital signature.

Certificate Authorities

A certificate authority is a computer or entity that creates and issues digital certificates. Inside of a digital certificate is information about the identity of a device, such as its IP address, fully qualified domain name (FQDN), and the public key of that device. The CA takes requests from devices that supply all of that information (including the public key generated by the computer making the request) and generates a digital certificate, which the CA assigns a serial number to. The CA then signs the certificate with its own digital signature. Also included in the final certificate is a URL that other devices can check to see whether this certificate has been revoked and the certificate's validity dates (the time window during which the certificate is considered valid). Also in the certificate is the information about the CA that issued the certificate and several other parameters used by PKI. This is illustrated in Figure 6-7, which shows the certificate for the website example.org.

Figure 6-7 *Example.org Certificate*

In Figure 6-7, you can see the CRL (certificate revocation list) Distribution Points URLs and other extensions such as the Certificate Authority Information Access and Online Certificate Status Protocol (OCSP) URLs.

Now let's go back to our scenario. Batman and Robin's computers can receive and verify identity certificates from each other (and thousands of others) by using a third-party trusted certificate authority, as long as the certificates are signed by a CA that is trusted by Batman and Robin. Commercial CAs charge a fee to issue and maintain digital certificates. One benefit of using a commercial CA server to obtain digital certificates for your devices is that most web browsers maintain a list of the more common trusted public CA servers, and as a result anyone using a browser can verify the identity of your web server by default without having to modify their web browser at all. If a company wants to set up its own internal CA and then configure each of the end devices to trust the certificates issued by this internal CA, no commercial certificate authority is required, but the scope of that CA is limited to the company and its managed devices, because any devices outside of the company would not trust the company's internal CA by default.

Root and Identity Certificates

A digital certificate can be thought of as an electronic document that identifies a device or person. It includes information such as the name of the person or organization, their address, and the public key of that person or device. There are different types of certificates, including root certificates (which identify the CA), and identity certificates, which identify devices such as servers and other devices that want to participate in PKI.

Root Certificate

A root certificate contains the public key of the CA server and the other details about the CA server. Figure 6-8 shows an example of one.

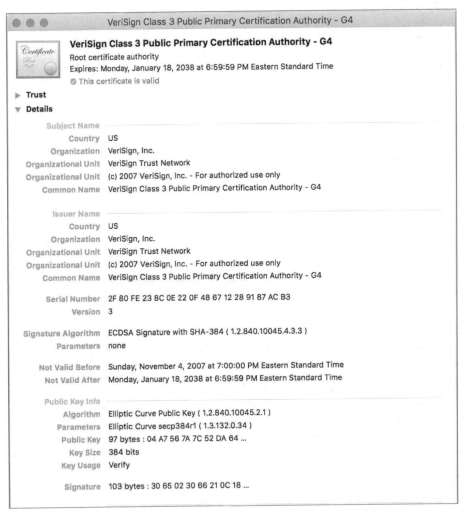

Figure 6-8 *A Root Certificate Example*

The output in Figure 6-8 can be seen on most browsers, although the location of the information might differ a bit depending on the browser vendor and version.

Here are the relevant parts of the certificate:

- **Serial number:** Issued and tracked by the CA that issued the certificate.

- **Issuer:** The CA that issued this certificate. (Even root certificates need to have their certificates issued from someone, perhaps even themselves.)

- **Validity dates:** The time window during which the certificate is considered valid. If a local computer believes the date to be off by a few years, that same PC may consider the certificate invalid due to its own error about the time. Using the Network Time Protocol (NTP) is a good idea to avoid this problem.

- **Subject of the certificate:** This includes the organizational unit (OU), organization (O), country (C), and other details commonly found in an X.500 structured directory (more on that later in the chapter, in "The Public Key Cryptography Standards" section). The subject of the root certificate is the CA itself. The subject for a client's identity certificate is the client.

- **Public key:** The contents of the public key and the length of the key are often both shown. After all, the public key is public.

- **Thumbprint algorithm and thumbprint:** This is the hash for the certificate. On a new root certificate, you could use a phone to call and ask for the hash value and compare it to the hash value you see on the certificate. If it matches, you have just performed out-of-band verification (using the telephone) of the digital certificate.

Identity Certificate

An identity certificate is similar to a root certificate, but it describes the client and contains the public key of an individual host (the client). An example of a client is a web server that wants to support Secure Sockets Layer (SSL) or a router that wants to use digital signatures for authentication of a VPN tunnel.

Basically, any device that wants to verify a digital signature must have the public key of the sender. So, as an example, let's say that you and I want to authenticate each other, and we both trust a common CA and have previously requested and received digital certificates (identity certificates) from the CA server. We exchange our identity certificates, which contain our public keys. We both verify the CA's signature on the digital certificate we just received from each other using the public key of the CA. In practice, this public key for the CA is built in to most of the browsers today for public CA servers. Once we verify each other's certificates, we can then trust the contents of those certificates (and most important, the public key). Now that you and I both have each other's public key, we can use those public keys to verify each other's digital signatures.

X.500 and X.509v3 Certificates

X.500 is a series of standards focused on directory services and how those directories are organized. Many popular network operating systems have been based on X.500, including Microsoft Active Directory. This X.500 structure is the foundation from which you see common directory elements such as CN=Batman (CN stands for common name), OU=engineering (OU stands for organizational unit), O=cisco.com (O stands for organization), and so on, all structured in an "org chart" way (that is, shaped like a pyramid). X.509 Version 3 is a standard for digital certificates that is widely accepted and incorporates many of the same directory and naming standards. A common protocol used to perform lookups from a directory is the Lightweight Directory Access Protocol (LDAP). A common use for this protocol is having a digital certificate that's used for authentication, and then based on the details of that certificate (for example, OU=sales in the certificate itself), the user can be dynamically assigned the access rights associated with that group in Active Directory or some other LDAP-accessible database. The concept is to define the rights in one place and then leverage them over and over again. An example is setting up Active Directory for the network and then using that to control what access is provided to each user after he or she authenticates.

As a review, most digital certificates contain the following information:

- **Serial number:** Assigned by the CA and used to uniquely identify the certificate
- **Subject:** The person or entity that is being identified
- **Signature algorithm:** The specific algorithm used for signing the digital certificate
- **Signature:** The digital signature from the certificate authority, which is used by devices that want to verify the authenticity of the certificate issued by that CA
- **Issuer:** The entity or CA that created and issued the digital certificate
- **Valid from:** The date the certificate became valid
- **Valid to:** The expiration date of the certificate
- **Key usage:** The functions for which the public key in the certificate may be used
- **Public key:** The public portion of the public and private key pair generated by the host whose certificate is being looked at
- **Thumbprint algorithm:** The hash algorithm used for data integrity
- **Thumbprint:** The actual hash
- **Certificate revocation list location:** The URL that can be checked to see whether the serial number of any certificates issued by the CA have been revoked

Authenticating and Enrolling with the CA

Using a new CA as a trusted entity, as well as requesting and receiving your own identity certificate from this CA, is really a two-step process, as demonstrated in Figure 6-9.

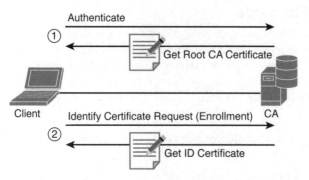

Figure 6-9 *Authenticating and Enrolling with the CA*

The following are the steps illustrated in Figure 6-9:

Step 1.   The first step is to authenticate the CA server (in other words, to *trust* the CA server). Unfortunately, if you do not have the public key for a CA server, you cannot verify the digital signature of that CA server. This is sort of like the chicken and the egg story, because you need the public key, which can be found in the root's CA certificate, but you cannot verify the signature on a certificate until you have the public key.

To get the ball rolling, you could download the root certificate and then use an out-of-band method, such as making a telephone call, to validate the root certificate. This can be done after downloading the root certificate and looking at the hash value by calling the administrators for the root CA and asking them to verbally tell you what the hash is. If the hash that they tell you over the phone matches the hash you see on the digital certificate (and assuming that you called the right phone number and talked with the right people), you know that the certificate is valid, and you can then use the public key contained in a certificate to verify future certificates signed by that CA. This process of getting the root CA certificate installed is often referred to as *authenticating the CA*. Current web browsers automate this process for well-known CAs.

Step 2.   After you have authenticated the root CA and have a known-good root certificate for that CA, you can then request your own identity certificate. This involves generating a public-private key pair and including the public key portion in any requests for your own identity certificate. An identity certificate could be for a device or person. Once you make this request, the CA can take all of your information and generate an identity certificate for you, which includes your public key, and then send this certificate back to you. If this is done electronically, how do you verify the identity certificate you got is really from the CA server that you trust? The answer is simple, because the CA has not only issued the certificate but has also signed the certificate. Because you authenticated the CA server earlier and you have a copy of its digital certificate with its public key, you can now verify the digital signature it has put on your own identity certificate. If the signature from the CA is valid, you also know that your certificate is valid so you can install it and use it.

Public Key Cryptography Standards

Many standards are in use for the PKI. Many of them have Public Key Cryptography Standards (PKCS) numbers. Some of these standards control the format and use of certificates, including requests to a CA for new certificates, the format for a file that is going to be the new identity certificate, and the file format and usage access for certificates. Having the standards in place helps with interoperability between different CA servers and many different CA clients.

Here are a few standards you should become familiar with; these include protocols by themselves and protocols used for working with digital certificates:

- **PKCS #1**: The RSA cryptography standard.
- **PKCS #3**: Diffie-Hellman key exchange.
- **PKCS #7**: This is a format that can be used by a CA as a response to a PKCS #10 request. The response itself will very likely be the identity certificate (or certificates) that had been previously requested.
- **PKCS #10**: This is a format of a certificate request sent to a CA that wants to receive its identity certificate. This type of request would include the public key for the entity desiring a certificate.
- **PKCS #12**: A format for storing both public and private keys using a symmetric password-based key to "unlock" the data whenever the key needs to be used or accessed.

Simple Certificate Enrollment Protocol

The process of authenticating a CA server, generating a public-private key pair, requesting an identity certificate, and then verifying and implementing the identity certificate can take several steps. Cisco, in association with a few other vendors, developed the Simple Certificate Enrollment Protocol (SCEP), which can automate most of the process for requesting and installing an identity certificate. Although it is not an open standard, it is supported by most Cisco devices and makes getting and installing both root and identity certificates convenient.

Revoking Digital Certificates

If you decommission a device that has been assigned an identity certificate, or if the device assigned a digital certificate has been compromised and you believe that the private key information is no longer "private," you could request from the CA that the previously issued certificate be revoked. This poses a unique problem. Normally when two devices authenticate with each other, they do not need to contact a CA to verify the identity of the other party. This is because the two devices already have the public key of the CA and can validate the signature on a peer's certificate without direct contact with the CA. So here's the challenge: If a certificate has been revoked by the CA, and the peers are not checking with the CA each time they try to authenticate the peers, how does a peer know whether the certificate it just received has been revoked? The answer is simple: It has to check and see. A digital certificate contains information on where an updated list of revoked certificates can be obtained. This URL could point to the CA server itself or to some other publicly available resource on the Internet. The revoked certificates are listed based on the serial number of the certificates, and if a peer has been configured to check for revoked certificates, it adds this check before completing the authentication with a peer.

If a certificate revocation list (CRL) is checked, and the certificate from the peer is on that list, the authentication stops at that moment. The three basic ways to check whether certificates have been revoked are as follows, in order of popularity:

- **Certificate revocation list (CRL):** This is a list of certificates, based on their serial numbers, that had initially been issued by a CA but have since been revoked and as a result should not be trusted. A CRL could be very large, and the client would have to process the entire list to verify a particular certificate is not on the list. A CRL can be thought of as the naughty list. This is the primary protocol used for this purpose, compared to OSCP and AAA. A CRL can be accessed by several protocols, including LDAP and HTTP. A CRL can also be obtained via SCEP.

- **Online Certificate Status Protocol (OCSP):** This is an alternative to CRLs. Using this method, a client simply sends a request to find the status of a certificate and gets a response without having to know the complete list of revoked certificates.

- **Authentication, authorization, and accounting (AAA):** Cisco AAA services also provide support for validating digital certificates, including a check to see whether a certificate has been revoked. Because this is a proprietary solution, it is not often used in PKI.

Using Digital Certificates

Digital certificates aren't just for breakfast anymore. They can be used for clients who want to authenticate a web server to verify they are connected to the correct server using HTTP Secure (HTTPS), Transport Layer Security (TLS), or Secure Sockets Layer (SSL). For the average user who does not have to write these protocols, but simply benefits from using them, they are all effectively the same, which is HTTP combined with TLS/SSL for the security benefits. This means that digital certificates can be used when you do online banking from your PC to the bank's website. It also means that if you use SSL technology for your remote-access VPNs, you can use digital certificates for authenticating the peers (at each end) of the VPN.

You can also use digital certificates with the protocol family of IPsec, which can also use digital certificates for the authentication portion.

In addition, digital certificates can be used with protocols such as 802.1X, which involves authentication at the edge of the network before allowing the user's packets and frames to progress through it. An example is a wireless network, controlling access and requiring authentication, using digital certificates for the PCs/users, before allowing them in on the network.

PKI Topologies

There is no one-size-fits-all solution for PKI. In small networks, a single CA server may be enough, but in a network with 30,000 devices, a single server might not provide the availability and fault tolerance required. To address these issues, let's investigate the options available to us for implementation of the PKI, using various topologies, including single and hierarchical. Let's start off with the single CA and expand from there.

Single Root CA

If you have one trusted CA, and you have tens of thousands of customers who want to authenticate that CA and request their own identity certificates, there might be too large of a demand on a single server, even though a single CA does not have to be directly involved in the day-to-day authentication that happens between peers. To offload some of the workload from a single server, you could publish CRLs on other servers. At the end of the day, it still makes sense to have at least some fault tolerance for your PKI, which means more than just a single root CA server.

Hierarchical CA with Subordinate CAs

One option for supporting fault tolerance and increased capacity is to use intermediate or subordinate CAs to assist the root CA. The root CA is the king of the hill. The root CA delegates the authority (to the subordinate CAs) to create and assign identity certificates to clients. This is called a *hierarchical PKI topology*. The root CA signs the digital certificates of its subordinate or intermediate CAs, and the subordinate CAs are the ones to issue certificates to clients. Figure 6-10 shows a hierarchical CA deployment with a root and three subordinate CAs.

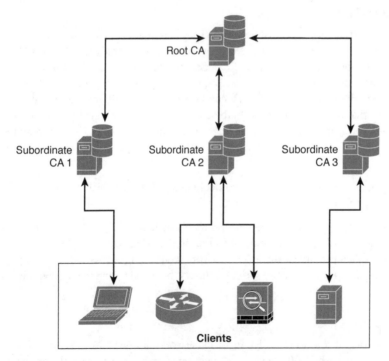

Figure 6-10   *Hierarchical CA Deployment with Subordinate CAs*

For a client to verify the "chain" of authority, a client needs both the subordinate CA's certificate and the root certificate. The root certificate (and its public key) is required to verify the digital signature of the subordinate CA, and the subordinate CA's certificate (and its public key) is required to verify the signature of the subordinate CA. If there are multiple levels of subordinate CAs, a client needs the certificates of all the devices in the chain, from the root all the way to the CA that issued the client's certificate.

Cross-certifying CAs

Another approach to hierarchical PKIs is called *cross-certification*. With cross-certification, you would have a CA with a horizontal trust relationship over to a second CA so that clients of either CA can trust the signatures of the other CA.

6

Exam Preparation Tasks

Review All Key Topics

Review the most important topics in the chapter, noted with the Key Topic icon in the outer margin of the page. Table 6-2 lists a reference of these key topics and the page numbers on which each is found.

Table 6-2   Key Topics

Key Topic Element	Description	Page
Section	Basic understanding of ciphers and keys	311
Section	Examples of block and stream ciphers	312
Section	Examples of symmetric and asymmetric algorithms	313
Section	Basic understanding of hashes	314
List	The three most popular types of hashes	316
Section	Explanation of HMAC	316
Section	The core benefits of digital signatures	317
Section	Define what are digital signatures	317
Section	Description of next-generation encryption protocols	321
Section	Description of IPsec and SSL	321
Section	Description of public-private key pairs	323
Section	Description of RSA, keys, and digital certificates	324
Section	Description of certificate authorities	324
Section	Description of root certificates	326
Section	Description of identity certificates	327
List	Public key cryptography standards	330
Section	Description of SCEP	330
List	Methods to check if certificates have been revoked	331

Complete Tables and Lists from Memory

Print a copy of Appendix B, "Memory Tables," (found on the book website), or at least the section for this chapter, and complete the tables and lists from memory. Appendix C, "Memory Tables Answer Key," also on the website, includes completed tables and lists to check your work.

Define Key Terms

Define the following key terms from this chapter, and check your answers in the glossary:

block ciphers, symmetric algorithms, asymmetric algorithms, hashing algorithms, digital certificates, certificate authority

Q&A

The answers to these questions appear in Appendix A, "Answers to the 'Do I Know This Already?' Quizzes and Q&A Questions." For more practice with exam format questions, use the exam engine on the website.

1. Which of the following files have the same contents based on their SHA checksum?

   bash-3.2$ shasum *

   b0f8ff8d3c376f802dd615e8a583d4df7306d02b cat.txt

   88e513e9186d5f71453115ce8ae3c16057c827d8 chair.txt

   b0f8ff8d3c376f802dd615e8a583d4df7306d02b chicken.txt

   1f95e28fc1aaef50f1987237a73c8b5f1429d375 dog.txt

   09bf76d43e9e04ab55884bf01740ea88fa15f4da table.txt

   a. cat.txt, dog.txt, and table.txt

   b. table.txt and chair.txt

   c. chicken.txt and cat.txt

   d. chicken.txt and dog.txt

2. Which of the following statements is true about collision attacks?

   a. A collision attack is an attack against databases that causes a collision of data and results in data corruption.

   b. A collision attack is a type of denial-of-service (DoS) attack.

   c. Collision attacks are a form of web application attack that leverage the collision of data types and data models.

   d. A collision attack is an attempt to find two input strings of a hash function that produce the same hash result.

3. Among MD5, SHA-1, and SHA-2, which is the most secure?

   a. SHA-1.

   b. SHA-2.

   c. MD5.

   d. They are all equally secure.

6

4. Certificate authorities can be deployed in a hierarchical way. Root CAs can delegate their authority to what type of CAs to create and assign identity certificates to clients?

   a. Sub-root CAs

   b. Subordinate CAs

   c. Client CAs

   d. Enrollment CAs

5. What is a certificate revocation list (CRL)?

   a. A list of root certificates of CA servers that can revoke certificates.

   b. A list of certificates, based on their serial numbers, that had initially been issued by a CA but have not been revoked and are trusted.

   c. A list of certificates, based on their serial numbers, that had initially been issued by a CA but have since been revoked and as a result should not be trusted.

   d. A list of serial numbers of CA servers that can participate in a certificate revocation process.

6. Which of the following is a format for storing both public and private keys using a symmetric password-based key to "unlock" the data whenever the key needs to be used or accessed?

   a. PKCS #12

   b. PKCS #10

   c. PKCS #7

   d. PKCS #2

7. Which of the following is a format of a certificate request sent to a CA that wants to receive its identity certificate? This type of request would include the public key for the entity desiring a certificate.

   a. PKCS #1

   b. PKCS #7

   c. PKCS #10

   d. PKCS #12

8. Which of the following are examples of symmetric encryption algorithms?

   a. AES

   b. IDEA

   c. Diffie-Hellman

   d. MD5

9. Which of the following are examples of asymmetric encryption algorithms?

   a. AES

   b. SHA

   c. Diffie-Hellman

   d. RSA

10. Which of the following are examples of hashing algorithms?

   a. SHA

   b. AES

   c. MD5

   d. RC4

6

This chapter covers the following topics:

- Identify VPN technologies

- Identify SSL VPNs

- Describe why VPNs are used

- Describe the uses of a hash algorithm

- Describe the uses of encryption algorithms

- Describe the security impact of commonly used hash algorithms

- Describe the security impact of commonly used encryption algorithms and secure communications protocols

CHAPTER 7

Introduction to Virtual Private Networks (VPNs)

In Chapter 6, "Fundamentals of Cryptography and Public Key Infrastructure (PKI)," you learned the fundamentals of cryptography, public key infrastructure (PKI), encryption and hashing algorithms, and what they apply to. This chapter covers virtual private networks and their related technologies.

"Do I Know This Already?" Quiz

The "Do I Know This Already?" quiz helps you identify your strengths and deficiencies in this chapter's topics. The nine-question quiz, derived from the major sections in the "Foundation Topics" portion of the chapter, helps you determine how to spend your limited study time. You can find the answers in Appendix A Answers to the "Do I Know This Already?" Quizzes and Q&A Questions.

Table 7-1 outlines the major topics discussed in this chapter and the "Do I Know This Already?" quiz questions that correspond to those topics.

Table 7-1 "Do I Know This Already?" Foundation Topics Section-to-Question Mapping

Foundation Topics Section	Questions Covered in This Section
What Are VPNs?	1–2
Site-to-site vs. Remote-Access VPNs	3–4
An Overview of IPsec	5–7
SSL VPNs	8–9

1. Which of the following are examples of protocols used for VPN implementations?

   a. TCP

   b. Secure Sockets Layer (SSL)

   c. UDP

   d. Multiprotocol Label Switching (MPLS)

   e. Internet Protocol Security (IPsec)

2. Which of the following VPN protocols do not provide data integrity, authentication, and data encryption?

   a. L2TP

   b. GRE

   c. SSL

   d. IPsec

   e. MPLS

3. VPN implementations are categorized into which of the following two general groups?

   a. Encrypted VPNs

   b. Non-encrypted VPNs

   c. Site-to-site (LAN-to-LAN) VPNs

   d. Remote-access VPNs

4. Which of the following is an example of a remote-access VPN client?

   a. Cisco Encrypted Tunnel Client

   b. Cisco AnyConnect Secure Mobility Client

   c. Cisco ASA Client

   d. Cisco Firepower Client

5. Which of the following attributes are exchanged in IKEv1 phase 1?

   a. Encryption algorithms

   b. Hashing algorithms

   c. Diffie-Hellman groups

   d. Vendor-specific attributes

6. Which of the following hashing algorithms are used in IPsec?

   a. AES 192

   b. AES 256

   c. Secure Hash Algorithm (SHA)

   d. Message Digest Algorithm 5 (MD5)

7. In IKEv1 phase 2, each security association (SA) is assigned which of the following?

   a. A unique security parameter index (SPI) value

   b. An IP address

   c. The DNS server IP address

   d. A public key

8. Which of the following statements is true about clientless SSL VPN?

   a. The client must use a digital certificate to authenticate.

   b. The remote client needs only an SSL-enabled web browser to access resources on the private network of the security appliances.

   c. Clientless SSL VPNs do not provide the same level of encryption as client-based SSL VPNs.

   d. Clientless SSL VPN sessions expire every hour.

9. Which of the following are some of the commonly used SSL VPN technologies?

   a. Tor browser

   b. Reverse proxy technology

   c. Port-forwarding technology and smart tunnels

   d. SSL VPN tunnel client (such as the AnyConnect Secure Mobility Client)

Foundation Topics

What Are VPNs?

Individuals and organizations deploy VPNs to provide data integrity, authentication, and data encryption to ensure confidentiality of the packets sent over an unprotected network or the Internet. VPNs are designed to avoid the cost of unnecessary leased lines. Individuals also use VPNs to remain anonymous online. Even threat actors use VPN technologies to encrypt data from compromised sites, command and control communications, and to maintain anonymity for the purposes of malfeasance in underground sites and darknet marketplaces.

Many different protocols are used for VPN implementations, including the following:

- Point-to-Point Tunneling Protocol (PPTP)
- Layer 2 Forwarding (L2F) protocol
- Layer 2 Tunneling Protocol (L2TP)
- Generic Routing Encapsulation (GRE)
- Multiprotocol Label Switching (MPLS)
- Internet Protocol Security (IPsec)
- Secure Sockets Layer (SSL)

NOTE L2F, L2TP, GRE, and MPLS VPNs do not provide data integrity, authentication, and data encryption. On the other hand, you can combine L2TP, GRE, and MPLS with IPsec to provide these benefits. Many organizations use IPsec or SSL VPNs as their preferred protocols because they support all three of these features.

Enterprises use VPNs to allow users and other networks to connect to network resources in a secure manner. On the other hand, individuals also use VPN services to maintain confidentiality when browsing the Internet and in combination with The Onion Router (Tor) to maintain anonymity. Tor was initially a worldwide network of servers developed with the United States Navy. It enables people to browse the Internet anonymously. Nowadays, Tor is maintained by a nonprofit organization dedicated to the development of online privacy tools. The Tor network masks your identity by "routing" your traffic across different Tor servers and then encrypting that traffic so it isn't traced back to you. It is important to know that Tor is not really a VPN.

Site-to-site vs. Remote-Access VPNs

Typically, VPN implementations are categorized into two general groups:

- **Site-to-site VPNs:** Enable organizations to establish VPN tunnels between two or more network infrastructure devices in different sites so that they can communicate over a shared medium such as the Internet. Many organizations use IPsec, GRE, and MPLS VPNs as site-to-site VPN protocols.

■ **Remote-access VPNs:** Enable users to work from remote locations such as their homes, hotels, and other premises as if they were directly connected to their corporate network.

In most cases, site-to-site VPN tunnels are terminated between two or more network infrastructure devices, whereas remote-access VPN tunnels are formed between a VPN head-end device and an end-user workstation or hardware VPN client.

Figure 7-1 illustrates a site-to-site IPsec tunnel between two sites: a site in New York (corporate headquarters) and a branch office in Raleigh, North Carolina.

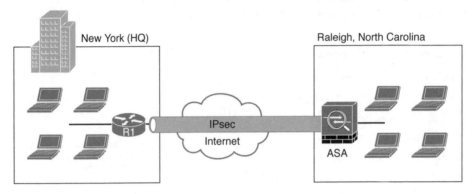

Figure 7-1 *Site-to-site VPN Example*

In Figure 7-1 a Cisco IOS router (R1) terminates an IPsec tunnel from the Cisco ASA firewall in the Raleigh office. Figure 7-2 shows an example of a remote-access VPN.

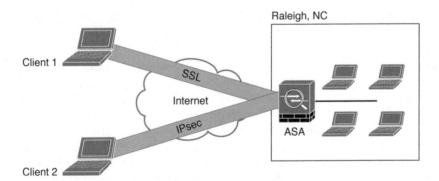

Figure 7-2 *Remote-Access VPN Example*

Two clients are connecting to the Cisco ASA in the Raleigh office in Figure 7-2. Client 1 is connecting using an SSL VPN, and client 2 is connecting using IPsec.

There are two main categories of remote-access VPNs:

■ **Clientless:** The user connects without a client, typically using a web browser. The major benefit of clientless SSL VPNs is that you do not need a client to be installed on your PC. One of the disadvantages is that only TCP-based applications are supported. Clientless

SSL VPNs are typically used in kiosks, shared workstations, mobile devices, and when users just want to encrypt web traffic.

- **Client based:** The user connects to the VPN terminating device (router, firewall, and so on) using a client. An example of a VPN client is the Cisco AnyConnect Secure Mobility Client.

An Overview of IPsec

IPsec uses the Internet Key Exchange (IKE) protocol to negotiate and establish secured site-to-site or remote-access VPN tunnels. IKE is a framework provided by the Internet Security Association and Key Management Protocol (ISAKMP) and parts of two other key management protocols—namely, Oakley and Secure Key Exchange Mechanism (SKEME).

IKE is defined in RFC 2409, "The Internet Key Exchange (IKE)." IKE version 2 (IKEv2) is defined in RFC 5996, "Internet Key Exchange Protocol Version 2 (IKEv2)."

IKE has two phases. Phase 1 is used to create a secure bidirectional communication channel between the IPsec peers. This channel is known as the ISAKMP security association (SA). Phase 2 is used to negotiate the IPsec SAs.

IKEv1 Phase 1

Within Phase 1 negotiation, several attributes are exchanged:

- Encryption algorithms
- Hashing algorithms
- Diffie-Hellman groups
- Authentication method
- Vendor-specific attributes

In Chapter 6, you learned the fundamentals of cryptography and the different encryption algorithms. The following are the typical encryption algorithms used in IPsec:

- Data Encryption Standard (DES): 64 bits long
- Triple DES (3DES): 168 bits long
- Advanced Encryption Standard (AES): 128 bits long
- AES 192: 192 bits long
- AES 256: 256 bits long

The hashing algorithms used in IPsec include the following:

- Secure Hash Algorithm (SHA)
- Message Digest Algorithm 5 (MD5)

The common authentication methods are preshared keys (where peers use a shared secret to authenticate each other) and digital certificates with the use of Public Key Infrastructure (PKI).

Small- and medium-sized organizations use preshared keys as their authentication mechanism. Many large organizations use digital certificates for scalability, centralized management, and additional security mechanisms.

You can establish a Phase 1 SA in main mode or aggressive mode. In main mode, the IPsec peers complete a six-packet exchange in three round trips to negotiate the ISAKMP SA, whereas aggressive mode completes the SA negotiation in three packet exchanges. Main mode provides identity protection if preshared keys are used. Aggressive mode offers identity protection only if digital certificates are employed.

NOTE Cisco products that support IPsec typically use main mode for site-to-site tunnels and use aggressive mode for remote-access VPN tunnels. This is the default behavior when preshared keys are employed as the authentication method.

Figure 7-3 illustrates the six-packet exchange in main mode negotiation.

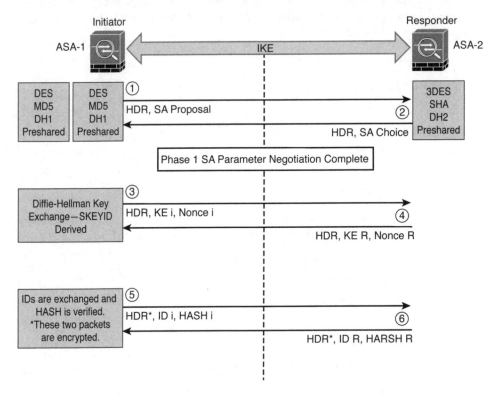

Figure 7-3 *IPsec Phase 1 Main Mode Negotiation*

In Figure 7-3, two Cisco ASAs are configured to terminate a site-to-site VPN tunnel between them. The Cisco ASA labeled as ASA-1 is the initiator, and ASA-2 is the responder. The following steps are illustrated in Figure 7-3:

1. ASA-1 (the initiator) has two ISAKMP proposals configured. In the first packet, ASA-1 sends its configured proposals to ASA-2.

2. ASA-2 evaluates the received proposal. Because it has a proposal that matches the offer of the initiator, ASA-2 sends the accepted proposal back to ASA-1 in the second packet.

3. The Diffie-Hellman exchange and calculation process is started. Diffie-Hellman is a key agreement protocol that enables two users or devices to authenticate each other's preshared keys without actually sending the keys over the unsecured medium. ASA-1 sends the Key Exchange (KE) payload and a randomly generated value called a *nonce*.

4. ASA-2 receives the information and reverses the equation, using the proposed Diffie-Hellman group/exchange to generate the SKEYID. The SKEYID is a string derived from secret material that is known only to the active participants in the exchange.

5. ASA-1 sends its identity information. The fifth packet is encrypted with the keying material derived from the SKEYID. The asterisk in Figure 7-3 is used to illustrate that this packet is encrypted.

6. ASA-2 validates the identity of ASA-1, and ASA-2 sends its own identity information to ASA-1. This packet is also encrypted.

IKE uses UDP port 500 for communication. UDP port 500 is employed to send all the packets described in the previous steps.

IKEv1 Phase 2

Phase 2 is used to negotiate the IPsec SAs. This phase is also known as *quick mode*. The ISAKMP SA protects the IPsec SAs because all payloads are encrypted except the ISAKMP header.

A single IPsec SA negotiation always creates two security associations—one inbound and one outbound. Each SA is assigned a unique security parameter index (SPI) value—one by the initiator and the other by the responder.

The security protocols (AH and ESP) are Layer 3 protocols and do not have Layer 4 port information, unlike TCP and UDP. If an IPsec peer is behind a PAT device, the ESP or AH packets are typically dropped. To work around this, many vendors, including Cisco Systems, use a feature called *IPsec pass-through*. The PAT device that is IPsec pass-through capable builds the translation table by looking at the SPI values on the packets.

Many industry vendors, including Cisco Systems, implement another feature called NAT Traversal (NAT-T). With NAT-T, the VPN peers dynamically discover whether an address translation device exists between them. If they detect a NAT/PAT device, they use UDP port 4500 to encapsulate the data packets, subsequently allowing the NAT device to successfully translate and forward the packets.

Another interesting point is that if the VPN router needs to connect multiple networks over the tunnel, it must negotiate twice as many IPsec SAs. Remember, each IPsec SA is unidirectional, so if three local subnets need to go over the VPN tunnel to talk to the remote network, then six IPsec SAs are negotiated. IPsec can use quick mode to negotiate these multiple Phase 2 SAs, using the single pre-established ISAKMP (IKEv1 Phase 1) SA. The number of IPsec SAs can be reduced, however, if source and/or destination networks are summarized.

Many different IPsec attributes are negotiated in quick mode, as shown in Table 7-2.

Table 7-2   IPsec Attributes

Attribute	Possible Values
Encryption	None, DES, 3DES, AES128, AES192, AES256
Hashing	MD5, SHA, null
Identity information	Network, protocol, port number
Lifetime	120–2,147,483,647 seconds
	10–2,147,483,647 kilobytes
Mode	Tunnel or transport
Perfect Forward Secrecy (PFS) group	None, 1, 2, or 5

In addition to generating the keying material, quick mode also negotiates identity information. The Phase 2 identity information specifies which network, protocol, and/ or port number to encrypt. Hence, the identities can vary anywhere from an entire network to a single host address, allowing a specific protocol and port.

Figure 7-4 illustrates the Phase 2 negotiation between the two routers that just completed Phase 1.

The following steps are illustrated in Figure 7-4.

1. ASA-1 sends the identity information, IPsec SA proposal, nonce payload, and (optionally) the Key Exchange (KE) payload if Perfect Forward Secrecy (PFS) is used. PFS is used to provide additional Diffie-Hellman calculations.

2. ASA-2 evaluates the received proposal against its configured proposal and sends the accepted proposal back to ASA-1, along with its identity information, nonce payload, and the optional KE payload.

3. ASA-1 evaluates the ASA-2 proposal and sends a confirmation that the IPsec SAs have been successfully negotiated. This starts the data encryption process.

IPsec uses two different protocols to encapsulate the data over a VPN tunnel:

■ Encapsulation Security Payload (ESP): IP Protocol 50

■ Authentication Header (AH): IP Protocol 51

ESP is defined in RFC 4303, "IP Encapsulating Security Payload (ESP)," and AH is defined in RFC 4302, "IP Authentication Header."

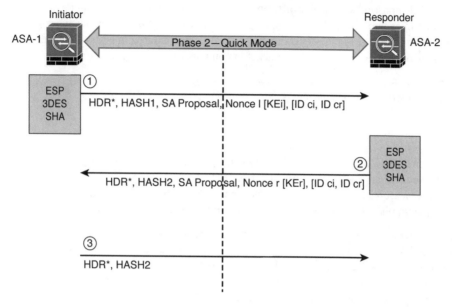

Figure 7-4   *IPsec Phase 2 Negotiation*

IPsec can use two modes with either AH or ESP:

- **Transport mode:** Protects upper-layer protocols, such as User Datagram Protocol (UDP) and TCP
- **Tunnel mode:** Protects the entire IP packet

Transport mode is used to encrypt and authenticate the data packets between the peers. A typical example is the use of GRE over an IPsec tunnel. Tunnel mode is employed to encrypt and authenticate the IP packets when they are originated by the hosts connected behind the VPN device. Tunnel mode adds an additional IP header to the packet, as illustrated in Figure 7-5.

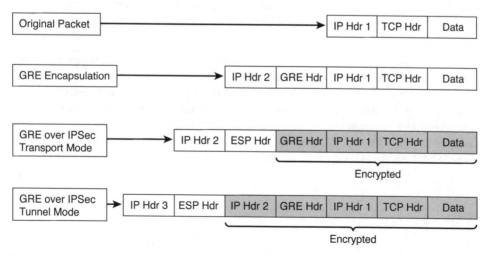

Figure 7-5   *Transport Mode vs. Tunnel Mode in IPsec*

Figure 7-5 demonstrates the major difference between transport mode and tunnel mode. It includes an example of an IP packet encapsulated in GRE and the difference when it is encrypted in transport mode versus tunnel mode. As demonstrated in Figure 7-5, tunnel mode increases the overall size of the packet in comparison to transport mode.

> **TIP**   Tunnel mode is the default mode in Cisco IPsec devices.

IKEv2

IKE version 2 (IKEv2) is defined in RFC 5996 and enhances the function of performing dynamic key exchange and peer authentication. IKEv2 simplifies the key exchange flows and introduces measures to fix vulnerabilities present in IKEv1. Both IKEv1 and IKEv2 protocols operate in two phases. IKEv2 provides a simpler and more efficient exchange.

Phase 1 in IKEv2 is IKE_SA, consisting of the message pair IKE_SA_INIT. IKE_SA is comparable to IKEv1 Phase 1. The attributes of the IKE_SA phase are defined in the Key Exchange Policy. Phase 2 in IKEv2 is CHILD_SA. The first CHILD_SA is the IKE_AUTH message pair. This phase is comparable to IKEv1 Phase 2. Additional CHILD_SA message pairs can be sent for rekey and informational messages. The CHILD_SA attributes are defined in the Data Policy.

The following differences exist between IKEv1 and IKEv2:

- IKEv1 Phase 1 has two possible exchanges: main mode and aggressive mode. There is a single exchange of a message pair for IKEv2 IKE_SA.

- IKEv2 has a simple exchange of two message pairs for the CHILD_SA. IKEv1 uses an exchange of at least three message pairs for Phase 2.

SSL VPNs

SSL-based VPNs leverage the SSL protocol. SSL, also referred to as Transport Layer Security (TLS), is a mature protocol that has been in existence since the early 1990s. The Internet Engineering Task Force (IETF) created TLS to consolidate the different SSL vendor versions into a common and open standard.

One of the most popular features of SSL VPN is the capability to launch a browser such as Google Chrome, Microsoft Internet Explorer, or Firefox and simply connect to the address of the VPN device, as opposed to running a separate VPN client program to establish an IPsec VPN connection. In most implementations, a clientless solution is possible. Users can access corporate intranet sites, portals, and email from almost anywhere. Even airport kiosks can establish clientless SSL VPN tunnels to access required resources. Because most people allow SSL (TCP port 443) over their firewalls, it is unnecessary to open additional ports.

The most successful application running on top of SSL is HTTP, because of the huge popularity of the World Wide Web. All the most popular web browsers in use today support HTTP over SSL/TLS (HTTPS). This ubiquity, if used in remote-access VPNs, provides some appealing properties:

- **Secure communication using cryptographic algorithms:** HTTPS/TLS offers confidentiality, integrity, and authentication.

- **Ubiquity:** The ubiquity of SSL/TLS makes it possible for VPN users to remotely access corporate resources from anywhere, using any PC, without having to preinstall a remote-access VPN client.

- **Low management cost:** The clientless access makes this type of remote-access VPN free of deployment costs and free of maintenance problems at the end-user side. This is a huge benefit for the IT management personnel, who would otherwise spend considerable resources to deploy and maintain their remote-access VPN solutions.

- **Effective operation with a firewall and NAT:** SSL VPN operates on the same port as HTTPS (TCP/443). Most Internet firewalls, proxy servers, and NAT devices have been configured to correctly handle TCP/443 traffic. Consequently, there is no need for any special consideration to transport SSL VPN traffic over the networks. This has been viewed as a significant advantage over native IPsec VPN, which operates over IP protocol 50 (ESP) or 51 (AH), which in many cases needs special configuration on the firewall or NAT devices to let traffic pass through.

As SSL VPN evolves to fulfill another important requirement of remote-access VPNs (namely, the requirement of supporting any application), some of these properties are no longer applicable, depending on which SSL VPN technology the VPN users choose. But overall, these properties are the main drivers for the popularity of SSL VPNs in recent years and are heavily marketed by SSL VPN vendors as the main reasons for IPsec replacement.

Today's SSL VPN technology uses SSL/TLS for secure transport and employs a heterogeneous collection of remote-access technologies such as reverse proxy, tunneling, and terminal services to provide users with different types of access methods that fit different environments. Subsequent chapters examine some commonly used SSL VPN technologies, such as the following:

- Reverse proxy technology
- Port-forwarding technology and smart tunnels
- SSL VPN tunnel client (AnyConnect Secure Mobility Client)
- Integrated terminal services

HTTPS provides secure web communication between a browser and a web server that supports the HTTPS protocol. SSL VPN extends this model to allow VPN users to access corporate internal web applications and other corporate application servers that might or might not support HTTPS, or even HTTP. SSL VPN does this by using several techniques that are collectively called *reverse proxy technology*.

A reverse proxy is a proxy server that resides in front of the application servers (normally web servers) and functions as an entry point for Internet users who want to access the corporate internal web application resources. To the external clients, a reverse proxy server appears to be the true web server. Upon receiving the user's web request, a reverse proxy relays the user request to the internal web server to fetch the content on behalf of the user and then relays the web content to the user with or without presenting additional modifications to the data.

Many web server implementations support reverse proxy. One example is the mod_proxy module in Apache. With so many implementations, you might wonder why you need an SSL VPN solution to have this functionality. The answer is that SSL VPN offers much more functionality than traditional reverse proxy technologies:

- SSL VPN can transform complicated web and some non-web applications that simple reverse proxy servers cannot handle. The content transformation process is sometimes called *webification*. For example, SSL VPN solutions enable users to access Windows or UNIX file systems. The SSL VPN gateway must be able to communicate with internal Windows or UNIX servers and "webify" the file access in a web browser–presentable format for the VPN users.

- SSL VPN supports a wide range of business applications. For applications that cannot be webified, SSL VPN can use other resource access methods to support them. For users who demand ultimate access, SSL VPN provides network-layer access to directly connect a remote system to the corporate network, in the same manner as an IPsec VPN.

- SSL VPN provides a true remote-access VPN package, including user authentication, resource access privilege management, logging and accounting, endpoint security, and user experience.

The reverse proxy mode in SSL VPN is also known as *clientless web access* or just *clientless access* because it does not require any client-side applications to be installed on the client machine. Client-based SSL VPN provides a solution where you can connect to the corporate network by just pointing your web browser to the Cisco ASA without the need of additional software being installed on your system.

The SSL VPN implementation on Cisco ASAs provides the most robust feature set in the industry. In the current software release, Cisco ASA supports all three flavors of SSL VPN:

- **Clientless:** In the clientless mode, the remote client needs only an SSL-enabled browser to access resources on the private network of the security appliances. SSL clients can access internal resources such as HTTP, HTTPS, and even Windows file shares over the SSL tunnel.

- **Thin client:** In the thin client mode, the remote client needs to install a small Java-based applet to establish a secure connection to the TCP-based internal resources. SSL clients can access internal resources such as HTTP, HTTPS, SSH, and Telnet servers.

- **Full Tunnel:** In the full tunnel client mode, the remote client needs to install an SSL VPN client first that can give full access to the internal private over an SSL tunnel. Using the full tunnel client mode, remote machines can send all IP unicast traffic such as TCP-, UDP-, or even ICMP-based traffic. SSL clients can access internal resources such as HTTP, HTTPS, DNS, SSH, and Telnet servers.

In many recent Cisco documents, clientless and thin client solutions are grouped under one umbrella and classified as *clientless SSL VPN*.

SSL VPN Design Considerations

Before you implement the SSL VPN services in Cisco ASA, you must analyze your current environment and determine which features and modes might be useful in your implementation. You have the option to install a Cisco IPSec VPN client or a Cisco AnyConnect VPN client, or you can go with the clientless SSL VPN functionality. Table 7-3 lists the major differences between the Cisco VPN client solution and the clientless SSL VPN solution. Clientless SSL VPN is an obvious choice for someone who wants to check email from a hotel or an Internet cafe without having to install and configure a Cisco VPN client.

Table 7-3   Contrasting Cisco VPN Client and SSL VPN

Feature	Cisco VPN Client	Clientless SSL VPN
VPN client	Uses Cisco VPN client software for complete network access.	Uses a standard web browser to access limited corporate network resources. Eliminates the need for separate client software.
Management	You must install and configure Cisco VPN client.	You do not need to install a VPN client. No configuration is required on the client machine.
Encryption	Uses a variety of encryption and hashing algorithms.	Uses SSL encryption native to web browsers.
Connectivity	Establishes a seamless connection to the network.	Supports application connectivity through a browser portal.
Applications	Encapsulates all IP protocols, including TCP, UDP, and ICMP.	Supports limited TCP-based client/server applications.

User Connectivity

Before designing and implementing the SSL VPN solution for your corporate network, you need to determine whether your users will connect to your corporate network from public shared computers, such as workstations made available to guests in a hotel or computers in an Internet kiosk. In this case, using a clientless SSL VPN is the preferred solution to access the protected resources.

VPN Device Feature Set

The features supported in a VPN device need to be taken into consideration when designing your VPN deployment. For instance, Cisco security appliances can run various features, such as IPsec VPN tunnels, routing engines, firewalls, and data inspection engines. Enabling the SSL VPN feature can add further load if your existing appliance is already running a number of features. You must check the CPU, memory, and buffer utilization before enabling SSL VPN.

Infrastructure Planning

Because SSL VPN provides network access to remote users, you have to consider the placement of the VPN termination devices. Before implementing the SSL VPN feature, ask the following questions:

- Should the Cisco ASA be placed behind another firewall? If so, what ports should be opened in that firewall?

- Should the decrypted traffic be passed through another set of firewalls? If so, what ports should be allowed in those firewalls?

Implementation Scope

Network security administrators need to determine the size of the SSL VPN deployment, especially the number of concurrent users that will connect to gain network access. If one Cisco ASA is not enough to support the required number of users, the use of Cisco ASA VPN load balancing must be considered to accommodate all the potential remote users.

The SSL VPN functionality on the ASAs requires that you have appropriate licenses. For example, if your environment is going to have 75 SSL VPN users, you can buy the SSL VPN license that can accommodate up to 100 potential users. The infrastructure requirements for SSL VPNs include, but are not limited to, the following options:

- **ASA placement:** If you are installing a new security appliance, determine the location that best fits your requirements. If you plan to place it behind an existing corporate firewall, make sure you allow appropriate SSL VPN ports to pass through the firewall.

- **User account:** Before SSL VPN tunnels are established, users must authenticate themselves to either the local database or to an external authentication server. The supported external servers include RADIUS (including Password Expiry using MSCHAPv2 to NT LAN Manager), RADIUS one-time password (OTP), RSA SecurID, Active Directory/ Kerberos, and Generic Lightweight Directory Access Protocol (LDAP). Make sure that SSL VPN users have accounts and appropriate access. LDAP password expiration is available for Microsoft and Sun LDAP.

- **Administrative privileges:** Administrative privileges on the local workstation are required for all connections with port forwarding if you want to use host mapping.

Exam Preparation Tasks

Review All Key Topics

Review the most important topics in the chapter, noted with the Key Topic icon in the outer margin of the page. Table 7-4 lists these key topics and the page numbers on which each is found.

Table 7-4   Key Topics

Key Topic Element	Description	Page
List	Describe clientless and client-based SSL VPNs	341
List	Compare remote access VPNs and site-to-site VPNs	341
List	Describe the phases of IPSec	343
List	Define and identify hashing algorithms used in VPNs	343
Table 7-2	Identify the different IPsec attributes	346
List	Compare IKEv1 and IKEv2	348
List	Identify SSL VPN technologies	349

Complete Tables and Lists from Memory

Print a copy of Appendix B, "Memory Tables," (found on the book website), or at least the section for this chapter, and complete the tables and lists from memory. Appendix C, "Memory Tables Answer Key," also on the website, includes completed tables and lists to check your work.

Define Key Terms

Define the following key terms from this chapter, and check your answers in the glossary:

IKE, Diffie-Hellman, IKEv1 vs. IKEv2

Q&A

The answers to these questions appear in Appendix A, "Answers to the 'Do I Know This Already?' Quizzes and Q&A Questions." For more practice with exam format questions, use the exam engine on the website.

1. Why can't ESP packets be transferred by NAT devices?

   a. Because ESP packets are too big to handle.

   b. Because the ESP protocol does not have any ports like TCP or UDP.

   c. Because ESP packets are encrypted.

   d. ESP is supported in NAT devices.

2. What is the difference between IPsec tunnel and transport mode?

  a. Tunnel mode uses encryption and transport mode uses TCP as the transport protocol.

  b. Tunnel mode uses encryption and transport mode uses UDP as the transport protocol.

  c. Transport mode protects upper-layer protocols, such as UDP and TCP, and tunnel mode protects the entire IP packet.

  d. Tunnel mode protects upper-layer protocols, such as UDP and TCP, and transport mode protects the entire IP packet.

3. Which of the following is true about Diffie-Hellman?

  a. Diffie-Hellman is a key agreement protocol that enables two users or devices to authenticate each other's preshared keys without actually sending the keys over the unsecured medium.

  b. Diffie-Hellman is an encapsulation protocol that enables two users or devices to send data to each other.

  c. Diffie-Hellman is a part of the RSA encryption suite.

  d. Diffie-Hellman has three phases, and the second and third are used to encrypt data.

4. Which of the following is not true about SSL VPNs?

  a. SSL VPNs are used in Cisco IOS routers as a site-to-site VPN solution.

  b. SSL VPNs are used in Cisco IOS routers as a remote access VPN solution.

  c. SSL VPNs are used in Cisco ASA firewalls as a remote access VPN solution.

  d. SSL VPNs can be client based or clientless.

5. Which of the following is not true about IKEv2?

  a. IKEv1 Phase 1 has two possible exchanges: main mode and aggressive mode. There is a single exchange of a message pair for IKEv2 IKE_SA.

  b. IKEv2 has a simple exchange of two message pairs for the CHILD_SA. IKEv1 uses an exchange of at least three message pairs for Phase 2.

  c. IKEv1 has a simple exchange of two message pairs for the CHILD_SA. IKEv2 uses an exchange of at least three message pairs for Phase 2.

  d. IKEv2 is used in VPN technologies such as FlexVPN.

6. Which of the following encryption protocols is the most secure?

  a. DES

  b. 3DES

  c. 4DES

  d. AES

7. Which of the following is not an SSL VPN technology or feature?

   a. Reverse proxy features

   b. Port-forwarding technology and smart tunnels

   c. NAT Traversal

   d. SSL VPN tunnel client (AnyConnect Secure Mobility Client)

8. Which browser is used by individuals to maintain anonymity on the Internet and to surf the dark web?

   a. OnionBrowser

   b. Tor

   c. Chrome

   d. Firefox

9. Which of the following are reasons why an attacker might use VPN technology?

   a. Attackers cannot use VPN technologies without being detected.

   b. To exfiltrate data.

   c. To encrypt traffic between a compromised host and a command and control system.

   d. To evade detection.

10. Which of the following are hashing algorithms?

   a. RSA

   b. MD5

   c. AES

   d. SHA

7

This chapter covers the following exam topics:

- Process and threads
- Memory allocation
- Windows registration
- Windows Management Instrumentation
- Handles
- Services
- Windows event logs

Windows-Based Analysis

The next area of focus for preparing for the SECFND is evaluating Windows-based systems. Other operating systems such as Linux and Mac OS X are covered in Chapter 9, "Linux- and Mac OS X–Based Analysis." We'll start with Windows based on its popularity in the business market space, although Apple continues to grow in popularity for enterprise mobile and desktop platforms.

The goal for this section is to understand the basics of how a system running Windows handles applications. This includes details from how memory is used to how resources are processed by the operating system. There are many versions of Windows between the current and older releases; however, the SECFND exam does not ask about or compare features among the various versions. The SECFND only focuses on the core concepts.

"Do I Know This Already?" Quiz

The "Do I Know This Already?" quiz helps you identify your strengths and deficiencies in this chapter's topics. The ten-question quiz, derived from the major sections in the "Foundation Topics" portion of the chapter, helps you determine how to spend your limited study time. You can find the answers in Appendix A Answers to the "Do I Know This Already?" Quizzes and Q&A Questions.

Table 8-1 outlines the major topics discussed in this chapter and the "Do I Know This Already?" quiz questions that correspond to those topics.

Table 8-1 "Do I Know This Already?" Foundation Topics Section-to-Question Mapping

Foundation Topics Section	Questions Covered in This Section
Process and Threads	1
Memory Allocation	2, 6
Windows Registration	3–4
Windows Management Instrumentation (WMI)	5
Handles	7–8
Services	9
Windows Event Logs	10

1. Which of the follow best describes Windows process permissions?

    a. User authentication data is stored in a token that is used to describe the security context of all processes associated with the user.

    b. Windows generates processes based on super user–level security permissions and limits processes based on predefined user authentication settings.

    c. Windows process permissions are developed by Microsoft and enforced by the host system administrator.

    d. Windows grants access to all processes unless otherwise defined by the Windows administrator.

2. Which of the following of the following is a true statement about a stack and heap?

    a. Heaps can allocate a block of memory at any time and free it at any time.

    b. Stacks can allocate a block of memory at any time and free it at any time.

    c. Heaps are best for when you know exactly how much memory you should use.

    d. Stacks are best when you don't know how much memory to use.

3. What is the Windows registry?

    a. A list of registered software on the Windows operating system

    b. Memory allocated to running programs

    c. A database used to store information necessary to configure the system for users, applications, and hardware devices

    d. A list of drivers for applications running on the Windows operating system

4. Which of the following is a function of the Windows registry?

    a. To register software with the application provider

    b. To load device drivers and start up programs

    c. To back up application registration data

    d. To log upgrade information

5. Which of the following statements is true?

    a. WMI is a command standard used by most operating systems.

    b. WMI cannot run on older versions of Windows such as Windows 98.

    c. WMI is a defense program designed to prevent scripting languages from managing Microsoft Windows computers and services.

    d. WMI allows scripting languages to locally and remotely manage Microsoft Windows computers and services.

6. What is a virtual address space in Windows?

    a. The physical memory allocated for processes

    b. A temporary space for processes to execute

    c. The set of virtual memory addresses that reference the physical memory object a process is permitted to use

    d. The virtual memory address used for storing applications

7. What is the difference between a handle and pointer?

   a. A handle is an abstract reference to a value, whereas a pointer is a direct reference.

   b. A pointer is an abstract reference to a value, whereas a handle is a direct reference.

   c. A pointer is a reference to a handle.

   d. A handle is a reference to a pointer.

8. Which of the following is true about handles?

   a. When Windows moves an object such as a memory block to make room in memory and the location of the object is impacted, the handles table is updated.

   b. Programmers can change a handle using Windows API.

   c. Handles can grant access rights against the operating system.

   d. When Windows moves an object such as a memory block to make room in memory and the location of the object is impacted, the pointer to the handle is updated.

9. Which of the following is true about Windows services?

   a. Windows services only function when a user has accessed the system.

   b. The Services Control Manager is the programming interface for modifying the configuration of Windows Services.

   c. Microsoft Windows services run in their own user session.

   d. Stopping a service requires a system reboot.

10. What is an IIS parser log used for?

   a. For logging specific Windows events

   b. For backing up Windows logs

   c. To generate alerts and log events

   d. To provide universal query access to text-based data such as logs

8

Foundation Topics

Windows was introduced by Microsoft in 1984 as a graphical user interface (GUI) for Microsoft DOS. Over time, Windows has matured in stability and capabilities with many releases, ranging from Windows 3.0 back in 1990 to the 2015 Windows 10 release. More current releases of Windows have offered customized options; for example, Windows Server was designed for provisioning services to multiple hosts, and Windows Mobile was created for Windows-based phones.

The Windows operating system architecture is made up of many components, such as the control panel, administrative tools, and software. The control panel permits users to view and change basic system settings and controls. This includes adding hardware and removing software as well as changing user accounts and accessibility options. Administrative tools are more specific to administrating Windows. For example, System Restore is used for rolling back Windows, and Disk Defragment is used to optimize performance. Software can be various types of applications, from the simple calculator application to complex programing languages.

As stated in the introduction of this chapter, the SECFND won't ask for specifics about each version of Windows; nor will it expect you to know every component within the Windows architecture. That would involve a ton of tedious detail that is out of scope for the learning objectives of the certification. The content covered in this chapter targets the core concepts you are expected to know about Windows. We will start with how applications function by defining processes and threads.

Process and Threads

Let's first run through some technical definitions of processes and threads. When you look at what an application is built from, you will find one or more processes. A *process* is a program that the system is running. Each process provides the required resources to execute a program. A process is made up of one or more *threads*, which are the basic units an operating system allocates process time to. A thread can be executed during any part of the application runtime, including being executed by another thread. Each process starts with a single thread, known as the *primary thread*, but can also create additional threads from any of its threads.

For example, the calculator application could run multiple processes when a user enters numbers to be computed, such as the process to compute the math as well as the process to display the answer. You can think of a thread as each number being called while the process is performing the computation that will be displayed by the calculator application. Figure 8-1 shows this relationship from a high-level view.

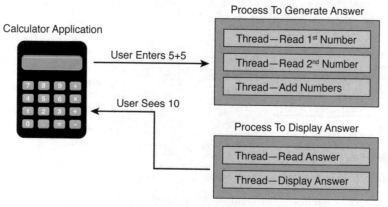

Figure 8-1   *Calculator Process and Thread Example*

Processes can be grouped together and managed as a unit called a *job object*, which can be used to control the attributes of those processes. Grouping processes together simplifies impacting those processes because any operation performed on a specific job object will impact all associated processes. A *thread pool* is a group of worker threads that efficiently execute asynchronous callbacks for the application. This is done to reduce the number of application threads and to manage the worker threads. A *fiber* is unit of execution that is manually scheduled by an application. Threads can schedule multiple fibers; however, fibers do not outperform properly designed multithreaded applications.

Whew, that's a lot of technical definitions to understand! Although these are the foundation concepts to be aware of, it is more important to understand how these items are generally used within Windows for security purposes. Knowing that a Windows process is a running program is important, but it's equally as import to understand that processes must have permission to run. This keeps processes from hurting the system as well as unauthorized actions from being performed. For example, the process to delete everything on the hard drive should have some authorization settings to avoid killing the computer.

Windows permissions are based on access control to process objects tied to user rights. This means that super users such as administrators will have more rights than other user roles. Windows uses tokens to specify the current security context for a process. This can be accomplished using the **CreateProcessWithTokenW** function.

Authentication is typically used to provision authorization to a user role. For example, you would log in with a username and password to authenticate to an access role that has specific user rights. Windows would validate this login attempt, and if authentication is successful, you will be authorized for a specific level of access. Windows stores user authentication data in a token that describes the security context of all processes associated with the user role. This means administrator tokens would have permission to delete items of importance whereas lower-level user tokens would provide the ability to view but not be authorized to delete.

Figure 8-2 ties this token idea to the calculator example, showing processes creating threads. The basic idea is that processes create threads, and threads validate whether they can run using an access token. In this example, the third thread is not authorized to operate for some reason, whereas the other two are permitted.

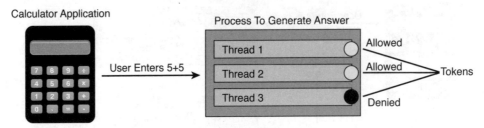

Figure 8-2 *Adding Tokens to the Threads Example*

It is important to understand how these components all work together when developing applications and later securing them. Threats to applications, known as *vulnerabilities*, could be abused to change the intended outcome of an application. This is why it is critical to include security at all stages of application development to ensure these and other application components are not abused. The next section reviews how processes and threads work within Windows memory.

The list that follows highlights the key process and thread concepts:

- A process is a program the system is running and is made of one or more threads.

- A thread is a basic unit an operating system allocates process time to.

- A job is a group of processes.

- A thread pool is a group of worker threats that efficiently execute asynchronous callbacks for the application.

- Processes must have permission to run within Windows.

- You can use a Windows token to specify the current security context for a process using the **CreateProcessWithTokenW** function.

- Windows stores data in a token that describes the security context of all processes associated with a particular user role.

Memory Allocation

Now that we have covered how applications function, let's look at where they are installed and how they run. Computer memory is any physical device capable of storing information in a temporary or permanent state. Memory can be volatile or nonvolatile. *Volatile memory* is memory that loses its contents when the computer or hardware storage device loses power. RAM is an example of volatile memory. That's why you never hear people say they are saving something to RAM. It's designed for application performance.

You might be thinking that there isn't a lot of value for the data stored in RAM; however, from a digital forensics viewpoint, the following data could be obtained by investigating RAM. (In case you're questioning some of the items in the list, keep in mind that data that is encrypted must be unencrypted when in use, meaning its unencrypted state could be in RAM. The same goes for passwords!)

- **Running processes:** Who is logged in
- **Passwords in cleartext:** Unencrypted data
- **Instant messages:** Registry information
- **Executed console commands:** Attached devices
- **Open ports:** Listening applications

Nonvolatile memory (NVRAM), on the other hand, holds data with or without power. EPROM would be an example of nonvolatile memory.

NOTE Memory and disk storage are two different things. Computers typically have anywhere from 1GB to 16GB of RAM, but they can have hundreds of terabytes of disk storage. A simple way to understand the difference is memory is the space applications use when they are running while storage is where applications store data for future use.

Memory can be managed in different ways, referred to as memory allocation or memory management. *Static memory allocation* is when a program allocates memory at compile time. *Dynamic memory allocation* is when a program allocates memory at runtime. Memory can be assigned in blocks representing portions of allocated memory dedicated to a running program. A program can request a block of memory, which the memory manager will assign to the program. When the program completes whatever it's doing, the allocated memory blocks are released and available for other uses.

Next up are stacks and heaps. A *stack* is memory set aside as spare space for a thread of execution. A *heap* is memory set aside for dynamic allocation (that is, where you put data on the fly). Unlike a stack, a heap doesn't have an enforced pattern for the allocation and deallocation of blocks. With heaps, you can allocate a block at any time and free it at any time. Stacks are best when you know ahead of time how much memory is needed, whereas heaps are better for when you don't know how much data you will need at runtime or if you need to allocate a lot of data. Memory allocation happens in hardware, in the operating system, and in programs and applications.

Processes function in a set of virtual memory known as *virtual address space*. The virtual address space for each process is private and cannot be accessed by other processes unless it is specifically shared. The virtual address does not represent the actual physical location of an object in memory; instead, it's simply a reference point. The system maintains a page table for each process that is used to reference virtual memory to its corresponding physical address space. Figure 8-3 shows this concept using the calculator example, where the threads are pointing to a page table that holds the location of the real memory object.

8

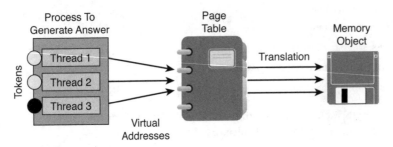

Figure 8-3 *Page Table Example*

The virtual address space of each process can be smaller or larger than the total physical memory available on the computer. A *working set* is a subset of the virtual address space of an active process. If a thread of a process attempts to use more physical memory than is currently available, the system will page some of the memory contest to disk. The total amount of virtual address space available to process on a specific system is limited by the physical memory and free space on the hard disks for the paging file.

We will now touch on a few other concepts of how Windows allocates memory. The ultimate result is the same, but the approach for each is slightly different. VirtualAlloc is a specialized allocation of OS virtual memory system; it allocates straight into virtual memory by reserving memory blocks. HeapAlloc allocates any size of memory requested, meaning it allocates by default regardless of size. Malloc is another memory allocation option, but it is more programming focused and not Windows dependent. It is not important for the SECFND to know the details of how each memory allocation option functions. The goal is just to have a general understanding of memory allocation.

The list that follows highlights the key memory allocation concepts:

- Volatile memory is memory that loses its contents when the computer or hardware storage device loses power.

- Nonvolatile memory (NVRAM) holds data with or without power.

- Static memory allocation is when a program allocates memory at compile time.

- Dynamic memory allocation is when a program allocates memory at runtime.

- A heap is memory set aside for dynamic allocation.

- A stack is the memory set aside as spare space for a thread of execution.

- A virtual address space is the virtual memory used by processes.

- A virtual address is a reference to the physical location of an object in memory. A page table translates virtual memory into its corresponding physical addresses.

- The virtual address space of each process can be smaller or larger than the total physical memory available on the computer.

Windows Registration

Now that we have covered what makes up an application and how it uses memory, let's look at Windows registration. Basically anything performed in Windows refers to or is recorded into the registry. Therefore, any actions taken by a user reference the Windows registry. The Windows registry is a hierarchical database for storing the information necessary to configure a system for one or more users, applications, and hardware devices.

Some functions of the Windows registry are to load device drivers, run startup programs, set environment variables, and store user settings and operating system parameters. You can view the Windows registry by typing the command **regedit** in the Run window. Figure 8-4 shows a screenshot of the Registry Editor window.

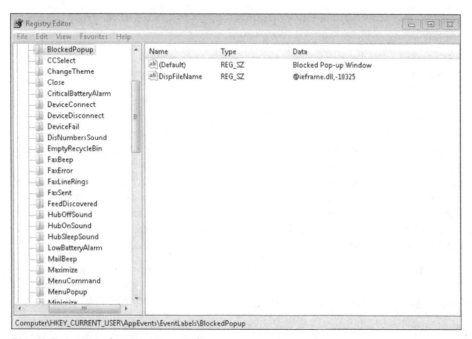

Figure 8-4 *Windows Registry Editor*

The registry is like a structured file system. The five hierarchal folders on the left are called hives and begin with HKEY (meaning the handle to a key). Two of the hives are real locations: HKEY_USERS (HKU) and HKEY_LOCAL_MACHINE (HKLM). The remaining three are shortcuts to branches within the HKU and HKLM hives. Each of the five main hives is composed of keys that contain values and subkeys. Values pertain to the operation system or applications within a key. The Windows registry is like an application containing folders. Inside an application, folders hold files. Inside the Windows registry, the hives hold values.

The following list defines the functions of the five hives within the Windows registry:

■ **HKEY_CLASSES_ROOT (HKCR):** HKCR information ensures that the correct program opens when it is executed in Windows Explorer. HKCR also contains further details on drag-and-drop rules, shortcuts, and information on the user interface. The reference location is HKLM\Software\Classes.

- **HKEY_CURRENT_USER (HKCU):** HKCU contains configuration information for any user who is currently logged in to the system, including user folders, screen colors, and control panel settings. The reference location for a specific user is HKEY_USERS. The reference for general use is HKU\.DEFAULT.

- **HKEY_CURRENT_CONFIG (HCU):** HCU stores information about the system's current configuration. The reference for HCU is HKLM\Config\profile.

- **HKEY_LOCAL_MACHINE (HKLM):** HKLM contains machine hardware-specific information that the operating system runs on. This includes a list of drives mounted on the system and generic configurations of installed hardware and applications. HKLM is a hive that isn't referenced from within another hive.

- **HKEY_USERS (HKU):** HKU contains configuration information of all user profiles on the system. This includes application configurations and visual settings. HKU is a hive that isn't referenced from within another hive.

Some interesting data points can be gained from analyzing the Windows registry. All registries contain a value called LastWrite time, which is the last modification time of a file. This can be used to identify the approximate date and time an event occurred. Autorun locations are registry keys that launch programs or applications during the boot process. Autorun is extremely important to protect because it could be used by an attacker for executing malicious applications. The most recently used (MRU) list contains entries made due to actions performed by the user. The purpose of the MRU list is to contain items in the event the user returns to them in the future. Think of the MRU list as how a cookie is used in a web browser. The UserAssist key contains a document of what the user has accessed.

Network settings, USB devices, and mounted devices all have registry keys that can be pulled up to identify activity within the operating system. Having a general understanding of Windows registration should be sufficient for questions found on the SECFND exam.

Key Topic

The list that follows highlights the key Windows registration concepts:

- The Windows registry is a hierarchical database used to store information necessary to configure the system for one or more users, applications, and hardware devices.

- Some functions of the registry are to load device drivers, run startup programs, set environment variables, and store user settings and operating system parameters.

- The five main folders in the Windows registry are called hives. Three of these hives are reference points inside of another primary hive.

- Hives contain values pertaining to the operation system or applications within a key.

Windows Management Instrumentation

The next topic focuses on managing Windows systems and sharing data with other management systems. *Windows Management Instrumentation (WMI)* is a scalable system management infrastructure built around a single, consistent, standards-based, extensible, object-oriented interface. Basically, WMI is Microsoft's approach to implementing Web-Based Enterprise Management (WBEM), which is a tool used by system management application developers for manipulating system management information. WMI uses the Common Information Model (CIM) industry standard to represent systems, applications, networks, devices, and other managed components. CIM is developed and maintained by the Distributed Management Task Force (DMTF).

It is important to remember that WMI is only for computers running Microsoft Windows. WMI comes preinstalled on all computers running Windows Millennium Edition (ME), Windows 2000, Windows XP, or Windows Server 2003; however, it can be downloaded to older systems running Windows 95, Windows 98, or Windows NT 4.0. Figure 8-5 shows a Windows computer displaying the WMI service.

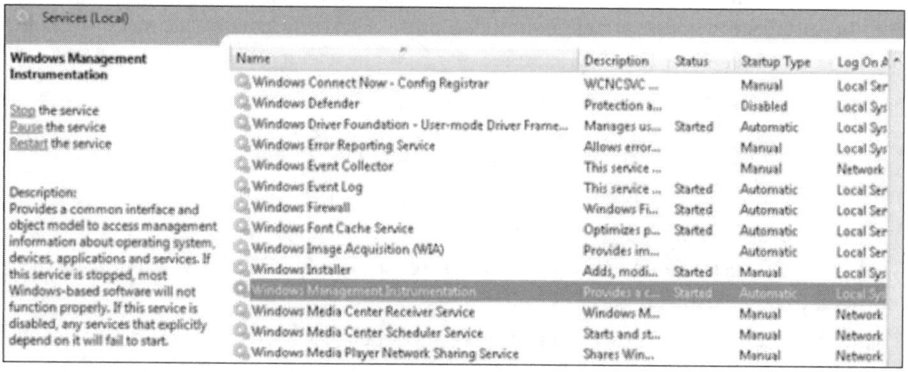

Figure 8-5 *Windows Computer Showing the WMI Service*

The purpose of WMI is to define a set of proprietary environment-independent specifications used for management information that's shared between management applications. WMI allows scripting languages to locally and remotely manage Microsoft Windows computers and services. The following list provides examples of what WMI can be used for:

- Providing information about the status of local or remote computer systems
- Configuring security settings
- Modifying system properties
- Changing permissions for authorized users and user groups
- Assigning and changing drive labels
- Scheduling times for processes to run
- Backing up the object repository
- Enabling or disabling error logging

Using WMI by itself doesn't provide these capabilities or display any data. You must pull this information using scripts and other tools. WMI can be compared to the electronics data of a car, where the car dashboard is the tool used to display what the electronics are doing. Without the dashboard, the electronics are there, but you won't be able to interact with the car or obtain any useful data. An example of WMI would be using a script to display the time zone configured on a Windows computer or issuing a command to change the time zone on one or more Windows computers.

When considering Windows security, you should note that WMI could be used to perform malicious activity. Malicious code could pull sensitive data from a system or automate malicious tasks. An example would be using WMI to escalate privileges so that malware can function at a higher privilege level if the security settings are modified. Another attack would be using WMI to obtain sensitive system information.

There haven't been many WMI attacks seen in the wild; however, Trend Micro published a whitepaper on one piece of WMI malware called TROJ_WMIGHOST.A. So although such attacks are not common, they are possible. WMI requires administrative permission and rights to be installed; therefore, a best practice to protect systems against this form of exploitation is to restrict access to the WMI service.

The list that follows highlights the key WMI concepts:

- WMI is a scalable system management infrastructure built around a single, consistent, standards-based, extensible, object-oriented interface.

- WMI is only for Windows systems.

- WMI comes preinstalled on many Windows systems. For older Windows versions, you may need to download and install it.

- WMI data must be pulled in with scripting or tools because WMI by itself doesn't show data.

Handles

In Microsoft Windows, a *handle* is an abstract reference value to a resource. Putting this another way, a handle identifies a particular resource you want to work with using the Win32 APIs. The resource is often memory, an open file, a pipe, or an object managed by another system. Handles hide the real memory address from the API user while permitting the system to reorganize physical memory in a way that's transparent to the program.

Handles are like pointers, but not in the sense of dereferencing a handle to gain access to some data. Instead, a handle is passed to a set of functions that can perform actions on the object the handle identifies. In comparison, a pointer contains the address of the item to which it refers, whereas a handle is an abstract of a reference and is managed externally. A handler can have its reference relocated in memory by the system without it being invalidated, which is impossible to do with a pointer because it directly points to something (see Figure 8-6).

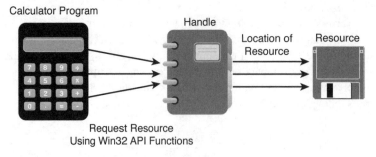

Figure 8-6 *Calculator Example Showing Handles*

An important security concept is that a handle not only can identify a value but also associate access rights to that value. Consider the following example:

```
int fd = open("/etc/passwd", O_RDWR);
```

In this example, the program is requesting to read the system password file "/etc/passwd" in read/write mode (noted as 0_RDWR). This means the program is asking to open this file with the specified access rights, which are read and write. If this is permitted by the operating system, it will return a handle to the user. The actual access is controlled by the operating system, and the handle can be looked at as a token of that access right provided by the operating system. Another outcome could be the operating system denying access, which means not opening the file or providing a handle. This shows why handles can be stored but never changed by the programmer—they are issued and managed by the operating system and can be changed on the fly by the operating system.

Handles generally end with ".h" (for example, WinDef.h) and are unsigned integers that Windows uses to internally keep track of objects in memory. When Windows moves an object, such as a memory block, to make room in memory and thus impacts the location of the object, the handles table is updated. Think of a handle as a pointer to a structure Windows doesn't want you to directly manipulate. That is the job of the operating system.

One security concern with regard to handles is a *handle leak*. This occurs when a computer program requests a handle to a resource but does not free the handle when it is no longer used. The outcome of this is a resource leak, which is similar to a pointer causing a memory leak. A handle leak could happen when a programmer requests a direct value while using a count, copy, or other operation that would break when the value changes. Other times it is an error caused by poor exception handling. An example would be a programmer using a handle to reference some property and proceeding without releasing the handle. If this issue continues to occur, it could lead to a number of handles being marked as "in use" and therefore unavailable, causing performance problems or a system crash.

The list that follows highlights the key handle concepts:

- A handle is an abstract reference value to a resource.
- Handles hide the real memory address from the API user while permitting the system to reorganize physical memory in a way that's transparent to the program.
- A handle not only can identify a value but also associate access rights to that value.
- A handle leak can occur if a handle is not released after being used.

Services

The next topic to tackle is Windows services, which are long-running executable applications that operate in their own Windows session. Basically, they are services that run in the background. Services can automatically kick off when a computer starts up, such as the McAfee security applications shown in Figure 8-7, and they must conform to the interface rules and protocols of the Services Control Manager.

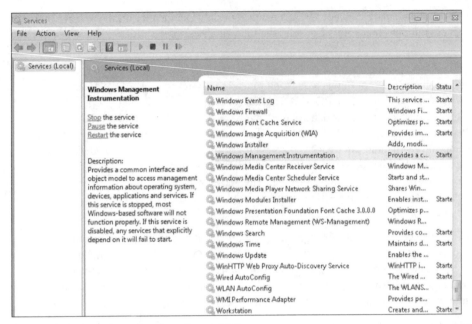

Figure 8-7 *Windows Services Control Manager*

Services can also be paused and restarted. Figure 8-7 shows some services started under the Status tab. You can see whether a service will automatically start under the Startup Type tab. To view the services on a Microsoft Windows system as shown in Figure 8-7, type **services. msc** in the Run window. This brings up the Services Control Manager.

Services are ideal for running things within a user security context, starting applications that should always be run for a specific user, and for long-running functionally that doesn't interfere with other users who are working on the same computer. An example would be monitoring whether storage is consumed past a certain threshold. The programmer could create a Windows service application that monitors storage space and set it to automatically start at bootup so it is continuously monitoring for the critical condition. If the user chooses not to monitor his system, he could open the Services Control Manager and change the startup type to Manual, meaning it must be manually turned on. Alternatively, he could just stop the service. The services inside the Services Control Manager can be started, stopped, or triggered by an event. Because services operate in their own user account, they can operate when a user is not logged in to the system, meaning that the storage space monitoring application could be set to automatically run for a specific user or for any other users, including when no user is logged in.

Windows administrators can manage services using the Services snap-in, Sc.exe, or Windows PowerShell. The Services snap-in is built into the Services Management Console and can connect to a local or remote computer on a network, thus enabling the administrator to perform some of the following actions:

- View installed services
- Start, stop, or restart services

- Change the startup type for a service
- Specify service parameters when available
- Change the startup type
- Change the user account context where the service operates
- Configure recovery actions in the event a service fails
- Inspect service dependencies for troubleshooting
- Export the list of services

Sc.exe, also known as the Service Control utility, is a command-line version of the Services snap-in. This means it can do everything the Services snap-in can do as well as install and uninstall services. Windows PowerShell can also manage Windows services using the following commands, also called cmdlets:

- **Get-Service:** Gets the services on a local or remote computer
- **New-Service:** Creates a new Windows service
- **Restart-Service:** Stops and then starts one or more services
- **Resume-Service:** Resumes one or more suspended (paused) services
- **Set-Service:** Starts, stops, and suspends a service, and changes its properties
- **Start-Service:** Starts one or more stopped services
- **Stop-Service:** Stops one or more running services
- **Suspend-Service:** Suspends (pauses) one or more running services

Other tools that can manage Windows services are Net.exe, Windows Task Manager, and MSConfig; however, their capabilities are limited compared to the other tools mentioned. For example, MSConfig can enable or disable Windows services, and Windows Task Manager can show a list of installed services as well as start or stop them.

Like other aspects of Windows, services are targeted by attackers. Microsoft has improved the security of services in later versions of the Windows operating system after finding various attack methods that compromise and completely own older versions of Windows. However, even the newer versions of Windows are not perfect, so best practice dictates securing (disabling) services such as the following unless they are needed:

- **TCP 53:** DNS Zone Transfer
- **TCP 135:** RPC Endpoint Mapper
- **TCP 139:** NetBIOS Session Service
- **TCP 445:** SMB Over TCP
- **TCP 3389:** Terminal Services
- **UDP 137:** NetBIOS Name Service
- **UDP 161:** Simple Network Management Protocol
- **TCP/UDP 389:** Lightweight Directory Access Protocol

In addition, you should enable host security solutions, such as the Windows Firewall services. Enforcing least privilege access as well as using restricted tokens and access control can reduce the damage that could occur if an attacker successfully compromises a Windows system's services. Basically applying best practices to secure hosts and your network will also help to reduce the risk of attacks against Microsoft Windows system services.

The list that follows highlights the key services concepts:

- Microsoft Windows services are long-running executable applications that operate in their own Windows session.

- Services Control Manager enforces the rules and protocols for Windows services.

- Services are ideal for running things within a user security context, starting applications that should always be run for a specific user, and for long-running functionally that doesn't interfere with other users who are working on the same computer.

- Windows administrators can manage services using the Services snap-in, Sc.exe, or Windows PowerShell.

Windows Event Logs

The final topic to address in this chapter is Windows event logs. Logs, as a general definition, are records of events that happened in your computer. The purpose of logging in Windows is to record errors and events in a standard, centralized way. This helps you track what happened and troubleshoot problems. The most common place for Windows logs is the Windows event log, which contains logs for the operating system and several applications, such as SQL Server and Internet Information Server (IIS). Logs are structured in a data format so they can be easily searched and analyzed. The tool commonly used to do this is the Windows Event Viewer.

The Windows event logging service records events from many sources and stores them in a single collection known as the event log. The event log typically maintains three event log types: Application, System, and Security log files. You can generally find the Windows event logs in the C:\Windowsystem3config directory. You can open the Windows Event Viewer to view these logs by simply searching for **Event Viewer** in the Run tab. Figure 8-8 shows an example of viewing logs in the Event Viewer. The panel on the left shows the Application, System, and Security log categories, whereas the panel on the right shows the actions.

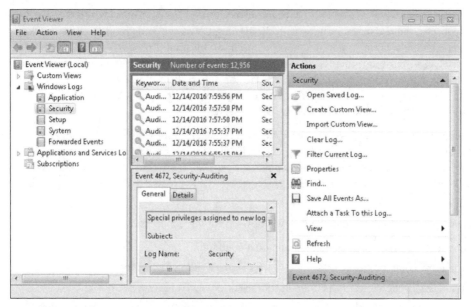

Figure 8-8 *Windows Event Viewer Example*

There are many panels in the Event Viewer as well as many different ways you can view the data. Although the SECFND exam won't have you dig through a Windows log, it is good practice to have a basic understanding of what type of data can be found in a log file. In general, you will find five event types when viewing Windows event logging:

- **Error:** Events that represent a significant problem such as loss of data or loss of functionality.

- **Warning:** Theses events are not significant, but may indicate a possible future issue.

- **Information:** Theses events represent the successful operation of an application, drive, or service.

- **Success Audit:** Theses events record audited security access attempts that were successful.

- **Failure Audit:** Theses events record audited security access attempts that failed.

Logs can eat up storage, so administrators should either set a time to have older logs deleted or export them to a storage system. Some security tools such as Security Information and Event Managers (SIEMs) can be used as a centralized tool for reading logs from many devices. The challenge for any system attempting to use a log is ensuring that the system is able to understand the log format.

If a system reading the file does not understand the file type or expects data in a specific format, weird results could happen or the system might reject the file. Administrators can adjust the system receiving the logs from Windows to accept the standard event format or use a parser in Windows to modify how the data is sent.

A log parser is a versatile tool that provides universal query access to text-based data such as event logs, the registry, the file system, XML files, CVE files, and so on. A parser works by you telling it what information you need and how you want it processed. The results of a query can be custom formatted in text-based output, or the output can be customized to a specialty target system such as SQL, SYSLOG, or a chart. Basically, a log parser gives you tons of flexibility for manipulating data. An example would be using a Windows IIS log parser to format event logs to be read by a SQL server.

It is important to protect logs because they are a critical tool for forensic investigations when an event occurs. Malicious users will likely be aware that their actions are logged by Windows and attempt to either manipulate or wipe all logs to cover their tracks. Savvy attackers will choose to only modify their impact to the log to avoid alerting administrators that an event has occurred.

The list that follows highlights the key Windows event log concepts:

- Logs are records of events that happen on a computer.

- The most common place for Windows logs is the Windows event log.

- Windows Event Viewer is a common tool used to view Windows event logs.

- You can generally find the Windows event logs in the C:\Windowsystem3config directory.

- Event logs typically maintain three event log types: Application, System, and Security log files

- Within the log types are generally five event types: Error, Warning, Information, Success Audit, and Failure Audit

- A log parser is a versatile tool that provides universal query access to text-based data.

Exam Preparation Tasks

Review All Key Topics

Review the most important topics in the chapter, noted with the Key Topic icon in the outer margin of the page. Table 8-2 lists these key topics and the page numbers on which each is found.

Table 8-2 Key Topics

Key Topic Element	Description	Page
List	Process and thread concepts	362
List	Memory allocation concepts	364
List	Four hives within a Windows Registry	366
List	WMI concepts	368
List	Key handle concepts	369
List	Key services concepts	372
List	Key Windows event log concepts	374

Define Key Terms

Define the following key terms from this chapter, and check your answers in the glossary:

process, Windows process permission, thread, job object, thread pool, fiber, static memory allocation, dynamic memory allocation, stack, heap, VirtualAlloc, virtual address space, HeapAlloc, Malloc, Windows registration, hives, Windows Management Instrumentation (WMI), handle, Microsoft Windows services, log parser

Q&A

The answers to these questions appear in Appendix A, "Answers to the 'Do I Know This Already?' Quizzes and Q&A Questions." For more practice with exam format questions, use the exam engine on the website.

1. Which is the best definition of a Windows process?

   a. A program that is running within Windows

   b. The basic unit an operating system allocates process time to

   c. A group of worker threads that efficiently execute asynchronous callbacks for the application

   d. A unit of execution that is manually scheduled by an application

8

2. Which statement about virtual address space is true?

    a. The virtual address space is shared by the system and referenced by a page table for each process.

    b. The virtual address space is private and cannot be accessed by other processes unless it is specifically shared.

    c. The virtual address represents the physical location of any object in memory.

    d. Virtual address space cannot be shared.

3. RAM is an example of which of the following?

    a. Magnetic storage

    b. Nonvolatile memory

    c. Volatile memory

    d. Removable storage

4. Which command is used to view the Windows Registry?

    a. winedit

    b. winreg

    c. regedit

    d. cntedit

5. Which of the following is not a Windows Registry hive?

    a. HKEY_LOCAL (HKLM)

    b. HKEY_CLASSES_ROOT (HKCR)

    c. HKEY_CURRENT_CONFIG (HCU)

    d. HKEY_USERS (HKU)

6. What does WMI stand for?

    a. Windows Management Instructions

    b. Windows Management Instrumentation

    c. Windows Monitor Instrumentation

    d. Windows Monitor Instructions

7. Which of the following is something WMI can't be used for?

    a. To schedule times for processes to run

    b. To assign and change drive label

    c. To uninstall an application

    d. To enable or disable error logging

8. What can cause a handle leak?

    a. A loop that leverages a handle

    b. A Windows compiler error

    c. A handle that's not released after being used

    d. A pointer to a handle

9. What is the command to bring up the Windows Services Control manager?

    a. cntmanage

    b. services.msc

    c. regedit

    d. services.exe

10. What tool can be used in Windows to format a log for a SQL server?

    a. SIEM

    b. Programing Language

    c. Event View

    d. Log Parser

References and Further Reading

https://msdn.microsoft.com/en-us/library/windows/desktop/ms681917(v=vs.85).aspx

http://la.trendmicro.com/media/misc/understanding-wmi-malware-research-paper-en.pdf

https://msdn.microsoft.com/en-us/library/d56de412%28v=vs.110%29.aspx

https://msdn.microsoft.com/en-us/library/windows/desktop/ms724457%28v=vs.85%29.aspx

https://msdn.microsoft.com/en-us/library/hk1k7x6x.aspx

https://support.microsoft.com/en-us/kb/256986

https://msdn.microsoft.com/en-us/library/aa394582%28v=vs.85%29.aspx

8

This chapter covers the following exam topics:

- Processes
- Forks
- Permissions
- Symlinks
- Daemons
- UNIX-based syslog
- Apache access logs

CHAPTER 9

Linux- and Mac OS X–Based Analysis

Now that we have covered Microsoft Windows, it's time to move on to Linux and Mac OS X. The focus in this chapter will be to understand how things work inside a UNIX environment. Learning how the UNIX environment functions will not only improve your technical skills but can also help you build a strategy for securing UNIX-based systems. You won't be expected to know every detail about the Linux or Mac OS X environments, so having an understanding of the topics covered in this chapter should be sufficient for the SECFND exam.

"Do I Know This Already?" Quiz

The "Do I Know This Already?" quiz helps you identify your strengths and deficiencies in this chapter's topics. The ten-question quiz, derived from the major sections in the "Foundation Topics" portion of the chapter, helps you determine how to spend your limited study time. You can find the answers in Appendix A Answers to the "Do I Know This Already?" Quizzes and Q&A Questions.

Table 9-1 outlines the major topics discussed in this chapter and the "Do I Know This Already?" quiz questions that correspond to those topics.

Table 9-1 "Do I Know This Already?" Foundation Topics Section-to-Question Mapping

Foundation Topics Section	Questions Covered in This Section
Processes	1–2
Forks	3
Permissions	4
Symlinks	6
Daemons	5, 7
UNIX-based syslog	8–9
Apache access logs	10

1. Which process type occurs when a parent process is terminated and the remaining child process is permitted to continue on its own?

    a. Zombie process

    b. Orphan process

    c. Rogue process

    d. Parent process

2. A zombie process occurs when which of the following happens?

   a. A process holds its associated memory and resources but is released from the entry table.

   b. A process continues to run on its own.

   c. A process holds on to associated memory but releases resources.

   d. A process releases the associated memory and resources but remains in the entry table.

3. What is the best explanation of a fork (system call) in UNIX?

   a. When a process is split into multiple processes

   b. When a parent process creates a child process

   c. When a process is restarted from the last run state

   d. When a running process returns to its original value

4. Which of the following shows giving permissions to the group owners for read and execute, giving file owner permission for read, write, and execute, and giving all others permissions for execute?

   a. -rwx-rx-x

   b. -rx-rwx-x

   c. -rx-x-rwx

   d. -rwx-rwx-x

5. Which is a correct explanation of daemon permissions?

   a. Daemons run at root-level access.

   b. Daemons run at super user–level access.

   c. Daemons run as the init process.

   d. Daemons run at different privileges, which are provided by their parent process.

6. Which of the following is not true about symlinks?

   a. A symlink will cause a system error if the file it points to is removed.

   b. Showing the contents of a symlink will display the contents of what it points to.

   c. An orphan symlink occurs when the link a symlink points to doesn't exist.

   d. A symlink is a reference to a file or directory.

7. What is a daemon?

   a. A program that manages the system's motherboard

   b. A program that runs other programs

   c. A computer program that runs as a background process rather than being under direct control of an interactive user

   d. The only program that runs in the background of a UNIX system

8. Which priority level of logging will be sent if the priority level is err?

    a. err

    b. err, warning, notice, info, debug, none

    c. err, alert, emerg

    d. err, crit, alert, emerg

9. Which of the following is an example of a facility?

    a. marker

    b. server

    c. system

    d. mail

10. Which security technology would be best for detecting a pivot attack?

    a. Virtual private network (VPN)

    b. Host-based antivirus

    c. NetFlow solution looking for anomalies within the network

    d. Application layer firewalls

9

Foundation Topics

Processes

As defined in the last chapter on Microsoft Windows, a *process* is a running instance of a program. How a process works in Linux and OS X is different and will be the focus of this chapter. The two methods for starting a process are starting it in the foreground and starting it in the background. You can see all the processes in UNIX by using the command **ps ()** in a terminal window, also known as a *shell*. What follows **ps** provides details of what type of processes should be displayed. For example, **a** would show all processes for all users, **u** would display the process's owner, and **x** would show processes not attached to a terminal. Figure 9-1 shows running the **ps aux** command on a Kali Linux installation. Notice that the **aux** command displays the processes, users, and owners.

```
root@kali:/# ps aux
USER         PID %CPU %MEM    VSZ   RSS TTY      STAT START   TIME COMMAND
root           1  0.0  0.2 202604  5132 ?        Ss   14:54   0:17 /sbin/init
root           2  0.0  0.0      0     0 ?        S    14:54   0:00 [kthreadd]
root           3  0.0  0.0      0     0 ?        S    14:54   0:00 [ksoftirqd/0]
root           5  0.0  0.0      0     0 ?        S<   14:54   0:00 [kworker/0:0H
root           7  0.0  0.0      0     0 ?        S    14:54   0:05 [rcu_sched]
root           8  0.0  0.0      0     0 ?        S    14:54   0:00 [rcu_bh]
root           9  0.0  0.0      0     0 ?        S    14:54   0:00 [migration/0]
root          10  0.0  0.0      0     0 ?        S    14:54   0:00 [watchdog/0]
root          11  0.0  0.0      0     0 ?        S    14:54   0:00 [watchdog/1]
root          12  0.0  0.0      0     0 ?        S    14:54   0:00 [migration/1]
```

Figure 9-1   *Running the ps aux Command*

Running a process in the foreground means you can't do anything else in that shell while the process is running. Running the process in the background (using the ampersand **&**) tells UNIX to allow you to do other tasks within the shell as the process is running. Here is an example of running the program "cisco" as a background process:

```
#The program cisco will execute in the background
./cisco &
```

The following types of processes can run in UNIX:

- Child process
- Init process
- Orphan process
- Zombie process
- Daemon process

We will now cover each of these briefly and go into a little more detail on the daemon process in a later section of this chapter because it has a few important concepts to cover for the SECFND exam. A process starts in the ready state and eventually executes when it is moved to the running state; this is known as *process scheduling*. Process scheduling is critical to keeping the CPU busy, delivering minimum response time for all programs, and keeping the system from crashing. This is achieved by using rules for moving processes in and out of the

CPU using two different scheduling tactics. The first is *non-preemptive scheduling*, which is when executing processes gives up CPU voluntarily. The other is *preemptive scheduling*, which is when the OS decides that another process has a greater importance and pre-empts the currently running process.

Processes can have a parent/child relationship. A *child process* is a process created by some other process during runtime. Typically, a child process is created to execute a task within an existing process, also known as a *parent process*. A parent process uses a *fork* system call to create child processes. Usually a shell is created that becomes the parent, and the child process executes inside of it. We examine the **fork** command in the next section of this chapter. All processes in UNIX have a parent except for the init process, which will be covered shortly. Each process is given an integer identifier, known as a *process identifier* (PID). The process schedule is giving a PID value of 0 and typically termed as *sched*. In Figure 9-1, notice the PIDs assigned to the various processes.

The init process is the first process during the boot sequence, meaning the init process does not have a parent process. The init process is another name for the schedule process; hence, its PID value is 1. Figure 9-2 shows a diagram of the init PID creating parent processes, which in turn are creating child processes.

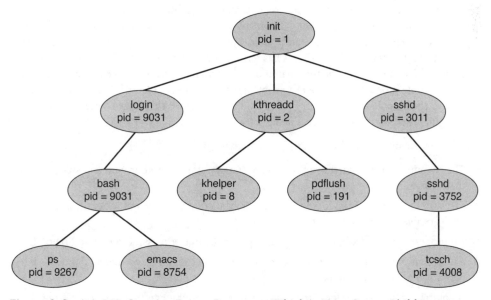

Figure 9-2   *init PID Creating Parent Processes, Which in Turn Create Child Processes*

In this diagram, a child process may receive some shared resources from its associated parent, depending on how the system is implemented. Best practice is to put restrictions in place to avoid the child process from consuming more resources than the parent process can provide, which would cause bad things to happen. The parent process can use the **Wait** system call, which pauses the process until the **Wait** returns. The parent can also issue a

Run system call, thus permitting the child to continue without waiting (basically making it a background task). A process can terminate if the system sees one of the following situations:

- The system doesn't have the resources to provide.

- The parent task doesn't need the task completed that is assigned to the child process.

- The parent stops, meaning the associated child doesn't have a parent process anymore. This can cause the system either to terminate the child process or to let it run as an orphan process.

- The **Exit** or **Kill** command is issued.

When the process ends, any associated system resources are freed up and any open files are flushed and closed. If a parent is waiting for a child process to terminate, a termination status and the time of execution are returned to the parent process. The same data can be returned to the init process if the process that ended was an orphan process.

An *orphan process* results when a parent process is terminated and the child process is permitted to continue on its own. Orphan processes become the child process of the init process; but they are still labeled as orphan processes because their parent no longer exists. The time between when the child process ends and the status information is returned to the parent, the process continues to be recorded as an entry in the process table. During this state, the terminated process becomes a *zombie process*, releasing the associated memory and resources but remaining in the entry table. Usually the parent will receive a SIGCHILD signal, letting it know the child process has terminated. The parent can then issue a **Wait** call that grabs the exit status of the terminated process and removes the process from the entry table. A zombie process can become a problem if the parent is killed off and not permitted to remove the zombie from the entry table. Zombie processes that linger around eventually become inherited by the init process and are terminated.

The list that follows highlights the key process concepts:

- The two methods for starting a process are starting it in the foreground and starting it in the background.

- The different types of processes in UNIX are the child process, init process, orphan process, zombie process, and daemon process.

- All processes in UNIX have a parent, except for the init process, which has a PID of 1.

- An orphan process results when a parent process is terminated and the child process is permitted to continue on its own.

- A zombie process is a process that releases its associated memory and resources but remains in the entry table.

Forks

A fork is when a parent creates a child process, or simply the act of creating a process. This means the **fork** command returns a process ID (PID). The parent and child processes run in separate memory spaces, and the child is a copy of the parent. The entire virtual space of the parent is replicated in the child process, including all the memory space. The child also inherits copies of the parent's set of open file descriptors, open message queue descriptors, and open directory streams.

To verify which process is the parent and which is the child, you can issue the **fork** command. The result of the **fork** command can be one of the following.

- A negative value (-1), indicating the child process was not created, followed by the number of the last error (or *errno*). One of the following could be the error:
  - **EAGAIN**: The system limited the number of threads for various reasons.
  - **EAGAIN Fork**: Failed to allocate the necessary kernel structures due to low memory.
  - **ENOMEN**: Attempt to create a child process in a PID whose init process has terminated.
  - **ENOSYS Fork**: The process is not supported on the platform.
  - **ERESTARTNOINTR**: The system call was interrupted by a signal and will be restarted.
- A zero, indicating a new child process was created.
- A positive value, indicating the PID of the child to its parent.

After the fork, the child and parent processes not only run the same program, but they resume execution as though both had made the system call. They will then inspect the system call's return value to determine their status and act accordingly. One thing that can impact a process's status is what permissions it has within its space to operate. We take a deeper look at UNIX permissions in the next section.

The list that follows highlights the key fork concepts:

- **A fork** is when a parent creates a child process.
- The **fork** command returns a process ID (PID).
- The entire virtual space of the parent is replicated in the child process, including all the memory space.

Permissions

UNIX and Mac OS X are different from other operating systems in that they are both multitasking and multiuser systems. *Multitasking* involves the forking concepts previously covered, and *multiuser* means more than one user can be operating the system at the same time. Yes, a laptop may only have one keyboard; however, that doesn't mean others can't connect to it over a network and open a shell to operate the computer. This functionality has always been included in the UNIX operating system since the times of large mainframe computers. However, this functionality can also be a bad thing if a malicious user gets shell access to the system, even when the system owner is logged in and doing daily tasks.

To ensure the practicality of offering multiuser access, it is important to have controls put in place for each user. These controls are known as *file permissions*. File permissions assign access rights for the owner of the file, members of the group of related users, and everybody else. Permissions can be granted to *read* a file, *write* to a file, and *execute* a file (meaning run the file as a program). You can see the permission settings of a file by typing the command **ls -l** (*filename*). This will return a long string of information, starting with the file's permission (such as **-rw-r---r--**). Example 9-1 demonstrates displaying the file permissions for a file called ninjatune1.png.

Example 9-1 *Displaying File Permissions for a File*

```
JOMUNIZ-M-91SU:documents jomuniz$ ls -l ninjatune1.png
-rwxrwxrwx@ 1 jomuniz  staff  90277  Oct  15  2013  ninjatune1.png
JOMUNIZ-M-91SU:documents jomuniz$
```

The first part of this output shows read, write, and execution rights, represented with the **rwx** statements. These are defined as follows:

- **read (r)**: Reading, opening, viewing, and copying the file are permitted.
- **write (w)**: Writing, changing, deleting, and saving the file are permitted.
- **execution (x)**: Executing and invoking the file is permitted. This includes permitting directories to have search access.

The second part of the output shows the file owner. The file owner in this example is "jomuniz," one of your friendly authors. The next item is the owner's group. In this example, we have a group called "staff." The last part is what everybody else has access to. This example shows all three parts—user jomuniz, group staff, and everybody else all have read, write, and execution rights to this file. Now let's look at Example 9-2, where we view the file rights for the bash program located in the /bin directory.

Example 9-2 *Displaying File Rights for a Program*

```
JOMUNIZ-M-91SU:/ jomuniz$ ls -l /bin/bash
-rxr-xr-x  1  root  wheel 628496 Jan 13  2016  /bin/bash
JOMUNIZ-M-91SU:/ jomuniz$
```

The first part of this output shows the user right settings for the file. The user is currently "root" and the group is "wheel." Everybody else has the access right to just execute this file. To break down the permissions further, let's look at the permissions statement **-rwx-xr-x**, broken down as follows:

- The opening **-** means a regular file. A **d** would indicate a directory.
- Next, **rwx** means read, write, and execution rights for the owner of the file.
- **-xr** means read and execution rights for the group owning the file.
- Finally, **-x** means execution rights for everybody else.

File permissions for a file or directory can be modified using the **chmod** command, which you use to specify the settings and the file or files you wish to modify (for example, using the command **chmod 700 the_file**). The number 700 represents a series of bits, which translates to the associated **rwx** privileges you find with the **ls** command. You can also add a **-v** to get a verbose response to the command (as in **chmod −v 700 the_file**). The math for permissions works like this:

Read (r) = 4

Write (w) = 2

Execution (x) = 1

Giving access to everybody would mean R=4 + W=2 + X=1, for a grand total of 7. That means the first digit of 7 represents the file owner having access to everything. The digits for the group and everybody else are 0, meaning no access. Therefore, the number 700 means the owner has access to everything while the group and everybody else have no access. The prior example used **−rwx-xr-r**. Here, the first number would again be 7, while **xr** would be 5 (R=4 + X=1) to represent read and execution access rights for the group. The last part is just read access, so that means R=4 for everybody else. This all translates **−rwx-xr-r** to the number 754. Therefore, to change the file permission to this, you would use the command **chmod 754 the_file**.

Table 9-2 represents a complete list of permission values. Note that this table would be used to compute the desired rights for the file owner, group, and everybody else, making it a three-digit number.

Table 9-2 List of Permission Values

Column Value	Permissions	Represented By
0	None	---
1	Execution-only	**--x**
2	Write	**-w-**
3	Execution and write	**-wx**
4	Read-only	**r--**
5	Read and execution	**r-x**
6	Read and write	**rw-**
7	Read, write, and execution	**rwx**

You can also be specific about whom you are granting rights to or removing rights from using the characters **a** (all), **u** (user), **g** (group), and **o** (others). For example, you can use the command **chmod g=r the_file** to change the group to read-only for the file. Another example would be the command **chmod a+x the_file**, which adds the execution privilege for all users. This means **=** gives a specific group a permission, **-** removes a permission, and **+** adds a permission. To see a few comparisons of using the complete

chmod command verses the shortened equivalent, check out the following list comparing the different approaches covered:

chmod a=rwx file.txt	is equivalent to **chmod 777 file.txt**	and also **rwxrwxrwx**
chmod o= file.txt	is equivalent to **chmod 770 file.txt**	and also **–rxrwx--**
chmod g=w file.txt	is equivalent to **chmod 740 file.txt**	and also **–rwx-w--**
chmod g+x file.txt	is equivalent to **chmod 754**	and also **–rwxr-xr-**
chmod o-r file.txt	is equivalent to **chmod 750 file.txt**	and also **–rwxr-x--**

All the previous **chmod** examples assume you are in the directory where the file is located. You may want to change files in another directory, which can be expressed in the **chmod** command as well. This is done by specifying the file path as directory/file.txt (verses just file. txt) so that the command knows where to look for the file.

NOTE   You need at least the minimal file permission execution (x) to access a directory. Without any permissions, you won't be able to access the directory.

File permissions in UNIX take a top-down approach, meaning that denying access for a directory will automatically include all subdirectories and files. For example, suppose you have the directory FILE_D with the permission **drwxr-xr-x** and a subdirectory SUBFILE_D with the permission **drwxr-xr-x**. Now suppose you want to deny read, write, and execution access for the group and everybody else without impacting the owner of FILE_D. In this case, you would use the command **chmod go-rwx FILE_D**, meaning **–rwx** removes access from FILE_D for the group and other users. This would also impact the subdirectory SUBFILE_D, even though SUBFILE_D's permissions are **drwxr-xr-x**, meaning groups and other users within SUBFILE would not have access to anything due to the parent fold FILE_D denying access, which flows down to SUBFILE.

The same concept works for whomever you assign rights to, meaning that if you give rights to the group and others in SUBFILE_D, this would *not* give the same rights to FILE_D. This is why sometimes an admin to a folder may give access to a file but not the folder it is contained in and find people with access rights to the file can't reach the file due to not being able to open the folder.

Another concept to touch upon is the *group*, which is the set of permissions for one or more users who are grouped together. When an account is created, the user is assigned to a group. For example, you might have a group called employees for all employees and another group called administrators for network operations. This allows you to grant the same level of permissions to an entire group verses having to do so for each user. Users can be members of one or more groups. You can view which groups a user is a member of and their user ID by using the command **id**. Figure 9-3 shows an example of user jomuniz, with the user ID of 501, being part of various groups with their associated numbers.

```
JOMUNIZ-M-91SU:~ jomuniz$ id
uid=501(jomuniz) gid=20(staff) groups=20(staff),12(everyone),61(localaccounts),7
9(_appserverusr),80(admin),81(_appserveradm),98(_lpadmin),33(_appstore),100(_lpo
perator),204(_developer),395(com.apple.access_ftp),398(com.apple.access_screensh
aring),399(com.apple.access_ssh)
```

Figure 9-3 *User ID Example*

If you own a file and are a member of more than one group, you can modify the group "ownership" of that file using the **chgrp** command. For example, the command **chgrp staff file.txt** would give the group "staff" permissions to file.txt. Note that this does not impact the individual ownership of the file. Ownership can only be changed by the file owner. The **chgrp** command just gives group permissions to the file, as in the previous example of giving the group "staff" access. To change the owner of the file, you can use the command **chown**. For example, you could use **chown Bob file.txt** to give Bob ownership of the file.

Sometimes changing the group or owner will require super user privileges, which provide the highest access level and should only be used for specific reasons, such as performing administrative tasks. Most UNIX distributions offer the command **su** (substitute user), which can give super user rights for short tasks. Doing this will require you to enter the super user's password. If successful, you will end up with a shell with super user rights. Typing **exit** will return you to your previous user permissions level.

Distributions such as Ubuntu offer the command **sudo**, which gives super user rights on an as-needed basis. Typically this is to execute a specific command, meaning you would type **sudo whatever_command** to execute the command with super user rights. The difference between **su** and **sudo** is that after entering **sudo**, you will be prompted for the user's password rather than the super user's password.

> **NOTE** Administrators should always proceed with caution when permitting super user and root-level permissions. All processes, including *background daemons*, should be limited to only the permissions required to successfully execute their purpose. Giving processes too much access could be a serious risk in case of a compromised process, which an attacker could use to gain full system access.

The list that follows highlights the key permissions concepts:

- File permissions assign access rights for the owner of the file, members of a group of related users, and everybody else.
- The command **chmod** modifies file permissions for a file or directory.
- Read (r) = 4, Write (w) = 2, Execute (x) = 1.
- A group is the set of permissions for one or more users grouped together.
- You can modify the group "ownership" of a file using the **chgrp** command.
- To change the owner of a file, you can use the command **chown**.
- File permissions in UNIX take a top-down approach, meaning denying access for a directory will automatically include all subdirectories and files.

- Super user privileges provide the highest access level and should only be used for specific reasons, such as performing administrative tasks.

- All processes, including background daemons, should be limited to only the permissions necessary to successfully accomplish their purpose.

Symlinks

The next topic we'll cover is how to link files together. A symlink (short for *symbolic link*, and sometimes called a "soft link") is any file that contains a reference to another file or directory in an absolute or relative path that affects pathname resolution. In short, a symlink contains the name for another file but doesn't contain actual data. From a command viewpoint, a symlink looks like a standard file, but when it's referenced, everything points to whatever the symlink is aimed at.

Let's look at an example of creating a file. Example 9-3 shows the **echo** command putting Vanilla Ice's lyric into a file called file1. You can see the contents of the file by using the **cat** command. After file1 is created, we create a symlink using the command **ln –s /tmp/file.1 / tmp/file.2** pointing file.2 to file.1. Finally, to verify both files, we use the command **ls –al / tmp/file*** to show both files.

Example 9-3   *Displaying File Rights for a Program*

```
[JOMUNIZ-M-91SU:~ jomuniz$ echo "Stop collaborate and listen" > /tmp/file.1
[JOMUNIZ-M-91SU:~ jomuniz$ cat /tmp/file.1
Stop collaborate and listen
[JOMUNIZ-M-91SU:~ jomuniz$ ln -s /tmp/file.1 /tmp/file.2
[JOMUNIZ-M-91SU:~ jomuniz$ ls -al /tmp/file*
-rw-r--r--  1 jomuniz  wheel  28 Jul 26 11:08 /tmp/file.1
Lrwxr-xr-x 1 jomuniz  wheel  11 Jul 26 11:09 /tmp/file.2 -> /tmp/file.1
JOMUNIZ-M-91SU:~ jomuniz$
```

Notice in Example 9-3 how the permissions for file.2 start with a "l," thus confirming the file is a symbolic link. The end of the statement also shows file.2 is referencing file.1 via the "->" symbol between the paths. To validate this, you can issue the **cat** command to view the contents of file.2, which are the contents from file.1, as shown in Example 9-4.

Example 9-4   *Displaying File Contents*

```
[JOMUNIZ-M-91SU:~ jomuniz$ cat  /tmp/file.2
Stop collaborate and listen
JOMUNIZ-M-91SU:~ jomuniz$
```

Because a symlink is just a reference, removing the symlink file doesn't impact the file it references. This means removing file.2 won't have any impact on file.1. If file.1 is removed, it will cause an *orphan symlink*, meaning a symlink pointing to nothing because the file it references doesn't exist anymore. For example, let's change file.1 to file.3 using the **mv** command. Example 9-5 shows this action. It then shows that there are now two files, file.2 symlinked to file.1 (even though file1 doesn't exist) and file.3. Example 9-5 also shows the results of attempting to view file.2 using the **cat** command. It returns "no such file or directory" because file.2 is now an orphan symlink. This shows how symlinks are interpreted at runtime, meaning that if we move file.3 back to file.1, file.2 would once again show Vanilla Ice's lyrics. One last key point is that unlike a hard link, a symlink can exist even if what it points to does not exist.

Example 9-5   *Displaying File Contents*

```
[JOMUNIZ-M-91SU:~ jomuniz$ mv /tmp/file.1 /tmp/file.3
[JOMUNIZ-M-91SU:~ jomuniz$ ls -al /tmp/file*
Lrwxr-xr-x  1 jomuniz  wheel  11 Jul 26 11:09 /tmp/file.2 -> /tmp/file.1
-rw-r--r--  1 jomuniz  wheel  28 Jul 26 11:08 /tmp/file.3
[JOMUNIZ-M-91SU:~ jomuniz$ cat /tmp/file.2
Cat:  /tmp/file.2: No such file or directory
JOMUNIZ-M-91SU:~ jomuniz$
```

The list that follows highlights the key symlink concepts:

- A symlink is any file that contains a reference to another file or directory.

- A symlink is just a reference. Removing the symlink file doesn't impact the file it references.

- An orphan symlink is a symlink pointing to nothing because the file it references doesn't exist anymore.

- A symlink is interpreted at runtime and can exist even if what it points to does not.

Daemons

We opened this chapter by explaining how processes can run in the foreground and background. When a process runs in the background, it is known as a *daemon*. Daemons are not controlled by the active user; instead they run unobtrusively in the background, waiting to be activated by the occurrence of a specific event or condition. UNIX systems usually have numerous daemons running to accommodate requests for services from other computers and responding to other programs and hardware activity. Daemon can be triggered by many things, such as a specific time, event, file being viewed, and so on. Essentially, daemons listen for specific things to trigger their response.

When initiated, a daemon, like any other process, will have an associated process identification number (PID). Daemons are system processes, so their parent is usually the *init* process, which has a PID value of 1 (but this is not always the case). Daemon processes are created by the system using the **fork** command, thus forming the process hierarchy covered previously in this chapter.

The following list shows some common daemons found in UNIX. You may notice that most daemon programs end with "d" to indicate they are a daemon.

- **xinetd:** The TCP/IP super server listening to ports assigned to processes listed in inetd. conf or einetd.config

- **corond:** Runs scheduled tasks

- **ftdp**: Used for file transfers
- **lpd**: Used for laser printing
- **rlogind**: Used for remote login
- **rshd**: Used for remote command execution
- **telnetd**: Used for telnet

Not all daemons are started automatically. Just like with other processes, daemons such as **binlogd, mysqld**, and **apache** can be set to not start unless the user or some event triggers them. This also means daemons, like any other program, can be terminated, restarted, and have their status evaluated. It is common for many daemons to be started at system boot; however, some are child processes that are launched based on a specific event. This all depends on the version of the system you are running.

The list that follows highlights the key daemon concepts:

- Daemons are programs that run in the background.
- From a permissions viewpoint, daemon's are typically created by the init process.
- A daemon's permissions level can vary depending on what is provided to it. Daemons should not always have super user–level access.
- Daemons are not controlled by the active user; instead, they run unobtrusively in the background, waiting to be activated by a specific event or condition.
- Not all daemons are started automatically.
- Children of the init process can be terminated and restarted.

UNIX-Based Syslog

UNIX-based systems have very flexible logging capabilities, enabling the user to record just about anything. The most common form of logging is the general-purpose logging facility called *syslog*. Most programs send logging information to syslog. Syslog is typically a daemon found under the /var/log directory. You can see the logs by typing **cd /var/log** followed by **ls** to view all the logs. Make sure you know the location of these files.

The *facility* describes the application or process that submits the log message. Table 9-3 provides examples of facilities. Not all of these are available in every version of UNIX.

Table 9-3 UNIX Facilities

Facility	Description
auth	For requesting name and password activity
authpriv	Same as auth but data is sent to a more secured file
console	Messages directed at the system console
cron	Cron system scheduler messages
daemon	Daemon catch-all messages
ftp	FTP daemon messages

Facility	Description
kern	Kernel-related messages
local0.local7	Local facilities defined per site
lpr	Line printing system messages
mail	Mail system messages
mark	Pseudo event used to generate timestamps in log files
news	Network News Protocol messages
ntp	Network Time Protocol messages
user	Regular user processes
uucp	UUCP subsystem

All messages are not treated the same. A *priority* is used to indicate the level of importance of a message. Table 9-4 summarizes the priority levels.

Table 9-4   UNIX Message Priorities

Priority	Description
emerg	Emergency condition, such as a system crashing
alert	Condition that should be dealt with immediately, such as a corrupted database
crit	Critical condition, such as a hardware failure
err	Standard error
warning	Standard warning
notice	No error condition but attention may be needed
info	Information message
debug	Messages used for debugging errors or programs
none	Specifies not to log messages

For the SECFND exam, you should know the different general log types. *Transaction logs* record all transactions that occur. For example, a database transaction log would log any modifications to the database. *Alert logs* record errors such as a startup, shutdown, space errors, and so on. Session logs track changes made on managed hosts during a web-based system manager session. Logging occurs each time an administrator uses web-based system management to make a change on a host. *Threat logs* trigger when an action matches one of the security profiles attached to a security rule. It is important to distinguish what type of log would go where for an event scenario. An example would be knowing that a system crash would be an alert log and that a malicious attack would be a threat log. Actions such as logging are triggered by selectors.

Selectors monitor for one or more facility and level combinations and, when triggered, perform some action. When a specific priority level is specified, the system will track everything at that level as well as anything higher. For example, if you use crit, you will see messages associated with crit, alert, and emerg. This is why enabling debug is extremely chatty because you are essentially seeing all messages.

Actions are the results from a selector triggering on a match. Actions can write to the log file, echo the message to the console or to other devices so users can read it, send a message to another syslog server, and perform other actions.

The configuration file /etc/syslog.conf controls what **syslogd** does with the log entries it receives. This file contains one line per action; the syntax for every line is a selector field followed by an action field. The syntax used for the selector field is **facility.level**, which is designed to match log messages from a facility at a level value or higher. Also, you can add an optional comparison flag before the level to specify more precisely what is being logged. The syslog.conf file can use multiple selector fields for the same action, separated by semicolons. The special character * sets a check to match everything. The action field points out where the logs should be sent. An example would be if something within the selector is triggered, sending a file to a remote host. Figure 9-4 shows a sample syslog.conf file.

```
*.err;kern.warning;auth.notice;mail.crit                 /dev/console
*.notice;authpriv.none;kern.debug;lpr.info;mail.crit;news.err   /var/log/messages
security.*                                      /var/log/security
auth.info;authpriv.info                         /var/log/auth.log
mail.info                                       /var/log/maillog
lpr.info                                        /var/log/lpd-errs
ftp.info                                        /var/log/xferlog
cron.*                                          /var/log/cron
!-devd
```

Figure 9-4   *Sample syslog.conf File*

Looking at this example, you can see that the first line shows that if the selector matches any message with a level of err or higher (**kern.warning**, **auth.notice**, and **mail.crit**), it will take the action of sending these logs to the /dev/console location. The fifth line down shows that if the selector sees all messages from mail at a level of info or above, it will take the action of having logs sent to /var/log/maillog. The syslog.conf file will vary from system to system, but this example should give you an idea of how the file is designed to work.

One common area of concern is managing logs. Many companies have log-retention requirements, such as storing logs for up to a year. Log files can grow very quickly, depending on how selectors and actions are set up, making it challenging to accommodate storage requirements as well as actually using the log information. Log management tools such as newsyslog attempt to mitigate this by periodically rotating and compressing log files. Newsyslog is not a system daemon and by default runs every hour. Figure 9-5 shows an example of a newsyslog file.

```
# logfilename              [owner:group]     mode count size when  flags [/pid_file] [sig_num]
/var/log/all.log                             600  7     *    @T00  J
/var/log/amd.log                             644  7     100  *     J
/var/log/auth.log                            600  7     100  @0101T JC
/var/log/console.log                         600  5     100  *     J
/var/log/cron                                600  3     100  *     JC
/var/log/daily.log                           640  7     *    @T00  JN
/var/log/debug.log                           600  7     100  *     JC
/var/log/kerberos.log                        600  7     100  *     J
/var/log/lpd-errs                            644  7     100  *     JC
/var/log/maillog                             640  7     *    @T00  JC
/var/log/messages                            644  5     100  @0101T JC
```

Figure 9-5 *Sample newsyslog File*

The output showcases the filename, file owner, permissions, when to rotate the file, optional flags, and programs to signal when a log is rotated. Looking at line 2 of Figure 9-5, you can see that the file to be rotated is /var/log/all.log. There is the option to show the owner and group, but this example just shows blank space. The mode field sets up the permissions on the log file whereas the count field depicts how many rotated log files should be kept. Basically this means line 2 shows the permission 600 and a file count of 7. The size field is used to trigger when the log should be rotated. This occurs when either the log's size is larger than the size field or when time has passed a marker in the field settings. Line 2 shows an asterisk (*), which tells newsyslog to ignore this field. The flag field gives extra instructions, such as how to compress the rotated file.

Logging can become extremely challenging to manage as more systems are generating logs. This is when centralized log management becomes the key to successful log management. Tons of centralized logging solutions are available, including free and open source as well as fancier enterprise offerings.

The general concept is the centralized log management solution must be capable of accepting logging information from the source sending the logs. Popular log management offerings have the ability to accept logs from a variety of systems; however, sometimes a system will generate logs in a unique format that requires tuning of how the message is read. Adjusting messages to an acceptable format for a centralized management system is known as "creating a custom parser." It is recommended that you identify all systems that potentially will generate log messages and validate whether they produce logging in a universally accepted format such as syslog. Logging has been around for a while, so in most cases, any relatively current centralized logging solution should be capable of accepting most common logging formats.

The list that follows highlights the key UNIX syslog concepts:

- The most common form of logging is the general-purpose logging facility called syslog.
- The default location of logs in UNIX is the /var/log directory.
- The facility describes the application or process that submits the log message.
- A priority is used to indicate the level of importance of the message.
- Transaction logs record all transactions that occur.
- Session logs track changes made on managed hosts during a web-based system manager session.
- Alert logs record errors such as a startup, shutdown, space errors, and so on.

- Threat logs trigger when an action matches one of the security profiles attached to a security rule.

- Selectors monitor for one or more facility and level combinations and, when triggered, perform some action.

- Actions are the result of a selector triggering on a match.

- The configuration file /etc/syslog.conf controls what **syslogd** does with the log entries it receives.

- Newsyslog attempts to mitigate log management by periodically rotating and compressing log files.

Apache Access Logs

One important aspect of logging is monitoring the activity and performance of a server. With regard to UNIX, Apache is a very popular option and therefore a topic on the SECFND exam. The focus for this section is on Apache logging, which is important for maintaining the health and security of such systems.

The Apache HTTP server provides a variety of different mechanisms for logging everything that happens on the server. Logging can include everything from an initial request to the final resolution of a connection, including any errors that may have happened during the process. Also, many third-party options complement the native logging capabilities; these include PHP scripts, CGI programs, and other event-sending applications.

In regard to errors, Apache will send diagnostic information and record any errors it encounters to the log file set by the **ErrorLog** directive. This is the first place you should go when troubleshooting any issues with starting or operating the server. You can use the command **cat**, **grep**, or any other UNIX text utility for this purpose. Basically, this file can answer what went wrong and how to fix it. The file is typically error_log on UNIX systems and error.log on OS X.

Another important log file is the access log controlled by the **CustomLog** directive. Apache servers record all incoming requests and all requests to this file. Basically, this file contains information about what pages people are viewing, the success status of a request, and how long the request took to respond.

Usually tracking is broken down into three parts: access, agent, and referrer. Respectively, these track access to the website, the browser being used to access the site, and the referring URL the site's visitor arrives from. It is very common to leverage Apache's *combined log format*, which combines all three of these logs into one log file. Most third-party software prefer a single log containing this information. The combined format typically looks like this:

```
LogFormat "%h %l %u %t  "%r" %>s %b "%{Referer}i" "%{User-Agent}i" combined
```

LogFormat starts the line by telling Apache that you define a log file type, which is *combined*. The following list explains the commands called by this file:

- **%h**: Logs the remote host
- **%l**: Remote log name

- **%u:** Remote user
- **%t:** The date and time of the request
- **%r:** The request to the website
- **%s:** The status of the request
- **%b:** Bytes sent for the request
- **%i:** Items sent in the HTML header

The full list of Apache configuration codes for custom logs can be found at http://httpd. apache.org/docs/2.0/mod/mod_log_config.html.

Like with any other UNIX system, Apache logging will most likely generate a lot of data very quickly, making it necessary to have proper rotation of logs. You have many options, including auto-removing files that are too big and archiving older copies of data for reference. In a crisis situation, you may manually move the files; however, a soft restart of Apache is required before it can begin to use the new logs for new connections. An automated method would use a program such as Logrotate. Logrotate can enforce parameters that you set such as certain date, size, and so on.

The list that follows highlights the key Apache access log concepts:

- Apache sends diagnostic information and records any errors it encounters to the ErrorLog log.
- Apache servers record all incoming requests and all requests to the access log file.
- The combined log format lists the access, agent, and referrer fields.

Exam Preparation Tasks

Review All Key Topics

Review the most important topics in the chapter, noted with the Key Topic icon in the outer margin of the page. Table 9-5 lists these key topics and the page numbers on which each is found.

Table 9-5   Key Topics

Key Topic Element	Description	Page
List	Summary of process types	382
List	Key process concepts	384
List	Key fork concepts	385
List	Read, write, and execution values	386
List	Key permission concepts	389
List	Key symlink concepts	391
List	Key daemon concepts	392
List	Key UNIX syslog concepts	395
List	Apache access log concepts	397

Complete Tables and Lists from Memory

Print a copy of Appendix B, "Memory Tables," (found on the book website), or at least the section for this chapter, and complete the tables and lists from memory. Appendix C, "Memory Tables Answer Key," also on the website, includes completed tables and lists to check your work.

Define Key Terms

Define the following key terms from this chapter, and check your answers in the glossary:

process, child process, fork, init process, orphan process, zombie process, file permissions, group, symlink, orphan symlink, daemon, facility, priority, selector, action, priority, transaction log, session log, alert log, threat log

Q&A

The answers to these questions appear in Appendix A, "Answers to the 'Do I Know This Already?' Quizzes and Q&A Questions." For more practice with exam format questions, use the exam engine on the website.

1. Which of the following statements is not true about a daemon process?

   a. A daemon is a process that runs in the background.

   b. A daemon's parent process is typically the init process.

   c. Daemons are controlled by the active user.

   d. Not all daemons are automatically started.

2. Apache will send diagnostic information and record any errors that it encounters to which of the following?

   a. ErrorLog

   b. Dump.txt

   c. syslog

   d. Accesslog

3. Which of the following explains the file permissions for **-rwx-rwx-x**?

   a. The owner has read, write, and execution permissions; the group has read, write and execution permissions; everybody else has read permission.

   b. The owner has read and execution permissions; the group has read, write, and execution permissions; everybody else has write permission.

   c. The owner has read, write, and execution permissions; the group has read, write, and execution permissions; everybody else has execution permission.

   d. The group has read, write, and execution permissions; the owner has read, write, and execution permissions; everybody else has execution permission.

4. Which is a true statement about a symlink?

   a. Deleting the symlink file deletes the file it references.

   b. Moving a file referenced by a symlink will cause a system error.

   c. Symlinks are the same as pointers.

   d. A symlink is also known as a soft link.

5. Which log type would be used for recording changes in a SQL database?

   a. Transaction logs

   b. Alert logs

   c. Session logs

   d. Threat logs

9

6. Which process has a PID of 1?

    a. Daemon

    b. Parent

    c. Child

    d. Init

7. When issuing the command **ls -l (filename)**, what is the correct order of user permissions?

    a. group, owner, everybody else

    b. everybody else, group, owner

    c. owner, everybody else, group

    d. owner, group, everybody else

8. Which command can change the file owner?

    a. file

    b. owner

    c. chown

    d. chmod

9. Which of the following explains Linux daemon permissions?

    a. Daemons get permissions from the init process.

    b. Daemons get permissions from a parent process.

    c. Daemons are always the highest level of permissions.

    d. Daemons and the init are the same thing.

10. Where is the UNIX log located?

    a. /var/log

    b. /dev/console

    c. /etc/log

    d. /config/log

References and Further Reading

http://man7.org/linux/man-pages/man2/fork.2.html

http://help.unc.edu/help/how-to-use-unix-and-linux-file-permissions/

https://www.freebsd.org/doc/handbook/configtuning-syslog.html

https://httpd.apache.org/docs/2.4/logs.html

This chapter covers the following topics:

- Antimalware and antivirus software

- Host-based firewalls and host-based intrusion prevention

- Application-level whitelisting and blacklisting

- System-based sandboxing

CHAPTER 10

Endpoint Security Technologies

This chapter describes different endpoint security technologies available to protect desktops, laptops, servers, and mobile devices. It covers details about antimalware and antivirus software, as well as what are host-based firewalls and host-based intrusion prevention solutions. You will also learn the concepts of application-level whitelisting and blacklisting, as well as system-based sandboxing.

"Do I Know This Already?" Quiz

The "Do I Know This Already?" quiz helps you identify your strengths and deficiencies in this chapter's topics. The eight-question quiz, derived from the major sections in the "Foundation Topics" portion of the chapter, helps you determine how to spend your limited study time. You can find the answers in Appendix A Answers to the "Do I Know This Already?" Quizzes and Q&A Questions.

Table 10-1 outlines the major topics discussed in this chapter and the "Do I Know This Already?" quiz questions that correspond to those topics.

Table 10-1 "Do I Know This Already?" Foundation Topics Section-to-Question Mapping

Foundation Topics Section	Questions Covered in This Section
Antimalware and Antivirus Software	1–3
Host-Based Firewalls and Host-Based Intrusion Prevention	4–5
Application-Level Whitelisting and Blacklisting	6–7
System-Based Sandboxing	8

1. What is a Trojan horse?

   a. A piece of malware that downloads and installs other malicious content from the Internet to perform additional exploitation on an affected system.

   b. A type of malware that executes instructions determined by the nature of the Trojan to delete files, steal data, and compromise the integrity of the underlying operating system, typically by leveraging social engineering and convincing a user to install such software.

   c. A virus that replicates itself over the network infecting numerous vulnerable systems.

   d. A type of malicious code that is injected into a legitimate application. An attacker can program a logic bomb to delete itself from the disk after it performs the malicious tasks on the system.

2. What is ransomware?

   a. A type of malware that compromises a system and then often demands a ransom from the victim to pay the attacker in order for the malicious activity to cease or for the malware to be removed from the affected system

   b. A set of tools used by an attacker to elevate his privilege to obtain root-level access in order to completely take control of the affected system

   c. A type of intrusion prevention system

   d. A type of malware that doesn't affect mobile devices

3. Which of the following are examples of free antivirus software? (Select all that apply.)

   a. McAfee Antivirus

   b. Norton AntiVirus

   c. ClamAV

   d. Immunet

4. Host-based firewalls are often referred to as which of the following?

   a. Next-generation firewalls

   b. Personal firewalls

   c. Host-based intrusion detection systems

   d. Antivirus software

5. What is an example of a Cisco solution for endpoint protection?

   a. Cisco ASA

   b. Cisco ESA

   c. Cisco AMP for Endpoints

   d. Firepower Endpoint System

6. What is a graylist?

   a. A list of separate things, such as hosts, applications, email addresses, and services, that are authorized to be installed or active on a system in accordance with a pre-determined baseline.

   b. A list of different entities that have been determined to be malicious.

   c. A list of different objects that have not yet been established as not harmful or malicious. Once additional information is obtained, graylist items can be moved onto a whitelist or a blacklist.

   d. A list of different objects that have not yet been established as not harmful or malicious. Once additional information is obtained, graylist items cannot be moved onto a whitelist or a blacklist.

7. Which of the following are examples of application file and folder attributes that can help with application whitelisting?

    a. Application store

    b. File path

    c. Filename

    d. File size

8. Which of the following are examples of sandboxing implementations?

    a. Google Chromium sandboxing

    b. Java Virtual Machine (JVM) sandboxing

    c. HTML CSS and JavaScript sandboxing

    d. HTML5 "sandbox" attribute for use with iframes

10

Foundation Topics

Antimalware and Antivirus Software

As you probably already know, computer viruses and malware have been in existence for a long time. On the other hand, the level of sophistication has increased over the years. There are numerous antivirus and antimalware solutions on the market designed to detect, analyze, and protect against both known and emerging endpoint threats. Before diving into these technologies, you should learn about viruses and malicious software (malware) and some of the taxonomy around the different types of malicious software.

The following are the most common types of malicious software:

- **Computer virus:** A malicious software that infects a host file or system area to perform undesirable actions such as erasing data, stealing information, and corrupting the integrity of the system. In numerous cases, these viruses multiply again to form new generations of themselves.

- **Worm:** Viruses that replicate themselves over the network, infecting numerous vulnerable systems. In most occasions, a worm will execute malicious instructions on a remote system without user interaction.

- **Mailer and mass-mailer worm:** A type of worm that sends itself in an email message. Examples of mass-mailer worms are Loveletter.A@mm and W32/SKA.A@m (a.k.a. the Happy99 worm), which sends a copy of itself every time the user sends a new message.

- **Logic bomb:** A type of malicious code that is injected into a legitimate application. An attacker can program a logic bomb to delete itself from the disk after it performs the malicious tasks on the system. Examples of these malicious tasks include deleting or corrupting files or databases and executing a specific instruction after certain system conditions are met.

- **Trojan horse:** A type of malware that executes instructions determined by the nature of the Trojan to delete files, steal data, or compromise the integrity of the underlying operating system. Trojan horses typically use a form of social engineering to fool victims into installing such software on their computers or mobile devices. Trojans can also act as backdoors.

- **Backdoor:** A piece of malware or configuration change that allows attackers to control the victim's system remotely. For example, a backdoor can open a network port on the affected system so that the attacker can connect and control the system.

- **Exploit:** A malicious program designed to "exploit" or take advantage of a single vulnerability or set of vulnerabilities.

- **Downloader:** A piece of malware that downloads and installs other malicious content from the Internet to perform additional exploitation on an affected system.

- **Spammer:** Systems or programs that send unsolicited messages via e-mail, instant messaging, newsgroups, or any other kind of computer or mobile device communication. Spammers use the type of malware that's sole purpose is to send these unsolicited messages, with the primary goal of fooling users into clicking malicious links, replying to emails or messages with sensitive information, or performing different types of scams.

The attacker's main objective is to make money.

- **Key logger:** A piece of malware that captures the user's keystrokes on a compromised computer or mobile device. It collects sensitive information such as passwords, PINs, personal identifiable information (PII), credit card numbers, and more.

- **Rootkit:** A set of tools used by an attacker to elevate his privilege to obtain root-level access to be able to completely take control of the affected system.

- **Ransomware:** A type of malware that compromises a system and then often demands a ransom from the victim to pay the attacker in order for the malicious activity to cease or for the malware to be removed from the affected system. The following are examples of ransomware:

  - Reveton

  - SamSam

  - Crypto Locker

  - CryptoWall

There are numerous types of commercial and free antivirus software, including the following:

- Avast!

- AVG Internet Security

- Bitdefender Antivirus Free

- ZoneAlarm PRO Antivirus + Firewall and ZoneAlarm Internet Security Suite

- F-Secure Anti-Virus

- Kaspersky Anti-Virus

- McAfee AntiVirus

- Panda Antivirus

- Sophos Antivirus

- Norton AntiVirus

- ClamAV

- Immunet AntiVirus

10

TIP   ClamAV is an open source antivirus engine sponsored and maintained by Cisco and non-Cisco engineers. You can download ClamAV from http://www.clamav.net. Immunet is a free community-based antivirus software maintained by Cisco Sourcefire. You can download Immunet from http://www.immunet.com.

There are numerous other antivirus software companies and products. The following link provides a comprehensive list and comparison of the different antivirus software available on the market: http://en.wikipedia.org/wiki/Comparison_of_antivirus_software.

Host-Based Firewalls and Host-Based Intrusion Prevention

Host-based firewalls are often referred to as "personal firewalls." Personal firewalls and host intrusion prevention systems (HIPSs) are software applications that you can install on end-user machines or servers to protect them from external security threats and intrusions. The term *personal firewall* typically applies to basic software that can control Layer 3 and Layer 4 access to client machines. HIPS provides several features that offer more robust security than a traditional personal firewall, such as host intrusion prevention and protection against spyware, viruses, worms, Trojans, and other types of malware.

Today, more sophisticated software is available on the market that makes basic personal firewalls and HIPS obsolete. For example, Cisco Advanced Malware Protection (AMP) for Endpoints provides more granular visibility and controls to stop advanced threats missed by other security layers. Cisco AMP for Endpoints takes advantage of telemetry from big data, continuous analysis, and advanced analytics provided by Cisco threat intelligence in order to detect, analyze, and stop advanced malware across endpoints.

Cisco AMP for Endpoints provides advanced malware protection for many operating systems, including the following:

- Windows
- Mac OS X
- Android

Attacks are getting very sophisticated, and they can evade detection of traditional systems and endpoint protection. Nowadays, attackers have the resources, knowledge, and persistence to beat point-in-time detection. Cisco AMP for Endpoints provides mitigation capabilities that go beyond point-in-time detection. It uses threat intelligence from Cisco to perform retrospective analysis and protection. Cisco AMP for Endpoints also provides device and file trajectory capabilities to allow the security administrator to analyze the full spectrum of an attack.

Cisco acquired a security company called Threat Grid that provides cloud-based and on-premises malware analysis solutions. Cisco integrated Cisco AMP and Threat Grid to provide a solution for advanced malware analysis with deep threat analytics. The Cisco AMP Threat Grid integrated solution analyzes millions of files and correlates them against hundreds of millions of malware samples. This provides a lot of visibility into attack campaigns and how malware is distributed. This solution provides security administrators with detailed reports of indicators of compromise and threat scores that help them prioritize mitigations and recovery from attacks.

In addition to host-based firewalls and HIPS, there are several solutions that provide hardware and software encryption of endpoint data. Several solutions provide capabilities to encrypt user data "at rest," and others provide encryption when transferring files to the corporate network.

When people refer to *email encryption*, they often are referring to encrypting the actual email message so that only the intended receiver can decrypt and read the message. To effectively protect your emails, however, you should make sure of the following:

- The connection to your email provider or email server is actually encrypted.
- Your actual email messages are encrypted.
- Your stored, cached, or archived email messages are also protected.

There are many commercial and free email encryption software programs. The following are examples of email encryption solutions:

- Pretty Good Privacy (PGP)
- GNU Privacy Guard (GnuPG)
- Secure/Multipurpose Internet Mail Extensions (S/MIME)
- Web-based encryption email services such as Sendinc and JumbleMe

S/MIME requires you to install a security certificate on your computer, and PGP requires you to generate a public and private key. Both require you to give your contacts your public key before they can send you an encrypted message. Similarly, the intended recipients of your encrypted email must install a security certificate on their workstation or mobile device and provide you with their public key before they send the encrypted email (so that you can decrypt it). Many email clients and web browser extensions for services such as Gmail provide support for S/MIME. You can obtain a certificate from a certificate authority in your organization or from a commercial service such as DigiCert or VeriSign. You can also obtain a free email certificate from an organization such as Comodo.

Many commercial and free pieces of software are available that enable you to encrypt files in an end-user workstation or mobile device. The following are a few examples of free solutions:

- **GPG:** GPG enables you to encrypt files and folders on a Windows, Mac, or Linux system.
- **The built-in Mac OS X Disk Utility:** Disk Utility enables you to create secure disks by encrypting files with AES 128-bit or AES 256-bit encryption.
- **TrueCrypt:** An encryption tool for Windows, Mac, and Linux systems.
- **AxCrypt:** A Windows-only file encryption tool.
- **BitLocker:** A full disk encryption feature included in several Windows operating systems.
- **Many Linux distributions such as Ubuntu:** Allow you to encrypt the home directory of a user with built-in utilities.
- **Mac OS X FileVault:** Supports full disk encryption on Mac OS X systems.

The following are a few examples of commercial file encryption software:

- Symantec Endpoint Encryption
- PGP Whole Disk Encryption
- McAfee Endpoint Encryption (SafeBoot)
- Trend Micro Endpoint Encryption

10

Application-Level Whitelisting and Blacklisting

Three different concepts are defined in this section:

- **Whitelist:** A list of separate things (such as hosts, applications, email addresses, and services) that are authorized to be installed or active on a system in accordance with a predetermined baseline.

- **Blacklist:** A list of different entities that have been determined to be malicious.

- **Graylist:** A list of different objects that have not yet been established as not harmful or malicious. Once additional information is obtained, graylist items can be moved onto a whitelist or a blacklist.

TIP   The National Institute of Standards and Technology (NIST) defines the concept of whitelisting and blacklisting applications in their special publication NIST.SP.800-167 (http://nvlpubs.nist.gov/nistpubs/SpecialPublications/NIST.SP.800-167.pdf).

Application whitelisting can be used to stop threats on managed hosts where users are not able to install or run applications without authorization. For example, let's imagine that you manage a kiosk in an airport where users are limited to running a web-based application. You may want to whitelist that application and prohibit running any additional applications in the system.

One of the most challenging parts of application whitelisting is the continuous management of what is and is not on the whitelist. It is extremely difficult to keep the list of what is and is not allowed on a system where there are hundreds of thousands of files with a legitimate need to be present and running on the system; however, several modern application whitelisting solutions are available that can help with this management nightmare. Several of these modern application whitelisting systems are quite adept at tracking what is happening on a system when approved changes are made and managing the whitelist accordingly. These solutions do this by performing system application profiling.

Different application file and folder attributes can help with application whitelisting. The following are a few examples:

- **File path:** The process to permit all applications contained within a particular path or directory/folder. This is a very weak attribute if used by itself because it allows any malicious files residing in such path/directory to be executed.

- **Filename:** This is also a weak attribute if used in isolation because an attacker could simply change the name of the file to be the same as a common benign file. It is recommended to combine path and filename attributes with strict access controls or to combine a filename attribute with a digital signature attribute.

- **File size:** Monitoring the file size assumes that a malicious version of an application would have a different file size than the original. However, attackers can also change the size of any given file. It is better to use attributes such as digital signatures and cryptographic hashes (MD5 or SHA).

Application blacklisting works by keeping a list of applications that will be blocked on a system, preventing such applications from installing or running on that system. One of the major drawbacks of application blacklisting is that the number, diversity, and complexity of threats are constantly increasing. This is why it is very important to implement modern systems with dynamic threat intelligence feeds such as the Cisco Firepower solutions. The Cisco Firepower solutions include the Security Intelligence feature, which allows you to immediately blacklist (block) connections, applications, and files based on the latest threat intelligence provided by the Cisco Talos research team, removing the need for a more resource-intensive, in-depth analysis.

Additionally, the security intelligence feature from Cisco Firepower next-generation IPS appliances and Cisco next-generation firewalls works by blocking traffic to or from IP addresses, URLs, or domain names that have a known-bad reputation. This traffic filtering takes place before any other policy-based inspection, analysis, or traffic handling.

> **NOTE**   For more information about the Cisco Firepower Security Intelligence Blacklisting feature, go to http://www.cisco.com/c/en/us/td/docs/security/firepower/60/configuration/guide/fpmc-config-guide-v60/Security_Intelligence_Blacklisting.html.

Some security professionals claim that, although whitelisting is a more thorough solution to the problem, it is not practical because of the overhead and resources required to create and maintain an effective whitelist.

System-Based Sandboxing

Sandboxing limits the impact of security vulnerabilities and bugs in code to only run inside the "sandbox." The goal of sandboxing is to ensure software bugs and exploits of vulnerabilities cannot affect the rest of the system and cannot install persistent malware in the system. In addition, sandboxing prevents exploits or malware from reading and stealing arbitrary files from the user's machine. Figure 10-1 shows an application without being run in a sandbox. The application has complete access to user data and other system resources.

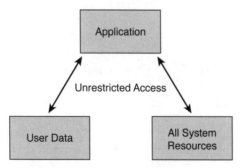

Figure 10-1   *Example Without a Sandbox*

Figure 10-2 shows the concept of a sandbox, where the application does not have access to user data or the rest of the system resources.

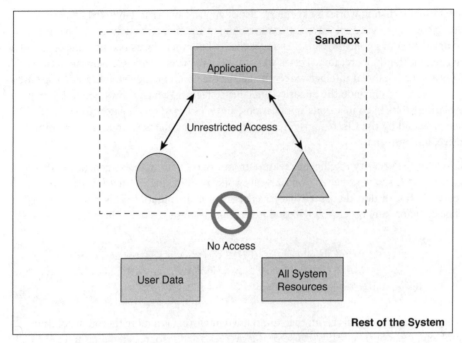

Figure 10-2 *Example with a Sandbox*

Several system-based sandboxing implementations are available. The following are a few examples:

■ Google Chromium sandboxing

■ Java JVM sandboxing

■ HTML5 "sandbox" attribute for use with iframes

Figure 10-3 illustrates the Google Chromium sandbox high-level architecture.

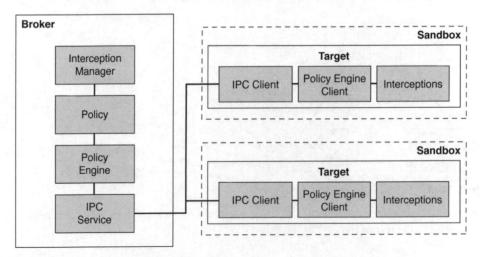

Figure 10-3 *Google Chromium Sandbox High-Level Architecture*

In Google Chromium's implementation, the target process hosts all the code that runs inside the sandbox and the sandbox infrastructure client side. The broker is always the browser process, and it is a privileged controller of the activities of the sandboxed processes. The following are the responsibilities of the broker:

- Detail the policy for each target process.
- Spawn the target processes.
- Host the sandbox policy engine service.
- Host the sandbox interception manager.
- Host the sandbox interprocess communication (IPC) service to the target processes. IPC is a collection of programming interfaces that allows the coordination of activities among different program processes that can run concurrently in an operating system.
- Perform the policy-allowed actions on behalf of the target process.

The broker should always outlive all the target processes that it spawned. The sandbox IPC is used to transparently forward certain API calls from the target to the broker. These calls are always evaluated against the predefined policy.

10

Exam Preparation Tasks

Review All Key Topics

Review the most important topics in the chapter, noted with the Key Topic icon in the outer margin of the page. Table 10-2 lists these key topics and the page numbers on which each is found.

Table 10-2   Key Topics

Key Topic Element	Description	Page
List	Examples of malicious software	406
Summary	Summary of host-based firewalls and host-based intrusion prevention systems (HIPSs)	408
Summary	Application whitelisting, blacklisting, and graylisting	410
Summary	System-based sandboxing	411

Complete Tables and Lists from Memory

There are no memory tables in this chapter.

Define Key Terms

Define the following key terms from this chapter, and check your answers in the glossary:

viruses, worms, mailers and mass-mailer worms, logic bombs, exploits, Trojan horses, backdoors, exploits, downloaders, spammers, key loggers, rootkits, ransomware

Q&A

The answers to these questions appear in Appendix A, "Answers to the 'Do I Know This Already?' Quizzes and Q&A Questions." For more practice with exam format questions, use the exam engine on the website.

1. What are worms?

   a. A type of malware that compromises a system and then often demands a ransom from the victim to pay the attacker in order for the malicious activity to cease or for the malware to be removed from the affected system.

   b. Viruses that replicate themselves over the network, infecting numerous vulnerable systems. On most occasions, a worm will execute malicious instructions on a remote system without user interaction.

   c. An exploit of a network infrastructure device vulnerability that installs a backdoor on the affected system.

   d. An exploit of a firewall vulnerability that installs a backdoor on the affected system.

2. What is ransomware?

   a. A type of malware that compromises a system and then often demands a ransom from the victim to pay the attacker in order for the malicious activity to cease or for the malware to be removed from the affected system.

   b. A type of malware that is installed on a stolen laptop or mobile device.

   c. A type of malware that compromises a system that has access to sensitive data and can replicate itself in other systems such as firewalls, IPSs, NetFlow collectors, and so on.

   d. A type of malware that compromises a system that has access to sensitive data and can replicate itself in other systems such as routers and switches.

3. Which of the following are examples of system-based sandboxing implementations? (Select all that apply.)

   a. Google Project Zero

   b. Google Chromium sandboxing

   c. Java JVM sandboxing

   d. Threat Grid

4. Which of the following are benefits of system-based sandboxing?

   a. It limits the development of an application inside of a region of memory.

   b. It limits the impact of security vulnerabilities and bugs in code to only run inside the "sandbox."

   c. It prevents software bugs and exploits of vulnerabilities from affecting the rest of the system and from installing persistent malware in the system.

   d. It limits the communication of kernel modules within the system, controlling the flow of information and data exchange.

5. What is a limitation of application whitelisting?

   a. The cost of application whitelisting technologies.

   b. The ability to interact with other systems.

   c. Scalability in low-power and low-resource IoT.

   d. The continuous management of what is and is not on the whitelist.

6. Cisco AMP for Endpoints takes advantage of which of the following?

   a. Telemetry from big data, continuous analysis, and advanced analytics provided by Cisco ESA and WSA in order to detect, analyze, and stop advanced malware across endpoints

   b. Advanced analytics provided by antivirus software in order to detect, analyze, and stop advanced malware across endpoints

   c. Telemetry from big data, continuous analysis, and advanced analytics provided by Cisco threat intelligence in order to detect, analyze, and stop advanced malware across endpoints

   d. Telemetry from big data, continuous analysis, and advanced analytics provided by Cisco next-generation firewalls in order to detect, analyze, and stop advanced malware across endpoints.

7. Which of the following is an example of a host-based encryption technology that can help protect files as well as email?

   a. Cisco AMP

   b. Protected Guided Privacy (PGP)

   c. Pretty Good Privacy (PGP)

   d. Cisco WSA

8. What is an application blacklist?

   a. A list of different entities that have been determined to be malicious

   b. A list of different entities that have been determined to be false positives

   c. A list of different malicious websites and hosts

   d. A list of different domains that are known to host malware

9. Which of the following is software that can enable you to encrypt files on your hard disk drive?

   a. BitCrypt

   b. CryptoWall

   c. CryptoLocker

   d. BitLocker

10. To effectively protect your emails, you should make sure of which the following?

   a. All your email messages are sent to a sandbox to be evaluated before reaching their destination.

   b. The connection to your email provider or email server is actually encrypted.

   c. Your actual email messages are encrypted.

   d. Your stored, cached, or archived email messages are also protected.

This chapter covers the following topics:

- Network telemetry
- Host telemetry

CHAPTER 11

Network and Host Telemetry

This chapter covers different network and host security telemetry solutions. Network telemetry and logs from network infrastructure devices such as firewalls, routers, and switches can prove useful when you're proactively detecting or responding to a security incident. Logs from user endpoints not only can help you for attribution if they are part of a malicious activity, but also for victim identification.

"Do I Know This Already?" Quiz

The "Do I Know This Already?" quiz helps you identify your strengths and deficiencies in this chapter's topics. The ten-question quiz, derived from the major sections in the "Foundation Topics" portion of the chapter, helps you determine how to spend your limited study time. You can find the answers in Appendix A Answers to the "Do I Know This Already?" Quizzes and Q&A Questions.

Table 11-1 outlines the major topics discussed in this chapter and the "Do I Know This Already?" quiz questions that correspond to those topics.

Table 11-1   "Do I Know This Already?" Foundation Topics Section-to-Question Mapping

Foundation Topics Section	Questions Covered in This Section
Network Telemetry	1–7
Host Telemetry	8–10

1. Why you should enable Network Time Protocol (NTP) when you collect logs from network devices?

   a. To make sure that network and server logs are collected faster.

   b. Syslog data is useless if it shows the wrong date and time. Using NTP ensures that the correct time is set and that all devices within the network are synchronized.

   c. By using NTP, network devices can record the time for certificate management.

   d. NTP is not supported when collecting logs from network infrastructure devices.

2. Cisco ASA supports which of the following types of logging? (Select all that apply.)

   a. Console logging

   b. Terminal logging

   c. ASDM logging

   d. Email logging

   e. External syslog server logging

3. Which of the following are examples of scalable, commercial, and open source log-collection and -analysis platforms? (Select all that apply.)

   a. Splunk

   b. Spark

   c. Graylog

   d. Elasticsearch, Logstash, and Kibana (ELK) Stack

4. Host-based firewalls are often referred to as which of the following?

   a. Next-generation firewalls

   b. Personal firewalls

   c. Host-based intrusion detection systems

   d. Antivirus software

5. What are some of the characteristics of next-generation firewall and next-generation IPS logging capabilities? (Select all that apply.)

   a. With next-generation firewalls, you can only monitor malware activity and not access control policies.

   b. With next-generation firewalls, you can monitor events for traffic that does not conform with your access control policies. Access control policies allow you to specify, inspect, and log the traffic that can traverse your network. An access control policy determines how the system handles traffic on your network.

   c. Next-generation firewalls and next-generation IPSs help you identify and mitigate the effects of malware. The FMC file control, network file trajectory, and Advanced Malware Protection (AMP) can detect, track, capture, analyze, log, and optionally block the transmission of files, including malware files and nested files inside archive files.

   d. AMP is supported by Cisco next-generation firewalls, but not by IPS devices.

6. Which of the following are characteristics of next-generation firewalls and the Cisco Firepower Management Center (FMC) in relation to incident management? (Select all that apply.)

   a. They provide a list of separate things, such as hosts, applications, email addresses, and services, that are authorized to be installed or active on a system in accordance with a predetermined baseline.

   b. These platforms support an incident lifecycle, allowing you to change an incident's status as you progress through your response to an attack.

   c. You can create your own event classifications and then apply them in a way that best describes the vulnerabilities on your network.

   d. You cannot create your own event classifications and then apply them in a way that best describes the vulnerabilities on your network

7. Which of the following are true regarding full packet capture?

    a. Full packet capture demands great system resources and engineering efforts, not only to collect the data and store it, but also to be able to analyze it. That is why, in many cases, it is better to obtain network metadata by using NetFlow.

    b. Full packet captures can be discarded within seconds of being collected because they are not needed for forensic activities.

    c. NetFlow and full packet captures serve the same purpose.

    d. Most sniffers do not support collecting broadcast and multicast traffic.

8. Which of the following are some useful attributes you should seek to collect from endpoints? (Select all that apply.)

    a. IP address of the endpoint or DNS hostname

    b. Application logs

    c. Processes running on the machine

    d. NetFlow data

9. SIEM solutions can collect logs from popular host security products, including which of the following?

    a. Antivirus or antimalware applications

    b. Cloud logs

    c. NetFlow data

    d. Personal firewalls

10. Which of the following are some useful reports you can collect from Cisco ISE related to endpoints? (Select all that apply.)

    a. Web Server Log reports

    b. Top Application reports

    c. RADIUS Authentication reports

    d. Administrator Login reports

Foundation Topics

Network Telemetry

The network can provide deep insights and the data to determine whether a cyber security incident has happened. This section covers the various types of telemetry features available in the network and how to collect such data. Even a small network can generate a large amount of data. That's why it is also important to have the proper tools to be able to analyze such data.

Network Infrastructure Logs

Logs from network devices such as firewalls, routers, and switches can prove useful when you're proactively detecting or responding to a security incident. For example, brute-force attacks against a router, switch, or firewall can be detected by system log (syslog) messages that could reveal the suspicious activity. Log collectors often offer correlation functionality to help identify compromises by correlating syslog events.

Syslog messages from transit network devices can provide insight into and context for security events that might not be available from other sources. Syslog messages definitely help to determine the validity and extent of an incident. They can be used to understand communication relationships, timing, and, in some cases, the attacker's motives and tools. These events should be considered complementary and used in conjunction with other forms of network monitoring already be in place.

Table 11-2 summarizes the different severity logging levels in Cisco ASA, Cisco IOS, Cisco IOS-XE, Cisco IOS-XR, and Cisco NX-OS devices.

Table 11-2   Syslog Severity Logging Levels

Level	System	Description
Emergency	0	System unusable messages
Alert	1	Immediate action required messages
Critical	2	Critical condition messages
Error	3	Error condition messages
Warning	4	Warning condition messages
Notification	5	Normal but significant messages
Information	6	Informational messages
Debugging	7	Debugging messages

Each severity level not only displays the events for that level but also shows the messages from the lower severity levels. For example, if logging is enabled for debugging (level 7), the router, switch, or firewall also logs levels 0 through 6 events.

Most Cisco infrastructure devices use syslog to manage system logs and alerts. In a Cisco router or switch, logging can be done to the device console or internal buffer, or the device can be configured to send the log messages to an external syslog server for storing. Logging to a syslog server is recommended because the storage size of a syslog server does not depend on the router's resources and is limited only by the amount of disk space available on the external syslog server. This option is not enabled by default in Cisco devices. In Figure 11-1, a router (R1) is configured with syslog and is sending all logs to a syslog server with the IP address of 10.8.1.10 in the management network.

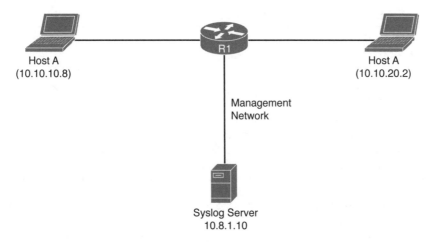

Figure 11-1 *Syslog Server Topology*

Network Time Protocol and Why It Is Important

Before you configure a Cisco device to send syslog messages to a syslog server, you need to make sure the router, switch, or firewall is configured with the right date, time, and time zone. Syslog data is useless if it shows the wrong date and time. As a best practice, you should configure all network devices to use Network Time Protocol (NTP). Using NTP ensures that the correct time is set and that all devices within the network are synchronized.

In Example 11-1, the router (R1) is configured to perform DNS resolution to the Cisco OpenDNS free DNS server 208.67.222.222 with the **ip name-server** command. Domain lookup is enabled with the **ip domain-lookup** command, and then finally the router is configured as an NTP client and synchronized with the NTP server 0.north-america.pool.ntp.org with the **ntp server** command.

Example 11-1 *Configuring NTP in a Cisco Router*

```
R1#configure terminal
Enter configuration commands, one per line.  End with CNTL/Z.
R1(config)#ip name-server 208.67.222.222
R1(config)#ip domain-lookup
R1(config)#ntp server 0.north-america.pool.ntp.org
```

> **TIP**   The pool.ntp.org project is a free and scalable virtual cluster of NTP servers deployed around the world that provide NTP services for millions of clients. You can obtain more information about these NTP servers at http://www.pool.ntp.org.

You can use the **show ntp status** command to display the status of the NTP service in the router, as demonstrated in Example 11-2.

Example 11-2 *show ntp status Command Output*

```
R1#show ntp status
Clock is synchronized, stratum 3, reference is 173.230.149.23
nominal freq is 1000.0003 Hz, actual freq is 1000.1594 Hz, precision is 2**19
ntp uptime is 131100 (1/100 of seconds), resolution is 1000
reference time is DB75E178.34FE24FB (23:55:36.207 UTC Sat Sep 3 2016)
clock offset is -1.8226 msec, root delay is 70.89 msec
root dispersion is 220.49 msec, peer dispersion is 187.53 msec
loopfilter state is 'CTRL' (Normal Controlled Loop), drift is -0.000159112 s/s
system poll interval is 64, last update was 6 sec ago.
```

You can use the **show ntp associations** command to display the NTP associations to active NTP servers, as demonstrated in Example 11-3.

Example 11-3 *show ntp associations Command Output*

```
R1#show ntp associations
  address         ref clock       st   when   poll reach  delay  offset   disp
*~173.230.149.23  127.67.113.92    2    11     64    1 69.829  -1.822 187.53
 * sys.peer, # selected, + candidate, - outlyer, x falseticker, ~ configured
```

To verify the time in the router, use the **show clock details** command, as demonstrated in Example 11-4.

Example 11-4 *show clock details Command Output*

```
R1#show clock detail
23:55:53.416 UTC Sat Sep 3 2016
Time source is NTP
```

In Example 11-4, you can see that the time source is NTP.

Configuring Syslog in a Cisco Router or Switch

Example 11-5 demonstrates how to configure syslog in a Cisco router or switch running Cisco IOS or Cisco IOS-XE software.

Example 11-5   *Configuring NTP in a Cisco Router*

```
R1#configure terminal
Enter configuration commands, one per line.  End with CNTL/Z.
R1(config)#logging host 10.8.1.10
R1(config)#logging trap warnings
R1(config)#service timestamps debug datetime msec localtime show-timezone
R1(config)#service timestamps log datetime msec localtime show-timezone
```

In Example 11-5, R1 is configured to send syslog messages to the syslog server with the IP address 10.8.1.10, as you saw previously in the topology shown in Figure 11-1. The **logging trap** command specifies the maximum severity level of the logs sent to the syslog server. The default value is informational and lower. The **service timestamps** command instructs the system to timestamp syslog messages; the options for the **type** keyword are **debug** and **log**.

You can display statistics and high-level information about the type of logging configured in a router or switch by invoking the **show log** command, as demonstrated in Example 11-6.

Example 11-6   *Output of the show log Command*

```
R1#show log
Syslog logging: enabled (0 messages dropped, 3 messages rate-limited, 0 flushes, 0
overruns, xml disabled, filtering disabled)
No Active Message Discriminator.
No Inactive Message Discriminator.
    Console logging: level informational, 74 messages logged, xml disabled,
                    filtering disabled
    Monitor logging: level debugging, 0 messages logged, xml disabled,
                    filtering disabled
    Buffer logging:  level debugging, 76 messages logged, xml disabled,
                    filtering disabled
    Exception Logging: size (8192 bytes)
    Count and timestamp logging messages: disabled
    Persistent logging: disabled

No active filter modules.
    Trap logging: level informational, 13 message lines logged
        Logging to 10.8.1.10  (udp port 514, audit disabled,
            link up),
            3 message lines logged,
            0 message lines rate-limited,
            0 message lines dropped-by-MD,
            xml disabled, sequence number disabled
            filtering disabled
        Logging Source-Interface:      VRF Name:

Log Buffer (8192 bytes):
```

11

```
*Mar  1 00:00:00.926: %ATA-6-DEV_FOUND: device 0x1F0
*Mar  1 00:00:10.148: %NVRAM-5-CONFIG_NVRAM_READ_OK: NVRAM configuration 'flash:/
nvram' was read from disk.
*Sep  3 22:24:51.426: %CTS-6-ENV_DATA_START_STATE: Environment Data Download in start
state
*Sep  3 22:24:51.689: %PA-3-PA_INIT_FAILED: Performance Agent failed to initialize
(Missing Data License)
```

The first highlighted line in Example 11-6 shows that syslog logging is enabled. The second highlighted line shows that the router is sending syslog messages to 10.8.1.10. The default syslog port in a Cisco infrastructure device is UDP port 514. You can change the port or protocol by using the **logging host** command with the **transport** and **port** keywords, as shown in Example 11-7.

Example 11-7   *Changing the Protocol and Port Used for Syslog*

```
logging host 10.8.1.10 transport tcp port 55
```

In the topology illustrated in Figure 11-1, the syslog server is a basic Ubuntu Linux server. Enabling syslog in Ubuntu is very simple. First, you edit the rsyslog.conf configuration file with your favorite editor. In Example 11-8, vim is used to edit the file.

Example 11-8   *Editing the rsyslog.conf File*

```
omar@omar:~$ sudo vim /etc/rsyslog.conf
```

Once you are in the file, you can uncomment the two lines shown in Example 11-9 to enable syslog in the default UDP port (514).

Example 11-9   *Enabling Syslog over UDP in the rsyslog.conf File*

```
module(load="imudp")
input(type="imudp" port="514")
```

Once you edit the rsyslog.conf configuration file, restart rsyslog with the **sudo service rsyslog restart** command. All of R1's syslog messages can now be seen in the server under /var/log/syslog.

Traditional Firewall Logs

The Cisco ASA supports the following types of logging capabilities:

- Console logging
- Terminal logging
- ASDM logging
- Email logging

- External syslog server logging
- External SNMP server logging
- Buffered logging

The followings sections detail each logging type.

Console Logging

Just like Cisco IOS and IOS-XE devices, the Cisco ASA supports console logging. Console logging enables the Cisco ASA to send syslog messages to the console serial port. This method is useful for viewing specific live events during troubleshooting.

TIP   Enable console logging with caution; the serial port is only 9600 bits per second, and the syslog messages can easily overwhelm the port. If the port is already overwhelmed, access the security appliance from an alternate method, such as SSH or Telnet, and lower the console-logging severity.

Terminal Logging

Terminal logging sends syslog messages to a remote terminal monitor such as a Telnet or SSH session. This method is also useful for viewing live events during troubleshooting. It is recommended that you define an event class for terminal logging so that your session does not get overwhelmed with the logs.

ASDM Logging

You can enable the security appliance to send logs to Cisco ASDM. This feature is extremely beneficial if you use ASDM as the configuration and monitoring platform. You can specify the number of messages that can exist in the ASDM buffer. By default, ASDM shows 100 messages in the ASDM logging window. You can use the **logging asdm-buffer-size** command to increase this buffer to store up to 512 messages.

Email Logging

The Cisco ASA supports sending log messages directly to individual email addresses. This feature is extremely useful if you are interested in getting immediate notification when the security appliance generates a specific log message. When an interesting event occurs, the security appliance contacts the specified email server and sends an email message to the email recipient from a preconfigured email account.

Using email-based logging with a logging level of notifications or debugging may easily overwhelm an email server or the Cisco ASA.

Syslog Server Logging

Cisco ASA supports sending the event logs to one or multiple external syslog servers. Messages can be stored for use in anomaly detection or event correlation. The security appliance allows the use of both TCP and UDP protocols to communicate with a syslog

11

server. You must define an external server to send the logs to it, as discussed later in the "Configuring Logging on the Cisco ASA" section.

SNMP Trap Logging

The Cisco ASA also supports sending the event logs to one or multiple external Simple Network Management Protocol (SNMP) servers. Messages are sent as SNMP traps for anomaly detection or event correlation.

Buffered Logging

The Cisco ASA allocates 4096 bytes of memory to store log messages in its buffer. This is the preferred method to troubleshoot an issue because it does not overwhelm the console or the terminal ports. If you are troubleshooting an issue that requires you to keep more messages than the buffer can store, you can increase the buffer size up to 1,048,576 bytes.

NOTE   The allocated memory is a circular buffer; consequently, the security appliance does not run out of memory as the older events get overwritten by newer events.

Configuring Logging on the Cisco ASA

You can configure logging in the Cisco ASA via the Adaptive Security Device Manager (ASDM) or via the command-line interface (CLI). To enable logging of system events through ASDM, go to **Configuration, Device Management, Logging, Logging Setup** and check the **Enable Logging** check box, as shown in Figure 11-2.

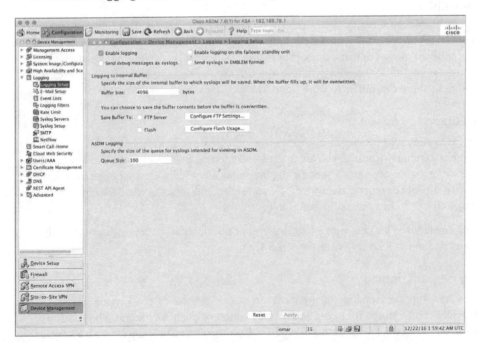

Figure 11-2   *Enabling Logging via ASDM*

This option enables the security appliance to send logs to all the terminals and devices set up to receive the syslog messages.

The security appliance does not send debug messages as logs, such as **debug icmp trace**, to a syslog server unless you explicitly turn it on by checking the **Send Debug Messages As Syslogs** check box. For UDP-based syslogs, the security appliance allows logging of messages in the Cisco EMBLEM format. Many Cisco devices, including the Cisco IOS routers and Cisco Prime management server, use this format for syslogging.

Example 11-10 shows the CLI commands used to enable syslog in the Cisco ASA.

Example 11-10   *Enabling Syslog in the Cisco ASA via the CLI*

```
ASA-1#configure terminal
ASA-1(config)#logging enable
ASA-1(config)#logging debug-trace
ASA-1(config)#logging host management 10.8.1.10
ASA-1(config)#logging emblem
```

After the logging is enabled, ensure that the messages are timestamped before they are sent. This is extremely important because in case of a security incident, you want to use the logs generated by the security appliance to backtrace. Navigate to **Configuration, Device Management, Logging, Syslog Setup** and choose the **Include Timestamp in Syslog** option. If you prefer to use the CLI, use the **logging timestamp** command, as shown in Example 11-11.

Example 11-11   *Enabling syslog Timestamps in the Cisco ASA via the CLI*

```
ASA-1(config)# logging timestamp
```

You can use the **show logging** command to display the logging configuration and statistics, as shown in Example 11-12.

Example 11-12   *Output of the show logging Command in the Cisco ASA*

```
ASA1# show logging
Syslog logging: enabled
    Facility: 20
    Timestamp logging: disabled
    Standby logging: disabled
    Debug-trace logging: enabled
    Console logging: disabled
    Monitor logging: disabled
    Buffer logging: disabled
    Trap logging: level informational, facility 20, 257 messages logged
        Logging to management 10.8.1.10
    Permit-hostdown logging: disabled
    History logging: disabled
```

11

```
Device ID: disabled
Mail logging: disabled
ASDM logging: disabled
```

Syslog in Large Scale Environments

Large organizations use more scalable and robust systems for log collection and analysis. The following are a few examples of scalable commercial and open source log-collection and -analysis platforms:

- Splunk
- Graylog
- Elasticsearch, Logstash, and Kibana (ELK) Stack

Splunk

The commercial log analysis platform Splunk is very scalable. You can customize many dashboards and analytics. Many large enterprises use Splunk as their central log collection engine. There are a few options available:

- **Splunk Light:** An on-premises log search and analysis platform for small organizations.
- **Splunk Enterprise:** An on-premises log search and analysis platform for large organizations. The Cisco Networks App for Splunk Enterprise includes dashboards, data models, and logic for analyzing data from Cisco IOS, IOS XE, IOS XR, and NX-OS devices using Splunk Enterprise. Splunk's Cisco Security Suite provides a single-pane-of-glass interface that's tailor made for your Cisco environment. Security teams can customize a full library of saved searches, reports, and dashboards to take full advantage of security-relevant data collected across Cisco ASA firewalls, Firepower Threat Defense (FTD), Cisco Web Security Appliance (WSA), Cisco Email Security Appliance (ESA), Cisco Identity Services Engine (ISE), and Cisco next-generation IPS devices.
- **Splunk Cloud:** A cloud service.
- **Hunk:** A Hadoop-based platform.

> **NOTE** You can obtain more information about Splunk by visiting the website http://www.splunk.com/.

Figure 11-3 shows the Cisco Security Overview dashboard that is part of the Cisco Security Suite app in Splunk Enterprise.

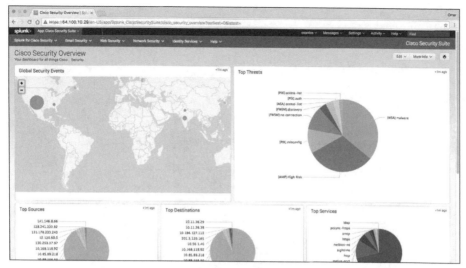

Figure 11-3   *Cisco Security Overview Dashboard*

Figure 11-4 shows the Top Sources, Top Destinations, and Top Services widgets that are part of the Cisco Security Suite app in Splunk Enterprise. It also shows the security event statistics by source type and by hosts.

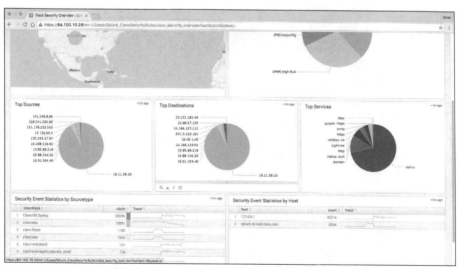

Figure 11-4   *Splunk Widgets and Event Statistics*

One of the capabilities of Splunk is to drill down to logs by searching source and destination IP addresses, source and destination ports, protocols, and services. Figure 11-5 shows the Firewall Event Search screen part of the Cisco Security Suite app in Splunk Enterprise.

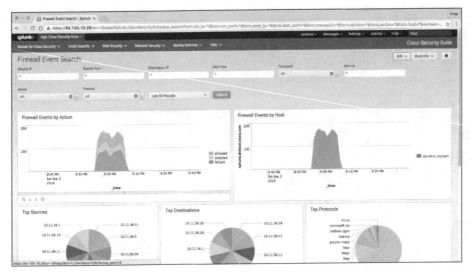

Figure 11-5 *Firewall Event Search Screen*

Splunk also provides high-level dashboards that include information about top threats and other network events. Figure 11-6 shows the Cisco Security Suite – Top Threats screen, where you can see the top threats and network device source of those events.

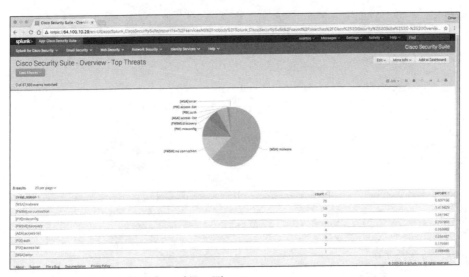

Figure 11-6 *Splunk Dashboard Top Threats*

In Splunk, you can click any of the items to drill down to each of the events. If you click the WSA events in the pie chart illustrated in Figure 11-6, the screen in Figure 11-7 is shown with the specific query/search for those events.

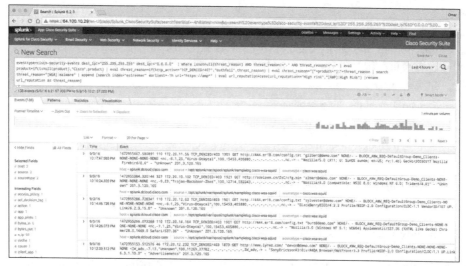

Figure 11-7   *WSA Malware Events*

That's one of the benefits of Splunk—being able to perform very granular and custom searches (search strings) to obtain information about network and security events. Figure 11-8 demonstrates how you can do a simple search by event type and event source. In the screen shown in Figure 11-8, the event type is **cisco-security-events** and the event source is set to any events by a Cisco ASA.

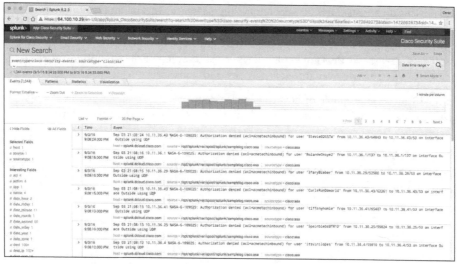

Figure 11-8   *Splunk Custom Searches*

11

Graylog

Graylog is a very scalable open source analysis tool that can be used to monitor security events from firewalls, IPS devices, and other network infrastructure devices. The folks at Graylog have many different examples and prepackaged installations including, but not limited to, the following:

- Prepackaged virtual machine appliances
- Installation scripts for Chef, Puppet, Ansible, and Vagrant
- Easy-to-install Docker containers
- OpenStack images
- Images that can run in Amazon Web Services
- Microsoft Windows servers and Linux-based servers

Graylog is fairly scalable and supports a multi-node setup. You can also use Graylog with load balancers. A typical deployment scenario when running Graylog in multiple servers is to route the logs to be sent to the Graylog servers through an IP load balancer. When you deploy a load balancer, you gain high availability and also scalability by just adding more Graylog servers/instances that can operate in parallel.

Graylog supports any syslog messages compliant with RFC 5424 and RFC 3164 and also supports TCP transport with both the octet counting and termination character methods. It also supports UDP as the transport, and it is the recommended way to send log messages in most architectures.

Several devices do not send RFC-compliant syslog messages. This might result in wrong or completely failing parsing. In that case, you might have to go with a combination of raw/plaintext message inputs that do not attempt to do any parsing. Graylog accepts data via inputs. Figure 11-9 shows the Graylog Input screen and several of the supported "inputs," including plaintext, Syslog from different devices, and transports (including TCP and UDP).

Figure 11-10 shows an example of how to launch a new Syslog UDP input. In this example, this syslog instance will be for Cisco firewalls and the port is set to the default UDP port 514.

NOTE You can obtain more information about Graylog by visiting the website https://www.graylog.org.

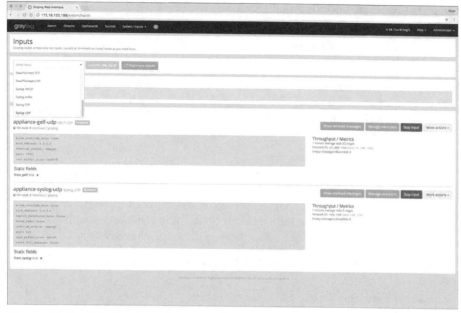

Figure 11-9   *Graylog Inputs*

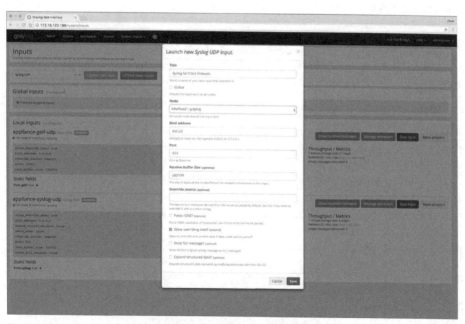

Figure 11-10   *Launching a New Graylog Syslog UDP Input*

Elasticsearch, Logstash, and Kibana (ELK) Stack

The Elasticsearch ELK stack is a very powerful open source analytics platform. ELK stands for Elasticsearch, Logstash, and Kibana.

Elasticsearch is the name of a distributed search and analytics engine, but it is also the name of the company founded by the folks behind Elasticsearch and Apache Lucene. Elasticsearch is built on top of Apache Lucene, which is a high-performance search and information retrieval library written in Java. Elasticsearch is a schema-free, full-text search engine with multilanguage support. It provides support for geolocation, suggestive search, auto-completion, and search snippets.

Logstash offers centralized log aggregation of many types, such as network infrastructure device logs, server logs, and also NetFlow. Logstash is written in JRuby and runs in a Java Virtual Machine (JVM). It has a very simple message-based architecture. Logstash has a single agent that is configured to perform different functions in combination with the other ELK components. There are four major components in the Logstash ecosystem:

- **The shipper:** Sends events to Logstash. Typically, remote agents will only run this component.
- **The broker and indexer:** Receive and index the events.
- **The search and storage:** Allow you to search and store events.
- **The web interface:** The web-based interface is called Kibana.

Logstash is very scalable because servers running Logstash can run one or more of these aforementioned components independently. Kibana is an analytics and visualization platform architected for Elasticsearch. It provides real-time summary and charting of streaming data, with the ability to share and embed dashboards.

Marvel and Shield are two additional components that can be integrated with ELK:

- **Marvel:** Provides monitoring of an Elasticsearch deployment. It uses Kibana to visualize the data. It provides a detailed explanation of things that are happening within the ELK deployment that are very useful for troubleshooting and additional analysis. You can obtain information about Marvel at http://www.elasticsearch.org/overview/marvel.
- **Shield:** Provides security features to ELK such as role-based access control, authentication, IP filtering, encryption of ELK data, and audit logging. Shield is not free, and it requires a license. You can obtain more information about Shield at http://www.elasticsearch.org/overview/shield.

Elasticsearch also provides integration with big data platforms such as Hadoop.

You can download each of the ELK components using the following links:

- **Elasticsearch:** https://www.elastic.co/downloads/elasticsearch
- **Kibana:** https://www.elastic.co/downloads/kibana
- **Logstash:** https://www.elastic.co/downloads/logstash

You can obtain information about how to install ELK and collect logs and NetFlow data with ELK at my GitHub repository, https://github.com/santosomar/netflow.

Next-Generation Firewall and Next-Generation IPS Logs

Next-generation firewalls, such as the Cisco ASA with FirePOWER services and Cisco Firepower Threat Defense (FTD), and next-generation IPS devices such as the Cisco Firepower Next-Generation IPS appliances provide a more robust solution to protect against today's threats. They provide a whole new game when analyzing security logs and events. This integrated suite of network security and traffic management products is also known as the Cisco Firepower System, and they all can be deployed either on appliances or as software solutions via virtual machines (VMs). In a typical deployment, multiple managed devices installed on network segments monitor traffic for analysis and report to a Firepower Management Center (FMC). The FMC is the heart of all reports and event analysis.

You can monitor events for traffic that does not conform to your access control policies. Access control policies allow you to specify, inspect, and log the traffic that can traverse your network. An access control policy determines how the system handles traffic on your network. The simplest access control policy directs its target devices to handle all traffic using its default action. You can set this default action to block or trust all traffic without further inspection, or to inspect traffic for intrusions and discovery data. A more complex access control policy can blacklist traffic based on IP, URL, and DNS Security Intelligence data, as well as use access control rules to exert granular control over network traffic logging and handling. These rules can be simple or complex, matching and inspecting traffic using multiple criteria; you can control traffic by security zone, network or geographical location, VLAN, port, application, requested URL, and user. Advanced access control options include decryption, preprocessing, and performance.

Each access control rule also has an action that determines whether you monitor, trust, block, or allow matching traffic. When you allow traffic, you can specify that the system first inspect it with intrusion or file policies to block any exploits, malware, or prohibited files before they reach your assets or exit your network.

Figure 11-11 shows the Content Explorer window of the Cisco FMC, including traffic and intrusion events from managed devices that include next-generation firewalls and next-generation IPS devices.

In Figure 11-11, you can also see high-level statistics and graphs of indicators of compromise detected in the infrastructure. Figure 11-12 shows the Network Information statistics of the Content Explorer window of the Cisco FMC. In this window, you can see traffic by operating system, connections by access control action, and traffic by source and destination IP addresses as well as source user and ingress security zone.

11

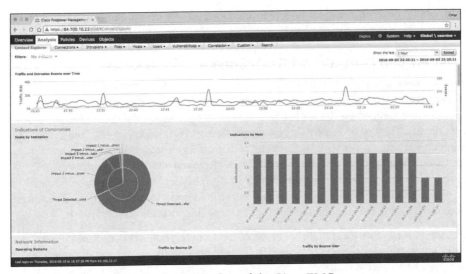

Figure 11-11 *Content Explorer Window of the Cisco FMC*

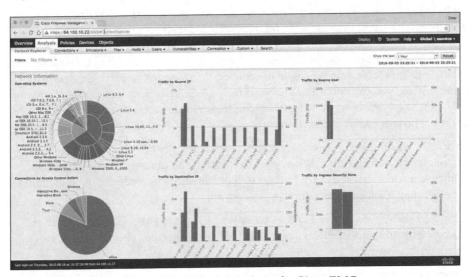

Figure 11-12 *Network Information Statistics in the Cisco FMC*

The FMC Context Explorer displays detailed, interactive graphical information in context about the status of your monitored network, including data on applications, application statistics, connections, geolocation, indications of compromise, intrusion events, hosts, servers, Security Intelligence, users, files (including malware files), and relevant URLs. Figure 11-13 shows application protocol information statistics on the Context Explorer in the FMC.

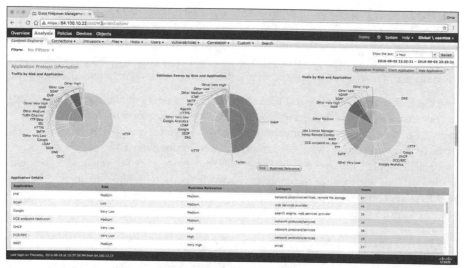

Figure 11-13 *Application Protocol Information in the Context Explorer of the Cisco FMC*

Figure 11-14 shows Security Intelligence information of the Context Explorer in the FMC, including Security Intelligence traffic by category, source IP, and destination IP. Figure 11-14 also shows high-level intrusion information by impact, as well as displays information about the top attackers and top users in the network.

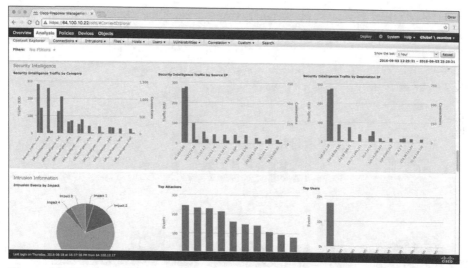

Figure 11-14 *Security Intelligence and Intrusion Information*

The FMC dashboard is highly customizable and compartmentalized, and it updates in real time. In contrast, the Context Explorer is manually updated, designed to provide broader context for its data, and has a single, consistent layout designed for active user exploration.

You can use FMC in a multidomain deployment. If you have deployed the FMC in a multidomain environment, the Context Explorer displays aggregated data from all subdomains when you view it in an ancestor domain. In a leaf domain, you can view data specific to that domain only. In a multidomain deployment, you can view data for the current domain and for any descendant domains. You cannot view data from higher-level or sibling domains.

You use the dashboard to monitor real-time activity on your network and appliances according to your own specific needs. Equally, you use the Context Explorer to investigate a predefined set of recent data in granular detail and clear context: for example, if you notice that only 15% of hosts on your network use Linux, but account for almost all YouTube traffic, you can quickly apply filters to view data only for Linux hosts, only for YouTube-associated application data, or both. Unlike the compact, narrowly focused dashboard widgets, the Context Explorer sections are designed to provide striking visual representations of system activity in a format useful to both expert and casual users of the FMC.

NOTE The data displayed depends on such factors as how you license and deploy your managed devices, and whether you configure features that provide the data. You can also apply filters to constrain the data that appears in all Context Explorer sections.

You can easily create and apply custom filters to fine-tune your analysis, and you can examine data sections in more detail by simply clicking or hovering your cursor over graph areas. For example, in Figure 11-15, the administrator right-clicks the pie chart under the **Intrusion Events by Impact** section and selects **Drill into Analysis**.

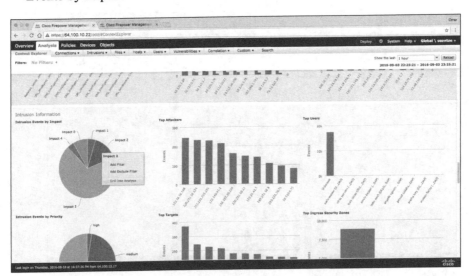

Figure 11-15 *Drilling Down into Analysis*

After the administrator selects **Drill into Analysis**, the screen shown in Figure 11-16 is displayed. This screen displays all events by priority and classification.

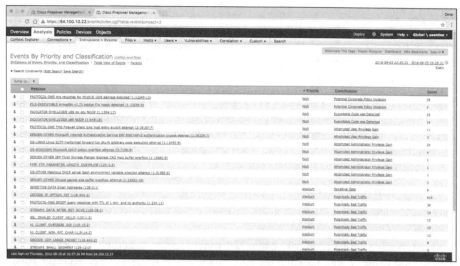

Figure 11-16 *FMC Events by Priority and Classification*

Depending on the type of data you examine, additional options can appear in the context menu. Data points that are associated with specific IP addresses offer the option to view host or whois information of the IP address you select. Data points associated with specific applications offer the option to view application information on the application you select. Data points associated with a specific user offer the option to view that user's profile page. Data points associated with an intrusion event message offer the option to view the rule documentation for that event's associated intrusion rule, and data points associated with a specific IP address offer the option to blacklist or whitelist that address.

Next-generation firewalls and next-generation IPS systems via the FMC also support an incident lifecycle, allowing you to change an incident's status as you progress through your response to an attack. When you close an incident, you can note any changes you have made to your security policies as a result of any lessons learned. Generally, an incident is defined as one or more intrusion events that you suspect are involved in a possible violation of your security policies. In the FMC, the term also describes the feature you can use to track your response to an incident.

Some intrusion events are more important than others to the availability, confidentiality, and integrity of your network assets. For example, the port scan detection can keep you informed of port-scanning activity on your network. Your security policy, however, may not specifically prohibit port scanning or see it as a high-priority threat, so rather than take any direct action, you may instead want to keep logs of any port scanning for later forensic study. On the other hand, if the system generates events that indicate hosts within your network have been compromised and are participating in distributed denial-of-service (DDoS) attacks, this activity is likely a clear violation of your security policy, and you should create an incident in the FMC to help you track your investigation of these events.

The FMC and next-generation firewalls and IPS systems are particularly well suited to supporting the investigation and qualification processes of the incident response process. You can create your own event classifications and then apply them in a way that best describes the vulnerabilities on your network. When traffic on your network triggers an event, that event is automatically prioritized and qualified for you with special indicators showing which attacks are directed against hosts that are known to be vulnerable. The incident-tracking feature in the FMC also includes a status indicator that you can change to show which incidents have been escalated.

All incident-handling processes should specify how an incident is communicated between the incident-handling team and both internal and external audiences. For example, you should consider what kinds of incidents require management intervention and at what level. Also, your process should outline how and when you communicate with outside organizations. You may ask yourself the following questions:

- Do I want to prosecute and contact law enforcement agencies?
- Will I inform the victim if my hosts are participating in a distributed denial-of-service (DDoS) attack?
- Do I want to share information with external organizations such as the U.S. CERT Coordination Center (CERT/CC) and the Forum of Incident Response and Security Teams (FIRST)?

The FMC has features that you can use to gather intrusion data in standard formats such as HTML, PDF, and comma-separated values (CSV) files so that you can easily share intrusion data with other entities. For instance, CERT/CC collects standard information about security incidents on its website that you can easily extract from FMC, such as the following:

- Information about the affected machines, including:
  - The hostname and IP
  - The time zone
  - The purpose or function of the host
- Information about the sources of the attack, including:
  - The hostname and IP
  - The time zone
  - Whether you had any contact with an attacker
  - The estimated cost of handling the incident
- A description of the incident, including:
  - Dates
  - Methods of intrusion
  - The intruder tools involved
  - The software versions and patch levels
  - Any intruder tool output
  - The details of vulnerabilities exploited
  - The source of the attack
  - Any other relevant information

You can also use the comment section of an incident to record when you communicate issues and with whom. You can create custom incidents in the FMC by navigating to **Analysis, Intrusions, Incidents,** as shown in Figure 11-17.

Figure 11-17   *Creating Custom Incidents in the FMC*

To help you identify and mitigate the effects of malware, the FMC file control, network file trajectory, and Advanced Malware Protection (AMP) can detect, track, capture, analyze, log, and optionally block the transmission of files, including malware files and nested files inside archive files.

> **NOTE**   You can also integrate the system with your organization's AMP for Endpoints deployment to import records of scans, malware detections, and quarantines, as well as indications of compromise (IOC).

The FMC can log various types of file and malware events. The information available for any individual event can vary depending on how and why it was generated. Malware events represent malware detected by either AMP for Firepower or AMP for Endpoints; malware events can also record data other than threats from your AMP for Endpoints deployment, such as scans and quarantines. For instance, you can go to **Analysis, Files, Malware Events** to display all malware events, as shown in Figure 11-18.

Retrospective malware events represent files detected by AMP whose dispositions have changed. The network file trajectory feature maps how hosts transferred files, including malware files, across your network. A trajectory charts file transfer data, the disposition of the file, and if a file transfer was blocked or quarantined. You can determine which hosts may have transferred malware, which hosts are at risk, and observe file transfer trends. Figure 11-19 shows the Network File Trajectory screen for the detection name Win.Trojan. Wootbot-199 that was listed in Figure 11-18.

11

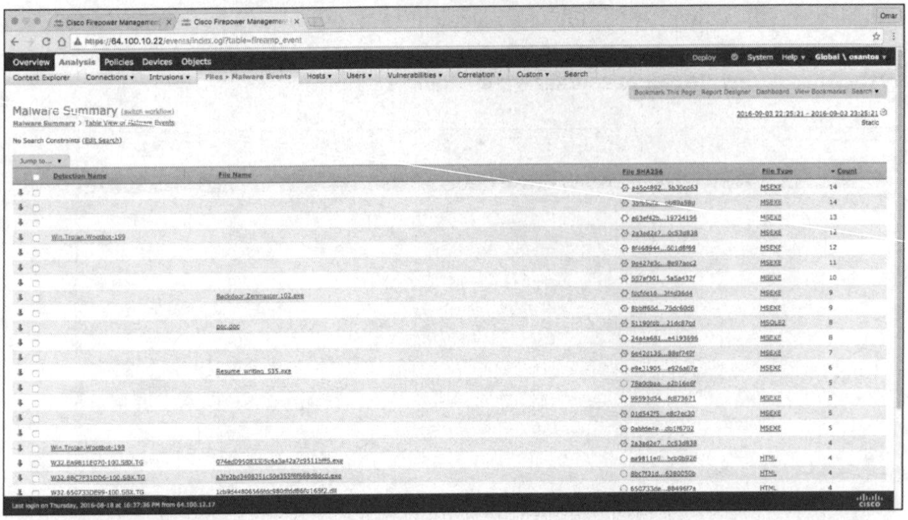

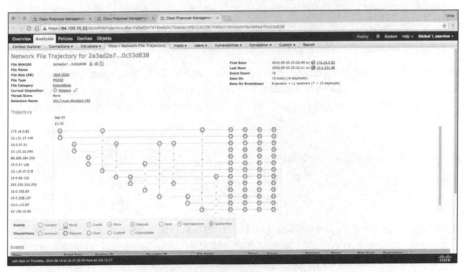

Figure 11-18 *FMC Malware Summary*

Figure 11-19 *Network File Trajectory*

You can track the transmission of any file with an AMP cloud-assigned disposition. The system can use information related to detecting and blocking malware from both AMP for Firepower and AMP for Endpoints to build the trajectory. The Network File Trajectory List page displays the malware most recently detected on your network, as well as the files whose trajectory maps you have most recently viewed. From these lists, you can view when each file was most recently seen on the network, the file's SHA-256 hash value, name, type, current file disposition, contents (for archive files), and the number of events associated with the file. The page also contains a search box that lets you locate files, either based on SHA-256 hash value or filename or based on the IP address of the host that transferred or received a file. After you locate a file, you can click the File SHA256 value to view the detailed trajectory map.

You can trace a file through the network by viewing the detailed network file trajectory. There are three components to a network file trajectory:

- **Summary information:** The summary information about the file, including file identification information, when the file was first seen and most recently seen on the network, the number of related events and hosts associated with the file, and the file's current disposition. From this section, if the managed device stored the file, you can download it locally, submit the file for dynamic analysis, or add the file to a file list.

- **Trajectory map:** Visually tracks a file from the first detection on your network to the most recent. The map shows when hosts transferred or received the file, how often they transferred the file, and when the file was blocked or quarantined. Vertical lines between data points represent file transfers between hosts. Horizontal lines connecting the data points show a host's file activity over time.

- **Related events:** You can select a data point in the map and highlight a path that traces back to the first instance the host transferred that file; this path also intersects with every occurrence involving the host as either sender or receiver of the file.

The Events table lists event information for each data point in the map. Using the table and the map, you can pinpoint specific file events, hosts on the network that transferred or received this file, related events in the map, and other related events in a table constrained on selected values.

NetFlow Analysis

In Chapter 2, "Network Security Devices and Cloud Services," you learned that NetFlow is a Cisco technology that provides comprehensive visibility into all network traffic that traverses a Cisco-supported device. NetFlow is used as a network security tool because its reporting capabilities provide nonrepudiation, anomaly detection, and investigative capabilities. As network traffic traverses a NetFlow-enabled device, the device collects traffic flow information and provides a network administrator or security professional with detailed information about such flows.

NetFlow provides detailed network telemetry that can be used to see what is actually happening across the entire network. You can use NetFlow to identify DoS attacks, quickly identify compromised endpoints and network infrastructure devices, and monitor network usage of employees, contractors, and partners. NetFlow is also often used to obtain network telemetry during security incident response and forensics. You can also take advantage of NetFlow to detect firewall misconfigurations and inappropriate access to corporate resources.

NetFlow provides detailed network telemetry that allows you to do the following:

- See what is actually happening across your entire network
- Regain control of your network, in case of a denial-of-service (DoS) attack
- Quickly identify compromised endpoints and network infrastructure devices
- Monitor network usage of employees, contractors, or partners

11

- Obtain network telemetry during security incident response and forensics
- Detect firewall misconfigurations and inappropriate access to corporate resources

NetFlow data can grow to tens of terabytes of data per day in large organizations, and it is expected to grow over the years to petabytes. However, many other telemetry sources can be used in conjunction with NetFlow to identify, classify, and mitigate potential threats in your network.

The Internet Protocol Flow Information Export (IPFIX) is a network flow standard led by the Internet Engineering Task Force (IETF). IPFIX was created to create a common, universal standard of export for flow information from routers, switches, firewalls, and other infrastructure devices. IPFIX defines how flow information should be formatted and transferred from an exporter to a collector. IPFIX is documented in RFC 7011 through RFC 7015 and RFC 5103. Cisco NetFlow Version 9 is the basis and main point of reference for IPFIX. IPFIX changes some of the terminologies of NetFlow, but in essence they are the same principles of NetFlow Version 9.

IPFIX is considered to be a push protocol. Each IPFIX-enabled device regularly sends IPFIX messages to configured collectors (receivers) without any interaction by the receiver. The sender controls most of the orchestration of the IPFIX data messages. IPFIX introduces the concept of templates, which make up these flow data messages to the receiver. IPFIX also allows the sender to use user-defined data types in its messages. IPFIX prefers the Stream Control Transmission Protocol (SCTP) as its transport layer protocol; however, it also supports the use of Transmission Control Protocol (TCP) or User Datagram Protocol (UDP) messages.

Traditional Cisco NetFlow records are usually exported via UDP messages. The IP address of the NetFlow collector and the destination UDP port must be configured on the sending device. The NetFlow standard (RFC 3954) does not specify a specific NetFlow listening port. The standard or most common UDP port used by NetFlow is UDP port 2055, but other ports such as 9555 or 9995, 9025, and 9026 can also be used. UDP port 4739 is the default port used by IPFIX.

NetFlow is supported in many different platforms, including the following:

- Numerous Cisco IOS and Cisco IOS-XE routers
- Cisco ISR Generation 2 routers
- Cisco Catalyst switches
- Cisco ASR 1000 series routers
- Cisco Carrier Routing System (CRS)
- Cisco Cloud Services Router (CSR)
- Cisco Network Convergence System (NCS)
- Cisco ASA 5500-X series next-generation firewalls
- Cisco NetFlow Generation Appliances (NGAs)
- Cisco Wireless LAN Controllers

Commercial NetFlow Analysis Tools

There are several commercial and open source NetFlow monitoring and analysis software packages in the industry. Two of the most popular commercial products are Lancope's Stealthwatch solution and Plixer Scrutinizer. Cisco acquired a company called Lancope. The Cisco Lancope's Stealthwatch solution is a key component of the Cisco Cyber Threat Defense (CTD) solution. One of the key benefits of Lancope's Stealthwatch is its capability to scale in large enterprises. It also provides integration with the Cisco Identity Services Engine (ISE) for user identity information. Cisco ISE is a security policy management and control system that you can use for access control and security compliance for wired, wireless, and virtual private network (VPN) connections.

The following are the primary components of the Lancope Stealthwatch solution:

- **Stealthwatch Management Console:** Provides centralized management, configuration, and reporting of the other Stealthwatch components. It can be deployed in a physical server or a virtual machine (VM). The Stealthwatch Management Console provides high-availability features (failover).

- **FlowCollector:** A physical or virtual appliance that collects NetFlow data from infrastructure devices.

- **FlowSensor:** A physical or virtual appliance that can generate NetFlow data when legacy Cisco network infrastructure components are not capable of producing line-rate, unsampled NetFlow data. Alternatively, the Cisco NetFlow Generator Appliance (NGA) can be used.

- **FlowReplicator:** A physical appliance used to forward NetFlow data as a single data stream to other devices.

- **Stealthwatch IDentity:** Provides user identity monitoring capabilities. Administrators can search on usernames to obtain a specific user network activity. Identity data can be obtained from the Stealthwatch IDentity appliance or through integration with the Cisco ISE.

NOTE   Lancope Stealthwatch also supports usernames within NetFlow records from Cisco ASA appliances.

Lancope's Stealthwatch solution supports a feature called network address translation (NAT) stitching. NAT stitching uses data from network devices to combine NAT information from inside a firewall (or a NAT device) with information from outside the firewall (or a NAT device) to identify which IP addresses and users are part of a specific flow.

One other major benefit of Lancope's Stealthwatch is its graphical interface, which includes great visualizations of network traffic, customized summary reports, and integrated security and network intelligence for drill-down analysis. Figure 11-20 shows the Security Insight Dashboard of Lancope's Stealthwatch Management Center (SMC).

11

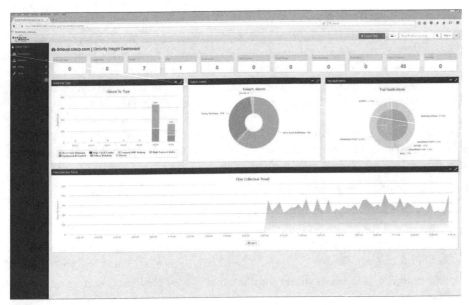

Figure 11-20   *Security Insight Dashboard*

Lancope's Stealthwatch allows you to drill into all the flows inspected by the system and search for policy violations, as demonstrated in Figure 11-21.

Figure 11-21   *Stealthwatch Policy Violations*

Figure 11-22 shows the detailed SMC's reporting and configuration graphical unit interface (GUI).

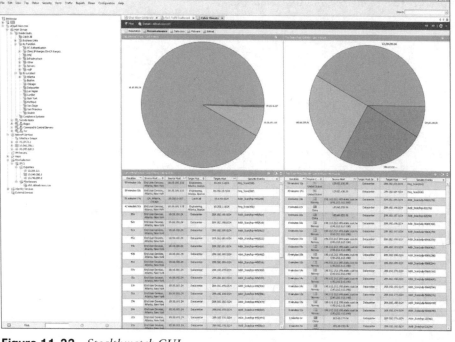

Figure 11-22   *Stealthwatch GUI*

Open Source NetFlow Analysis Tools

The number of open source NetFlow monitoring and analysis software packages is on the rise. You can use these open source tools to successfully identify security threats within your network. Here are a few examples of the most popular open source NetFlow collection and analysis toolkits:

■ NFdump (sometimes used with NfSen or Stager)

■ SiLK

■ ELK

NFdump is a set of Linux-based tools that support NetFlow Versions 5, 7, and 9. You can download NFdump from http://nfdump.sourceforge.net and install it from source. Alternatively, you can easily install NFdump in multiple Linux distributions such as Ubuntu using **sudo apt-get install nfdump**.

Routers, firewalls, and any other NetFlow-enabled infrastructure devices can send NetFlow records to NFdump. The command to capture the NetFlow data is **nfcapd**. All processed NetFlow records are stored in one or more binary files. These binary files are read by NFdump and can be displayed in plaintext to standard output (stdout) or written to another file. Example 11-13 demonstrates how the **nfcapd** command is used to capture and store NetFlow data in a directory called netflow. The server is configured to listen to port 9996 for NetFlow communication.

11

Example 11-13 *Using the nfcapd Command*

```
omar@server1:~$ nfcapd -w -D -l netflow -p 9996
omar@server1:~$ cd netflow
omar@server1:~/netflow$ ls -l
total 544
-rw-r--r-- 1 omar omar  20772 Sep 18 00:45 nfcapd.201609180040
-rw-r--r-- 1 omar omar  94916 Sep 18 00:50 nfcapd.201609180045
-rw-r--r-- 1 omar omar  84108 Sep 18 00:55 nfcapd.201609180050
-rw-r--r-- 1 omar omar  78564 Sep 18 01:00 nfcapd.201609180055
-rw-r--r-- 1 omar omar 106732 Sep 18 01:05 nfcapd.201609180100
-rw-r--r-- 1 omar omar  73692 Sep 18 01:10 nfcapd.201609180105
-rw-r--r-- 1 omar omar  76996 Sep 18 01:15 nfcapd.201609180110
-rw-r--r-- 1 omar omar    276 Sep 18 01:15 nfcapd.current
```

Flows are read either from a single file or from a sequence of files. In Example 11-13, a series of files was created by the **nfcapd** daemon. Example 11-14 shows the command options of the **nfcapd** daemon command.

Example 11-14 *nfcapd Daemon Command Options*

```
omar@ server1:~$ nfcapd  -h
usage nfcapd [options]
-h              this text you see right here
-u userid       Change user to username
-g groupid      Change group to groupname
-w              Sync file rotation with next 5min (default) interval
-t interval     set the interval to rotate nfcapd files
-b host         bind socket to host/IP addr
-j mcastgroup   Join multicast group <mcastgroup>
-p portnum      listen on port portnum
-l basdir       set the output directory. (no default)
-S subdir       Sub directory format. see nfcapd(1) for format
-I Ident        set the ident string for stat file. (default 'none')
-H              Add port histogram data to flow file.(default 'no')
-n Ident,IP,logdir  Add this flow source - multiple streams
-P pidfile      set the PID file
-R IP[/port]    Repeat incoming packets to IP address/port
-s rate         set default sampling rate (default 1)
-x process      launch process after a new file becomes available
-z              Compress flows in output file.
-B bufflen      Set socket buffer to bufflen bytes
-e              Expire data at each cycle.
-D              Fork to background
-E              Print extended format of netflow data. for debugging purpose only.
-T              Include extension tags in records.
```

```
-4                Listen on IPv4 (default).
-6                Listen on IPv6.
-V                Print version and exit.
```

Example 11-15 demonstrates how to use the **nfdump** command to process and analyze all files that were created by **nfcapd** in the netflow directory.

Example 11-15   *Processing and Displaying the nfcapd Files with nfdump*

```
omar@server1::~$ nfdump -R netflow -o extended -s srcip -s ip/flows
Top 10 Src IP Addr ordered by flows:
Date first seen          Duration Proto    Src IP Addr    Flows(%)
   Packets(%)         Bytes(%)        pps      bps   bpp
2016-09-11 22:35:10.805    2.353 any      192.168.1.140   1582(19.5)
   0(-nan)           0(-nan)         0        0     0
2016-09-11 22:35:10.829    2.380 any      192.168.1.130   875(10.8)
   0(-nan)           0(-nan)         0        0     0
2016-09-11 22:35:10.805    2.404 any      192.168.1.168   807( 9.9)
   0(-nan)           0(-nan)         0        0     0
2016-09-11 22:35:11.219    1.839 any      192.168.1.142   679( 8.4)
   0(-nan)           0(-nan)         0        0     0
2016-09-11 22:35:10.805    2.258 any      192.168.1.156   665( 8.2)
   0(-nan)           0(-nan)         0        0     0
2016-09-11 22:35:10.805    2.297 any      192.168.1.205   562( 6.9)
   0(-nan)           0(-nan).        0        0     0
2016-09-11 22:35:10.805    2.404 any      192.168.1.89    450( 5.5)
   0(-nan)           0(-nan)         0        0     0
2016-09-11 22:35:11.050    1.989 any      10.248.91.231   248( 3.1)
   0(-nan)           0(-nan)         0        0     0
2016-09-11 22:35:11.633    1.342 any      192.168.1.149   234( 2.9)
   0(-nan)           0(-nan)         0        0     0
2016-09-11 22:35:11.040    2.118 any      192.168.1.157   213( 2.6)
   0(-nan)           0(-nan)         0        0     0

Top 10 IP Addr ordered by flows:
Date first seen          Duration Proto    IP Addr        Flows(%)
   Packets(%)         Bytes(%)        pps      bps   bpp
2016-09-11 22:35:10.805    2.353 any      192.168.1.140   1582(19.5)
   0(-nan)           0(-nan)         0        0     0
2016-09-11 22:35:10.805    2.353 any      10.8.8.8        1188(14.6)
   0(-nan)           0(-nan)         0        0     0
2016-09-11 22:35:10.805    2.297 any      192.168.1.1     1041(12.8)
   0(-nan)           0(-nan)         0        0     0
2016-09-11 22:35:10.829    2.380 any      192.168.1.130   875(10.8)
   0(-nan)           0(-nan)         0        0     0
2016-09-11 22:35:10.805    2.404 any      192.168.1.168   807( 9.9)
   0(-nan)           0(-nan)         0        0     0
```

11

```
2016-09-11 22:35:11.219      1.839 any       192.168.1.142    679( 8.4)
  0(-nan)          0(-nan)        0         0    0
2016-09-11 22:35:10.805      2.258 any       192.168.1.156    665( 8.2)
  0(-nan)          0(-nan)        0         0    0
2016-09-11 22:35:10.805      2.297 any       192.168.1.205    562( 6.9)
  0(-nan)          0(-nan)        0         0    0
2016-09-11 22:35:10.825      2.277 any       10.190.38.99     467( 5.8)
  0(-nan)          0(-nan)        0         0    0
2016-09-11 22:35:10.805      2.404 any       192.168.1.89     450( 5.5)
  0(-nan)          0(-nan)        0         0    0

Summary: total flows: 8115, total bytes: 0, total packets: 0, avg bps: 0, avg
  pps: 0, avg bpp: 0
Time window: 2016-09-11 22:35:10 - 2016-09-11 22:35:13
Total flows processed: 8115, Blocks skipped: 0, Bytes read: 457128
Sys: 0.009s flows/second: 829924.3   Wall: 0.008s flows/second: 967222.9
```

In Example 11-15, you can see the top talkers (top hosts that are sending the most traffic in the network). You can refer to the **nfdump** man pages for details about usage of the **nfdump** command (using the **man nfdump** command).

NfSen is the graphical web-based front end for NFdump. You can download and obtain more information about NfSen at http://nfsen.sourceforge.net.

The SiLK analysis suite is a very popular open source command-line Swiss army knife developed by CERT. Administrators and security professionals combine these tools in various ways to perform detailed NetFlow analysis. SiLK includes numerous tools and plug-ins.

The SiLK Packing System includes several applications (daemons) that collect NetFlow data and translate it into a more space-efficient format. SiLK stores these records into service-specific binary flat files for use by the analysis suite. Files are organized in a time-based directory hierarchy. The following are the SiLK daemons:

- **flowcap**: Listens to flow generators and stores the data in temporary files.

- **rwflowpack**: Processes flow data either directly from a flow generator or from files generated by flowcap. Then it converts the data to the SiLK flow record format.

- **rwflowappend**: Appends flow records to hourly files organized in a time-based directory tree.

- **rwsender**: Watches an incoming directory for files, moves the files into a processing directory, and transfers the files to one or more **rwreceiver** processes.

- **rwreceiver**: Receives and processes files transferred from one or more **rwsender** processes and stores them in a destination directory.

- **rwpollexec**: Monitors a directory for incoming files and runs a user-specified command on each file.

- **rwpackchecker:** Reads SiLK flow records and checks for unusual patterns that may indicate data file corruption.

- **packlogic-twoway and packlogic-generic:** Plug-ins that **rwflowpack** may use when categorizing flow records.

SiLK's Python Extension (PySiLK) can be used to read, manipulate, and write SiLK NetFlow records in Python. PySiLK can be deployed as a standalone Python program or to write plug-ins for several SiLK applications. SiLK Python plug-in (silkpython.so) can be used by PySiLK to define new partitioning rules for **rwfilter**; new key fields for **rwcut, rwgroup,** and **rwsort**; and fields in **rwstats** and **rwuniq**.

Counting, Grouping, and Mating NetFlow Records with Silk

The following are the tools included in SiLK used for counting, grouping, and mating NetFlow records:

- **rwcount:** Used to count and summarize NetFlow records across time (referred to as time bins). Its output includes counts of bytes, packets, and flow records for each time bin.

- **rwuniq:** User-specified key unique record attributes. It can print columns for the total byte, packet, and/or flow counts for each bin. **rwuniq** can also count the number of individual values for a field.

- **rwstats:** Summarizes NetFlow records just like **rwuniq**, but sorts the results by a value field to generate a Top-N or Bottom-N list and prints the results.

- **rwtotal:** Summarizes NetFlow records by a specified key and prints the sum of the byte, packet, and flow counts for flows matching such a key. **rwtotal** is faster than **rwuniq** because it uses a fixed amount of memory; however, it has a limited set of keys.

- **rwaddrcount:** Organizes NetFlow records by the source or destination IPv4 address and prints the byte, packet, and flow counts for each IP.

- **rwgroup:** Groups NetFlow records by a user-specified key that includes record attributes, labels the records with a group ID that is stored in the Next-Hop IP field, and writes the resulting binary flows to a file or to standard output.

- **rwmatch:** Matches records as queries and responses, marks mated records with an identifier that is stored in the Next-Hop IP field, and writes the binary flow records to the output.

Elasticsearch ELK stack is a very powerful open source NetFlow analytics platform. Previously in this chapter, you learned that ELK stands for Elasticsearch, Logstash, and Kibana.

11

Big Data Analytics for Cyber Security Network Telemetry

NetFlow data, syslog, SNMP logs, server and host logs, packet captures, and files (such as executables, malware, and exploits) can be parsed, formatted, and combined with threat intelligence information and other "enrichment data" (network metadata) to perform analytics. This process is not an easy one; this is why Cisco created an open source framework for big data analytics called Open Security Operations Center (OpenSOC). OpenSOC was later replaced by Apache Metron (Incubating). You can find additional information about Apache Metron at http://metron.incubator.apache.org/.

OpenSOC was created by Cisco to attack the "big data problem" for their Advanced Threat Analytics (ATA) offering, formerly known as Managed Threat Defense (MTD). Cisco has developed a fully managed service delivered by Cisco Security Solutions to help customers protect against known intrusions, zero-day attacks, and advanced persistent threats. Cisco has a global network of security operations centers (SOCs) ensuring constant awareness and on-demand analysis 24 hours a day, 7 days a week. They needed the ability to capture full packet-level data and extract protocol metadata to create a unique profile of the customer's network and monitor it against Cisco threat intelligence. As you can imagine, performing big data analytics for one organization is a challenge; Cisco has to perform big data analytics for numerous customers, including very large enterprises. The goal with OpenSOC and now Apache Metron is to have a robust framework based on proven technologies to combine machine learning algorithms and predictive analytics to detect today's security threats.

The following are some of the benefits of these frameworks:

- The ability to capture raw network packets, store those packets, and perform traffic reconstruction
- Collect any network telemetry, perform enrichment, and generate real-time rules-based alerts
- Perform real-time search and cross-telemetry matching
- Automated reports
- Anomaly detection and alerting
- Integration with existing analytics tools

NOTE   Metron is open sourced under the Apache license.

These frameworks use technologies such as the following:

- Hadoop
- Flume
- Kafka
- Storm
- Hive
- Elasticsearch
- HBase
- Third-party analytic tool support (R, Python-based tools, Power Pivot, Tableau, and so on)

The challenges of big data analytics include the following:

- Data capture capabilities
- Data management (curation)

- Storage
- Adequate and real-time search
- Sharing and transferring of information
- Deep-dive and automated analysis
- Adequate visualizations

Big data has become a hot topic due to the overabundance of data sources inundating today's data stores as applications proliferate. These challenges will become even bigger as the world moves to the Internet of Everything (IoE), a term coined by Cisco. IoE is based on the foundation of the Internet of Things (IoT) by adding network intelligence that allows convergence, orchestration, and visibility across previously disparate systems. IoT is the networked connection of physical objects. IoT is one of many technology transitions that enable the IoE.

The goal is to make networked connections more relevant by turning information into actions that create new capabilities. The IoE consists of many technology transitions, including the IoT. The key concepts are as follows:

- **Machine-to-machine connections:** Including things such as IoT sensors, remote monitoring, industrial control systems, and so on
- **People-to-people connections:** Including collaboration technologies such as TelePresence, WebEx, and so on
- **Machine-to-people connections:** Including traditional and new applications

Big data analytics for cyber security in an IoE world will require substantial engineering to address the huge data sets. Scalability will be a huge challenge. In addition, the endless variety of IoT applications presents a security operational challenge. We are starting to experience these challenges nowadays. For instance, on the factory floor, embedded programmable logic controllers (PLCs) that operate manufacturing systems and robots can be a huge target for bad actors. Do we know all the potential true indicators of compromise so that we can perform deep-dive analysis and perform good incident response?

The need to combine threat intelligence and big data analytics will be paramount in this ever-changing world.

Configuring Flexible NetFlow in Cisco IOS and Cisco IOS-XE Devices

Flexible NetFlow provides enhanced optimization of the network infrastructure, reduces costs, and improves capacity planning and security detection beyond other flow-based technologies available today. Flexible NetFlow supports IPv6 and Network-Based Application Recognition (NBAR) 2 for IPv6 starting in Cisco IOS Software Version 15.2(1)T. It also supports IPv6 transition techniques (IPv6 inside IPv4).

Flexible NetFlow tracks different applications simultaneously. For instance, security monitoring, traffic analysis, and billing can be tracked separately, and the information customized per application.

Flexible NetFlow allows the network administrator or security professional to create multiple flow caches or information databases to track. Conventionally, NetFlow has a single cache, and all applications use the same cache information. Flexible NetFlow supports the collection of specific security information in one flow cache and traffic analysis in another. Subsequently, each NetFlow cache serves a different purpose. For instance, multicast and security information can be tracked separately and the results sent to two different collectors. Figure 11-23 shows the Flexible NetFlow model and how three different monitors are used. Monitor 1 exports Flexible NetFlow data to Exporter 1, Monitor 2 exports Flexible NetFlow data to Exporter 2, and Monitor 3 exports Flexible NetFlow data to Exporter 1 and Exporter 3.

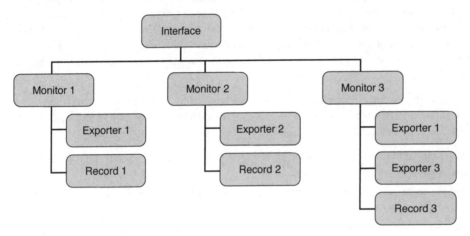

Figure 11-23 *Flexible NetFlow Model*

The following are the Flexible NetFlow components:

- Records
- Flow monitors
- Flow exporters
- Flow samplers

In Flexible NetFlow, the administrator can specify what to track, resulting in fewer flows. This helps to scale in busy networks and use fewer resources that are already taxed by other features and services.

Records are a combination of key and non-key fields. In Flexible NetFlow, records are appointed to flow monitors to define the cache that is used for storing flow data. There are seven default attributes in the IP packet identity or "key fields" for a flow and for a device to determine whether the packet information is unique or similar to other packets sent over the network. Fields such as TCP flags, subnet masks, packets, and number of bytes are *non-key fields*. However, they are often collected and exported in NetFlow or in IPFIX.

There are several Flexible NetFlow key fields in each packet that is forwarded within a NetFlow-enabled device. The device looks for a set of IP packet attributes for the flow and determines whether the packet information is unique or similar to other packets. In Flexible NetFlow, key fields are configurable, which enables the administrator to conduct a more granular traffic analysis.

Table 11-3 lists the key fields related to the actual flow, device interface, and Layer 2 services.

Table 11-3   Flexible NetFlow Key Fields Related to Flow, Interface, and Layer 2

	Flow	Interface	Layer 2
Fields	Sampler ID	Input	Source VLAN
	Direction	Output	Destination VLAN
	Class ID		Dot1q Priority
			Source MAC Address
			Destination MAC Address

Table 11-4 lists the IPv4- and IPv6-related key fields.

Table 11-4   Flexible NetFlow IPv4 and IPv6 Key Fields

	IPv4	IPv6
Fields	IP (Source or Destination)	IP (Source or Destination)
	Prefix (Source or Destination)	Prefix (Source or Destination)
	Mask (Source or Destination)	Mask (Source or Destination)
	Minimum-Mask (Source or Destination)	Minimum-Mask (Source or Destination)
	Protocol	Protocol
	Fragmentation Flags	Traffic Class
	Fragmentation Offset	Flow Label
	Identification	Option Header
	Header Length	Header Length
	Total Length	Payload Length
	Payload Size	Payload Size
	Packet Section (Header)	Packet Section (Header)
	Packet Section (Payload)	Packet Section (Payload)
	Time to Live (TTL)	DSCP
	Options bitmap	Extension Headers
	Version	Hop-Limit
	Precedence	Length
	DSCP	Next-Header
	TOS	Version

11

Table 11-5 lists the Layer 3 routing protocol–related key fields.

Table 11-5 Flexible NetFlow Layer 3 Routing Protocol Key Fields

	Routing
Fields	Source or Destination AS (autonomous system)
	Peer AS
	Traffic Index
	Forwarding Status
	Input VRF Name
	IGP Next Hop
	BGP Next Hop

Table 11-6 lists the transport-related key fields.

Table 11-6 Flexible NetFlow Transport Key Fields

	Transport
Fields	Destination Port
	Source Port
	ICMP Code
	ICMP Type
	IGMP Type (IPv4 only)
	TCP ACK Number
	TCP Header Length
	TCP Sequence Number
	TCP Window-Size
	TCP Source Port
	TCP Destination Port
	TCP Urgent Pointer

Table 11-7 lists the Layer 3 routing protocol–related key fields.

Table 11-7 Flexible NetFlow Layer 3 Routing Protocol Key Fields

	Application
Fields	Application ID

Table 11-8 lists the multicast-related key fields.

Table 11-8   Flexible NetFlow Multicast Key Fields

	Multicast
Fields	Replication Factor (IPv4 only)
	RPF Check Drop (IPv4 only)
	Is-Multicast

There are several non-key Flexible NetFlow fields. Table 11-9 lists the non-key fields that are related to counters such as byte counts, number of packets, and more. Network administrators can use non-key fields for different purposes. For instance, the number of packets and amount of data (bytes) can be used for capacity planning and also to identify denial-of-service (DoS) attacks, in addition to other anomalies in the network.

Table 11-9   Flexible NetFlow Counters Non-key Fields

	Counters
Fields	Bytes
	Bytes Long
	Bytes Square Sum
	Bytes Square Sum Long
	Packets
	Packets Long
	Bytes Replicated
	Bytes Replicated Long
	Packets Replicated
	Packets Replicated Long

Table 11-10 lists the timestamp-related non-key fields.

Table 11-10   Flexible NetFlow Timestamp Non-key Fields

	Timestamp
Fields	sysUpTime First Packet
	sysUpTime First Packet
	Absolute First Packet
	Absolute Last Packet

11

Table 11-11 lists the IPv4-only non-key fields.

Table 11-11   Flexible NetFlow IPv4-Only Non-key Fields

	IPv4 Only
Fields	Total Length Minimum
	Total Length Maximum
	TTL Minimum
	TTL Maximum

Table 11-12 lists the IPv4 and IPv6 non-key fields.

Table 11-12   Flexible NetFlow IPv4 and IPv6 Non-key Fields

	IPv4 and IPv6
Fields	Total Length Minimum
	Total Length Maximum

Flexible NetFlow includes several predefined records that can help an administrator or security professional start deploying NetFlow within their organization. Alternatively, they can create their own customized records for more granular analysis. As Cisco evolves Flexible NetFlow, many popular user-defined flow records could be made available as predefined records to make them easier to implement.

The predefined records guarantee backward compatibility with legacy NetFlow collectors. Predefined records have a unique blend of key and non-key fields that allows network administrators and security professionals to monitor different types of traffic in their environment without any customization.

NOTE   Flexible NetFlow predefined records that are based on the aggregation cache schemes in legacy NetFlow do not perform aggregation. Alternatively, the predefined records track each flow separately.

As the name indicates, Flexible NetFlow gives network administrators and security professionals the flexibility to create their own records (user-defined records) by specifying key and non-key fields to customize the data collection. The values in non-key fields are added to flows to provide additional information about the traffic in the flows. A change in the value of a non-key field does not create a new flow. In most cases, the values for non-key fields are taken from only the first packet in the flow. Flexible NetFlow enables you to capture counter values such as the number of bytes and packets in a flow as non-key fields.

Flexible NetFlow adds a new NetFlow v9 export format field type for the header and packet section types. A device configured for Flexible NetFlow communicates with the collector using NetFlow v9 export template fields.

In Flexible NetFlow, *flow monitors* are applied to the network device interfaces to perform network traffic monitoring. Flow data is collected from the network traffic and added to the flow monitor cache during the monitoring process based on the key and non-key fields in the flow record.

The entities that export the data in the flow monitor cache to a remote system are called *flow exporters*. Flow exporters are configured as separate entities. Flow exporters are assigned to flow monitors. An administrator can create several flow exporters and assign them to one or more flow monitors. A flow exporter includes the destination address of the reporting server, the type of transport (User Datagram Protocol [UDP] or Stream Control Transmission Protocol [SCTP]), and the export format corresponding to the NetFlow version or IPFIX.

> **NOTE**   You can configure up to eight flow exporters per flow monitor.

Flow samplers are created as separate components in a router's configuration. Flow samplers are used to reduce the load on the device that is running Flexible NetFlow by limiting the number of packets that are selected for analysis.

Flow sampling exchanges monitoring accuracy for router performance. When you apply a sampler to a flow monitor, the overhead load on the router of running the flow monitor is reduced because the number of packets that the flow monitor must analyze is reduced. The reduction in the number of packets that are analyzed by the flow monitor causes a corresponding reduction in the accuracy of the information stored in the flow monitor's cache.

The following is guidance for a step-by-step configuration for how to enable and configure Flexible NetFlow in Cisco IOS and Cisco IOS-XE devices. Figure 11-24 shows the configuration steps in a sequential graphical representation.

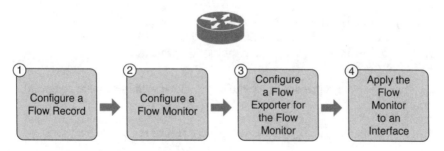

Figure 11-24   *Flexible NetFlow Configuration Steps*

The configuration steps are as follows:

Step 1.   Configure a flow record.

Step 2.   Configure a flow monitor.

Step 3.   Configure a flow exporter for the flow monitor.

Step 4.   Apply the flow monitor to an interface.

The topology shown in Figure 11-25 is used in the following examples.

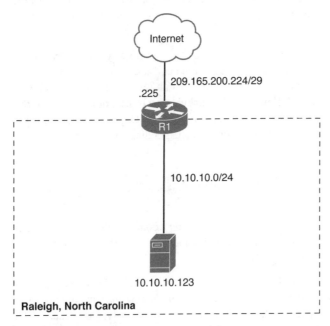

Figure 11-25 *Flexible NetFlow Model*

A Cisco router (R1) at the Raleigh, North Carolina branch office is configured for Flexible NetFlow. The outside network is 209.165.200.224/29, and the inside network is 10.10.10.0/24.

The following are the steps required to configure a customized flow record.

> **NOTE**   There are hundreds of possible ways to configure customized flow records. The following steps can be followed to create one of the possible variations. You can create a customized flow record depending on your organization's requirements.

Step 1.   Log in to your router and enter into enable mode with the **enable** command:

```
R1>enable
```

Step 2.   Enter into configuration mode with the **configure terminal** command:

```
R1#configure terminal
Enter configuration commands, one per line.  End with CNTL/Z.
```

Step 3.   Create a flow record with the **flow record** command. In this example, the record name is R1-FLOW-RECORD-1. After you enter the **flow record** command, the router enters flow record configuration mode. You can also use the **flow record** command to edit an existing flow record:

```
R1(config)# flow record R1-FLOW-RECORD-1
```

Step 4.   (Optional) Enter a description for the new flow record:

```
R1(config-flow-record)# description FLOW RECORD 1 for basic traffic
analysis
```

Step 5.   Configure a key field for the flow record using the **match** command. In this example, the IPv4 destination address is configured as a key field for the record:

```
R1(config-flow-record)# match ipv4 destination address
```

The output of the **match ?** command shows all the primary options for the key field categories that you learned earlier in this chapter:

```
R1(config-flow-record)# match ?
  application  Application fields
  flow         Flow identifying fields
  interface    Interface fields
  ipv4         IPv4 fields
  ipv6         IPv6 fields
  routing      Routing attributes
  transport    Transport layer fields
```

Step 6.   Configure a non-key field with the **collect** command. In this example, the input interface is configured as a non-key field for the record:

```
R1(config-flow-record)#collect interface input
```

The output of the **collect ?** command shows all the options for the non-key field categories that you learned earlier in this chapter:

```
R1(config-flow-record)# collect ?
  application  Application fields
  counter      Counter fields
  flow         Flow identifying fields
  interface    Interface fields
  ipv4         IPv4 fields
  ipv6         IPv6 fields
  routing      Routing attributes
  timestamp    Timestamp fields
  transport    Transport layer fields
```

Step 7.   Exit configuration mode with the **end** command and return to privileged EXEC mode:

```
R1(config-flow-record)# end
```

11

NOTE   You can configure Flexible NetFlow to support NBAR with the **match application name** command under Flexible NetFlow flow record configuration mode.

You can use the **show flow record** command to show the status and fields for the flow record. If multiple flow records are configured in the router, you can use the **show flow record** *name* command to show the output of a specific flow record, as shown in Example 11-16.

Example 11-16 *show flow record Command Output*

```
R1# show flow record R1-FLOW-RECORD-1
flow record R1-FLOW-RECORD-1:
 Description:        Used for basic traffic analysis
 No. of users:      0
 Total field space: 8 bytes
 Fields:
   match ipv4 destination address
   collect interface input
```

Use the **show running-config flow record** command to show the flow record configuration in the running configuration, as shown in Example 11-17.

Example 11-17 *show running-config flow record Command Output*

```
R1# show running-config flow record
Current configuration:
!
flow record R1-FLOW-RECORD-1
 description Used for basic traffic analysis
 match ipv4 destination address
 collect interface input
!
```

The following are the steps required to configure a flow monitor for IPv4 or IPv6 implementations. In the following examples, a flow monitor is configured for the previously configured flow record.

Step 1.   Log in to your router and enter into enable mode with the **enable** command:

```
R1>enable
```

Step 2.   Enter into configuration mode with the **configure terminal** command:

```
R1# configure terminal
Enter configuration commands, one per line.  End with CNTL/Z.
```

Step 3   Create a flow monitor with the **flow monitor** command. In this example, the flow monitor is called R1-FLOW-MON-1:

```
R1(config)# flow monitor R1-FLOW-MON-1
```

Step 4.   (Optional) Enter a description for the new flow monitor:

```
R1(config-flow-monitor)# description monitor for IPv4 traffic in NY
```

Step 5.   Identify the record for the flow monitor:

```
R1(config-flow-monitor)# record netflow R1-FLOW-RECORD-1
```

In the following example, the **record ?** command is used to see all the flow monitor record options:

```
R1(config-flow-monitor)# record ?
  R1-FLOW-RECORD-1  Used for basic traffic analysis
  netflow           Traditional NetFlow collection schemes
  netflow-original  Traditional IPv4 input NetFlow with origin ASs
```

Step 6.   Exit configuration mode with the **end** command and return to privileged EXEC mode:

```
R1(config-flow-record)# end
```

You can use the **show flow monitor** command to show the status and configured parameters for the flow monitor, as shown in Example 11-18.

Example 11-18   *show flow monitor Command Output*

```
R1# show flow monitor
Flow Monitor R1-FLOW-MON-1:
  Description:      monitor for IPv4 traffic in NY
  Flow Record:      R1-FLOW-RECORD-1
  Cache:
    Type:           normal (Platform cache)
    Status:         not allocated
    Size:           200000 entries
    Inactive Timeout:  15 secs
    Active Timeout:   1800 secs
    Update Timeout:   1800 secs
```

Use the **show running-config flow monitor** command to display the flow monitor configuration in the running configuration, as shown in Example 11-19.

Example 11-19   *show running-config flow monitor Command Output*

```
R1# show running-config flow monitor
Current configuration:
!
flow monitor R1-FLOW-MON-1
 description monitor for IPv4 traffic in NY
 record R1-FLOW-RECORD-1
 cache entries 200000
```

Complete the following steps to configure a flow exporter for the flow monitor to export the data that is collected by NetFlow to a remote system for further analysis and storage. This is an optional step. IPv4 and IPv6 are supported for flow exporters.

> **NOTE**   Flow exporters use UDP as the transport protocol and use the NetFlow v9 export
> format. Each flow exporter supports only one destination. If you want to export the data
> to multiple destinations, you must configure multiple flow exporters and assign them to the
> flow monitor.

Step 1.   Log in to the router and enter into enable and configuration mode, as you learned in previous steps.

Step 2.   Create a flow exporter with the **flow exporter** command. In this example, the exporter's name is NC-EXPORTER-1:

```
R1(config)# flow exporter NC-EXPORTER-1
```

Step 3.   (Optional) Enter a description for the exporter:

```
R1(config-flow-exporter)# description exports to North Carolina Collector
```

Step 4.   Configure the export protocol using the **export-protocol** command. In this example, NetFlow v9 is used. You can also configure legacy NetFlow v5 with the **netflow-v5** keyword or IPFIX with the **ipfix** keyword. IPFIX support was added in Cisco IOS Software Release 15.2(4)M and Cisco IOS XE Release 3.7S:

```
R1(config-flow-exporter)# export-protocol netflow-v9
```

Step 5.   Enter the IP address of the destination host with the **destination** command. In this example, the destination host is 10.10.10.123:

```
R1(config-flow-exporter)# destination 10.10.10.123
```

Step 6.   You can configure the UDP port used by the flow exporter with the **transport udp** command. The default is UDP port 9995.

Step 7.   Exit the Flexible NetFlow flow monitor configuration mode with the **exit** command and specify the name of the exporter in the flow monitor:

```
R1(config)# flow monitor R1-FLOW-MON-1
R1(config-flow-monitor)# exporter NC-EXPORTER-1
```

You can use the **show flow exporter** command to view the configured options for the Flexible NetFlow exporter, as demonstrated in Example 11-20.

Example 11-20   *show flow exporter Command Output*

```
R1# show flow exporter
Flow Exporter NC-EXPORTER-1:
  Description:          exports to North Carolina Collector
  Export protocol:     NetFlow Version 9
  Transport Configuration:
    Destination IP address: 10.10.10.123
    Source IP address:   209.165.200.225
    Transport Protocol:  UDP
    Destination Port:    9995
    Source Port:         55939
```

```
    DSCP:                     0x0
    TTL:                      255
    Output Features:          Used
```

You can use the **show running-config flow exporter** command to view the flow exporter configuration in the command-line interface (CLI), as demonstrated in Example 11-21.

Example 11-21 *show running-config flow exporter Command Output*

```
R1# show running-config flow exporter
Current configuration:
!
flow exporter NC-EXPORTER-1
 description exports to North Carolina Collector
 destination 10.10.10.123
```

You can use the **show flow monitor name R1-FLOW-MON-1 cache format record** command to display the status and flow data in the NetFlow cache for the flow monitor, as demonstrated in Example 11-22.

Example 11-22 *show flow monitor name R1-FLOW-MON-1 cache format record Command Output*

```
R1# show flow monitor name R1-FLOW-MON-1 cache format record
  Cache type:                        Normal (Platform cache)
  Cache size:                        200000
  Current entries:                        4
  High Watermark:                         4
  Flows added:                          132
  Flows aged:                            42
    - Active timeout   (  3600 secs)      3
    - Inactive timeout (    15 secs)     94
    - Event aged                          0
    - Watermark aged                      0
    - Emergency aged                      0
IPV4 DESTINATION ADDRESS:    10.10.20.5
ipv4 source address:         10.10.10.42
trns source port:            25
trns destination port:       25
counter bytes:               34320
counter packets:             1112
IPV4 DESTINATION ADDRESS:    10.10.1.2
ipv4 source address:         10.10.10.2
trns source port:            20
trns destination port:       20
counter bytes:               3914221
counter packets:             5124
```

```
IPV4 DESTINATION ADDRESS:    10.10.10.200
ipv4 source address:         10.20.10.6
trns source port:            32
trns destination port:       3073
counter bytes:               82723
counter packets:             8232
```

A flow monitor must be applied to at least one interface. To apply the flow monitor to an interface, use the **ip flow monitor** *name* **input** command in interface configuration mode, as demonstrated in Example 11-23.

Example 11-23 *Applying the Flow Monitor to an Interface*

```
R1(config)# interface GigabitEthernet0/0
R1(config-if)# ip flow monitor R1-FLOW-MON-1 input
```

In Example 11-23, the flow monitor R1-FLOW-MON-1 is applied to interface GigabitEthernet0/0.

Example 11-24 shows the complete configuration.

Example 11-24 *Flexible NetFlow Configuration*

```
flow record R1-FLOW-RECORD-1
 description Used for basic traffic analysis
 match ipv4 destination address
 collect interface input
!
!
flow exporter NC-EXPORTER-1
 description exports to North Carolina Collector
 destination 10.10.10.123
!
!
flow monitor R1-FLOW-MON-1
 description monitor for IPv4 traffic in NY
 record R1-FLOW-RECORD-1
 exporter NC-EXPORTER-1
 cache entries 200000
!
interface GigabitEthernet0/0
 ip address 209.165.200.233 255.255.255.248
 ip flow monitor R1-FLOW-MON-1 input
```

Starting with Cisco IOS Software Version 15.2(4)M and Cisco IOS XE Software Version 3.7S, a feature was added to enable you to send export Flexible NetFlow packets using the

IPFIX export protocol. This feature is enabled with the **export-protocol ipfix** subcommand under the flow exporter. Example 11-25 shows how the Flexible NetFlow IPFIX Export Format feature is enabled in the flow exporter configured in the previous example (Example 11-24).

Example 11-25 *Flexible NetFlow Configuration*

```
flow exporter NC-EXPORTER-1
 description exports to North Carolina Collector
 destination 10.10.10.123
  export-protocol ipfix
```

Cisco Application Visibility and Control (AVC)

The Cisco Application Visibility and Control (AVC) solution is a collection of services available in several Cisco network infrastructure devices to provide application-level classification, monitoring, and traffic control. The Cisco AVC solution is supported by Cisco Integrated Services Routers Generation 2 (ISR G2), Cisco ASR 1000 Series Aggregation Service Routers (ASR 1000s), and Cisco Wireless LAN Controllers (WLCs). The following are the capabilities that Cisco AVC combines:

- Application recognition
- Metrics collection and exporting
- Management and reporting systems
- Network traffic control

Cisco AVC uses existing Cisco Network-Based Application Recognition Version 2 (NBAR2) to provide deep packet inspection (DPI) technology to identify a wide variety of applications within the network traffic flow, using Layer 3 to Layer 7 data. NBAR works with QoS features to help ensure that the network bandwidth is best used to fulfill its main primary objectives. The benefits of combining these features include the ability to guarantee bandwidth to critical applications, limit bandwidth to other applications, drop selective packets to avoid congestion, and mark packets appropriately so that the network and the service provider's network can provide QoS from end to end.

Cisco AVC includes an embedded monitoring agent that is combined with NetFlow to provide a wide variety of network metrics data. Examples of the type of metrics the monitoring agent collects include the following:

- TCP performance metrics such as bandwidth usage, response time, and latency
- VoIP performance metrics such as packet loss and jitter

These metrics are collected and exported in NetFlow v9 or IPFIX format to a management and reporting system.

NOTE In Cisco IOS routers, metrics records are sent out directly from the data plane when possible to maximize system performance. However, if more complex processing is required on the Cisco AVC-enabled device, such as if the user requests that a router keep a history of exported records, the records may be exported from the route processor at a lower speed.

As previously mentioned, administrators can use QoS capabilities to control application prioritization. Protocol discovery features in Cisco AVC show you the mix of applications currently running on the network. This helps you define QoS classes and policies, such as how much bandwidth to provide to mission-critical applications and how to determine which protocols should be policed. Per-protocol bidirectional statistics are available, such as packet and byte counts, as well as bit rates.

After administrators classify the network traffic, they can apply the following QoS features:

- Class-based weighted fair queuing (CBWFQ) for guaranteed bandwidth
- Enforcing bandwidth limits using policing
- Marking for differentiated service downstream or from the service provider using the type of service (ToS) bits or DSCPs in the IP header
- Dropping policy to avoid congestion using weighted random early detection (WRED)

Network Packet Capture

Full packet capture can be very useful to see exactly what's happening on the network. In a perfect world, network security administrators would have full packet capture enabled everywhere. However, this is not possible because packet capture demands great system resources and engineering efforts, not only to collect the data and store it, but also to be able to analyze it. That is why, in many cases, it is better to obtain network metadata by using NetFlow, as previously discussed in this chapter.

Packet capture tools are called *sniffers*. Sometimes you hear the phrase "sniffer traces," which means the same thing as "packet captures." Packet captures are very helpful when someone wants to re-create an attack scenario or when doing network forensics. Logging all packets that come and leave the network may be possible with proper filtering, storage, indexing, and recall capabilities. You can also opt for a rolling or constant packet capture deployment, with the option of searching historical data in more long-term storage. Broadcast, multicast, and other chatty network protocols can also be filtered to reduce the total size packet captures.

Encryption can also cause problems when analyzing data in packet captures, because you cannot see the actual payload of the packet. The following are some pros and cons of full packet capture:

- Packet captures provide a full, historical record of a network transaction or an attack. It is important to recognize that no other data source offers this level of detail.
- Packet capture data requires understanding and analysis capabilities.
- Collecting and storing packet captures takes a lot of resources. Depending on your environment, this can be fairly expensive.

The following are a few examples of the many commercial and open source packet capture utilities (sniffers) available:

■ tcpdump, which is an open source packet capture utility that runs on Linux and Mac OS X systems

■ Wireshark, which is one of the most popular open source packet capture utilities used by many professionals

■ Netscout enterprise packet capture solutions

■ Solarwinds Deep Packet Inspection and Analysis

tcpdump

tcpdump is an open source packet capture utility that runs on Linux and Mac OS X systems. It provides good capabilities for capturing traffic to and from a specific host.

In Example 11-26, tcpdump is invoked to capture packets to and from cisco.com. The system that is connecting to cisco.com is 192.168.78.3.

Example 11-26 *Example of tcpdump to cisco.com*

```
bash-3.2$ sudo tcpdump host cisco.com
tcpdump: data link type PKTAP
tcpdump: verbose output suppressed, use -v or -vv for full protocol decode
listening on pktap, link-type PKTAP (Packet Tap), capture size 262144 bytes
02:22:03.626075 IP 192.168.78.3.59133 > www1.cisco.com.http: Flags [S], seq
1685307965, win 65535, options [mss 1460,nop,wscale 5,nop,nop,TS val 29606499 ecr
0,sackOK,eol], length 0
02:22:03.655776 IP www1.cisco.com.http > 192.168.78.3.59133: Flags [S.], seq
1635859801, ack 1685307966, win 32768, options [mss 1380], length 0
02:22:03.655795 IP 192.168.78.3.59133 > www1.cisco.com.http: Flags [.], ack 1, win
65535, length 0
02:22:06.044472 IP 192.168.78.3.59133 > www1.cisco.com.http: Flags [P.], seq 1:6, ack
1, win 65535, length 5: HTTP: get
02:22:06.073700 IP www1.cisco.com.http > 192.168.78.3.59133: Flags [.], ack 6, win
32763, length 0
02:22:13.732096 IP 192.168.78.3.59133 > www1.cisco.com.http: Flags [P.], seq 6:8, ack
1, win 65535, length 2: HTTP
02:22:13.953418 IP www1.cisco.com.http > 192.168.78.3.59133: Flags [.], ack 8, win
32761, length 0
02:22:15.029650 IP 192.168.78.3.59133 > www1.cisco.com.http: Flags [P.], seq 8:9, ack
1, win 65535, length 1: HTTP
02:22:15.059947 IP www1.cisco.com.http > 192.168.78.3.59133: Flags [P.], seq 1:230,
ack 9, win 32768, length 229: HTTP
02:22:15.060017 IP 192.168.78.3.59133 > www1.cisco.com.http: Flags [.], ack 230, win
65535, length 0
02:22:15.089414 IP www1.cisco.com.http > 192.168.78.3.59133: Flags [F.], seq 230, ack
9, win 5840, length 0
02:22:15.089441 IP 192.168.78.3.59133 > www1.cisco.com.http: Flags [.], ack 231, win
65535, length 0
```

11

```
02:22:15.089527 IP 192.168.78.3.59133 > www1.cisco.com.http: Flags [F.], seq 9, ack
231, win 65535, length 0

02:22:15.119438 IP www1.cisco.com.http > 192.168.78.3.59133: Flags [.], ack 10, win
5840, length 0
```

In Example 11-26, you can see high-level information about each packet that was part of the transaction. On the other hand, you can obtain more detailed information by using the **−nnvvXSs 1514** option, as demonstrated in Example 11-27.

Example 11-27 *Example of tcpdump to cisco.com Collecting the Full Packet*

```
bash-3.2$ sudo tcpdump -nnvvXSs 1514 host cisco.com
tcpdump: data link type PKTAP
tcpdump: listening on pktap, link-type PKTAP (Packet Tap), capture size 1514 bytes
02:29:32.277832 IP (tos 0x10, ttl 64, id 36161, offset 0, flags [DF], proto TCP (6),
length 64, bad cksum 0 (->5177)!)
    192.168.78.3.59239 > 72.163.4.161.80: Flags [S], cksum 0x5c22 (incorrect ->
0x93ec), seq 1654599046, win 65535, options [mss 1460,nop,wscale 5,nop,nop,TS val
30002554 ecr 0,sackOK,eol], length 0
        0x0000:  188b 9dad 79c4 ac87 a318 71e1 0800 4510   ....y.....q...E.
        0x0010:  0040 8d41 4000 4006 0000 c0a8 4e03 48a3   .@.A@.@.....N.H.
        0x0020:  04a1 e767 0050 629f 2d86 0000 0000 b002   ...g.Pb.-.......
        0x0030:  ffff 5c22 0000 0204 05b4 0103 0305 0101   ..\"............
        0x0040:  080a 01c9 cd7a 0000 0000 0402 0000        .....z........
02:29:32.308046 IP (tos 0x0, ttl 243, id 28770, offset 0, flags [none], proto TCP (6),
length 44)
    72.163.4.161.80 > 192.168.78.3.59239: Flags [S.], cksum 0xca59 (correct), seq
1699681519, ack 1654599047, win 32768, options [mss 1380], length 0
        0x0000:  ac87 a318 71e1 188b 9dad 79c4 0800 4500   ....q.....y...E.
        0x0010:  002c 7062 0000 f306 fb79 48a3 04a1 c0a8   .,pb.....yH.....
        0x0020:  4e03 0050 e767 654f 14ef 629f 2d87 6012   N..P.geO..b.-.'.
        0x0030:  8000 ca59 0000 0204 0564                  ...Y.....d
02:29:32.308080 IP (tos 0x10, ttl 64, id 62245, offset 0, flags [DF], proto TCP (6),
length 40, bad cksum 0 (->ebaa)!)
    192.168.78.3.59239 > 72.163.4.161.80: Flags [.], cksum 0x5c0a (incorrect ->
0x61c7), seq 1654599047, ack 1699681520, win 65535, length 0
        0x0000:  188b 9dad 79c4 ac87 a318 71e1 0800 4510   ....y.....q...E.
        0x0010:  0028 f325 4000 4006 0000 c0a8 4e03 48a3   .(.%@.@.....N.H.
        0x0020:  04a1 e767 0050 629f 2d87 654f 14f0 5010   ...g.Pb.-.eO..P.
        0x0030:  ffff 5c0a 0000                            ..\...
02:29:35.092892 IP (tos 0x10, ttl 64, id 42537, offset 0, flags [DF], proto TCP (6),
length 45, bad cksum 0 (->38a2)!)
    192.168.78.3.59239 > 72.163.4.161.80: Flags [P.], cksum 0x5c0f (incorrect ->
0x7c47), seq 1654599047:1654599052, ack 1699681520, win 65535, length 5: HTTP, length: 5
        get
        0x0000:  188b 9dad 79c4 ac87 a318 71e1 0800 4510   ....y.....q...E.
```

```
        0x0010:  002d a629 4000 4006 0000 c0a8 4e03 48a3   .-.)@.@.....N.H.
        0x0020:  04a1 e767 0050 629f 2d87 654f 14f0 5018   ...g.Pb.-.eO..P.
        0x0030:  ffff 5c0f 0000 6765 740d 0a                ..\...get..
02:29:35.123164 IP (tos 0x0, ttl 243, id 34965, offset 0, flags [none], proto TCP (6),
length 40)
    72.163.4.161.80 > 192.168.78.3.59239: Flags [.], cksum 0xe1c6 (correct), seq
1699681520, ack 1654599052, win 32763, length 0
        0x0000:  ac87 a318 71e1 188b 9dad 79c4 0800 4500   ....q.....y...E.
        0x0010:  0028 8895 0000 f306 e34a 48a3 04a1 c0a8   .(.......JH.....
        0x0020:  4e03 0050 e767 654f 14f0 629f 2d8c 5010   N..P.geO..b.-.P.
        0x0030:  7ffb e1c6 0000                             ......
***output omitted for brevity***
```

There are many different parameters and options in tcpdump, which you learn about in more detail in the tcpdump man page (which can be accessed by the **man tcpdump** command.)

> **TIP**   The following site provides a good list of examples when using tcpdump: https://danielmiessler.com/study/tcpdump.

Wireshark

Wireshark is one of the most popular open source packet analyzers because it supports many features and a huge list of common and uncommon protocols with an easy-to-navigate GUI. Wireshark can be downloaded from http://www.wireshark.org. The installation setup is very simple, and within a few clicks, you will be up and running with Wireshark on a Mac OS X or Microsoft Windows machine.

Wireshark provides the user with really good filtering capability. Filters in Wireshark are like conditionals that software developers use while writing code. For example, you can filter by source or destination IP address, protocol, and so on. Wireshark provides the following two types of filtering options:

- **Capture filters:** Used before starting the capture.
- **Display filters:** Used during the analysis of captured packets. Display filters can also be used while capturing because they do not limit the packets being captured; they just restrict the visible number of packets.

Figure 11-26 shows a screen capture of Wireshark.

11

> **TIP**   If you are new to packet capture and sniffing, Wireshark's website has several sample packet captures you can play with. Go to https://wiki.wireshark.org/SampleCaptures.

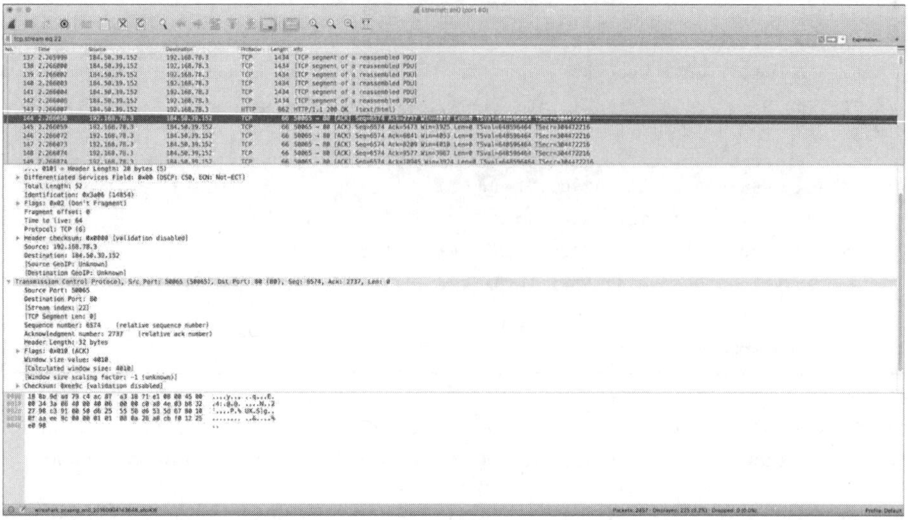

Figure 11-26 *The Wireshark Packet Sniffer*

Cisco Prime Infrastructure

Cisco Prime Infrastructure is a network management platform that you can use to configure and monitor many network infrastructure devices in your network. It provides network administrators with a single solution for provisioning, monitoring, optimizing, and troubleshooting both wired and wireless devices. This platform comes with many dashboards and graphical interfaces that can be used to monitor anomalies in the network. It also provides a RESTful API so you can integrate it with other systems you may use in your network operations center (NOC) or security operations center (SOC).

The Prime Infrastructure platform is organized into a lifecycle workflow that includes the following high-level task areas:

- **Dashboards:** Provide a quick view of devices, performance information, and various incidents.

- **Monitor area:** Used to monitor your network on a daily basis and perform other day-to-day or ad hoc operations related to network device inventory and configuration management.

- **Configuration:** Allows you to create reusable design patterns, such as configuration templates, in the Design area. You may use predefined templates or create your own. Patterns and templates are used in the deployment phase of the lifecycle.

- **Inventory:** Allows you to perform all device management operations such as adding devices, running discovery, managing software images, configuring device archives, and auditing configuration changes on devices.

- **Maps:** Allows you to display network topology and wireless maps.

- **Services:** Allows you to access mobility services, AVC services, and IWAN features.

- **Report:** Allows you to create reports, view saved report templates, and run scheduled reports.

■ **Administration:** Used for making system-wide configurations and data collection settings as well as managing access control.

Figure 11-27 shows the overview dashboard of Cisco Prime Infrastructure.

Figure 11-27   *Cisco Prime Infrastructure Overview Dashboard*

In Figure 11-27, you can see different widgets that include information about the overall network health and high-level statistics, including the following:

■ Reachability metrics for ICMP, APs, and controllers

■ Summary metrics for all alarms and rogue alarms

■ Metrics for system health, WAN link health, and service health

■ Coverage areas, including links to APs not assigned to a map

■ Client counts by association/authentication

■ Top CPU, interface, and memory utilization

■ Network topology

■ Summary metrics for all alarms and rogue alarms

■ Metrics for system health, WAN link health, and service health

■ Alarms graph

■ Top alarm and event type graphs

■ Top N applications

■ Top N clients

■ Top N devices with the most alarms

■ Top N servers

Figure 11-28 shows the devices managed by the Cisco Prime Infrastructure platform.

11

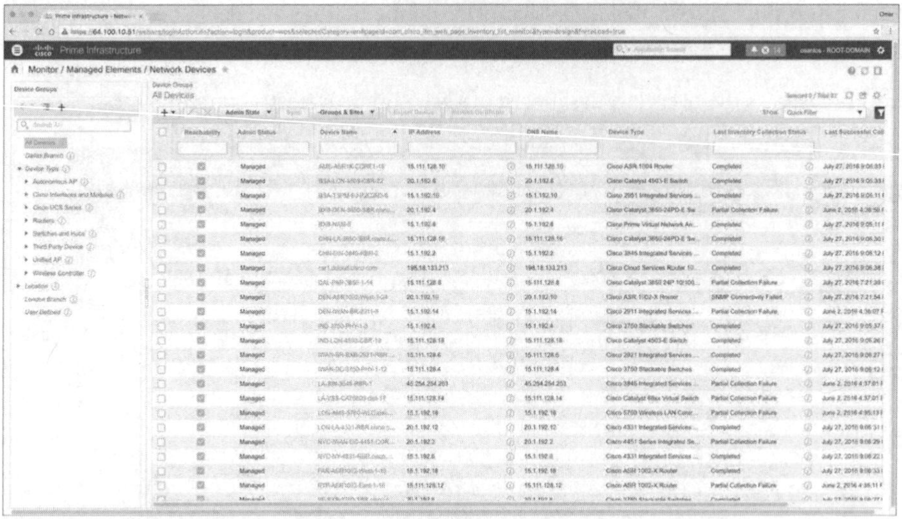

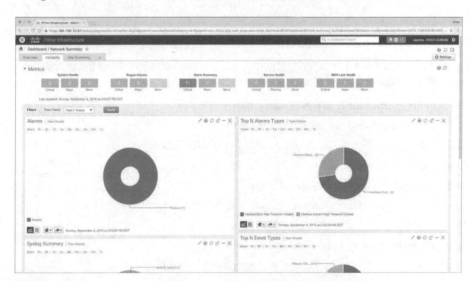

Figure 11-28   *Cisco Prime Infrastructure Network Devices*

Figure 11-29 shows the Cisco Prime Infrastructure incidents dashboard.

Figure 11-29   *Cisco Prime Infrastructure Incidents Dashboard*

The Incidents dashboard illustrated in Figure 11-29 includes widgets that report the following:

- Alarm summary metrics for all alarms and rogue alarms
- Health metrics for system health, WAN link health, and service health
- Alarms graphs
- Top alarm and event type graphs

In Cisco Prime Infrastructure, you can run a report to determine whether any Cisco device is affected by a vulnerability disclosed by the Cisco Product Security Incident Response Team (PSIRT) by going to **Reports, PSIRT and EoX**. On that screen, you can also see whether any field notices also affect any of your devices, as well as create reports about whether any Cisco device hardware or software in your network has reached its end of life (EoL). This can help you determine product upgrade and substitution options. In Figure 11-30, the PSIRT report shows many devices affected by many vulnerabilities published by the Cisco PSIRT. These types of reports accelerate the assessment of known vulnerabilities in an infrastructure in a very effective manner.

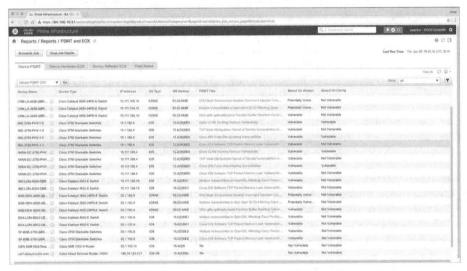

Figure 11-30   *Cisco Prime Infrastructure PSIRT Report*

Host Telemetry

Telemetry from user endpoints, mobile devices, servers, and applications is also crucial when protecting, detecting, and reacting to security incidents and attacks. The following sections go over several examples of this type of telemetry and their use.

Logs from User Endpoints

Logs from user endpoints not only can help you for attribution if they are part of a malicious activity, but also for victim identification. However, how do you determine where an endpoint and user are located? If you do not have sophisticated host or network management systems, it's very difficult to track every useful attribute about user endpoints. This is why it is important what type of telemetry and metadata you collect as well as how you keep such telemetry and metadata updated and how you perform checks against it.

The following are some useful attributes you should seek to collect:

- Location based on just the IP address of the endpoint or DNS hostname
- Application logs
- Processes running on the machine

You can correlate those with VPN and DHCP logs. However, these can present their own challenges because of the rapid turnover of network addresses associated with dynamic addressing protocols. For example, a user may authenticate to a VPN server, drop his connection, re-authenticate, and end up with a completely new address.

The level of logs you want to collect from each and every user endpoint depends on many environmental factors, such as storage, network bandwidth, and also the ability to analyze such logs. In many cases, more detailed logs are used in forensics investigations.

For instance, let's say you are doing a forensics investigation on an Apple Mac OS X device; in that case, you may need to collect hard evidence on everything that happened on that device. In the case of a daily monitoring of endpoint machines, you will not be able to inspect and collect information about the device and the user in the same manner you would when doing a forensics investigation. For example, for that same Mac OS X machine, you may want to take a top-down approach while investigating files, beginning at the root directory, and then move into the User directory, which may have a majority of the forensic evidence.

Another example is dumping all the account information on the system. Mac OS X contains a SQLite database for the accounts used on the system. This includes information such as email addresses, social media usernames, and descriptions of the items.

On Windows, events are collected and stored by the Event Logging Service. This keeps events from different sources in event logs and includes chronological information. On the other hand, the type of data that will be stored in an event log is dependent on system configuration and application settings. Windows event logs provide a lot of data for investigators. Some items of the event log record, such as Event ID and Event Category, help security professionals get information about a certain event. The Windows Event Logging Service can be configured to store very granular information about numerous objects on the system. Almost any resource of the system can be considered an object, thus allowing security professionals to detect any requests for unauthorized access to resources.

Typically, what you do in a security operations center (SOC) is monitor logs sent by endpoint systems to a security information management (SIM) and security event management (SEM) system—otherwise known as a SIEM system. You already learned one example of a SIEM: Splunk.

A SIM mainly provides a way to digest large amount of log data, making it easy to search through collected data. SEMs are designed to consolidate and correlate large amounts of event data so that the security analyst or network administrator can prioritize events and react appropriately. Numerous SIEM vendors tend to specialize in SIM or SEM despite the fact that they may offer both event and information management features. SIEM solutions can collect logs from popular host security products, including the following:

- Personal firewalls
- Intrusion detection/prevention systems
- Antivirus or antimalware
- Web security logs (from a web security appliance)

- Email security logs (from an email security appliance)
- Advanced malware protection logs

There are many other host security features, such as data-loss prevention and VPN clients. For example, the Cisco AnyConnect Secure Mobility Client includes the Network Visibility Module (NVM), which is designed to monitor application use by generating IPFIX flow information.

The AnyConnect NVM collects the endpoint telemetry information, including the following:

- The endpoint device, irrespective of its location
- The user logged in to the endpoint
- The application that generates the traffic
- The network location the traffic was generated on
- The destination (FQDN) to which this traffic was intended

The AnyConnect NVM exports the flow records to a collector (such as the Cisco Lancope Stealthwatch system). You can also configure NVM to get notified when the VPN state changes to connected and when the endpoint is in a trusted network. NVM collects and exports the following information:

- Source IP address
- Source port
- Destination IP address
- Destination port
- A Universally Unique Identifier (UDID) that uniquely identifies the endpoint corresponding to each flow
- Operating system (OS) name
- OS version
- System manufacturer
- System type (x86 or x64)
- Process account, including the authority/username of the process associated with the flow
- Parent process associated with the flow
- The name of the process associated with the flow
- A SHA-256 hash of the process image associated with the flow
- A SHA-256 hash of the image of the parent process associated with the flow
- The DNS suffix configured on the interface associated with the flow on the endpoint
- The FQDN or hostname that resolved to the destination IP on the endpoint
- The total number of incoming and outgoing bytes on that flow at Layer 4 (payload only)

Mobile devices in some cases are treated differently because of their dynamic nature and limitations such as system resources and restrictions. Many organizations use Mobile Device

Management (MDM) platforms to manage policies on mobile devices and to monitor such devices. The policies can be applied using different techniques—for example, by using a sandbox that creates an isolated environment that limits what applications can be accessed and controls how systems gain access to the environment. In other scenarios, organizations install an agent on the mobile device to control applications and to issue commands (for example, to remotely wipe sensitive data). Typically, MDM systems include the following features:

- Mandatory password protection
- Jailbreak detection
- Remote wipe
- Remote lock
- Device encryption
- Data encryption
- Geolocation
- Malware detection
- VPN configuration and management
- Wi-Fi configuration and management

The following are a few MDM vendors:

- AirWatch
- MobileIron
- Citrix
- Good Technology

MDM solutions from these vendors typically have the ability to export logs natively to Splunk or other third-party reporting tools such as Tableau, Crystal Reports, and QlikView.

You can also monitor user activity using the Cisco Identity Services Engine (ISE). The Cisco ISE reports are used with monitoring and troubleshooting features to analyze trends and to monitor user activities from a central location. Think about it: Identity management systems such as the Cisco ISE keep the keys to the kingdom. It is very important to monitor not only user activity, but also the activity on the Cisco ISE itself.

The following are a few examples of user and endpoint reports you can run on the Cisco ISE:

- AAA Diagnostics reports provide details of all network sessions between Cisco ISE and users. For example, you can use user authentication attempts.
- The RADIUS Authentications report enables a security analyst to obtain the history of authentication failures and successes.
- The RADIUS Errors report enables security analysts to check for RADIUS requests dropped by the system.
- The RADIUS Accounting report tells you how long users have been on the network.

- The Authentication Summary report is based on the RADIUS authentications. It tells the administrator or security analyst about the most common authentications and the reason for any authentication failures.

- The OCSP Monitoring Report allows you to get the status of the Online Certificate Status Protocol (OCSP) services and provides a summary of all the OCSP certificate validation operations performed by Cisco ISE.

- The Administrator Logins report provides an audit trail of all administrator logins. This can be used in conjunction with the Internal Administrator Summary report to verify the entitlement of administrator users.

- The Change Configuration Audit report provides details about configuration changes within a specified time period. If you need to troubleshoot a feature, this report can help you determine if a recent configuration change contributed to the problem.

- The Client Provisioning report indicates the client-provisioning agents applied to particular endpoints. You can use this report to verify the policies applied to each endpoint to verify whether the endpoints have been correctly provisioned.

- The Current Active Sessions report enables you to export a report with details about who was currently on the network within a specified time period.

- The Guest Activity report provides details about the websites that guest users are visiting. You can use this report for security-auditing purposes to demonstrate when guest users accessed the network and what they did on it.

- The Guest Accounting report is a subset of the RADIUS Accounting report. All users assigned to the Activated Guest or Guest Identity group appear in this report.

- The Endpoint Protection Service Audit report is based on the RADIUS accounting. It displays historical reporting of all network sessions for each endpoint.

- The Mobile Device Management report provides details about integration between Cisco ISE and the external Mobile Device Management (MDM) server.

- The Posture Detail Assessment report provides details about posture compliancy for a particular endpoint. If an endpoint previously had network access and then suddenly was unable to access the network, you can use this report to determine whether a posture violation occurred.

- The Profiled Endpoint Summary report provides profiling details about endpoints that are accessing the network.

Logs from Servers

Just like with endpoints, it is very important that you analyze server logs. This can be done by analyzing simple syslog messages, or more specific web or file server logs. It does not matter whether the server is a physical device or a virtual machine.

For instance, on Linux/UNIX-based systems, you can review and monitor logs stored under /var/log. Example 11-28 shows a snippet of the syslog of a Linux-based system where you can see postfix database messages on a system running the gitlab code repository.

Example 11-28 *Syslog on a Linux system*

```
Sep  4 17:12:43 odin postfix/qmgr[2757]: 78B9C1120595: from=<gitlab@odin>, size=1610,
nrcpt=1 (queue active)
Sep  4 17:13:13 odin postfix/smtp[5812]: connect to gmail-smtp-in.l.google.
com[173.194.204.27]:25: Connection timed out
Sep  4 17:13:13 odin postfix/smtp[5812]: connect to gmail-smtp-in.l.google.
com[2607:f8b0:400d:c07::1a]:25: Network is unreachable
Sep  4 17:13:43 odin postfix/smtp[5812]: connect to alt1.gmail-smtp-in.l.google.
com[64.233.190.27]:25: Connection timed out
Sep  4 17:13:43 odin postfix/smtp[5812]: connect to alt1.gmail-smtp-in.l.google.
com[2800:3f0:4003:c01::1a]:25: Network is unreachable
Sep  4 17:13:43 odin postfix/smtp[5812]: connect to alt2.gmail-smtp-in.l.google.
com[2a00:1450:400b:c02::1a]:25: Network is unreachable
```

You can also check the audit.log for authentication and user session information. Example 11-29 shows a snippet of the auth.log on a Linux system, where the user (omar) initially typed his password incorrectly while attempting to connect to the server (odin) via SSH.

Example 11-29 *audit.log on a Linux System*

```
Sep  4 17:21:32 odin sshd[6414]: Failed password for omar from 192.168.78.3 port 52523
ssh2
Sep  4 17:21:35 odin sshd[6422]: pam_ecryptfs: Passphrase file wrapped
Sep  4 17:21:36 odin sshd[6414]: Accepted password for omar from 192.168.78.3 port
52523 ssh2
Sep  4 17:21:36 odin sshd[6414]: pam_unix(sshd:session): session opened for user omar
by (uid=0)
Sep  4 17:21:36 odin systemd: pam_unix(systemd-user:session): session opened for user
omar by (uid=0)
```

Web server logs are also important and should be monitored. Of course, the amount of activity on these logs can be very overwhelming—thus the need for robust SIEM and log management platforms such as Splunk, Naggios, and others. Example 11-30 shows a snippet of a web server (Apache httpd) log.

Example 11-30 *Apache httpd Log on a Linux System*

```
192.168.78.167 - - [02/Apr/2016:23:32:46 -0400] "GET / HTTP/1.1" 200 3525 "-"
"Mozilla/5.0 (Macintosh; Intel Mac OS X 10_11_3) AppleWebKit/537.36 (KHTML, like
Gecko) Chrome/48.0.2564.116 Safari/537.36"
192.168.78.167 - - [02/Apr/2016:23:32:46 -0400] "GET /icons/ubuntu-logo.png HTTP/1.1"
200 3689 "http://192.168.78.8/" "Mozilla/5.0 (Macintosh; Intel Mac OS X 10_11_3)
AppleWebKit/537.36 (KHTML, like Gecko) Chrome/48.0.2564.116 Safari/537.36"
192.168.78.167 - - [02/Apr/2016:23:32:47 -0400] "GET /favicon.ico HTTP/1.1" 404 503
"http://192.168.78.8/" "Mozilla/5.0 (Macintosh; Intel Mac OS X 10_11_3) AppleWeb-
Kit/537.36 (KHTML, like Gecko) Chrome/48.0.2564.116 Safari/537.36"
192.168.78.167 - - [03/Apr/2016:00:37:11 -0400] "GET / HTTP/1.1" 200 3525 "-"
"Mozilla/5.0 (Macintosh; Intel Mac OS X 10_11_3) AppleWebKit/537.36 (KHTML, like
Gecko) Chrome/48.0.2564.116 Safari/537.36"
```

Exam Preparation Tasks

Review All Key Topics

Review the most important topics in the chapter, noted with the Key Topic icon in the outer margin of the page. Table 11-13 lists these key topics and the page numbers on which each is found.

Table 11-13   Key Topics

Key Topic Element	Description	Page
Summary	Understanding network infrastructure logs and their sources	422
Summary	Analyzing traditional firewall logs	426
Summary	Analyzing syslog and logging in large scale environments	430
Summary	Analyzing next-generation firewall and next-generation IPS logs	437
Summary	Using the Cisco FMC to analyze next-generation firewall and next-generation IPS events	441
Summary	Understanding and analyzing NetFlow data	445
Summary	Understanding Application Visibility and Control (AVC)	469
Summary	Analyzing network packet captures	470
Summary	Analyzing server logs	481

Complete Tables and Lists from Memory

Print a copy of Appendix B, "Memory Tables," (found on the book website), or at least the section for this chapter, and complete the tables and lists from memory. Appendix C, "Memory Tables Answer Key," also on the website, includes completed tables and lists to check your work.

Define Key Terms

Define the following key terms from this chapter, and check your answers in the glossary:

NetFlow, tcpdump, Wireshark

11

Q&A

The answers to these questions appear in Appendix A, "Answers to the 'Do I Know This Already?' Quizzes and Q&A Questions." For more practice with exam format questions, use the exam engine on the website.

1. Which of the following are open source packet-capture software? (Select all that apply.)

   a. WireMark

   b. Wireshark

   c. tcpdump

   d. udpdump

2. Which of the following is a big data analytics technology that's used by several frameworks in security operation centers?

   a. Hadoop

   b. Next-generation firewalls

   c. Next-generation IPS

   d. IPFIX

3. Which of the following is not a host-based telemetry source?

   a. Personal firewalls

   b. Intrusion detection/prevention

   c. Antivirus or antimalware

   d. Router syslogs

4. Why can encryption cause problems when you're analyzing data in packet captures?

   a. Because encryption causes fragmentation

   b. Because encryption causes packet loss

   c. Because you cannot see the actual payload of the packet

   d. Because encryption adds overhead to the network, and infrastructure devices cannot scale

5. What is Cisco Prime Infrastructure?

   a. A next-generation firewall

   b. A network management platform you can use to configure and monitor many network infrastructure devices in your network

   c. A NetFlow generation appliance

   d. A next-generation IPS solution

6. In what location (directory) do Linux-based systems store most of their logs, including syslog?

   a. /opt/logs

   b. /var/log

   c. /etc/log

   d. /dev/log

7. Cisco AVC uses which of the following technologies to provide deep packet inspection (DPI) technology to identify a wide variety of applications within the network traffic flow, using Layer 3 to Layer 7 data?

   a. Cisco NetFlow

   b. IPFIX

   c. Cisco AMP

   d. Cisco Network-Based Application Recognition Version 2 (NBAR2)

8. NBAR works with which of the following technologies to help ensure that the network bandwidth is best used to fulfill its main primary objectives?

   a. Quality of Service (QoS)

   b. IPFIX

   c. Snort

   d. Antimalware software

9. Traditional Cisco NetFlow records are usually exported via which of the following methods?

   a. IPFIX records

   b. TLS packets

   c. UDP packets

   d. HTTPS packets

10. Which of the following is not a NetFlow version?

   a. Version 5

   b. Version 7

   c. Version 9

   d. IPFIX

11

This chapter covers the following topics:

- Security monitoring and encryption

- Security monitoring and network address translation

- Security monitoring and event correlation time synchronization

- DNS tunneling and other exfiltration methods

- Security monitoring and Tor

- Security monitoring and peer-to-peer communication

CHAPTER 12

Security Monitoring Operational Challenges

There are several security monitoring operational challenges, including encryption, network address translation (NAT), time synchronization, Tor, and peer-to peer communications. This chapter covers these operational challenges in detail.

"Do I Know This Already?" Quiz

The "Do I Know This Already?" quiz helps you identify your strengths and deficiencies in this chapter's topics. The ten-question quiz, derived from the major sections in the "Foundation Topics" portion of the chapter, helps you determine how to spend your limited study time. You can find the answers in Appendix A Answers to the "Do I Know This Already?" Quizzes and Q&A Questions.

Table 12-1 outlines the major topics discussed in this chapter and the "Do I Know This Already?" quiz questions that correspond to those topics.

Table 12-1 "Do I Know This Already?" Foundation Topics Section-to-Question Mapping

Foundation Topics Section	Questions Covered in This Section
Security Monitoring and Encryption	1–2
Security Monitoring and Network Address Translation	3
Security Monitoring and Event Correlation Time Synchronization	4
DNS Tunneling and Other Exfiltration Methods	5–6
Security Monitoring and Tor	7–8
Security Monitoring and Peer-to-Peer Communication	9–10

1. Which of the following are benefits of encryption?

   a. Malware communication

   b. Privacy

   c. Malware mitigation

   d. Malware identification

2. Why can encryption be challenging to security monitoring?

   a. Encryption introduces latency.

   b. Encryption introduces additional processing requirements by the CPU.

   c. Encryption can be used by threat actors as a method of evasion and obfuscation, and security monitoring tools might not be able to inspect encrypted traffic.

   d. Encryption can be used by attackers to monitor VPN tunnels.

3. Network address translation (NAT) introduces challenges in the identification and attribution of endpoints in a security victim. The identification challenge applies to both the victim and the attack source. What tools are available to be able to correlate security monitoring events in environments where NAT is deployed?

   a. NetFlow

   b. Cisco Lancope Stealthwatch System

   c. Intrusion Prevention Systems (IPS)

   d. Encryption protocols

4. If the date and time are not synchronized among network and security devices, logs can become almost impossible to correlate. What protocol is recommended as a best practice to deploy to mitigate this issue?

   a. Network address translation

   b. Port address translation

   c. Network Time Protocol (NTP)

   d. Native Time Protocol (NTP)

5. What is a DNS tunnel?

   a. A type of VPN tunnel that uses DNS.

   b. A type of MPLS deployment that uses DNS.

   c. DNS was not created for tunneling, but a few tools have used it to encapsulate data in the payload of DNS packets.

   d. An encryption tunneling protocol that uses DNS's UDP port 53.

6. Which of the following are examples of DNS tunneling tools? (Select all that apply.)

   a. DeNiSe

   b. dns2tcp

   c. DNScapy

   d. DNStor

7. What is Tor?

   a. An encryption protocol.

   b. A hashing protocol.

   c. A VPN tunnel client.

   d. Tor is a free tool that enables its users to surf the Web anonymously.

8. What is a Tor exit node?

   a. The encrypted Tor network

   b. The last Tor node or the "gateways" where the Tor encrypted traffic "exits" to the Internet

   c. The Tor node that performs encryption

   d. The Tor browser installed in your system in order to "exit" the Internet

9. What is a SQL injection vulnerability?

   a. A type of vulnerability where an attacker can insert or "inject" a SQL query via the input data from the client to the application or database

   b. A type of vulnerability where an attacker can "inject" a new password to a SQL server or the client

   c. A type of DoS vulnerability that can cause a SQL server to crash

   d. A type of privilege escalation vulnerability aimed at SQL servers

10. What are examples of peer-to-peer (P2P) tools?

    a. LionShare

    b. P2P NetFlow

    c. Napster

    d. Peercoin

12

Foundation Topics

Security Monitoring and Encryption

Encryption has great benefits for security and privacy, but the world of incident response and forensics can present several challenges. Even law enforcement agencies have been fascinated with the dual-use nature of encryption. When protecting information and communications, encryption has numerous benefits for everyone from governments and militaries to corporations and individuals. On the other hand, those same mechanisms can be used by threat actors as a method of evasion and obfuscation. Historically, even governments have tried to regulate the use and exportation of encryption technologies. A good example is the Wassenaar Arrangement, which is a multinational agreement with the goal of regulating the export of technologies like encryption.

Other examples include events around law enforcement agencies such as the U.S. Federal Bureau of Investigation (FBI) trying to force vendors to leave certain investigative techniques in their software and devices. Another example is the alleged U. S. National Security Agency (NSA) backdoor in the Dual Elliptic Curve Deterministic Random Bit Generator (Dual_EC_DRBG) that allows cleartext extraction of any algorithm seeded by this pseudorandom number generator.

Some folks have bought into the idea of "encrypt everything." However, encrypting everything would have very serious consequences, not only for law enforcement agencies, but also for incident response professionals. Something to remember about the concept of "encrypt everything" is that the deployment of end-to-end encryption is difficult and can leave unencrypted data at risk of attack.

Many security products (including next-generation IPSs and next-generation firewalls) can intercept, decrypt, inspect, and re-encrypt or even ignore encrypted traffic payloads. Some people consider this a man-in-the-middle (MITM) matter and have many privacy concerns. On the other hand, you can still use metadata from network traffic and other security event sources to investigate and solve security issues. You can obtain a lot of good information by leveraging NetFlow, firewall logs, web proxy logs, user authentication information, and even passive DNS (pDNS) data. In some cases, the combination of these logs can make the encrypted contents of malware payloads and other traffic irrelevant. Of course, this is as long as you can detect their traffic patterns to be able to remediate an incident.

It is a fact that you need to deal with encrypted data, but in transit or "at rest" on an endpoint or server. If you deploy web proxies, you'll need to assess the feasibility in your environment of MITM secure HTTP connections.

> **TIP** It is important to recognize that from a security monitoring perspective, it's technically possible to monitor some encrypted communications. However, from a policy perspective, it's an especially different task depending on your geographical location and local laws around privacy.

Security Monitoring and Network Address Translation

In Chapter 2, "Network Security Devices and Cloud Services," you learned that Layer 3 devices, such as routers and firewalls, can perform network address translation (NAT). The router or firewall "translates" the "internal" host's private (or real) IP addresses to a publicly routable (or mapped) address. By using NAT, the firewall hides the internal private addresses from the unprotected network and exposes only its own address or public range. This enables a network professional to use any IP address space as the internal network. A best practice is to use the address spaces that are reserved for private use (see RFC 1918, "Address Allocation for Private Internets").

> **NOTE**   Cisco uses the terminology of *real* and *mapped* IP addresses when describing NAT. The real IP address is the address that is configured on the host, before it is translated. The mapped IP address is the address that the real address is translated to.

Static NAT allows connections to be initiated bidirectionally, meaning both to the host and from the host.

NAT can present a challenge when you're performing security monitoring and analyzing logs, NetFlow, and other data, because device IP addresses can be seen in the logs as the "translated" IP address versus the "real" IP address. In the case of port address translation (PAT), this could become even more problematic because many different hosts can be translated to a single address, making the correlation almost impossible to achieve.

Security products, such as the Cisco Lancope Stealthwatch system, provide features that can be used to correlate and "map" translated IP addresses with NetFlow. This feature in the Cisco Lancope Stealthwatch system is called *NAT stitching*. This accelerates incident response tasks and eases continuous security monitoring operations.

Security Monitoring and Event Correlation Time Synchronization

In Chapter 11, "Network and Host Telemetry," you learned that server and endpoint logs, NetFlow, syslog data, and any other security monitoring data is useless if it shows the wrong date and time. This is why as a best practice you should configure all network devices to use Network Time Protocol (NTP). Using NTP ensures that the correct time is set and all devices within the network are synchronized. Also, another best practice is to try to reduce the amount of duplicate logs. This is why you have to think and plan ahead as to where exactly you will deploy NetFlow, how you will correlate it with other events (like syslog), and so on.

DNS Tunneling and Other Exfiltration Methods

Threat actors have been using many different nontraditional techniques to steal data from corporate networks without being detected. For example, they have been sending stolen credit card data, intellectual property, and confidential documents over DNS using tunneling. As you probably know, DNS is a protocol that enables systems to resolve domain names (for example, cisco.com) into IP addresses (for example, 72.163.4.161). DNS is not intended

12

for a command channel or even tunneling. However, attackers have developed software that enables tunneling over DNS. These threat actors like to use protocols that traditionally are not designed for data transfer, because they are less inspected in terms of security monitoring. Undetected DNS tunneling (otherwise known as DNS exfiltration) represents a significant risk to any organization.

In many cases, malware can use Base64 encoding to put sensitive data (such as credit card numbers, PII, and so on) in the payload of DNS packets to cyber criminals. The following are some examples of encoding methods that could be used by attackers:

- Base64 encoding
- Binary (8-bit) encoding
- NetBIOS encoding
- Hex encoding

Several utilities have been created to perform DNS tunneling (for the good and also for the bad). The following are a few examples:

- **DeNiSe:** A Python tool for tunneling TCP over DNS.
- **dns2tcp:** Written by Olivier Dembour and Nicolas Collignon in C, dns2tcp supports KEY and TXT request types.
- **DNScapy:** Created by Pierre Bienaimé, this Python-based Scapy tool for packet generation even supports SSH tunneling over DNS, including a SOCKS proxy.
- **DNScat or DNScat-P:** This Java-based tool created by Tadeusz Pietraszek supports bidirectional communication through DNS.
- **DNScat (DNScat-B):** Written by Ron Bowes, this tool runs on Linux, Mac OS X, and Windows. DNScat encodes DNS requests in NetBIOS encoding or hex encoding.
- **Heyoka:** This tool, written in C, supports bidirectional tunneling for data exfiltration.
- **Iodine:** Written by Bjorn Andersson and Erik Ekman in C, Iodine runs on Linux, Mac OS X, and Windows, and can even be ported to Android.
- **Nameserver Transfer Protocol (NSTX):** Creates IP tunnels using DNS.
- **OzymanDNS:** Written in Perl by Dan Kaminsky, this tool is used to set up an SSH tunnel over DNS or for file transfer. The requests are Base32 encoded, and responses are Base64-encoded TXT records.
- **psudp:** Developed by Kenton Born, this tool injects data into existing DNS requests by modifying the IP/UDP lengths.
- **Feederbot and Moto:** Attackers have used this malware using DNS to steal sensitive information from many organizations.

Some of these tools were not created with the intent of stealing data, but cyber criminals have used them for their own purposes.

Security Monitoring and Tor

Many people use tools such as Tor for privacy. Tor is a free tool that enables its users to surf the Web anonymously. Tor works by "routing" IP traffic through a free, worldwide network consisting of thousands of Tor relays. Then it constantly changes the way it routes traffic in order to obscure a user's location from anyone monitoring the network.

> **NOTE**   Tor's name is an acronym of the original software project's name, "The Onion Router."

The use of Tor also makes security monitoring and incident response more difficult, because it's hard to attribute and trace back the traffic to the user. Different types of malware are known to use Tor to cover their tracks.

This "onion routing" is accomplished by encrypting the application layer of a communication protocol stack that's "nested" just like the layers of an onion. The Tor client encrypts the data multiple times and sends it through a "network or circuit" that includes randomly selected Tor relays. Each of the relays decrypts "a layer of the onion" to reveal only the next relay so that the remaining encrypted data can be routed on to it.

Figure 12-1 shows a screenshot of the Tor browser. You can see the Tor circuit when the user accessed cisco.com from the Tor browser. It first went to a host in the Netherlands, then to hosts in Sweden and France, and finally to cisco.com.

Figure 12-1   *The Tor Browser*

A Tor exit node is basically the last Tor node or the "gateway" where the Tor encrypted traffic "exits" to the Internet. A Tor exit node can be targeted to monitor Tor traffic. Many organizations block Tor exit nodes in their environment. The Tor project has a dynamic list of Tor exit nodes that makes this task a bit easier. This Tor exit node list can be downloaded from https://check.torproject.org/exit-addresses.

12

NOTE   Security products such as the Cisco Next-Generation Firepower software provide the capability to dynamically learn and block Tor exit nodes.

Security Monitoring and Peer-to-Peer Communication

Peer-to-peer (P2P) communication involves a distributed architecture that "divides tasks" between participant computing peers. In a P2P network, the peers are equally privileged, which is why it's called a "peer-to-peer" network of nodes.

P2P participant computers or nodes reserve a chunk of their resources (such as CPU, memory, disk storage, and network bandwidth) so that other "peers" or participants can access those resources. This is all done without the need of a centralized server. In P2P networks, each peer can be both a supplier as well as a consumer of resources or data. A good example was the music-sharing application Napster back in the 1990s.

P2P networks have been used to share music, videos, stolen books, and other data; even legitimate multimedia applications such as Spotify use a peer-to-peer network along with streaming servers to stream audio and video to their clients. There's even an application called Peercoin (also known as PPCoin) that's a P2P crypto currency that utilizes both proof-of-stake and proof-of-work systems.

Universities such as MIT and Penn State have even created a project called LionShare, which is designed to share files among educational institutions globally.

From a security perspective, P2P systems introduce unique challenges. Malware has used P2P networks to communicate and also spread to victims. Many "free" or stolen music and movie files usually come with the surprise of malware. Additionally, like any other form of software, P2P applications are not immune to security vulnerabilities. This, of course, introduces risks for P2P software because it is more susceptible to remote exploits, due to the nature of the P2P network architecture.

Exam Preparation Tasks

Review All Key Topics

Review the most important topics in the chapter, noted with the Key Topic icon in the outer margin of the page. Table 12-2 lists these key topics and the page numbers on which each is found.

Table 12-2 Key Topics

Key Topic Element	Description	Page
Summary	Understanding the challenges that encryption introduces to security monitoring	490
Summary	Understanding the challenges that NAT introduces to security monitoring	491
Summary	The importance of network time synchronization for security monitoring and event correlation	491
Summary	Understanding DNS tuneling and other data exfiltration methods	491
Summary	Understanding the challenges that Tor introduces to security monitoring	493
Summary	Understanding the challenges that peer-to-peer communication introduces to security monitoring	494

Define Key Terms

Define the following key terms from this chapter, and check your answers in the glossary:

Tor, Tor exit node, peer-to-peer (P2P) communication

Q&A

The answers to these questions appear in Appendix A, "Answers to the 'Do I Know This Already?' Quizzes and Q&A Questions." For more practice with exam format questions, use the exam engine on the website.

1. What is Tor?

   a. Tor is The Onion Router and is a free tool that enables its users to surf the Web anonymously.

   b. Tor is The Onion Router and is a free tool that enables its users to send email in an encrypted way using PGP.

   c. Tor is The Onion Router and is a free tool that enables its users to route packets anonymously by leveraging the EIGRP or OSPF routing protocol.

   d. Tor is The Onion Router and is a free tool that enables its users to route packets anonymously by using BGP.

12

2. Why does NAT present a challenge to security monitoring?

    a. NAT can present a challenge when performing security monitoring and analyzing logs because data can be encrypted as a result of the network address translation.

    b. NAT can present a challenge when performing security monitoring and analyzing logs because data can be dropped as a result of the network address translation.

    c. NAT can present a challenge when performing security monitoring and analyzing logs, NetFlow, and other data because device IP addresses can be seen in the logs as the "translated" IP address versus the "real" IP address.

    d. NAT can present a challenge when performing security monitoring and analyzing logs because data can be fragmented as a result of the network address translation.

3. What is a Tor exit node?

    a. A Tor exit node is the first Tor node or the "gateway" where the Tor encrypted traffic "exits" to the Internet.

    b. A Tor exit node is the last Tor node or the "gateway" where the Tor encrypted traffic "exits" to the Internet.

    c. A Tor exit node is the Tor node or the "gateway" where the Tor browser connects first.

    d. A Tor exit node is an Internet routing entity that can define how the Tor browser exits the common Internet and connects to the darknet.

4. Which of the following is an example of a DNS tunneling tool?

    a. dig

    b. nslookup

    c. DNScapy

    d. DNSSEC

5. Which of the following is an example of an encoding mechanism used by threat actors?

    a. Base24 encoding

    b. GRE tunnels

    c. Hex tunnels

    d. Base64 encoding

6. Why should NTP be enabled in infrastructure devices and for security monitoring?

    a. Using NTP ensures that the correct time is set and that all devices within the network are synchronized. Also, it helps to reduce the amount of duplicate logs.

    b. Using NTP ensures that the network tunneling protocol is implemented with the correct encryption algorithms.

    c. Using NTP ensures that the network tunneling protocol is implemented with the correct hashing algorithms.

    d. Using NTP ensures that the network tunneling protocol is implemented with the correct DNS names and NetFlow records.

This chapter covers the following topics:

- Types of attacks
- Types of vulnerabilities

CHAPTER 13

Types of Attacks and Vulnerabilities

The sophistication of cyber security attacks is increasing every day. In addition, there are numerous types of cyber security attacks and vulnerabilities. This chapter covers the most common.

"Do I Know This Already?" Quiz

The "Do I Know This Already?" quiz helps you identify your strengths and deficiencies in this chapter's topics. The eight-question quiz, derived from the major sections in the "Foundation Topics" portion of the chapter, helps you determine how to spend your limited study time. You can find the answers in Appendix A Answers to the "Do I Know This Already?" Quizzes and Q&A Questions.

Table 13-1 outlines the major topics discussed in this chapter and the "Do I Know This Already?" quiz questions that correspond to those topics.

Table 13-1 "Do I Know This Already?" Foundation Topics Section-to-Question Mapping

Foundation Topics Section	Questions Covered in This Section
Types of Attacks	1–5
Types of Vulnerabilities	6–8

1. Which of the following are examples of vulnerability and port scanners? (Select all that apply.)

    a. SuperScan

    b. nmap

    c. Nexpose

    d. Nessus

2. How do UDP scans work?

    a. By establishing a three-way handshake.

    b. By sending SYN packets to see what ports are open.

    c. UDP scans have to rely on ICMP "port unreachable" messages to determine whether a port is open. When the scanner sends a UDP packet and the port is not open on the victim's system, that system will respond with an ICMP "port unreachable" message.

    d. By sending ICMP "port unreachable" messages to the victim.

3. What is a phishing attack?

  a. A phishing attack is the act of incorporating malicious ads on trusted websites, which results in users' browsers being inadvertently redirected to sites hosting malware.

  b. A phishing attack uses SQL injection vulnerabilities in order to execute malicious code.

  c. This is a type of denial-of-service (DoS) attack where the attacker sends numerous phishing requests to the victim.

  d. This is a type of attack where the attacker presents a link that looks like a valid, trusted resource to a user. When the user clicks it, he is prompted to disclose confidential information such as his username and password.

4. What is a backdoor?

  a. A backdoor is a social engineering attack to get access back to the victim.

  b. A backdoor is a privilege escalation attack designed to get access from the victim.

  c. A backdoor is an application or code used by an attacker either to allow future access or to collect information to use in further attacks.

  d. A backdoor is malware installed using man-in-the-middle attacks.

5. What is an amplification attack?

  a. An amplification attack is a form of directed DDoS attack in which the attacker's packets are sent at a much faster rate than the victim's packets.

  b. An amplification attack is a form of reflected attack in which the response traffic (sent by the unwitting participant) is made up of packets that are much larger than those that were initially sent by the attacker (spoofing the victim).

  c. An amplification attack is a type of man-in-the-middle attack.

  d. An amplification attack is a type of data exfiltration attack.

6. What is a buffer overflow?

  a. A buffer overflow is when a program or software cannot write data in a buffer, causing the application to crash.

  b. A buffer overflow is when a program or software sends the contents of the buffer to an attacker.

  c. A buffer overflow is when an attacker overflows a program with numerous packets to cause a denial-of-service condition.

  d. A buffer overflow is when a program or software puts more data in a buffer than it can hold or when a program tries to put data in a memory location past a buffer.

7. What is a cross-site scripting (XSS) vulnerability?

    a. A type of web application vulnerability where malicious scripts are injected into legitimate and trusted websites

    b. A type of cross-domain hijack vulnerability

    c. A type of vulnerability that leverages the crossing of scripts in an application

    d. A type of cross-site request forgery (CSRF) vulnerability that is used to steal information from the network

8. What is a SQL injection vulnerability?

    a. A type of vulnerability where an attacker can insert or "inject" a SQL query via the input data from the client to the application or database

    b. A type of vulnerability where an attacker can "inject" a new password to a SQL server or the client

    c. A type of DoS vulnerability that can cause a SQL server to crash

    d. A type of privilege escalation vulnerability aimed at SQL servers

13

Foundation Topics

Types of Attacks

As you probably already know, most attackers do not want to be discovered, so they use a variety of techniques to remain in the shadows when attempting to compromise a network. The following sections list the most common types of attacks carried out by threat actors.

Reconnaissance Attacks

Reconnaissance attacks include the discovery process used to find information about the network, users, and victims. It could include scans of the network to find out which IP addresses respond, and further scans to see which ports on the devices at these IP addresses are open. This is usually the first step taken to discover what is on the network and to determine what vulnerabilities to exploit.

Scans can be passive or active. A passive scan can be carried by an attacker just researching information about the victim's public records, social media sites, and other technical information, such as DNS, whois, and so on. The attacker can use tools such as Maltego to accelerate this "research." Active scans are carried by tools called "scanners." The following are a few commercial and open source application and vulnerability scanners:

- AppScan by IBM
- Burp Suite Professional by PortSwigger
- Hailstorm by Cenzic
- N-Stalker by N-Stalker
- Nessus by Tenable Network Security
- NetSparker by Mavituna Security
- NeXpose by Rapid7
- nmap open source scanner
- NTOSpider by NTObjectives
- ParosPro by MileSCAN Technologies
- QualysGuard Web Application Scanning by Qualys
- Retina Web Security Scanner by eEye Digital Security
- Sentinel by WhiteHat
- Veracode Web Application Security by Veracode
- VUPEN Web Application Security Scanner by VUPEN Security
- WebApp360 by nCircle
- WebInspect by HP
- WebKing by Parasoft
- WebScanService by Elanize KG
- Websecurify by GNUCITIZEN

TIP   Be aware that attacks are not launched only from individuals outside your company. They are also launched from people and devices inside your company who have current, legitimate user accounts. This vector is of particular concern these days with the proliferation of organizations allowing employees to use their personal devices—known as "bring your own device" (BYOD)—to seamlessly access to data, applications, and devices on the corporate networks. Perhaps the user is curious, or maybe a backdoor is installed on the computer on which the user is logged in. In either case, it is important to implement a security policy that takes nothing for granted and to be prepared to mitigate risk at several levels.

There are different types of port- and network-scanning techniques. The following are the most common:

- **Basic port scan:** Involves scanning a predetermined TCP/UDP port by sending a specifically configured packet that contains the port number of the port that was selected. This is typically used to determine what ports are "open" or available in a given system.

- **TCP scan:** A TCP-based scan of a series of ports on a machine to determine port availability. If a port on the machine is listening, then the TCP "connect" is successful in reaching that specific port. Earlier you learned that nmap is an open source scanner; nmap refers to TCP scans as "connect scans," which is named after the UNIX **connect()** system call. If the scanner finds that a port is open, the victim operating system completes the TCP three-way handshake. In some cases, the port scanner will close the connection to avoid a denial-of-service condition.

  TCP SYN scan is one of the most common types of TCP scanning, and it is also referred to as "half-open scanning" because it never actually opens a full TCP connection. The scanner sends a SYN packet, and if the target responds with a SYN-ACK packet, the scanner typically responds with an RST packet.

  Another TCP scan type is TCP ACK. This type of scan does not exactly determine whether the TCP port is open or closed; instead, it checks whether the port is filtered or unfiltered. TCP ACK scans are typically used when trying to see if a firewall is deployed and its rule sets. There are also TCP FIN packets that in some cases can bypass legacy firewalls because closed ports may cause a system to reply to a FIN packet with a corresponding RST packet due to the nature of TCP.

- **UDP scan:** Because UDP is a connectionless protocol and does not have a three-way handshake like TCP, the UDP scans have to rely on ICMP "port unreachable" messages to determine if the port is open. When the scanner sends a UDP packet and the port is not open on the victim, the victim's system will respond with an ICMP "port unreachable" message. This type of scanning will be affected by firewalls and ICMP rate limiting.

- **Strobe scan:** Typically used by an attacker to find the ports that he or she already knows how to exploit. Strobe scans execute on a more confined level.

- **Stealth scan:** Designed to go undetected by network auditing tools.

Example 13-1 shows a basic nmap scan against a Linux machine (172.18.104.139).

13

Example 13-1 *Nmap Scanner Example*

```
bash-3.2$ sudo nmap -sS 172.18.104.139
Password: ****************
Starting Nmap 7.12 ( https://nmap.org ) at 2016-09-06 11:13 EDT
Nmap scan report for 172.18.104.139
Host is up (0.024s latency).
Not shown: 995 closed ports
PORT     STATE SERVICE
22/tcp   open  ssh
25/tcp   open  smtp
80/tcp   open  http
110/tcp  open  pop3
143/tcp  open  imap
Nmap done: 1 IP address (1 host up) scanned in 1.26 seconds
```

In Example 13-1, the host (172.18.104.139) is listening to TCP ports 22, 25, 80, 110, and 143.

Example 13-2 shows how to perform a "ping sweep" using nmap to see what systems are present in a given subnet (in this example, 172.18.104.129/29).

Example 13-2 *Nmap Ping Sweep Example*

```
bash-3.2$ nmap -sP 172.18.104.129/29
Starting Nmap 7.12 ( https://nmap.org ) at 2016-09-06 11:22 EDT
Nmap scan report for 172.18.104.129
Host is up (0.0071s latency).
Nmap scan report for 172.18.104.130
Host is up (0.0076s latency).
Nmap scan report for 172.18.104.132
Host is up (0.0076s latency).
Nmap scan report for 172.18.104.133
Host is up (0.0079s latency).
Nmap scan report for 172.18.104.134
Host is up (0.0074s latency).
Nmap scan report for 172.18.104.135
Host is up (0.011s latency).
Nmap done: 8 IP addresses (6 hosts up) scanned in 3.75 seconds
```

NOTE Additional examples and details about all the different nmap scanner options can be obtained at http://linuxcommand.org/man_pages/nmap1.html.

Social Engineering

Social engineering attacks leverage the weakest link, which is the human user. If the attacker can get the user to reveal information, it is much easier for the attacker to cause harm rather than using some other method of reconnaissance. This could be done through email or mis-direction of web pages, which results in the user clicking something that leads to the attacker gaining information. Social engineering can also be done in person by an insider or outside entity or over the phone.

A primary example is attackers leveraging normal user behavior. Suppose for a second that you are a security professional who is in charge of the network firewalls and other secu-rity infrastructure equipment in your company. An attacker could post a job offer for a very lucrative position and make it very attractive to you, the victim. Let's say that the job description lists benefits and compensation far beyond what you are already making at your company. You decide to apply for the position. The criminal (attacker) then schedules an interview with you. Because you are likely to "show off' your skills and work, he may ask you how you configured the firewalls and other network infrastructure devices for your company. You might disclose information about the firewalls used in your network, how you configured them, how they were designed, and so on. This gives the attacker a lot of knowledge about the organization without even performing any type of scanning or recon-naissance on the network.

Other social engineering techniques include the following:

- **Phishing:** Where the attacker presents a link that looks like a valid, trusted resource to a user. When the user clicks it, he is prompted to disclose confidential information such as his username and password.

- **Pharming:** The attacker uses this technique to direct a customer's URL from a valid resource to a malicious one that could be made to appear as the valid site to the user. From there, an attempt is made to extract confidential information from the user.

- **Malvertising:** The act of incorporating malicious ads on trusted websites, which results in users' browsers being inadvertently redirected to sites hosting malware.

A security-aware culture must include ongoing training that consistently informs employees about the latest security threats, as well as policies and procedures that reflect the over-all vision and mission of corporate information security. This emphasis on security helps employees understand the potential risk of social engineering threats, how they can prevent successful attacks, and why their role within the security culture is vital to corporate health. Security-aware employees are better prepared to recognize and avoid rapidly changing and increasingly sophisticated social engineering attacks, and are more willing to take ownership of security responsibilities.

Official security policies and procedures take the guesswork out of operations and help employees make the right security decisions. Such policies include the following:

- **Password management:** Guidelines such as the number and type of characters that each password must include, how often a password must be changed, and even a simple dec-laration that employees should not disclose passwords to anyone (even if they believe they are speaking with someone at the corporate help desk) will help secure information assets.

- **Two-factor authentication:** Authentication for high-risk network services such as modem pools and VPNs should use two-factor authentication rather than fixed passwords.

13

- **Antivirus/antiphishing defenses:** Multiple layers of antivirus defenses, such as at mail gateways and end-user desktops, can minimize the threat of phishing and other social engineering attacks.

- **Change management:** A documented change-management process is more secure than an ad hoc process, which is more easily exploited by an attacker who claims to be in a crisis.

- **Information classification:** A classification policy should clearly describe what information is considered sensitive and how to label and handle it.

- **Document handling and destruction:** Sensitive documents and media must be securely disposed of and not simply thrown out with the regular office trash.

- **Physical security:** The organization should have effective physical security controls such as visitor logs, escort requirements, and background checks.

Privilege Escalation Attacks

Privilege escalation is a type of attack and also a type of vulnerability. Privilege escalation is the process of taking some level of access (whether authorized or not) and achieving an even greater level of access (elevating the user's privileges). An example is an attacker who gains user-mode access to a firewall, router, or server and then uses a brute-force attack against the system that gives him administrative access.

Backdoors

When threat actors gain access to a system, they usually want future access as well, and they want it to be easy. A backdoor application can be installed by the attacker to either allow future access or collect information to use in further attacks.

Many backdoors are installed by users clicking something without realizing that the link they clicked or the file they opened is a threat. Backdoors can also be implemented as a result of a virus, worm, or malware.

Code Execution

When threat actors gain access to a system, they also might be able to take several actions. The type of action depends on the level of access the threat actor has, or can achieve, and is based on permissions granted to the account compromised by the attacker. One of the most devastating actions available to an attacker is the ability to execute code within a device. Code execution could result in an adverse impact to the confidentiality, integrity, and availability of the system or network.

Man-in-the Middle Attacks

A man-in-the-middle attack results when attackers place themselves in line between two devices that are communicating, with the intent of performing reconnaissance or manipulating the data as it moves between the devices. This can happen at Layer 2 or Layer 3. The main purpose is eavesdropping, so the attacker can see all the traffic.

If this happens at Layer 2, the attacker spoofs Layer 2 MAC addresses to make the devices on a LAN believe that the Layer 2 address of the attacker is the Layer 2 address of its default gateway. This is called "ARP poisoning." Frames that are supposed to go to the default gateway are forwarded by the switch to the Layer 2 address of the attacker on the same network. As a courtesy, the attacker can forward the frames to the correct destination so that the client will have the connectivity needed, and the attacker now sees all the data between the two devices. To mitigate this risk, you could use techniques such as dynamic Address Resolution Protocol (ARP) inspection (DAI) on switches to prevent spoofing of the Layer 2 addresses.

The attacker could also implement the attack by placing a switch into the network and manipulating the Spanning Tree Protocol (STP) to become the root switch (and thus gain the ability to see any traffic that needs to be sent through the root switch).

A man-in-the-middle attack can occur at Layer 3 by placing a rogue router on the network and then tricking the other routers into believing that this new router has a better path. This could cause network traffic to flow through the rogue router and again allow the attacker to steal network data. You can mitigate attacks such as these in various ways, including using routing authentication protocols and filtering information from being advertised or learned on specific interfaces.

A man-in-the-middle attack can occur by compromising the victim's machine and installing malware that can intercept the packets sent by the victim and sending them to the attacker. This type of malware can capture packets before they are encrypted if the victim is using SSL/TLS/HTTPS or any other mechanism.

To safeguard data in motion, one of the best things you can do is to use encryption for the confidentiality of the data in transit. If you use plaintext protocols for management, such as Telnet or HTTP, an attacker who has implemented a man-in-the-middle attack can see the contents of your cleartext data packets, and as a result will see everything that goes across his device, including usernames and passwords that are used. Using management protocols that have encryption built in, such as Secure Shell (SSH) and Hypertext Transfer Protocol Secure (HTTPS), is considered a best practice, and using VPN protection for cleartext sensitive data is also considered a best practice.

Denial-of-Service Attacks

Denial-of-service (DoS) and distributed DoS (DDoS) attacks have been around for quite some time now, but there has been heightened awareness of them over the past few years. DDoS attacks can generally be divided into the following three categories:

- Direct DDoS attacks
- Reflected
- Amplification DDoS attacks

Direct DDoS

Direct DDoS attacks occur when the source of the attack generates the packets, regardless of protocol, application, and so on, that are sent directly to the victim of the attack.

13

Figure 13-1 illustrates a direct DDoS attack.

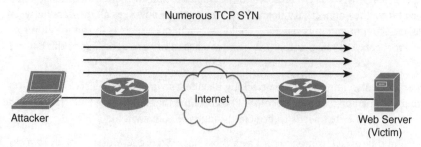

Figure 13-1 *Direct DDoS Attack*

In Figure 13-1, the attacker launches a direct DoS to a web server (the victim) by sending numerous TCP SYN packets. This type of attack is aimed at flooding the victim with an overwhelming number of packets, oversaturating its connection bandwidth or depleting the target's system resources. This type of attack is also known as a "SYN flood attack."

Cyber criminals also can use DDoS attacks to produce added costs to the victim when the victim is using cloud services. In most cases, when you use a cloud service such as Amazon Web Services (AWS), you pay per usage. Attackers can launch DDoS to cause you to pay more for usage and resources.

Another type of DoS is caused by exploiting vulnerabilities such as buffer overflows to cause a server or even network infrastructure device to crash, subsequently causing a denial-of-service condition.

Botnets Participating in DDoS Attacks

Many attackers use botnets to launch DDoS attacks. A *botnet* is a collection of compromised machines that the attacker can manipulate from a command and control (CnC) system to participate in a DDoS, send spam emails, and perform other illicit activities. Figure 13-2 shows how a botnet is used by an attacker to launch a DDoS attack.

In Figure 13-2, the attacker sends instructions to the CnC; subsequently, the CnC sends instructions to the bots within the botnet to launch the DDoS attack against the victim.

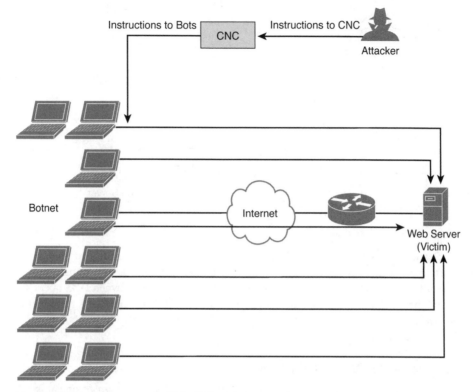

Figure 13-2 *Botnets and a DDoS Attack*

Reflected DDoS Attacks

Reflected DDoS attacks occur when the sources of the attack are sent spoofed packets that appear to be from the victim, and then the sources become unwitting participants in the DDoS attacks by sending the response traffic back to the intended victim. UDP is often used as the transport mechanism because it is more easily spoofed due to the lack of a three-way handshake. For example, if the attacker (A) decides he wants to attack a victim (V), he will send packets (for example, Network Time Protocol [NTP] requests) to a source (S) that thinks these packets are legitimate. The source then responds to the NTP requests by sending the responses to the victim, who was never expecting these NTP packets from the source (see Figure 13-3).

13

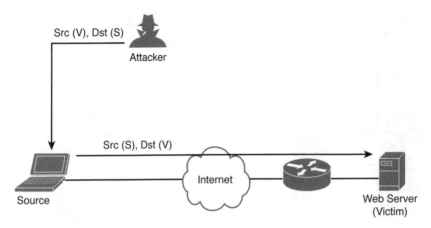

Figure 13-3 *Reflected DDoS Attacks*

An amplification attack is a form of reflected attack in which the response traffic (sent by the unwitting participant) is made up of packets that are much larger than those that were initially sent by the attacker (spoofing the victim). An example of this is when DNS queries are sent and the DNS responses are much larger in packet size than the initial query packets. The end result is that the victim's machine gets flooded by large packets for which it never actually issued queries.

Attack Methods for Data Exfiltration

There are many different attack methods for data exfiltration. One of the most popular is to use DNS tunneling. Cisco is seeing it used more and more for malware-based data exfiltration out of enterprise networks. An example of this technique is described in detail in a Cisco Talos post at http://blog.talosintel.com/2016/06/detecting-dns-data-exfiltration.html.

Attackers can encapsulate chucks of data into DNS packets to steal sensitive information such as PII information, credit card numbers, and much more. The following are a few examples of DNS tunneling tools used by attackers to exfiltrate data:

- **DNS2TCP**: Uses the KEY, TXT DNS record types. More information can be found at http://www.aldeid.com/wiki/Dns2tcp.
- **DNScat-P**: Uses the A and CNAME DNS record types. More information can be found at http://tadek.pietraszek.org/projects/DNScat/.
- **Iodine Protocol v5.00**: Uses the NULL DNS record type. More information can be found at http://code.kryo.se/iodine/.
- **Iodine Protocol v5.02**: Uses the A, CNAME, MX, NULL, SRV, and TXT DNS record types. More information can be found at http://code.kryo.se/iodine/.
- **OzymanDNS**: Uses the A and TXT DNS record types. More information can be found at http://dankaminsky.com/2004/07/29/51/.
- **SplitBrain**: Uses the A and TXT DNS record types. More information can be found at http://www.splitbrain.org/blog/2008-11/02-dns_tunneling_made_simple.

■ **TCP-Over-DNS:** Uses the CNAME and TXT DNS record types. More information can be found at http://www.sans.org/reading-room/whitepapers/dns/detecting-dns-tunneling-34152.

■ **YourFreedom:** Uses the NULL DNS record type. More information can be found at http://your-freedom.net/.

There are many other tools and DNS tunneling techniques. The following is a good reference that includes many additional types of tools and DNS exfiltration attacks:

https://www.sans.org/reading-room/whitepapers/dns/detecting-dns-tunneling-34152

DNS tunneling may be detected by analyzing the DNS packet payload or by using traffic analysis such as byte count and frequency of the DNS requests.

ARP Cache Poisoning

Threat actors can attack hosts, switches, and routers connected to your Layer 2 network by poisoning the ARP caches of systems connected to the subnet and by intercepting traffic intended for other hosts on the subnet. Cisco switches support a feature called "dynamic ARP inspection" that validates ARP packets and intercepts, logs, and discards ARP packets with invalid IP-to-MAC address bindings. This feature also protects the network from certain man-in-the-middle attacks. The dynamic ARP inspection feature ensures that only valid ARP requests and responses are relayed by performing the following:

■ Intercepting all ARP requests and responses on untrusted ports.

■ Verifying that each of the intercepted packets has a valid IP-to-MAC address binding before updating the local ARP cache or before forwarding the packet to the respective destination host.

■ Dropping invalid ARP packets.

■ Determining if an ARP packet is valid based on IP-to-MAC address bindings stored in a trusted database. This database is called the "DHCP snooping binding database."

On Cisco IOS switches, you can enable dynamic ARP inspection on a per-VLAN basis with the **ip arp inspection vlan** *vlan-range* global configuration command. In environments without DHCP configured, dynamic ARP inspection can validate ARP packets against user-configured ARP access control lists (ACLs) for hosts with statically configured IP addresses. You can use the **arp access-list acl-name global configuration** command to define the ACL.

The following are some additional Layer 2 security best practices for securing your infrastructure:

■ Select an unused VLAN (other than VLAN 1) and use that for the native VLAN for all your trunks. Do not use this native VLAN for any of your enabled access ports.

■ Avoid using VLAN 1 anywhere, because it is the default.

■ Administratively configure switch ports as access ports so that users cannot negotiate a trunk and disable the negotiation of trunking (no Dynamic Trunking Protocol [DTP]).

13

- Limit the number of MAC addresses learned on a given port with the port security feature.

- Control spanning tree to stop users or unknown devices from manipulating it. You can do so by using the BPDU Guard and Root Guard features.

- Turn off Cisco Discovery Protocol (CDP) on ports facing untrusted or unknown networks that do not require CDP for anything positive. (CDP operates at Layer 2 and may provide attackers information you would rather not disclose.)

- On a new switch, shut down all ports and assign them to a VLAN that is not used for anything other than a parking lot. Then bring up the ports and assign correct VLANs as the ports are allocated and needed.

Several other Layer 2 security features can be used to protect your infrastructure:

- **Port Security:** Limits the number of MAC address to be learned on access switch posts.

- **BPDU Guard:** If BPDUs show up where they should not, the switch will protect itself.

- **Root Guard:** Controls which ports are not allowed to become root ports to remote switches.

- **Dynamic ARP inspection:** This feature was covered earlier in this section.

- **IP Source Guard:** Prevents spoofing of Layer 3 information by hosts.

- **802.1X:** Authenticates and authorizes users before allowing them to communicate to the rest of the network.

- **DHCP snooping:** Prevents rogue DHCP servers from impacting the network.

- **Storm control:** Limits the amount of broadcast or multicast traffic flowing through the switch.

- **Access control lists:** Layer 3 and Layer 2 ACLs for traffic control and policy enforcement.

Spoofing Attacks

A spoofing attack is when an attacker impersonates another device to execute an attack. The following are a few examples of spoofing attacks:

- **IP address spoofing attack:** The attacker sends IP packets from a fake (or "spoofed") source address in order to disguise itself. DDoS attacks typically use IP spoofing to make the packets appear to be from legitimate source IP addresses.

- **ARP spoofing attack:** The attacker sends spoofed ARP packets across the Layer 2 network in order to link the attacker's MAC address with the IP address of a legitimate host. The best practices covered in the previous section help mitigate ARP spoofing attacks.

- **DNS server spoofing attack:** The attacker modifies the DNS server in order to reroute a specific domain name to a different IP address. DNS server spoofing attacks are typically used to spread malware.

Route Manipulation Attacks

There are different route manipulation attacks, but one of the most common is the BGP hijacking attack. BGP is a dynamic routing protocol used to route Internet traffic. The BGP hijacking attack can be launched by an attacker by configuring or compromising an edge router to announce prefixes that have not been assigned to his or her organization. If the malicious announcement contains a route that is more specific than the legitimate advertisement or presents a shorter path, the victim's traffic may be redirected to the attacker. In the past, threat actors have leveraged unused prefixes for BGP hijacking in order to avoid attention from the legitimate user or organization.

Password Attacks

The following are a few examples of the most common password attacks:

- **Password-guessing attack:** This is the most common type of password attack, but some of these techniques may be very inefficient. Threat actors can guess passwords locally or remotely using either a manual or automated approach. Several tools can automate the process of password guessing, such as the following:

  - **Hydra:** http://www.thc.org
  - **TSGrinder:** http://www.hammerofgod.com/download.htm
  - **SQLRecon:** http://www.sqlsecurity.com/DesktopDefault.aspx?tabid=26

  These automated password attack tools and crackers leverage different techniques. Some use a method called "the brute-force attack," where the attacker tries every possible combination of characters for a password. Another technique they use is a password-guessing attack called a "dictionary attack." Because most passwords consist of whole words, dates, and numbers, these tools use a dictionary of words, phrases, and even the most commonly used passwords (such as qwerty, password1, and so on). Other tools such as John the Ripper (http://www.openwall.com/john) and Cain & Abel (http://www.oxid.it) can take a hybrid approach from brute-force and dictionary attacks.

- **Password-resetting attack:** In many cases, it is easier to reset passwords than to use tools to guess them. Several cracking tools just attempt to reset passwords. In most cases, the attacker boots from a floppy disk or CD-ROM to get around the typical Windows protections. Most password resetters contain a bootable version of Linux that can mount NTFS volumes and help the attacker locate and reset the administrator's password.

- **Password cracking:** These attacks work by taking a password hash and converting it to its plaintext original. In this case, the attacker needs tools such as extractors for hash guessing, rainbow tables for looking up plaintext passwords, and password sniffers to extract authentication information. The concept of rainbow tables is that the attacker computes possible passwords and their hashes in a given system and puts the results into a lookup table called a "rainbow table." This allows an attacker to just get a hash from the victim system and then just search for that hash in the rainbow table to get the plaintext password. To mitigate rainbow table attacks, you can disable LM hashes and use long and complex passwords.

13

- **Password sniffing:** The threat actor just sniffs authentication packets between a client and server and extracts password hashes or enough authentication information to begin the cracking process.
- **Password capturing:** This is typically done by using key loggers or Trojan horses.

Wireless Attacks

The following are a few examples of wireless-specific attacks:

- **Installing a rogue access point:** The attacker basically installs an access point and can create a backdoor and obtain access to the network and its systems.
- **Jamming wireless signals and causing interference:** The purpose of this attack is to cause a full or partial denial-of-service condition in the wireless network.
- **Evil twin attack:** This is done when the attacker is trying to create rogue access points so as to gain access to the network or steal information. Basically the attacker purchases a wireless access point, plugs it into the network, and configures it exactly the same as the existing network.
- **War driving:** This is a methodology used by attackers to find wireless access points wherever they may be. The term *war driving* is used because the attacker can just drive around and get a very huge amount of information over a very short period of time.
- **Bluejacking:** The attacker sends unsolicited messages to another device via Bluetooth.
- **IV attack:** The attacker can cause some modification on the Initialization Vector (IV) of a wireless packet that is encrypted during transmission. The goal of the attacker is to obtain a lot of information about the plaintext of a single packet and generate another encryption key that then can be used to decrypt other packets using the same IV.
- **WEP/WPA attack:** WEP and several versions of WPA are susceptible to different vulnerabilities and are considered weak.
- **WPS attack:** This attack is carried out with WPS password-guessing tools to obtain the WPS passwords and use them to gain access to the network and its data.

Types of Vulnerabilities

Understanding the weaknesses and vulnerabilities in a system or network is a huge step toward correcting these vulnerabilities or putting in appropriate countermeasures to mitigate threats against them. Potential network vulnerabilities abound, with many resulting from one or more of the following:

- Policy flaws
- Design errors
- Protocol weaknesses
- Misconfiguration
- Software vulnerabilities
- Human factors
- Malicious software

- Hardware vulnerabilities
- Physical access to network resources

Cisco and others have created databases that categorize threats in the public domain. The Common Vulnerabilities and Exposures (CVE) is a dictionary of publicly known security vulnerabilities and exposures. A quick search using your favorite search engine will lead you to the website. Also, the National Vulnerability Database (NVD) is a repository of standards-based vulnerability information; you can do a quick search for it, too. (URLs change over time, so it is better to advise you to just do a quick search and click any links that interest you.)

The following are examples of the most common types of vulnerabilities:

- **API abuse:** These are vulnerabilities that are aimed to attack flaws in application programmable interfaces (APIs).
- **Authentication and authorization bypass vulnerabilities:** These vulnerabilities are used to bypass authentication and authorization mechanisms of systems within a network.

- **Buffer overflow:** A buffer overflow occurs when a program or software puts more data in a buffer than it can hold or when a program tries to put data in a memory location past a buffer. This is done so data outside the bounds of a block of allocated memory can corrupt other data or crash the program or operating system. In a worst-case scenario, this could lead to the execution of malicious code. There is a wide variety of ways buffer overflows can occur and, unfortunately, there are many error-prone techniques often used to prevent them.

A buffer overflow vulnerability typically involves many memory manipulation functions in languages such as C and C++, where the program does not perform bounds checking and can easily overwrite the allocated bounds of such buffers. A perfect example is a **strncpy()** function, which can cause vulnerabilities when used incorrectly.

Let's take a look at Figure 13-4, where the sample code shows a buffer that includes a small chunk of data (HELLO WORLD).

```
struct my_struct{
        char my_buffer[14];
        struct my_struct*next_struct;
};
```

Figure 13-4   *A Buffer Example*

An attacker can take advantage of this vulnerability and send data that can put data in a memory location past that buffer, as shown in Figure 13-5.

13

```
struct my_struct{
        char my_buffer[14];
        struct my_struct*next_struct;
};
```

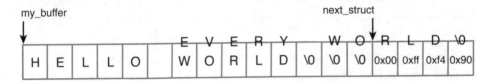

Figure 13-5 *A Buffer Overflow*

In Figure 13-5, the attacker sent data (EVERY WORLD) that was more than the buffer could hold, causing it to subsequently write to the adjacent memory location. Of course, this example is a very simplistic one, but it represents how an attacker could then write instructions to the system and potentially cause a local or remote code execution. In several of these attacks, the attacker writes "shellcode" to invoke instructions and manipulate the system.

- **Cross-site scripting (XSS) vulnerability:** A type of web application vulnerability where malicious scripts are injected into legitimate and trusted websites. An attacker can launch an attack against an XSS vulnerability using a web application to send malicious code (typically in the form of a browser-side script) to a different end user. XSS vulnerabilities are quite widespread and occur anywhere a web application uses input from a user within the output it generates without validating or encoding it. There are several types of XSS vulnerabilities (reflected, stored, and so on). Cisco has a document that explains all the different types of XSS vulnerabilities available at https://supportforums.cisco.com/document/13113946/what-are-cross-site-scripting-xss-vulnerabilities.

- **Cross-site request forgery (CSRF) vulnerability:** A vulnerability that forces an end user to execute malicious steps on a web application. This is typically done after the user is authenticated to such an application. CSRF attacks generally target state-changing requests, and the attacker cannot steal data because he or she has no way to see the response to the forged request. CSRF attacks are carried by being combined with social engineering.

- **Cryptographic vulnerability:** A vulnerability or flaw in a cryptographic protocol or its implementation.

- **Deserialization of untrusted data vulnerability:** To use or cause malformed data or unexpected data to abuse an application logic, cause a DoS attack, or to execute arbitrary code.

- **Double free:** A vulnerability typically in C, C++, and similar languages that occurs when free() is called more than once with the same memory address as an argument.

- **Insufficient entropy:** A vulnerability where a cryptographic application does not have proper entropy. For example, pseudo-random number generators (PRNGs) can be susceptible to insufficient entropy vulnerabilities and attacks when they are initialized.

- **SQL injection vulnerability:** Attackers can insert or "inject" a SQL query via the input data from the client to the application or database. Attackers can exploit SQL injector vulnerabilities in order to read sensitive data from the database, modify or delete database data, execute administration operations on the database, and even issue commands to the operating system.

There are many more types of vulnerabilities. OWASP provides good references to different types of vulnerabilities and how to mitigate them at https://www.owasp.org.

The OWASP Foundation is a not-for-profit charitable organization dedicated to educating organizations to "develop, acquire, operate, and maintain applications that can be trusted." They maintain many different resources that security professionals use to learn about different attacks and vulnerabilities, and how to protect against them.

13

Exam Preparation Tasks

Review All Key Topics

Review the most important topics in the chapter, noted with the Key Topic icon in the outer margin of the page. Table 13-2 lists these key topics and the page numbers on which each is found.

Table 13-2   Key Topics

Key Topic Element	Description	Page
List	Different types of port and network scanning techniques	502
Summary	What is phishing, pharming, and malvertising?	505
Summary	What are privilege escalation attacks?	506
Summary	What are backdoors?	506
Summary	What are man-in-the-middle attacks?	506
Summary	What are direct, reflected, and amplification DDoS attacks?	507
Summary	What are botnets?	508
Summary	What is DNS tunneling and how it is used for data exfiltration?	510
Summary	What is ARP cache poisoning?	511
List	Different types of password attacks	513
Summary	Defining and understanding different types of security vulnerabilities	514
Summary	What are buffer overflows?	515
Summary	What is XSS?	516
Summary	What is CSRF?	516
Summary	What are SQL injection vulnerabilities?	517
Summary	What is OWASP?	517

Define Key Terms

Define the following key terms from this chapter, and check your answers in the glossary:

SQL injection, CSRF, XSS, buffer overflow, war driving, rainbow tables, DNS tunneling, botnet, backdoors

Q&A

The answers to these questions appear in Appendix A, "Answers to the 'Do I Know This Already?' Quizzes and Q&A Questions." For more practice with exam format questions, use the exam engine on the website.

1. Which of the following describes a rainbow table?

   a. An attacker creates a table of mathematical calculations that can be used to perform cryptanalysis of encryption algorithms.

   b. An attacker creates a table of mathematical calculations that can be used to perform cryptanalysis of hashing algorithms.

   c. An attacker computes possible passwords and their hashes in a given system and puts the results into a lookup table.

   d. An attacker computes possible hashing algorithms used in an encrypted channel and puts the results into a lookup table.

2. Which of the following is a methodology used by attackers to find wireless access points wherever they may be?

   a. War driving

   b. Wireless LWAP scanning

   c. Wireless driving

   d. Wireless Aironet scanning

3. Which of the following is a type of web application vulnerability where malicious scripts are injected into legitimate and trusted websites?

   a. Buffer overflow

   b. Cross-site scripting (XSS)

   c. Cross-site injection (XSI)

   d. SQL injection

4. Which of the following is a type of vulnerability that attackers can exploit to read sensitive data from the database, modify or delete database data, execute administration operations on the database, and even issue commands to the operating system?

   a. SQL injection

   b. SQL buffer overflow

   c. SQL drop

   d. SQL bomb

5. Which one of the following attacks results when attackers place themselves in line between two devices that are communicating, with the intent of performing reconnaissance or manipulating the data as it moves between the devices?

   a. Man-in-the-path

   b. Man-in-the-middle

   c. Routing protocol attacks

   d. Routing injection attacks

13

6. Which of the following is a type of vulnerability where an attacker can use or cause malformed data or unexpected data to abuse an application's logic, cause a DoS attack, or execute arbitrary code?

    a. Deserialization of untrusted data

    b. Serialization of untrusted data

    c. Deserialization of encrypted data

    d. Serialization of encrypted data

7. Which of the following is a type vulnerability that describes when a program or software puts more data in a buffer than it can hold or when a program tries to put data in a memory location past a buffer?

    a. Buffer deserialization

    b. Buffer injection

    c. Cross-site buffer injection

    d. Buffer overflow

8. What type of attack is done when the attacker tries to create rogue access points so as to gain access to the network or steal information?

    a. SSID injection

    b. Evil twin

    c. War driving

    d. LWAP injection

9. Which of the following is an attack where threat actors can attack hosts, switches, and routers connected to your Layer 2 network by poisoning the ARP caches of systems connected to the subnet and by intercepting traffic intended for other hosts on the subnet?

    a. ARP cache injection

    b. ARP cache poisoning

    c. DHCP snooping

    d. ARP snooping

10. Cisco switches support a feature that validates ARP packets and intercepts, logs, and discards ARP packets with invalid IP-to-MAC address bindings. What is this feature called?

    a. DHCP cache snooping

    b. ARP cache poisoning

    c. ARP cache snooping

    d. Dynamic ARP inspection

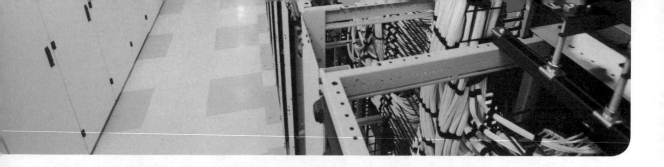

This chapter covers the following topics:

Describe the following concepts as they relate to security evasion techniques:

- Encryption and tunneling

- Resource exhaustion

- Traffic fragmentation

- Protocol-level misinterpretation

- Traffic substitution and insertion

- Pivoting

CHAPTER 14

Security Evasion Techniques

The last chapter provided an overview of some common methods malicious parties and contracted penetration testers use to breach networks. In summary, an attacker looks to abuse a vulnerability to accomplish something; however, there is another element that can make or break the success of the attack. That missing element is *stealth*, meaning attackers must also consider the amount of exposure an attack may cause as well as the expected countermeasures if the attack is noticed by the target's defense measures.

In this chapter, we look at how attackers obtain stealth as well as the tricks used to negatively impact detection and forensic technologies. An example of this concept is a robber kicking in a door verses picking a lock when breaking into a house. Both methods will accomplish the same goal of gaining access to the property. The difference is that kicking in a door will be louder and leave a mess behind that will quickly attract attention, whereas picking a lock is slower but leaves little evidence and is much quieter, which is why it is the more common choice for a robbery. Another example would be the robber picking the lock and setting off the alarm system every few days before actually attempting to enter the property. The idea is that the people monitoring the system will assume the attempt following multiple false alarms is another false alarm, thus giving the attacker access without concern for the alarm attracting attention to his or her actions. This ignoring the alarm behavior can be seen in some neighborhoods with car alarms that continually go off on their own.

"Do I Know This Already?" Quiz

The "Do I Know This Already?" quiz helps you identify your strengths and deficiencies in this chapter's topics. The ten-question quiz, derived from the major sections in the "Foundation Topics" portion of the chapter, helps you determine how to spend your limited study time. You can find the answers in Appendix A Answers to the "Do I Know This Already?" Quizzes and Q&A Questions.

Table 14-1 outlines the major topics discussed in this chapter and the "Do I Know This Already?" quiz questions that correspond to those topics.

Table 14-1   "Do I Know This Already?" Foundation Topics Section-to-Question Mapping

Foundation Topics Section	Questions Covered in This Section
Encryption and Tunneling	1–2
Resource Exhaustion	3
Traffic Fragmentation	4–5
Protocol-Level Misinterpretation	6
Traffic Timing, Substitution, and Insertion	7–8
Pivoting	9–10

1. Which of the following is when the attacker sends traffic slower than normal, not exceeding thresholds inside the time windows the signatures use to correlate different packets together?

   a. Traffic insertion

   b. Protocol manipulation

   c. Traffic fragmentation

   d. Timing attack

2. Which of the following would give an IPS the most trouble?

   a. Jumbo packets

   b. Encryption

   c. Throughput

   d. Updates

3. Which type of attack is when an IPS receives a lot of traffic/packets?

   a. Resource exhaustion

   b. DoS (denial of service)

   c. Smoke and mirrors

   d. Timing attack

4. Which of the following is not an example of traffic fragmentation?

   a. Modifying routing tables

   b. Modifying the TCP/IP in a way that is unexpected by security detection devices

   c. Modifying IP headers to cause fragments to overlap

   d. TCP segmentation

5. What is the best defense for traffic fragmentation attacks?

   a. Deploying a passive security solution that monitors internal traffic for unusual traffic and traffic fragmentation

   b. Deploying a next-generation application layer firewall

   c. Configuring fragmentation limits on a security solution

   d. Deploying a proxy or inline security solution

6. Which of the following is a TCP-injection attack?

   a. Forging a TCP packet over an HTTPS session

   b. Replacing legitimate TCP traffic with forged TCP packets

   c. The addition of a forged TCP packet to an existing TCP session

   d. Modifying the TCP/IP in a way that is unexpected by security detection

7. A traffic substitution and insertion attack does which of the following?

    a. Substitutes the traffic with data in a different format but with the same meaning

    b. Substitutes the payload with data in the same format but with a different meaning, providing a new payload

    c. Substitutes the payload with data in a different format but with the same meaning, not modifying the payload

    d. Substitutes the traffic with data in the same format but with a different meaning

8. Which of the following is not a defense against a traffic substitution and insertion attack?

    a. Unicode de-obfuscation

    b. Using Unicode instead of ASCII

    c. Adopting the format changes

    d. Properly processing extended characters

9. Which of the following is not a defense against a pivot attack?

    a. Content filtering

    b. Proper patch management

    c. Network segmentation

    d. Access control

10. Which security technology would be best for detecting a pivot attack?

    a. Virtual private network (VPN)

    b. Host-based antivirus

    c. NetFlow solution looking for anomalies within the network

    d. Application layer firewalls

Foundation Topics

Encryption and Tunneling

A very simple definition of encryption in the context of the SECFND exam is "to hide or encode something so the content is protected from unwanted parties." The content could be network traffic, such as a virtual private network (VPN) between two systems encrypting traffic to prevent eavesdropping on a conversation. Encryption could also mean rendering a file unreadable unless the user is able to decrypt the file. Although encryption might sound like something very positive, attackers can use it to hide data when leaving a victim's network after successfully breaching it or to mask an attack from a security defense tool. For example, encrypting an attack would hide it from many signature-based detection technologies such as an Intrusion Prevention System (IPS).

Starting with protecting data in transit, the use of *virtual private networks (VPNs)* is a common method for providing security for network traffic. A VPN can exist between two or more locations; this is known as a *site-to-site VPN*. Its purpose is to connect two or more locations in a secure manner over an unsecure medium. An example is an organization having two locations in different countries. A site-to-site VPN could be set up so that someone at location A could plug in his or her laptop and access resources at location B without any network changes. This means that communication between sites A and B travels over an encrypted tunnel. Any unwanted parties who attempt to capture and view the traffic would be unable to decipher it because they don't have the ability to decrypt the traffic. Figure 14-1 illustrates how a typical site-to-site VPN session functions.

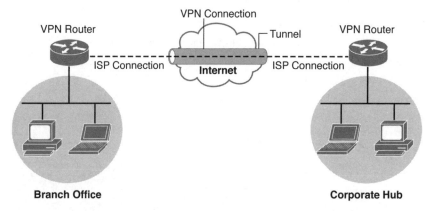

Figure 14-1 *Site-to-Site Example*

Another form of VPN technology involves securing traffic from a specific host to another location known as a *remote-access VPN*. As with a site-to-site VPN, the traffic between the host and remote connection is encrypted to prevent eavesdropping. The two forms of remote-access VPN are *client based* and *clientless*. Client-based remote-access VPN requires a hardware or software client to establish, maintain, and terminate the VPN connection. This approach is typically used for employees and other users who require a certain level of access to a remote location on a continuous basis. VPN security policy can be enforced to ensure the proper access level is maintained. An example of a remote-access VPN technology is Cisco AnyConnect; however, there are many other open source and commercial options. Figure 14-2 shows an example of a typical remote-access VPN session.

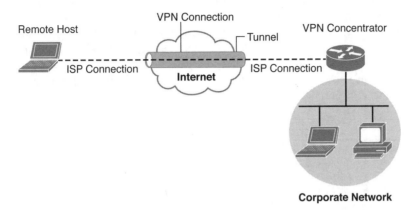

Figure 14-2 *Remote-Access VPN Example*

Cisco AnyConnect offers many security features to ensure the right person, device, or level of access is provisioned to the end user. Here's a remote-access VPN example: Suppose user Joey needs to access the Cisco network, so he launches a remote-access VPN. Joey's computer is then evaluated for specific checks, such as making sure that antivirus and system software are running the latest versions and that certain applications are not installed. Also, multifactor authentication can be enforced using a password combined with a valid certificate before access is permitted. The access that is permitted might be on a specific VLAN that limits access to email and certain web resources. Figure 14-3 shows an example of the Cisco AnyConnect client providing a connection from Joey's laptop to the remote location titled RTP.

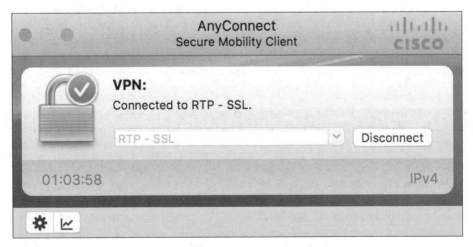

Figure 14-3 *AnyConnect VPN Client*

Clientless VPN, also known as a *secure portal*, does not require software on the end device. This is typically accomplished by providing access to a portal that keeps services within the secured container and wipes the history of the session from the device once the session is terminated. Typically, the portal is opened when an authorized user accesses it using an Internet browser and then is later terminated once the user logs out of the portal or the web browser is closed. Administrators can provision and monitor specific access inside the container such as links to websites, provide a terminal to manage network devices, and so on. Clientless VPNs are common solutions for temporary access from unsecure devices such as a shared computer in a hotel or airport terminal. Figure 14-4 shows an example of setting up a Cisco clientless VPN portal.

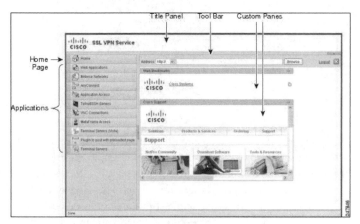

Figure 14-4   *Cisco Clientless VPN Portal*

An example of using a clientless VPN would be when user Joey wants to check his email from his friend's computer. That computer is not considered a trusted system by Joey's company policy, so a direct connection to the internal network is not permitted. A clientless portal is an alternative option Joey can access. This option requires authentication and a scan of the system he is on for specific items before access is permitted to specific resources. If Joey's temporary untrusted computer passes the policy checks, he can access a secure portal that has a link to his Outlook email. Once Joey closes his Internet browser, a popup will inform him that his browser history will be erased and the secure session will be closed.

Secure Shell (SSH) encrypts traffic between a client and an SSH server. SSH was developed as a secure alternative to Telnet, because Telnet is vulnerable to man-in-the-middle attacks due to its lack of encryption. The most common use of SSH is protecting traffic between an administrator remotely accessing and administrating network device command-line terminals.

SSH uses public-key cryptography to authenticate the remote computer and permit it to authenticate the user. A number of cryptographic algorithms can be used to generate SSH keys, such as Rivest, Shamir, and Adelman (RSA), Digital Signature Algorithm (DSA), and Elliptic Curve Digital Signature Algorithm (ECDSA). Essentially, the components of an SSH system are the SSH server, clients, and keys. The industry TCP port used for SSH servers is 22. Many sources can be found online for learning more details about how to develop an SSH solution. Building an SSH solution, however, is out of scope for the SECFND exam.

Attackers can use SSH to hide traffic, such as creating a reverse SSH tunnel from a breached system back to an external SSH server, hiding sensitive data as the traffic leaves the network. Figure 14-5 provides an example of how a typical SSH session functions.

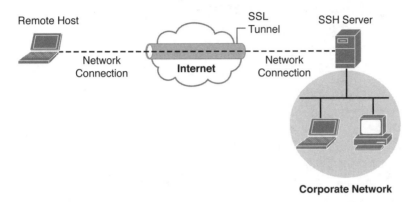

Figure 14-5   *SSH VPN Example*

There are many use cases where an attacker breaches a network and launches some form of a VPN session. An example is using Hak5's LAN Turtle USB adaptor, which can be configured to auto-launch a reverse SSH tunnel to a cloud storage server, essentially creating a cloud-accessible back door to a victim's network. Figure 14-6 shows a LAN Turtle plugged into a laptop.

Figure 14-6   *Hak5's LAN Turtle*

It is challenging for an administrator to identify the LAN Turtle because it sits on a trusted system and does not require an IP address of its own to provide the reverse encrypted tunnel out of the network. Figure 14-7 shows an example of a LAN Turtle plugged into a server, providing an encrypted tunnel to an attacker's remote server. This would represent a physical attack that leads to a back door for external malicious parties to access.

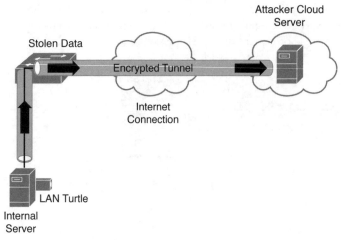

Figure 14-7   *LAN Turtle SSH Tunnel*

The LAN Turtle is just one example of the many tools available that can be planted on a network to create an unauthorized back door. The people at www.pwnieexpress.com develop various types of hacking tools designed to look like office items, such as power strips and printer plugs. Most of their tools offer various forms of encrypting access to the compromised network using LAN, wireless, and VPN technologies to accomplish the goal. The Pwnie Express team even offers a Raspberry Pi image, turning a Raspberry Pi into a remotely accessible penetration tool for under US$50. You can learn more at http://blog. pwnieexpress.com/post/24967860602/raspberry-pwn-a-pentesting-release-for-the.

Another encryption concept is hiding the actual data. There are many techniques for doing this, such as enterprise file encryption technologies that encrypt files and control access to opening them. An example is having a software agent installed on a server that specifies which files should be encrypted. When a file is removed that should be encrypted, it is tagged and encrypted, with access only provided to people within a specific authentication group. People within that group can use a host-based agent that auto-logs them in to the file, or they could be sent to an online portal to authenticate to gain access to the file.

The term *data at rest* means data that is placed on a storage medium. Data-at-rest security requirements typically refer to the ability to deny all access to stored data that is deemed sensitive and at risk of being exposed. Typically this is done by encrypting data and later removing all methods to unencrypt the data. Examples include hard disk encryption where a hard drive is encrypted, making it impossible to clone. The same concept can be applied to file encryption technology, where the data owner can expire access to the file, meaning all users won't be able to unencrypt it.

Many attackers abuse encryption concepts such as file and protocol encryption to hide malicious code. An example would be an attack happening from a web server over SSL encryption to hide the attack from network intrusion detection technologies. This works because a network intrusion detection tool uses signatures to identify a threat, which is useless if the traffic being evaluated is encrypted. Another example would be encoding a malicious file with a bunch of pointless text, with the goal of confusing an antivirus application. Antivirus applications also use signatures to detect threats, so adding additional text to malicious code could possibly change the code enough to not be tied to a known attack when evaluated by a security tool.

Key Encryption and Tunneling Concepts

The list that follows highlights the key encryption and tunneling concepts:

- A VPN is used to hide or encode something so the content is protected from unwanted parties.

- Encryption traffic can be used to bypass detection, such as by an IPS.

- The two forms of remote-access VPN are client based and clientless.

- A site-to-site VPN connects two or more networks.

- SSH connects a host to an SSH server and uses public-key cryptography to authenticate the remote computer and permit it to authenticate the user.

- File encryption technology protects files from unauthorized users.

Next, we will look at exhausting resources to bypass detection and gain unauthorized access to systems and networks.

Resource Exhaustion

Resource exhaustion is a type of denial-of-service attack; however, it can also be used to evade detection by security defenses. A simple definition of *resource exhaustion* is "consuming the resources necessary to perform an action." For example, a service can be a website, such as one of the authors' blog called www.thesecurityblogger.com. The server hosting this website can only provide services to a certain number of systems using digital communication, meaning the server will fail if too many systems access a specific resource at the same time. One denial-of-service attack tool that can exhaust the available resources of the server hosting such a website is called Slowloris, which can be found at http://chers. org/slowloris. This tool holds connections by sending partial HTTP requests to the website. The tool continues sending several hundred subsequent headers at regular intervals to keep sockets from closing, thus overwhelming the target's resources. This causes the website to be caught up with existing requests, thus delaying responses to legitimate traffic. Figure 14-8 shows the Slowloris tool being used against the www.thesecurityblogger.com website.

```
   .   .        ..  ..::cccc:..::ccoocc:. ............ ..  . ..::::.::::::::ccco
 Welcome to Slowloris - the low bandwidth, yet greedy and poisonous HTTP client
Defaulting to port 80.
Defaulting to a 5 second tcp connection timeout.
Defaulting to a 100 second re-try timeout.
Defaulting to 1000 connections.
Multithreading enabled.
Connecting to                    com:80 every 100 seconds with 1000 sockets:
            Building sockets.
            Building sockets.
            Building sockets.
            Building sockets.
            Building sockets.
            Building sockets.
            Building sockets.
            Building sockets.
            Building sockets.
            Building sockets.
```

Figure 14-8 *Slowloris attack against thesecurityblogger.com*

When it comes to bypassing access-control security, resource exhaustion attacks can consume all processes to force a system to fail open, meaning to permit access to unauthorized systems and networks. This attack can be effective against access-control technologies that administrators typically configure to fail open if a service failure is detected. The same approach could be used to exhaust systems that have tracking capabilities, such as intrusion detection tools or other network sensors, causing a blackout period for an attacker to abuse without being recorded. Attackers will use resource exhaustion attacks against logging systems they identify during an attack, knowing many administrators do not have the skills or understanding to defend against resource exhaustion attacks and therefore will be unable to prevent the monitoring blackouts from occurring. This also prevents the evidence required for a forensic investigation from being collected, thus legally protecting the attacker from being incriminated by a future post-breach investigation. The most common example of a resource exhaustion attack involves sending a bunch of traffic directly at the IPS.

Defensive strategies should be implemented in order to prevent resource exhaustion attacks. The first defense layer, which involves having checks for unusual or unauthorized methods of requesting resources, is usually built in by the vendor. The idea is to recognize when an attack is being attempted and to deny the attacker further access for a specific amount of time so that the system resources can sustain the traffic without impacting service. One simple method to enforce this effect involves using *throttling*, which is limiting the amount of service a specific user or group can consume, thus enforcing an acceptable amount of resource consumption. Sometimes these features need to be enabled before they can be enforced, so best practice is to validate whether resource exhaustion defenses exist within a security solution.

The list that follows highlights the key resource exhaustion concepts:

- Resource exhaustion refers to consuming the resources necessary to perform an action.
- Attackers use resource exhaustion to bypass access control and security detection capabilities. A common example is sending a ton of traffic at an IPS.
- Resource exhaustion can be used to render logging unusable.
- Throttling is a method to prevent resource exhaustion by limiting the amount of processes that can be consumed at one time.

Now let's look at dicing up and modifying the traffic to bypass detection. This is known as traffic fragmentation.

Traffic Fragmentation

Network technologies expect traffic to move in a certain way. This is known as the *TCP/IP suite*. Understanding how this works can help you identify when something is operating in an unusual manner. Fragmenting traffic is a method of avoiding detection by breaking up a single Internet Protocol (IP) datagram into multiple, smaller-size packets. The goal is to abuse the fragmentation protocol within IP by creating a situation where the attacker's intended traffic is ignored or let through as trusted traffic. The good news is that most modern intrusion detection systems (IDSs) and intrusion prevention systems (IPSs) are aware of this attack

14

and can prevent it. Best practice is to verify that your version of IDS/IPS has traffic fragmentation detection capabilities.

IPS products should be able to properly reassemble packets to evaluate whether there is malicious intent. This includes understanding the proper order of the packets. Unfortunately, attackers have various techniques they can use to confuse an IPS solution during its reassembly process. An example of this involves using a TCP segmentation and reordering attack that is designed to confuse the detection tool by sending traffic in an uninspected method with the hope it can't properly reassemble the traffic and identify it as being malicious. Security devices that can't perform traffic reassembly will automatically fail to prevent this attack. Some security devices will fail when the attacker reorders or fragments the traffic with enough tweaks to accomplish the bypass.

Another example of a fragmentation attack involves using overlapping fragments. This attack works by setting the offset values in the IP header so that they do not match up, thus causing one fragment to overlap another. The confusion could cause the detection tool to ignore some traffic, letting malicious traffic slip through.

Best practice for avoiding traffic fragmentation attacks is verifying with your security solution provider that the solution is capable of detecting traffic fragmentation. Solutions that operate in full proxy type modes are not susceptible to this type of attack (for example, content filters and inline security devices).

The list that follows highlights the key traffic fragmentation concepts:

- Traffic fragmentation attacks modify the TCP/IP traffic in a way that is unexpected by security detection devices; the goal is to confuse the detection functions.
- Using TCP segmentation and reordering attacks is one way to modify traffic to bypass detection.
- Causing fragments to overlap by modifying IP headers is another type of traffic fragmentation attack.
- Proxies and in-line security devices can help prevent traffic fragmentation attacks.

Like with TCP/IP traffic, protocols can also be modified to bypass security devices. Let's look at how this works.

Protocol-Level Misinterpretation

A *protocol* is a set of rules or data structures that governs how computers or other network devices exchange information over a network. Protocols can be manipulated to confuse security devices from properly evaluating traffic since many devices and applications expect network communication to follow the industry-defined rules when a protocol is used. The key is understanding how the protocol should work and attempting to see if the developer of the receiving system defined defenses such as limitations on what is accepted, a method to validate what is received, and so on. The second key piece is identifying what happens when a receiving system encounters something it doesn't understand (meaning seeing the outcome of a failure). A security device misinterpreting the end-to-end meaning of network protocols could cause traffic to be ignored, dropped, or delayed, all of which could be used to an attacker's advantage.

Another example of a protocol-level misinterpretation is abusing the "time to live" (TTL) of traffic. TTL is a protocol within a packet that limits the lifespan of data in a computer network. This prevents a data packet from circulating indefinitely. Abusing TTL works by first sending a short TTL value with the goal of passing the security receiver, assuming it will be dropped by a router later. This dropping occurs after the security device (meaning between the target and the security device) due to the TTL equaling a value of zero before the packet can reach its intended target. The attacker follows up the first packet with a TTL that has too high a value, with the goal of looking like duplicate traffic to the security device so that the security device will ignore it. By having the longer TTL, the packet will make it all the way to the host because now it has a high enough TTL value while being ignored by the network security solutions. Figure 14-9 shows an example of how this attack works. The first packet has a TTL value of 1, meaning it will hop past the security device but be dropped by the router due to having a value equal to 0. The second packet has a large enough TTL to make it to the host, yet if it's the same data, the security device will assume it's a duplicate, thus giving the attacker the ability to sneak in data.

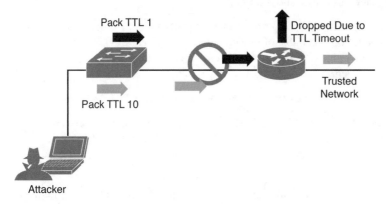

Figure 14-9 *TTL Manipulation Attack*

Like with IP fragmentation attacks, the good news is that many security solutions are aware of this form of attack and have methods to validate and handle protocol manipulation. Best practice is to verify with your security solution providers whether their products are aware of protocol-level misinterpretation attacks.

The list that follows highlights the key protocol misinterpretation concepts:

■ Protocols can be manipulated to confuse security devices from properly evaluating traffic.

■ TCP checksum and time-to-live protocols can be manipulated to first look like one thing and later to look like something else, with the goal of tricking the security defenses.

Now let's look at another evasion technique that takes a different approach to modifying network traffic.

14

Traffic Timing, Substitution, and Insertion

A traffic timing attack is when the attacker evades detection by performing his or her actions slower than normal while not exceeding thresholds inside the time windows the detection signatures use to correlate different packets together. A traffic timing attack can be mounted against any correlating engine that uses a fixed time window and a threshold to classify multiple packets into a composite event. An example of this attack would be sending packets at a slower rate than the detection system would be tuned to alarm to via sampling, making the attack unacceptably long in the eyes of the detection system.

A *traffic substitution and insertion attack* involves substituting the payload data with data in a different format but that has the same meaning, with the goal of it being ignored due to not being recognized by the security device. Some methods for changing the format include exchanging spaces with tabs, using Unicode instead of ASCII strings or characters in HTTP requests, modifying legitimate shell code with exploit code, and abusing case-sensitive communication. Most security devices can decode traffic; however, this attack is successful when a flaw is found in the decoding process. An example of a traffic substitution and insertion attack would be hiding malicious code by using Latin characters, knowing that the receiver will translate the code into ASCII. If this vulnerability exists, the security device will translate the text without verifying whether it is a threat, thus permitting the attack into the environment.

Defending against traffic timing attacks as well as substitution and insertion attacks once again requires features typically found in many security products offered by leading security vendors. Security features need to include the ability to adapt to changes in the timing of traffic patterns as well as changes in the format, to properly process extended characters, and to perform Unicode de-obfuscation. Unicode decoding examples include identifying ambiguous bits, double-encoding detection, and multidirectory delimiters. It is recommended that you verify with your trusted security solution provider whether your security solution has these detection capabilities.

The list that follows highlights the key traffic substitution and insertion concepts:

- Traffic timing attacks are when the attacker evades detection by performing his or her actions slower than normal while not exceeding thresholds inside the time windows the detection signatures use to correlate different packets together.

- A traffic substitution and insertion attack substitutes the payload with data in a different format but that has the same meaning.

- Some methods to accomplish a traffic substitution and insertion attack include exchanging spaces with tabs, using Unicode instead of ASCII, and abusing case-sensitive communication.

- Security products can stop this type of attack by being able to adapt to format changes, properly processing extended characters, and providing Unicode de-obfuscation.

One final evasion technique we will cover is pivoting inside a network.

Pivoting

Although cyber attacks can vary in nature, one common step in the attack process, according to the "kill chain" concept first introduced by Lockheed Martin, is the idea of establishing a foothold in the target network and attempting to pivot to a more trusted area of the network. Establishing a foothold means breaching the network through exploiting a vulnerability and creating access points into the compromised network. The challenge for the attacker is the level of access granted with the exploit. For example, breaching a guest system on a network would typically mean gaining access to a guest network that is granted very limited access to network resources. An attacker would want to pivot from the guest network to another network with more access rights, such as the employee network. In regards to the kill chain, a pivot would be an action taken to start the sequence over once the attacker reached the "action" point. As illustrated in Figure 14-10, the attacker would first perform reconnaissance on other systems on the same network as the compromised system, weaponize an attack, and eventually move through the attack kill chain with the goal of gaining command and control abilities on other systems with greater network access rights.

Figure 14-10   *The Lockheed Martin Kill Chain*

Usually privileges and available resources on a network are grouped together into silos; this is known as *network segmentation*. Access to each network segment is typically enforced through some means of network access control. Figure 14-11 demonstrates the concept of segmentation and access control, where printers, guests, and a trusted network are on different network segments.

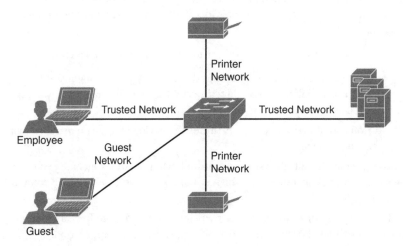

Figure 14-11   *Example of Segmentation*

Pivoting, also known as *island hopping*, means to attack other systems on the same network. The idea is to identify a system with higher level access rights, such as administrator.

This is also known as a form of *privilege escalation*. Identifying other systems with different levels of network access privileges can also be used to provide more doorways into the network in the event the original breach is closed, to identify systems to leverage for another form or attack, to hide data by using multiple systems as exit points from the network, and so on. It is also important to understand that privilege escalation can occur within a system. This involves breaching a server with a guest account and then later obtaining root access in order to provide more resource rights on that system. Figure 14-12 shows an attacker pivoting through a vulnerable system sitting on a trusted network. This could be accomplished by identifying a vulnerability on the employee's laptop, placing a remote-access tool (RAT) on it, and then remotely connecting to the system to use it to surf inside the trusted network. The pivot is when the threat actor first gains access to the employee computer and "pivots" from that system to another system on the same network to gain further access to the target network.

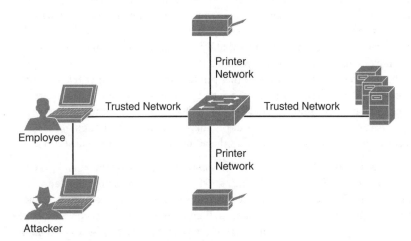

Figure 14-12   *Example of Pivoting*

There are different methods for pivoting across a network. The first involves using the existing network connections and ports available on the compromised system, essentially turning that system into a proxy pivot point. Although this provides some access, the attacker would be limited to the available TCP and UDP ports on the compromised system. A second approach that provides full access is setting up a VPN connection from the compromised system to the trusted network, giving the attacker full access by having all ports available from the attacker's system to the point of VPN termination.

Figure 14-13 shows an example of using a system connected to two networks as a pivot point for a remote attack. I have found that many organizations are vulnerable to this type of attack during assessments, meaning their host systems aren't disabling wireless connections made to a network through a device's Ethernet port.

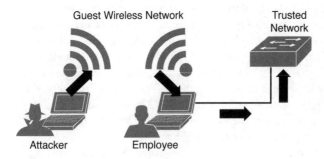

Figure 14-13   *Pivoting Through a Compromised Host*

Defending against pivoting can be addressed a few ways. The first method is to enforce proper network access control and segmentation by limiting what can access specific network segments and filtering access to only what is required to operate the business within those segments. This approach limits the available systems an attacker can pivot to as well as what new network services would become available by breaching other systems on the same network. For example, if all printers are limited to a specific network segment and one printer is breached, the attacker could only attack other printers and access printer-related traffic. We find pivoting occurs when a poor security architecture is implemented, such as putting all devices on the same network segment and not validating what can plug into a network. There are many penetration-testing stories about organizations that forgot about an older, vulnerable system sitting on the same network as the administrators and critical servers.

Cisco Identity Services Engine (ISE) is the Cisco flagship identity management and policy enforcement solution designed for address pivoting risks. An example is providing an employee named Julie limited access to specific resources due to her device being an iPhone, which doesn't require the same access as her laptop. Figure 14-14 represents how ISE would identify user Julie and limit her access to only specific resources. Different access would be provisioned to her printer, laptop, and desk phone, depending on each device's posture status and how the administrators configured the ISE solution. This is just one of the many ways ISE dramatically simplifies enforcing segmentation through a centralized policy.

Figure 14-14   *Cisco Identity Services Engine (ISE)*

Another defense strategy is to provide proper endpoint security practices such as patch management, antivirus, breach detection technologies, and so on. Typically systems are breached though a vulnerability, where a payload such as a remote-access tool (RAT) is delivered to give access to an unwanted remote party. Preventing the breach stops the attacker from having access to the network.

NetFlow security products such as Cisco Stealthwatch can be used to identify unusual traffic, giving you a "canary in the coalmine" defense. An example of this concept in regard to Stealthwatch would be an attacker compromising an employee's system and using it to pivot into the network. If Julie is in the sales department and she starts scanning the network and accessing critical systems for the first time, it probably means something bad is happening, regardless of whether she is authorized to do so. Although NetFlow might not be able to tell you *why* the situation is bad at first, it can quickly alarm you that something bad is happening so that you can start to investigate the situation—just like miners would do when they noticed the canary had died in the coalmine.

NetFlow security doesn't require a lot of storage, is supported by most vendors, and can be enabled on most device types (routers, switches, wireless apps, virtual switching traffic, data center traffic, and so on). It essentially turns the entire network into a security sensor grid. Figure 14-15 shows the Cisco Stealthwatch dashboard for various internal threats, including suspicious systems that might be infected with malware based on how they are scanning other systems (perhaps to identify new systems to infect).

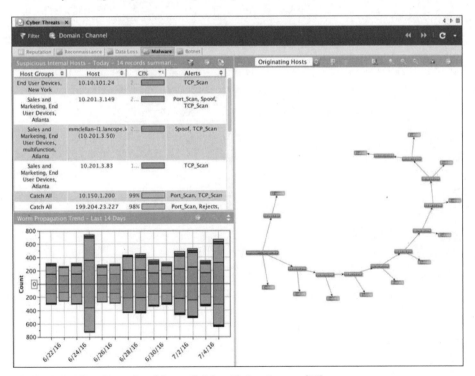

Figure 14-15 *Cisco Stealthwatch Identifying Internal Threats*

The list that follows highlights the key pivot concepts:

■ Pivoting in terms of cyber attacks (also known as *island hopping*) means to attack other systems on the same network with the goal of gaining accessing to that system.

■ Best practice is to have networks segmented and to control access between each segment.

■ A common goal for a pivot attack is to escalate the attacker's privileges. This is commonly accomplished by jumping from one system to another system with greater network privileges.

■ Defending against pivoting can be accomplished by providing proper access control, network segmentation, DNS security, reputation security, and proper patch management.

■ NetFlow is a great sensor-based tool for detecting unauthorized pivoting occurring within the network.

Exam Preparation Tasks

Review All Key Topics

Review the most important topics in the chapter, noted with the Key Topic icon in the outer margin of the page. Table 14-2 lists these key topics and the page numbers on which each is found.

Table 14-2   Key Topics

Key Topic Element	Description	Page
List	Encryption and tunneling concepts	531
List	Resource exhaustion concepts	532
List	Traffic fragmentation concepts	533
List	Protocol misinterpretation concepts	534
List	Traffic substitution and Insertion concepts	535
List	Pivot concepts	540

Complete Tables and Lists from Memory

Print a copy of Appendix B, "Memory Tables," (found on the book website), or at least the section for this chapter, and complete the tables and lists from memory. Appendix C, "Memory Tables Answer Key," also on the website, includes completed tables and lists to check your work.

Define Key Terms

Define the following key terms from this chapter, and check your answers in the glossary:

Virtual private network (VPN), remote-access VPN, traffic timing attack, clientless VPN, Secure Shell (SSH), resource exhaustion attack, traffic fragmentation attack, protocol misinterpretation attack, traffic substitution and insertion attack, pivoting, site-to-site VPN

Q&A

The answers to these questions appear in Appendix A, "Answers to the 'Do I Know This Already?' Quizzes and Q&A Questions." For more practice with exam format questions, use the exam engine on the website.

1. What is SSH used for?

    a. Remote access

    b. To provide a client-based VPN solution for remote users

    c. Managing network equipment remotely

    d. Preventing man-in-the-middle attacks by securing traffic between the client and server

2. Which of the following is a true statement?

   a. A remote access VPN must include a host installed on the client.

   b. A clientless VPN can connect multiple concentrators together.

   c. A remote access VPN may include a host installed on the client.

   d. A clientless VPN installs software on the host to establish the VPN connection.

3. Which of the following is not a possible outcome of a resource exhaustion attack?

   a. Corrupting applications by modifying their code

   b. A denial of server on the target system

   c. Bypassing access control security

   d. Causing blackouts in network monitoring

4. Which of the following is not a technique used to confuse an IPS from assembling fragmenting packets?

   a. Encrypting traffic

   b. TCP segmentation and reordering attack

   c. Overlapping fragments

   d. Sending traffic in very slow method

5. Which of the following is the best explanation of an overlapping fragment attack?

   a. This attack works by setting the offset values in the IP header to match up, causing one fragment to overlap another.

   b. This attack works by setting the TCP values in the IP header to not match up, causing one fragment to overlap another.

   c. This attack works by setting the UDP values in the IP header to match up, causing one fragment to overlap another.

   d. This attack works by setting the offset values in the IP header to not match up, causing one fragment to overlap another.

6. Which of the following best describes a timing attack?

   a. Sending a ton of traffic to render the system or data useless

   b. Sending traffic in a method that is slower than the system can accept

   c. Sending traffic slowly enough where the system can accept it but overlooks it

   d. Sending the traffic over different protocols

7. Which of the following is an example of a traffic substitution and insertion attack?

   a. Inputting more characters than requested

   b. Using functions and classes

   c. Changing spaces with tabs

   d. Inputting wildcard characters

8. Which of the following is not a method used to pivot a network?

   a. Exploiting a host on the same network

   b. Creating a back door to the network

   c. VLAN hopping

   d. Exploiting a network server

9. Which is the best answer to explain why Cisco Identity Services Engine would reduce the risk of pivoting to a higher, trusted network?

   a. ISE ensures systems have the latest antivirus updates prior to permitting access to the network.

   b. ISE can unify and enforce the LAN, wireless, and VPN access control policies into one secure policy.

   c. ISE can profile devices, providing greater detail on which ones can access what resources.

   d. ISE enforces network segmentation.

10. Which of the following statements is not true about SSH?

   a. SSH uses TCP port 22.

   b. SSH is composed of an SSH server, clients, and keys.

   c. SSH uses asymmetric encryption.

   d. SSH encrypts traffic between a client and an SSH server.

References and Further Reading

informationassurance.regis.edu/ia-programs/resources/blog/cybersecurity-pivot

www.pwnieexpress.com/

www.cisco.com/go/ise

www.cisco.com/go/wsa

www.opendns.com

www.lancope.com

www.incapsula.com/ddos/attack-glossary/slowloris.html

www.thesecurityblogger.com

CHAPTER 15

Final Preparation

The first 14 chapters of this book covered the technologies, protocols, design concepts, and considerations required to be prepared to pass the CCNA Cyber Ops 210-250 SECFND exam. Although these chapters supplied the detailed information, most people need more preparation than just reading the first 14 chapters of this book. This chapter details a set of tools and a study plan to help you complete your preparation for the exam.

This short chapter has two main sections. The first section lists the exam preparation tools useful at this point in the study process. The second section lists a suggested study plan now that you have completed all the earlier chapters in this book.

> **NOTE** Note that Appendix B, "Memory Tables," and Appendix C, "Memory Tables Answer Key," exist as soft-copy appendixes on the website for this book, which you can access by going to www.pearsonITcertification.com/register, registering your book, and entering this book's ISBN: 9781587147029.

Tools for Final Preparation

This section lists some information about the available tools and how to access them.

Pearson Cert Practice Test Engine and Questions on the Website

Register this book to get access to the Pearson IT Certification test engine (software that displays and grades a set of exam-realistic, multiple-choice questions). Using the Pearson Cert Practice Test Engine, you can either study by going through the questions in Study mode or take a simulated (timed) SECFND exam.

The Pearson Test Prep practice test software comes with two full practice exams. These practice tests are available to you either online or as an offline Windows application. To access the practice exams that were developed with this book, please see the instructions in the card inserted in the sleeve in the back of the book. This card includes a unique access code that enables you to activate your exams in the Pearson Test Prep software.

Accessing the Pearson Test Prep Software Online

The online version of this software can be used on any device with a browser and connectivity to the Internet, including desktop machines, tablets, and smartphones. To start using your practice exams online, simply follow these steps:

Step 1. Go to: http://www.PearsonTestPrep.com.

Step 2. Select **Pearson IT Certification** as your product group.

Step 3. Enter your email/password for your account. If you don't have an account on PearsonITCertification.com or CiscoPress.com, you will need to establish one by going to PearsonITCertification.com/join.

Step 4. In the **My Products** tab, click the **Activate New Product** button.

Step 5. Enter the access code printed on the insert card in the back of your book to activate your product.

Step 6. The product will now be listed in your My Products page. Click the **Exams** button to launch the exam settings screen and start your exam.

Accessing the Pearson Test Prep Software Offline

If you wish to study offline, you can download and install the Windows version of the Pearson Test Prep software. There is a download link for this software on the book's companion website, or you can just enter this link in your browser:

http://www.pearsonitcertification.com/content/downloads/pcpt/engine.zip

To access the book's companion website and the software, simply follow these steps:

Step 1. Register your book by going to PearsonITCertification.com/register and entering the ISBN: 9781587147029.

Step 2. Respond to the challenge questions.

Step 3. Go to your account page and select the **Registered Products** tab.

Step 4. Click the **Access Bonus Content** link under the product listing.

Step 5. Click the **Install Pearson Test Prep Desktop Version** link under the Practice Exams section of the page to download the software.

Step 6. Once the software finishes downloading, unzip all the files on your computer.

Step 7. Double-click the application file to start the installation; then follow the onscreen instructions to complete the registration.

Step 8. Once the installation is complete, launch the application and select **Activate Exam** button on the My Products tab.

Step 9. Click the **Activate a Product** button in the Activate Product Wizard.

Step 10. Enter the unique access code found on the card in the sleeve in the back of your book and click the **Activate** button.

Step 11. Click **Next** and then the **Finish** button to download the exam data to your application.

Step 12. You can now start using the practice exams by selecting the product and clicking the **Open Exam** button to open the exam settings screen.

Note that the offline and online versions will sync together, so saved exams and grade results recorded on one version will be available to you on the other as well.

Customizing Your Exams

Once you are in the exam settings screen, you can choose to take exams in one of three modes:

- Study mode
- Practice Exam mode
- Flash Card mode

Study mode allows you to fully customize your exams and review answers as you are taking the exam. This is typically the mode you would use first to assess your knowledge and identify information gaps. Practice Exam mode locks certain customization options, as it is presenting a realistic exam experience. Use this mode when you are preparing to test your exam readiness. Flash Card mode strips out the answers and presents you with only the question stem. This mode is great for late-stage preparation when you really want to challenge yourself to provide answers without the benefit of seeing multiple-choice options. This mode will not provide the detailed score reports that the other two modes will, so it should not be used if you are trying to identify knowledge gaps.

In addition to these three modes, you will be able to select the source of your questions. You can choose to take exams that cover all of the chapters or you can narrow your selection to just a single chapter or the chapters that make up specific parts in the book. All chapters are selected by default. If you want to narrow your focus to individual chapters, simply deselect all the chapters and then select only those on which you wish to focus in the Objectives area.

You can also select the exam banks on which to focus. Each exam bank comes complete with a full exam of questions that cover topics in every chapter. The two exams printed in the book are available to you as well as two additional exams of unique questions. You can have the test engine serve up exams from all four banks or just from one individual bank by selecting the desired banks in the exam bank area.

There are several other customizations you can make to your exam from the exam settings screen, such as the time of the exam, the number of questions served up, whether to randomize questions and answers, whether to show the number of correct answers for multiple-answer questions, and whether to serve up only specific types of questions. You can also create custom test banks by selecting only questions that you have marked or questions for which you have added notes.

Updating Your Exams

If you are using the online version of the Pearson Test Prep software, you should always have access to the latest version of the software as well as the exam data. If you are using the Windows desktop version, every time you launch the software, it will check to see if there are any updates to your exam data and automatically download any changes that were made since the last time you used the software. This requires you to be connected to the Internet at the time you launch the software.

Sometimes, due to many factors, the exam data might not fully download when you activate your exam. If you find that figures or exhibits are missing, you may need to manually update your exams.

To update a particular exam you have already activated and downloaded, simply select the **Tools** tab and select the **Update Products** button. Again, this is only an issue with the desktop Windows application.

If you wish to check for updates to the Pearson Test Prep exam engine software, Windows desktop version, simply select the **Tools** tab and select the **Update Application** button. This will ensure you are running the latest version of the software engine.

Premium Edition

In addition to the free practice exam provided on the website, you can purchase additional exams with expanded functionality directly from Pearson IT Certification. The Premium Edition of this title contains an additional two full practice exams and an eBook (in both PDF and ePub format). In addition, the Premium Edition title also has remediation for each question to the specific part of the eBook that relates to that question.

Because you have purchased the print version of this title, you can purchase the Premium Edition at a deep discount. There is a coupon code in the book sleeve that contains a one-time-use code and instructions for where you can purchase the Premium Edition.

To view the premium edition product page, go to www.informit.com/title/9781587147029.

The Cisco Learning Network

Cisco provides a wide variety of CCNA Cyber Ops preparation tools at a Cisco Systems website called the Cisco Learning Network. This site includes a large variety of exam preparation tools, including sample questions, forums on each Cisco exam, learning video games, and information about each exam.

To reach the Cisco Learning Network, go to www.cisco.com/go/learnnetspace, or just search for "Cisco Learning Network." You must use the logon you created at Cisco.com. If you do not have such a logon, you can register for free. To register, simply go to Cisco.com, click **Register** at the top of the page, and supply some information.

Memory Tables

Like most *Official Cert Guides* from Cisco Press, this book purposely organizes information into tables and lists for easier study and review. Rereading these tables can be very useful before the exam. However, it is easy to skim over the tables without paying attention to every detail, especially when you remember having seen the table's contents when reading the chapter.

Instead of just reading the tables in the various chapters, this book's Appendixes B and C give you another review tool. Appendix B lists partially completed versions of many of the tables from the book. You can open Appendix B (a PDF available on the book website after registering) and print the appendix. For review, you can attempt to complete the tables. This exercise can help you focus on the review. It also exercises the memory connectors in your brain; plus it makes you think about the information without as much information, which forces a little more contemplation about the facts.

Appendix C also a PDF located on the book website, lists the completed tables to check yourself. You can also just refer to the tables as printed in the book.

Chapter-Ending Review Tools

Chapters 1 through 14 each have several features in the "Exam Preparation Tasks" and "Q&A" sections at the end of the chapter. You might have already worked through these in each chapter. It can also be useful to use these tools again as you make your final preparations for the exam.

Suggested Plan for Final Review/Study

This section lists a suggested study plan from the point at which you finish reading through Chapter 14 until you take the 210-250 SECFND exam. Certainly, you can ignore this plan, use it as is, or just take suggestions from it.

The plan uses five steps:

Step 1. **Review key topics and DIKTA questions:** You can use the table that lists the key topics in each chapter, or just flip through the pages looking for key topics. Also, reviewing the "Do I Know This Already" (DIKTA) questions from the beginning of the chapter can be helpful for review.

Step 2. **Complete memory tables:** Open Appendix B from the book's website and print the entire thing, or print the tables by major part. Then complete the tables.

Step 3. **Review the "Q&A" sections:** Go through the Q&A questions at the end of each chapter to identify areas where you need more study.

Step 4. **Use the Pearson Cert Practice Test engine to practice:** The Pearson Cert Practice Test engine on the book's companion website can be used to study using a bank of unique exam-realistic questions available only with this book.

Summary

The tools and suggestions listed in this chapter have been designed with one goal in mind: to help you develop the skills required to pass the 210-250 SECFND exam. This book has been developed from the beginning to not just tell you the facts but to also help you learn how to apply the facts. Regardless of your experience level leading up to when you take the exams, it is our hope that the broad range of preparation tools, and even the structure of the book, helps you pass the exam with ease. We hope you do well on the exam.

Answers to the "Do I Know This Already?" Quizzes and Q&A Questions

Answers to the "Do I Know This Already?" Quizzes

Chapter 1

1. A. The transport layer is concerned with end-to-end communication and provides multiplexing through the use of sockets.

2. C. CSMA/CD allows stations to detect a collision. When that occurs, each station waits a random time, called the backoff time, before retransmitting.

3. A. Hubs and repeaters simply regenerate the signal and transmit to all ports.

4. A. A MAC address table includes information about the MAC address and the port where the frame should be forwarded.

5. A and B. A wireless LAN controller provides station authentication, QoS, security management. and other management services.

6. A. The Identification field is used by the receiving host to recognize fragments belonging to the same original IP packet.

7. A. Address Resolution Protocol (ARP) is used to request a MAC address given a known IP address.

8. A. A DNS resolver sends recursive queries to the configured DNS server.

9. A. A /25 network has 7 bits reserved for host addressing. The number of hosts can be found as follows: $2^7 - 2 = 126$. Two addresses need to be removed because they are used for the network ID and broadcast address.

10. B. A /64 network allows 64 bits to be used for host addressing.

11. A. SLAAC is a protocol used to generate an IPv6 address.

12. A. TCP requires a connection to be established through a three-way handshake before transmitting data.

13. B. The TCP window is used for flow control.

Chapter 2

1. B, C, D. Firewalls, traditional and next-generation intrusion prevention systems (IPSs), and anomaly detection systems are network security devices that provide enforcement and network visibility.

2. A, C, E, F. ACEs can classify packets by inspecting Layer 2 protocol information such as EtherTypes; Layer 3 protocol information such as ICMP, TCP, or UDP; Layer 3 header information such as source and destination IP addresses; and Layer 4 header information such as source and destination TCP or UDP ports.

3. A, B. Application proxies, or proxy servers, are devices that operate as intermediary agents on behalf of clients that are on a private or protected network. Clients on the protected network send connection requests to the application proxy to transfer data to the unprotected network or the Internet.

4. C, D. Static NAT allows connections to be initiated bidirectionally, meaning both to the host and from the host. Also, NAT is often used by firewalls; however, other devices such as routers and wireless access points provide support for NAT.

5. B, D. Cisco ASA 5500-X and the Cisco Firepower 4100 Series are next-generation firewalls.

6. B, C, D, E, F. Cisco Cloud Email Security (CES), Cisco AMP Threat Grid, Cisco Threat Awareness Service (CTAS), OpenDNS, and CloudLock are examples of cloud-based security solutions.

7. A, C, D, E. The Cisco ISR routers, Cisco ASA, Cisco WSA, and Cisco AnyConnect have connectors for CWS.

8. B, C, D, E. There are different versions of NetFlow. Depending on the version of NetFlow, the router can also gather additional information, such as the type of service (ToS) byte, the differentiated services code point (DSCP), the device's input interface, TCP flags, byte counters, and start and end times.

9. C. One of the main differences between NetFlow and full-packet capture is the cost and the amount of data that needs to be analyzed. In a lot of scenarios and in most cases, you don't need heavyweight packet capture technology everywhere throughout your network if you have an appropriate NetFlow collection and analysis ecosystem.

10. B. Cisco CloudLock is designed to protect organizations of any type against data breaches in any cloud environment or application through a highly configurable cloud-based DLP architecture.

Chapter 3

1. C. One of the primary benefits of a defense-in-depth strategy is that even if a single control (such as a firewall or IPS) fails, other controls can still protect your environment and assets.

2. A, C, E, F. Understanding the management, control, user/data, and services planes is crucial for a defense-in-depth strategy.

3. C, D, E, F. SQL injection, command injection, XSS, and CSRF are all examples of vulnerabilities.

4. D. CVE is a standard for identifying vulnerabilities to make it easier to share data across tools, vulnerability repositories, and security services.

5. B. Threat intelligence's primary purpose is to inform business decisions regarding the risks and implications associated with threats.

6. C. Collaborative Research Into Threats (CRITs) is an open source feed for threat data. Learn more at https://crits.github.io.

7. C. CVSS is a standards-based scoring method that conveys vulnerability severity and helps determine the urgency and priority of response.

8. A, B, D. The following are a few examples of PII:

   - The individual's name
   - Social security number
   - Biological or personal characteristics, such as an image of distinguishing features, fingerprints, x-rays, voice signature, retina scan, and geometry of the face
   - Date and place of birth
   - Mother's maiden name
   - Credit card numbers
   - Bank account numbers
   - Driver's license number
   - Address information, such as email addresses or street addresses, and telephone numbers for businesses or personal use

9. B, C. The principle of least privilege states that all users—whether they are individual contributors, managers, directors, or executives—should be granted only the level of privilege they need to do their job, and no more. It also applies to programs or processes running on a system. These programs or processes should have the capabilities they need to "get their job done," but no root access to the system.

10. D. A runbook is a collection of procedures and operations performed by system administrators, security professionals, or network operators.

11. A, B, C. Chain of custody is the way you document and preserve evidence from the time you started the cyber forensics investigation to the time the evidence is presented at court. It is extremely important to be able to show clear documentation of the following:

   - How the evidence was collected
   - When it was collected
   - How it was transported
   - How is was tracked
   - How it was stored
   - Who had access to the evidence and how it was accessed

Chapter 4

1. B. A *subject* is the active entity that requests access to a resource.

2. B. Authentication is the process of proving one's identity.

3. A and C. Password and PIN code are examples of authentication by knowledge.

4. C. False rejection rate (FRR) refers to when the system rejects a valid user that should have been authenticated.

5. B. In military classification, the Secret label is usually associated with severe damage to the organization.

6. A. Encryption and storage media access controls are commonly used to protect data at rest.

7. A. The asset owner and senior management are ultimately responsible for the security of the assets.

8. A and B. Preventive and Deterrent access controls are controls used to prevent a breach.

9. B. Attribute-based access control (ABAC) uses subject, object, and environmental attributes to make an access decision.

10. A. MAC offers better security compared to DAC because the operating system ensures compliance with the organization's security policy.

11. A and B. Classification and category are typically found in a security label.

12. C. Role-based access control (RBAC) uses the role or function of a subject to make access decisions.

13. C. Host-based IDS can detect attacks using encryption, because it can see the decrypted payload on the host.

14. B. Host-based antimalware can detect attacks using encryption, because it can see the decrypted payload on the host.

15. D. A security group access list (SGACL) implements access control based on a security group tag (SGT) assigned to a packet. The SGT could be assigned, for example, based on the role of the user.

16. C. TACACS+ encrypts the TACACS+ message payload.

17. A. Cisco TrustSec uses MACSec to provide link-level encryption.

Chapter 5

1. C. Access rights are provided during the privileges provisioning phase.

2. B. System-generated passwords are created by the system by following the constraints embedded in the security policy.

3. B. An asynchronous token system uses a challenge-response mechanism.

4. A. An entity is uniquely identified by its distinguish name (DN).

5. A. The advantage of SSO is that the user authenticates once and he is granted access to organization resources.

6. B. One of the critical functions of an SIEM compared to a normal log collector is the log correlation capability.

7. A. An asset inventory results in a list of assets owned by the organization.

8. B, C, D. A cloud-based MDM provides more flexibility and scalability, and it is easier to maintain.

9. B. MDM solutions typically provide PIN lock enforcement capabilities.

10. A. A security baseline configuration is a configuration that has been formally reviewed and approved and cannot be changed without a formal request.

11. A. A standard change is a low-risk change that might not require the full change management process.

12. A. With a white box approach, all information about the systems is known prior to the start of the penetration assessment.

13. C. In a responsible disclosure approach, the information about how to exploit a vulnerability is not disclosed.

14. A, B, D. Verifying that the patch works correctly is done *after* the patch has been deployed.

Chapter 6

1. A, B, C. Common methods that ciphers use include substitution, polyalphabetic, and transposition.

2. A, B, D. AES, 3DES, and Blowfish are examples of symmetric block cipher algorithms. DSA and ElGamal are examples of asymmetric algorithms.

3. B, C, D. The three most popular types of hashes are Message Digest 5 (MD5), Secure Hash Algorithm 1 (SHA-1), and Secure Hash Algorithm 2 (SHA-2).

4. A and B. A digital signature provides three core benefits: authentication, data integrity, and nonrepudiation.

5. A and C. A key pair is a set of two keys that work in combination with each other as a team, and if you use the public key to encrypt data using an asymmetric encryption algorithm, the corresponding private key is used to decrypt the data.

6. A and D. Inside of a digital certificate is information about the identity of a device, such as its IP address, fully qualified domain name (FQDN), and the public key of that device or person.

7. C. A root certificate contains the public key of the CA server and the other details about the CA server.

8. B and C. PKCS #10 and PKCS #12 are public key standards you should become familiar with. They include protocols by themselves and protocols used for working with digital certificates. PKCS #10 defines the format of a certificate request sent to a CA that wants to receive its identity certificate. This type of request would include the public key for the entity desiring a certificate. PKCS #12 is a standard that defines the format for storing both public and private keys using a symmetric password-based key to "unlock" the data whenever the key needs to be used or accessed.

Chapter 7

1. B, D, E. MPLS, IPsec, SSL, PPTP, and GRE are examples of protocols used for VPN implementations.

2. A, B, E. L2TP, GRE, and MPLS VPNs do not provide data integrity, authentication, and data encryption.

A

3. C and D. VPN implementations are categorized into two general groups: Site-to-site VPNs, which enable organizations to establish VPN tunnels between two or more network infrastructure devices in different sites so that they can communicate over a shared medium such as the Internet, and remote-access VPNs, which enable users to work from remote locations such as their homes, hotels, and other premises as if they were directly connected to their corporate network.

4. B. The Cisco AnyConnect Secure Mobility Client is an example of a remote-access VPN client.

5. A, B, C, D. Encryption algorithms, hashing algorithms, Diffie-Hellman groups, the authentication method, and vendor-specific attributes are all exchanged in IKEv1 phase 1.

6. C and D. SHA and MD5 are hashing algorithms used in IPsec. AES 192 and AES 256 are not hashing algorithms; they are encryption algorithms.

7. A. Each SA is assigned a unique security parameter index (SPI) value—one by the initiator and the other by the responder.

8. B. In the clientless mode, the remote client needs only an SSL-enabled web browser to access resources on the private network of the security appliances.

9. B, C, D. Reverse proxy technology, port-forwarding technology and smart tunnels, and an SSL VPN tunnel client (such as the AnyConnect Secure Mobility Client) are some of the commonly used SSL VPN technologies.

Chapter 8

1. A. Although the other answers are somewhat correct, Answer A is the most specific and correct definition of process permissions as they relate to Windows.

2. A. Answer A is the best comparison of a heap and stack.

3. C. Answer C is the correct definition of the Windows registry.

4. B. Some of the functions of the Windows registry are to load device drivers, run start-up programs, set environmental variables, and store user settings and operating system parameters.

5. D. Answer D is the correct explanation of WMI.

6. C. Answer C is the best explanation of virtual address space in Windows.

7. A. Answer A is the correct explanation of a pointer and handle.

8. A. Answer A is a correct statement. Answer B is incorrect because programmers don't change handles. Answer C is incorrect because the OS provides handles. Answer D is incorrect because a pointer and handle are different things.

9. C. Windows services run in their own session and therefore can operate with or without a user logged in.

10. D. Answer D is the correct explanation of a log parser.

Chapter 9

1. B. An orphan process results when a parent process is terminated and the remaining child process is permitted to continue on its own.

2. D. A zombie process occurs when a process releases the associated memory and resources but remains in the entry table.

3. B. A fork occurs when a parent process creates a child process.

4. A. Answer A represents the file owner being given rwx permissions, the file owner rx permissions, and all others x permissions.

5. D. Answer D is correct. Best practice is to avoid giving daemons root or super user access because that level of access could be abused. Typically the init process is used to create daemons.

6. A. Symlinks can run even though the data they reference doesn't exist.

7. C. Answer C is the best answer in this case. There can be multiple daemon programs, making Answer D incorrect. Although a daemon can be a parent program, that isn't the best explanation, making answer B incorrect. Answer A is incorrect because daemons are not tasked to just manage a mother board.

8. D. Answer D represents err and every level above it.

9. D. Mail is an example of a facility.

10. C. NetFlow would be the best security technology for detecting a pivot attack.

Chapter 10

1. B. A Trojan horse is a type of malware that executes instructions determined by the nature of the Trojan to delete files, steal data, and compromise the integrity of the underlying operating system. Trojan horses typically use a form of social engineering to fool victims into installing such software on their computers or mobile devices.

2. A. Ransomware is a type of malware that compromises a system and then often demands a ransom from the victim to pay the attacker in order for the malicious activity to cease or for the malware to be removed from the affected system.

3. C and D. ClamAV and Immunet are free. The rest are commercial-based antivirus software.

4. B. Host-based firewalls are often referred to as "personal firewalls."

5. C. Cisco AMP for Endpoints is an example of a Cisco solution for endpoint protection. Cisco ASA is a network firewall, Cisco ESA is an email security appliance, and Firepower Endpoint System does not exist.

6. C. A graylist is a list of different objects that have not yet been established as not harmful or malicious. Once additional information is obtained, graylist items can be moved onto a whitelist or a blacklist.

   A whitelist is a list of separate things, such as hosts, applications, email addresses, and services, that are authorized to be installed or active on a system in accordance to a predetermined baseline. A blacklist is a list of different entities that have been determined to be malicious.

7. B, C, D. File path, filename, and file size are examples of application file and folder attributes that can help with application whitelisting.

8. A, B, D. Google Chromium sandboxing, JVM sandboxing, and the HTML5 "sandbox" attribute for use with iframes are all examples of sandboxing implementations.

Chapter 11

1. B. Syslog data is useless if it shows the wrong date and time. As a best practice, you should configure all network devices to use the Network Time Protocol (NTP). Using NTP ensures that the correct time is set and that all devices within the network are synchronized.

2. A, B, C, D, E. All of these logging capabilities are supported in Cisco ASA.

3. A, C, D. Splunk, Graylog, and ELK Stack are examples of commercial and open source log-collection and -analysis platforms.

4. B. Host-based firewalls are often referred to as "personal firewalls."

5. B and C. You can monitor events for traffic that does not conform with your access control policies. Access control policies allow you to specify, inspect, and log the traffic that can traverse your network. An access control policy determines how the system handles traffic on your network. To help you identify and mitigate the effects of malware, the FMC file control, network file trajectory, and Advanced Malware Protection (AMP) can detect, track, capture, analyze, log, and optionally block the transmission of files, including malware files and nested files inside archive files.

6. B and C. Next-generation firewalls and next-generation IPS systems via the FMC support an incident lifecycle, allowing you to change an incident's status as you progress through your response to an attack. When you close an incident, you can note any changes you have made to your security policies as a result of any lessons learned. Generally, an incident is defined as one or more intrusion events that you suspect are involved in a possible violation of your security policies. The FMC and next-generation firewalls and IPS systems are particularly well suited to supporting the investigation and qualification procedures of the incident response process. You can create your own event classifications and then apply them in a way that best describes the vulnerabilities on your network.

7. A. Full packet capture demands great system resources and engineering effort, not only to collect the data and store it, but also to be able to analyze it. That is why, in many cases, it is better to obtain network metadata by using NetFlow.

8. A, B, C. IP address or DNS hostname, application logs, and processes running on the system are some useful attributes you should seek to collect from endpoint systems.

9. A and D. Antivirus or antimalware applications and personal firewalls produce good security telemetry on endpoints.

10. A, B, D. The Cisco ISE Administrator Logins report provides an audit trail of all administrator logins. The web server log reports and top application reports provide additional contextual information that you can collect from Cisco ISE to help you investigate security incidents.

Chapter 12

1. B. Privacy is one of the main benefits of encryption. The rest of the answers are either not valid or not a benefit.

2. C. Encryption can be used by threat actors as a method of evasion and obfuscation, and security monitoring tools might not be able to inspect encrypted traffic.

3. B. A few security products, such as the Cisco Lancope Stealthwatch system, provide features such as NAT stitching to use NetFlow with other data in the network and be able to correlate and "map" translated IP addresses. This accelerates incident response tasks and eases continuous security monitoring operations.

4. C. NTP is recommended as a best practice to synchronize the "clock" (date and time) of all network infrastructure devices, servers, and other endpoints.

5. B. DNS was not created for tunneling, but a few tools have used it to encapsulate data in the payload of DNS packets. Threat actors have been using many different untraditional techniques to steal data from corporate networks without being detected. For example, they have been sending stolen credit card data, intellectual property, and confidential documents over DNS using tunneling.

6. A, B, C. DeNiSe, dns2tcp, and DNScapy are examples of DNS tunneling tools. They were originally not created for malicious purposes, but they have been used by attackers to steal data from victims for years.

7. D. Tor is a free tool that enables its users to surf the Web anonymously. Tor has been used by nonmalicious users to keep their activity private, but also by malicious threat actors to carry out their attacks and perform other illicit activities.

8. B. A Tor exit node is basically the last Tor node or the "gateway" where the Tor encrypted traffic "exits" to the Internet. A Tor exit node can be targeted to monitor Tor traffic. Many organizations block Tor exit nodes in their environment. The Tor project has a dynamic list of Tor exit nodes that make this task a bit easier. This Tor exit node list can be downloaded from https://check.torproject.org/exit-addresses.

9. A. Attackers can insert or "inject" a SQL query via the input data from the client to the application or database. Attackers can exploit SQL injector vulnerabilities to read sensitive data from the database, modify or delete database data, execute administration operations on the database, and even issue commands to the operating system.

10. A, C, D. LionShare, Napster, and Peercoin are examples of P2P tools. P2P NetFlow does not exist.

Chapter 13

1. B, C, D. Nexpose, Nessus, and nmap are all vulnerability and port scanners.

2. C. Because UDP is a connectionless protocol and does not have a three-way handshake like TCP, the UDP scans have to rely on ICMP "port unreachable" messages to determine whether a port is open. When the scanner sends a UDP packet and the port is not open on the victim's system, that system will respond with an ICMP "port unreachable" message.

3. D. In phishing attacks, the attacker presents a link that looks like a valid, trusted resource to a user. When the user clicks it, he is prompted to disclose confidential information such as his username and password.

4. C. A backdoor is an application or code used by an attacker either to allow future access or to collect information to use in further attacks.

5. B. An amplification attack is a form of reflected attack in which the response traffic (sent by the unwitting participant) is made up of packets that are much larger than those that were initially sent by the attacker (spoofing the victim).

6. D. A buffer overflow is when a program or software puts more data in a buffer than it can hold or when a program tries to put data in a memory location past a buffer. This is done so that data outside the bounds of a block of allocated memory can corrupt other data or crash the program or operating system. In a worst-case scenario, a buffer overflow can lead to the execution of malicious code.

7. A. XSS is a type of web application vulnerability where malicious scripts are injected into legitimate and trusted websites. An attacker can launch an attack against an XSS vulnerability using a web application to send malicious code (typically in the form of a browser-side script) to a different end user.

8. A. Attackers can insert or "inject" a SQL query via the input data from the client to the application or database. Attackers can exploit SQL injection vulnerabilities to read sensitive data from the database, modify or delete database data, execute administration operations on the database, and even issue commands to the operating system.

Chapter 14

1. D. This example represents adjusting the timing of traffic, which is a timing attack.

2. B. Encryption would be the biggest challenge because traffic cannot be evaluated by the IPS for threats.

3. A. Resource exhaustion is when the attacker sends a ton of traffic with the goal of consuming available resources. This could generate a bunch of alarms and render the system useless.

4. A. Modifying routing would not cause a traffic fragmentation error on a security detection device.

5. D. Proxies and inline security devices can help prevent traffic fragmentation attacks. Protocols can be manipulated to confuse security devices from properly evaluating traffic. TCP Checksum and Time-to-Live protocols can be manipulated to first look like one thing and then later look like something else, with the goal of tricking the security defenses.

6. C. Answer C is correct because this does not modify the legitimate traffic and act over HTTP. Answer A is incorrect because this doesn't work over HTTPS. Answer B is incorrect because this attack doesn't modify the legitimate traffic. Answer D doesn't provide enough detail.

7. C. Answer C is the best answer. Answers A and D do not include a payload, meaning there isn't an associated attack. Answer B is incorrect because if the same payload is used, it will be detected by most security solutions. Answer C would be formatted to bypass detection but not modify the attacker payload.

8. B. Using Unicode instead of ASCII can cause a traffic substitution and insertion attack.

9. A. Content filtering is a method for controlling what type of content is available to users. This is not a method of preventing a pivot attack. Answer B is a way to harden systems to avoid lateral movement through system exploitation. Answers C and D both represent methods to control what can access other systems on the network and lateral movement.

10. C. NetFlow can be used to detect unusual network patterns such as internal pivoting. Answer A is an encryption technology that can be used once a pivot has occurred. Answer B is typically a signature-based security solution that can prevent a host from exploiting another host, but this is not the best answer. Answer D could help but is typically used for controlling what traffic can and can't pass. Answer D, in its current state, is too vague, but it would be a good defense using segmentation. However, this doesn't necessarily mean it is the best solution for pivot detection.

Answers to the Q&A Questions

Chapter 1

1. B. A router mainly operates at the Network layer.

2. A and B. In full-duplex mode, a station can transmit and receive at the same time. This prevents collisions form happening.

3. D. Because no Layer 3 device is involved, there is only one broadcast domain.

4. A. A trunk link is used to transport multiple VLANs.

5. A. Multilayer switch includes Layer 3 functionality.

6. C. CAPWAP is used between a LAP and the WLC.

7. A and B. LAP includes real-time functionalities such as channel encryption and the TX/RX of frames.

8. A and B. Class B allows $2^{16} - 2$ host addresses. C is incorrect because it allows a maximum of 254 usable addresses.

9. D. A /29 network can have six hosts, whereas /30 can have only two.

10. C. OSPF is a routing protocol of the type link state.

11. A. Because OSPF nodes have a full view of the topology, the problem of count to infinity is avoided.

12. A and C. These are the correct alternative ways that the IPv6 address can be written.

13. C. NDP uses NA/NS messages to provide functionality similar to ARP.

14. A. 2345:0:0:0:0500.11FF.FE11.2222 is the correct answer.

15. A. Iterative queries are used between DNS servers.

16. B. A TCP client will start a connection by sending a TCP SYN packet.

17. A, B, C. A network socket includes a protocol, IP address, and port.

Chapter 2

1. B. ACLs are the heart of a traditional stateful firewall, and they are based on source and destination IP addresses, source and destination ports, and protocol information.

2. C. A traditional IPS is a network security appliance or software technology that inspects network traffic to detect and prevent security threats and exploits.

3. B. NetFlow provides information about network flows and sessions.

4. B. DLP stands for *data loss prevention* and is a software or cloud solution for making sure that corporate users do not send sensitive or critical information outside the corporate network.

5. C and D. ACLs inspect and apply policies based on source and destination IP addresses as well as source and destination ports and protocol information.

6. B and C. OpenDNS and CloudLock are Cisco cloud security solutions.

7. D. Cisco pxGrid is used to enable the sharing of contextual-based information from a Cisco ISE session directory to other policy network systems, such as Cisco IOS devices and the Cisco ASA.

8. A. Heuristic-based algorithms may require fine tuning to adapt to network traffic and minimize the possibility of false positives.

9. C. DMZs provide security to the systems that reside within them, with different security levels and policies between them. DMZs can have several purposes; for example, they can serve as segments on which a web server farm resides or as extranet connections to business partners.

10. C. Full packet captures take more storage resources in comparison to NetFlow, syslog, and other network logs.

Chapter 3

1. B and C. A vulnerability is an exploitable weakness in a system or its design. Vulnerabilities can be found in protocols, operating systems, applications, hardware, and system designs. An exploit is software or a sequence of commands that takes advantage of a vulnerability in order to cause harm to a system or network.

2. A. Exploit kits can be uploaded and can run from web servers in order to spread malware and compromise other systems.

3. A and C. Angler and Blackhole are examples of exploit kits.

4. C. A threat is any potential danger to an asset.

5. A. IoC stands for indicator of compromise.

6. A and B. Threat intelligence feeds typically include information such as indicators of compromise, known malicious domains, IP addresses of attacking systems, and other types of information.

7. D. Chain of custody is the way you document and preserve evidence from the time you start the cyber forensics investigation to the time the evidence is presented in court.

8. A. Decompilers are programs that take an executable binary file and attempt to produce readable high-level language code from it.

9. D. Mean time to repair (MTTR), mean time between failures (MTBF), and mean time to discover a security incident are all examples of metrics that can measure the effectiveness of a runbook.

10. B. PHI stands for protected health information.

Chapter 4

1. C. In the authorization phase, access is granted to a resource.

2. A, B, C. Uniqueness, nondescriptiveness, and secured issuance are characteristics of a secure identity.

3. D. Strong authentication is obtained by the combination of at least two methods.

4. A. The asset owner assigns the classification.

5. A. Clearing ensures protection against simple and noninvasive data-recovery techniques.

6. A. Security training is a type of administrative control.

7. A. Dropping a packet prevents a security incident from occurring.

8. C. A fence is an example of physical deterrent control.

9. A. A capability table is user centric and includes several objects with user access rights.

10. B. The RADIUS exchange happens between the NAS and the authentication server.

11. C. Diameter allows for the exchange of nodes' capabilities.

12. C. 802.1x allows authorization policy to be downloaded and enforced at the access device.

13. B. EAPoL messages are transmitted between the supplicant and the authenticator.

14. B. SXP can be used to exchange SGT between an access device with only Cisco TrustSec capability on software and a device with Cisco TrustSec hardware support.

15. D. An isolated port can only communicate with the promiscuous port.

16. A. An IPS may add latency due to its packet-processing engine.

17. A. Network-based antimalware can block malware before it enters the network. Answers C and D are true for host-based antimalware as well. Answer B applies only to host-based antimalware.

18. A. Location is part of the environmental attributes.

19. B. MAC uses security labels for access decisions.

20. B. Strict control over the access to resources is one of the main advantages of MAC.

21. A. In a DAC model, the object owner grants authorization permission over the objects he owns.

Chapter 5

1. A and B. A secure digital identity should be a unique and nondescriptive security issuance.

2. A. A periodic privileges review is needed to make sure each user has the correct level of privileges after any event that could require the assignment of different privileges.

3. A, B, D. Access can be revoked due to job termination, change of the job, or a violation of security policy.

4. B and C. Asset classification and Asset disposal are responsibilities of the asset owner.

5. A. Answer A is correct in this case.

6. C is the most correct answer.

7. A. Configuration records are stored in a configuration management database (CMDB).

8. D. Active vulnerability scanners probes the target system.

9. C. Agent based deployment model gives automatic patch installation capabilities.

10. A. The syslog PRI is obtained by multiplying the facility code by 8 and adding the severity code.

11. D. Log normalization extracts relevant attributes from logs received in different formats and stores them in a common data model or template.

12. A, B, C. SIEM provides correlation, archiving, normalization, aggregation, and reporting for logs.

13. A and B. Cisco ISE and an MDM server are typically found in a Cisco BYOD architecture.

14. A. After the RFC is closed, the configuration database is updated with the new configuration.

15. B and D. Vulnerability scanners usually work with known vulnerabilities and can work in passive and active modes.

16. A. An OVAL definition is an XML file that contains information about how to check a system for the presence of vulnerabilities.

Chapter 6

1. C. The files chicken.txt and cat.txt have the same SHA checksum; subsequently, they have the same contents.

2. D. A collision attack is an attempt to find two input strings of a hash function that produce the same hash result. This is because hash functions have an infinite input length and a predefined output length.

3. B. SHA-2 is more secure than SHA-1 and MD5.

4. B. Root CAs can delegate their authority to subordinate CAs.

5. C. A CRL is a list of certificates, based on their serial numbers, that had initially been issued by a CA but have since been revoked and as a result should not be trusted. A CRL could be very large, and the client would have to process the entire list to verify a particular certificate is not on the list. A CRL can be thought of as the naughty list, and is the primary protocol used for this purpose.

6. A. PKCS #12 is a format for storing both public and private keys using a symmetric password-based key to "unlock" the data whenever the key needs to be used or accessed.

7. C. PKCS #10 is a format of a certificate request sent to a CA that wants to receive its identity certificate.

8. A and B. AES and IDEA are both examples of symmetric encryption algorithms.

9. C and D. Diffie-Hellman and RSA are both examples of asymmetric encryption algorithms.

10. A and C. SHA and MD5 are both examples of hashing algorithms.

Chapter 7

1. B. ESP packets cannot be successfully translated (NATed) because ESP does not have any ports.

2. C. IPsec transport mode protects upper-layer protocols, such as UDP and TCP, and tunnel mode protects the entire IP packet.

3. A. Diffie-Hellman is a key agreement protocol and it enables users or devices to authenticate each other using preshared keys without actually sending the keys over the unsecured medium.

4. A. SSL is not supported for Cisco site-to-site VPN tunnels.

5. C. IKEv1 has a simple exchange of two message pairs for the CHILD_SA. IKEv2 uses an exchange of at least three message pairs for Phase 2.

6. D. AES is more secure than DES and 3DES. 4DES does not exist.

7. C. NAT Traversal is an IPsec feature and specification.

8. B. The Tor browser is used by individuals to keep themselves anonymous on the Internet and it is also used to browse the dark web.

9. B, C, D. Attackers use VPN to exfiltrate data, encrypt traffic between a compromised host and a command and control system, and to evade detection.

10. B and D. MD5 and SHA are hashing algorithms. RSA and AES are encryption algorithms.

Chapter 8

1. A. Answer A is the best definition of a Windows process. Answer B describes a thread, Answer C describes a thread pool, and Answer D describes a fiber.

2. B. Answer B is the only correct statement. Virtual address space is not shared unless it is specified. It is a reference to the physical location and not the actual physical location of an object in memory.

3. C. RAM is an example of volatile memory.

4. C. The command **regedit** is used to view the Windows Registry.

5. A. HKEY_LOCAL (HKLM) is not a Windows Registry hive.

6. B. Windows Management Instrumentation is the correct name.

7. C. WMI can't be used to uninstall an application.

8. C. A handle that's not released after being used is an example of how a handle leak could occur.

9. B. The correct command is **services.msc**.

10. D. The Log Parser is a common Windows tool that can be used to adjust logs for this purpose.

Chapter 9

1. C. Daemons are not controlled by the active user.

2. A. ErrorLog is the correct file that Apache sends error data to.

3. C. Remember that rwx stands for read, write, and execution, and the order is owner, group, and everybody else.

4. D. Soft link is another name for a symlink.

5. A. Transaction logs is the best answer. If an error occurred, then an alert log would be generated.

6. D. Init has a PID of 1. Note that init is not a daemon. This will be important for the exam.

7. D. The correct format is owner, group, everybody else.

8. C. The correct command is **chown**.

9. B. Answer B is correct. Answer A is typically how daemons are created; however, sometimes they are not created by the init process. Usually init creates daemons.

10. A. The default location is /var/log.

Chapter 10

1. B. Worms are viruses that replicate themselves over the network, infecting numerous vulnerable systems.

2. A. Ramsomware is a type of malware that compromises a system and then often demands a ransom from the victim to pay the attacker in order for the malicious activity to cease or for the malware to be removed from the affected system.

3. B and C. Google Chromium sandboxing and Java JVM sandboxing are examples of system-based sandboxing implementations.

4. B and C. Answers B and C are both benefits of system-based sandboxing.

5. D. A limitation of whitelisting is the need to continuously manage what is and is not on the whitelist. It is extremely difficult to keep a list of what is and is not allowed on a system where there are hundreds of thousands of files with a legitimate need to be present and running on the system.

6. C. Cisco AMP for Endpoints takes advantage of telemetry from big data, continuous analysis, and advanced analytics provided by Cisco threat intelligence in order to detect, analyze, and stop advanced malware across endpoints.

7. C. Pretty Good Privacy (PGP) is an example of a host-based encryption technology that can help protect files as well as email.

8. A. An application blacklist is a list of different entities that have been determined to be malicious.

9. D. BitLocker is software for encrypting files on a hard disk drive.

10. B, C, D. Answers B, C, and D represent actions you should take to ensure your emails are protected.

Chapter 11

1. B and C. Wireshark and tcpdump are examples of open source packet capture software.

2. A. Hadoop is a big data analytics technology that's used by several frameworks in security operation centers and many scenarios.

3. D. Router syslogs are not a host-based telemetry source. Router syslogs are a network-based telemetry source.

4. C. Encryption can cause problems in an SOC because you cannot see the actual payload of the packet.

5. B. Cisco Prime Infrastructure is a network management platform you can use to configure and monitor many network infrastructure devices in your network. It provides network administrators with a single solution for provisioning, monitoring, optimizing, and troubleshooting both wired and wireless devices.

6. B. Linux-based systems store most of their logs (including syslog) in /var/log.

7. D. NBAR2 is used by Cisco AVC to provide deep packet inspection.

8. A. QoS can be used with NBAR2 to help ensure that the network bandwidth is best used.

9. C. Cisco NetFlow records are usually exported using UDP packets.

10. D. IPFIX is not a NetFlow version, it is a flow based standard based on NetFlow version 9.

Chapter 12

1. A. The Onion Router (Tor) is both free and enables its users to surf the Web anonymously.

2. C. Answer C correctly states the challenge NAT presents to security monitoring.

3. B. A Tor exit node is the last Tor node or the "gateway" where the Tor encrypted traffic "exits" to the Internet.

4. C. DNScapy is an example of a DNS tunneling tool.

5. D. Base64 encoding is an example of an encoding mechanism used by threat actors.

6. A. The Network Time Protocol (NTP) ensures that the correct time is set and that all devices within the network are synchronized.

Chapter 13

1. C. In a rainbow table, an attacker computes possible passwords and their hashes in a given system and puts the results into a lookup table.

2. A. War driving is a technique used by attackers to find wireless access points and wireless routers wherever they may be.

3. B. XSS is one of the most common types of web application vulnerabilities where the attacker uses malicious scripts and injects them into legitimate and trusted websites.

4. A. SQL injection vulnerabilities are used by attackers to read sensitive data from the database, modify or delete database data, execute administration operations on the database, and even issue commands to the operating system.

5. B. A man-in-the-middle attack results when attackers place themselves in line between two devices that are communicating, with the intent of performing reconnaissance or manipulating the data as it moves between the devices.

6. A. Deserialization of untrusted data vulnerabilities is used by attackers to use or cause malformed data or unexpected data to abuse an application's logic, cause a DoS attack, or execute arbitrary code.

7. D. A buffer overflow is when a program or software puts more data in a buffer than it can hold or when a program tries to put data in a memory location past a buffer.

8. B. In an evil twin attack the attacker tries to create rogue access points so as to gain access to the network or steal information.

9. B. ARP cache poisoning is an attack where threat actors can attack hosts, switches, and routers connected to your Layer 2 network by poisoning the ARP caches of systems connected to the subnet and by intercepting traffic intended for other hosts on the subnet.

10. D. Dynamic ARP inspection is a feature in Cisco switches that validates ARP packets and intercepts, logs, and discards ARP packets with invalid IP-to-MAC address bindings.

Chapter 14

1. D. Answer D is the best answer. Answer A doesn't have enough information. Answer B is incorrect in that a client isn't required. Answer C is correct, but it's not the only use for SSH.

2. C. A remote-access VPN can be client or clientless, thus making Answer C correct.

3. A. Consuming resources typically slows down or prevents a system from operating properly. This usually doesn't corrupt the actual application, just its ability to function due to low available resources.

4. A. Encrypting traffic hides the traffic from the IPS rather than confusing it, which is the tactic used in the other answers.

5. D. Answer D is the correct explanation of an overlapping fragment attack.

6. C. Answer C is the correct explanation of a timing attack.

7. C. Answer C is an example of a traffic substitution and insertion attack. Answers A and D are input validation attacks. Answer B is a coding practice.

8. B. Answer B is a method of establishing a foothold on a network. However, this does not provide new access to the network, meaning the attacker isn't pivoting to another network resource.

9. D. Segmentation is the best approach listed for reducing the risk of a compromised system to be able to attack another system with higher, trusted network access.

10. C. SSH uses public-key encryption.

A

A

access control   Access control is the process of granting, preventing, or revoking access to an object.

access point   A wireless access point provides connectivity between the distribution network and the wireless client.

accounting   Accounting is the process of auditing and monitoring user operations on a resource.

ACL   Stateful and traditional firewalls can analyze packets and judge them against a set of predetermined rules called access control lists (ACLs). They inspect the following elements within a packet: source address, destination address, source port, destination port, and protocol. ACLs are typically configured in firewalls, but they also can be configured in network infrastructure devices such as routers, switches, wireless access controllers (WLCs), and others.

action   The result from a selector triggering on a match.

alert log   Records errors such as a startup, shutdown, space errors, and so on.

AMP   Advanced malware protection—a Cisco solution for detecting and mitigating malware in the corporate network.

antivirus and antimalware   The terms *antivirus* and *antimalware* are generally used interchangeability to indicate software that can be used to detect and prevent the installation of computer malware and in some cases quarantine affected computers or eradicate the malware and restore the operation of the system.

asset   Anything that has value for the organization. In simple terms an asset can be any organization resource, including personnel, hardware, software, building, and data.

asset classification   In information security, refers to the process of classifying an asset or data based on the potential damage a breach to the confidentiality, integrity, or availability of that data could cause.

asset handling   In information security, refers to procedures and technologies that allow the secure storage, use, and transfer of an asset.

asset inventory   The collection and storage of information about assets, such as, location, security classification, and owner.

asset management   In information security, refers to policies, processes, and technologies to manage and protect organization assets during their lifecycle.

asset ownership   The process of assigning an owner to an asset. Each asset within the organization needs an owner. The owner is responsible for the security of the asset during its lifecycle.

asymmetric algorithms   Encryption algorithms that use two different keys: a public key and a private key. Together they make a key pair.

attribute-based access control   ABAC is an access control model where the access decision is based on the attributes or characteristics of the subject, object, and environment.

authentication   The process of proving the identity of an entity.

authorization   The process of providing access to a resource with specific access rights.

autonomous access point   Access points that implement both real-time and management functions. These are autonomous and thus work in a standalone mode. Each AP needs to be configured singularly.

B

backdoor   A piece of malware or configuration change that allows an attacker to control the victim's system remotely. For example, a backdoor can open a network port on the affected system so that the attacker can connect and control the system. A backdoor application can be installed by the attacker either to allow future access or to collect information to use in further attacks.

block cipher   A symmetric key cipher that operates on a group of bits called a block. A block cipher encryption algorithm may take a 64-bit block of plaintext and generate a 64-bit block of ciphertext. With this type of encryption, the same key is used to encrypt and decrypt.

botnet   A collection of compromised machines that the attacker can manipulate from a command and control (CnC) system to participate in a DDoS, send spam emails, or perform other illicit activities.

buffer overflow   Occurs when a program or software puts more data in a buffer than it can hold or when a program tries to put data in a memory location past a buffer. This is done so that data outside the bounds of a block of allocated memory can corrupt other data or crash the program or operating system. In a worst-case scenario, this can lead to the execution of malicious code. There is a wide variety of ways buffer overflows can occur and, unfortunately, there are many error-prone techniques often used to prevent them.

C

certificate authority   A system that generates and issues digital certificates to users and systems.

change   Any modification, addition, or removal of an organizational resource, for example, of a configuration item. A common categorization includes Standard, Emergency and Normal change.

change management   Change management is concerned with all policies, processes, and technologies that handle a change on an asset lifecycle.

child process   A process created by some other process during runtime.

Classless Inter Domain Routing (CIDR)   IP address assignment that uses prefix notation to determine the network prefix. This allows for more flexible IP address allocation compared to a classless schema.

clientless VPN   Provides remote access services without requiring a host client. Typically this is based on providing access to a secure network segment also known as a "sandbox."

collision domain   A network link or section that is shared between the transmitting and receiving stations. When multiple stations transmit information at the same time, a collision occurs due to the overlapping signal over the transport mechanism (example radio frequencies or wire). A typical example of a collision domain is a shared Ethernet bus.

Common Vulnerabilities and Exposures (CVE)   A dictionary of vulnerabilities and exposures in products and systems maintained by MITRE. A CVE-ID is the industry standard method to identify vulnerabilities.

Common Vulnerability Scoring System (CVSS)   An industry standard used to convey information about the severity of vulnerabilities.

Configuration Item (CI)   An identifiable part of the system that is the target of the configuration control process.

configuration management   A process concerned with all policies, processes, and technologies used to maintain the integrity of the configuration of a given asset.

configuration management database   A database that stores configuration items and configuration records.

Configuration Record   A collection of attributes and relationship of a configuration item.

connectionless communication   A type of communication that does not require a communication channel to be established before data is transmitted or an acknowledgement is sent from the receiving station. UDP is an example of a protocol using connectionless communication.

connection-oriented communication   A type of communication that requires a communication channel to be established before data is transmitted. TCP is an example of a connection-oriented protocol.

CSRF Cross-site request forgery is a vulnerability that forces an end user to execute malicious steps on a web application. This is typically done after the user is authenticated to the application. CSRF attacks generally target state-changing requests, and the attacker cannot steal data because he or she has no way to see the response to the forged request. CSRF attacks are generally combined with social engineering when carried out.

D

daemon A process that runs in the background.

Diffie-Hellman A key agreement protocol that enables two users or devices to authenticate each other's preshared keys without actually sending the keys over the unsecured medium.

digital certificate A digital entity used to verify that a user is who he or she claims to be, and to provide the receiver with the means to encode a reply. Digital certificates also apply to systems, not just individuals.

directory Repository used by an organization to store information about users, systems, networks, etc. Information stored in directories can be used with the purpose of identifying and authenticating users, as well to apply security policies and authorization.

Directory Service Directory Services use directories to provide an organization with a way to manage identity, authentication, and authorization services.

discretionary access control DAC is an access control model where the access decision and permission are decided by the object owner.

DLP Data loss prevention is a software or cloud solution for making sure that corporate users do not send sensitive or critical information outside the corporate network.

DNS tunneling Attackers can encapsulate chucks of data into DNS packets to steal sensitive information such as PII information, credit card numbers, and much more.

Domain Name System Includes an architecture and protocol that enable several functions. The most important function is the resolution of IP addresses provided a fully qualified domain name (FQDN).

downloader A piece of malware that downloads and installs other malicious content from the Internet to perform additional exploitation on an affected system.

Dynamic Host Configuration Protocol (DHCP) A protocol used to assign IP addresses dynamically to devices.

dynamic MAC address learning A mechanism that helps populate the MAC address table. When a switch receives an Ethernet frame on a port, it notes the source MAC address and inserts an entry in the MAC address table, marking that MAC address as reachable from that port.

dynamic memory allocation A program that allocates memory at runtime.

E

Enterprise Mobile Management (EMM)   Includes policies, processes and technologies to allow the secure management of mobile devices. Technologies that enable BYOD, Mobile Device Management (MDM), and Mobile Applications Management (MAM) are examples of areas covered by an organization EMM.

Ethernet   Ethernet is a protocol used to provide transmission and services for physical and data link layers, and it is described in the IEEE 802.3 standards collection. Ethernet is part of the larger IEEE 802 standards for LAN communication. Another example of IEEE 802 standards is 802.11, which covers wireless LANs.

Ethernet broadcast domain   A broadcast domain is formed by all devices connected to the same LAN switches. Broadcast domains are separated by network layer devices such as routers. An Ethernet broadcast domain is sometimes also called a subnet.

exploit   A malicious program designed to "exploit" or take advantage of a single vulnerability or set of vulnerabilities. An exploit can be software or a sequence of commands that takes advantage of a vulnerability in order to cause harm to a system or network.

F

facility   The application or process that submits the log message.

Federated SSO   A further evolution of a single sign-on (SSO) model within one organization is a model where a user could authenticate once and then has access to resources across multiple organizations, which are not managed under the same IAM system.

fiber   A unit of execution that is manually scheduled by an application.

file permissions   Used to assign access rights for the owner of the file, members of the group of related users, and everybody else.

fork   A command that creates child processes.

full duplex   In full duplex mode, two devices can transmit simultaneously because there is a dedicated channel allocated for the transmission. Because of that, there is no need to detect collisions or to wait before transmitting. Full duplex is called "collision free" because collisions cannot happen.

G

group   A set of permissions for one or more users grouped together.

H

half duplex   In half duplex mode, two Ethernet devices share a common transmission medium. The access is controlled by implementing Carrier Sense Multiple Access with Collision Detection (CSMA/CD). With CSMA/CD, a device has the ability to detect whether there is a transmission occurring over the shared medium.

handle   An abstract reference value to a resource.

hashing algorithm   An algorithm used to verify data integrity.

heap   Memory set aside for dynamic allocation, meaning where you put data on the fly.

HeapAlloc   Allocates any size of memory that is requested, meaning it allocates by default

hives   Hierarchal folders within the Windows registry.

host-based intrusion prevention system   An HIPS is a specialized software that interacts with the host operating system to provide access control and threat protection. In most cases, it also includes network detection and protection capabilities on the host network interface cards. If there is no prevention capabilities but the system can only detect threats, it is referred to as a host-based intrusion detection system (HIDS).

I

identification   The process of providing identity to the access control policy enforcer.

Identity and Access Management (IAM)   A collection of policies, processes, and technology to manage identity, authentication, and authorization to organization resources.

init process   The first process during the boot sequence.

IKE   IPsec uses the Internet Key Exchange (IKE) protocol to negotiate and establish secured site-to-site or remote-access VPN tunnels. IKE is a framework provided by the Internet Security Association and Key Management Protocol (ISAKMP) and parts of two other key management protocols—namely, Oakley and Secure Key Exchange Mechanism (SKEME).

IKEv1 vs. IKEv2   IKEv1 Phase 1 has two possible exchanges: main mode and aggressive mode. There is a single exchange of a message pair for IKEv2 IKE_SA. IKEv2 has a simple exchange of two message pairs for the CHILD_SA. IKEv1 uses an exchange of at least three message pairs for Phase 2.

information or data owner   The person who maintains ownership and responsibility over a specific piece or subset of data. Part of the responsibility of this role is to determine the appropriate classification of the information, ensure that the information is protected with controls, to periodically review classification and access rights, and to understand the risk associated to the information he or she owns. Together with senior management, the information or data owner holds the responsibility for the security on the asset.

Internet protocol   The most used Layer 3 protocol. It comes in two versions: IPv4 and IPv6.

IP address   A 32-bit (IPv4) or 128-bit (IPv6) identifier used to allow two devices to communicate at Layer 3 using IP.

IP address resolution   Defines the methods for a host to find the Ethernet MAC address provided for an IP address. For IPv4, this is done using ARP. IPv6 uses NDP instead.

IPS   An intrusion prevention system is a network security appliance or software technology that inspects network traffic to detect and prevent security threats and exploits.

ITU-T X.500   A collection of standards including information on directories organization and protocols to access the information within the directories.

J

job object   Processes grouped together to be managed as a unit.

K

key logger   A piece of malware that captures the user's keystrokes on a compromised computer or mobile device. It collects sensitive information such as passwords, PINs, personal identifiable information (PII), credit card numbers, and more.

L

LAN bridge   Unlike a LAN hub, which just regenerates a signal, a LAN bridge typically implements some frame-forwarding decision based on whether or not a frame needs to reach a device on the other side of the bridge.

LAN hub   The role of the LAN hub or repeater is uniquely to regenerate a signal and transmit it to all its ports. This type of topology is a typical half duplex transmission mode and, as in the case of an Ethernet bus, defines a single collision domain.

LAN switch   A device that allows multiple stations to connect in full duplex mode. This creates a separate collision domain for each of the ports, so collisions cannot happen.

LDAP   Lightweight Directory Access Protocol is based on X.500 and maintains the same directory structure and definition. It simplifies the directory queries and it has been designed to work with the TCP/IP stack.

lightweight access point   A LAP is an access point that implements only the real-time functions and works together with a management device called a wireless LAN controller (WLC), which provides the management functions. The communication between LAPs and the WLC is done using the control and provision of wireless access point (CAPWAP).

local area network   LAN describes a collection of devices, protocols, and technologies that are operating and located nearby each other. It can be wired if cables are used to connect devices or wireless if the communication occurs over radio waves.

log parser   A versatile tool that provides universal query access to text-based data.

logic bomb   A type of malicious code that is injected into a legitimate application. An attacker can program a logic bomb to delete itself from the disk after it performs the malicious tasks on the system. Examples of these malicious tasks include deleting or corrupting files or databases and executing a specific instruction after certain system conditions are met.

logs collection   The process of collecting and organizing logs for analysis. A log collector is a software which is able to receive logs from multiple sources and in some cases offers storage capabilities and logs analysis functionality.

M

MAC address   To transmit a frame, Ethernet uses source and destination addresses. The Ethernet addresses are called MAC addresses, or Extended Unique Identifiers (EUI) in the new terminology, and they are either 48 bits (MAC-48 or EUI-48) or 64 bits (MAC-64 or EUI-64) if we consider all MAC addresses for the larger IEEE 802 standard.

MAC address table   A table that keeps the link between a MAC address and the physical port of the switch where frames for that MAC address should be forwarded.

mailer and mass-mailer worm   A type of worm that sends itself in an email message. Examples of mass-mailer worms are Loveletter.A@mm and W32/SKA.A@m (a.k.a. the Happy99 worm), which sends a copy of itself every time the user sends a new message.

Malloc   A standard C and C++ library function that allocates memory to a process using the C runtime heap.

mandatory access control   MAC is an access control model where the access decision is enforced by the access policy enforcer (for example, the operating system). MAC uses security labels.

Microsoft Windows service   A long-running executable application that operates in its own Windows session.

Mobile Device Management (MDM)   MDM manages the deployment, operations, and monitoring of mobile devices used to access organization resources. It is used to enforce organizational security policy on mobile devices.

multilayer switch   A switch that integrates Layer 3 functionality.

N

NetFlow   NetFlow is a Cisco technology that provides comprehensive visibility into all network traffic that traverses a Cisco-supported device. NetFlow is used as a network security tool because its reporting capabilities provide nonrepudiation, anomaly detection, and investigative capabilities. As network traffic traverses a NetFlow-enabled device, the device collects traffic flow information and provides a network administrator or security professional with detailed information about such flows.

NetFlow provides detailed network telemetry that can be used to see what is actually happening across the entire network. You can use NetFlow to identify DoS attacks, quickly identify compromised endpoints and network infrastructure devices, and monitor network usage of employees, contractors, and partners. NetFlow is also often used to obtain network telemetry during security incident response and forensics.

network address translation   NAT is often used by firewalls; however, other devices such as routers and wireless access points provide support for NAT. By using NAT, the firewall hides the internal private addresses from the unprotected network, and exposes only its own address or public range. This enables a network professional to use any IP address space as the internal network.

network-based intrusion prevention system   An NIPS is a specialized networking device deployed at important network segments that has visibility into all traffic entering or exiting a segment. NIPS has prevention capabilities, that is, is able to prevent a threat to reach the target. If there is only detection capabilities then the system is called network-based intrusion detection system (NIDS).

network firewall   A firewall that provides key features used for perimeter security. The primary task of a network firewall is to deny or permit traffic that attempts to enter or leave the network based on explicit preconfigured policies and rules. Firewalls are often deployed in several other parts of the network to provide network segmentation within the corporate infrastructure and also in data centers.

O

One Time Password   A password, randomly generated, that can be used only once.

orphan process   A child process that's permitted to continue on its own after its parent process is terminated.

orphan symlink   A symlink pointing to nothing because the file that it references doesn't exist anymore.

OSI model   The Open System Interconnection (OSI) model is an alternative to the TCP/IP model proposed by ISO. It is organized in layers, each describing a different function of a communication or computing device. While it is much more complete then the TCP/IP model, it is also more complex.

P

Password Management   Collection of processes, policies, and technologies that help an organization and users to improve the security of their password authentication systems. It includes policies and technologies around password creation, password storage, and password reset.

Patch Management   The process of identifying, acquiring, installing, and verifying patches for products and systems.

peer-to-peer (P2P) communication   The distributed architecture that "divides tasks" between participant computing peers. In a P2P network, the peers are equally privileged, which is why it's called a "peer-to-peer" network of nodes.

Penetration Assessment   Also called Pen test, it is used to test an exploit of a vulnerability. Besides trying to exploit known vulnerabilities, penetration test may also be able to find unknown vulnerabilities in a system.

pivoting   Also known as island hopping, pivoting means to attack other systems on the same network.

priority   Indicates the level of importance of the message.

private IP address   An address that cannot be routed over the Internet.

process   A running instance of a program.

protocol misinterpretation attack   An attack where protocols are manipulated to confuse security devices from properly evaluating traffic.

R

rainbow table   The concept of a rainbow table is that the attacker computes possible passwords and their hashes in a given system and puts the results into a lookup table called a "rainbow table." This allows an attacker to just get a hash from the victim system and then just search for that hash in the rainbow table to get the plaintext password. To mitigate rainbow table attacks, you can disable LM hashes and use long and complex passwords.

ransomware   A type of malware that compromises a system and then often demands a ransom from the victim to pay the attacker in order for the malicious activity to cease or for the malware to be removed from the affected system.

remote access VPN   Connects a remote host to a trusted network.

Request For Change (RFC)   A formal request for a change that usually includes the high level description of the change, the reason for the change, and other information.

resource exhaustion attack   An attack that consumes the resources necessary to perform an action.

role-based access control   RBAC is an access control model where the access decision is based on the role or function of the subject.

rootkit   A set of tools used by an attacker to elevate his privilege to obtain root-level access in order to completely take control of the affected system.

router   A router or IP gateway is a Layer 3 device that performs packet routing. It has two or more interfaces connected to a network segment—either a LAN segment or a WAN segment. Although a router is usually classified as Layer 3, most of modern routers implement all layers of the TCP/IP model; however, their main function is to route packets at Layer 3.

routing protocol   A protocol that allows the exchange of information about an IP packet forwarding path. If the protocol operates within the organization boundary, it is called an interior gateway protocol (IGP); if it operates between organizations, it is called an exterior gateway protocol (EGP). Most common IGP routing protocols are based on three models: Distance Vector, Link-State, and Hybrid. The most common IGPs are RIPv2 (RIPng for IPv6), OSPFv2 and v3, EIGRP (with IPv6), and IS-IS. The most common EGP is BGP.

routing table   A routing table or routing database is somewhat similar to a MAC address table. A routing table contains two main pieces of information: the destination IP or network and the next-hop IP address, which is the IP address of the next device where the IP packet should be sent.

S

Secure Shell (SSH)   Encrypts traffic between a client and SSH server and uses public-key cryptography to authenticate the remote computer and permit it to authenticate the user.

Security baseline configuration   A set of attributes and configuration items related to a system which has been formally reviewed and approved. It can be changed only with a formal change process.

Security Information and Event Manager (SIEM)   A specialized device or software for security event management. It typically includes logs collection, normalization, aggregation and correlation capabilities, and built-in reporting.

selector   Monitors for one or more facility and level combinations and, when triggered, performs some action.

session log   Tracks changes made on managed hosts during a web-based system manager session.

Single Sign-On (SSO)   An authentication system that allows users to authenticate with only one system and only once to get access to organization resources.

site-to-site VPN   Connects one or more hosts over a secure connection.

spammer   An attacker who uses the type of malware whose sole purpose is to send unsolicited messages with the primary goal of fooling users into clicking on malicious links or replying to emails or such messages with sensitive information. The attacker seeks to perform different types of scams with the main objective being to make money.

SQL injection   An attack where the attacker inserts or "injects" a SQL query via the input data from the client to the application or database. An attacker can exploit SQL injection vulnerabilities in order to read sensitive data from the database, modify or delete database data, execute administration operations on the database, and even issue commands to the operating system.

stack   Memory set aside as spare space for a thread of execution.

stateless address auto configuration (SLAAC)   A method of IPv6 address configuration.

static memory allocation   When a program allocates memory at compile time.

subject/object   A subject is defined as any active entity that requests access to a resource, also called the object. The subject usually performs the request on behalf of a principal. An object is defined as the passive entity that is, or contains, the information needed by the subject.

symlink   Any file that contains a reference to another file or directory.

symmetric algorithm   An encryption algorithm that uses the same key to encrypt and decrypt the data.

T

tcpdump   An open source packet capture utility.

TCP/IP model   A layered model at the base of most of the modern communication networks.

thread   A basic unit an operating system allocates process time to.

thread pool   A group of worker threads that efficiently execute asynchronous callbacks for the application.

threat   Any potential danger to an asset. If a vulnerability exists but has not yet been exploited or, more importantly, it is not yet publicly known, the threat is latent and not yet realized. If someone is actively launching an attack against your system and successfully accesses something or compromises your security against an asset, the threat is realized. The entity that takes advantage of the vulnerability is known as the malicious actor, and the path used by this actor to perform the attack is known as the threat agent or threat vector.

threat actor   An individual or group of individuals that performs an attack or is responsible for a security incident that impacts or has the potential of impacting an organization or individual.

threat log   A log that triggers when an action matches one of the security profiles attached to a security rule.

Tor   Tor is a free tool that enables its users to surf the Web anonymously. Tor works by "routing" IP traffic through a free, worldwide network consisting of thousands of Tor relays. It then constantly changes the way it routes traffic in order to obscure a user's location from anyone monitoring the network. Tor's name was created from the acronym for the original software project name, "The Onion Router."

Tor exit node   Basically the last Tor node or the "gateway" where the Tor encrypted traffic "exits" to the Internet.

traffic fragmentation attack   A method of avoiding detection by breaking up a single Internet Protocol or IP datagram into multiple smaller size packets.

traffic substitution and insertion attack   Substituting the payload data with data in a different format but with the same meaning, with the goal of being ignored due to not being recognized by the security device.

traffic timing attack   An attack in which the attacker performs actions slower than normal while not exceeding thresholds inside the time windows the detection signatures use to correlate different packets together.

transaction log   Records all transactions that occur.

transport protocol socket   A socket that's a combination of three pieces of information: the host IP address, a port number, and the transport layer protocol. The first two items are sometimes grouped together under the notion of "socket address."

Trojan horse   A type of malware that executes instructions, determined by the nature of the Trojan, to delete files, steal data, or compromise the integrity of the underlying operating system. Trojan horses typically use a form of social engineering to fool victims into installing such software on their computers or mobile devices. Trojans can also act as backdoors.

trunk   A connection between two switches using a VLAN.

V

variable-length subnet mask (VLSM)   An IP address schema that uses a variable-length prefix or subnet mask to improve efficiency in the IP address allocation.

virtual address space   The virtual memory used by processes.

VirtualAlloc   A specialized allocation of OS virtual memory that allocates straight into virtual memory via reserved blocks.

virtual private network (VPN)   Used to hide or encode something so that the content is protected from unwanted parties.

virus   Malicious software that infects a host file or system area to perform undesirable actions such as erasing data, stealing information, and corrupting the integrity of the system. In numerous cases, the virus multiplies again to form new generations of itself.

VLAN   A virtual LAN is a virtually separated subnet created on a switch. The switch uses a VLAN ID to tag traffic and keep the broadcast domain separated.

vulnerability   An exploitable weakness in a system or its design. Vulnerabilities can be found in protocols, operating systems, applications, hardware, and system designs. Vulnerabilities abound, with more discovered every day.

vulnerability management   The process of identifying, analyzing, prioritizing, and remediating vulnerabilities in software and hardware.

vulnerability scanner   Software that can be used to identify vulnerabilities on systems.

W

war driving   This is a methodology used by attackers to find wireless access points wherever they may be. The term *war driving* comes from the fact that the attacker can just drive around and get a huge amount of information over a very short period of time.

Windows Management Instrumentation (WMI)   A scalable system management infrastructure that was built around a single consistent, standards-based, extensible, object-oriented interface.

Windows process permission   User authentication data that is stored in a token and used to describe the security context of all processes associated with the user.

Windows registration   A hierarchical database used to store information necessary to configure the system for one or more users, applications, and hardware devices requested, meaning it allocates by default.

wireless LAN   A LAN that uses radio frequency as its medium.

Wireshark   An open source packet capture sniffer.

worm   A virus that replicates itself over the network, infecting numerous vulnerable systems. In most occasions, a worm will execute malicious instructions on a remote system without user interaction.

X

XSS   A type of web application vulnerability where malicious scripts are injected into legitimate and trusted websites. An attacker can launch an attack against an XSS vulnerability using a web application to send malicious code (typically in the form of a browser-side script) to a different end user. XSS vulnerabilities are quite widespread and occur anywhere a web application uses input from a user within the output it generates without validating or encoding it. There are several types of XSS vulnerabilities: reflected, stored, and so on.

Z

zombie process   A terminated process that releases its associated memory and resources but still remains in the entry table.

Index

C

J-K

M

O

Q-R

S

T

U

W

CISCO

Connect, Engage, Collaborate

The Award Winning Cisco Support Community

Attend and Participate in Events

Ask the Experts
Live Webcasts

Knowledge Sharing

Documents
Blogs
Videos

Top Contributor Programs

Cisco Designated VIP
Hall of Fame
Spotlight Awards

Multi-Language Support

https://supportforums.cisco.com